ETHICS IN ACTION

ETHICS IN ACTION

A CASE-BASED APPROACH

Peggy Connolly, Becky Cox-White,
David R. Keller, and Martin G. Leever

WILEY-BLACKWELL

A John Wiley & Sons, Ltd., Publication

This edition first published 2009
© 2009 Peggy Connolly, Becky Cox-White, David R. Keller, and Martin G. Leever

Blackwell Publishing was acquired by John Wiley & Sons in February 2007.
Blackwell's publishing program has been merged with Wiley's global Scientific,
Technical, and Medical business to form Wiley-Blackwell.

Registered Office
John Wiley & Sons Ltd, The Atrium, Southern Gate, Chichester, West Sussex,
PO19 8SQ, United Kingdom

Editorial Offices
350 Main Street, Malden, MA 02148-5020, USA
9600 Garsington Road, Oxford, OX4 2DQ, UK
The Atrium, Southern Gate, Chichester, West Sussex, PO19 8SQ, UK

For details of our global editorial offices, for customer services, and for information
about how to apply for permission to reuse the copyright material in this book
please see our website at www.wiley.com/wiley-blackwell.

The right of Peggy Connolly, Becky Cox-White, David R. Keller, and Martin G. Leever
to be identified as the authors of this work has been asserted in accordance with the
Copyright, Designs and Patents Act 1988.

Library of Congress Cataloging-in-Publication Data

Connolly, Peggy.
Ethics in action : a case-based approach / Peggy Connolly . . . [et al.].
    p. cm.
  Includes bibliographical references and index.
   ISBN 978–1–4051–7098–7 (hardcover : alk. paper) — ISBN 978–1–4051–7097–0
(pbk. : alk. paper) 1. Ethics—Textbooks. I. Title.
BJ1012.C66 2009
170—dc22

                                                            2008031718

A catalogue record for this book is available from the British Library.

Set in 10.5/12.5pt Galliard by Graphicraft Limited, Hong Kong
Printed in Singapore by Ho Printing Pte Ltd

01   2009

This book is dedicated to Robert F. Ladenson, without whom countless marvelous events and fulfilling relationships would never have come into existence.

CONTENTS

ABOUT THE AUTHORS

Peggy Connolly chairs the national case-writing committee for the Intercollegiate Ethics Bowl and serves on the Central DuPage Hospital Ethics Committee. She has served on a number of Institutional Review Boards and Animal Care and Use Committees. Dr Connolly has contributed to two volumes of the NATO Science Series: *Science Education: Talent Recruitment and Public Understanding* (2003); and *Science Education: Best Practices of Research Education Training for Students Under 21* (2005); and to the 2007 volume of the NATO Programme for Security through Science: *Science Education: Models and Networking of Student Research Training Under 21*. Dr Connolly is a Fellow of the American Association for the Advancement of Science. Her areas of specialty in ethics include research, genetics, and biomedical ethics.

Becky Cox-White is Professor of Philosophy, and Bioethics Project Director for the Center for Applied and Professional Ethics (CAPE), at California State University, Chico, where she teaches moral theory, biomedical ethics, and issues in altruism. She has served on a number of institutional bioethics committees and institutional review boards. Dr White is the author of two books, *Competence to Consent* (Georgetown University Press, 1994), and, with Joel A. Zimbelman, *Moral Dilemmas in Community Healthcare* (Pearson/Longman, 2005). Her current research interests include allocation of health resources, disability, and teaching ethics.

David R. Keller is Professor of Philosophy, Director of the Center for the Study of Ethics, and Chair of the Environmental Studies Program at Utah Valley University. His first book, *The Philosophy of Ecology: From Science to Synthesis* (co-authored with ecologist Frank Golley), was published in 2000 by the University of Georgia Press. He served as editor of *Teaching Ethics*, the journal of the International Society for Ethics Across the Curriculum, from Spring 2006 to Fall 2007. He has contributed to *The International Global Studies Encyclopedia, Classics of Philosophy: The Twentieth Century*, and Terra Nova Books' *Writing on Air*. He has published in the journals *BioScience, Humanitas, Teaching Ethics, Environmental Ethics, Interdisciplinary Humanities, Ethics and the Environment, Ecosystem Health, Essays in Philosophy, Process Papers, Encyclia*, and *Journal of the Utah Academy*. He has also served as Dean of the School of Humanities, Arts, and Social Sciences, Administrator and Chair of the Institutional Review Board, and Assistant Vice-President for Academic Affairs at Utah Valley University.

Martin G. Leever is Associate Professor of Philosophy and Chair of the Department of Philosophy at the University of Detroit Mercy, where he teaches ethical theory, healthcare ethics, and the history of philosophy. He served as President of the Medical Ethics Resource Network of Michigan in 2004–7 and currently chairs the Archdiocesan Healthcare Ethics Advisory Committee in Detroit. His research and publications have focused on ethical issues in the professions, with particular attention to social work and medicine. Dr Leever is co-author of *Ethical Child Welfare Practice* (Child Welfare League of America, 2002) and serves as an ethics consultant to various hospital and social service agencies in the Detroit area. He has BA and MA degrees from Marquette University and a PhD from Loyola University of Chicago.

FOREWORD

Robert F. Ladenson

Ethics in Action: A Case-based Approach is intended for any reader who wants to develop critical abilities in the area of ethical decision-making. Reflecting this broad purpose, the book includes thought-provoking case studies on personal relationships, public discourse, healthcare choices, community issues, public policy, and exercise of the full range of rights and responsibilities of citizens in a democracy. The approach taken in this book to critical thinking about ethical decisions grew, in large part, out of the involvement of all the authors with the Intercollegiate Ethics Bowl (IEB), an academic competition that I originated in 1993 at the Illinois Institute of Technology in Chicago. Each author has played an important part in the development and growth of the IEB into a major educational activity in which, by 2007, 85 colleges and universities throughout the United States were taking part. (Ethics Bowl competitions modeled on the IEB now also take place in Canada, Puerto Rico, Turkey, and the Philippines.) I am honored by the decision each author made to devote a substantial part of his or her already full professional life to working on the IEB, and immensely gratified that their work together has led to the production of this superb book.

The following two points are critical underlying premises of the IEB. First, the positions people take on complex, ambiguous, and difficult-to-resolve ethical issues tend strongly to reflect such factors as an individual's politics, personal values, childhood background, economic status, gender, or religion. No one may reasonably assume that ethical thinking invariably proceeds from a neutral standpoint, absolutely uninfluenced by these kinds of factors. A critical aspect of ethical decision-making thus consists largely of attempting to view from the inside other ethical positions besides those to which one feels most strongly drawn. It involves not only an awareness of the arguments advanced on behalf of those opposed positions, but also of concerns that motivate the arguments and even, to some extent, an appreciation of their force.

Second, despite the highly viewpoint-dependent aspects of complex, ambiguous, and difficult-to-resolve ethical issues, the appropriate rules, principles, and ideals for thinking about such matters have a rational basis and relate to one another in terms of a rationally systematic structure. For this reason, philosophical theories of ethics can provide an important conceptual resource for defining what makes an issue an *ethical* issue and, when ethical decisions must be made, for helping identify relevant considerations and avoiding clearly unethical alternatives.

The approach to critical thinking about ethical decisions in *Ethics in Action: A Case-based Approach* incorporates and develops the above two points. In this regard, the authors demonstrate, with many detailed examples, how different individuals, applying the approach in a given case, could arrive at different conclusions about it. The authors' examples, however, also make the following point apparent: even in cases of deep ethical disagreement, the matters in dispute can be identified, debated, and discussed within a wider framework of agreed-upon rules, principles, ethically relevant considerations, and ideals at the core of ethical thinking. *Ethics in Action: A Case-based Approach* provides immensely valuable insight and guidance on how to do so.

PREFACE

Our immersion in practical and theoretical moral problem-solving has convinced us that moral dilemmas are an ineluctable part of everyone's life; that persons of good will struggle with moral quandaries on a regular basis; that good will is not a sufficiently powerful tool to insure success in moral problem-solving; and that many, many people – both inside and outside colleges and universities – would welcome an accessible method that would enable them to identify and work toward the resolution of these inescapable moral challenges. Hence this book.

Since the mid-1990s we have been active – indeed, immersed – in the National Intercollegiate Ethics Bowl. We have watched thousands of students construct and defend solutions to scores of moral dilemmas, have been engaged in constructing cases that articulate those dilemmas, and have composed those cases to bring them alive for students. The cases incorporated in this volume continue our efforts to delineate the complexities of moral problems arising in everyday life, be they in personal, professional, or social arenas. We have encouraged our own students (they might say that we drove them mercilessly) to search out and embrace problem-solving strategies that enabled them to address these conundrums with all the nuances and richness they deserve.

We have also worked with colleagues in medicine, science, education, government, and research to identify practical applications of moral principles and meaningful solutions to real-world ethical issues. Each of these environments gave further testimony to the ubiquity of moral challenges.

Herein we present 40 moral dilemmas – some culled from personal and professional experience and others drawn from daily media accounts – that demonstrate the prevalence of moral quandaries in all aspects of life: in personal and professional relationships, at the beginning and end of life, in nature and invention, in our communities, and in the world at large. Perhaps, however, the greatest strength of the book lies in its disciplined application of a systematic method for resolving moral dilemmas, regardless of their particulars. In applying this method, designed by Eric H. Gampel, PhD, to cases in this book, we hope to inculcate in the reader an habitual approach that will be ready-to-hand whenever a moral conundrum arises. Of course, we anticipate that students will find the book useful; but our hope is that its utility will extend – as do the dilemmas detailed herein – beyond the halls of the academy. Because ethical dilemmas are ever-present in our lives, and thoughtful discourse about them is

often absent, abilities leading to the recognition and resolution of moral dilemmas are particularly valuable. As public discussions of ethical issues have become
common media fare, an increasing number of persons are both interested in,
and motivated to acquire or refine, moral problem-solving skills. If this book
helps a few more people address the dilemmas that niggle at them in the wee,
small hours of the night, we will count it a success.

One word about style. The first case(s) in each chapter are fully analyzed,
providing an example of what a thorough approach should look like. The cases
that follow present only two competing analyses, such as might be quickly
advanced by principled persons of good will who happen to disagree about the
better solution to a moral problem. The final case(s) in each chapter are left un-
analyzed, giving the reader the opportunity to start from the very beginning
in resolving a case. These successive approaches, we anticipate, will aid readers in
developing and refining their own moral problem-solving skills.

Academics interested in learning more about the Intercollegiate Ethics Bowl
are referred to the Bowl's website: http://ethics.iit.edu/eb/index.html. We
have included the current (January 2008) rules at the end of the book. Note,
however, that the rules are constantly under revision; the website will contain
the most recent version.

ACKNOWLEDGMENTS

All the authors owe an immense debt of gratitude to Robert F. Ladenson, PhD, JD. As the originator of the Intercollegiate Ethics Bowl (IEB), he has given us the opportunity to do what, as moral theorists, we love to do: put our ideas into action. His enthusiasm pulled us into this activity in so many rewarding ways: as team coaches, judges, and moderators for the competition, and as colleagues in a project that is both timely and critical for a society embroiled in so many moral issues. His gracious support enabled us to expand our knowledge and our practical, professional, and pedagogical skills. Truly, without him we would be lesser persons than we have become.

Our unstinting appreciation goes, next, to Brian Schrag, PhD, Executive Director of the Association for Practical and Professional Ethics (APPE). Without his efforts to incorporate the IEB into his organization's annual meeting, the competition would never have seen the enormous popularity and growth that it currently enjoys; and we would not have been moved to produce this volume.

Special gratitude goes to Lida Anestidou, PhD, DVM, without whose initiative and vision this book would not have come into existence.

The authors thank the writers who have graciously contributed their time and the benefit of their experience and collective wisdom to writing cases for the national IEB. In doing so, they inspired us and this book: Ruth Ann Althaus, Lida Anestidou, Christina Bellon, Anthony Brinkman, Elaine Englehardt, Lawrence Hinman, Robert F. Ladenson, Robert Boyd Skipper, and Christine Weigel.

Thanks are also due to all our colleagues in APPE who have served as judges and moderators for the IEB competition each year. Generously donating their time and expertise, these professionals have listened to students argue their positions, have studiously examined the cases about which students deliberate, and have posed thoughtful questions designed to draw out the nuances of the cases and to assist students to see more fully and with greater clarity the implications of their postulated solutions. Again, without them we would never have seen the potential for this work.

We owe thanks beyond measure to all the students who have competed in the regional and the national IEBs since 1997. They have demonstrated, time and time again, that progress can be made on the thorniest dilemmas if they are approached with an open mind and with a resolve to answer the tough questions.

Finally, our appreciation goes to Jeff Dean, our Blackwell editor, for his advice, encouragement, and patience throughout the process, and to Sarah Dancy for her first-rate editing of the original manuscript.

In addition, each of us owes personal debts of gratitude.

Peggy Connolly thanks Erica and Cailin Sandvig, and the Connolly and Langseth families for their unfailing support and encouragement; Christopher Sandvig, whose commitment to integrity is as constant as the sunrise; Carl Waltenbaugh for undaunted courage and personal sacrifice in defending ethical principles; Heidi Malm, Tim Murphy, and Tom May for years of stimulating and provocative discussions; Ronald M. Green and the Dartmouth College ELSI Institute; and the Reverend David Anderson and members of the Central DuPage Hospital Ethics Committee for their dedicated pursuit of wisdom and compassion.

Becky Cox-White wishes to thank her husband Kelly White for his endless patience and wry sense of humor, and her daughter Kathryn White for putting things in perspective. The California State University at Chico funded a full semester's leave to work on this project; and the CSUC College of Humanities and Fine Arts and the Department of Philosophy provided additional support. Helen Marsden, Researcher, School of Management, University of South Australia, Adelaide, was an invaluable resource in providing background material for the case on plagiarism. Troy Jollimore, CSU Chico, was instrumental in imaginings of the case on emergency contraception (which, in an earlier version, was published in *Teaching Ethics*); Joel Zimbelman, CSU Chico, has been an invaluable resource for thinking about applied ethics in general and aid-in-dying in particular; and Dennis Rothermel, CSU Chico, has rerouted many possible distractions. Finally, Daphne and Diogenes were reliable sources of comic relief.

David Keller thanks Kurt Torben Bernhard, Asia Ferrin, Matt Gowans, Ali Jahromi, Blakely Neilson, Nissa Roper, and Sam Taylor for case study research assistance; E. Charles Brummer for detailed comments on the science of plant-breeding for the genetically modified rice case study; and Becky Cox-White for invaluable constructive criticism of his overview of the basic ethical theory chapter. David Rothenberg provided inspiration for the title of the Goshute case study. Don LaVange's precise calculations of the distance of the proposed Goshute-PFS siting from downtown Salt Lake City and the campus of Utah Valley University are most appreciated. An earlier version of the Goshute case study appeared in *Teaching Ethics* 1/1 (2001): 79–87. Portions of earlier versions of "Utah Valley Versus State College?" appeared in *Academe* 91/5 (2005) and *Academe* 93/5 (2007). And most importantly, gratitude to Anina Merrill, who, during the long hours of work on this project, provided unflagging support on the Keller-Merrill home front.

Martin Leever is grateful for the helpful comments both from the other authors of this book and from his colleagues at the University of Detroit Mercy, especially Beth Oljar, Jim Tubbs, Roy Finkenbine, and Victoria Mantzopoulos. He would also like to thank the Mellon Foundation for the course release that allowed him to focus on this project.

INTRODUCTION

Peggy Connolly

We are confronted on a daily basis with ethical dilemmas. Many situations present clear incidents of unethical behavior: athletes using illegal steroids to gain a competitive and economic advantage; governments manipulating scientific reports to fit their environmental policies; medical students practicing pelvic examinations on anesthetized women who have not consented to participate in medical education. Other situations pose challenging quandaries where the appropriate action is not easily determined: continuing or withdrawing artificial life support; telling a friend about a partner's infidelity; using private means to procure a transplant organ for a child. While the application of ethical theory may suggest a morally plausible response, theory alone is often inadequate to address the everyday dilemmas created by the complexities of multiple roles, societal realities, and competing loyalties. Should a parent leave a sick child alone or stay at home with the child and risk losing the job that provides health insurance? Is it morally permissible to pay protection money to stay in business and provide for one's family? Is it ethically acceptable to create a child to be a donor for another?

Whether deliberative or unconscious, satisfying or distressing, decisions about moral issues are ubiquitous in daily life, affecting choices and behavior in public and private spheres. People often seek answers to perplexing ethical questions by turning to law, religion, etiquette, or other familiar sources that guide behavior. While these institutions are essential to a well-ordered society and frequently offer excellent counsel, and although to some extent all are mutually intertwined, ethics is not the same as law, religion, or courtesy.

For thousands of years, people have attempted to define ethical conduct and articulate expectations that guide moral behavior. Communities, religions, governments, social institutions, and professions have all been based in part on ethical practices. Yet still we seek for wise and just answers to the challenging moral dilemmas of daily life. Intelligent, reasonable, and deeply caring individuals hold diametrically opposing and mutually exclusive perspectives. We continue to be challenged to find ways to acknowledge others' perspectives respectfully, and to honor those who hold them, even when it is not possible to accommodate their positions.

Some laws attempt to codify moral behavior; other laws attempt to correct it; yet still other laws may preserve an unfair privilege or advantage. While most religions are concerned with developing goodness in their followers, others require conversion and resort to violent or coercive methods to achieve that end or remove the recalcitrant non-believer. Followers of a religion are not required to examine other belief systems, but to accept on faith the fundamental beliefs of the doctrine. Even while courtesy encourages respectful treatment of others and their values, rules of behavior can be exclusionary, truth is not always required, and harmonious social accord rather than pursuit of goodness sometimes shapes mores.

Despite the prevalence of ethical challenges in daily life, few people have had training in moral reasoning. This problem is not new. Nearly 2,500 years ago, Plato addressed this issue in a conversation between Socrates and Alcibiades in the dialogue, "Alcibiades." Socrates lamented that people disagree, often with harmful results, about issues of justice and injustice: the Trojan War was fought over a disagreement about justice. He concluded that people who disagree strongly over issues of justice and injustice have not bothered to take the time to understand the complexities of the dilemma. He chastised his pupil for neither bothering to learn about justice and injustice himself nor learning from a teacher, but instead relying on his own unexamined opinions for authority (Plato 1997: ll. 1.109a–1.112d).

Still, today, although students who enroll in ethics classes may be exposed to ethical theory, they may have limited opportunities for examining its practical application to the complexities of everyday moral situations. Those who have never studied philosophy are nevertheless confronted with ethical dilemmas in their daily lives. The perennial challenge of how to respond to practical moral dilemmas remains (Ladenson 2001: 63–78).

Practical Difficulties in Solving Moral Problems

Understanding moral issues is difficult. People often fail to recognize moral dilemmas and, when they do, are uncertain how to respond. No single set of ethical principles encompasses all the dimensions and complexities of moral challenges for all people in all places at all times. What constitutes ethically justifiable action is affected by changes in technology, social and political environments, and human understanding. It varies among cultures, belief systems, and the nature and extent of one's experience. Perceptions of and responses to ethical dilemmas may be skewed by the conflict between moral interests and self-interest.

Consider, for example, the perception of death. The concept of death has changed with the development of technologies that can significantly prolong the dying process. Changes in the legal system and the standards of care in medical practice have redefined death (in the United States) from cessation of heartbeat to cessation of brain activity. Individuals' experience of intractable pain in the face of incurable disease or fatal injury has changed perceptions about the morality of withholding and withdrawing artificial life-support. Yet strong disagreement about the definition of death persists. Despite the medical and legal definitions of death as cessation of brain activity, some cultures and religions believe death occurs only when the heart stops beating. Furthermore, historic prejudices and the current practice of insurance companies in dictating terms of care have created mistrust of the medical establishment. Even if patients and providers agree on a definition of death, patients (or families) may suspect the motives behind the recommendations and challenge decisions to withdraw treatment when brain death occurs, creating moral dilemmas involving professional ethics, conflicting responsibilities, and competing interests.

Sometimes, acceptance of evolving ethical principles comes with the recognition that what was once considered the best response to a certain type of moral dilemma is no longer appropriate or adequate. For many years physician paternalism was the accepted ethical approach to decision-making in healthcare. Over time, the perspective that the physician was unequivocally the most appropriate judge of what was best for the patient was replaced by the principle of autonomy. The practical outcomes of establishing the principle of autonomy as paramount were the derivative right of patients to make decisions about their medical care and physicians' responsibility to provide patients with the information they need to make appropriate decisions.

The Purpose of This Book

Ethical dilemmas directly impact our personal lives and, at times, require timely responses. Imagine that your community is beset with mounting ethnic tension, fueled by increasing numbers of immigrants, stresses on education and social services, economic concerns, and insensitive law-enforcement. Your neighbor rents out a small house to several immigrant families who are crowded together in the dwelling. The children are largely unsupervised. You are concerned for the safety and welfare of the children, but are afraid that if you report your concerns, the families will face disruption, eviction, and even greater hardships.

We might strive to develop an informed perspective about a social issue we care about but have limited ability to influence. Should the United States, for example, pay opium poppy farmers the same amount they could make in profits from selling their crop if, instead of harvesting the poppies, they were to destroy them?

We might foresee a situation where conflicting factors obscure an easy answer, yet the dilemma nonetheless requires a decision. Your child has suffered through several rounds of harsh chemotherapy and will have cumulative life-long debilitation because of it. The cancer is in remission now, but if it recurs, will you insist on additional chemotherapy, despite your child's desperate pleas to forgo future treatments?

This book features cases drawn from real-world ethical challenges, written by members of the National Intercollegiate Ethics Bowl case-writing team. It addresses a wide variety of topics reflecting ethical dilemmas that confront people in everyday life: in the arts, the environment, government, interpersonal and social relationships, healthcare, education, and business. Each dilemma, presented as a case study, offers an opportunity for moral reflection and problem-solving. The first (and sometimes second) case in each chapter is analyzed from three perspectives. The first perspective articulates a position that an individual might hold and argues for a particular solution. The second perspective offers an alternative resolution, often in opposition to the solution advocated in the first perspective. The third perspective evaluates both previous analyses and demonstrates that, although both have merit, neither is complete in and of itself. Further moral reasoning and practical application of ethical principles identify a morally preferable solution. Other cases offer only the first two perspectives – leaving the task of comparative analysis and construction of a third perspective for the reader. Still other cases are presented without any analyses, giving the reader the challenge of analyzing the case – as most persons must in their own experience – from the beginning. Each chapter of the book contains examples of all three approaches.

An array of everyday moral dilemmas is introduced; tools are presented to enable the reader to understand the multiple perspectives that these dilemmas demonstrate, and guidance is provided to enable the reader to work through the dilemmas and, ultimately, achieve a resolution. Ethical dilemmas are, by their nature, complex, ambiguous, and challenging. Cases that are controversial, difficult to resolve, morally troublesome, and likely to evoke serious disagreement were deliberately chosen for inclusion in this book. Some cases are vague, with incomplete information or facts open to interpretation. The authors' purpose is not to confuse or mislead; but as most cases are drawn from real life, speculation is not offered about intent, belief, and other aspects that cannot be verified. Factual uncertainty reflects the reality of many ethical challenges people face: if complete information were available, often the solution to the ethical dilemma would be evident. If it were known for a fact that vaccinations are harmless, for example, the controversy over mandatory childhood inoculation that pits public health concerns against parental rights might evaporate.

The problem-solving method adopted herein begins with the seeming intractability of moral conflict, demonstrates the value of discourse in moral problem-solving, and identifies a systematic approach to moral reasoning that guides the reader through the process of moral deliberation such that an ethically justifiable resolution is identified.

Moral Reasoning

Moral reasoning is a theoretical exercise, and yet the study of ethics is not intended primarily to be the examination of theories of reasoning in a scholarly or sterile environment, but a reflective structure for arriving at decisions that inform moral choices and actions.

Logic and emotion both play a crucial role in developing personal ethics, and persons make decisions through both intuition and analytical reasoning (Cushman et al. 2006: 1082–4). Judgment, an intrinsic component of moral decision-making, combines subjective and objective reflection. Sometimes we feel a sense of moral outrage, concern, or revulsion regarding a situation, and yet are unable to articulate why we find it ethically repugnant. In the face of practiced persuasion, we may not readily be able to confute a position that disquiets our scruples. We cannot explain our conviction logically, even to ourselves, much less defend our point of view to others. Ethicists refer to this inexplicable feeling of wrongness, without an identifiable ethical principle or rationale on which to form a judgment, as the "yuk factor," or "argument from repugnance" (Kass 1997: 17–26; Midgley 2000: 8–10). It would be regrettable to dismiss emotional responses as flawed or inferior: our intuitions may have profound legitimacy and, in time, we may be able to justify our initial emotional reactions. However, it is equally untenable to fail to acknowledge that emotional judgment may be based on bias, habit, discomfort with change, lack of experience, or other reasons having little to do with the nature of an action or its consequences. Although the "yuk factor" may shape an initial moral position, repugnance alone is inadequate for moral justification. Recall that in the first half of the twentieth century, repugnance, under the moral guise of scientific good of society, resulted in thousands of vulnerable populations – ethnic minorities, the impoverished, the blind, the deaf, and the homeless – being involuntarily sterilized in Lynchburg, Virginia. It is imperative to strive to understand the principles that underlie a sense of revulsion to determine whether the emotional reaction is an indicator of genuine moral significance or an expression of personal prejudice. Systematically and logically examining ethical issues can better help persons to draw those distinctions, and provides a process for developing understanding.

Opinions, feelings, and beliefs, while significant to the individual, in and of themselves do not provide adequate and defensible support for moral reasoning. Yet, moral reasoning without the benefit of experience, sensibility, and personal judgment – and foundation in ethical theory – has limited practical application. Often, more than one moral principle is relevant in a particular situation, and equally relevant principles can come into conflict with each other. Imagine that one brother needs a kidney and his sister is the best donor candidate. It might be argued from a duty perspective that his sister, with two good kidneys, is morally obligated to donate one to her brother. Conversely, it might be argued from a libertarian perspective that enforced benevolence is a form of violence and therefore, because it creates harm, is morally wrong. Or consider the case of Robin Hood and his proclivity to rob the rich and distribute this wealth to the poor. A utilitarian viewpoint might support this redistribution, which creates the greatest good for the greatest number, as ethically appropriate. However, the universalization principle, which holds that an action is ethical only if it is acceptable for everyone to act in the same manner, would conclude that Robin Hood's actions, however well intended, are not ethically justifiable.

A challenge of ethical discourse, then, is to understand that mutually exclusive moral theories may be applied to the same dilemma, argued logically and eloquently, and result in diametrically opposing, but equally reasonable, resolutions. This is a reality of ethical discussion, even within a framework of moral reasoning. Numerous ethical principles and moral theories provide useful starting points for a rational approach for examining ethical dilemmas; but none is perfect for all situations, and some are more relevant than others for particular disciplines or in particular contexts.

Despite numerous informal approaches to moral reasoning, a systematic method is necessary if ethical theories are to be applied in a non-arbitrary fashion to dilemmas drawn from actual events. Thus, this volume includes an approach for analyzing ethical dilemmas developed by Eric H. Gampel in "A Framework for Moral Reasoning" (see chapter 2). Gampel's approach offers a sound methodology for case analyses and it is for this reason that we have chosen to use it. Through the generous permission of Pearson-Longman (the publisher of Gampel's piece), we have included herein this thorough, practical, useful, and tested method for critical and nuanced moral analysis both in the classroom and in the outside world.

Although this book may be used as a text in applied ethics courses, it is also written for the large number of ordinary people interested in becoming more effective ethical decision-makers in personal relationships, professional practice, public discourse, healthcare choices, community relations, and public policy, and in exercising the full range of rights and responsibilities of citizens in a democracy.

The potential advantages of increasing one's ability for moral reasoning are many. In becoming proficient in ethical decision-making, individuals may replace polarizing, judgmental, and mutually exclusive positions characterizing political debate with respectful appreciation of alternative viewpoints. They may come to understand, and, thus, be more tolerant of, different perspectives, values, and experiences – and the people who embrace them. Increasing the willingness to listen to those with other opinions, replacing attempts at coercion with respectful exchanges of ideas to share the richness of others' experiences and beliefs, striving to understand the ethical complexities and consequences of a broad range of issues, and becoming more effective at teaching children to make ethical decisions are all potential outcomes of increasing one's abilities in moral reasoning.

In the face of competing values and pressures from multiple self-interested sources, courage is often required to live by one's moral choices. Courage is developed from the confidence of deep conviction derived from reflective examination of issues within the context of personal values and moral reasoning. This book aids readers in developing the skills that will lead to an appropriate courage of one's convictions.

RESOURCES

Cushman, F., Young, L., and Hauser, M. (2006) The role of conscious reasoning and intuition in moral judgment: testing three principles of harm. *Psychological Science* 17 (12): 1082–9.

Kass, L. R. (1997) The wisdom of repugnance. *New Republic* 216 (22): 17–26.

Ladenson, R. F. (2001) The educational significance of the ethics bowl. *Teaching Ethics* 1 (1): 63–78.

Midgley, M. (2000) Biotechnology and monstrosity: why we should pay attention to the "Yuk Factor." *The Hastings Center Report* 30 (5): 7–15.

Plato (1997) Alcibiades. *Plato: Complete Works*, ed. J. M. Cooper, trans. D. S. Hutchinson. Indianapolis, IN: Hackett.

PART I

ETHICAL REASONING

1

A BRIEF OVERVIEW OF BASIC ETHICAL THEORY

David R. Keller

Ethics is the philosophical study of *morality*. Although we use the words synonymously in everyday discourse, in philosophy it is important to distinguish the two.

Morality is the behavior of making *value* judgments regarding how we should best live our lives. Two points follow. First, judgments presuppose freedom of choice; the entire edifice of ethics is erected on the assumption that value judgments are made by moral agents voluntarily, who therefore are responsible for those choices. This assumption leads into a whole debate about determinism versus free will that I cannot address here.[1] Second, value judgments differ from judgments of ordinary preference, such as how spicy we like our food or what color of clothing we prefer to wear. Moral judgments involve interconnected conceptions of goodness, rightness, the class of beings worthy of moral consideration, and virtue.

Moral judgments presuppose the acceptance of some highest moral good (*summum bonum*). This might be obedience to God, acting in accordance with duty, realizing one's unique individual potential, affirming relationships based on care and empathy, or maximizing overall collective happiness. Humans live their lives and make daily choices with an eye to some ideal of moral goodness. Moral judgments commend some actions as right and condemn other actions as wrong, depending on the moral good to be affirmed. Moral judgments also presuppose a class of beings judged to be worthy of moral consideration: humans, all beings capable of suffering, all living things, entire ecosystems, etc. Moral judgments depend on the virtue of moral agents, namely, whether the character and actions of moral agents affirm or deny moral goodness, rightness, and the beings helped or harmed by the moral agents involved.

All humans make moral judgments; we cannot avoid it.[2] That ability, or responsibility, is the distinguishing and wondrous feature of *humanness*. The German philosopher Immanuel Kant marveled: "Two things fill the mind with ever new and increasing admiration and reverence, the more often and more steadily one reflects on them: *the starry heavens above me and the moral law within me*" (2006:

133). Moral awareness makes humans moral agents. With awareness – what Kant called moral law – comes responsibility, a responsibility that cannot be shirked even with focused determination. If you wake up tomorrow and say to yourself, "I will not make value judgments today," you will shortly fail. By choosing not to choose, you have chosen. And you will judge the characters and actions of family, friends, peers, and strangers before noon. As French philosopher Jean-Paul Sartre put it: "In one sense choice is possible, but what is not possible is not to choose. I can always choose, but I ought to know that if I do not choose, I am still choosing" (2003: 235). Sartre meant that, as agents capable of moral awareness and reflection, we are also responsible – whether we want the responsibility or not – for the effects our actions have on others. Not making a choice or not taking an action does not free us of moral responsibility. Inaction has its own moral repercussions.

This issue of unavoidable responsibility brings to the fore the issue of identifying the class of beings worthy of moral consideration. Judgments that involve how best to live our lives are *moral* judgments because they affect beings to which we as moral agents have responsibilities. We are not morally culpable for choices we make regarding things that are not worthy of moral consideration, like rocks: choosing sandstone over limestone for the walkway to the front door is not an overtly moral decision because the stone that will be cut into slabs is not a proper object of moral consideration. But injuring a friend or kicking your dog for barking are actions that are open to moral judgment, and you are morally culpable for them because your friend and your dog (many people think) are worthy of moral consideration.

If a being is worthy of moral consideration, then other moral agents have a duty either to help that being or, at minimum, not to harm them. The toughest moral choices involve situations that require deciding between two mutually exclusive moral duties, such as telling the truth and avoiding harm. Suppose your elderly grandmother spends most of her waking hours worrying about her grandchildren. As one of those grandchildren, you are aware that telling her the truth about your life – your lingering doubts about medical school, the possibility of your girlfriend's pregnancy, your credit card debt – would cause her acute distress. If you just say, "Grandma, my life is going great, it couldn't be better" (which is not true) and leave it at that, she will be relieved of her worry for you. If you do not tell the whole truth, which is a form of deception, you avoid harm; if you act honestly and tell the truth in full detail, you will most likely cause harm in the form of some kind of distress.

Moral agents frequently face much more difficult decisions. Imagine a nation at war. The enemy has captured both a military officer and a civilian. The officer knows the location of a submarine armed with nuclear weapons which, when used against the enemy, will likely turn the course of the war and result in victory for the officer's forces. The enemy is aware that the officer knows, and threatens to torture the civilian to death in gruesome fashion unless the officer discloses the information. The officer faces an *ethical dilemma*. He has two conflicting moral duties: to uphold his duty as a military officer and protect the military and the nation from further harm at the enemy's hands; and to the civilian, a citizen of the officer's own nation whom he also is sworn to protect. Acting either way will violate one or more duties the officer is responsible for upholding. If he avoids one horn of the dilemma, he will be impaled on the other. Ethical dilemmas should not be confused with moral problems in which the right thing to do is obvious, but in which doing it is difficult. For example, admitting publicly that you have made an egregious and embarrassing error, such as violating the public trust by misusing funds or admitting to infidelity, is hard to do. It is a lot easier not to fess up to one's errors.

Ethics and Religion

Moral judgments can be made in several ways. You could simply flip a coin: heads, tell Grandma the truth; tails, don't give Grandma the full story. Or you could fast and meditate, hoping to have a mystical experience that will reveal the morally preferable option. Or you could follow your gut instincts. The problem with flipping a coin, trying to have a mystical (what theologians describe as a "fideistic") experience, or following your instincts is that these ways of making moral decisions ignore other resources that characterize humanity: reason and religious faith. As alternatives to the above approaches, therefore, you could systematically analyze the situation using the principles of rationality (the approach of ethics, to be explained shortly); or you could use faith as the basis for making moral judgments (the approach of religion).

The distinctively human traits of reason and faith are the primary sources of moral insight. So the question naturally arises: What is the relation between the two? Basing moral judgments on religion, as a conduit of faith, usually means deferring to some kind of authority, whether that authority is a person (such as a prophet, priest, imam, seer, shaman, and so forth) or scripture (such as the Upanishads, Bhagavad-Gita, I-Ching, Torah, New Testament, Qur'ān, Book of Mormon, and others). In either case, the source of authority is assumed to give an avenue of insight into the unseen order of things behind the everyday world, whether that unseen order is structured by God (as is believed in the West) or by a cycle of reincarnation (as is believed in the East). Within the Western tradition, which is the focus of this essay, the question becomes: How does divinity, as the source of faith, determine moral goodness and right action?

Plato posed that question 25 centuries ago in a dialogue called the *Euthyphro*. Socrates asks Euthyphro: Is something good because the gods will it? Or do the gods will it because it is good? (lines 11a–b). The former question answered in the affirmative implies that divine will is the criterion for moral goodness. The latter question answered in the affirmative implies that divinity adheres to some external standard of goodness. There is a big difference between the two, which Socrates stresses but Euthyphro seems to miss: actions are morally reprehensible either because – and only because – of divine intentionality, or because there are independent moral standards with which God complies. For example, is torturing babies wrong only because God thinks it so? And if at some future time God should change His mind, would torturing babies then become morally acceptable? Or is torturing babies wrong in and of itself, independent of what God judges?

Divine Command theory represents the former alternative. On this theory, there is no moral standard independent of God: what is right is what God approves, and what is wrong is what God disapproves. Without divine imperatives, there would be no morality (Harris 2003: 5). This is especially true in the three great Abrahamic monotheistic traditions (Judaism, Christianity, and Islam) that posit God as the source of morality. These religions hold God's will to be the standard of moral goodness, the *summum bonum* of all morality. "The Good," Swiss theologian Emil Brunner (1889–1966) wrote, "has its basis and its existence solely in the will of God" (1947: 53). Extending this line of argument, American theologian Carl Henry (1913–2003) directly repudiated Socrates' implication that moral standards are independent of divine will: "There exists no intrinsic good that is distinguishable from the will of God and to which God must conform" (1957: 212). For this reason, Divine Command theory invalidates the very possibility of an autonomous secular morality independent of God's existence (ibid.: 210).

The Bible itself, however, contradicts Henry's contention. As described in Genesis 3: 5 and 3: 22, human moral awareness was brought when the forbidden fruit of the tree of knowledge was eaten, and this knowledge is passed from each human generation to the next (Harris 2003: 55). Thus, the source of knowledge of good and evil is natural, not supernatural. Moral knowledge as described in the Bible has earthly, not divine, origins, as Henry asserted.

Whether or not the Old Testament buttresses Divine Command theory, there remains the challenge of discerning God's will. Two possible arbiters stand out: scripture and ecclesiastical authority. The difficulty for ethics is that God's will is not always easily discernible, even within a single religious tradition. Here is an example. An orthodox Jewish teenager is wondering whether he should enroll in the nearby state college and get a public secular education after graduating from a private Talmudic high school. He may recall the advice of Proverbs 4: 5–8: "Get wisdom; get insight; do not forget, nor turn away from the word of my mouth. Do not forsake her, and she will keep you; love her, and she will guard you. The beginning of wisdom is this: Get wisdom, and whatever else you get, get insight. Prize her highly." But then he remembers the warning of the very next book of the Hebrew Bible: "For in much wisdom is much vexation, and those who increase knowledge increase sorrow" (Ecclesiastes 1: 18). If the teenager were an evangelical Christian, he might recall God's admonition in the New Testament: "I will destroy the wisdom of the wise, and the discernment of the discerning I will thwart" (1 Corinthians 1: 19). The decision to pursue higher education is perhaps one of the most important decisions in a teenager's life, whether an orthodox Jew or an evangelical Christian. As such, it is likely a moral decision, albeit one in which the Word of God as transmitted through the Bible does not offer much practical guidance.

The Divine Command theorist may conclude that authoritative guidance is needed. Unfortunately, deference to ecclesiastical leadership is no less problematic than deference to scriptural authority. For example, the slavery debate that raged before the American Civil War evoked Christian support for both abolition and slavery (Swartley 1983: 31–64). The then governor of South Carolina, James H. Hammond, called slavery "an established, as well as an inevitable human condition of human society" (*The Pro-slavery Argument*: 107). According to Hammond, neither Christ nor any of his apostles ever "hinted at such a thing as its termination on earth. . . . It is impossible, therefore, to suppose that Slavery is contrary to the will of God. It is equally absurd to say that American Slavery differs in form or principle from that of the chosen people. We accept the Bible terms as the definition of our Slavery, and its precepts as the guide of our conduct" (ibid.: 107–8). The Princeton-educated Presbyterian minister, Albert Barnes, on the other hand, saw "conclusive proof that Christianity was not designed to extend and perpetuate slavery, but that the spirit of the Christian religion is against it: and that the fair application of the Christian religion would remove it from the world, *because* it is an evil, and is displeasing to God . . . it is there-fore wrong" (1969: 375, 365).

The predicament for the Divine Command theorist is that there is no way of resolving these incommensurable interpretations of divine will without resorting to reason – or violence. If we wish to avoid violence, we should focus on the latter alternative to Socrates' conundrum: if some action (like torturing babies or enslaving human beings) is reprehensible for reasons that are independent of God's will, and those reasons are discoverable through critical thinking, then discerning divine will is unnecessary for the practice of ethics. That is, if God wills something as morally permissible or impermissible because it is wrong in and of itself, then morality need not be based on religion. Critics of Divine Command theory argue that, as Socrates alluded, morality should be based on *reason* because that is God's own approach.

Within the Western tradition, the much more common religious approach to morality is Natural Law theory. The Catholic theologian and philosopher Thomas Aquinas (1225–74) viewed reason as *complementing* faith. Aquinas gives Natural Law theory a robust treatment in his gigantic *Summa Theologica*. Through reason, humans discover laws that ultimately emanate from God. These laws are of four kinds:

1 Eternal Law
2 Divine Law
3 Natural Law
4 Human Law

In a section of the *Summa* called "Treatise on Law," Aquinas defines Eternal Law as the law by which God operates the Universe: all laws derive from Eternal Law (Question 93 Third Article; 1981: 1005). Since all that God does is done with a purpose, "the law denotes a kind of plan directing acts towards an end" (ibid.). All things have imprinted on them laws that govern them: acorns grow into oaks, tadpoles into frogs, infants into adults. Acorns do not grow into tad-poles nor infants into oaks, because doing so would contravene the purposes

laid down by Eternal Law. All laws, as functions of Eternal Law, are thus manifestations of God's will and are discoverable by reason (Question 90 First Article;
ibid.: 993) through comprehension of God's purpose.

Divine Law is the body of Eternal Law that God has revealed to humans, for
example as transmitted through prophets and/or scripture. The source of
Divine Law is thus revelation. In contrast, the source of Natural Law is reason.
Divine Law forms the basis of religion, whereas Natural Law is the basis for
philosophy. What is crucial to note is that while religion and philosophy address
two distinct arenas of human wisdom, they are complementary, not contradictory. Their difference lies in the avenues through which truth is transmitted; their
difference is epistemological, not ontological.

Natural Law is humans' interpretation of Eternal Law through the exercise of
reason (Question 94 Second Article; ibid.: 1009). Reason enables the discovery
of the precepts of Eternal Law, and the discovery of these precepts constitutes
the body of Natural Law. Natural Law is therefore, by definition, the same for
all humans. Human Law is a portion of Natural Law codified for the practical
purpose of governing specific communities (Question 95 Third and Fourth Articles;
ibid.: 1015, 1016). Human Law varies spatiotemporally from polis to polis and
from state to state, but since all specific bodies of Human Law derive from
universal Natural Law, Human Law is always consistent with Natural Law. And
just because something is not against Human Law, it may still be against Natural
Law, because the particular body of Human Law may not include within it
all the precepts of Natural Law. As a mere portion of Natural Law, Human
Law cannot prohibit all that Natural Law prohibits (Question 96 Second
Article; ibid.: 1018).

Herein lies a basis for ethics. The consistency or inconsistency of Human Law
with Eternal Law by way of Natural Law as determined by rational analysis
provides the basis for normativity – civil law and ethics. If Human Law is based
on "right reason" (Question 93 Third Article; ibid.: 1005), then it is consistent
with Eternal Law via Natural Law and consequently is ethical; if it is inconsistent, it is unethical. The challenge is discovering the consistency of Human Law
with Eternal Law by way of an analysis of Natural Law. In this way, Eternal Law
provides the basis of morality. Ethics, in Aquarian terms, is the rational exercise
of discovering Natural Law as a window to Eternal Law and evaluating Human
Law according to that assessment (Question 93 Sixth Article; ibid.: 1007).

When the dictates of Natural Law seem straightforward and universally
binding on all moral agents – such as the dictum that injuring beings worthy of
moral consideration is wrong unless some supervening factor suggests otherwise
– the supplication of Human Law to Natural Law appears obvious. Eternal Law
sometimes appears ambiguous, however, because seemingly rational arguments
can be made for contradictory interpretations of Natural Law, such as in the
case of slavery mentioned above. If the Bible is taken as an indication of Eternal
Law on the subject, the advice is murky. The apostle Paul claims that slavery is
founded on "the sound words of our Lord Jesus Christ and the teaching that
is in accordance with godliness" (1 Timothy 6: 1–6), but elsewhere "slave traders"
are described as "godless and sinful" as well as "unholy and profane" (1 Timothy

1: 9–10). In this case, one *interpretation* of Divine Law as transmitted through scripture must be in error. The solution for the Natural Law theorist is to turn to reason in an attempt to discern, in this case, the philosophical spirit of the teachings of Christ. If this is taken to represent an egalitarian spirit under which we are all equal in the eyes of God, as Barnes suggested, then the inequality of the ownership of one human being by another, as goatherds own goats, is contrary to divine intention. Therefore slavery is unethical.

The difference for ethics between Divine Command and Natural Law theories is that the latter explicitly links human reason with divine intentionality while the former does not. Divine Command theory is fideism (i.e., faith exists independently of and is irrelevant to reason), and its logical outcome is irrationalism (since one can ascribe to the dictates of morality only by embracing faith absolutely). Natural Law theory preserves the role of rationality in discerning God's will and treats the making of moral decisions as a rational process. This makes sense if one believes that God would make nothing in vain. With regard to the brain, as Kant said, "no organ is to be found for any end unless it be the most fit and the best adapted for that end" (1985: 8 [395]). Many pious people believe that God must have had a purpose in giving humans brains that facilitate logical thinking, and that purpose is to ground the capacity for ethical inquiry. On the Natural Law approach, then, reason complements and enhances faith.

Religion plays an important role in the moral life of many people and is indispensable in helping them make moral decisions. From the standpoint of ethics, religion may be indispensable in making moral decisions, but moral judgments inspired by religion must never run contrary to reason. Knowledge of good and bad, right and wrong, virtue and villainy is available to all rational beings of all religions – or no religion.

Ethics in the Western Intellectual Tradition

All cultures have normative systems based in law and custom to adjudicate conflicts. The details of these systems vary from culture to culture, time to time, and place to place. All add in unique ways to the moral maturity of humanity as a whole and, for that reason, the moral systems of all cultures merit study.

Such breadth and depth of scope is not possible here. We must limit our attention to the Western tradition from which stem mainstream European and American cultures. The Western (or Occidental) tradition has its origins in Greek and Hebrew antiquity and is the foundation on which Roman and European cultures were built; the Eastern (or Oriental) tradition originates in ancient Chinese and Indian civilizations and is the foundation for Asian culture. The Western tradition is so named because the Grecian peninsula is west of those early civilizations with written histories centered on the eastern end of the Mediterranean Sea and Mesopotamia, and is contrasted with civilizations to the east, in Asia. This dualism between East and West, itself the product of Western thinking, excludes the abundantly interesting cultures of Aboriginal Australia, Africa, Arabia, Native (South, Central, North) America, and Oceania.

Most Western philosophers have modeled the process of moral decision-making on reason, with the notable exceptions of some British philosophers: the third Earl of Shaftesbury (1671–1713), Samuel Clarke (1675–1729), Francis Hutcheson (1694–1746), Adam Smith (1723–90), and, most significantly, the Scottish David Hume (1711–76). In *An Enquiry Concerning the Principles of Morals* and elsewhere, Hume emphasizes the importance of emotion (what he calls "sentiment") in ethics. Eroticism holds that moral decisions spring from emotion rather than rational analysis. It should not go unnoticed, however, that Hume arrives at this position using razor-sharp reason and crystal-clear prose.

Most philosophers base ethics squarely on reason. To meet the minimum standards of rationality, reasoning should be comprehensive, consistent, coherent, and verifiable (these categories are modeled after Ferré 1998: 2–4). Applied to morality, these four criteria constitute the standards for ethics.

Comprehensive reasoning must incorporate all relevant information into the theory and not leave out obviously relevant information. Ethical theories must articulate (1) what is to be valued as the *summum bonum*, (2) what actions are to be morally demanded, morally forbidden, and merely morally permissible (right), (3) the class of beings worthy of moral consideration (discussed in detail below), and (4) the conditions under which the interests of those beings may legitimately be transgressed. For example, a theory of capital punishment that claims that all human life is good must forbid the death penalty unless it can be justified in terms of some additional consistent and coherent value embraced by the theory. Perhaps criteria could be identified to support a belief that one forfeits his or her claim to moral consideration by behaving in a particularly heinous way, such as torturing an innocent child to death. A theory that both claimed to value all human life and permitted capital punishment but failed to justify that practice would not be sufficiently comprehensive. In another example, a theory of animal ethics that claims all sentient life is intrinsically valuable and worthy of moral consideration must forbid the taking of animal life unless some other supervening considerations become relevant, such as looming starvation or finding a cure for a deadly disease through animal experimentation.

A *consistent* theory is not logically contradictory. For example, consider the following argument made in one of my classes: "All human life is inherently valuable, and thus fetuses, who are potential human beings, are inherently valuable. Women who terminate their pregnancies are thus guilty of murder and ought to receive the death penalty." At face value, this argument is blatantly inconsistent. If all human life is inherently valuable and must not be harmed, then the woman who terminates a pregnancy has the same claim not to be killed. A theory that claims *all* human life is intrinsically valuable and also forbids abortion must – *other things being equal* – forbid capital punishment. Simultaneously allowing and forbidding the taking of human life is inconsistent and hence irrational. The claim that a woman who terminates her pregnancy should receive the death penalty fails to meet the standard of consistency, and therefore does not meet the standard for ethical reasoning.

Here, however, inconsistency could be easily avoided by stipulating that *no innocent life should be taken*. This argument would be consistent on account of the distinction between innocent fetuses and guilty adults. But if it is noted that the public policy of capital punishment always results in the death of innocent persons, then the argument again suffers from inconsistency.

A *coherent* theory must link all involved concepts in a unified and integrated whole. For instance, mixing astrology (fulfilling one's cosmic destiny as a member of a standing militia) with constitutional law (the Second Amendment of the US Constitution) in a theory about gun ownership would be flirting with incoherence. Yet such an argument would not necessarily be internally inconsistent. A theory might be incoherent, in the sense that its parts do not cohere very well, but still be consistent, in the sense that its parts are not straightforwardly self-contradictory.

A *verifiable* theory is applicable to the real world and is supported by empirical evidence (or at minimum is not observably contradicted). For example, if capital punishment is justified by the assertion "the death penalty reduces the rate of violent crime," that assertion ought to be verified by actual demographic data and should not be impugned by data to the contrary. Similarly, the assertion "pre-emptive war is prudent foreign policy" ought to be supported by concrete examples of how this policy is more empirically adequate than detente.

Socrates (470–399 BCE) – at least as depicted by Plato (428–347 BCE) – is considered to be the first ethicist of the Western intellectual tradition and an exemplar of logical reasoning about moral problems and living by his conclusions. He accomplished this in two ways. First, he made himself the object of rational inquiry. Philosophers before Socrates typically concerned themselves with the ultimate constitution of nature. In refocusing philosophy on himself, Socrates asked the questions: What are human beings? How ought human beings to live? "For," Socrates says to Thrasymachus in the *Republic*, "it is no ordinary matter that we are discussing, but the right conduct of life" (line 352d). Second, Socrates applied methods of rational inquiry to moral problems, what we have defined as the practice of ethics.

After recounting, in the *Apology*, Socrates' prosaic defense of himself for allegedly corrupting the youth of Athens and fabricating his own gods (line 23c), in the *Crito* Plato describes the Socratic method of working through a moral problem using reason. As Socrates is awaiting execution, his friend Crito visits the prison at daybreak and pleads with Socrates to escape, claiming that if he does not he will be harming himself by playing into the hands of his enemies and deserting his own children. Crito and others will lose a friend, and Socrates will create adverse public opinion because the people of Athens will think of Crito and others as bad friends who were too cheap to bribe the guards and facilitate escape (lines 44b–46a). Crito bases his plea on public perception, and many of us would find it compelling. Rather than examining Crito's reasons themselves, though, Socrates focuses on Crito's root rationale for considering the opinions of others in questions of morality. In this conversation, the two agree that one should pay attention to good opinion and reject bad opinion. For example, Socrates says, the athlete in training ought to listen to the expert (i.e., the coach) rather than the non-experts, who might very well instruct the athlete to push too hard and injure his body. Good advice, in terms of the athletic performance, improves the body; bad advice harms the body. Then Socrates draws an analogy: the soul is like the body. Therefore, in questions of ethics, such as escape, heeding the advice of the many, who are non-experts, might damage the soul. Socrates states that he appreciates Crito's concern, but cannot take public opinion seriously on the issue of escape from prison (lines 46b–48b).

Socrates has discovered, through conversations with the most prominent and powerful people of Athens, that there is no obvious "expert" on ethics, such as coaches are to athletes. So Socrates must decide his course of action himself, and he does so by analyzing the various harms caused by escape. As the foundation for discussion, Socrates and Crito lay down two premises that are themselves the conclusions of arguments from prior discussions: (1) one ought never to do harm, and (2) one ought to keep one's promises. From these premises, Socrates builds the following argument (lines 48c–54e): As an Athenian, he has agreed by tacit consent to live under the laws of Athens insofar as he could have left freely at any time but has chosen to stay.[3] Socrates owes his very existence to the laws which provided the social structure for 'his parents to marry, form a family, raise him, and educate him. It follows that he is squarely within the scope of the laws' authority by his own choice. Socrates is capable of vitiating the social structure of Athens by denying the authority of the laws that frame the social structure. Therefore, if he escapes, he would be harming, at minimum, his friends and family through harming the integrity of laws that give Athens its civil structure. To the Greek mind, the polis was the very foundation of human existence, and threatening it would be an abomination (Hamilton 1993: 143). But more important, he would be harming his soul by committing an unethical act. The act of escape would be unethical because it would precipitate harm to various other beings worthy of moral consideration, such as his friends and family and fellow citizens. Socrates concludes that unethical actions harm the soul, while ethical actions benefit the soul. If he escapes, he benefits his body but harms his soul by compromising his moral integrity; if he does not escape, he harms his body but benefits his soul.

Socrates demonstrates ethics in action. First, his reasoning is comprehensive. He carefully and methodically catalogues and itemizes the various kinds of harms that escaping might incur in light of the good of avoiding harm to his body versus the good of avoiding harm to his soul. Second, his reasoning is coherent. The parts of his argument are all connected by the themes of harm and upholding one's promises. Third, Socrates' reasoning is consistent. In fact, consistency forms the backbone of his argument. He concludes that while his promise to live according to the laws of Athens will result in harm to his own body, it is an acceptable outcome in light of the fact that abiding by his promise will not harm his soul, which is the more important consideration. The commitment to abide by his promise led to the necessity of accepting the verdict, dubious as it is. Fourth, Socrates' reasoning has an element of verifiability insofar as he catalogues the concrete outcomes of alternate actions, including various degrees of harm: to the polis generally, to his friends and family and own body specifically, and, most significantly, to his own soul (not to mention the unpleasant reality for him of living in exile and being unable to practice philosophy). These outcomes are empirically observable in terms real-world repercussions.

Most readers of the *Crito*, especially those who read the *Apology* first, would judge prima facie that escape is warranted given the ludicrous nature of the charges against Socrates and the disproportionality between the alleged crime and the punishment. Yet, through careful, logical reasoning, Socrates arrives at the opposite conclusion. His reasoned, logical approach to the quandary of escape epitomizes the philosophical approach to the study of morality – that is, ethics.

Normative Ethics and Metaethics

Ethics can be divided into two broad categories: *normative ethics* and *metaethics* (Nielsen 1967: 118–19). Normative ethics refers to actual ethical theories; metaethics is concerned with questions about those ethical theories. To understand the difference, it is instructive to draw an analogy with religion. On one hand, we know that there are many different religions around the world; for example, a variety of animistic religions, Zoroastrianism, Buddhism, Taoism, Jainism, Hinduism, Judaism, Christianity, and Islam. These religions consist of actual practices by which people lead their lives. When we study the different religions, we ask questions about actual doctrines and actual daily practices of the people who live by them.

On the other hand, we can also ask questions about religion in general, above and beyond the actual practices and doctrines of specific religions. We can, for example, ask: Is there only one "true" religion? Or, can there be more than one "true" religion? These questions are *meta*religious insofar as they are questions about religion in general rather than about any specific religion.

Metareligion sheds light on metaethics. Metaethics asks questions about ethics generally rather than about the details of specific ethical theories. The paramount metaethical question concerns *relativism*: Do ethical standards apply to all people in all places at all times, regardless of culture, or are moral standards determined by culture and relative to culture, differing from nation to nation and generation to generation? The former position is *metaethical objectivism* (or *metaethical realism*), which holds that ethical standards have real, objective existence independent of the contingencies of human culture; the latter position is *metaethical relativism*, which holds that ethical standards have no real, objective existence independent of the contingencies of human culture.

One version of metaethical objectivism, formulated by Jeremy Bentham and John Stuart Mill, insists that ethically correct action is embedded in human psychology. Human psychology is universal across culture and, as a result, does not hinge on the contingencies of culture; yet the precise psychological necessities of human happiness (camaraderie, satiation, shelter, security, salvation) may vary. Happiness has been a perennial theme in ethics from Aristotle (384–322 BCE) through Henry Sidgwick (1838–1900), and on these theories standards are not socially conditional (hence objective), nor are they immutable (hence not *absolute*).

This subtlety makes it crucial to distinguish objectivist psychologically oriented theories from *metaethical absolutism*. Metaethical absolutism is a particular, more stringent, variation of metaethical objectivism. Metaethical absolutism asserts that there is but one – and only one – ethically correct action per moral category (veracity, beneficence, respect, etc.): period. Not only are social specificities blocked from ethical reasoning by the absolutists; so too are the vagaries of human psychology. Divine Command theorists such as Augustine and Immanuel Kant defend metaethical absolutism.

Ethical relativism is the theory that morality, in the form of values and norms of good behavior, changes from culture to culture, and different moral systems may even be inconsistent. Thus, morally good or bad behavior are determined by the culture in question ("when in Rome, do as the Romans do"). Morally good behavior, on this theory, changes from culture to culture. This raises the problem of cross-cultural moral tolerance.

Imagine that you live in an apartment building in Queens, New York and have befriended the mother of a Muslim family down the hall. The parents emigrated from Sudan and are eager to be assimilated into American culture, but they also want to maintain their African traditions in the upbringing of their children. In college, you learned about the practice of clitorectomy, or female genital circumcision, which has its origins in ancient tribal African cultures and is now practiced by some African Muslims, primarily in Egypt, Ethiopia, Mali, Somalia, and Sudan. Clitorectomy involves, at minimum, the removal of a portion of a female's external genitalia. You are shocked but not surprised when the mother tells you over tea one afternoon that the family intends to carry out a ritual clitorectomy on their 12-year-old daughter. You argue that the practice is mutilation and will impair the daughter's ability to experience normal orgasm; plus, you point out, the practice is illegal under US law. The mother, apparently offended at your lack of tolerance and understanding of their culture, counters, "You just don't understand our culture," and says that the practice has ancient origins and ensures the daughter's "purity" for marriage by reducing the likelihood of premarital sexual intercourse. She voluntarily admits that although it is not mentioned in the Qur'an, clitorectomy has been a sacred Islamic practice for centuries. Unfazed by the illegality of the practice, the mother states that laws against female genital circumcision are nothing more than Western cultural imperialism and must be dismissed by devout Sudanese Muslims.

After the heated and uncomfortable discussion, you walk down the hall telling yourself that you are adamantly opposed to clitorectomy because it violates the right of each individual to maintain the integrity of his or her body. Regardless of cultural tradition, the procedure is morally unconscionable. And since it is illegal in the United States, reporting the family's plan to a social worker might very well forestall the procedure. But you wonder if it is your place to judge the beliefs and practices of this reverent and seemingly good family; perhaps you should just keep quiet. You wonder if you would think differently if you lived in Khartoum rather than Queens. If morality transcends cultural practices – that is, if the right to bodily integrity is an *ethical* and not merely a *moral* right – then the locality and laws should have no bearing on the rightness or wrongness of clitorectomy. What should you do?

The challenge of relativism is that, on one hand, we want to be tolerant of people and cultures different from our own (especially in the United States, where we pride ourselves on pluralism), but, on the other hand, we want the right to condemn cultures that we think are blatantly immoral. This tension arises in the case study on Japanese whaling given in chapter 7 (Case 27: "Straits of Strife: Japanese Whaling, Cultural Relativism, and International Politics"), where, on one hand, the Japanese believe whaling to be an inherent part of their island culture, and, on the other, Western environmentalists believe it to be an unconscionable form of animal cruelty.

Ethical objectivism and ethical relativism generate tension. Although we strive to be tolerant, at the same time we are, by our very nature, judgmental. One possible solution to this quandary would be to appeal to positive law rooted in an objective ethical principle such as the right of every person to physical and psychological integrity: for example, the *Universal Declaration of Human Rights* (1948). Using this as our model, we might say that certain social practices, such as burial or marriage rituals, may properly vary from culture to culture as long as they do not violate universal human rights. Possession of such rights could be based on the criteria of rationality, free will, capacity for speech, being aware of oneself as a subject in the world, ability to experience pleasure and pain, etc., which determine the scope of moral consideration discussed below.[4] This solution blends objectivism and relativism into a reasonable and workable system.

Types of Normative Ethics

Normative ethics comprises the actual ethical theories. Normative ethics can be divided broadly into two categories: *virtue ethics* and *rule ethics*. Virtue ethics emphasizes the personality traits – the *character* – of the morally good person; rule ethics emphasizes adherence to guidelines of conduct. Generally speaking, ancient Greek philosophers took the virtue approach to ethics. In the *Republic*, Socrates describes the makeup of the character, or "soul," of the person of moral excellence, or *virtue* (*arête*). The "soul" (the Greek word is *psyche*) has three parts or, more accurately, aspects: the rational part seeks knowledge, including knowledge of moral goodness; the spirited part is vain and desires honor; and the appetitive part covets material gain and is inclined to satisfy physical pleasures (lines 436–45).[5] The "cardinal virtues" corresponding to these three aspects of the human psyche are wisdom, courage, and temperance. Moral excellence (justice) is a fourth, supreme, cardinal virtue that consists of each part of the soul functioning in harmony with the others, according to reason (lines 443d–e).[6] Justice of the soul – in contemporary terms what we would call psychological harmony or balance – is the *summum bonum* of human conduct. The person of virtue subjugates the spirited and appetitive parts of the soul to the rule of reason. Reason keeps the desire for honor and gratification in check, resulting in a well-ordered soul.

Aristotle was the first philosopher to use the word *ethics* (*ethike*). For Aristotle, the *summum bonum* of ethics was happiness, and reason played the central role. By "happiness," Aristotle meant not mere pleasure but a general sense of well-being (*eudaimonia*) – presaging the difference between Mill's qualitative hedonism and Bentham's quantitative hedonism, discussed below. Aristotle, like Plato, parsed the human soul into parts. In the *Nicomachean Ethics*, Aristotle (line 1098a) identifies different aspects of the soul, each with a certain function: one of nutrition and growth (which we share with plants and nonhuman animals), one of sense perception and locomotion (which we share with nonhuman animals), and reason (which is unique to us). Since "Nature . . . makes nothing in vain" (*Politics*: line 1253a8), reason must have some role in the realization of virtuous character.

Rationality is the mark of virtuous character because actions should express right reason (*Nicomachean Ethics*: line 1103b28). The person of virtuous character is able to determine accurately the "mean" between two vices – a vice of deficiency and a vice of excess (ibid.: lines 1106b36–1107a3). Philosophers refer to this principle as the Doctrine of the Mean. Thus the virtue of bravery is the mean between cowardice (a vice of deficiency) and foolhardiness (a vice of excess), as determined by reason. Ethics requires that a person with experience and practical wisdom uses reason to evaluate the support for alternative moral actions and acts accordingly. Choices in ethics "depend on particular facts," Aristotle notes, "and the decision rests with [the] perception" (line 1109b23) of the person with virtuous character informed by right reason.

Augustine (354–430) elucidated Plato's ideal of the well-ordered soul in Christian terms. In *The City of God*, Augustine writes: "If we were irrational animals, we should desire nothing beyond the proper arrangement of the body's parts and the satisfaction of our appetites. . . . But because there is in man a rational soul, he subordinates all that he has in common with the beasts to the peace of that rational soul" (1998: 940–1). Whereas for Plato a well-ordered soul is an end in and of itself, for Augustine a well-ordered soul is a means to a higher end beyond individual happiness. That higher end is obedience to God, à la Divine Command theory.

Augustine distinguishes between two types of people: those who are selfish (egoistic) and those who are selfless (unegoistic). The principle of conduct of the former type is autonomy; the principle of conduct of the latter type is heteronomy, or deference to authority. For Augustine, heteronomy is morally right and autonomy is morally wrong because acting autonomously is disobedient to God and commits the sin of hubris. Augustine uses this distinction to elucidate two types of societies (or "cities"): the City of God and the City of Man. The history of civilization, Augustine argues, is the history of the interaction of these two groups:

> Though there are a great many nations throughout the world, living according to different rites and customs, and distinguished by many different forms of language,

arms and dress, there nonetheless exist only two orders, as we may call them, of human society; and, following our Scriptures,[7] we may rightly speak of these as two cities. The one is made up of men who live according to the flesh, and the other of those who live according to the spirit. Each desires its own kind of peace, and, when they have found what they sought, each lives in its own kind of peace. (Ibid.: 581)

These two cities are idealized categories; actual cities are mixtures of the two: citizens of the City of God are identified not by political boundaries but, rather, by conduct and character. What distinguishes the two types of cities are their citizens. The principle of conduct of citizens of the City of God (i.e., the Christian city) is love of God. The principle of conduct of citizens of the City of Man (i.e., the pagan city) is love of self. Citizens of the City of God, using free will, turn to God in accordance to Divine Law; citizens of the City of Man, using free will, turn away from God in violation of Divine Law. Therefore, virtuous character is exemplified by persons who acquiesce to God's will, and debauched character is exemplified by persons who defy God's will.

Skeptics of supernaturalism will find Augustinian ethics problematic with regard to the standard of adequacy: Augustine founded his ethics on crucial supernaturalistic tenets that are not empirically verifiable. Nonetheless, virtue ethics is directly relevant in cases where moral agents stand either to improve or to damage their moral integrity, depending on the choices they make and the actions they take – an idea reminiscent of the *Crito*.

Some feminist philosophers have recently emphasized the virtue of caring for others. The Western tradition, they point out, has been characterized by a mis-guided emphasis on moral agents as discrete, atomistic selves. On the atomistic ontology of the self, individuals are discrete beings who make moral judgments about other individuals in a cool and detached way. This ontology of self is overtly masculine in that it emphasizes autonomy and sets the stage for competition in the marketplace. The failing of this ontology of self is that it does not appreci-ate the importance of the webs of relationships that constitute the social fabric into which individuals are woven. Feminist ontology of self emphasizes inter-dependence over autonomy. It is not so much that selves *have* relationships (the masculine model) as that selves *are* relationships (the feminine model).

American philosopher of education Nel Noddings highlights the importance in ethics of the ability to nurture reciprocal relationships of empathy and care. An ethics of care arises out of "that relation in which we respond . . . out of love or natural inclination. The relation of natural caring [is] the human condition that we, consciously or unconsciously, perceive as 'good.' It is that condition toward which we long and strive, and it is our longing for caring – to be in that special relation – that provides the motivation for us to be moral" (1984: 5). Persons of virtue are able to intuit the complexity of relationships that bind us together and act accordingly: "Many persons who live moral lives do not approach moral problems formally. Women, in particular, seem to approach moral problems by placing themselves as nearly as possible in concrete situations and assuming personal responsibility for the choices to be made. They define themselves in terms of caring" (ibid.: 8). Noddings's *summum bonum* is care, and the sign of moral virtue is the ability to create, nurture, and maintain relationships.

In virtue ethics, moral character is gauged in terms of some other notion of goodness. These notions vary widely: harmony of the soul (Plato), living a life of well-being in accordance with reason (Aristotle), obedience to God (Augustine), willingness to take a "leap of faith" (Kierkegaard), radical individuality (Nietzsche), and capacity for care (Noddings) are among them. Virtue ethics holds up role models that moral agents should emulate – "do as the Buddha would do" or "do as Jesus would do" (Johnson 2003).

The premise of virtue ethics is that the person of good character will have a predilection to do the right thing (although in specific circumstances may fail to do so). That is why we sometimes say that someone "acted out of character." Or the virtuous person may act according to one virtue rather than another when the two conflict. The virtuous person is able to use practical wisdom to determine the correct course of action when all things are considered.

What passes for a virtue of character is to some degree culturally relative (MacIntyre 1984: 131): some cultures may prize unflinching resolve and stoic forbearance, while others may not. American philosopher Martha Nussbaum asserts that some virtues, however, are cross-cultural and have withstood the test of time. Nussbaum (1993) identifies the virtues of honesty (the disposition to avoid deceit), fidelity (the disposition to keep one's promises, to be true to one's word), compassion (the disposition to assuage the suffering of others), courage (the disposition to remain faithful to what one believes, even when doing so poses risks), and integrity (the disposition to be true to one's values). In chapter 2 of this volume, Eric H. Gampel acknowledges the significance of these personal virtues in the process of moral reasoning by including virtue as a fundamental ethical principle for moral problem solving.

Many modern philosophers have found virtue ethics abstruse and have taken a new approach to ethics by formulating specific *rules* instead of worrying about the psychology of the morally good person.[8] In contrasting ancient with modern approaches, English philosopher Henry Sidgwick remarked in the late nineteenth century that ancient and medieval moral philosophers conceived of ethics as being:

> attractive rather than imperative. . . . For the chief characteristics of ancient ethical controversy as distinguished from modern may be traced to the employment of a generic notion instead of a specific one in expressing the common moral judgments on actions. Virtue or Right action is commonly regarded as only a species of the Good: and so, on this view . . . the first question that offers itself, when we endeavour to systematise conduct, is how to determine the relation of this species of good to the rest of the genus. It was on this question that the Greek thinkers argued, from first to last. (1962: 105–6)

More effective, the reasoning goes, would be to come up with moral rules or authoritative prescriptions (ibid.: 106) with the force of law.

An obvious way to formulate rules is by analyzing the *consequences* that altern-ative actions produce. On this approach, once the *summum bonum* is agreed on, rules effective in producing that good can be formulated. This good might be acting according to God's will (Divine Command theory), good will (deonto-logy), individual determination (existentialism), individual pleasure (egoistic hedonism), the rational escape from the state of nature (social contractarianism), or collective pleasure of society measured as a whole (utilitarianism). For the moment, we shall focus on utilitarianism, deontology, and social contractarianism.

Utilitarianism

Jeremy Bentham (1748–1832), in *The Principles of Morals and Legislation*, wastes no time in citing psychological hedonism as the starting point for ethics: "Nature has placed mankind under the governance of two sovereign masters, *pain* and *pleasure*" (1988: 1). On this foundation, Bentham immediately lays a consequentialist framework: "It is for [pain and pleasure] alone to point out what we ought to do, as well as to determine what we shall do. On the one hand the standard of right and wrong, on the other the chain of causes and effects, are fastened to their throne" (ibid.). An act is morally correct insofar as it produces the greatest amount of pleasure (or at least mitigates pain). But an individual's act is not to be calculated in terms of the pleasure or pain produced for that individual alone, but *collectively*.[9] The method of ethics turns into a cost/benefit analysis (ibid.: 29–32) that later commentators dubbed the "hedonistic calcu-lus." Moral agents should act to produce the most units of pleasure ("hedons"), collectively, as possible.

While Bentham measured pleasure quantitatively, his successor, John Stuart Mill (1806–73), characterized it as also differing qualitatively. In *Utilitarianism*, Mill notes that "it is quite compatible with the principle of utility to recognize the fact that some kinds of pleasure are more desirable and more valuable than others. It would be absurd that, while in estimating all other things quality is considered as well as quantity, the estimation of pleasure should be supposed to depend on quantity alone" (2001: 8). Mill identifies morally good action by the consequences it produces. The desirable consequence is happiness, which varies in both quantity and quality. The Principle of Utility weaves all these threads together in one moral rule by which alternative actions may be judged: "The creed which accepts as the foundation of morals 'utility' or the 'greatest happi-ness principle' holds that actions are right in proportion as they tend to promote happiness, wrong as they tend to produce the reverse of happiness. By happi-ness is intended pleasure and the absence of pain; by unhappiness, pain and the privation of pleasure" (ibid.: 7). Mill argues, in Aristotelian fashion, that all human beings desire pleasure (happiness) and the avoidance of pain. Diverging here from Bentham, Mill insists that ethics must consider both mental pleasure and phys-ical pleasure.

While the case could be made that mental pleasures are more instrumentally (extrinsically) valuable than physical pleasures (as they are safer, more durable, and less likely to lead to unpleasant after-effects, like hangovers or infection by sexually transmitted diseases), the better case to be made is that mental pleasures are actually more intrinsically valuable. Mill uses the "competent judge criterion" to make this argument. A competent judge is a person who has had experiences of roughly the same type (e.g., being a spectator of two several-hour-long events, such as watching the Daytona 500 in a sports bar and listening to a live performance of Stravinsky's *The Rite of Spring* at the London Philharmonic) and, after assessing the relative merits and demerits of each, decidedly prefers one over the other. As Mill puts it: "Of two pleasures, if there be one to which all or almost all who have experience of both give a decided preference, irrespective of any feeling of moral obligation to prefer it, that is the more desirable pleasure" (ibid.: 8). Mill believed certain pleasures are more mentally satisfying, and hence better. He is renowned for saying: "It is better to be a human being dissatisfied than a pig satisfied; better to be Socrates dissatisfied than a fool satisfied. And if the fool, or the pig, are of a different opinion, it is because they only know their own side of the question" (ibid.: 10).

We can see that egoism and utilitarianism share the psychological foundation of hedonism – the pursuit of pleasure and the avoidance of pain. The difference between egoism and utilitarianism is that egoism is individualistic hedonism and utilitarianism is collective hedonism. Bentham's utilitarianism is quantitative collective hedonism, however, and Mill's utilitarianism is qualitative collective hedonism.

In Mill's formulation of utilitarianism, there are two ways to implement the Principle of Utility: one is to assess alternate actions of each particular situation that arises in the course of one's life, and the other is to generate general rules calculated to create the greatest good in the long run. Interestingly, these two approaches are not always commensurate. One may decide that in a particular instance it is better to lie (or at least when talking to Grandma not to divulge the whole truth), while one may also decide that as a rule it is better to tell the whole truth despite the fact that in particular instances the greatest good will not result. Commentators have named these two approaches act-utilitarianism and rule-utilitarianism, respectively. Mill himself alludes to both approaches; he says at one point that an agent should consider whether actions would be "generally injurious" (ibid.: 19) – evoking a rule-utilitarian methodology – but remarks later that there will always be exceptions to generalized rules, and that the moral agent must therefore consider each situation individually (ibid.: 24) – evoking an act-utilitarian methodology. The debate about the relative merits of each approach is the topic of an enduring discussion in ethics.

Mill treats the sociopolitical implications of utilitarianism in greater detail in *On Liberty*, which states that a principle of liberty governs the political dynamics of individuals with the collective (1978: 1, 73). This principle deals with two spheres of individual actions: private actions that have no discernible public repercussion, and those that do. In the first case, if the idiosyncrasies of a chosen lifestyle are of no consequence to others, society has no right to limit liberty: "There is no room for entertaining any such question when a person's conduct affects the interests of no persons besides himself, or need not affect them unless they like. . . . In all such cases, there should be perfect freedom, legal and social, to do the action and stand the consequences" (ibid.: 73–4).

The most obvious instances of actions of the second sphere involve violent harm to others, either intentional or negligent, that fully justify punishment and abrogation of liberty (ibid.: 77). Harm to others can also be transmitted non-violently, such as by smoking cigarettes in public places. Less overt are transgressions of social duty and violation of the public trust that justify some kind of limitation of liberty: "When a person disables himself, by conduct purely self-regarding, from the performance of some definite duty incumbent to the public, he is guilty of a social offense. No person ought to be punished simply for being drunk; but a soldier or a policemen should be punished for being drunk on duty" (ibid.: 79–80).

The least obvious grounds for the limitation of liberty by society concern instances in which an individual, through harm to him- or herself, also exacts some sort of social cost. According to Mill, each individual has the right to liberty up to the point at which exercising that right infringes on the similar right of others to liberty and the pursuit of happiness. This principle is the under-pinning of liberal democracy – that is, democracy based on the value of liberty – and is the political justification for paternalism. Paternalistic laws limit freedom at that the point at which one person's actions interfere with the liberties of others and inhibit their ability to pursue happiness. Mandatory motorcycle helmet laws and bans against cigarette smoking in public are common paternalistic laws. The intent of these laws is to save society from footing the bill for foolish individual behavior.

The principle of liberty is analyzable in terms of utilitarianism. If individual choice, no matter how odd and eccentric, brings happiness to the agent and does not result in any significant harm to the collective, there is no ethical basis for limiting liberty. If the social cost trumps individual happiness, limitation of freedom is warranted. Or if choice brings happiness to an individual at a cost to others affected by those actions, liberty may be limited even by incarceration. A recurrent theme of the case studies in this book is the tension between individual liberty and the common good. Mill's ethics provide an outstanding resource for analyzing the dynamics of these tensions.

In the next chapter in this volume, Eric H. Gampel evokes the central lesson of utilitarianism – namely, the necessity of producing good and avoiding bad consequences – and then identifies three utilitarian moral principles: non-maleficence, beneficence, and utility. The principle of nonmaleficence prohibits harm. The principle of beneficence dictates help. More commonly, when the outcomes of an action are mixed, the principle of utility states that the ratio of harm to help should be kept as low as possible once the outcomes for all those affected are taken into consideration. Thus, an action is correct insofar as it produces the greatest ratio of benefit to harm, or the smallest ratio of harm to benefit, of all alternative actions.

In summary, the importance of the attention paid by utilitarianism to consequences cannot be overestimated. One of the very few certainties in ethics is that, *ceteris paribus*, good outcomes are better than bad outcomes. Even critics of utilitarianism admit the importance of outcomes; disagreement arises regarding the relationship of outcomes to other moral values, such as duty.

Deontology

Kant (1724–1804) believed that ethics must be built on law – not civil law, but rational law. He adopted the Christian emphasis of the importance of conformity to law but made reason, not God, its source. In order to achieve the nomothetic certainty attained by science, Kant grounded his ethics on the inherent properties of rationality. By deriving moral principles from the innate cognitive structure of all rational beings, he developed an ethical theory that is universally binding on all rational beings in all places at all times. The details of particular situations are thus irrelevant for ethics, for they have nothing to do with the universal dictates of reason. Herein lies the Kantian dismissal of relativism: ethics, by definition, is not relative to culture or to any contingencies of the human condition, but is grounded in the dictates of reason.

Since the ingredients for happiness change from person to person, Kant rejected any attempt to found ethics on happiness or the consequentialism that hedonism entails. The problem with grounding ethics on happiness, as Aristotle, Bentham, and Mill did, is that there is no *necessary* connection between happiness and morality. One might be happy and immoral (think of Alex in Anthony Burgess's *A Clockwork Orange*) or unhappy and moral (think of Viktor Frankl in Nazi concentration camps). Kant argues in the *Groundwork of the Metaphysics of Morals* that the *summum bonum* for ethics is not happiness but *good will* – that is, good intentions. The greatest good for the greatest number of people may be produced accidentally for the wrong reasons (such as the hope for fame and fortune) rather than from pure, morally good intentions. In Kant's view,

> [Nothing] can be regarded as good without qualification, except a good will. Intelligence, wit, judgment, and whatever talents of the mind one might want to name are doubtless in many respects good and desirable, as are such qualities of temperament as courage, resolution, perseverance. But they can also become extremely bad and harmful if the will, which is to make use of these gifts of nature and which in its special constitution is called virtue, is not good. . . . A good will is good not because of what it effects or accomplishes, nor because of its fitness to attain some proposed end; it is good only through its willing, i.e., it is good in itself. (1985: 7 [393])

Good will – acting on good intentions – is the only unqualified moral good. Other qualities of character are good if and only if a person has good will. Charisma or intelligence may be good or bad, depending on the leader who possesses it. A good will is good not because of the results it produces, as Mill asserted, but is good in and of itself. "Like a jewel," the will "shine[s] by its own light as something which has its full value in itself," regardless of whether the person is able to realize his or her good intentions (ibid.: 8 [394]).

A good will acts in accordance with *duty* (ibid.: 9 [397]), and this is the basis for defining Kant's ethical theory as "deontology" (from the ancient Greek word *deon*, meaning "duty"). Whereas acting on inclination is contingent on the particulars of a given situation, acting in accordance with duty is acting in accordance with moral law. The difference between duty and inclination marks the difference between ethically praiseworthy action and merely praiseworthy action. Kant uses the example of a shopkeeper. If the shopkeeper does not overcharge a child inexperienced in commercial transactions, it makes a difference whether the shopkeeper refrains out of fear of being discovered and punished or out of a sense of duty to charge the fair market price (ibid.: 10 [397]). The former action might be done in accordance with duty yet not done out of a sense of duty. In this volume, the duty to refrain from exploiting persons inexperienced in certain types of transactions, such as commercial transactions, arises in the bio-piracy case study, "Only God Can Make a Tree: Patenting Indigenous Plants" (see chapter 7).

Reason prescribes acting from duty and proscribes acting from inclination. To elaborate, Kant offers three summary propositions: (1) moral action emanates from duty, not inclination; (2) actions have moral worth due not to the results they produce but to the goodness of the will; and (3) duty is the necessity of acting out of respect for moral law (ibid.: 12–13 [399–400]). What is needed is a test to determine whether the intentions motivating an action flow from a sense of duty and are in agreement with moral law.

The test must take the form of an imperative that commands moral agents to act in accordance with duty. Kant identifies two types of imperatives: hypothetical and categorical (ibid.: 25 [414]). Hypothetical imperatives take an "if . . . then" form: If you want to achieve X, then do Y. If you want to score well on the LSAT (X), for example, then study for it (Y). But since moral law must be universally (i.e., categorically) binding, hypothetical imperatives cannot be moral laws. Hypothetical imperatives are practical imperatives for those who want to achieve certain ends; since not all of us want to attend law school, the advice about studying for the LSAT is not universally applicable. Therefore the deontologist could say that utilitarianism is a system of hypothetical imperatives, and hence has nothing to do with morality.

Laws are laws insofar AS they are universal (ibid.: 34 [426]). Moral law is universal and legislates that moral agents act always in accordance with duty. The moral imperative must hold categorically – taking the form of "Do Y!" – and must not be contingent on any extraneous circumstances. Hence the Categorical Imperative for ethics: "Act only on that subjective statement of intention through which you can at the same time will that it should become a universal moral law" (ibid.: 30 [421]). Now think of yourself for a moment. As a rational being, you recognize that the value of your existence extends beyond your use-value for other people. Your existence is value independent of the instrumental value you also happen to have for other people's needs or desires; that is, you have intrinsic value in and of yourself. Since you cannot will, as a general rule, that rational beings have value only to the extent that they are valuable for others' ends, it follows that the first formulation of the Categorical

Imperative entails a second: "Act in such a way that you treat humanity, whether in your own person or in the person of another, always at the same time as an end and never simply as a means" (ibid.: 36 [429]). Since rational beings exist as ends in themselves, each rational being is intrinsically valuable and ought never to have this value denied. The second instantiation of the Categorical Imperative provides the rationale for the inherent respect for persons and provides the bulwark against the utilitarian rationale for forsaking individual rights for the common good.

An agent capable of conformity to the Categorical Imperative recognizes as a logical consequence that just as one ought not be a means to others' ends, neither can others be a means to one's own ends. This reciprocal recognition of oneself and others comprising a community bound by moral law means that each agent is at once legislator and citizen, drafting and obeying those laws simultaneously:

> For all rational beings stand under the law that each of them should treat himself and all others never merely as means but always at the same time as an end in himself. Hereby arises a systematic union of rational beings through common objective laws, i.e., a kingdom that may be called a kingdom of ends (certainly only an ideal), inasmuch as these laws have in view the very relation of such beings to one another as ends and means.
>
> A rational being belongs to the kingdom of ends as a member when he legislates in it universal laws while also being himself subject to these laws. He belongs to it as sovereign, when as legislator he is himself subject to the will of no other. (Ibid.: 39–40 [433])

The class of rational agents that at once wills and obeys universal moral law constitutes a community – the "kingdom of ends" – and circumscribes the scope of beings worthy of moral consideration. If one recognizes the universally binding strength of the Categorical Imperative, one is a citizen of the Kingdom of Ends. Citizens of the Kingdom of Ends are both sovereigns and vassals of moral laws. Thankfully, all citizens of the Kingdom of Ends will draft the exact same set of laws as prescribed by the Categorical Imperative.

Reciprocity of respect is a key part of Kant's ethics. Moral law entails the recognition of the reciprocity of mutual respect among all members of the Kingdom of Ends, and requires each member of the community to help every other member achieve individual goals as long as pursuing those goals does not conflict with moral law. Kant makes reciprocity of respect explicit in *The Metaphysics of Morals*: "Any action is *right* if it can coexist with everyone's freedom in accordance with a universal law, or if on its maxim the freedom of choice of each can coexist with everyone's freedom in accordance with a universal law" (1996: 24). Ethics is thus pre-eminently *public* insofar as calculations of alternate actions need to be constantly referenced to the moral community, the Kingdom of Ends – a theme that can be traced through every case study in this book.

The way to use the Categorical Imperative is to take a subjective statement of intention and universalize it. If it can logically be universalized, it passes the test and can be acted on. If a contradiction occurs in the process of universalizing a subjective statement of intention, it does not pass the test and must be rejected. Kant gives four examples (1985: 30–2 [422–3]), which are of two types:

straightforward logical contradictions and inconsistencies in the treatment of members of the Kingdom of Ends. Kant's first two examples illustrate straightforward logical contradictions. Consider example two. Suppose your subjective statement of intention is: (i) "When I need money, I will lie in order to get it." Universalized, according to the Categorical Imperative, the subjective statement of intention becomes: (ii) "When anyone is in need of money, anyone should lie in order to get it." Statement (i) implies a world in which people generally tell the truth (World T), for that is only the kind of world that would enable lying in order to get money. Statement (ii) implies a world in which no one tells the truth (World not-T). Therefore, the subjective statement of intention is a straightforward logical contradiction when universalized.

Now consider example one. Someone is suffering from depression and considering suicide. The universalized subjective statement of intention would be: "If anyone is depressed and fails to see any value or purpose in continued existence, then he or she should end his/her life." Willing suicide is a logical contradiction because one cannot simultaneously will to respect oneself (World R) and will to disrespect oneself by destroying oneself (World not-R).

Examples three and four illustrate the other complication in universalization. They are not logical contradictions like examples one and two, because some subjective statements of intention are consistent but problematic. In example three the universalized subjective statement of intention, "I will squander my unique talents" (athleticism, musicality, religiosity, etc.), for instance, makes sense in a world in which everybody squanders their natural aptitudes (World S). There is no logical inconsistency between the world implied by the subjective statement of intention and the world implied by the universalization. Instead there is a different kind of problem: the universalization results in unacceptable disrespect within the framework of the Kingdom of Ends. One cannot will to squander one's natural talents or refuse to help others in need (as in example four) because both the subjective statement of intention and the universalized imperative would fail to recognize rational moral agents as intrinsically valuable ends in themselves. Given these illustrations, it is clear that consequences do matter for Kant, but they are not the sole determining factors of morality as in Utilitarianism.

Kant's contribution to ethics is the idea that people are bound in a moral community. The glue that binds this community is mutual respect: each person commands respect from others and accedes to others' commands for respect. As utilitarianism did, deontology gave rise to several moral principles: specifically, respect for autonomy and individual rights. Citizens of the Kingdom of Ends deserve to be respected as autonomous and self-determining individuals. Citizens of the Kingdom of Ends have rights that cannot be transgressed for the ends of others or even for the common good.

Social contractarianism

The third major rule-based ethical theory is social contractarianism, outlined by John Locke (1632–1704) and Jean-Jacques Rousseau (1712–78), but initially

and most importantly by the English philosopher Thomas Hobbes (1588–
1650). Unlike the ancient Greeks, who thought of political bodies as *natural*
products of human association, Hobbes believed that political bodies are
artificial constructions (1996: 7) aimed at resolving disputes so that humans
might live together as peaceably as possible. In *Leviathan*, Hobbes gives a hypothetical explanation of how humans beings came together out of an anarchic
"state of nature" to form civil society. He does not intend his outline to be a
literal historical account, but rather a philosophical justification for civil society,
and an ethical justification for civil societies to censure and punish those who
do not heed the social contract.

Hobbes's ethical theory, like utilitarianism, rests on a psychological foundation. This foundation is one of egoism, unlike Mill's appeal to the common good
(or unegoism). According to Hobbes, all humans want to achieve their goals,
which brings us into strife with one another, since all inevitably compete for the
same things, such as mates, shelter, food, and luxuries (ibid.: 83). In our natural state, each of us is predisposed to engage in continual warfare, and each of
us has a natural right to do whatever we can to protect ourselves and attain our
goals; egoistically, anything else would be irrational. While all persons have a
natural right to protect themselves and their property, continually exercising this
right causes relentless aggression, which makes civilization itself impossible. In
humans' natural state:

> [T]here is no place for industry; because the fruit thereof is uncertain: and conse-
> quently no culture of the earth; no navigation, nor use of the commodities that
> may be imported by sea; no commodious building; no instruments of moving, and
> removing such things as require much force; no knowledge of the face of the earth;
> an account of time; no arts; no letters; no society; and which is worst of all,
> continual fear, and danger of violent death; and the life of man, solitary, poor, nasty,
> brutish, and short. (Ibid.: 84)

Egoistic prudence mandates individuals to get out of this grim state of incessant
barbarity. Fortunately, the discovery of the Laws of Nature, which are dictates
of reason, makes this possible. The fundamental Law of Nature, a precept of
egoism, states that people cannot act contrary to self-interest. "It is a precept,
or general rule of reason, that every man, ought to endeavour peace, as far as
he has hope of obtaining it; and when he cannot obtain it, that he may seek,
and use, all helps, and advantages of war" (ibid.: 87; italics omitted). The Second
Law of Nature prescribes the willingness, if others are willing as well, to forswear
the natural right to engage in violence and to transfer this right to a "sovereign"
who is not party to the social contract. This second law is the foundation for a
"social contract" that directs a mutual transfer of the forsworn natural rights to
a sovereign (ibid.: 89).

A covenant, or pact, is needed to back up the contract and establish a
commonwealth, or civil society. The covenant charges those involved in the
contract to promise each other to make the contract permanent and to trust
that others will do so as well (ibid.). The Third Law of Nature logically follows:

"that men perform their covenants made: without which, covenants are in vain, and but empty words" (ibid.: 95; italics omitted). Once the covenant is secured, the contractarians's natural right to exercise violence is transferred to a sovereign leader, and a civil government is formed (ibid.: 114). Only the government has the right to judge citizens' guilt or innocence and mete out punishment (ibid.: 120). Citizens no longer possess a right of retribution; those who take retribution into their own hands are vigilantes.

Ethics thus lays the foundation for political *justice*. Upholding one's covenant is ethical; breaking one's covenant is unethical. Justice has no existence prior to the state (as it does for Plato, Aristotle, Augustine, and Aquinas); justice is the a posteriori product of the establishment of a commonwealth, and distinguishes Hobbes's modern method from those of his ancient and medieval predecessors.

Interestingly, because communities are complex networks of individuals and subgroups, covenants within communities can collide. In this volume, in the case study in chapter 5 on the murder of an infant, "Deadly Secrets: Releasing Confidential Medical Records to Law-Enforcement Officers," the apparent covenant of privacy between Planned Parenthood and women seeking its services collides with the covenant of public safety between law-enforcement officials and the community. In the case study on the student arrested for writing an essay with violent images (chapter 8), "Words Fail: Institutional Responses to Creative Violence," the apparent covenant between teachers and families to implement pedagogical methods that actualize students' creative potential collides with a concomitant covenant of teachers and families to prohibit students from inciting violence.

In *A Theory of Justice*, the American philosopher John Rawls (1921–2002) greatly enhances and refines social contractarianism. Rather than assuming anything about the actual historical human condition, Rawls appeals to a hypothetical "original position." The original position is an imaginary assembly of rational persons who have not yet entered into a social contract to form a civil society. In this hypothetical situation, these rational persons have no knowledge or inclination of what accidental attributes they may possess in real life – whether they might be rich or poor, black or white, bright or dim, talented or not, religious or nonreligious (1971: 12). Rawls calls this lack of knowledge about one's real position in a real society after the formation of a social contract a "veil of ignorance." Rawls's idea is that, in this situation, moral agents will not focus on the specifics of social organization, but instead on untainted abstract principles of justice on which the political structure should be devised (ibid.: pp. 136–7). As biological beings, we do not have control over "accidents of natural endowment" (ibid.: 15), but as moral agents we do have the power to mitigate these inequalities as much as possible within a just political framework.

Rawls assumes that the moral agents entering the social contract are both rational and reasonable: rational insofar as each citizen is able to identify and pursue his or her own good (ibid.: 408), reasonable insofar as each is able to get along with others (i.e., the contractarians are not antisocial). In the original position, it is rational and reasonable to agree collectively on two principles of justice on which civil society is to be founded. The first is an equal liberty principle that holds that "each person is to have an equal right to the most extensive basic liberty compatible with similar liberty for others" (ibid.: 60). The second is a difference and equal opportunity principle that holds that "social and economic inequalities are to be arranged so that they are both (a) reasonably expected to be to everyone's advantage, and (b) attached to positions and offices open to all" (ibid.). Inequalities in the distribution of wealth are justified if those inequalities redound to the good of the least well off (e.g., paying physicians higher wages so that the rest will benefit from quality healthcare).

It should be noted that Rawls's ethics, though generally cast in the framework of social contract theory, has consequentialist as well as deontological elements. For example, moral agents in the original position, behind a veil of ignorance, are to choose principles of justice according to a duty to secure well-being for all those involved without knowing the material conditions of those people. At the same time, though, those principles are to be chosen with an eye to producing the most favorable consequences for all those involved. If some citizens end up in a state of poverty and squalor and these disadvantages cannot be justified by the given social arrangements of society as a whole, then the social arrangements are unjust and the social contract is unethical.

Social contractarianism is directly relevant to many of the case studies examined in this book, particularly in public policy issues where discrimination on the basis of some attribute irrelevant to the social contract – race, religion, sex, income – is an issue.

The three pioneering theories of modern ethics – utilitarianism, deontology, and social contractarianism – are not without serious problems. Each theory has been energetically criticized and defended, and all are subjects of book-length treatments. Let us look briefly at some of the common criticisms of each theory.

Feminist philosophers have criticized all three theories because they overemphasize reason. Through empirical studies, American psychologist Carol Gilligan (1982) concludes that women tend to make moral judgments not through reason and adherence to rigid and abstract principles but, rather, on relationships and how webs of relationships are effected by moral actions. Building on Gilligan's research, philosopher Annette Baier (1986: 249) argues that there is little hope of melding the mainstream obsession with rigid principles in Western ethics with the empirical lessons of Gilligan's research. Ethics based on cool reason and detached analysis ignores morally relevant considerations such as compassion, caring, empathy, and love. In Baier's estimation:

> [Modern philosophers have] managed to relegate to the mental background the web of trust tying most moral agents to one another, and to focus their philosophical attention . . . single-mindedly on cool, distanced relations between more or less free and equal adult strangers. . . . Relations between equals and nonintimates will *be* the moral norm for adult males whose dealings with others are mainly business or restrained social dealings with similarly placed males. But for lovers, husbands, fathers, the ill, the very young, and the elderly, other relationships with their moral potential and perils will loom larger. (Ibid.: 248)

In reaffirming the importance of sentiment, feminist moral philosophy echoes the emotivism of Hume and rejects the rationalism of Kant. In Noddings's view, "An ethic built on caring is . . . characteristically and essentially feminine[;] . . . an ethic of caring arises . . . out of our experience as women, just as the traditional logical approach to ethical problems arises more obviously from masculine experience" (1984: 8).

Aside from emotivists' and feminists' sweeping condemnation of ethical theory as being obsessed with reason, each ethical theory is the target of more distinct criticisms. Utilitarianism, in particular, has been criticized on the bases that it justifies injustice and overlooks special relationships. The first allegation has manifold permutations, but the most significant problem might be called the "majority/minority" problem: the good of individuals or groups of individuals constituting a minority can be justifiably sacrificed for the collective good using the Principle of Utility. A mundane example is this: Farmer John has been cultivating land owned by his family for five generations; he feels close to the land, and farming is his raison d'être. A population surge has ignited the expansion of exurbia into the bucolic community where Farmer John resides, bringing with it traffic and congestion. City planners have drafted a proposal to build a six-lane connector highway right through the middle of Farmer John's fields. Farmer John is unwilling to sell his land at any price, so the city planners intend to take the land by eminent domain. According to the Principle of Utility, if taking his land will cause five thousand units of pain to Farmer John but building the road will create ten thousand units of pleasure (in the form of convenience) – one unit for each of the ten thousand people who will be able to get home more quickly at the end of a long workday – then public policy is clear: take Farmer John's land! Even though the ratio of his individual suffering to the suffering of each commuter who cannot get home quite as fast is five thousand to one, the collective benefit outweighs the individual cost two to one. The problem with this, a deontologist would reflexively retort, is that Farmer John has the *right* to keep his land, regardless of the will of the majority. He has done nothing wrong and does not deserve to suffer. (Similar arguments condoning slavery could be made using the Principle of Utility.) One thing is clear: the cost/benefit methodology of utilitarianism makes it amenable to economic analysis, and consequently it often serves as a "moral" rationale for public policy. Our culture is distinctively utilitarian. Note again, though, that the concept of fairness (getting what one deserves) did not apply to Farmer John because Farmer John did nothing wrong but was caused overt harm by public policy decisions.

The second problem is the impersonal nature of utilitarianism: it does not consider special relationships. Say you are a parent and your teenage son will soon be graduating from high school – theoretically. But your son skips school, doesn't study, barely passes his classes, stays up late drinking and smoking and playing video games and sleeps until noon the next day, hangs out with unsavory types, and generally, at least in your view, lacks motivation, focus, and purpose. This is vexing because you had hoped that he would attend a prestigious private college, for which you are well able to pay. You harbor a lingering idealism from the heady days of the 1960s, optimistic that individuals can initiate social change and make the world a better place. As an engaged citizen worried about injustice and human suffering, you believe it is your obligation to try to make the world a better place. You had hoped that your son would become a physician, social activist, or civil rights lawyer – someone who would improve the human condition. Just down the street is a young woman who is the same age as your son. Unlike your son, she is focused, driven to achieve, and exemplifies a social consciousness you admire. She told you yesterday in her family's dry-cleaning business that she would like to study medicine, join Doctors Without Borders or the Peace Corps, and work in free health clinics in Africa. Unfortunately, her family cannot afford post-secondary education and she will likely spend her adult life running the family business.

Assume that, given your finite income, you cannot send both your son and the neighbor to college, and that it is crystal clear to you that sending your son will result in no social benefit whatsoever and a legacy of public intoxication arrests. On the other hand, sending the young woman to college would result in significant social good. According to the Principle of Utility, you should let you own son waste his life playing video games and smoking marijuana and send the neighbor to college. Critics of utilitarianism note that parents have special obligations to their own children over other children, a relationship that the Principle of Utility fails to recognize.

Deontology, as articulated by Kant, is also subject to pointed criticisms. One that looms large is the problem of ethical absolutism. If ethical rules are absolute, then there should be no ambiguity in adhering to them in any given situation. Unfortunately for ethical absolutism, adherence to one exceptionless imperative sometimes seems to violate another. Consider the following example. Suppose you are on a ski vacation in Utah and are riding the aerial tramway at Snowbird. Suddenly, a snowboarder rips open his baggy jacket and shouts, "Save the red squirrel! No ski resorts! Earth first!" Under his jacket you see an explosive vest. With one deft move you could jab your ski pole in his neck from behind, subverting his ability to detonate the blast and saving all 119 persons onboard – and most likely killing him. You recall from your college Introduction to Ethics course that killing him would violate the categorically binding imperative never to take a human life. You use your keen intellect to do a lighting-quick Kantian calculation, reasoning that the subjective statement of intention, "I should act as to prevent the loss of human life whenever possible," can be universalized into another categorically binding imperative: "Anyone should act to prevent the loss of human life whenever possible." As a moral agent, you confront two mutually exclusive absolute moral duties. Mill's advice would be unequivocal: kill the deranged ecological saboteur. Kant would say that if the young man sets off the blast, the moral turpitude of murder rests on his shoulders, not yours: the proximate cause of death would be the actions of the eco-terrorist, not your failure to take his life. But the price you pay for this moral courage is death (yours and the other 118 persons on the tram). So is adhering to a categorical prohibition against taking a human life the right thing to do in this situation?

Social contractarianism is problematic with regard to the standard of comprehensiveness. It lays the foundation for ethical relations between rational individuals but is technically silent on obligations to nonrational beings. Beings that seem worthy of moral consideration, such as nonhuman animals (on the basis of their capacity to suffer) and profoundly retarded persons (on the basis of respect for people), are excluded from the social contract on the basis that they lack rationality and hence cannot be party to a mutually agreed-on social pact. This cannot justify treating profoundly retarded persons unequally from normal persons or harming nonhuman animals and causing suffering. "Unless some way can be found to remedy this difficulty," American philosopher James Rachels remarked, "the verdict must be that the basic idea of the theory is deeply flawed" (1986: 138).

In summary, the three great theories of modern ethics – utilitarianism, deontology, and social contractarianism – are problematic, yet no ethical analysis could be considered comprehensive if it did not take into consideration their central principles. Even if the consequences of one action are horrendous compared with its alternative, the moral agent should at least take pause to consider acting against duty; even if one's duty is crystal clear, the moral agent should at least pause to consider the consequences of that action.

To use the language of Gampel's CARVE schema, outlined in chapter 2, we will all be faced with problems that require us to determine the scope of moral consideration of the beings involved and consider:

C: the consequences of various alternatives, including inaction, both for individuals and for the common good;
A: which actions will best respect persons or their autonomy;
R: the presence, nature, and comparative strength of intrinsic rights;
V: how different actions may develop virtuous character in and affect the moral integrity of the persons involved – whether as agents or as patients;
E: the relationship of individuals with civil society as a whole and whether agents ought to treat others equally or fairly (i.e., justly).

In short, we must learn to CARVE moral dilemmas (a process to which we will turn in the next chapter) from the varied topography of the human condition into problems we can grapple with to the best of our abilities.

In the hyperbolic example of the snowboarding eco-terrorist, and many actual situations, both consequences and duties must be taken into consideration in ethical dilemmas. If you respect *autonomy* and the *right* of the eco-terrorist independently of the details of this particular situation, you could be criticized for turning a blind eye to the *consequences* of not incapacitating him. If you kill him, you carry the moral burden of taking a human life. Of course, you might justifiably conclude that the terrorist has violated the social contract through his threat of violence, and thus has relinquished his right to equal treatment and respect. Since adherence to all principles is not possible in this situation, the only rational way to proceed is through a careful analysis of all the relevant moral principles and their relative weight in the context of the problem. A framework for such an analysis is outlined by Gampel.

Beyond the nuance of theory itself is the metaethical question: Which methodology (virtue ethics or rule ethics) is primary? The answer is that while virtue and rule ethics are two types of ethical theories, they are interrelated. For example, if you are a parent raising children, you want to help them develop virtues. In order to do that, you probably impose some set of rules (don't lie, don't harm, don't steal). Virtue ethics thus presupposes rules: it is hard to know which dispositions (virtues) to cultivate without reference to some kind of rules.

An individual who lacks virtue will have no motivation to follow rules and may choose instead to ignore them. There is no reason to subscribe to rules unless you have a disposition to do so. Rule ethics thus presupposes virtuous character. In Aristotelian ethics, for example, the Doctrine of the Mean is unmistakably rule-like, and it takes a person of virtue (practically wise) to discern the mean. In Augustinian ethics, persons with good character have the proclivity to adhere to rules reflecting God's will (as outlined in the Decalogue, for instance). These rules provide a blueprint for developing good character. In Kantian ethics, there would be no motivation to observe moral law unless one possessed the virtue of good will. Although seldom noticed by those who study Kant, Kantian justifications of a particular action involve a virtue-ethics dimension insofar as acting in accordance to duty requires good intentions.

So while the distinction between virtue ethics and rule ethics has pedagogical value, in the end it is an artificial dichotomy. Virtue ethics and rule ethics are pieces of a whole.

The Scope of Ethics: Who (or What) Matters?

Ethical theories provide conceptual frameworks to help moral agents make decisions and to guide their actions. Yet the questions remain: What is the proper subject-matter of ethics? Exactly *who* or *what* should be counted in ethical deliberations and actions? What attribute or essence defines the class of beings worthy of moral consideration?

From Socrates to Sartre, philosophers of the Western tradition have held that humans, and humans only, are the proper subject-matter of ethics; that is, only humans are worthy of moral consideration. Rationality is the attribute that defines the class of beings worthy of moral consideration. This human-centered, or "anthropocentric," bias holds that rationality is the necessary condition for demanding moral consideration. Socrates espoused a human-centered perspective when he claimed, while walking with a companion outside the city walls of Athens, "Trees and open country won't teach me a thing, whereas people in the town do" (*Phaedrus*: line 230d). In suggesting, obliquely but repeatedly, that a "human being" is a "rational animal," Aristotle distinguished humans from nonhuman animals, conferring on us special status. Two millennia later, the French philosopher René Descartes (1596–1650) argued that rationality is a function of the immortal soul. Thinking and speaking are functions of the soul. Humans possess immortal souls that nonhumans lack. "The reason why animals do not speak as we do is not that they lack the organs," Descartes explained, "but that they have no thoughts" (1991: 303). Since only humans have immortal souls, humans have no more ethical obligations to nonhumans than they have to machines – a view of nonhuman animals that is at the foundation of modern factory farming.

Kant agreed with Descartes that we have no direct ethical duties to nonhuman animals, but disagreed that we have *no* ethical obligations to animals whatsoever. He believed that we have duties to some nonrational beings that transcend utility:

> If a dog, for example, has served his master long and faithfully, that is an analogue of merit; hence I must reward it, and once the dog can serve no longer, must look after him to the end, for I thereby cultivate my duty to humanity, as I am called on to do; so if the acts of animals arise out of the same *principium* from which human actions spring, and the animal actions are analogues of this, we have duties to animals, in that we thereby promote the cause of humanity. (1997: 212)[10]

The way we treat nonhumans, that is, will likely affect the way we treat fellow humans, "for he who is cruel to animals becomes hard also in his dealing with men" (ibid.). "Thus our duties to animals are indirectly duties to humanity" (ibid.: 213). Treating nonhumans "inhumanly" may not be wrong per se, but mistreating nonhumans will lead to the mistreatment of fellow humans, a direct violation of the Categorical Imperative framed in the Kingdom of Ends.

The thoroughgoing anthropocentrism of Western ethics was not called into question until the mid-to-late twentieth century, and the last several decades have marked a sea change in ethical thinking. Contemporary philosopher Tom Regan (1983) argues that the standard of rationality (and allied criterion of speech) for moral consideration is too narrow. It should be widened, he says, to include "subjects-of-a-life." A subject-of-a-life is any being with an awareness of itself as a subject in the world. Chimpanzees looking in mirrors are an example of Regan's concept. They understand that the image in front of them is not another chimpanzee but is *them* (Gallup 1970), indicating that they have an awareness of themselves as subjects in the world of chimpanzees.

Other animal ethicists argue that this scope, albeit wider than anthropocentrism, is still too narrow because it applies only to mammals distinguished by highly centralized nervous systems. Philosopher Peter Singer insists that Bentham was absolutely right in pegging the criterion for moral consideration not to rationality, as Descartes and Kant did, but to the capacity to suffer, the ability to experience pain. Singer (2002: 7) quotes Bentham approvingly:

> The day *may* come when the rest of the animal creation may acquire those rights which never could have been withholden from them but by the hand of tyranny. . . . It may one day come to be recognized that the number of the legs, the villosity of the skin, or the termination of the *os sacrum* [the end of the spinal cord], are reasons equally insufficient for abandoning a sensitive being to the same fate. What else is it that should trace the insuperable line? Is it the faculty of reason, or, perhaps, the faculty of discourse? But a full-grown horse or dog is beyond comparison a more rational, as well as a more conversable animal, than an infant of a day, or a week, or even a month, old. But suppose the case were otherwise, what would it avail? The question is not, Can they *reason*? nor, Can they *talk*? but, Can they *suffer*? (Bentham 1988: 311n.)

In formulating animal ethics, Singer did not invent a new class of beings worthy of moral consideration; he creatively and consistently applied the Principle of Utility to nonhuman animals.

The consequences for ethics of this move are profound: the scope of moral consideration is not limited to human individuals or subjects-of-a-life, but encompasses any being capable of suffering. This includes, most obviously, the higher mammals included in Regan's theory, but also other vertebrates, such as poultry, that may not exhibit much in the way of self-awareness but that can experience pain.

The animal ethics of Regan and Singer reject the traditional narrow scope of anthropocentrism and lay the groundwork for non-anthropocentric ethics. For Singer and Regan, rationality and the ability to speak and write are no more ethically relevant than skin color or degree of hairiness. While this direction is an improvement on the myopic focus of mainstream Western ethics, Paul Taylor (1986) believes that it *still* does not go far enough. Every entity that has inherent value – that is, value in and of itself independent of any instrumental value the entity might have for others – is worthy of moral consideration. An entity has inherent value if it exhibits goal-directed (teleological, in the jargon of philosophy) activity. An entity that exhibits goal-directed activity may be helped to achieve its ends or harmed.

All living things meet this standard of inherent value because all organisms have an end – namely, to live and flourish. All living things are worthy of moral consideration: "All organisms, whether conscious or not, are teleological centers of life in the sense that each is a unified, coherently ordered system of goal-oriented activities that has a constant tendency to protect and maintain the organism's existence" (ibid.; 122). Thus the locus of moral consideration for Taylor is not being human (Kant), being a subject-of-a-life (Regan), or being sentient (Bentham and Singer), but rather being alive. This ethic is thus *biocentric* – centered on life.

Pathogens, such as bacteria and other micro-organisms, are living things (viruses are borderline cases), so the biocentrist must provide a method for adjudicating mutually exclusive interests of the biota. For example, the eradication of *Mycobacterium tuberculosis*, the bacterium which causes tuberculosis, is a necessary condition for the flourishing of *Homo sapiens*. The Principle of Self-Defense makes it "permissible for moral agents to protect themselves against dangerous or harmful organisms by destroying them" (ibid. 1986: 264–5), such as killing *Mycobacterium tuberculosis*.

As Singer reconfigured utilitarianism to meet the demands of non-anthropocentrism posed by nonhuman suffering, so Taylor reconfigured deontology to meet the demands of non-anthropocentrism posed by the goal-directed activity of all living things, essentially granting a new type of citizenship in Kant's Kingdom of Ends for nonrational living things:

> In addition to and independently of whatever moral obligations we might have toward our fellow humans, we also have duties that are owed to wild living things in their own right. . . . Our duties toward the Earth's non-human forms of life are

grounded on their status as entities possessing inherent worth. They have a kind of value that belongs to them by their very nature, and it is this value that makes it wrong to treat them as if they existed as mere means to human ends. It is for *their* sake that their good should be promoted or protected. Just as humans should be treated with respect, so should they. (Ibid.: 13)

Taylor's biocentric ethics points to a major difference between being a moral agent and being morally considerable: moral agents are aware of themselves (as in Kant and Regan) and aware of their moral obligations to other beings (explicit in the thinking of Socrates, Mill, and Kant). Other entities are not moral agents but nonetheless are worthy of moral consideration. A damning fallacy of anthropocentric ethics is associating the *class of moral agents* with the *class of beings deserving of moral respect*. Some beings such as frogs, cats, babies, profoundly retarded persons, and even sociopaths are not moral agents, but still demand inclusion in moral calculations. Moral agents are thus obligated, out of a sense of duty, to respect all beings with inherent value, whether or not those beings also happen to be moral agents themselves.

Biocentric ethics holds that moral agents have two sets of duties: one set to other moral agents, and the other set to all entities who are not moral agents themselves but are nonetheless worthy of moral consideration.

The foregoing theories are all individualistic; that is, all root the locus of moral consideration in individual beings. The American ecologist Aldo Leopold (1887–1948), who opposed individualism in ethics, fomented a revolution. He argued that it is not individual organisms that are the proper locus of moral consideration, but rather *entire ecological communities*. This holistic emphasis in ethics departs from 2,500 years of Western ethics. It is perhaps telling that such a revolution would come from an ecologist, not a philosopher.

In *A Sand County Almanac* Leopold points out that during the evolution of the Western tradition, moral consideration has been expanded to include individuals of previously excluded groups, such as blacks and women. "During the three thousand years which have since elapsed, ethical criteria have been extended to many fields of conduct, with corresponding shrinkages in those judged by expediency only" (1960: 202). (If Leopold had not been several decades ahead of his time, he might have included the categories of sentient beings and living beings discussed above.) Just as the domain of moral consideration has expanded to include more human individuals, Leopold argues it should be further expanded to include entire ecological communities, or ecosystems. Leopold calls this new moral philosophy Land Ethics.[11]

As parts of ecosystems, human beings are citizens not only of human communities but also of larger biotic communities. Our dual citizenship fundamentally alters the relationship of humans to ecosystems: "a land ethic changes the role of *Homo sapiens* from conqueror of the land-community to plain member and citizen of it" (ibid.: 204). Ecosystems are not simply something to conquer, to tame, to order; indeed, humans ought to act with honor and respect as citizens of biotic communities.

Leopold explicitly addresses the tension between environmental ethics and economics – a common theme throughout the present book. The major obstacle to achieving an ecological ethic, he notes, is the economic worldview. Currently, human relations with ecosystems are guided only by human economic interests. To understand Leopold, it is useful to refer back to the source of the economic ethic that is the source of his pillory, the theory of the creation of private property outlined by English philosopher John Locke. In *The Second Treatise of Government*, Locke (1987: 16–30) conjectures that God gave humankind the Earth in common for use as a natural resource for our well-being. Each individual "owns" his or her own body, and labor is a function of the body. Once one applies one's labor to the unproductive pool of natural resources to make it productive – by clearing forest, moving rocks, plowing the soil, and planting crops – one is entitled to the fruits of that labor. Through work, humans pull resources out of the common pool and secure the products of that labor for themselves as private property. This is the essence of private property, and it is based on the fundamental assumption that the value of natural resources is latent, in the sense that the value in resources must be actualized by human labor. Nature itself has no inherent value; human beings, through labor, can transform the latent resource value of ecosystems into useful products. Humans should "release" as much value from ecosystems as possible through development.

In the economic model, the value of ecosystems is its resource value, its instrumental value as property. In the ecological model, ecosystems are living things with value above and beyond economic value. In a word, ecosystems have intrinsic value as biotic communities in which we are citizens. The problem with economic ethics is that they are ill-suited to recognize non-economic (read: "ecological") types of value. "A system of conservation based solely on economic self-interest is hopelessly lopsided," Leopold claims in *A Sand County Almanac*. "It tends to ignore, and thus eventually to eliminate, many elements in the land community that lack commercial value, but that are (as far as we know) essential to its healthy functioning" (1960: 214). The triumph of achieving an ethical relationship with ecosystems requires recognizing the intrinsic value that ecological systems have far beyond their mere Lockean economic value.

All poignant and powerful ethical theories are reducible to one memorable maxim (e.g., Aristotle's Doctrine of the Mean; the Golden Rule of Jesus, Hillel, and Confucius; Mill's Principle of Utility; Kant's Categorical Imperative). Leopold provides a similar summarization of ecological ethics: "A thing is right when it tends to preserve the integrity, stability, and beauty of the biotic community. It is wrong when it tends otherwise" (ibid.: 224–5).

The American philosopher J. Baird Callicott (1989) has fleshed out the nuances of Leopold's insights in greater detail than any other scholar. Building on Leopold's insights, Callicott argues in *In Defense of the Land Ethic* that the entire enterprise of mainstream Occidental moral philosophy – including Singer's and Regan's animal ethics and Taylor's biocentric ethics – has been wrongly based on individualism and must be abandoned. Individual organisms should not be thought of as having intrinsic value or rights because individuals do not really affect ecosystems. An individual organism, qua member of a species, has value insofar as it contributes to the overall integrity and stability of the larger biotic community (ibid.: 39). Individuals have extrinsic value for ecosystems;

ecosystems have intrinsic value that deserves and demands recognition by moral agents.

Environmental ethics, beginning with the holistic revolution of ecological theory and continuing through animal ethics to biocentrism, has tended to focus almost exclusively on the natural – that is, nonhuman – environment. Very recently, philosophers have begun to call this focus into question and suggest a need to reintroduce human-constructed environments as a legitimate subject-matter for ethics of the environment. The Australian philosopher Warwick Fox, for example, notes that "just as traditional, anthropocentrically focused forms of ethics have exhibited a major blind spot in their theorizing with respect to the non-human world, so the development of environmental ethics has thus far exhibited a major blind spot of its own" (2000: 2), namely, the human-constructed environment. As noted at the outset of this chapter, ethics is all about how we ought best to live our lives. This must include questions about how we build our cities and homes, and how we move things around the globe from one place to another. This recognition, in a profound sense, brings ethics full circle from the Greeks' human-centered focus to the non-anthropocentrism of ecosystem, animal, and life-centered ethics and back to the human.

The story of ethics in the West is a story about refocusing the lens of moral consideration. The narrative began with human beings as the only characters on stage, and the play continued that way, with minor exceptions, for more than 2,000 years. Eventually, nonhuman animals entered the scene, followed by entire ecosystems and the totality of living things. Most recently, the human-built environment has re-entered the drama. The question Socrates posed to his peers inside the city walls of Athens remains to this day: How should we best live our lives?

Conclusion

Either by divine plan (Augustine 1998) or evolutionary design (Wilson 1980), human beings are moral agents. Every day we judge, of ourselves and others, character and action. Making moral judgments constitutes nothing less than the essence, the defining feature, of what it means to be *human*.

Nowadays it is common to equate morality with private life. While it is certainly true that each moral agent must cultivate virtues to best live his or her life, as Socrates did by example, ethics is pre-eminently a public affair. No moral agent lives in a normative vacuum, for we are intricately bound in a social fabric by relationships of reciprocity. Whatever we do – and do not do – affects other beings worthy of consideration and respect.

With awareness comes responsibility, though sometimes the gravity of this responsibility seems a crushing weight we wish we did not have to bear. Part of this responsibility is determining which beings demand recognition and which do not. Historically, the class of beings possessing rights has typically been limited to certain categories of humans. In Western culture, the boundaries of this class have ranged from property-owning males, in Greek antiquity, to white males, in colonial America. More recently the boundary of moral consideration has been enlarged to include all human beings, regardless of race, religion, sex or gender, socioeconomic status, and other attributes accidental to core humanness. Within the last few decades, moral philosophers have widened the scope of moral consideration to include sentient mammals, all living things, or even entire ecosystems. If indeed the moral community includes more than the human community, then as moral agents it is our duty to respect nonhuman beings – a radical departure from 2,500 years of anthropocentrism.

Many moral problems that at first glance seem simple to solve turn out to be tremendously complicated. The case studies contained in this book are intended to reflect this aspect of moral problems, to reflect the variety and complexity of moral conundrums that each of us, as moral agents, faces in the private and public dimensions of our lives. It is tempting to deal with the dizzying intricacies of moral choices by painting the human condition in stark black and austere white, to fall back onto the ordinary dualisms of good and evil, right and wrong, moral and immoral, righteous and depraved; in short, to succumb to the absolutism of extremism. Since moral problems are characterized by inherent ambiguity (Beauvoir 1976), negligence in acknowledging ambiguity – thinking rigidly of morality in terms of either/or rather than both/and – precipitates intolerance and violence. For ethics, absolutism fails.

Some kind of moral compass is needed to help us navigate the variegated terrain of our daily lives and keep the distant horizon in focus. The pivot point of this compass may be faith, intuition, or reason; most likely it is a combination of all three. The latter pivot point we have defined as *ethics*. Ethics, based on the four criteria of comprehensiveness, coherence, consistency, and adequacy, is an exceptionally effective way of making moral decisions.

Ethical thinking requires practical wisdom. Practical wisdom is the sum of the capacity to reason plus worldly experience. The person of practical wisdom is tolerant of ambiguity and has an acute ability to discern myriad shades of moral gray. Since it is doubtful that a single ethical system can be superimposed on the rolling topography of the human condition, the person of practical wisdom must decide whether it is best to proceed through the valley of virtue, over the summit of duty, or along the ridgeline of consequences.

Ethics is not about making decisions for the sake of being decisive. It is about the quality of those decisions, about not just living, but, as Socrates said, living well.

NOTES

1   French philosopher Baron Paul d'Holbach (1723–89) notoriously embraced determinism and denied free will: "Man's life is a line that nature commands him to describe on the surface of the earth, without his ever being able to swerve from it, even for an instant. . . . Nevertheless, in spite of the shackles by which he is bound, it is pretended he is a free agent, or that independent of the causes by which he is moved,

he determines his own will, and regulates his own condition. . . . Man . . . is not a free agent in any one instant of his life" (1999: 135, 145). If d'Holbach and other determinists are right, the study of ethics is all for naught because moral actions and value judgments about them are determined by antecedent conditions.

2   This statement assumes a benchmark of normalcy; some human beings, for one cause or another, may not be moral agents insofar as they can not make moral judgments. Laws against capital punishment for mentally retarded persons and children reflect this distinction.

3   This is not a social contract insofar as Socrates did not enter an agreement with other individuals; rather, he simply agreed to live under the authority of the laws by not leaving the city walls (see lines 51d–52d).

4   The relativist could protest that the notion of universal human rights is an unwarranted attempt to foist universal standards on all human cultures, but in doing so would need to argue that flourishing is *not* an intrinsic human good.

5   To translate *psyche* as "soul" is misleading in that *psyche* refers to the essence of humanness, or the capacity for ideation, but not necessarily to an immaterial soul as we tend to think of today.

6   Plato saw a close parallel between the soul and the state (*Republic*, lines 434d ff). The state, like the soul, has three parts, or classes of people; when these classes function according to the wisdom of the rulers and are not meddling in each other's business, they exhibit political virtue, or justice (ibid.: 685).

7   See Ephesians 2: 19 and Philippians 3: 20.

8   It is useful to divide the Western tradition into four periods: ancient, medieval, modern, and postmodern (i.e., the contemporary period). The modern period begins approximately with the Renaissance, continues through the Enlightenment, and extends into the twentieth century, when postmodern thinkers began questioning the fundamental tenets of modernism, such as epistemic objectivity.

9   Interestingly, Bentham (1988: 311n.) argued that many nonhuman animals have the capacity to suffer just as humans do and should therefore have their pleasures and pains included in the scope of moral considerability. Peter Singer (2002) extends Bentham's argument in his theory for the ethical treatment of sentient animals elaborated in the section "The Scope of Ethics."

10   These remarks were not published by Kant but are taken from a transcription of a lecture on ethics taken by a student at Albertina University in Königsberg in 1784.

11   "Land Ethics" is technically a misnomer, because the term refers to all living systems, including aquatic systems. Leopold spent most of his life scouting the interior of the North American continent, so, biographically speaking, it is easy to understand his choice of words.

REFERENCES

Aquinas, T. (1981) *Summa Theologica*, vol. II (Part 1 of the Second Part), trans. Fathers of the English Dominican Province. Notre Dame, IN: Christian Classics.

Aristotle (1941) *The Basic Works of Aristotle*, ed. R. McKeon. New York: Random House.

Augustine (1998) *The City of God Against the Pagans*, ed. and trans. R. W. Dyson. Cambridge: Cambridge University Press.

Baier, A. (1986) Trust and antitrust. *Ethics* 96 (2): 231–60.

Barnes, A. (1969) *An Inquiry into the Scriptural Views of Slavery*. Detroit, MI: Negro History Press.

Beauvoir, S. de (1976) *The Ethics of Ambiguity*, trans. B. Frechtman. New York: Citadel Press.

Bentham, J. (1988) *The Principles of Morals and Legislation*. Amherst, NY: Prometheus Books.

Brunner, E. (1947) *The Divine Imperative*, trans. O. Wyon. Philadelphia, PA: Westminster Press.

Callicott, J. B. (1989) *In Defense of the Land Ethic: Essays in Environmental Philosophy*. Albany, NY: State University of New York Press.

d'Holbach, Baron P. (1999) *The System of Nature*, vol. I, trans. H. D. Robinson. London: Clinamen Press.

Descartes, R. (1991) *The Philosophical Writings of Descartes*. Vol. III: *The Correspondence*, trans. J. Cottingham, R. Stoothoff, D. Murdoch, et al. New York: Cambridge University Press.

Ferré, F. (1998) *Knowing and Value: Toward a Constructive Postmodern Epistemology*. Albany, NY: State University Press of New York.

Fox, W. (ed.) (2000) *Ethics and the Built Environment*. New York: Routledge.

Gallup, G. C., Jr. (1970) Chimpanzees: self-recognition. *Science* 167 (3914): 86–7.

Gampel, E. H. (2005) A framework for moral reasoning. In B. C. White and J. A. Zimbelman (eds.), *Moral Dilemmas in Community Health Care: Cases and Commentaries*. New York: Pearson/Longman, pp. 1–27.

Gilligan, C. (1982) *In a Different Voice: Psychological Theory and Women's Development*. Cambridge, MA: Harvard University Press.

Hamilton, E. (1993) *The Greek Way*. New York: W. W. Norton.

Harris, M. J. (2003) *Divine Command Ethics: Jewish and Christian Perspectives*. New York: Routledge Curzon.

Henry, C. F. H. (1957) *Christian Personal Ethics*. Grand Rapids, MI: Eerdmans.

Hobbes, T. (1996) *Leviathan*, ed. J. C. A. Gaskin. New York: Oxford University Press.

Hume, D. (1988) *An Enquiry Concerning the Principles of Morals*, ed. J. B. Schneewind. Hackett Publishing.

Johnson, R. (2003) Virtue and right. *Ethics* 113 (4): 810–34.

Kant, I. (1985) *Grounding for the Metaphysics of Morals*, 2nd edn., trans. J. W. Ellington. Indianapolis, IN: Hackett Publishing. (Numbers in brackets in all *Grounding* citations indicate pagination of *Kants Gesammelte Schriften*, Königlichen Preussischen Academie der Wissenschaften edn. (Berlin: Walter de Gruyter, 1911), the standard reference text of Kant's works.)

Kant, I. (1996) *The Metaphysics of Morals*, trans. M. Gregor. New York: Cambridge University Press.

Kant, I. (1997) *Lectures on Ethics*, trans. P. Heath. New York: Cambridge University Press.

Kant, I. (2006) *Critique of Practical Reason*, trans. M. Gregor. New York: Cambridge University Press.

Kierkegaard, S. (1992) *Concluding Unscientific Postscript to Philosophical Fragments*, ed. and trans. H. V. Hong and E. H. Hong. Princeton, NJ: Princeton University Press.

Leopold, A. (1960) *A Sand County Almanac and Sketches Here and There*. New York: Oxford University Press.

Locke, J. (1987) *The Second Treatise of Government*, ed. T. Peardon. New York: Macmillan Publishing Company.

MacIntyre, A. (1984) *After Virtue: A Study in Moral Theory*, 2nd edn. Notre Dame, IN: University of Notre Dame Press.

Mill, J. S. (1978) *On Liberty*. Indianapolis, IN: Hackett Publishing.

Mill, J. S. (2001) *Utilitarianism*, 2nd edn., ed. G. Sher. Indianapolis, IN: Hackett Publishing.

New Oxford Annotated Bible (2001) New Revised Standard Version, 3rd edn. New York: Oxford University Press.

Nielsen, K. (1967) Problems of ethics. In P. Edwards (ed.), *The Encyclopedia of Philosophy*, vol. III. New York: Macmillan and Free Press, pp. 117–34.

Nietzsche, F. (1989) *On the Genealogy of Morals*, trans. W. Kaufmann and R. J. Hollingdale. New York: Vintage Books.

Noddings, N. (1984) *Caring: A Feminine Approach to Ethics and Moral Education*. Berkeley, CA: University of California Press.

Nussbaum, M. (1993) Non-relative virtues: an Aristotelian approach. In M. Nussbaum and A. Sen (eds.), *The Quality of Life*. New York: Oxford University Press, pp. 1–6.

Plato (2005) *Plato: The Collected Dialogues*, ed. E. Hamilton and H. Cairns. Princeton, NJ: Princeton University Press.

The Pro-slavery Argument, as Maintained by the Most Distinguished Writers of the Southern States (1968) New York: Negro Universities Press.

Rachels, J. (1986) *The Elements of Moral Philosophy*. New York: Random House.

Rawls, J. (1971) *A Theory of Justice*. Cambridge, MA: Belknap Press of Harvard University Press.

Regan, T. (1983) *The Case for Animal Rights*. Berkeley, CA: University of California Press.

Rousseau, J.-J. (2006) *The Social Contract*, trans. M. Cranston. New York: Penguin Books.

Sartre, J.-P. (2003) Existentialism is a humanism. In F. Baird and W. Kaufmann, W. (eds.), *Philosophical Classics: From Plato to Derrida*, 4th edn. Upper Saddle River, NJ: Prentice-Hall.

Sidgwick, H. (1962) *The Methods of Ethics*, 7th edn. Chicago: University of Chicago Press (orig. pub. 1874).

Singer, P. (2002) *Animal Liberation*. New York: HarperCollins.

Swartley, W. M. (1983) *Slavery, Sabbath, War, and Women: Case Issues in Biblical Interpretation*. Scottsdale, PA: Herald Press.

Taylor, P. W. (1986) *Respect for Nature: A Theory of Environmental Ethics*. Princeton, NJ: Princeton University Press.

United Nations General Assembly (1948) *Universal Declaration of Human Rights*. Resolution 217 A (III). New York: United Nations.

Wilson, E. O. (1980) *Sociobiology*. Cambridge, MA: Belknap Press of Harvard University Press.

2

A FRAMEWORK FOR MORAL REASONING

A Note to the Reader

The reader will quickly note that Eric H. Gampel's "A Framework for Moral Reasoning" is constructed exclusively in terms of health care ethics. This singular focus might suggest that the piece has scant utility beyond that limited arena. We wish quickly to disabuse the reader of that worry. We have chosen Gampel's piece because of its exceptionally helpful *process* for moral problem-solving, a process that is easily applied to moral dilemmas across the content spectrum. Gampel's approach to analysis and justification (the AJ method) of resolutions to moral dilemmas is content-neutral; it enables persons to assess moral conundrums that arise in business, international relations, education – indeed, in any particular domain – as fruitfully as in biomedical ethics.

But why is *any process* required? As a practical matter, having a standard decision-making process to use when facing moral dilemmas facilitates their resolution. A systematic approach reminds one to include *all* necessary steps: (1) to seek out and incorporate relevant empiric data (essential for understanding the full nature of the dilemma); (2) to search for alternatives that might eliminate the dilemma altogether; (3) to list carefully the reasons in favor of and against *both* sides of the dilemma (crucial to avoiding bias and short-sightedness); (4) to recognize the ubiquitous use of assumptions (necessary to keeping moral problem-solvers humble and open-minded) by articulating both *value assumptions* that represent and are derived from normative ethical theories and *factual assumptions* about data that are unavailable – *both of which may be contested* (critical to thorough moral consideration); and (5) to justify one's postulated solution so as to *demonstrate the reasoning* behind it.

We have chosen Gampel's framework because it incorporates *and* systematizes these five essential aspects of moral problem-solving. Not only does he explicitly remind problem-solvers to seek out relevant facts and acknowledge assumptions on which a justification depends; his CARVE principles incorporate the contributions of *all* serious normative ethical theories. His process creates and structures an environment for discussion and judgment that will help problem-solvers avoid many common pitfalls: information deficits (Step 1), overlooking possible options that dissolve dilemmas (Step 2), incomplete surveys of moral reasons that play a role in dilemmas at hand (Step 3), failure to acknowledge assumptions that may prove erroneous or biased (Step 4), and using rational analysis to justify one's position to an intelligent opponent (Step 5). This thorough approach will enable concerned persons to reach resolutions that are morally and rationally supported. In short, Gampel's *process* encourages solutions that are unlikely to be capricious, arbitrary, or biased, and are likely to be relevant, sensible, and practicable.

Three notes of explanation are needed. In the case studies in this book, we have altered Gampel's process in two ways. First, while he recommends listing only a few pros and cons – specifically, those in terms of which the dilemma is stated – we believe that listing *all* identifiable, non-trivial pros and cons more effectively illustrates the complexity and nuances of many of these dilemmas. As a result, our lists are often much longer than recommended by Gampel. Second, we have incorporated much of the analysis, begun by Gampel in Step 4, into Step 5. Our rationale for this revision is the belief that this approach more closely reflects the typical form a justification takes, whether in a written or oral argument. While most people will – as, indeed, they should – assess reasons prior to reaching a conclusion, most typically fold those assessments into the justification itself.

As an aid to readers analyzing cases – specifically, in identifying which ethical principles are relevant to issues in a particular case – we include in Step 3 ('Listing pros and cons') letters at the end of each pro or con that correspond with Gampel's CARVE principles. We also include in Step 5 ('Justification') numbers that refer back to the pros and cons listed in Step 3.

Finally, as readers may find a discrete list of CARVE principles useful, we provide this here:

CARVE
  (C): Consequences
    (C-B): Consequences: beneficence
    (C-NM): Consequences: nonmaleficence
    (C-U): Consequences: utility
  (A): Autonomy
    (RFP): Respect for persons
  (R): Rights
  (V): Virtues
  (E/F): Justice
    (J-E): Justice: equality
    (J-F): Justice: fairness

A FRAMEWORK FOR MORAL REASONING

Eric H. Gampel

This [chapter] offers a systematic framework for reasoning about the kinds of ethical issues that come up in health care contexts. Following an introduction to the topic of ethics, we examine the major moral principles that are especially important to medical ethics. A five-step procedure for analyzing and resolving ethical issues that incorporates those principles is then described. The procedure offers a principled alternative to the appeals to gut instinct, tradition, and politics that all too often characterize ethical problem-solving. Finally we discuss the fields of moral theory and moral philosophy – areas for further study that can also improve ethical decision-making.

Ethics and Health Care

Ethical issues involve matters of right and wrong, good and bad, virtue and vice, rights and responsibilities. When we take the *moral point of view*,[1] we evaluate human actions and characters morally, making judgments such as "Sara was *wrong* to unplug Uncle John from the respirator before the rest of the family could arrive"; or "Steve has a *right* to a pay raise after all he has done for the company." We will refer to these as "moral" or "ethical" judgments.[2] Of course, the moral point of view is not the only point of view we can take: we can also consider whether something is cost-effective, legal, conducive to self-interest, in accord with applicable policy, beautiful, educational, interesting, and so on. But the moral point of view can be identified through four distinguishing features.

First, it is mostly about *how we ought to treat people* – including, in some cases, how we ought to treat ourselves. The moral point of view is especially concerned with whether actions or persons harm others, violate their rights, are unfair, or otherwise mistreat someone. Second, the moral point of view is *normative and prescriptive*; its primary task is not a description of what the world is like, but a prescription of what people ought to do (or what a person's character ought to be like). The purpose of the moral point of view is to guide action, not simply to describe how things are. Third, the moral point of view often *overrides* other considerations, especially those of self-interest. This does not mean that the moral point of view always prevails, only that we often judge that it *should* prevail.[3] Fourth, the moral point of view is *universalizable*, leading us to make moral judgments we expect others to share, even if they come from very different cultural or religious backgrounds. This is most clear in the case of very general moral claims, such as the wrongness of deliberate harm, or of not giving people what they deserve. Of course, there are also moral claims we take to be *subjective* or relative to a cultural context, such as whether honoring parents requires letting them choose your marriage partner, or whether to show respect through a handshake or by spitting at the ground. But there still seems a universal core: even if *how* we honor parents or show respect differs across cultures and communities, the importance of having *some* customary manner of doing so is a universal and uncontroversial human value.

For some ethical issues there is not much controversy at all – just about everyone agrees on what would be the morally right (or wrong) thing to do. These include most of the actions forbidden by criminal and civil law in all cultures – murder, theft, assault, negligence, fraud. In health care contexts, such actions sometimes involve physicians, nurses, or other health care professionals (HCPs) who have become clearly "corrupt" – stealing medications for personal use, providing inappropriate therapies for personal gain, writing ghost prescriptions to sell drugs on the black market, and so on. These kinds of ethical issues do not usually call out for analysis or careful reasoning – we know what is morally right, have passed laws to enforce it, and need only keep watch that any who violate the laws are prosecuted.

But other ethical issues are less clear-cut. Should the truth be told when it will do harm to tell it? Do the bonds of friendship mean we must protect a friend or colleague, even in his or her unethical behavior? How far must we sacrifice our own interests to help others, and in what ways? When our jobs seem to require acts about which we have ethical reservations, should we ignore the job's requirements and do what we believe to be morally right? Not everyone agrees about these kinds of ethical issues – they involve controversial questions about the shape of our ethical duties. Partly for that reason, it is common for there to be no laws, rules, or policies governing the more controversial ethical issues – or for there to be uncertainty regarding how to interpret, or whether to follow, any legal or institutional requirements. This is where clarity and careful ethical reasoning are important. We all must make choices involving ethical issues, and those choices stem from and help define our characters and our values. Moreover, the choices are often made in social contexts of friendships, families, and professional life, in ways that affect other people, are seen by others, and establish patterns of behavior for ourselves and others to follow. So how we resolve the less clear-cut ethical issues matters – to us as individuals, to those directly affected by our actions, and sometimes to a broader community as well.

Health care is filled with these less clear-cut ethical issues, where law, policy, and widely shared moral rules do not settle the question of what we should do. For instance, if family members of a dying woman disagree about whether it is time to unplug her from a respirator, how should the decision be resolved? If a patient does not consent to a beneficial treatment, should a nurse try to further inform and persuade the patient, or simply let the patient's decision stand? When not all can receive a scarce medical resource, such as an organ or simply a health professional's time and attention, what criteria should be used to select those who receive it? . . .

The Hippocratic tradition of medical ethics, beginning in ancient Greek times, sought to establish certain ethical principles and virtues that would help physicians navigate the less clear ethical waters. For instance, physicians were often told "above all, do no harm" – an important reminder in the days when little was known about how to cure and the use of untried and risky measures was a daily temptation. In general, the Hippocratic tradition handled ethical issues "in-house," with an emphasis on developing virtuous character and good general dispositions. Physicians trained students to follow the time-tested ways, developing the bedside manner and character traits of a virtuous physician: a dedication to helping patients, a devotion to medical learning, respect for patient confidentiality, and loyalty to fellow physicians. This approach worked well enough, perhaps, when most physicians were general practitioners, working with patients whom they knew intimately for long periods of time. But in modern medicine, the explosions of technology and specialization since the 1960s have meant that health professionals often work in teams, and meet their patients for the first time as referrals. In addition, patients now come from diverse cultural, religious, moral, and linguistic backgrounds, increasing the possibilities for misunderstanding and moral disagreement.

In this modern context of health care, the number and complexity of ethical issues has also increased, and has led to the establishment of health care ethics as a field of study in its own right. Since the 1960s, a regular stream of books and articles has been published, ethics committees have been formed, and policies have been developed, all to come up with better ways to handle the kinds of ethical issues that arise in modern medicine. Individual HCPs must still navigate by their own moral compasses, but there is a scholarly background of medical ethics that has been shaped by a self-conscious and wide-ranging ethical reflection.

Major Moral Principles

Modern health care is subject to a plethora of explicit laws, rules, and policies. For instance, only 20 years ago physicians just talked informally to the terminally ill about whether they would want ventilation support or other life-sustaining measures. Today, there are multipage advance directive forms, such as living wills and powers of attorney for health care, along with laws requiring that hospitals tell patients about the forms. As a result, most hospitals have implemented policies requiring staff to obtain patient signatures indicating they have been informed about the availability of advance directives.

Many such rules and policies were established in the name of ethics: to ensure that medical professionals treat patients well, acting with compassion and respect for individual rights. But the rules and policies are still not the "court of last appeal" when considering what it would be ethical to do. For one thing, the rules can change, even dramatically, as evidenced by the rise of advance directives. More significantly, the rules sometimes conflict with other moral ideas. For instance, one might question whether it is humane to insist on every patient's "right" to fill out a form about when he or she would like life-sustaining treatments withheld. What about a frightened patient facing a low-risk surgery, whose fear is exacerbated by considering the extremely unlikely situations addressed by advance directives? What about patients whose ability to think clearly is compromised by the anxiety of a medical emergency, by illness, or by medications? Might it be best not to worry about advance directives for such patients, at least low-risk ones? Should one perhaps "bend" legal or administrative rules, for instance getting signatures indicating patients have been informed about advance directives by simply offering the signature in a stack of paperwork, without explaining the nature or purpose of advance directives?

So HCPs cannot (and generally do not) just blindly follow the rules or the "standard" procedure: they reflect on the situation and evaluate what would be best, given the specific circumstances. For behind the rules and standard procedures, and behind the changes made in them over the years, are other, more fundamental moral ideas and values. The field of bioethics has developed a short and useful list of the kinds of fundamental moral principles significant to medical contexts.[4] The following list has been organized around the acronym CARVE as a memory aid:[5]

1   *Consequences* (C): promote the best possible consequences for all those affected by your action. This very broad moral principle includes three subprinciples regarding the health and well-being of persons:
   (a)   *The principle of nonmaleficence* (NM): refrain from causing unnecessary harm. This principle reminds HCPs to take due care not to subject patients to unnecessary risks, or to harm patients through their own negligence.
   (b)   *The principle of positive beneficence* (B): take action to benefit others. This principle identifies the goal of medicine: to help improve the health and well-being of individual patients.
   (c)   *The principle of utility* (U): act so as to produce the best possible outcome for the welfare of the group as a whole, when some people are harmed while others benefit. This principle directs HCPs to look beyond their individual patients, considering how a decision might be affecting other patients, family, and the general public. As a result, utility allows trade-offs in which an individual patient's well-being might be sacrificed for the greater good, as in quarantines, mandatory inoculations, and violations of confidentiality that are required to protect third parties.
2   *Respect for Autonomy* (A): respect and promote the self-determination of competent persons. This is the principle behind rules of informed consent and truth-telling, since both seek to help patients make their own decisions about the course of their health care. The principle requires both letting patients make their own decisions and giving them the information about risks, benefits, and burdens that is relevant to their decisions.
3   *Rights* (R): respect individual moral rights, such as rights to freedom and confidentiality. This principle directs HCPs to consider not just the legal but the moral rights of patients.
4   *Virtues* (V): act in accord with good character, expressing such virtues as honesty, courage, fidelity, integrity, and compassion. This principle focuses on the character, motives, and intentions of HCPs and patients.

5   *Equality* (E): treat people with equal consideration and respect, being fair and
     not discriminating on the basis of morally irrelevant features (such as income,
     race, or gender).[6] Note that when equality and fairness are at issue, people
     often speak of "justice" and "injustice," as they do when important moral
     rights are at stake.

These principles as stated are completely uncontroversial, in the sense that
everyone grants their relevance to the practice of medicine. Any controversy stems
from the details of their interpretation, application, or relative priority. People
have different views about how to define harms, benefits, competence, rights,
virtue, and fairness, as well as about how to weigh those different considerations. But the principles provide a shared and systematic way of identifying the
concerns important to health care ethics, a basis for further discussion and reflection.
Even in today's diverse environments of care, with persons from widely different cultural and religious backgrounds, the principles can serve – with a few caveats
– as common touchstones for reasoning about ethical issues.

What people agree on is *not* that the CARVE principles are exhaustive or
absolute, but that they are prima facie obligations on practitioners – presumpt-
ive obligations that give moral reasons for action, though reasons that might
be outweighed by other considerations (including competing moral principles
from the CARVE list). This distinguishes the principles from *absolute* obligations,
which hold independently of context and may never be outweighed. Some
people take the Ten Commandments to be morally absolute; what makes the
CARVE principles different, and much less controversial, is that they are offered
for health care contexts only as prima facie obligations that identify the kinds of
moral considerations we should take into account.

The result is that when a moral issue comes up in a health care environment,
progress can be made in discussions or in personal reflection by considering how
the CARVE principles apply to the situation. (You will see examples of the use
of these principles in this [chapter], and in the commentaries throughout this
book.) The principles cannot serve as a litmus test or simple decision procedure,
of course, and HCPs are quite often faced with too little time to engage in detailed
ethical analysis. But in many cases there is time, and analysis can always be done
in retrospect, as HCPs seek to understand and improve on how situations are
handled. The CARVE principles help identify the major values at stake – a first
step in understanding a moral issue. Sometimes this is simple, as when a single
CARVE principle is clearly the primary and decisive consideration to take into
account. But often one is blind to aspects of a case that are important, and going
through all the CARVE principles can bring the other aspects to one's awareness. Indeed, people tend to emphasize one or another principle in their own
personal and professional ethical lives: some people pride themselves on their
compassion, others on their respect for individual rights. Those long-standing
emphases can function as biases, albeit well-intentioned ones, that blind people
to the other moral considerations relevant to health care ethics. Going through
CARVE, making sure one sees all the ethical dimensions of a case, can thus be
a useful corrective device.

The use of CARVE can also help overcome other kinds of prejudices and biases learned from one's upbringing or training as a health care professional. For instance, until fairly recently physicians were trained under a paternalistic model, according to which physicians were to do what was best for the patient even if it meant protecting them from the truth, or not granting them full decision-making power. This model was based on a long-standing medical tradition, learned directly from one's teachers, and it was associated with a cluster of gut feelings: compassion for the vulnerable patient, a sense of expertise, and feelings of authority, privilege, and integrity. This paternalistic model has been overthrown in recent decades, mainly on the grounds that it conflicts with two CARVE principles: the rights and autonomy of patients. Many physicians resisted the change for quite a while, since it went against deeply rooted instincts about the nature of the compassionate, virtuous physician. But antipaternalists argued that true compassion requires being responsive to the patient's need for autonomy, and that true integrity requires respecting the patient's rights. The point is that a blind following of one's gut feelings risks making one unable to see the possibility of such arguments. Of course, the paternalistic model could itself be defended on the basis of CARVE principles – giving primacy to the principles of beneficence and nonmaleficence. So having the list of CARVE principles is not going to resolve the question of whether physicians should be paternalistic. But the CARVE principles help articulate the ethical controversy, and they bring one's attention away from the gut feelings inculcated by professional training toward the deeper values at stake.

A Procedure for Moral Reasoning: The AJ Method

The major moral principles are useful tools in moral reflection. The principles help identify the values behind different choices, ensure one has not missed important moral considerations, and provide a common vocabulary for discussions with others. But questions about how to interpret, apply, and weigh the principles are inevitable. As in any case where judgment is involved, there is no substitute for experience and practice in developing good moral reasoning skills: seeing many cases, making tough moral decisions, observing and living with the results. This book provides many cases on which to practice. You may well find that after reading a case, you have a "gut instinct," an intuitive sense of what should or should not be done. The CARVE principles should help you identify the values behind that instinctive position. But after reading some of the commentaries, or discussing the case with others, you will usually find that your intuition needs further support: there are moral arguments and CARVE principles on the other side; and you could imagine an intelligent and decent person having a different "gut instinct" about the case, based on a different understanding of the CARVE principles or their relative importance. Here it would be useful to analyze the case and the moral arguments more carefully, to better understand and possibly reevaluate your initial position.

The procedure for moral reasoning described below involves five simple steps to take when faced with an ethical issue.[7] Going through these steps involves carefully analyzing the ethical issue, and then justifying a position on how to best handle it; we will thus call the method the "Analysis and Justification Method" (or the "AJ Method"). This is not the only possible method of ethical reasoning, and it is not strictly followed by HCPs, ethicists, or other professionals involved in the field of biomedical ethics (lawyers, clergy, etc.). But the AJ Method incorporates most of the elements to be found in any good attempt to analyze and justify a position on a biomedical issue. We thus offer this method as a useful guide. Simply reading through it can help further develop your skills in ethical reasoning, and it can be used more formally to structure group discussions, individual reflection, or essays on ethical issues.

The first four steps in the AJ Method are "neutral" ones, involving a careful analysis of the issue with which all parties should agree; only the last step involves taking a stand on the moral issue, and that step requires explaining and justifying (to oneself or others) why one set of reasons outweighs those on the other side. Going through the procedure does not guarantee avoiding mistakes or coming up with the right view – no procedure can guarantee that everyone thinks clearly and insightfully, and there may even be more than one reasonable stand on a moral question. But the recommended procedure does provide a framework that helps one to minimize mistakes, and to better understand the deeper issues involved. The procedure is thus a way to expand your moral imagination, urging you to take into account more of the moral factors involved in an issue, and making your judgments more subtle, complex, and well-grounded.

Step 1: Information-gathering (IG)

The very first step in tackling an ethical issue is to make sure one fully understands the factual elements of the situation, as well as any background information important to the issue. In bioethics this usually means learning as much as possible about: (1) the *medical circumstances* involved; (2) the *implications* of different decisions for the lives of patients and their families (consequences); (3) the *history* of the situation, especially elements that are important to applying the CARVE principles of rights, virtue, and equality; (4) any relevant *laws or institutional policies*; (5) *economic* considerations; and (6) the *cultural and psychological* dimensions of the situation, especially as they affect the determination of competency and the application of the CARVE principle of autonomy. In hospital bioethics committees, investigating these various kinds of information about a specific case means having extensive discussions with HCPs, families, and patients; in academic contexts, this may mean more scholarly research on factors relevant to the ethical issue under consideration.

As an example, if a family is in disagreement over whether to end life support, we need to be sure we really understand (1) the medical circumstances: What is the medical condition, who made the diagnosis and prognosis, how sure are they, and are there any differing opinions? We also should consider (2) the implications of a decision: What does ending life support really mean for the patient and the family? Does the patient have any prospect of enjoying a sustained life, or would we be causing needless suffering to keep the patient alive (non-maleficence)? If life support were to continue, would family members be unduly postponing their lives or their grieving (utility)? In addition, we ought to be acquainted with (3) the history: What led to the current disagreement amongst family members? Have they all always felt as they do, or has there been an evolution in their views as the case progressed? How have medical staff dealt with the family over time (virtue, equality)? Of course, we need to also know about (4) law and policy: Who has the *legal* decisional power within the family, as a legal proxy if there is a power of attorney, or as next of kin? What is the policy of the institution about family disagreements: is there a clear directive or informal norm allowing delays until a family works out its disagreements? Is there room under law or policy for questioning decisional power in a case like this one – for example, are there questions about motive or competence which are clearly relevant to applying law or policy (rights)? What are the penalties, if any, for going against the legal or policy mandates? Would jobs be lost, or civil suits likely to succeed against the institution? This raises the matter of (5) economic considerations: What would be the economic burdens of continued treatment, or the risk assessments regarding the likelihood of being sued (utility)? Would continued life support take money from an estate, and are some family members concerned about that? Finally, we should consider (6) the cultural and psychological dimensions of the situation: Are there religious differences between family members leading to their disagreement? Is there evidence of what the patient would have wanted (autonomy)? Do some family members want to avoid the guilt of going along with a decision to end life support? Is there a rift in the family that leads inevitably to fights, no matter the issue at hand? These various questions need to be explored to make progress in figuring out how the situation should be handled.

Step 2: Creative problem-solving (CPS)

The ideal way of dealing with a tough ethical dilemma is to come up with a creative plan of action that avoids the ethically troubling alternatives, while still solving the problem that created the dilemma. This requires a strategy that cannot be reasonably objected to on moral grounds. In health care contexts, this is often where ethical reflection begins and, with a little good fortune, ends: in a creative strategy which all parties recognize to be consistent with each of the CARVE principles and (thus) ethically untroubling.

For instance, if an expensive, medically recommended procedure is not covered by a patient's insurance, and the patient cannot afford to pay for it, there is an apparent dilemma: forgo the procedure, risking the patient's health, or provide the procedure anyway, billing the patient while knowing payment will never be forthcoming, requiring that others absorb the costs (through higher charges for medical services, government reimbursements, or decreased profits). If we choose to forgo the procedure, we are violating the principles of beneficence and perhaps equality; but if we provide the procedure without expecting the patient to pay, we are arguably violating the rights of those who would have to absorb the costs – perhaps other patients who would be paying higher charges, or taxpayers, or shareholders, depending on how the costs would be absorbed. This is a dilemma about the demands of *justice*, with claims of fairness and rights on both sides. A creative solution would avoid the moral problem – which means finding a way to provide good health care to the patient without requiring that others absorb the costs, thereby not violating any major moral principles. But how?

Here a bit of creative (and optimistic) thinking is in order. Perhaps there is another medical procedure, covered by the patient's insurance, which is a reasonable alternative to the one that is not covered? Or perhaps further negotiations with the insurance agency can convince it to extend the coverage in this instance? Or maybe the funds can be found elsewhere – an organized charity, or a fund-raising campaign by family and friends? If any of these strategies worked, ethical controversy would be avoided; the problem would be solved.

This stage of moral reasoning is perhaps the most important one for the everyday practice of health care. People in the health care professions are very talented at it, and take it to be a major part of their jobs. Psychology and counseling are quite often at the center stage in such creative problem-solving, since ethical dilemmas are often raised by conflicts amongst patients, family, medical staff, and insurance companies, and those conflicts may be dissolved through good dialogue, further information, and various other practical strategies (e.g., participation in a support group, viewing of informational videos, etc.). When conflicts between the parties can be resolved, the dilemma goes away; everyone agrees on the proper course of care. But this is not always the case: sometimes HCPs cannot find successful creative solutions, and must face the hard choice between morally troubling options.

Step 3: Listing pros and cons (PC)

Faced with the hard choice, one must explore the moral reasons for and against each of the morally troubling choices, the moral "pros and cons." To keep track of the various ethical considerations, one can construct a simple list of the main options, and the reasons for or against each option. As mechanical as such a procedure seems, keeping track of all of the important moral arguments can make a tremendous difference in the quality of moral reasoning. In a group setting, it ensures all participants have their reasons written down and addressed, and in personal decision-making it provides a map of the relevant moral reasons for further analysis. In addition, this is the point where the CARVE principles are especially useful. After going through the moral reasons you take to be obvious, go through each CARVE principle and see what it would lead you to consider important about the case. This often brings out moral factors you miss at first glance, given your own initial bias about the case, or your specific moral perspective. Even if a consideration seems trivial, if it is backed by a CARVE principle perhaps it deserves further thought. The resulting list of moral reasons has the following form (with the CARVE principles included in parentheses to identify the general values behind each reason):

	Pros	Cons
1st option	1. Reason for 1st option (CARVE principle)	3. Reason against 1st option (CARVE principle)
2nd option	2. Reason for 2nd option (CARVE principle)	4. Reason against 2nd option (CARVE principle)

The goal at this stage is to provide a map of the moral reasons for further reflection, a map that will be neutral in an important sense: people who disagree about which option is best could still accept the map as identifying the main moral considerations important to the case. Usually it is best not to list trivial reasons, since that can clutter up the chart, and to keep the options to two or three. Note that not every pro/con box needs to be filled; as long as there is a reason or argument listed on each diagonal (in a two-option chart), each option has something in the chart that is in its favor. Also, be prepared for cases where a reason could fit either as a pro for one option or a con against an alternative. For instance, one might argue for providing surgery based on the fact that it could save the patient's life (a pro), or against forgoing surgery because the patient could die (a con). Rather than double-entering this basic idea, it is best to list the reason one place or the other but not both.

Step 4: Analysis (A)

The next step is the most challenging and difficult one, where the *strengths* of the various reasons in the pro/con list are evaluated. The key here is to be thorough, seriously considering whether each reason is a strong one, taken independently or in comparison to other reasons on the pro/con list. One way to do this is to keep in mind the question: *What assumptions are necessary to consider the reason extremely important?*

Some assumptions will be (1) *factual*, in the sense of not directly involving moral values. They would involve the sort of factual information to be invest-igated in Step 1, but it may be that there is no good evidence or agreement about the factual issue involved, so that different persons might make different assumptions about it.[8] In bioethics such assumptions are typically about the like-lihood of an outcome, the long-term consequences of a decision, or the true motivations or intentions of the parties. In contrast, other assumptions will be (2) about the deeper *values and moral principles* at stake, and their relative importance. For instance, if one is considering a complicated rehabilitative surgery to give a disabled patient full use of his arms, one might be making factual assumptions about the degree of risk or the likelihood of success, or one might be making a value assumption about whether it is worth risking a patient's life to improve its quality in this way. Thus, a reason should be considered a strong one only if it is *quite likely to protect or promote an important value.* These two judgments, of likelihood and importance, rest on factual and value assumptions that need to be examined.

This is especially apparent when people from different religious or cultural backgrounds are involved in a case or its analysis, since such differences often go along with radically different assumptions. For instance, some people from certain religious traditions assume that spiritual strategies of healing have a very good chance of success. So when physicians admit that an illness is not easily treated with a proven cure, some religious people forgo the recommended but uncertain medical strategies in favor of their spiritual approach. Note that this choice is based on a factual assumption by the religious persons that spiritual strategies have good prospects for curing. The assumption is not factual in the sense of provable, but it is factual in the sense that it has to do with the factual outcomes involved, not with the weighting of values. Alternatively, a religious person might place more value on reverence for life itself, apart from the quality of the life. This could lead to avoiding surgical risks, on the basis of a different value assumption from the one made by a person who counts life not to be worth living, once its quality drops sufficiently.

Notice that this analysis step is still "neutral," in the sense that people who disagree about which option is best can agree on the analysis. At this stage one is only further exploring the reasons, considering what might lead a person to view a reason as especially strong (or weak), and raising questions about the factual and value assumptions thus unearthed. This means that even before making up one's mind about a case, or taking a position in a discussion, the proposed method requires one to *imaginatively put oneself in the shoes of those who weigh the reasons in different ways.* Nevertheless, this can bring to light the more vulnerable or unsupported assumptions, thus leading into the next step of taking a position and defending it. For instance, if an assumption that is crucial to considering a reason a strong one is factual, one can ask if there is any good evidence for it, or if one would be making a mere guess. If one would be guessing, is it reasonable to base a morally significant decision on such a guess? Alternatively, if an assumption is evaluative or moral in nature, one can ask if there are any good moral reasons for that assumption: why should we interpret rights or autonomy in the requisite way, and what moral assumptions are built into that way of interpreting the value? This process helps one to see which are the more and less reasonable weightings of the reasons, since some of the assumptions are likely to look more plausible than others.

In addition, looking at the assumptions behind the evaluation of reasons helps identify what really lies at the core of disagreements about which option is best. In this context a useful question is: *What difference in basic assumptions can explain why reasonable people might disagree about the strength of a reason?*

Once again, sometimes the differing assumptions will be about the factual elements of a case – what is the likelihood of a certain outcome, how a patient will accommodate to a certain outcome. At other times the assumptions will be about the values at stake. But it is important to identify the real source of a difference in perspective about the case.

People in health care contexts often focus their discussions and arguments on the strictly factual aspects of bioethics dilemmas: on what the chances are for recovery, on the likely outcome for various parties, on the relevant psychological and legal factors, or on the long-term consequences of a given decision. These are matters about which HCPs can offer their expert judgments, and such matters are reasonably comfortable to discuss. But restricting the conversation to factual matters risks ignoring the underlying value issues at stake, and it is at least equally important to consider those issues. Indeed, there is sometimes little or no good evidence for some of the factual predictions on which people base their arguments, raising the question of whether their positions are really based on something else, specifically on *value assessments* that are more difficult to defend. For instance, one might argue for the rehabilitative surgery mentioned above on the grounds that it is safe and quite likely to succeed, when the real reason is that one doesn't much value a life of disability. So it is important in this analysis step to question any factual assumptions for which there is no real evidence, in case a deeper value commitment is really at work, and then to consider whether that value commitment can be adequately supported.

Step 5: Justification (J)

At this point one has identified the relevant moral reasons, the moral principles on which they depend, and the factual and value assumptions being made by those who take one or another reason to be especially significant. This means one should have a good understanding of the ethical issue, why people might disagree about it, and usually a sense of which option has stronger moral support, in light of the reasons, principles, and assumptions one has determined to be most important or plausible. The next step is to work through a systematic justification of the morally preferable option. The key to a successful justification is this:

> Identify why the reasons for one option are more convincing than the reasons on the other side, based on a reasonable assessment of the factual and value issues important to the case.

Working out a systematic justification can be done in different spirits – simply to test one's initial view, or as a final defense of one's position. It can also be done in different contexts: as a presentation at a meeting, in conversation with friends, as a series of notes on paper for oneself, or in a formal essay for sharing with others. In any of these cases, it is always important to cover all the reasons someone could consider significant – that is, all the reasons listed in the pro/con chart. Here is an outline of this process that can aid in constructing presentations or written work:

I *Introduction*: Briefly introduce the moral issue, and indicate the option your analysis has shown to be morally preferable.

II   *Support*: For each reason in the pro/con chart that supports the option you prefer, write a paragraph explaining what your analysis has shown about the reason. Identify why it is strong or important (if it is), and discuss and defend any factual or value assumptions behind that judgment. (Note: the reasons that "support" an option include (a) the pros for the option, and (b) the cons against the alternative options, since those provide indirect support by working against the alternatives.)

III   *Defense*: For each reason in the pro/con chart that goes against the option you prefer, write a paragraph detailing what your analysis has shown about the reason. Identify why it is weak or unimportant, and discuss and defend any factual or value assumptions behind that judgment. (Note: the reasons that "go against" an option include (a) the cons directly against it, and (b) the pros that attempt to support the alternative options.)

IV   *Summary*: Summarize the reasoning. Review the most important reason favoring the better option, and remind the reader why the main reason against that option is not as significant.

This format ensures that every reason from the pro/con list is carefully presented and evaluated. All too often, presentations and written justifications simply put forward the supporting side, including the reasons against alternative views, without explaining why the reasons on the other side, against one's position, are not just as important. That can lead to parties speaking past one another, or to a kind of tunnel vision when working through moral dilemmas on one's own. A way to avoid this is always to keep in mind a reasonable critic, one who disagrees with your position but is willing to hear your reasons and be convinced if the reasons are good ones. What could sway such a person to weight the reasons as you would? Here the key is to further defend the factual and value assumptions behind your weighting of reasons. What is your evidence for the factual assumption about which someone might initially disagree? What kinds of moral argument can support a value assumption about the importance of one moral principle, as compared to the other principles at issue in the case? Why might someone disagree, and what mistake or misunderstanding lies behind that disagreement?

A Sample Case Study

. . . [I]t may be useful to review the framework described in this chapter by considering how the CARVE principles and the AJ Method might be used systematically to tackle a sample case. Here is the case:

> Following an auto accident Ms. A and her four children are admitted to a small rural hospital. Three of the children are doing well, but the fourth, a young girl, was dead on arrival. Ms. A suffers from broken ribs and internal bleeding; she is fully conscious, and deeply distraught over her children. She repeatedly asks how they are doing.

Ms. A's physician, Dr. B, assures her that her children are fine, and writes an order in the chart specifying that Ms. A is not to be told of the child's death until morning, at which time her condition will have stabilized and her husband will have arrived to support her. Ms. A's nurse, Ms. C, understands the physician's concerns but worries that patients have a right to the truth and, in any case, thinks it would be horrible to have to look her patient in the eye and repeat a lie of such magnitude.[9] After the physician has gone, Ms. A asks, "Tell me the truth, are my children all OK, and why can't I see them?" Ms. C wonders whether she shouldn't tell this mother what she so clearly wants to know.

In this case, the right thing to do is not obvious at first glance: if Ms. C tells the truth it might cause Ms. A's condition to worsen, perhaps causing her death; but faced with a direct question, the only other option seems to be to tell a lie, one of great magnitude. Telling the truth is responsive to Ms. A's rights and autonomy, but it threatens to violate nonmaleficence, arguably the most important principle governing the care of patients. So this is a genuine moral dilemma, one worth wrestling with.

Step 1: Information-gathering

The most crucial information here concerns the risk to Ms. A: how serious is that risk, and thus what are the chances that we are violating nonmaleficence if we give Ms. A the news of her daughter's death? Investigating this requires more information about Ms. A's *medical condition*, and the potential *implications* of telling her the bad news: how likely is it that being told the bad news would threaten her life or complicate the recovery process? These could be discussed with Dr. B, Ms. C, and other medical experts, if available, and we could do general research on traumatic injury cases, to understand the kinds of injuries involved and the kinds of threats such injuries make to continued survival. We could then look for any studies about the implications of psychological or emotional stress on the relevant physiological conditions involved in traumatic injuries, such as blood pressure and heart rate. Perhaps there is good evidence in the medical or psychological literature that emotional stress or grief has a dramatic effect on such physiological conditions, and thus evidence that there is a substantial risk to Ms. C if she is told the bad news. Or perhaps there is evidence that there are no such dramatic effects (e.g., a study indicating that there are no known cases where emotional trauma was causally important to a patient's death).

We might also investigate the *history* of the persons involved here and their relationships. Does Ms. A have a good and trusting relationship with Dr. B and/or Nurse C? Do Dr. B and Nurse C have high regard amongst other HCPs and patients, or do they have a history of questionable decision-making? Was Ms. A promised by medical staff that she would be kept informed about her children – for example, if she protested their absence at some point? These historical factors affect how to apply the principles of rights, virtue, and equality (fairness), and they could substantially shape a decision about what to do.

As for the *law and policy* issues, these are probably quite complex, since the contemplated lie (normally against law and policy) is in defense of a life, which law and policy often explicitly or implicitly allow as an exception. But there might be relevant case law worth exploring, or a history of cases at the specific institution, and these might concern not only the general question of informing at-risk patients, but also the question of the role of nurses in withholding such information on physicians' orders.

It is unlikely that *economic* considerations are crucial here, though it might be worth looking into a risk assessment regarding a potential suit by Ms. A or her survivors should we make one choice or another. But it would clearly be important to know more about Ms. A's *cultural and psychological* situation, if possible. Is she someone prone to extreme emotional reactions, or more even-keeled? Is she from a cultural or religious tradition that might affect her way of seeing the loss of a child, or the event of having been lied to about her child?

Step 2: Creative problem-solving

The information gathered in Step 1 might resolve the case: perhaps there is clearly no risk to Ms. A's health, and the physician is simply misinformed. But more likely, the information has only enriched our understanding without clearly resolving the issue. So the next strategy is to find a way out of the dilemma of whether to tell such a terrible lie, or risk killing Ms. A with the truth.

A natural thought is for Ms. C to try to avoid doing either, for instance trying to redirect Ms. A's concern by saying "we need to worry about *you* right now." This would not be a lie, and it might avoid causing Ms. A emotional distress. Alternatively, Ms. C could simply pretend ignorance of the children's condition, which would involve a lie, but arguably a less troublesome one than saying that all the children are fine. Notice, however, that these techniques could actually cause Ms. A to become more irritated and anxious about not receiving the answers she is seeking, which may still risk causing her condition to worsen. So the strategies might be worth trying, but if they do lead to psychological frustration and physiological decline, the nurse would still be faced with the question of whether to ease the anxiety by telling the lie.

Another creative strategy would be to find other family or close friends to support Ms. A before telling her the truth. One could even make sure her husband is on the phone, having been informed of the situation – and perhaps he could help assess whether Ms. A would be able to handle the news, with his knowledge of how she deals with emotional difficulties. But notice that these sorts of strategies still involve acting against the physician's orders, a moral concern involving virtue and rights, so they do not completely avoid the dilemma.

Another possibility would be to medicate Ms. A so that she is unable to ask or worry about her children. Of course, this may be an unreasonable option, given Ms. A's condition, but it may be that induced sleep would be medically advantageous, in which case it is a solution that would avoid the dilemma.

Step 3: Listing the pros and cons

Let us suppose these creative strategies all fail, or face serious moral objections, so Ms. C faces just two primary options: telling Ms. A about the death of her daughter, or lying and saying her daughter is still alive. Of course, there are lots of different ways of telling the truth – bluntly and insensitively, or with care and compassion. And there are different ways of lying: saying her daughter is perfectly OK, saying you are unsure how she is doing, or saying she is in surgery. The differences are important to consider, but for simplicity, we can speak of two options, telling the truth and lying, keeping in mind that there are various ways of exercising each of the options.

The question then is which of the two options is the better one, and to make progress in answering it we can list the pros and cons, putting down the obvious ones first. In favor of telling the truth is that the mother has a right to know about the condition of her own child, which involves the CARVE principle of rights. But in favor of lying to her, despite her apparent right to know, is the consideration that the physician has instructed the nurse to do so, and ordinarily nurses should follow physicians' orders. This involves the CARVE principle of virtue, since it is appealing to a general trait of character that nurses should have: a tendency to respect and follow the instructions of the physicians in charge of their patients' care. Against that idea is of course the thought that lying is wrong, a violation of the autonomy and rights of patients; but against telling the truth is the thought that doing so could seriously harm the mother, given her vulnerable medical condition. This leaves us with the following chart of basic moral pros and cons, with the related CARVE principles in parentheses:

	Pros	Cons
Tell the truth	1. Ms. A has a right to know about her child (Rights)	3. It could cause her condition to worsen (Nonmaleficence)
Lie	2. Dr. B has instructed Ms. C not to tell Ms. A about the daughter's death (Virtue)	4. Lying is wrong (Autonomy, Rights)

To be systematic, let us consider each of the CARVE principles in more detail, to see if we have missed anything. Nonmaleficence is represented by reason #3, the concern not to harm the mother with the news. Beneficence might lead one to try to comfort Ms. A with the lie, but that concern, while morally relevant in most contexts, is trivial in this one, and so it need not be included. Utility requires looking to all those persons affected by one's choices, and that means considering others besides the mother, something not yet incorporated in the pro/con list. Who else might be affected? The other children, of course, if the mother is harmed by hearing the news. There is also a larger concern about the effects of lying on the reputation of health care professionals. If the lie is told, the mother may come to distrust and resent those who lied to her, and that sentiment is one she may share with others. This could harm the reputation of the profession – however important and well-intentioned the lie may have been – leading to future patients not trusting medical professionals, which could mean withholding information or even refraining from seeking medical assistance (at least until it is urgent, and perhaps too late). These are significant concerns overlooked in the first list, and worth adding as a separate reason against lying (see below).

As for the principle of respect for autonomy, it also goes against lying to Ms. A; in misinforming, one would be manipulating Ms. A's view of the world for one's own purposes.[10] This is already reflected in the chart for reason #4. Autonomy might also tell in favor of Ms. C making her own moral decision, rather than just following the physician's directions, which would undercut the importance of reason #2. That is worth noting, but it is something that can be considered later since it concerns an evaluation of the strength of a reason rather than a new reason altogether. Rights are represented – the right to know the truth about your children, and the right not to be lied to. Virtue appears, as the idea that a good nurse should follow a physician's orders. But notice that virtue can also cut the other way: it is not obvious that the virtue of obedience should override virtues of honesty and integrity in the nursing profession. So it would be worth inserting this idea into the chart, especially since Ms. C's own concern, as reflected in the case description, seems to have to do with the matter of her own personal integrity in participating in the lie (see below). Finally, equality (and the related concept of fairness) does not seem directly relevant, unless one speaks of the unfairness of lying to the mother, something better captured by the idea of her rights. The revised pro/con list then reads:

	Pros	Cons
Tell the truth	1. Ms. A has a right to know about her child (Rights)	3. It could cause her condition to worsen (Nonmaleficence)
Lie	2. Dr. B has instructed Ms. C not to tell Ms. A about the daughter's death (Virtue)	4. Lying is wrong (Autonomy, Rights)
		5. May contribute to loss of trust in the medical profession (Utility)
		6. Violates the nurse's honesty and integrity (Virtue)

Step 4: Analysis

All the reasons listed in the chart are morally relevant, and have some moral force. What assumptions must be made to consider any one reason substantially stronger than another?

The most obvious place to start is with *factual assumptions* about how likely the truth is to cause the mother serious harm. One might assume that there is a significant risk, on the grounds that this must be why the doctor wanted to wait until the morning, or based on general knowledge of the effects of emotional stress on the physiology of those under critical care. But is this sufficient evidence? Alternatively, one could argue that it is just as likely the doctor simply wanted to wait so the husband could deal with the mother and her emotional reaction, rather than having to deal with it himself.

If we are forced to admit uncertainty about the likelihood of harm, it raises the question of what the "default" position should be when one is uncertain about causing harm, which can involve *value assumptions* worth exploring. For instance, one might be assuming that even a slight chance of causing death is a powerful, overwhelming moral consideration, based on the idea that the most significant moral principle for health care is to avoid harm (nonmaleficence). Note that this is an assumption about values, not an assumption about the facts: people who *agree* about the chance of causing death could *disagree* about its moral importance. For why think nonmaleficence should override prohibitions on lying, or considerations of rights and autonomy? In recent years more emphasis has been put on respecting the rights and autonomy of patients, even when doing so means that patients may be harmed by hearing bad news, or be allowed to make poor choices. Why not extend this argument to cases where risk of death is involved? Here it might be useful to consider what led to the increased importance of autonomy and rights in health care, and whether the reasons extend to the current kind of case.

Alternatively, one might assume patient's rights and autonomy are so important that they can only be overridden if there is *clear and convincing evidence* of its necessity to avoid serious harm. What could justify putting the burden of proof on the side of the paternalist here? Is this based on a suspicion of the motives of physicians, or on a prioritization of principles of autonomy and rights? If the former, what is the evidence; if the latter, what considerations (or examples) might be used to show that the patient's welfare should not be the sole or main focus of health care ethics? One way to think about this is to notice that there is a chance the mother will die even if lied to, and then she would die under the false belief that her daughter was fine. Is that a terrible thing, suggesting that there is something important about knowing (and telling) the truth regardless of the consequences? Or is it a mercy that the mother did not have to spend her last hours agonizing over the loss of her child, and perhaps her own responsibility for the death?

Similar factual and value assumptions lie behind assessments of the other reasons in the chart. Why think a nurse should follow a physician's orders (reason #2), even when those conflict with the nurse's own moral judgment? Is that based on a factual assumption about the role of nurses in medical practice, and the worry that if nurses were to second-guess physicians' orders it would undermine that role and thereby cause patients harm? What is the evidence for that? If one assumes nurses should follow their own moral compass, valuing integrity and professional autonomy over obedience to physicians, what justifies that assumption? Again, is it based on assumptions about what would work better for the health care profession, for example that nurses are needed in certain cases to advocate for patients or protect them against mistaken or unethical conduct by physicians? What justifies that assumption? Or perhaps there are value assumptions at the root of this question of virtue: perhaps anyone, in any job, should always consider his or her own own moral compass, at least when asked by superiors to do things which would be a serious violation of one's own moral conscience. Perhaps that is a view based simply on the dignity of human beings, on their ultimate autonomy to live by their own values.

Another reason worth examining is #4, that lying is wrong. Some people assume all lies are serious moral violations, while others take beneficent and "white" lies to be morally legitimate.[11] What is behind these differing assumptions? In the case at hand, all would agree the lie is one of great magnitude or import, so it isn't a trivial or white lie, but arguably it is a beneficent lie, designed to save a life. What assumption must be made to think this beneficence sufficient to justify the lie? Is the assumption that lying is wrong based on the belief that it typically is harmful to persons to lie? Is that the essence of the wrongness of lying? Or is lying an interference with rights not so easily overridden by considerations of utility? What assumption must one make to think lying is wrong independent of such utility considerations? If no one is harmed by a lie – indeed, if people are helped – what is left to make the lie wrong?

Step 5: Justification

At this point, having worked through the analysis, one should be better prepared to determine which option is morally preferable. There may be room for reasonable people to disagree about the current case, but let us consider the position that the nurse should lie to the mother, waiting until the morning and the arrival of her husband to tell her of her loss. A simple justification, fitting the recommended format, and with minimal information-gathering involved, could be offered as follows:

I. Introduction
Faced with Ms. A's continual request for information about her children, Ms. C should follow the physician's orders and tell Ms. A her children are fine, seeking to calm the mother and help her make it through the night, when she will be in a more stable and safer condition to receive the news about her loss.

II. Support
The most significant reason for this course of action is the need to protect Ms. A from harm (reason #3). Telling Ms. A of the death of her child could cause her condition to worsen, and increase the risk that she will die. These are reasonably likely consequences, given that she is likely to feel substantial grief and anguish about her involvement, and those emotions are well known to cause physiological stresses that threaten those under critical care. The likelihood is further supported by the physician's order, written in the chart, which indicates the seriousness of the threat in the eyes of the physician. It is not for a nurse to

second-guess such a medical judgment. Moreover, it is extremely important that a nurse not cause such harms, or take substantial risk of doing so. That is the primary ethical command in health care, since its purpose is defined by the goal of tending to the well-being of patients.

Another reason for telling this difficult lie is that the nurse is on orders from the doctor to do so (reason #2). This is not a trivial reason, since physicians are in a clear line of command over nurses. It is an important virtue of nurses that they respect and obey the directives of physicians, since that is their nursing role and generally reflects the differences in levels of education, training, and expertise. Nevertheless, it must be admitted that there is also an important role for nursing autonomy, even on medical questions about which the nurse is especially experienced, and certainly on ethical questions, since a physician's medical training is no guarantee of superior ethical instincts. In addition, respect for moral integrity requires that nurses be considered free to consult their own moral conscience. So if a nurse believes that following a physician's orders would involve a serious violation of ethics, it should be open to the nurse not to do so. As a result, this reason is not a strong one in this case: the nurse has serious reservations, and the existence of a physician's orders does not alone settle what to do.

[Notice: each supporting reason listed in the chart above has been considered, although the author says one of the reasons is not a very important one. The goal is to represent one's own genuine views, not to simply use any reason that one can.]

III. Defense

A significant reason against lying is the simple idea that lying is wrong, a violation of patients' rights and their autonomy (reason #4). For this reason to prevail, in the face of the risk to Ms. A's life, we would need to assume that considerations of rights and autonomy are of equal or greater import than ones of welfare in health care contexts. But what could justify such an assumption? The central mission of medicine is by any lights to serve patient well-being, and any rights or other moral rules are themselves best understood in the service of that mission. It is true that in recent years medical paternalism and its prioritization of patient welfare over autonomy has become less accepted, cut back by various rules and laws about informed consent and the rights of patients. But the history of these changes shows that the new rules and laws were developed precisely because they were seen as necessary to protect patients. Thus informed consent rules have their birth in the discovery of the abuse of patients in medical research (most importantly in the case of the Tuskegee Syphilis Study). And many of the other rules are due to the decline of the family doctor and the rise of bureaucratic, specialized medicine, where the familiarity and trust crucial to a paternalistic model are far more rare. So while there are some good utility reasons for taking rights and autonomy seriously, they do not extend to situations where a person's unwanted and preventable death might be the result. In such a context, one should always look to the ultimate mission of medicine, and err on the side of life.

Another argument against lying is that the mother has a right to know information about her own daughter (reason #1). This is true, but there is the question of timing. The mother has the right to know at some point, but not necessarily right away, in a situation where knowing could endanger her health (or that of others). The right to know is like the right to free speech: it generally holds, but not when someone wants to yell "fire" in a crowded theatre. Telling the mother the truth immediately would be like yelling "fire," possibly leading to serious harm or death, and so we need not do so.

There are also concerns about whether lying in this case, or in cases like this one, could lead to a decrease in trust and respect for the medical profession (reason #5). Again, this is an important consideration, but not a crucial one. The mother will learn the truth in the morning, and it can be explained that the delay was to protect her own life given her unstable condition. Some mothers would focus on the loss of their child, and forget, forgive, or even be grateful for the beneficent lie. Others may be indignant and severely upset, but it is doubtful that would last very long. The chance that Ms. A will reject the paternalistic justification, leading to a long-term distrust of the medical profession that leads to her not seeking necessary care, is fairly small – and worth risking in face of the alternative of definitely risking her health and survival this very night.

Finally, the point can be raised that for the nurse to tell a lie goes against the virtues of honesty and integrity – virtues which we would want nurses to cultivate (reason #6). Here the key is to recognize that those virtues, like all virtues, need to be evaluated in context. Honesty is important, as a basic disposition to tell the truth, but there are exceptions where telling the truth can be a vice. That is obvious when it comes to truths which are confidential or inappropriate, but it also means that there are some cases where lying is consistent with virtue, as in the trivial cases of white lies to put people at ease in social situations ("fine, how are you?"). As for integrity, if the nurse thinks through the arguments put forward here, she would recognize the moral legitimacy of the lie, and thus it would not violate her integrity to do so. So the virtues of honesty and integrity are insufficient to undermine the beneficent lie in this case, as important as they are in other contexts.

IV. Summary
As difficult as it may be for Ms. C, she should tell Ms. A that her children are doing well, to help increase Ms. A's chances of getting through the night. The sole reason is to avoid worsening Ms. A's condition with the terrible news of her child's death. Though telling the lie flies in the face of many ordinary moral norms, it is justified by the motive behind it – protecting the well-being of the patient – and the primacy of that motive in the mission of health care.

Further Steps: Moral Theory and Moral Philosophy

This use of the above framework – the CARVE principles, and the five-step AJ Method – may lead different people to different conclusions about the morally best way to handle ethical issues, in health care contexts and elsewhere. The advantage of using the framework is that it helps make each person's reasoning more complete, subtle, and complex, but it does not ensure that all reasonable people will end up agreeing with one another. Perhaps nothing can do that, but some have tried, and in closing let us briefly consider two additional stages in the process of moral reflection.

The first is the realm of *moral theory*, in which we step beyond our judgments about specific ethical issues and develop a more general moral outlook.[12] This is a natural and common theoretical step, as we seek to organize our moral ideas and make them more coherent, usually by basing them on a set of more fundamental moral principles or values. The theoretically simplest way of doing this is to find a *single* moral principle on which all our moral judgments can be based. One example of such an approach is a moral theory called *utilitarianism*. Someone who has committed to a utilitarian moral theory takes the CARVE principle of utility to be the most fundamental principle for moral thinking. This means that a utilitarian takes concern for the welfare of all to be the deepest, most general, and most important moral consideration, lying at the base of all other thoughts about right and wrong, goodness and evil, virtue and vice. For instance, *why* should we respect individual rights, or the choices and autonomy of individuals? The answer, according to a utilitarian, is that doing so generally involves more benefit than it involves harm: people do not like being interfered with, and generally fare better if left to their own devices. Yet in some cases – such as when the rich want to keep all their income despite the health care needs of the poor, or when a sick person is fearful of life-saving surgery – the utilitarian would set aside claims of rights and autonomy to do what would be best for all concerned. So a utilitarian offers a general answer to the question of what is morally right or wrong in any given situation: it is the choice, of the alternatives, that would promote the most general welfare for all who might be affected by one's choice.[13] Sometimes the benefits and harms are difficult to calculate, so there can be moral controversies based on different factual assumptions; but if utilitarianism is right, there is no basis for a dispute over fundamental values; we should all share a fundamental concern for promoting the general welfare, and that value will decide any questions about whether to follow a certain moral rule or value in a given case. John Stuart Mill is the most well-known historical proponent of this moral theory, a theory which has had tremendous influence on moral and political thinking in the Western world.[14]

Of course, there are other influential moral theories, which prioritize different moral principles, and that's the rub: to enter into moral theory is to enter the realm of controversy all over again, though at a more general level. For instance, those following the philosophy of Immanuel Kant prioritize a version of respect for autonomy over utility.[15] On a Kantian view, the most fundamental moral idea is that we should recognize other moral agents as rational beings – as able to think and evaluate and reason for themselves – and we should respect the dignity of all such rational beings. This means putting far less emphasis on how people *feel*, and more on how they *reason*; less emphasis on promoting health or well-being, and more on respecting individuals; less emphasis on good *outcomes*, more on *duties*. Kantians thus embrace the idea of absolute restrictions on how we can treat other persons. As a result, they reject the utilitarian idea that we should treat persons in ways that promote the general welfare, for that may involve an insult to the dignity of an individual we may be using as a means to greater good. Instead, Kantians seek to base all moral reflection on some idea of respect for the autonomy and dignity of rational beings. There are different versions of Kantianism, based on different ways of fleshing out this basic idea of respect for autonomy, and there is controversy over which of the different approaches is best. But like utilitarianism, Kantianism has been quite influential in Western ethical thought, helping create the recent emphasis in health care ethics on informed consent procedures, as well as having an influence on moral and political thought more generally.

There are also moral theories that reject the attempt to base all ethical thought on a single principle, while still seeking to provide a coherent story about what it is to take a moral point of view. One approach, called *pluralism*, insists that none of the major moral principles is fundamental; different principles have more or less importance in different contexts, with only our moral intuition to judge which principle should prevail in a given case.[16] Other theories stress the importance of virtue, and the development of a virtuous character, rather than the application of principles or rules.[17] Traditional virtue theorists have sought to further develop Aristotle's ancient theory of virtue, while some feminists have argued that the virtue of caring for others should be understood as the organizing idea for moral theory.[18]

To enter moral theory is to investigate these various alternative moral theories, and the kinds of arguments that have been offered for thinking one or another provides a better sense of how to organize and improve ethical reflection. The advantage of engaging in moral theory is that the focus can be on the general value disagreements, which may lead to progress on the larger questions of how to understand and prioritize basic moral principles and values. But a disadvantage is that one may lose a sense of why the value disagreements matter. One may only see what is truly at stake in taking on a general moral outlook if one considers individual decisions about cases and specific moral judgments. Those who study and write about moral theory usually handle this quandary by seeking what John Rawls has defined as "reflective equilibrium" – by adjusting their moral theory in light of considered judgments about individual cases, and vice versa, until there is an overall coherence between the moral theory and what the theorist thinks, on reflection, is the morally best approach to individual cases.[19] This reflective equilibrium may not fit perfectly with some intuitions or gut instincts about cases, due to considerations at the more general level introduced by the moral theory; but one is searching for the most coherent fit one can find between theory and specific moral beliefs. Once again, however, even if you do find a moral theory that is in reflective equilibrium with your various considered judgments about cases, other people may find that a different and competing moral theory is in reflective equilibrium with their own considered judgments. So how can the difference over moral theory be resolved, once the same level of reflective equilibrium has been reached by each party to the dispute?

Moral philosophy is the field of study that seeks to make further progress through the most abstract kinds of questions about the nature of moral thought and discourse.[20] What is the relationship between our different moral concepts of the right, the good, and the virtuous? What would it mean to have a good argument for one moral theory or judgment over another? Is it a matter of finding absolute certainty, or is some kind of intuitive probability sufficient? What would be the ultimate grounds of such a judgment? Indeed, what are we even doing when we make an ethical claim? As G. E. Moore put it, how can we know what is good if we do not first figure out what we mean when we talk about good?[21] What kind of judgment is it that something is good, or that an act is morally wrong? Is ethical judgment the ascription of an objective property, like the property of being red or of weighing two pounds?[22] Or are ethical judgments subjective, matters of personal taste or emotion that make no claims to objectivity, as when we judge a fashion or a musical style to be good or desirable?[23] Yet could a mere difference in subjective tastes be the essence of disagreements about whether patients have a right to refuse treatments, or whether the rich and famous should be given priority in organ transplants?

This level of moral reflection, while quite abstract and seemingly detached, can sometimes enter into practical ethical thinking, A common example is when someone argues against interfering in the affairs of another person or culture, on the grounds that we and they have different ethical judgments, and it is not for us to impose our ethical judgments on them, since ethical judgments are merely relative. This line of reasoning argues from a relativist position in moral philosophy to the conclusion that we should respect the moral views of others. Note though the paradox: the ethical conclusion about respecting others is not taken to be a relative one, so there must be at least some ethical norms that are not relative. This provides an example of how reflections at the most general level of moral philosophy sometimes enter into everyday ethical life, for better or for worse.

The upshot is that there is no end to the process of reflecting on moral questions. Which kinds of reflection are most important is itself a matter of controversy, as is even the question of whether reflection is itself a good thing. This essay has offered a fairly uncontroversial approach, emphasizing principles and basic reasoning steps useful in evaluating moral issues and justifying one's position. The CARVE principles and the AJ Method procedure are more than enough for most of us, busy as we are, to make our moral choices and get on with our lives. But for those who seek to go further, moral theory and moral philosophy are ways to deepen and enrich one's understanding of the moral domain.

NOTES

1   Kurt Baier, *The Moral Point of View: A Rational Basis of Ethics* (Ithaca, NY: Cornell University Press, 1958).
2   Some writers have made distinctions between "the moral" and "the ethical," with the moral being more closely tied to everyday notions of guilt, punishment, and

explicit social rules. We will follow the more common usage and take *moral* and *ethical* to be roughly synonymous.

3 The judgment that moral considerations should prevail is an overall normative assessment, not a narrowly moral one, a sense of what would be best "all things considered."

4 See Tom L. Beauchamp and James F. Childress, *Principles of Biomedical. Ethics*, 4th edn. (New York: Oxford University Press, 1994), pp. 28–40.

5 This version of the list of principles, and the acronym, is from Becky Cox-White and Eric H. Gampel, "Resolving moral dilemmas: a case-based method," *HEC Forum* 8, no. 2 (1996): 89–90.

6 The Principle of Equality does allow unequal treatment if people are different in a way that *is* morally relevant. As an obvious example, emergency room personnel may treat a person with a jammed finger "differently" from one in cardiac arrest, treating the latter more quickly and more intensively than the former, without being in violation of the Principle of Equality.

7 The use of a similar method in teaching is discussed in Eric Gampel, "A method for teaching ethics," *Teaching Philosophy* 19, no. 4 (1996): 371–83.

8 The "facts" in this sense are not known or provable, but we might find that our own views presuppose that the facts are a certain way.

9 This case is adapted from B. Tate, *The Nurse's Dilemma* (Geneva: International Council of Nurses, 1977). The discussion is based on White and Gampel, note 5, above.

10 The principle of autonomy is usually understood to prohibit misinforming while requiring the provision of accurate information. Both involve shaping a person's choices, but misinformation does so in a way that serves one's own purposes – even if one's purpose is beneficence – and thus counts as a kind of manipulation, whereas informing a person as to the facts simply allows the person to make a decision in light of all the relevant information.

11 Sisela Bok, *Lying: Moral Choice in Public and Personal Life* (New York: Vintage Books, 1989).

12 For an accessible overview of moral theory, see James Rachels, *The Elements of Moral Philosophy*, 2nd edn. (New York: McGraw-Hill, 1993).

13 This is a version of utilitarianism called "act utilitarianism," since we are applying the principle of utility to the individual act to see if it is morally best. A different suggestion is that we should follow the rules that would, if generally followed, promote the greatest overall welfare. See Richard B. Brandt, *A Theory of the Right and the Good* (Oxford: Oxford University Press, 1979), pp. 271–305.

14 John Stuart Mill, *Utilitarianism* (New York: Bobbs-Merrill, 1957).

15 For a good historical survey of Kantian and other moral theories, see T. C. Denise, S. P. Peterfreund, and N. P. White (eds.), *Great Traditions in Ethics*, 9th edn. (Belmont, CA: Wadsworth, 1999).

16 William Ross, *The Right and the Good* (Oxford: Oxford University Press, 1932).

17 For an overview of virtue ethics, see Rachels, note 12 above, pp. 159–79.

18 Nel Noddings, *Caring: A Feminine Approach to Ethics and Moral Education* (Berkeley: University of California Press, 1984).

19 John Rawls, *A Theory of Justice* (Cambridge, MA: Harvard University Press, 1971), pp. 20–1, 46–50.

20 For an overview that emphasizes these more abstract questions, see Gilbert Harman, *The Nature of Morality* (New York: Oxford University Press, 1977).

21 C. E. Moore, *Principia Ethica* (Cambridge: Cambridge University Press, 1993).

22 Moore defended this sort of objectivity of ethical properties in *Principia Ethica*. For a defense of ethical objectivity in the tradition of virtue ethics and natural law, see John Finnis, *Natural Law and Natural Rights* (Oxford: Clarendon Press, 1980). In the Kantian tradition, see Christine Korsgaard, *Sources of Normativity* (Cambridge: Cambridge University Press, 1996).

23 For an account that emphasizes ethical attitudes and emotions, see Allan Gibbard, *Wise Choices, Apt Feelings* (Cambridge, MA: Harvard University Press, 1990). Another kind of subjectivism has been developed by Simon Blackburn, who draws an analogy between subjective color judgments and ethical judgments; see "How to be an ethical anti-realist," in *Essays in Quasi-Realism* (Oxford: Oxford University Press, 1993).

PART II

CASES AND COMMENTARIES

3

THE EYE OF THE BEHOLDER

Ethical Issues in the Arts

Case One: Monumental Controversies – The FDR Memorial

Case Two: Fire Sale – Destroying Privately Owned Works of Art

Case Three: What Price Immortality? – The *Body Worlds* Exhibition

Case Four: Finders Keepers, Losers Weepers? – Returning Antiquities to Their
   Countries of Origin

Case Five: Faux Paws – The Genetically Engineered Bunny

The arts fire the imagination, nourish the spirit, stir the emotions, and challenge
the intellect. Art, in all its forms, is intrinsically interwoven with personal and
cultural perceptions of meaning and expressions of identity. The power, meaning, and importance of art are often a curious blend of private and public interests. Common – but also idiosyncratic – threads of identity, value, ownership,
traditions, and dignity run through quandaries posed by the creation, display,
and preservation of art that are examined in the first set of cases. Competing
conceptions of the arts as entertainment, as knowledge, as mechanisms for appreciating the human condition, as "belonging" (in various senses of the word) to
populations vs. individuals, as goods for sale, as priceless heritage – to mention
only a few of these competing conceptions – raise numerous ethical questions.

Should individuals have the right to determine how they are portrayed in public art? Is dignity compromised when the human body is exposed as a means of
entertainment – even if the "owners" of these bodies consent? Do private owners
of beloved or historically significant works of art bear any responsibility for
their stewardship? When is possession (mere) ownership? Is altering a life form
in pursuit of artistic fulfillment creativity or exploitation? These and other dilemmas are considered in "The Eye of the Beholder: Ethical Issues in the Arts."

CASE ONE: MONUMENTAL CONTROVERSIES – THE FDR MEMORIAL

The FDR Memorial in Washington, DC, honors President Franklin Delano Roosevelt, the 32nd President of the United States. Visitors travel through his presidency, wandering along pathways of the beautiful park-like memorial where symbolic sculptures, secluded alcoves, waterfalls, and pools mark significant events of his time in office. Compared with the park, the entrance is simple: an open plaza, empty except for a 10-foot statue of President Roosevelt in a wheelchair.

The statue was not part of the original design; in fact, it is the antithesis of the original plan. A robust athlete, Franklin Delano Roosevelt was stricken with polio at the age of 39, leaving him crippled and confined to a wheelchair, his legs withered and virtually useless. President Roosevelt never denied his limitations. He campaigned vigorously for a polio vaccine, and visited the Warm Springs rehabilitation center annually. However, he went to great lengths to conceal his disability, and few Americans were aware that he was impaired. For deeply personal and symbolic reasons, he did not want to appear disabled. He believed his physical impairment would appear to be a symbol of weakness when the country – and the world – needed a strong leader. President Roosevelt's personal appearances were staged so he never appeared in a wheelchair, with braces, or with any apparent disability. His braces were painted to match the color of his pants so they wouldn't show when he was seated. Except for his fireside chats, President Roosevelt insisted on standing for all public appearances, and podiums were reinforced to bear his full weight. His wishes were honored to such an extent that, by unspoken agreement, the press didn't photograph him in motion. Almost all photographs taken of President Roosevelt during his public life show him seated behind a desk, visible only from the chest upwards. The few photographs of him in a wheelchair, taken by family and close friends, were not released until decades after his death. When FDR Memorial designer Lawrence Halprin tried to find photos of President Roosevelt in a wheelchair, only four were found in more than 10,000 taken of him during his presidency (Stein 2004: 36–7). Why is it, then, that the first thing people are intended to notice in the public monument to honor President Roosevelt is his infirmity – the one thing he took such pains to hide?

Controversies surrounding the FDR Memorial erupted almost from its inception. In 1946, a little over a year after his death, Congress approved the concept of a memorial honoring President Roosevelt. Disagreements over design and funding stalled the project for 30 years. Three decades later, in 1975, the Franklin Delano Roosevelt Memorial Commission finally approved Lawrence Halprin's proposal for the memorial. A year later, the District of Columbia Commission of Fine Arts, a separate body that regulates public art in Washington, DC, also granted its approval for the design. More delays followed, and work on the monument finally began in 1991. Bowing to pressure from advocacy groups, the final design did not include images of President Roosevelt's ever-present cigarette holder, nor of Eleanor Roosevelt's fox fur (Struck 1997b: A01).

Ironically, President Franklin Roosevelt had himself been involved in a controversy over the monument to one of his predecessors, President Thomas Jefferson. John Russell Pope designed two presidential memorials: one for President Jefferson and one for President Theodore Roosevelt. The Thomas Jefferson Memorial Commission approved Pope's design for the Jefferson Memorial in 1936. After Pope's death the following year, the Commission of Fine Arts recommended that two of his former associates modify Pope's original design, despite his widow's plea against this happening, and substitute the design Pope had created for a memorial to President Theodore Roosevelt. When the Memorial Commission circumvented the process and appealed directly to President Franklin Roosevelt, the president settled the controversy by allowing Pope's former associates to modify his design. Critics decried the undemocratic and un-Jeffersonian process used to select a design for his memorial, and the use of the designer's work in a way he had neither intended nor approved (NPSDI 2004). Partly because of the furor surrounding the Jefferson Memorial design, President Roosevelt requested that any monument to himself be a simple, unadorned, desk-sized block of granite placed in front of the National Archives (Gabor 1997: 106).

Conscious of the controversies other monuments aroused, Lawrence Halprin put considerable thought into creating one that would unite people. Speaking before a joint session of Congress on December 8, 1941, President Roosevelt asked Congress to declare war, calling the previous day, when Pearl Harbor was attacked, "a date which will live in infamy" (Roosevelt 1941). Although Halprin served in World War II on a destroyer that was split in two by a Kamikaze pilot, he deliberately chose not to use President Roosevelt's famous quote on the monument, to avoid giving offense to former wartime enemies (Struck 1997a: A01). Halprin designed the memorial park with the disabled community in mind, including in his initial design a statue of President Roosevelt in an exact replica of the wheelchair he used, and depicting the president's disability in granite. He designed the park to be wheelchair-accessible. Halprin's aim was to maintain historical accuracy while honoring the former president by showing him as he allowed himself to be seen (PBS 1997).

As the project neared completion in the mid-1990s, disability advocates threatened to delay the monument's completion and disrupt its dedication. Protesters requested that the original design be changed to depict the president more prominently in a wheelchair. Although room three of the original design included Halprin's statue of President Roosevelt seated in his wheelchair, advocates contended that this did not show his impairment conspicuously enough. President Roosevelt's many great accomplishments, achieved despite his disability, made him a powerful symbol for the disability community. To fail to emphasize his physical impairment, they charged, fictionalized history. Disability advocates asked that an oversized statue of President Roosevelt, seated in a large wheelchair, be prominently displayed at the entrance of the memorial. Protestors staged rallies, promising continued demonstrations until their request was granted. Proponents of the original design argued that the memorial was intended to be not only a monument to history, but also a memorial to honor President Roosevelt. To depict him in a way that he would find personally objectionable would dishonor him and reflect the political era in which the monument was built, rather than the one it was meant to represent. Accusations of revisionism and political correctness flew back and forth (Stein 2004: 51).

President Clinton accommodated the wishes of the disability advocates: a week prior to the dedication, he met with disability advocates and acceded to their demands for the modification of the statue (Stout 1997: B8). At his request, on the evening of May 1, 1997, the Senate approved the addition of the statue, and sent the legislation to the House. The following day President Clinton dedicated the FDR Memorial, more than two decades after its approval and half a century after its conception. Two months after the memorial's dedication, on July 24, President Clinton signed Public Law 10529, to provide "an addition of a permanent statue, base relief, or other similar structure to the [FDR Memorial] to provide recognition of the fact that President Roosevelt's leadership in the struggle by the United States for peace, well-being, and human dignity was provided while the President used a wheelchair" (USDI 1997). Four months later, on September 12, Secretary of the Interior Bruce Babbitt announced the formation of a committee to determine "where and how an addition to the memorial will recognize that President Roosevelt used a wheelchair while leading the Nation through some of its most difficult times" (USDI 1997). Lawrence Halprin agreed to work with the committee to create an appropriate addition to the memorial, and a commission was appointed in September 1997 to work with the memorial's designer to incorporate the changes (USDI 1997). Over the next four years, disability advocates raised $1.65 million for the statue. In January 2001, the oversized bronze figure of President Roosevelt, seated in a wheelchair, was placed prominently at the entrance of the memorial.

Were advocates for the disabled morally justified in threatening to disrupt the dedication of the FDR Memorial if President Clinton did not agree to include in the memorial a statue prominently depicting President Roosevelt in a wheelchair?

Perspective One

A statue of President Roosevelt in his wheelchair should be the first image to be seen by visitors to the FDR Memorial. We base this position on appeals to consequences and justice.

Not only was it morally permissible for disability advocates to insist that President Roosevelt be prominently depicted in a wheelchair, despite his insistence that his disability be kept from the public, it was also morally imperative. The benefits that would accrue to persons with impairments, and to all of society, were many and significant. These included recognition that disability does not prevent unparalleled accomplishment; inspiration to persist, despite challenges; and knowledge that worth is measured by what a person can do, and not what a person cannot do. Insisting that President Roosevelt's physical limitations be publicly acknowledged proclaimed the message that discrimination against persons with disabilities is not to be tolerated.

Moreover, these benefits would not be accompanied by any harms. We consider "harm," as Honderich does, to be an action that negatively affects others or their interests, or that leaves individuals worse off than they would have been but for the action, or that is intended to deprive an individual of pleasure or a right, or that has negative consequences (Honderich 2005: 359–60). By any of these characterizations of harm, we can see that President Roosevelt – being dead – was beyond harm. Further, the knowledge of his disability did not diminish his reputation and accomplishments, but enhanced them. Nor was anyone else harmed. In sum, a consequential analysis demonstrates that depicting President Roosevelt in his wheelchair generated numerous benefits and no harms. Since the consequences of this approach were uniformly positive, advocates for the disabled were morally justified in insisting that the president be conspicuously depicted in his wheelchair.

Failing to show President Roosevelt's impairment would not, however, correct historic harms to the disabled: discrimination, lack of opportunity, ostracism. For centuries, disabled individuals have been marginalized, abused, discriminated against, and thwarted in their attempts to fulfill their potential. Despite laws to remove obstacles, and policies to insure equity and access, contrived barriers still circumscribe the ability of many to participate fully in the activities of society and share in its resources. Moreover, these obstructions are undeserved and, thus, unfair and unjust. For society to continue to tolerate so great an injustice, an injustice created and sustained by prejudicial perception, is morally indefensible. President Franklin Roosevelt was perhaps the world's most respected leader at a time of unparalleled global turmoil, despite being disabled. He demonstrated that disability need not affect ability, and so is a particularly powerful symbol of hope and inspiration for disabled individuals.

In conclusion, public demonstration, even if it diminishes others' pleasure or infringes on their choices, is justified if it results in greater good for greater numbers and if it rectifies injustice. Advocates for the disabled were justified in threatening to disrupt the FDR Memorial dedication ceremony.

Perspective Two

Advocates for the disabled were not morally justified in threatening to disrupt the dedication of the FDR Memorial if President Clinton did not agree to have a statue of President Roosevelt in his wheelchair incorporated into the FDR Memorial. We base this position on an appeal to autonomy.

The golden rule, a fundamental principle of most moral theories and religious traditions, requires that we treat others as we want to be treated, and to refrain from doing to others what we would not wish to have done to us. Surely we would want others to respect our wishes regarding how we are publicly portrayed, particularly if, like President Roosevelt, we have clearly made our wishes known and demonstrated through consistent effort the sincerity of our desires. President Roosevelt clearly did not want his disability to be shown publicly. Not only did his family and friends honor his request, but, in an era of greater civility, even the news media respected his wishes.

The principle of autonomy justifies choices of individuals both to define and protect their identity and their dignity, and entails that others refrain from undermining those choices. These choices are fundamental to our self-concept. How we define ourselves and how we choose to let the world see us are important to who we are as persons. The right of self-determination absolves us of any obligation to become an unwilling symbol for others, no matter how noble the intention or good the cause.

The rights of freedom of speech and assembly come with the responsibility to respect the mutual rights of others to free speech and assembly. The exercise of the freedom of speech requires more than the opportunity to talk: it also necessitates an environment of respect. This imposes on others the responsibility not to interfere with this right by disruptive actions or irrelevant intrusions. Freedom of assembly entails not only the right to gather with others, but the responsibility to respect the intentions for which others come together, and not contravene their purposes by imposing an agenda of self-interest.

In conclusion, the principle of autonomy prohibited advocates for the disabled from threatening to disrupt the FDR Memorial dedication ceremony if the request to prominently depict President Roosevelt in a wheelchair had been denied.

Perspective Three

This dilemma is a moral conflict between consequences and justice, on the one hand, and autonomy, rights, and equality of consideration and respect on the other. The two perspectives are mutually exclusive. Yet each offers compelling and morally justifiable reasons for addressing a conflict between consequences and autonomy, and among justice and rights and equality, and weighing relative rights and responsibilities, as well as harms and benefits between an individual and society. These principles are not always in conflict, but, as this case demonstrates, at times they may be. What are the implications of each response?

Step 1: Information-gathering

Implications

- Will including the statue advance progress towards equality that has eluded the disabled community throughout history?

- Would disrupting the dedication cause future gatherings to be more closely controlled, diminishing rights of free speech and assembly?
- How is the public likely to react to disruption of the memorial service by disability activists?
- Would backlash in response to disruption reverse progress already made in opportunities for and perceptions of the abilities of the disabled community?

History

- Have memorials often raised controversies? If so, how have these been resolved and what were the justifications for these resolutions?
- How have disabled individuals been treated through history?

Legal

- Have laws been adequate to insure equity for the disabled?

Psychosocial

- Would disrupting the ceremony have raised awareness of the barriers that still exist for the disabled?
- Will the inclusion of a statue in the FDR Memorial of President Roosevelt in a wheelchair serve as an inspiration to others who struggle in a society that judges competence by traits other than capability?
- If advocates had not spoken out, would a moment to advance opportunities for the disabled have been missed?
- If President Roosevelt were alive today, would he choose to be represented with his wheelchair?

Step 2: Creative problem-solving

Any creative solution will have to achieve the specified benefits for currently disabled persons while respecting the autonomous choice of President Roosevelt. While achieving the benefits was unlikely to occur prior to the dedication, President Clinton's advocacy for eliminating barriers for disabled individuals through legislation was an important step. Signing the legislation at the FDR Memorial was a highly visible response to concerns raised by advocates for the disabled. Just as Interior Secretary Bruce Babbitt advanced the formation of a committee to consider an addition to the FDR Memorial, what other issues of interest to the disabled community could be addressed, with similar support, with advocates for the disabled participating and leading these efforts? However, much of the creative solution to address this situation lies outside the agency of the individuals involved. While it might be agreed that it is the obligation of all conscionable individuals to end discrimination and maltreatment directed at the disabled, there may be differing opinions on the best way to do so. As this case demonstrates, making the appropriate moral choice is often difficult.

Step 3: Listing pros and cons

Options	Pros	Cons
Advocates for the disabled should disrupt the dedication of the FDR Memorial if the request to prominently depict President Roosevelt in a wheelchair isn't honored.	1. Raises awareness of challenges to disabled (C-B) 2. Inspires others with disabilities (C-B) 3. Increases opportunities for persons with disabilities (C-B, C-U, J-E) 4. Increases tolerance for persons with disabilities (C-B, J)	5. Turbulent public gathering (C-NM, C-U, R) 6. Restrictions on speech and assembly (C-NM, C-U, R) 7. Backlash (C-NM, C-U) 8. President Roosevelt is treated as a means to an end (C-NM, A, J-E) 9. Invades President Roosevelt's privacy (R)
Advocates for the disabled should not disrupt the dedication of FDR Memorial if the request to prominently depict President Roosevelt in a wheelchair is not honored.	10. President Roosevelt's wishes honored (A)	11. Missed opportunity to raise awareness, create change for the disability community (C-B, C-U, J-E, J-F)

Both options are persuasive, but which carries greater moral justification?

Step 4: Analysis

Factual assumptions

- Different times and circumstances create different perspectives and mores. What was considered appropriate to reveal or disclose about an individual at the time of President Roosevelt's death in 1945 reflects a different ethos from today.
- History incorporates not only facts, but also interpretations.
- Society is best served when all its members are able to make full use of their talents.
- Discrimination is not accidental: it is created by prejudice, fear, and indifference.

Value assumptions

- All individuals should have equitable opportunities to develop and use their abilities and contribute to society.
- Public leaders should have the right to privacy in their personal lives, and control of their public image, as long as this protection does not affect their leadership responsibilities.
- People's wishes about how they will be depicted in a public monument honoring them should be respected.

Step 5: Justification

Compelling arguments exist both for and against the moral justification of the disability advocates' threat to disrupt the FDR Memorial dedication ceremony. In balancing consequences and justice against autonomy, rights, and equality of consideration and respect, we find the latter to be more persuasive.

Historically, controversies abound in the design of public monuments. Early in President Franklin Roosevelt's first term, the New Deal's Public Works of Art Project commissioned more than two dozen unemployed artists to paint a series of murals depicting California's cultural history on the walls of San Francisco's Coit Tower. One of the murals included images of *The Daily Worker* newspaper and a copy of Karl Marx's *Das Kapital*. Angry vigilantes threatened to storm Coit Tower and destroy the offending communistic mural, while irate citizens condemned the expenditure of public money on un-American art. As a result of the mural controversies, the building was closed during the summer of 1934 (SFAI 2007).

Maya Lin was a 20-year-old Yale University student when her design for the Vietnam Veterans Memorial was submitted. Despite the elegant and profoundly moving simplicity of Lin's design, detractors criticized her youth, ethnicity, and inexperience, and argued for a traditional heroic sculpture by a more seasoned artist (Mock 1995).

Particularly controversial are monuments hewn into the Black Hills of South Dakota. Sculptor Gutzon Borglum used drills and dynamite to carve the faces of Presidents George Washington, Thomas Jefferson, Abraham Lincoln, and Theodore Roosevelt into the granite bluff of Mount Rushmore. Many take pride in Mount Rushmore's colossal presidential sculptures, which symbolize the strength of the United States and the vision, courage, and tenacity of its leaders. Others call the sculpture an abomination that scars the most sacred site of the Great Sioux Nation.

Mount Rushmore is in the heart of the Black Hills, land granted to the Sioux in the Fort Laramie Treaty of 1851, but reclaimed when General George Custer's 7th Cavalry discovered gold there in 1874. Despite efforts to drive tribes from their lands and annihilate their members, culminating with the Sell or Starve Bill (Indian Appropriations Act) of 1876, surviving tribal members chose to starve rather than leave or sell their sacred lands. Finally, in 1888 Congress stripped the tribe of ownership to gain control of the gold-rich Black Hills (Inouye 1988: 10). In 1927, a mere 39 years later, work began on the Mount Rushmore sculptures. In 1939, Chief Henry Standing Bear of the Oglala Sioux approached Korczak Ziolkowski, a sculptor who had worked on the Mount Rushmore memorial, and asked him to carve a sculpture honoring Chief Crazy Horse. Chief Crazy Horse, a Lakota Sioux born in the Black Hills, was a hero revered not only for his fearlessness in protecting his tribe, but also for his compassion for the elderly, widowed, and orphaned. Henry Standing Bear and other chiefs wanted the world to recognize that Native Americans also had great heroes. However, not all Native Americans agreed with the chiefs (House Resolution 482 2005). Russell Means and other Native American activists criticized the monument as further desecrating sacred land and the Lakota spirit. Crazy Horse would allow neither his photograph to be taken, nor sketches to be made of him. The Lakota place greater value on community than on individual achievement. Opponents of the monument argued that singling out Crazy Horse to be depicted on a monument, especially as he wanted no images made of himself, dishonored both the man and his culture (Roberts 2001: 38). Yet even as controversies delayed construction of these monuments, they generated public discussion and raised awareness of moral dilemmas and the inherently conflicting interests they identify.

Controversies also pervade the historical treatment of persons with disabilities. During President Franklin Roosevelt's lifetime, more than half the states in the United States passed laws allowing sterilization of those considered to be a burden on society. Between 1927 and 1972 more than 70,000 young people, whom the government decreed unfit to reproduce, were sexually sterilized (Eadie 1993). Many state and municipalities enforced "Ugly Laws." These ordinances prohibited people who were maimed or considered unsightly from being seen in public or exposing themselves to others (*UAB v. Garrrett* 2000: 2a). It is not surprising that President Roosevelt fiercely hid his disability in a society of such intolerance. Although the 1990 Americans with Disabilities Act addressed many inequities, discrimination against 50 million disabled Americans persisted (Stein 2004: 51). Until 1999, disabled individuals had to choose between employment and healthcare, as, once employed, they often became ineligible for Medicaid or Medicare. President Clinton signed the Ticket to Work and Work Incentives Improvement Act of 1999 into law at the FDR Memorial in December 1999. This legislation greatly improved employment opportunities for the disabled, and benefited both the economy and society (Public Law 106–70).

The principle of consequences, which judges an act by its outcomes, justifies the protestors' demonstration on the basis of beneficence and utility. The disability advocates' threats to disrupt the FDR Memorial dedication ceremony raised awareness of the barriers that still exist for disabled individuals. The protesters' actions resulted in the inclusion in the memorial of a strikingly visible statue of President Roosevelt in a wheelchair. The statue is an inspiration to those who struggle in a society that judges competence by traits other than capability. While inclusion of the statue cannot harm President Roosevelt, it does benefit countless others. Does the benefit that disabled individuals receive by progress toward removing physical and attitudinal barriers that hinder them from reaching their full potential outweigh the harm to President Roosevelt by the denial of his autonomous choice to preserve his public image?

Harm can be analyzed in terms of its relative maleficence. Of the three types of harm – actions, omissions, and using persons as means to another's ends – the greater harms are those caused by actions rather than omissions, when the injury is the means to a goal rather than a foreseeable side affect, and when the victim is physically present (as opposed to there being no physical contact with the victim) (Cushman et al. 2006: 1086–8). Erecting a statue of President Roosevelt is a deliberate action, rather than an omission, and the action is a means to a goal. However, as the former president is dead, he cannot be harmed. Thus, it may be argued that the benefits to the disabled community are more persuasive, and beneficence holds sway (Reasons ##1, 2, 3).

The principle of utility, however, requires that individuals forsake the full measure of their own benefit when failing to do so causes harm to others or prevents maximizing benefit. This principle extends special protection to the interests of the majority (Driver 2007: 44). In placing benefit to the community above benefit to the individual, utility promotes civil societies by encouraging concern for the welfare of all its members or of the group considered collectively, by promoting greater tolerance and acceptance of all citizens (Reason #4). President Roosevelt wished to conceal his disability. However, the powerful public evidence that his physical limitations had no affect on his extraordinary abilities is of great value to members of the disabled community as well as to the larger society, particularly to the segment that equates disability with inability. Society benefits from the dismantling of barriers based on prejudice, fear, indifference, and thoroughgoing selfishness. A public memorial that prominently expresses both President Roosevelt's accomplishments and his physical limitation may help to overcome those negative perceptions and social barriers. This will benefit individuals who will have greater opportunities to develop and use their abilities to contribute to society, and to the society that will benefit from the contributions of all its members. The benefits gained by removing barriers to disabled persons outweigh an individual's right to place personal preferences above societal good.

Throughout history, disabled individuals have suffered discrimination and persecution: forced confinement to institutions, imposed sterilization, loss of parental rights, lack of employment opportunity, diminished educational options, and limited access to buildings, public spaces, recreational areas, and transportation (*UAB v. Garrrett* 2000). Even today, disabled individuals bear many of the same social and emotional burdens, imposed on them by a prejudiced society. The right to personal identity and self-development for all individuals is a global issue. Article 22 of the 1948 Universal Declaration of Human Rights states: "Everyone, as a member of society, has the right to social security and is entitled to realization, through national effort and international co-operation and in accordance with the organization and resources of each State, of the economic, social and cultural rights indispensable for his dignity and the free development of his personality" (Van Der Heijden and Tahzib-Lie 1998: 236). The threat of disrupting the ceremony resulted in progress towards justice – in the forms of equality of consideration and of fairness – that has eluded the disability community throughout history. Fairness, according to philosopher John Rawls, requires that each individual have equal access to liberty and opportunity, with inequalities arranged to favor the least advantaged (Driver 2007: 112–13; Honderich 2005: 464). Failing to use the dedication ceremony to raise awareness of continued discrimination against disabled persons would result in a lost opportunity to create change (Reason #11).

The appeals to consequences and justice make a compelling case to support disability advocates threat to disrupt the ceremony. Let us consider the other perspective.

Preserving the balance between the interests of the individual and the interests of others is an ongoing, ever-present, and difficult challenge. Societies are formed as a way of organizing services, distributing burdens and benefits, and avoiding chaos. In choosing to become part of a society, individuals bind themselves to mutually agreed-upon rules for living together. When individuals choose their self-interest and desires over the good of others, beneficence and utility are compromised and society suffers, particularly individual members who are already disadvantaged by inequitable distribution of burdens and benefits.

But harm to society can also stem from deliberately acting against an individual's expressed and explicit wishes. In some circumstances there is a legal right to control the image of an individual after death; but this right is often more concerned with financial gain from use of the person's image than with protection of the individual's identity. Protecting the financial interests of the use of a person's image, but disregarding the individual's personal choices, particularly of an individual being publicly honored, indicates a society that tolerates exploitation (Reason #8).

Kantian moral theory is grounded on the principles of moral universalizability, autonomy, and respect for persons (Hill 2000). Moral universalizability, or Kant's Categorical Imperative, requires that we act only in ways that we would permit to become universal laws (Boylan 2000: 92–9). Respect for persons requires that individuals be treated as significant in themselves, and not merely as a means to others' ends. Only actions that support the status of individuals as free and rational beings are morally justifiable. Is there any compelling moral justification in forcing President Roosevelt to become a symbol for a purpose that, while eminently worthy, portrays him in a way he consistently and diligently fought to avoid? Kantian moral theory argues that there is not, that doing so disrespects President Roosevelt by using him as a mere means to achieve others' goals.

Using President Roosevelt as a metaphor for Herculean achievement in the face of physical disability, thus disregarding the extraordinary lengths he went to in order to hide his infirmity in public, deprives him of autonomy regarding his own person (Reasons ##8, 9). Many people, including some of his descendants, believe that, were he alive today, President Roosevelt would actively promote the image of disability as an inconvenience rather than a limitation, and would agree to be a visible symbol of accomplishment and leadership for the disabled community. However, these claims that President Roosevelt would choose to publicize his condition are speculative, with even his grandchildren divided on the issue. His oldest grandson, Curtis, who lived in the White House with his grandparents for a time, feels strongly that his grandfather would not want a statue to show that he was disabled (Gabor 1997: 106). Another grandson, David, agreed that the design should not be changed to include a second and very prominent statue of his grandfather in a wheelchair. David Roosevelt, a member of the Franklin Delano Roosevelt Memorial Commission, noted that the commission approved a design that included several depictions of the president's disabilities, but chose not to make them the memorial's focus (Stout 1997: B8). On the other side of the debate, President Roosevelt's granddaughter, Anne, believes he would have wanted such a statue (PBS 1997). Both positions are based on personal knowledge of the former president: the first reaffirms that his wishes would not change, even in a different social environment; the other assumes they would. Yet, assumptions that President Roosevelt would have changed his mind are clearly subjective. Ample evidence confirms that his decision was informed and uncoerced, and so met the requirements for autonomous choice.

Kant was adamantly against making moral arguments by appealing to hypothetical consequences; not only does this undermine autonomy and respect, but – given the unpredictability of outcomes based on subjective speculation – this appeal is often mistaken. All individuals have equal claim to freedom and, hence, to autonomy. Because substituting one's own judgment for another's fails to respect autonomy (Reason #10), doing so is morally impermissible. Public figures have the right to some privacy if it does not affect their ability to govern (Reason #8). By disregarding his clear and repeated desire to hide the fact that President Roosevelt was impaired, and using that very condition to promote their own agenda, however noble the cause, advocates for the disabled used the president as a means to further their cause. In doing so, they denied the fundamental respect due to him as a person (Reason #9).

To make this point differently, consider Norma McCorvey. Ms. McCorvey became known as Jane Roe, to protect her identity as the plaintiff in the 1973 Supreme Court case, *Roe v. Wade*, which affirmed a woman's right to make reproductive decisions about her own body. Although Ms. McCorvey never had an abortion – she placed her baby for adoption – she became the symbol of a woman's right to decide when and whether to bear a child. In 1997, she became an outspoken opponent of abortion, expressing regret for her involvement in *Roe v. Wade* (*McCorvey v. Hill* 2004). Protecting life and protecting the right of autonomy regarding one's own body are both worthy endeavors. Supporters of reproductive choice and anti-abortionists now both hail Norma McCorvey as a hero.

Now suppose, many years in the future, that both groups decide to erect a statue of Ms. McCorvey to recognize the role she played in furthering their goals. Neither claims of historical accuracy nor her value as a symbol are morally supportable reasons for using her identity without her permission – because both groups would portray Ms. McCorvey inaccurately and, given her change of beliefs, in ways to which she would object. Just as there is a moral imperative to refrain from memorializing Norma McCorvey in a manner she might find objectionable, there is a moral obligation to refrain from depicting President Roosevelt, to advance the goals and interests of others, in a way he clearly did not want to be portrayed (Reasons ##8, 9).

Justifying the action to disregard the autonomous and well-known decisions of the deceased has other consequences; consider a will, for example. Imagine that you leave in your will a sizeable amount to an animal rights organization for their fight against the use of animals in laboratory research. After your death, your heirs have appealed to overturn the provisions of the will so the money can be used to construct a research facility that studies the disease that caused your demise. The facility will be named in your honor. It will use laboratory animals in research. Are your heirs morally justified in using your legacy and your name in a manner that is the exact opposite of your known wishes, by substituting their judgment, goals, and interests for yours? They are not.

The question of autonomy, as it applies to truth-telling and free decision-making in recording and interpreting history, raises intriguing issues. Disability advocates charge that failure to depict President Roosevelt as unmistakably impaired is a falsification of history (Stein 2004: 51). Others contend that showing him in a way he never allowed himself to be seen is a falsification of his identity. All of history, even faithfully chronicled and factually portrayed eyewitness events, is interpreted. Who has the right to interpret history and decide how it will be memorialized?

As part of the withdrawal of Russian troops stationed in former Soviet bloc countries until the early 1990s, countries such as Poland, Estonia, and Hungary agreed to maintain Soviet cemeteries and memorials. How these should be preserved is disputed. The governments of Russia and Poland are at odds over Russian memorials within Poland's borders. More than half a million Soviet army soldiers died liberating Poland from Nazi rule. Hundreds of thousand of these soldiers are buried in Poland, in cemeteries carefully maintained at the expense of Polish taxpayers. However, Poland is demanding its right to remove Soviet monuments and replace them with their own. Although the Soviet army freed Poland from Nazi brutality, the "liberators" became tyrants, plundering Poland and subjugating and terrorizing its citizens for half a century. The people of Tallinn, Estonia's capital, removed the statue of a Russian soldier from their main square. The government of Vladimir Putin retaliated with economic sanctions. What Russia saw as the desecration of a memorial to a brave soldier, the Estonians saw as removal from cultural memory of a monument to the "unknown rapist." Hungary, likewise "liberated" from Nazi oppression only to suffer under Soviet dictatorship for 45 years, plans to remove a Soviet memorial from Liberty Square near the Hungarian Parliament (Hundley 2007: 23). Poland, Estonia, and Hungary claim the right to interpret their own history, define their own cultural identity, and determine what aspects of their identity they will honor and publicly memorialize. The domination of Eastern Europe that was a source of pride to Soviet Russia was the cause of suffering for those who lived under Soviet rule. Each perspective reflects truth. Poland, Estonia, and Hungary have the autonomous right to honor the aspects of their histories and identities in the manner they choose. They are not required to serve Russia's goals. Nor is President Roosevelt required to accommodate his identity to others' interpretation of truth, nor serve their goals in the way he is honored.

The social contract in the United States allows freedom of speech and assembly, but assumes civility in the expression of these rights. Likewise, Article 1 of the Universal Declaration of Human Rights protects freedom of speech and assembly, but requires that "all human beings . . . act towards one another in a spirit of brotherhood" (Van Der Heijden and Tahzib-Lie 1998: 17). The threat of the activists to disrupt a ceremony meant to honor President Roosevelt resulted in the desired outcome for the protestors. Confrontations staged to take advantage of large public gatherings, however, do not always turn out as well. Violating the social contract by antagonism, discourtesy, or other disruptive tactics may bring about the desired results, but may also carry the cost of resentment, license for further disruption, disrespect, social unrest, and physical harm. If public gatherings became an opportunity to protest or promote an agenda, rights are undermined as respect and civility erode (Reasons ##5, 6). Moreover, those who cause such disruptions may see support for their causes erode (Reason #7).

On September 17, 2006, an audiotape of a closed-door meeting of top Hungarian government officials was leaked to the public. The recording included a statement by Hungarian Prime Minister Ferenc Gyurcsány that the government had been lying to the people about the economic situation in order to win the election. In addition, the tape also recorded many instances of Prime Minister Gyurcsány using obscenities. The tape was played on Hungarian radio, and led to increasingly large demonstrations against the government throughout the following months (BBC News 2006).

Monday, October 23, 2006, marked the 50th anniversary of the 1956 Hungarian Revolution. National ceremonies to bring the Hungarian people together to celebrate the courage of the country's resistance fighters and the end of decades of repression and occupation that followed the uprising had been planned for years. The crowds that turned out for the ceremonies included elderly survivors, families, and little children. Protestors targeted this day for particularly intense protests against the Gyurcsány government. The commemoration to honor fallen heroes, recognize survivors, and celebrate hard-won freedom was marred by demonstrators and subsequent police actions to restore order. To control the protestors, police used water cannon and tear gas. Demonstrators expropriated a national day of remembrance and thanksgiving and transmuted it into its antithesis: a night of intimidation and pugnacity.

If every group felt morally justified in hijacking an event that had been planned and sponsored by another party for another purpose in order to benefit from the public exposure that seizing the limelight would garner, the result would be chaos. The original focus would be redirected and diluted. The disruption would divert attention from the person being honored or the event being commemorated to the protestors. Future gatherings might be more closely controlled, diminishing rights of free speech and assembly. Exploiting the situation to impose an agenda of personal interests robs both the individuals being honored and society of respect, and infringes on the people's right to speak and assemble peacefully (Reasons ##5, 6).

Finally, equality, understood as equal consideration and respect, does not support the protesters' threat to disrupt the ceremony. We would not want to be memorialized in a way we specifically, emphatically, and constantly fought against. We would not want our identity in the form of an image that we did not allow to be seen publicly, commandeered to become a symbol and used as a means to an end. Respect is denied when others are allowed to determine our identity in pursuit of their own interests. It is unlikely that we would desire this for ourselves and it is therefore morally unjustifiable to allow this exploitation of others. Disability advocates must honor President Roosevelt's desire to be portrayed without prominent reference to his disability (Reasons ##8, 10).

In conclusion, society is best served when all its members are able to make full use of their talents: acting to secure equity for all is justifiable. However, those actions must not infringe on the rights of others. The benefits that might be realized and the justice that might be brought about for disabled individuals by disability advocates' demonstrations did not outweigh the disregard for autonomy, rights, and respect due to President Roosevelt. Although their intentions and goal were noble and just, their method was not morally justifiable.

Note that this dilemma raises additional concerns about other troubling conflicts. If we look at different aspects of this particular case, we could ask – and moral problem-solvers would have to consider – a different question. So let us do that now.

Responsibilities of the President of the United States include defending the Constitution and preventing social unrest. As leader of the country, the president also bears the responsibility for promoting civic virtues such as tolerance and justice, and for demonstrating respect and integrity. President Clinton had a positive duty to fulfill the obligations of his position (Fox and DeMarco 2001: 245–7; Honderich 2005: 224), but this put him on the horns of a dilemma, requiring him to decide if memorials are to inspire the living, or honor the dead.

Was it morally justifiable for President Clinton to agree to the request to place a statue of President Roosevelt in a wheelchair in a prominent location as part of the FDR Memorial?

What tools will you use to analyze this moral dilemma?

Perspective One-A

- President Clinton's decision to have a statue of President Roosevelt in a wheelchair prominently placed at the entrance to the FDR Memorial was morally justified.

Perspective Two-A

- President Clinton should not have agreed to have a statue of President Roosevelt in a wheelchair placed in a prominent location as part of the FDR Memorial.

Perspective Three-A

- You decide, based on your analysis, what the appropriate response would be.

Options	Pros	Cons
President Clinton agrees that the FDR Memorial will prominently depict President Roosevelt in a wheelchair, as requested by advocates for the disabled.		
President Clinton supports the artist's original design for the FDR Memorial that depicts President Roosevelt in the manner in which FDR chose to portray himself.		

Additional Issues to Consider

Other moral issues are raised by this case. How would you analyze the following questions in the context of moral theories?

Q From a moral point of view, should a statue of Crazy Horse be carved into the Black Hills?

Options	Pros	Cons
A statue of Crazy Horse should be carved into the Black Hills.		
A statue of Crazy Horse should not be carved into the Black Hills.		

Q From a moral point of view, should the public have the right to modify an artist's work after his death to accommodate contemporary perspectives?

Options	Pros	Cons
The public has the right to modify art after an artist's death to reflect contemporary mores and perspectives.		
The public does not have the right to modify art after an artist's death to reflect contemporary mores and perspectives.		

Q Does it matter what President Roosevelt wanted?

Options	Pros	Cons
Posterity is obligated to honor President Roosevelt's wishes about how he is portrayed.		
The wishes of a deceased leader should have no influence on how that person may be used in a meaningful and symbolic way.		

REFERENCES

BBC News (2006) We lied to win, says Hungary PM (September 18). Available at: http://news.bbc.co.uk/2/hi/europe/5354972.stm (accessed October 13, 2007).

Boylan, M. (2000) *Basic Ethics*. Upper Saddle River, NJ: Prentice Hall.

Centers for Medicare and Medicaid Services (2006) *A Report on the Status of the State Medicaid Infrastructure Grants Program as of December 31, 2005*. Baltimore, MD: United States Department of Health and Human Services, pp. 1–13.

Cushman, F., Young, L., and Hauser, M. (2006) The role of conscious reasoning and intuition in moral judgment: testing three principles of harm. *Psychological Science* 17 (12): 1082–9.

Driver, J. (2007) *Ethics: The Fundamentals.* Series in Fundamentals of Philosophy. Oxford: Blackwell Publishing, pp. 40–60, 112–13.

Eadie, B. (Producer) (1993) The Lynchburg story: Eugenic sterilization in America (video). Salem, NY: Worldview Pictures.

Fox, R. M., and DeMarco, J. P. (2001) *Moral Reasoning: A Philosophical Approach to Applied Ethics,* 2nd edn. Fort Worth, TX: Harcourt.

Gabor, A. (1997) Even our most loved monuments had a trial by fire. *Smithsonian* 28 (2): 96–106.

Hill, T. E., Jr. (2000) Kantianism. In H. LaFollette (ed.), *The Blackwell Guide to Ethical Theory.* Oxford: Blackwell Publishing, pp. 240–5.

Honderich, T. (ed.) (2005) *The Oxford Companion to Philosophy,* new edn. Oxford: Oxford University Press.

House Resolution 482 [109th Congress] (2005) *Expressing the sense of the House of Representatives that a commemorative postage stamp should be issued to honor sculptor Korczak Ziolkowski.*

Hundley, T. (2007) Russia seeing red as Soviet history snubbed. *Chicago Tribune* (July 24): 23.

Inouye, D. (1988) 1986 Black Hills hearing on S. 1453. *Wicazo Sa Review* 4 (1): 10–13.

McCorvey v. Hill, No. 03–10711 (5th Circuit, September 14, 2004).

Mock, F. L. (1995) Maya Lin – a strong clear vision: the story of the Viet Nam Veterans Memorial and its inspiring creator (video). Santa Monica, CA: Sanders and Mock Productions.

NPSDI (National Park Service Department of the Interior) (2004) *Thomas Jefferson Memorial: Building the Memorial* (22 December). Available at: www.nps.gov/ archive/thje/memorial/building.htm (accessed October 13, 2007).

PBS Online Newshour (1997) F.D.R. remembered (1 May). Available at: www. pbs.org/newshour/bb/remember/1997/fdr_5-1.html (accessed October 13, 2007).

Public Law 106–170 (Approved December 19, 1999; amended June 30, 2004) Tax Relief Extension Act of 1999 (or The Ticket to Work and Work Incentives Improvement Act of 1999). Available at: ssa.gov/OP_Home/comp2/F106-170.html (accessed May 22, 2008).

Roberts, C. (2001) Russell Means. *The Progressive* (September 1), 36–9. Available at: www.thefreelibrary.com/The+Progressive/2001/September/1-p56 (accessed October 13, 2007).

Roosevelt, F. D. (1941) To the Congress of the United States. Speech delivered to a joint session of Congress (December 8). Available at: www.umkc.edu/lib/ spec-col/ww2/PearlHarbor/fdr-speech (accessed February 12, 2007).

SFAI (San Francisco Art Institute) (2007) *SFAI Offers Diego Rivera His Second Commission in the US.* Available at: www.sfai.edu/page.aspx?page=35&navID= 79&sectionID=2 (accessed October 13, 2007).

Stein, S. (2004) The president's two bodies: stagings and restagings of FDR and the new deal body politic. *American Art* 18 (1): 32–57.

Stout, D. (1997) Clinton calls for sculpture of Roosevelt in wheelchair. *New York Times* (April 24): B8.

Struck, D. (1997a) The FDR memorial's deeper meaning. *Washington Post* (May 1): A01.

Struck, D. with J. Mann, R. H. Melton, and L. Wheeler (1997b) Clinton dedicates memorial, urges Americans to emulate FDR. *Washington Post* (May 3): A01.

University of Alabama at Birmingham Board of Trustees v. Patricia Garrett 99 US 1240 11 (2000).

USDI (United States Department of the Interior) (1997) Press release: Babbitt announces appointment of FDR memorial committee: the committee will help determine how an addition to the memorial will show that FDR used a wheelchair (September 12). Available at: www.doi.gov/news/archives/fdr.html (accessed October 13, 2007).

Van Der Heijden, B., and Tahzib-Lie, B. (eds.) (1998) *Reflections on the Universal Declaration of Human Rights.* The Hague: Martinus Nijhoff.

CASE TWO: FIRE SALE – DESTROYING PRIVATELY OWNED WORKS OF ART

Besieged for two years by the troops of his twin brother, the Assyrian king Ashurbanipal, and realizing that defeat was imminent, Sardanapalus (Shamash-shum-ukin) commanded the destruction of his treasures and the deaths of his wife, concubines, servants, and horses. He ordered fire to be set to his palace, took poison, and then committed himself and all his possessions to a fire that burned for 15 days (Carr-Gomm 2001: 223; Saggs 1988: 106–7). The Greek legend of the last king of Babylon, who ruled in the seventh century BCE, inspired romantic writer Lord Byron's drama *Sardanapalus.* Six years later, Eugène Delacroix painted the romanticized *Death of Sardanapalus,* based on Byron's play. In Delacroix's painting, the doomed king reclines languidly on his opulent bed, which had been placed over his funeral pyre. Sardanapalus watches impassively as his favorite concubines and horses are killed, and his wealth is piled around him on the pyre, ensuring that no one else will enjoy his treasures (Hagen and Hagen 2000: 380–5; Piper 2000: 328).

Ryoei Saito, the former chairman of Daishowa Paper, paid a record $82.5 million for Vincent van Gogh's *Portrait of Dr Gachet,* and $78.1 million for Pierre-Auguste Renoir's *Le Moulin de la Galette.* Mr Saito stunned the art world when he announced that the paintings would be burned with him when he was cremated. Following the auction, the paintings were shipped to a secret climate-controlled storeroom in the Tokyo area. Mr Saito viewed them for a few hours, then locked them securely away, allowing no one, not even members of his family, to view them. His son was aware of only one time over the following six years that the paintings were removed from storage: his father had them hung in a restaurant for the evening while he entertained a guest from Sotheby's Auction House for dinner. Three years after he purchased the paintings, Mr Saito ran into financial and legal difficulty, including conviction and a suspended sentence for bribing officials. When he died in 1996, his fortune was gone. The paintings were saved from the Sardanapalian destruction that Mr Saito had announced would be their fate when they were claimed as collateral against his debts (Kleiner 2000: 45–6; Saltzman 1999: 321, 324).

Although the paintings apparently were not cremated with Ryoei Saito, it is not certain what did happen to them. Did Mr Saito's heirs take possession of them? Did a bank or other creditor receive them as collateral? Were they secretly sold? Were they secretly destroyed? Have they passed into the holdings of Daishowa Paper Corporation? Despite efforts by the art community to locate them, their whereabouts remain a mystery (Saltzman 1999: 329).

Ryoei Saito's declared intention to have two treasured and extremely valuable pieces of art destroyed following his death raises provocative questions about moral decision-making in the art world. Who decides what is valuable? When does the worth of a work of art pass from the insignificant bargain-basement price paid to struggling artists to the exorbitant prices commanded at an art auction? What is the difference between a painting that never emerges from the obscurity of a street market and the painting that inflames the passion to possess? For that matter, what is the difference between a painting that never emerges from a private, climate-controlled vault and a masterpiece that is destroyed? Does humankind have any moral interest in the disposition of significant, but privately owned, artworks, or any moral standing to claim that they remain intact, even if unavailable to the public at large?

Is it morally justifiable for the owner of a significant and valuable work of art to destroy it, eliminating the masterpiece and access to it forever?

Perspective One

Owners of significant works of art have the right to do with their possessions what they will, even destroying masterpieces if they so desire. This position is supported by appeals to the moral principles of consequences, respect for autonomy, and rights.

Destroying a work of art, even an extremely valuable one, does not compromise anyone's well-being. The harm, if any is indeed caused, is hypothetical. Do we miss what we have never seen? Millions of pieces of art are accessible to the public, and to claim harm if access to *all* other artwork is restricted is unrealistic and outlandish. Interfering with the right of individuals to do as they wish with their legally acquired goods in a legally permissible manner would cause a greater and actual harm. Social order is undermined when people are not secure in their possessions, nor free to act in accordance with their own self-interest. Since most people would not choose to live under these conditions, such a society would compromise utility.

It is true that destroying a valuable and irreplaceable work of art eliminates the possibility of future generations' access to the original work for study or pleasure. It can be argued that such destruction undermines utility by removing something that has the potential to give happiness to many people. But valuable objects are destroyed all the time, inadvertently, maliciously, or by design. Buildings are torn down, primeval forests are developed or clear-cut, animals are hunted for sport, and canvases are painted over. Taste in art changes over time:

a thing of beauty is not necessarily a joy forever. There is no guarantee that what is considered priceless today will be deemed valuable in the future. Even museums, charged with the preservation and conservation of artwork, sometimes sell or trade very valuable pieces to allow for other acquisitions or priorities. Sometimes these transactions are with private collectors, resulting in loss of public access to these treasures. Sometimes curators, pressed for space, store pieces away indefinitely. In short, many pieces are not available for public viewings, and for many reasons.

Individuals should be free to determine how they will use their possessions for their own happiness. They are not morally obligated to use them for the benefit or pleasure of others. Requiring this would compromise both autonomy and the right of owners to determine what they legally may do with their legitimately acquired personal belongings.

Protecting utility, autonomy, and personal and property rights guarantees each individual's right to strive for personal happiness and to make choices in accordance with personally meaningful values. In conclusion, the moral principles of consequences (harms and utility), respect for autonomy, and rights support the prerogative of Mr Saito and other owners of important works of art to do with their masterpieces what they will.

Perspective Two

Owners of consequential works of art have a responsibility to protect masterpieces that, although privately owned, are invaluable and irreplaceable components of a common cultural heritage. This position is supported by the moral principles of consequences, virtue, and justice as fairness.

The destruction of art masterpieces such as *Portrait of Dr Gachet* and *Le Moulin de la Galette* would generate profound harms. These two paintings are recognized throughout the world as great treasures, not primarily because of their cost, but because of their exquisite quality and their significance in the evolution of artistic concepts and perceptions. Conversely, it is difficult to see how burning the paintings would create a benefit to either Mr Saito or his heirs, unless destroying the paintings would put his heirs in a more favorable situation regarding inheritance taxes. Even if that were the case, the negative consequences that would result from destroying irreplaceable masterpieces far outweigh the benefit to so few. The balance between harm and benefit does not justify destruction of valuable artwork.

Willfully destroying something that is cherished by millions, whether a valuable piece of art treasured for its beauty or history, colossal second-century statues of Buddha revered as spiritual symbols, or desirable public land expropriated for its commercial value solely to accommodate the pleasure or goals of a few, is not acting in accordance with virtue. In contrast to virtuous action, deliberate destruction of a valued treasure demonstrates vices that include arrogance, greed, insensitivity, and selfishness. According to Harris (2002: 192) virtue theory includes societal as well as individual ethics. Virtuous societies promote self-actualization and opportunities for experiences to encourage self-development. Individual members of society have a responsibility to contribute to its character. Destroying priceless artwork is contrary to the development of a virtuous society.

Justice as fairness requires social obligations of the wealthy. Social and economic inequalities exist in large part because of chance circumstances of social class and geography of birth, and not always or necessarily due to the merits or efforts of individuals. Many who work hard are impoverished, through no fault of their own. The world's resources and wealth are disproportionately controlled by a relatively few individuals, and the resultant benefits and burdens are disproportionate as well. Given these inequities, justice is achieved by actions that reasonable individuals would agree provide some measure of benefit for all, but particularly for the least advantaged (Rawls 1971: 138–42). Only a small portion of the holdings of large museums is on display at any one time, as the major part of a museum's collection is usually in storage or on loan and inaccessible to the public. Many other works are in private collections, so also unavailable to the public. Although most people will never be able to view most of the world's great art, and some might argue that the destruction of two masterpieces among so many would be a negligible loss, it is unlikely that most reasonable persons would perceive the destruction of valuable artwork as contributing to the welfare of society. Justice as fairness would not support their destruction.

To summarize, the responsibility of private owners to protect their significant art treasures, and to refrain from destroying that artwork is supported by the moral appeals to consequences (nonmaleficence and beneficence), virtue, and justice as fairness.

Perspective Three

The case before us that presents the issue of deliberate destruction of privately owned treasures of cultural significance illustrates a moral dilemma between appeals to autonomy and justice, and between rights and virtues. It also demonstrates a not infrequent ethical quandary in which a moral principle, in this case the principle of consequences, appears to support conflicting perspectives. What information do we need to consider in determining which of these conflicting tensions has the greatest moral authority?

Step 1: Information-gathering

History

- What contribution did the works of van Gogh and Renoir make to the evolution of artistic concepts?
- Why are *Portrait of Dr Gachet* and *Le Moulin de la Galette* considered to be significant pieces of art?

Economic considerations

- Does the purchase of art for financial investment purposes carry social responsibility to preserve it for its aesthetics and value as cultural heritage?

Cultural and psychological information

- Did cultural values influence Mr Saito's actions?
- What motives may have influenced Mr Saito's request? Do motives matter?
- Does art enhance people's lives?
- What is lost when artwork is destroyed?

Step 2: Creative problem-solving

Art collectors should consider themselves as guardians, rather than private owners, of significant works of art. This would foster a perception of their role as conservators who are entrusted with the legacy of humankind's cultural heritage, thereby discouraging destruction of important works of art.

Step 3: Listing pros and cons

Options	Pros	Cons
Private art collectors may destroy their significant pieces of art if they so desire.	1. Preserves owners' autonomy (A) 2. Supports property rights (R).	3. The world loses a valuable cultural treasure forever (C-U) 4. Denies others happiness that art provides (C-B, C-U) 5. Eliminates possibility of studying the original (C-U) 6. Promotes culture of entitlement of the rich (J-E) 7. Demonstrates vices of insensitivity, arrogance (V) 8. Promotes selfishness and greed (V, C-NM)
Private art collectors are prohibited from destroying important artwork in their collections.	9. Promotes society in which general welfare is considered (V-concern, C-U). 10. Demonstrates generosity (V)	11. Social pressure intimidates owners (C-NM) 12. Compromises self-determination of owners (A)

Step 4: Analysis

Factual assumptions

- Beauty enhance people's lives: art nourishes the human spirit.
- Some art has particular significance beyond its aesthetic value: as an example of an artistic concept or art's evolution, as a visual record of history, or as an important cultural symbol.
- Most great art is unique: once destroyed it is lost to the world forever.

Value assumptions

- People who own great art masterpieces should protect them.
- People should not have the absolute right to decide how they will enjoy the financial rewards of their labor.
- The wealthy should not have greater access than the disadvantaged to the cultural heritage of humankind.
- Although it currently may not be universally accessible in the public domain, great art should not be destroyed, thus eliminating the possibility that it will ever again be publicly accessible.

Step 5: Justification

Private art collectors, like Ryoei Saito, should not destroy art masterpieces that they own, but should take upon themselves the role of guardian of the cultural legacy of humankind. In doing so, owners would retain the rights of property ownership while contributing to social benefit by preserving those treasures for the future. This position is supported by moral appeals to consequences, virtues, and justice.

Vincent van Gogh and Pierre-Auguste Renoir were two of the leading Impressionists, a small group of artists whose esthetic vision revolutionized art. Breaking with traditional depictions of formalized heroic, religious, or mythical scenes, the Impressionists painted ordinary people engaging in everyday pleasurable activities, seeming to catch their subjects by surprise in unguarded moments. The Impressionists often painted outside, developing novel techniques to capture in their painting the effects of natural light at different times of day. Their realistic portrayals of specific moments expressed time and emotion as dynamic forces that shaped reality. They sought to convey the concept that art is subjective for both artist and viewer. The Impressionists promoted art not as a moralistic instructive tool, but as a creative intellectual pleasure, meant to elicit sensations and emotions, and to be enjoyed and interpreted by the viewer (Walther 2006: 94–9; Wilkins et al. 1994: 446–9).

Although most of the Impressionists suffered chronic poverty and the ridicule of the established artistic elite of France, they lived in – or rather created – an intellectually exciting time for artists. The Impressionists met in Paris cafés, their dismal lodgings little better than the *cafés de nuit* where the homeless could seek shelter for the night (Wilkins et al. 1994: 460). There the artists explored novel techniques, such as using whitewashed canvas rather than a dark base, integrated new perspectives and influences such as photography and the bold simplicity of Japanese prints, and embraced technical advances such as synthetic paint and resealable paint tubes (Hagen and Hagen 2000: 442–5; Piper 2000: 351; Wilkins et al. 1994: 449). Despite rejection by the tastemaker juries of the French Salon (the official body authorized to select artists whose work was deemed worthy to be exhibited and purchased), the Impressionists changed the way art was created and how the world experienced art (Walther 2006: 58). Among Impressionist paintings, *Le Moulin de la Galette* and *Portrait of Dr Gachet* are considered two of the most significant masterpieces: *Le Moulin de la Galette* for it's embodiment of the principles of pure Impressionism; *Portrait of Dr Gachet* as the bridge between Impressionism and Modern Art, and innovation in portraiture that revealed character as much as it captured likeness.

Renoir and van Gogh, like other Impressionists, used dabs of color or created small areas of layered paint, an "optical mixture" (Hoving 2006: 151). The optical mixture, created by applying tiny bits of unmixed pure colors to the canvas, allows the subject to be perceived only at a distance when the viewer's eye mixes the colors (Walther 2006: 97). The thick, bold, fluid brushwork that creates the surface of Impressionist painting is almost as essential to the painting as is its subject (Piper 2000: 346; Wilkins et al. 1994: 449). Such subtleties cannot be perceived from replications. If you have ever had the pleasure of comparing Japanese wood block prints, for example, from the first print of the series through the last, you will see what a great difference is achieved in the end by minute changes in the process: changes such as intensity and definition that cannot be perceived by viewing even high-quality reproductions. How much more is lost in replication of a textured three-dimensional medium such as oil! The consequence of destroying absolutely the possibility for future artists, art scholars, and ordinary people to understand how subtle emphases on color and definition changed perception of art and influenced its development would be the permanent loss of a priceless element of cultural heritage (Reasons ##3, 4, 5).

Portrait of Dr Gachet, van Gogh's last portrait, was painted three weeks before the painter committed suicide (Saltzman 1999: 180). The painting represents a crucial development in portraiture. It was the culmination of van Gogh's philosophy and experiments on portraiture, and is considered by some to be one of Western art's most significant examples of this genre. Tormented by debilitating emotional turmoil throughout most of his life, van Gogh questioned life's purpose and agonized over its suffering and transience. He sought to reveal the dignity of the spirit in the image of his subject's face, to capture not merely the appearance of the face, but the essence of the soul (Piper 2000: 363; Pool 1967: 179–80). He tried to create a comforting feeling of eternity and hope through portraiture:

> And in my pictures I want to say something consoling, as music does. I want to paint men and women with a touch of the eternal which the halo used to

symbolize, and which we seek to confer by the actual radiance and vibration of our colourings. . . . Ah! portraiture, portraiture with the thought, the soul of the model in it, that is what I think must come. (van Gogh 1888)

A soul in constant agitation over his inability to ease the suffering he saw around him, van Gogh was highly sensitive to his subjects' internal feelings and external struggles. This constant tension made him an anguished man, but an innovative artist (Abbate 1972: 104, 110). His earlier works were Impressionist, but as his work moved toward Expressionism, he became one of the first Post-Impressionist artists, and the harbinger of Fauvism. Expressionism uses vivid color and deliberate distortion to express intense personal feeling, while Fauvism uses boldly brilliant color to express wild, primitive emotion. Expressionism and Fauvism are the significant bridges between Impressionism, and Modern and Abstract Art (Piper 2000: 360, 390; Wilkins et al. 1994: 460, 513).

Le Moulin de la Galette, one of Renoir's largest and most significant works, captures the richly exquisite details of the popular Monmartre open-air dance hall. On Sunday afternoons and evenings, working girls would come to the lively Moulin de la Galette to dance with their beaux, or in the hope of finding a beau. As he did in other paintings, Renoir included fellow painters and friends in the foreground of this work (Pool 1967: 155–6). The loss of this work would not only represent the loss of a beautiful painting, but also the loss of a visual record of history.

Renoir was greatly influenced by both his contemporaries and the Old Masters. His art evolved in subtle ways through these simultaneous influences. When Renoir and Monet began painting outdoors together in natural light, the similarities in their subjects and technique rendered their work almost indistinguishable. As each developed individually as a painter, their work grew markedly unique. Monet softened his paintings with diffused light to capture the ephemera of a specific, fleeting moment in time. Renoir began to bring greater definition to his subjects as he toured museums to revisit the works of Renaissance and ancient painters (Abbate 1972: 57–9). These visits reawakened his appreciation for the elegance of precise delineation, and inspired him to blend traditional formats with Impressionism, using more formal poses and sharply detailed figures against an unfocused impressionistic background (Piper 2000: 347, 351). Although Renoir moved away from strictly impressionistic art, he and Claude Monet are credited with articulating the guiding principles of Impressionism (Walther 2006: 690). The importance of their body of work is not exclusively the value of the art for its beauty, but also as documentation of the process of how artistic styles develop and diverge.

The history of *Portrait of Dr Gachet* is as almost as significant as the work itself. Van Gogh gave the painting to his brother Theo, whose widow sold it several years later (Saltzman 1999: 80). It passed through 13 different owners, including Frankfurt's Städtische Galerie, whose director, George Swarzenski, astutely assessed Germany's Nazi political climate and hid the painting in 1933 (ibid.: 161). It remained safely hidden for five years before the Nazis confiscated it and included it in a traveling exhibition of degenerate Expressionist art (ibid.). Hermann

Goering sold the painting in 1937 for $53,000, and it was later smuggled out of Germany (ibid.: 192). The banking Kramarsky family eventually purchased the painting, and sent it ahead to New York when they escaped from Amsterdam before the Nazis invaded the Netherlands (ibid.: 211–12). Over the next 50 years, the Kramarsky family frequently loaned the work to New York's Metropolitan Museum (ibid.: xix). In 1990, the painting was auctioned by Christie's New York auction house, the winning bid placed by Mr Saito's representative (ibid.: 311). In addition to the painting's value as a beautiful work of art and as an example of artistic innovation and transition, *Portrait of Dr Gachet* holds special historical significance. The painting was sought by the ruthlessly repressive Nazi regime as an example of "degenerate" art. Originally slated for destruction, it was saved by heroic efforts. Destroying it would trivialize those efforts and demonstrate a callous insensitivity for the abuses suffered by victims of the Holocaust (Reason #7).

The moral dilemma at the heart of this case is based on Mr Saito's statement that he would destroy the paintings. Let us consider another explanation for his statement that he intended the paintings to be burned with him on his funeral pyre. Values are culturally relative. In the particular case of Mr Saito, lack of awareness of Japan's cultural values may have created unfair perceptions that an understanding of other traditions might have prevented. It is customary in Japanese society to keep valued possessions stored in secure locations, to be taken out on rare occasions and ceremoniously displayed for the pleasure of esteemed guests. After witnessing the furor aroused by his comment that he would burn the two paintings, a spokesman for Mr Saito explained that the comment was a figure of speech that the Japanese understood indicated his great appreciation for the picture, while Westerners misunderstood his meaning when they interpreted his comment literally (Saltzman 1999: 322, 324). We do not know with certainty that Mr Saito actually intended to burn the paintings, nor do we know why he bought them. Perhaps he did so for a personal reason that may not be immediately apparent.

Art may be an object of beauty to many people, but to some it is primarily an investment. In the year following Mr Saito's purchase of the van Gogh and Renoir paintings, the Japanese economy plunged into a downward spiral. As a result, Mr Saito could not afford to pay the $23,000,000 capital gains tax due on the profit from property he sold to raise funds to buy the paintings (Saltzman 1999: 324). It was speculated that Mr Saito considered destroying the paintings to lower inheritance taxes that would be charged to his family upon his death. (Note that this is one of those situations that we warned you about in the Introduction, where there is incomplete information about intention and personal circumstances. Don't get tangled up in the hypothetical, but focus on the essence of the moral dilemma.) If buying, then destroying, a priceless treasure has meaning or benefit for an individual, what greater right do others have to dictate how that possession should be used (Reasons ##1, 2, 11, 12)? Those who support property rights claim that people cannot be deprived of property they do not own. Neither do they have a legitimate claim to share in others' benefits or possessions without some contribution. Such claims to an interest in another's property can only be supported in the context of justice as fairness when there is a legitimate right of ownership (Narveson 2000: 310–12). In this case, the public has no such interest.

One may find this position somewhat persuasive, and may sympathize with such a great reversal of fortune, yet still legitimately question who would benefit from the destruction of the paintings, and who would bear the burden of harm. No one is likely to benefit from the destruction, except Mr Saito's heirs. The burden would be borne by the rest of the world. The threat of harm (loss of the paintings forever) was generated by the desire of one very wealthy man to acquire objects valued by many others for his exclusive pleasure and use (Reason #8). The harm of the loss of the paintings would be exacerbated by imposing the burden of Mr Saito's investment misadventure on those who had nothing to do with his acquisition of extravagant luxuries (Reason #6). While in the interest of liberty and property rights justice does not demand that disparities of wealth be eliminated, it does require that everyone benefit (Rawls 1971: 141). Accordingly, destroying the paintings would undermine the moral principles of consequences ((nonmaleficence, beneficence) and justice.

Acting in accordance with virtue means acting with good intentions, motivated by the ideal of morally right behavior, and seeking to develop good character rather than acting from a sense of duty. Persons are judged morally worthy based not on their actions, but on the virtues and intentions that direct their actions (Harris 2002: 182–3). While Mr Saito's actions display some virtues such as self-reliance, competitiveness, and ambition, these are concerned more with self-realization than with the welfare of others. These virtues, in excess, can become vices: self-absorption, materialism, and callousness.

Aristotle (2003) warned against the particular vice of squandering money on self-indulgence that results in financial ruin and destroys moral character through greed and excess (Reason #8). He calls those who are excessively self-indulgent the worst of characters, as they simultaneously demonstrate numerous vices (1119b31–4). Although Aristotle does not directly identify these "several vices," greedy, imprudent, selfish, materialistic, self-absorbed, and irresponsible might reasonably describe this behavior. Aristotle does, however, go on to describe the vices associated with lack of generosity that often accompanies self-indulgence: pettiness, vulgarity, and ostentation (1122a30–3). He criticizes those who seek admiration through a pretentious display of wealth as simultaneously ostentatious and parsimonious, failing both in stewarding their wealth and using it to benefit others (1123a20–1, 1123a25–7). Private art collectors who seek only their own pleasure and status through collecting masterpieces fail to act in accordance with virtue.

If, on the other hand, private art collectors were to act as guardians of cultural heritage, enjoying the pleasure of ownership while at the same time preserving artworks for future generations, they could instead demonstrate numerous virtues: generosity, justice, kindness, unselfishness, caring, and respectfulness (Reason #10). In addition, this individual demonstration of virtue would set a moral tone that would contribute to the development of a virtuous society. Masterpieces, although privately held, would not be permanently lost to the public domain.

Does justice require that art be in the public domain? Russia addressed this question by making public access to art a priority. Until the Bolshevik revolution, the visual and performing arts had been the exclusive privilege of the Russian aristocracy, largely paid for by the toil of serfs. Leaders of the new social order were committed to providing ordinary workers with the same experience of beauty and culture enjoyed in the past by wealthy members of Russian society. Cultural centers were established in workers' neighborhoods (Murrell 1995: 131). According to Julia Husen, a native teacher of Russian language and culture, after the 1917 Revolution visual and performing arts were made accessible as part of daily life for ordinary people. Soviet communism saw universal access to art and music as a means of just distribution of the country's wealth of cultural heritage. The government heavily subsidized symphony and ballet tickets, so that even the poorest could attend performances (Reason #9). "People's Palaces," the dazzling Russian metro stations of Moscow and St Petersburg, were designed not only to showcase the wealth and power of the Soviet Union and celebrate the diversity of the Soviet states, but also to lift the spirits of working people by the daily experience of beauty (J. A. Husen, personal conversation, 2007). The best artists and architects were invited from throughout the Soviet Union to create sumptuous metro stations, designed as gilded palaces with huge rooms and soaring vaults that were illuminated by glittering chandeliers. Stations were filled with magnificent statues, gold leaf, beautiful stained-glass windows, marble floors and pillars, precious metals, intricate mosaics, friezes, and elegant caryatids and atlases. The floor of Byelorusskaya Station is tiled to appear as a Byelorussian carpet. Avtovo Station's 16 cut-glass pillars stand in tribute to technology. The ceiling of Komsomolskaya Station is embedded with tiny mosaic tiles, crafted in ancient Byzantine techniques (Kokker and Selby 2002: 74–5; Kornyushov and Selby 1998: 124–5). While cultural heritage has been destroyed – often deliberately – in many of the world's revolutions, Soviet Russia acknowledged access to its artistic treasures as a fundamental right of the people.

The art world is not the only realm facing the threat of intellectual loss. The preservation of scientific archives, specifically the original private documents of leading scientists, raises concerns not unlike those of the art world. Laboratory notebooks, preliminary drafts of manuscripts, correspondence with fellow scientists, and other primary documents are invaluable sources that reveal how some of the world's greatest scientific minds developed concepts and brought about breakthrough discoveries. In recent years, as scientists and the public realized how valuable these documents were, a mad scramble ensued to collect them and reap their commercial benefits. Few public scientific institutions or libraries had the available resources to pay the competitive prices demanded, so collections were sold piecemeal (Rinaldi 2006: 571, 573). Ironically, the quest for financial gain undermined the documents' scientific value. As individual archives were broken up to sell bits and pieces of science history, the scientific integrity of the collections was destroyed, and with it the priceless opportunity to see the thinking processes of consummate scientific minds (Reasons ##3, 5). The enormity of this loss cannot be overstated.

Mr Saito's right to destroy his own property does not override his more compelling moral responsibility to preserve valuable objects of humankind's cultural heritage. The deliberate destruction, for personal pleasure or gain, of priceless and beloved works of art is morally unjustifiable. In conclusion, the moral principles of consequences, virtue, and justice prohibit the deliberate destruction of *Le Moulin de la Galette* and *Portrait of Dr Gachet*.

Additional Issues to Consider

Q Should private ownership of art or cultural artifacts be forbidden?

Q Should private parties be allowed to own art or cultural artifacts, only if they agree to transfer them to public institutions (e.g., museums) when they no longer wish to keep them, or upon their deaths?

Q Should all significant art be jointly owned by individuals and public institutions, but private individuals allowed to keep and display them according to their own desires?

REFERENCES

Abbate, F. (ed.) (1972) *Impressionism: Its Forerunners and Influences*. London: Octopus Books.
Aristotle (2003) *The Ethics of Aristotle: The Nichomachean Ethics*, trans. J. A. K. Thomson; rev. trans. Hugh Tredennick. New York: Penguin Books.
Carr-Gomm, S. (2001) *Hidden Symbols in Art*. London: Duncan Baird.
Hagen, R.-M., and Hagen, R. (2000) *What Great Paintings Say – Old Masters in Detail*. Köln, Germany: Taschen.
Harris, C. E., Jr. (2002) *Applying Moral Theories*, 4th edn. Toronto: Wadsworth.
Hoving, T. (2006) *Master Pieces: The Curator's Game*. New York: W. W. Norton.
Kleiner, C. (2000) Van Gogh's vanishing act. *US News and World Report* 129 (4): 45–6.
Kokker, S., and Selby, N. (2002) *St Petersburg*. Melbourne: Lonely Planet.
Kornyushov, S., and Selby, N. (1998) *Moscow*, English edn. Moscow: Art-Rodnik.
Murrell, K. B. (1995) *St Petersburg*. London: Flint River Press.
Narveson, J. (2000) Libertarianism. In H. Lafollette (ed.), *The Blackwell Guide to Ethical Theory*. Oxford: Blackwell Publishing.
Piper, D. (2000) *The Illustrated History of Art*. London: Chancello Press (Bounty Books).
Pool, P. (1967) *Impressionism*. New York: Frederick A. Praeger.
Rawls, J. (1971) A theory of justice. In L. H. Newton (ed.), *Ethics in America*, 2nd edn. Upper Saddle River, NJ: Prentice Hall.
Rinaldi, A. (2006) Private ownership of public heritage. *EMBO Reports* 7 (6): 571–5.
Saggs, H. W. F. (1988) *The Babylonians*. London: Folio Society.
Saltzman, C. (1999) *Portrait of Dr Gachet: The Story of a van Gogh Masterpiece, Money, Politics, Collectors, Greed, and Loss*. New York: Penguin.

Van Gogh, V. (1888) Letter to Theo van Gogh (September 3). Available at: http://webexhibits.org/vangogh/letter/18/531 (accessed May 31, 2007).

Walther, I. F. (2006) *Impressionism*. China: Taschen.

Wilkins, D. G., Shultz, B., and Linduff, K. M. (1994) *Art Past, Art Present*, 2nd edn. New York: Harry N. Abrams, Inc.

CASE THREE: WHAT PRICE IMMORTALITY? – THE *BODY WORLDS* EXHIBITION

In 1995 an entirely new form of public display – *Body Worlds* – opened in Tokyo, Japan. A collection of human bodies whose skin had been removed so that underlying muscles, nerves, and tendons could be revealed, *Body Worlds* provided an opportunity for the public to see what heretofore had been the province of physicians and undertakers: the inside of the human body.

Body Worlds is the brainchild of physician Gunther von Hagens. Using his patented process, "plastination," he preserves the bodies (as well as organs and fetuses) by "removing water and fats from the tissue and replacing these with polymers" (*Body Worlds* 2006b: para 2). This process renders the bodies dry and odorless, while retaining the natural coloration of the various body parts. After the bodies have been posed in lifelike positions – running, riding bicycles, playing chess – they are "cured" with heat or gases, to make them rigid. After the curing, the bodies hold their positions indefinitely.

Body Worlds has been an enormous success. By the end of 2006 it had been seen by more than 20 million visitors in Asia, Canada, Europe, and the United States. The original collection has become three collections, each with different themes. At least six "copy-cat" collections have sprung up. More than 7,000 living persons have signed forms indicating that, upon their deaths, they wish to have their bodies plastinated and used for medical and public education. Dr von Hagens has made millions of dollars.

According to the *Body Worlds* website:

> The exceptional success of the exhibits is to a great extent due to its educational value. They are structured in such a way that visitors experience it much as they would a three-dimensional textbook: anatomy as the foundation of the body is laid out in an educational and elucidating fashion. Visitors learn about the body's functions; they also realize how highly sophisticated and beautiful, and yet how fragile the body is. (2006b: para 2)

In fact, the advertised purpose of these exhibitions is educational:

> The objectives of the IfP [Institute for Plastination] can be summarized as follows:
> (1) Improving overall anatomical instruction
> The IfP produces high-quality educational specimens for anatomical instruction at universities and other teaching institutions.

(2) Improving awareness of medical issues, particularly among the general public
The IfP produces plastinates aimed at educating non-medical professionals and restores
public access to the anatomy of the human body. (Body Worlds 2002)

This purpose seems to have been widely achieved. According to exit polls, "Three-quarters say it's informative and educational" (Russell 2007: para 35), while the CEO of the California Science Center notes that visitors "really get a chance to understand . . . how the body functions and what can go wrong with it" (Ulaby 2006: para 5). One hoped-for extension of this educational endeavor is an appreciation of the human body in all its complexity and possibility, which also seems to have been achieved: One visitor says: "*Body Worlds* profoundly changed my attitudes toward my own body, towards life and death. I feel myself in a different way, more intensely" (Stern 2003: para 8). Dr Eric Jolly, President of the Science Museum of Minnesota, reports: "This is an astounding exhibit, unlike anything I'd ever seen before. When I first saw this in Chicago I was struck by how inspiring it is for my own healthcare. How it could bring others to have aspirations to work in health and allied health fields. And how awesome the human body is in its architecture" (Cunningham 2006: para 8).

Many of the persons who have signed consent forms to donate their bodies for plastination and exhibition after their deaths indicate a desire to contribute to medical and general education. Others believe the plastination process insures their own "immortality," or at least offers the possibility of transcending death that would otherwise end their existence on this earth.

Nonetheless, *Body Worlds* and its imitators (e.g., *Bodies . . . The Exhibition*; *The Universe Within*) have their detractors. Many critics charge that the purpose of such exhibitions is not educational, but sensational. They object to poses that seem to mock the deceased (one body is posed holding his internal organs in one of his hands) or are designed to shock viewers' sensibilities (a pregnant woman reclining, with her fetus still present within her and on display). Various "playful" or casual poses suggest a commodification of the human body – that is, seeing the human body not as an object of reverence but as an object to be "used" according to the desires of its "owner." Megan Stern (2003: para 4) compares the posing of bodies to the posing of Barbie dolls, manipulating the bodies as objects to be played with. Linda Schulte-Sasse (2006: 378–9) charges that the repetitive manipulations of the bodies to simulate athletes reifies a morbid fascination with bodily perfection and perpetuates a perfection myth that many persons/viewers will only poorly approximate. These concerns are particularly troubling as body exhibitions proliferate, suggesting that the body as art is a "fashion" (ibid. 2006: 382–3) or, put differently, a currently popular commodity that consumers willingly pay to see.

Some persons find the exhibition of dead bodies to be inherently disrespectful, objecting to any public display of a dead body (a concern that is more problematic to some cultures than to others). And when *Body Worlds* was on exhibit in Los Angeles, a fetus was stolen.

Finally, a serious and ongoing concern is the lingering question about the sources of the bodies on display. Exhibitors have been accused (though not formally charged) with using bodies of executed Chinese prisoners (i.e., bodies of persons

who did not consent to plastination and display). The charge that *Bodies* . . .
The Exhibition used corpses of political prisoners (e.g., members of Falun Gong)
is particularly troubling (BBC 2006: para 1), given ongoing concerns about China's
record of human rights abuses. Gunther von Hagens earlier returned seven
bodies to China when bullet holes in their skulls were discovered (Mohseni 2006).
Von Hagens also admits to using unclaimed bodies, as well as body parts
donated to medical schools in the past (Allen 2007: 24); in such cases, persons
had no chance to consent to this particular use of their bodies or body parts.

From the moral point of view, is the use of human bodies in exhibitions such
as *Body Worlds* morally justifiable?

Perspective One

The use of bodies in exhibitions such as *Body Worlds* is morally permissible. This
position is supported by appeals to consequences, respect for autonomy, and
(in Western democracies) to the right of privacy.

Consider, first, the consequences of the anatomical exhibitions for particular
individuals. Many of the persons who viewed the show recorded their thoughts
in a comment book available in the halls in which the presentations were seen.
These comments were almost universally positive, and indicated that the second
goal of the Institute for Plastination was resoundingly achieved. Viewers *did* express
a heightened appreciation for the workings of the human body and for the implications of their behaviors for their health. One high school student wrote,
"I had better take care of this body of mine," while a senior citizen commented,
"I have learned more about my body in an hour than in all the preceding
83 years" (Lara 2005: paras 25, 26). Many visitors spoke of experiencing a sense
of wonder at the body's complexity (see, also, Maienschein and Creath 2007:
27). Robin Russell, writing for *The United Methodist Reporter Interactive*,
observes that "[v]oices are hushed with reverence and awe" and that "experiencing a sense of mortality is one of the strongest impressions visitors take away.
Sometimes, there's also a religious epiphany" (2007: para 32). Physician Neil
Wenger, a member of the Ethics Committee that evaluated the propriety of
bringing *Body Worlds* to the California Science Center, waxed eloquent: "Every
physician, at one time or another[,] is struck by the sheer elegance and intricacy
of the human body. But, few laypersons get a chance to experience such
wonder. This exhibit is a rare opportunity for the layperson to share in this
privileged view of ourselves" (California Science Center 2004–5: 7). And, as Jon
Mooallem (2005) reminds us, *Body Worlds* is only the latest in such up-close and
personal experiences:

> I began to think of "The Universe Within" as a kind of secular reliquary – like
> Rome's crypt of Santa Maria della Concezione, where room-sized mosaics have been
> fashioned from the bones of thousands of Capuchin monks; or St. Catherine's glass-
> encased hand in Siena; or the slumped body of St. Boniface in Prague. The believer

was meant to feel earnestly, if not qualifiably, inspired in the presence of these relics. Seeing a cadaver hitchhiking or a plastinate lung – a *real* lung for crissakes! – filled me with a not so dissimilar, almost religious exuberance. (para 16)

The evidence indicates that viewers did have significantly positive educational experiences. Nine out of ten persons rated the experience as good or very good, suggesting a personal benefit was achieved during the visit. As millions of persons have now seen the shows, the extent of these benefits is enormous. Further, if persons – as a result of seeing these exhibits – do become more respectful, and therefore more careful, of their bodies, widespread health benefits will accrue to individuals (as well as to society more generally). One Methodist minister suggested that donating one's body to such exhibitions was no different from donating one's organs for transplant: in both cases one's body serves as an aid to the well-being of others (Russell 2007: para 49).

Respect for autonomous choice supports the appeal to consequences. To date, more than 7,000 living persons have signed consents directing that, upon their deaths, their bodies be donated to *Body Worlds*. The right to privacy – that is, the right to grant access of others to one's body, when coupled with autonomous choices to donate, support these public demonstrations.

Perspective Two

The use of bodies in exhibitions such as *Body Worlds* is not morally permissible. Although effects on visitors have not been studied formally, any public display of human bodies raises discomfort (Burns 2007a: 14). All societies demonstrate evidence of a belief that corpses should be treated with respect (Allen 2006; Barilan 2006: 235–6). Just as societies have moral norms that specify what counts as inappropriate treatment of living persons, so they have guidelines about the inappropriate treatment of dead persons (Burns 2007a: 17–18). Typically, the body "goes away" – into the ground (burial), an urn (cremation), or back to the universe (burning without collection of the ashes). The *Body World* bodies are now (and perhaps will forever be) somewhere other than their "assigned" location (Barilan 2006: 239). Unlike cadavers used by modern medical students, which are buried after studies are completed (often following a funeral service that the students attend), these publicly displayed bodies are in cultural limbo, a status that elicits discomfort in the minds of others. Further, dead bodies cannot help but remind us of those who, until recently, animated the bodies. Perhaps these unsettling facts explain some of the behavior noted by one commentator: "[T]he exhibit guards were yelling about cell phones and cameras and visitors were laughing and making off-color comments about the bodies. No solemnity; . . . no anatomy lessons underway" (Guyer 2007: 30).

In spite of widespread respect typically shown to corpses (whatever form that respect may take), the relationship between society and dead bodies has a check-ered history. In the sixteenth century, when Belgian anatomist Andreas Vesalius (apparently) originated the practice of flaying dead bodies and of posing skeletons to demonstrate the relationships between muscles, bones and movement, acquiring dead bodies for scientific examination was illegal. To obtain bodies for dissection and study, early anatomists and medical students resorted to grave-robbing. (In contemporary ethical language, corpses were used for educational purposes without their prior consent, autonomous or otherwise.)

A lingering consequence of this past is a widespread, jaundiced view of "using" human bodies, no matter however allegedly noble the purpose. The human body, even when dead, is not a mere *thing* – that is, something to be put to good use, or, for that matter, any use: "[T]he human cadaver should [not] be regarded as an object of art, entertainment, or education *like any other* object (e.g., like a wax model . . .) because of its exceptional meaning" (Burns 2007b: W1). Moreover, any "use" of a dead body counts as an unwarranted desecration of something that commands respect (see, also, Kass 1985). At least some commentators have found that "[t]he exhibit is flashy and sexy; it is disquieting and disrespectful. Why does the cadaver of a child in the 'family' group give a thumbs-up sign? . . . Why *are* cadavers wearing hats and scarves?" (Guyer 2007: 30) Moreover, as the particular exhibits become less scientific and more "playful" or "whimsical" – as, for example, those that use more *undissected* whole bodies, the purposes of the exhibition began to look less like education and more like entertainment (Jones and Whitaker 2007: 28).

These subtle changes in the content of the program raise slippery slope issues: If the purpose is not (or is not so much, or, eventually – the argument goes – not at all) education, to what other uses may dead bodies be put? A bone-smuggling racket was recently uncovered in India (Majumdar 2007). One laboratory in Michigan advertises, via its website, products for performing plastination, as well as "hundreds of what appear to be body parts. It's unclear whether just anybody can buy items from this site with a Visa card, but one sees the possibilities. Can a possible, permanent installation of a fiberglass Uncle Ned at the family Wurlitzer be far behind?" (Lara 2005: para 16) Even if one believes that their educational value can justify public exhibitions of dead bodies, such a claim is unlikely to be successfully defended for personal uses thereof.

But even assuming that these exhibits have educational or artistic utility, other concerns persist. Laurie Zoloth asks: "What exactly is engaged by the gaze toward the naked, dead body, normally a gaze reserved for lovers, morticians, and doctors entirely?" (2005: 7). She wonders whether the "detached" gaze of the healthcare professional can – or should – be encouraged in the lay viewer, especially the many schoolchildren who are seeing the exhibit. Some moral concern attaches to the fact that we have no idea how to answer her query, in part because the precise effects on the millions of viewers can only be imagined. Exactly what goes through the minds of children who view the exhibits is anybody's guess. Are younger children likely to wonder if the bodies are persons they know? family members? grandparents? In a population too young to contemplate the questions of finitude and its meaning for life, is the lifelike red tissue just another example of violence to others? Further, the thorough nakedness of the bodies is undoubtedly unsettling to many. While teachers and parents might get some sense of children's impressions or concerns, one should not assume that all will be addressed, if only because children – especially younger children – may be unable to articulate them. Y. Michael Barilan reports (2006: 246) that Gunther von Hagens has indicated a plan to plasticize a male and female body engaging in sexual intercourse. If this plan were publicized, what (if any) effect would it have on viewers? On young viewers?

In short, while short-term consequences, as reported by viewers, are mixed, the *long-term* consequences of public exhibitions of dead bodies simply cannot be known – or even guessed at. But good cultural and psychological accounts suggest that many of these consequences will be negative, perhaps significantly so.

Advocates note that thousands of persons, upon seeing and being impressed by these exhibitions, have autonomously chosen to donate their bodies for use in future exhibitions. Putting aside the question of possible coercive (psychological) influences, one has to wonder whether genuinely *informed* consent is possible. Persons whose bodies are currently on display might have consented to the use of their postmortem bodies for medical education, but they quite likely did not foresee (and could not then have imagined) that their bodies would be put to use in public, touring exhibitions. This unconsented-to use of one's remains in what some call "freak shows" seems morally dubious; put another way, "it's unlikely a man somewhere in China volunteered specifically to be the skinless fellow riding a bike" (Mooallem 2005: para 20). Did the pregnant woman, reclining on a couch with her fetus still in place, imagine that her unborn child would become part of this exhibit? Would she have consented had she considered this possibility? The point is that those who are reasonably well informed still cannot possibly imagine all future scenarios sufficiently to avoid having their bodies used in ways to which they would object. How many would consent if they knew they might become one half of a copulating couple?

Interestingly, many people purportedly donate to achieve immortality. If so, they are likely to be disappointed, as von Hagens (and others) assure them that their anonymity will be protected. Many of the bodies are presented in such a way that determining the identity of the living person would be difficult, if not impossible. Surely persons whose organs (only) are used would not be identifiable. On the other hand, persons who donate after being assured of anonymity might be distressed to discover that: "These are not skeletons or mummies but recognizable humans with . . . often enough face left to make things unsettling" (Mooallem 2005: para 10). A horrifyingly ironic possibility is that those wishing anonymity will be identifiable, while those wishing immortality will not be. In either case, one worries that anonymity undercuts the uniqueness of each human, making all the bodies on display somehow interchangeable – just one among others, nothing special (Burns 2007a: 19).

Finally, autonomous choices that undermine other important values need not be respected (Burns 2007b: W1; Barilan 2006: 243ff). Just as one need not respect a friend's autonomous choice to rob a bank, one need not respect an autonomous choice that will contribute to the disrespect of humanity in general or of particular (now dead) humans. Persons who make disrespectful autonomous choices should be educated, not permitted to act on their morally mistaken decisions (Allen 2007: 24). Robin Lovin, Professor of Ethics at Southern Methodist University, charges: "[T]urn[ing] the body of another person into an anonymous exhibit, a kind of entertainment for which admission might be charged, shows little respect for the person" (Russell 2007: para 45). Those who think these shows are not a commercial undertaking might be surprised to learn that by 2005 Gunther von Hagen had "taken in an estimated billion dollars" (Lara 2005: para 10).

In sum, serious potential long-term consequences may offset the alleged short-term positive consequences often touted to result from seeing these exhibitions. Particularly worrisome is the threat to the dignity of human persons. As a result, the appeal to consequences gives, at best, ambiguous support to public demonstrations such as *Body Worlds*. Further, choices to participate may or may not be/have been autonomous. But even if future consents are autonomous, should such exhibitions be shown to be egregiously harmful to human dignity, autonomous participation need not have the final word.

Body Worlds (and similar) exhibitions should not be allowed.

Additional Issues to Consider

Q Should *Body Worlds* (and similar) exhibitions be allowed to be shown in schools?

Q Should *Body Worlds* (and similar) exhibitions be allowed to be shown in schools, as long as students have reached a certain age?

Q Should *any* similar graphic art works be limited to particular populations or environments?

REFERENCES

Allen, A. (2006) Body ethics, body aesthetics. *Philadelphia Inquirer* (March 12). Available at: www.law.upenn.edu/cf/faculty/aallen/moralist/BodyEthics031206.pdf (accessed October 5, 2007).

Allen, A. (2007) No dignity in *Body Worlds*: a silent minority speaks. *The American Journal of Bioethics* 7 (4): 24–5. Available at: http://dx.doi.org/10.1080/15265160701220667 (accessed June 12, 2007).

Barilan, Y. (2006) Bodyworlds and the ethics of using human remains: a preliminary discussion. *Bioethics* 20 (5): 233–47.

BBC (2006) Body parts shows to need licences. Available at: http://news.bbc.co.uk/1/hi/health/4772739.stm (accessed October 5, 2007).

Body Worlds (2002) The anatomical exhibition of real human bodies: mission & objectives. Available at: www.bodyworlds.com/en/institute_for_plastination/mission_objectives.html (accessed October 5, 2007).

Body Worlds (2006a) The anatomical exhibition of real human bodies: the plastination process. Available at: www.bodyworlds.com/en/plastination/plastination_process.html (accessed October 5, 2007).

Body Worlds (2006b) The anatomical exhibition of real human bodies: the unparalleled success. Available at: http://www.bodyworlds.com/en/exhibitions/unparalleled_ success.html (accessed October 5, 2007).

Burns, L. (2007a) Gunther von Hagens' *Body Worlds*: selling beautiful education. *The American Journal of Bioethics* 7 (4): 12–23. Available at: http://dx.doi.org/10.1080/ 15265160701220659 (accessed June 12, 2007).

Burns, L. (2007b) Response to open peer commentaries on "Gunther von Hagens' *Body Worlds*: selling beautiful education": signed, sealed, delivered. *The American Journal of Bioethics* 7 (4): W1–W3. Available at: http://dx.doi.org/10.1080/ 15265160701307647 (accessed June 12, 2007).

California Science Center (2004–5) *Body Worlds*: the anatomical exhibition of real human bodies: summary of ethical review. Available at: www.bodyworlds.com/Downloads/ ethics_summary.pdf (accessed October 5, 2007).

Cunningham, G. (2006) Minnesota Public Radio (May 5). A new way to view the body. Available at: http://minnesota.publicradio.org/display/web/2006/05/05/body-worlds/ (accessed October 5, 2007).

Guyer, R. (2007) Metamorphosis: beautiful education to smarmy edutainment. *The American Journal of Bioethics* 7 (4): 30–1. Available at: http://dx.doi.org/10.1080/ 15265160701220683 (accessed June 12, 2007).

Jones, D., and Whitaker, M. (2007) The tenuous world of plastinates. *The American Journal of Bioethics* 7 (4): 27–9. Available at: http://dx.doi.org/10.1080/ 15265160701220709 (accessed June 12, 2007).

Kass, L. (1985) Thinking about the body. *The Hastings Center Report* 15 (1): 20–30.

Lara, A. (2005) Seeing dead people. *San Francisco Chronicle* (March 27). Available at: www.sfgate.com/cgi-bin/article.cgi?f=/c/a/2005/03/27/PKGIIBT7G61.DTL&hw= Seeing+dead+people&sn=001&sc=1000 (accessed October 5, 2007).

Maienschein, J., and Creath, R. (2007) *Body Worlds* as education and humanism. *The American Journal of Bioethics* 7 (4): 26–7. Available at: http://dx.doi.org/ 10.1080/15265160701220733 (accessed June 12, 2007).

Majumdar, B. (2007) Police uncover human bone smuggling racket. *Reuters Limited*. Available at: www.netscape.com/viewstory/2007/06/19/police-uncover-human-bone-smuggling-racket/?url=http%3A%2F%2Fnews.yahoo.com%2Fs%2Fnm%2F20070619% 2Findia_nm%2Findia303804&frame=true (accessed June 21, 2007).

Mohseni, Y. (2006) Body snatchers. *Discover Magazine* 27 (April 2). Available at: http://discovermagazine.com/2006/apr/cover/?searchterm=Body%20Snatchers (accessed October 5, 2007).

Mooallem, J. (2005) I see dead people. *Salon.com* (June 5). Available at: http:// dir.salon.com/story/ent/feature/2005/06/05/universe_within/index.html (accessed October 5, 2007).

Russell, R. (2007) *Body Worlds* prompts reflection on mortality. *The United Methodist Reporter – Interactive*. Available at: http://www.umportal.org/article.asp?id=1729 (accessed July 22, 2007).

Schulte-Sasse, L. (2006) Advise and consent: on the Americanization of *Body Worlds*. *BioSocieties* 1 (4): 369–84.

Stern, M. (2003) Shiny, happy people: '*Body Worlds*' and the commodification of health. *Radical Philosophy* 118 (March/April). Available at: www.radicalphilosophy.com/ default.asp?channel_id=2187&editorial_id=11213 (accessed October 5, 2007).

Ulaby, N. (2006) Cadavers exhibit prompts ethical questions. Cadaver exhibits are part
    science, part sideshow. *National Public Radio.* Available at: www.npr.org/templates/
    story/story.php?storyId=5553329 (accessed October 5, 2007).
Zoloth, L. (2005) The gaze toward the beautiful dead: considering ethical issues raised by
    the *Body Worlds* exhibit. *Atrium* 1 (Spring). Available at: http://bioethics.northwestern.
    edu/atrium/atriumissue1.pdf (accessed October 5, 2007).

CASE FOUR: FINDERS KEEPERS, LOSERS WEEPERS? – RETURNING ANTIQUITIES TO THEIR COUNTRIES OF ORIGIN

Machu Picchu

In 2005 Alejandro Toledo, President of Peru, threatened to sue Yale University
to force the return to his country of Incan artifacts excavated at Machu Picchu.[1]
In 1911 Hiram Bingham III, a Yale University Professor of History, had been
led by a Peruvian native to that ancient city. Although the particulars of agreements between Bingham and the Peruvian government are ambiguous and disputed, Yale University claims that Bingham received permission from the
then-Peruvian president, Augusto Leguia, to remove artifacts from Machu
Picchu and take them – permanently – to Yale for study and safe-keeping. The
university further claims that "the civil code of 1852, which was in effect at the
time of the Bingham expeditions, gave Yale title to the artifacts at the time of
their excavation and ever since" (Harman 2005: para 8). When Bingham
returned in 1912 to excavate the city further and harvest its cultural artifacts,
the Peruvians had undergone a change of heart: the government now demanded
that any artifacts removed from the site must be returned to Peru within eigh-
teen months (Lubow 2007).

Ninety years later, the Peruvians ran out of patience and wanted the artifacts
returned. Although Yale has, in fact, returned many of the artifacts, the university keenly desired to retain those contained in a stunning traveling collection:
Machu Picchu: Unveiling the Mystery of the Incas. This exhibition was shown in
six cities to audiences in excess of one million visitors before returning to Yale's
Peabody Museum of Natural History. Yale argued that without the expertise of
their scholars, the pieces would have not been restored to their present condition; indeed, the pieces may have been destroyed had they been left in Machu
Picchu. Because the labor of Yale's scholars is responsible for the pieces' current
value, Yale claimed that their possession of them should be continued.

Sabina

In 2006 the Boston Museum of Fine Arts returned "over 13 archaeological
treasures to Italy that cultural officials . . . say were looted from Italian soil"

(Povoledo 2006: para 1). Of particular interest to the Italians was "a majestic statue of Sabina, the wife of the second-century Emperor Hadrian" (ibid.: para 4). Although Sabina and the other pieces returned to Italy were acquired in "good faith," museum officials determined that their return was appropriate. Italian officials praised the Boston museum negotiators for valuing cultural heritage over owner-ship of property. They further expressed hope that the return would encourage others – both institutions and individuals – in possession of items important to Italian history to return those items to their country of origin. (Italy has long suffered from tomb robbers' illicit acquisitions and sales of cultural artifacts, depriv-ing their population of important historical representations of their culture.)

The Rosetta Stone

The Rosetta Stone, carved in 196 BCE, is a stone with writing on it in two lan-guages (Egyptian and Greek), using the three scripts – hieroglyphic (used for religious records), demotic (used for common communications), and Greek (used by rulers of Egypt during that era) – that were in use in Egypt at the time the stone was carved. Discovered in 1799 by Napoleonic troops in the seaside town of Rosetta, the stone provided the key to deciphering ancient Egyptian hiero-glyphs, a project that had taxed scholars for centuries (The Rosetta Stone n.d.(a)). The stone was constructed following a military campaign against fac-tions resisting the control of Egypt by the Greeks, of whom Ptolemy V was king:

> It appears that it was decided that the best way to emphasize the legitimacy of the
> 13-year-old Ptolemy V in the eyes of the Egyptian elite was to re-emphasize his
> traditional royal credentials with a coronation ceremony in the city of Memphis,
> and to affirm his royal cult throughout Egypt. This second aim was done through
> a series of priestly decrees, of which the Rosetta Stone is by far the best-known
> example. It is a version of the decree issued at the city of Memphis. (The Rosetta
> Stone n.d.(b))

Upon its discovery, the stone was initially taken to the Institut de l'Egypte in Cairo, founded by Napoleon Bonaparte in 1798. Following their defeat of the French in 1801, the English laid claim to (among other artifacts) the Rosetta Stone, and it was moved to The British Museum in 1802, where it has resided ever since (ibid.) and where it is "seen by more of the museum's 5.5 million annual visitors than any other single object" (Vallely 2003: para 2).

Between 1822 and 1824, French Egyptologist Jean François Champollion was able to determine the meaning and import of the hieroglyphs, ultimately determining that the stone contained one message, written in three different languages. The result of his translations eventuated in a "code book" that served to guide translations of other ancient texts (ibid.).

In 2005, Zahi Hawass, Egypt's chief archaeologist and secretary general of Egypt's Supreme Council of Antiquities, requested that UNESCO (United Nations Educational, Scientific and Cultural Organization) assist the country in reacquiring some of their most significant cultural artifacts, including the Rosetta Stone. He has ardently pursued this goal since that time.

Common themes

Although the Peruvian, Italian, and Egyptian artifacts differ in many ways, the most important argument supporting their return is identical: the artifacts constitute part of the countries' cultural heritage. As "patrimonial goods," the artifacts are among "those which have a special meaning for society because they are a testimony of history. Patrimonial goods are a reference of social identity and cohesion, providing society with a sense of belonging at local, regional and international levels" (Government of Chile n.d.: para 12). Patrimonial goods include anthropological, archaeological, paleontologic, and historical or artistic goods of a country or a community/society (ibid.). According to *The Web Journal on Cultural Patrimony* (n.d.), patrimonial goods can also incorporate immaterial heritage (i.e., cultures per se), as well as the disciplines of "archaeology, history, art, art history, architecture, architectural history, civil engineering, urban planning, computer science, physics, geophysics, chemistry and biology as applied to cultural and environmental patrimony, geology, anthropology, ethnology, geography, economics, and languages and literature such as oral history and traditions."

According to political, popular, and scholarly representatives of these countries (and of proponents of returning patrimonial objects in the art and archeological world at large), the contributions of these artifacts to their cultural heritage cannot be overstated. The absence of these (and many other) pieces in the museums and historical sites of their countries of origin constitutes a sad lacuna of tragic proportions. That citizens of a country should have to travel abroad to view their own history strikes many as ludicrous; those without fiscal resources to travel will simply never be able to view their own cultural treasures. Further, since many of the works were acquired or retained illicitly, proponents of their return argue that the current possessors have no morally legitimate claim to their continued possession.

Given the historical and cultural significance of these (and, of course, many other) pieces, the propriety of their return may seem self-evident. Nonetheless, many scholars, museum directors, and governments have demurred. Among their reasons for retaining various artifacts are the claims that some pieces have been legitimately acquired; that these acquisitions, had they not been restored and carefully preserved by the institutions currently holding them, would quite likely have been destroyed or irreparably damaged; that the pieces are much better appreciated in their current locations than they would be were they returned to their countries of origin; and that the return of these artifacts would set a dangerous precedent that would throw cultural institutions into chaos and call into question the legitimate (and often contractually guaranteed) cultural exchanges between countries (Vallely 2003). Finally, the return of cultural patrimony to their countries of origin would decimate the collections of many of the world's finest museum collections (Lubow 2007).

From a moral point of view, should cultural artifacts be returned to their countries of origin?

Perspective One

Although countries currently in possession of artifacts from other countries may choose to return them, from a moral point of view these artifacts need not be returned to their countries of origin.

First, the consequences of returning these artifacts would be overwhelmingly negative. Museum directors note that the artifacts are preserved in controlled environments that minimize further deterioration or damage. These pieces were rescued from their original environments, where they were subject to mistreatment that, if left unaddressed, would have resulted in the destruction and deterioration – perhaps obliteration – of these priceless objects (Atwood 2004). Because of continuing environmental degradation in some of the countries of origin, returning the objects would expose them to the sorts of ongoing degradation from which they were originally rescued. Extant antiquities are finite in number and constitute a non-renewable resource which should be carefully excavated, restored, and preserved. Since not every person, institution, town, or country has these capabilities, the role of current possessors as stewards for scarce and precious resources should be recognized (Warren 1989: 6–7, 19–21). In short, persons who care about the preservation of these objects should leave them in institutions that are best prepared to conserve them (Gayford 2006).

Second, the present sites make the pieces much more widely accessible than the sites to which they would be returned (ibid.). According to Vivian Davies, Egyptian curator for the British Museum: "The Rosetta Stone is the centrepiece of the British Museum's Egyptology collection. If it were to be moved to the Cairo Museum, which has less than half the British Museum's number of visitors, it would be seen by far fewer people" (Vallely 2003: para 20). Neil MacGregor, director of the British Museum, expands on this idea: "The British Museum is one of the great cultural achievements of mankind: it is very important that there is a place where all the world can store its achievements. I personally don't see any difference between Greek visual culture and the visual culture of Italy and Holland, which is also spread around the world" (ibid.: para 19). As an added benefit, "[museum] displays generally illustrate the geography and geology of the nation in question, demonstrate its technological achievements, regale its monarchy and/or political leaders, and recount its history. . . . These national displays also usually include some depiction of the cultural forms of the people who live in the country: their clothing, their housing, their treasured possessions, their lifestyle, and their customs" (Hendry 2005: 5–6). In short, the artifacts are located in cultural and historical contexts that makes the viewing in its entirety educational and provides an example of cultural diversity to the thousands or (depending on the location of the display) millions of visitors.

A derivative positive effect of this accessibility is the thriving tourist trade that springs therefrom. For example, Peru profits greatly from a thriving tourist interest in Machu Picchu, an interest that has been sparked in large part by exposure elsewhere to artifacts that lead to a desire to see the city itself. The economic hardship that would follow repatriation of the artifacts would be disastrous for Peru's economy.

Third, acceding to requests for returns would set a dangerous precedent: the nullification of all previous contracts regarding the acquisition of invaluable, albeit culturally specific, artifacts. First the Rosetta Stone, then everything else in the British Museum's Egyptian collection will disappear (or, so goes the worst case scenario) (BBC News 2007: para 5).

In short, retaining the artifacts in their current locations has the positive consequences of preserving the pieces, making them accessible to many more viewers, and honoring socially critical legal contracts. In fact, these exact concerns prompted the Vatican to refuse to return to Athens the fragments it holds of Greece's Parthenon (Lorenzi 2007).

The principle of autonomy provides additional support for allowing countries currently in possession of cultural artifacts to keep them. Although countries and individuals often petition for the return of artifacts which were stolen from them, in many cases (including the three cited above) many holders demonstrate evidence of having acquired the pieces with the permission of the governments (through their duly appointed representatives) that were in power at the time the relics were transferred. This is to say that they came by the works legally and, thus, should be neither castigated nor punished for possessing them (Warren 1989). Regardless of the particular historic conditions that were present at the time of the transactions, the governments in question ceded possession and control of the pieces to others. That contemporary governments or their representations rue these earlier decisions is not sufficient moral reason to overturn them. They can, of course, petition for the return of artifacts; but if the current owners demur, the earlier autonomous decisions to transfer possession of the pieces must stand.

Finally, the principle of justice (as fairness) supports leaving the artifacts where they now reside. Because of the attention devoted to them by scholars or restorers associated with these institutions, the pieces have been returned to (near) original condition. Given their role in saving, restoring, and protecting these artworks, the museums deserve to keep them on site (i.e., retain them fairly). As the seventeenth-century philosopher John Locke noted, persons are morally entitled to retain materials with which they have "mixed their labour" (1980 [1690]: ch. V; see also Warren 1989: 3–4, 7). Committing one's resources – time, money, knowledge, skill – to improve an object gives one a right to claim it as personal property, and to resist the claims of others to acquire the object. Moreover, had earlier discoverers/restorers not mixed their labor to acquire or restore these objects, they may not have been discovered or preserved at all. Thus, those who are responsible for the current state of the artifacts can justly (fairly) claim possession.

In a broader sense, one can argue that antiquities belong to humanity in general. Anthropologist Jaime King argues: "[C]ultural property is the property of humankind as a whole since it represents the achievement of a part of all humankind that cannot be set apart from other achievements, in other geographical places" (1989: 199). The past belongs – if the past can be said to "belong" to anyone – to the whole of humanity. (See Warren 1989: 5–6 for this argument.)

Geographical loci of artifacts are accidents of history and, thus, do not in any meaningful sense belong to the persons, institutions, or governments who – equally accidentally – inhabit those regions now. As a result, all persons have an equal interest in the discovery and preservation of such objects; justice requires that they be in the hands of those who can and will take the best care of them.

In conclusion, the appeals to positive consequences, autonomy, and justice support the retention by current holders of cultural artifacts.

Perspective Two

Countries currently in possession of artifacts from other countries must, from a moral point of view, return them to their countries of origin.

Beginning with a consideration of consequences, we note that patrimonial objects have symbolic significance for the peoples of the countries of origin: "Patrimonial goods . . . have special meaning for society because they are a testimony of history. Patrimonial goods are a reference of social identity and cohesion, providing society with a sense of belonging at local, regional and international levels. Any loss in this sense is both irreversible and non-retrievable" (Government of Chile n.d.: para 12). One example of such significance comes from the Italian town of Aidone, where residents are hoping that a statue of Aphrodite will soon be returned to them from the Getty Museum in California. According to Beatrice Basile, the art supervisor for the province, the region has suffered egregiously from illegal excavations and plundering of its archaeological sites. According to Basile: "[The statue has] given an identity to the people in Aidone, who feel very strongly that this is a restitution that in some way would compensate for a collective loss to their society" (Povoledo 2007b: para 12).

Cultural artifacts are also an important source of pride for countries and peoples, particularly if the country's history is more impressive than their current circumstances (Lubow 2007; Rothstein 2006). As noted by David Ugarte, of the Peruvian National Culture Institute: "This is our patrimony. This is everything to us – proof that even though today we are poor, our ancestors lived great and proud" (Harman 2005: para 7). An inspiring history can serve to motivate contemporary people to work to regain their once-illustrious society, according to Eliane Karp-Toledo, an anthropologist and the wife of ex-Peruvian President Toledo (ibid.; see also Atwood 2004). Or, as Zahi Hawass, head of the Egyptian Supreme Council of Antiquities, put it: "the past is important to our future" (Handwerk 2006). According to UNESCO, "the illicit import, export and transfer of ownership of cultural property is one of the main causes of the impoverishment of the cultural heritage of the countries of origin" (UNESCO 1970: Article 2). Because of this significance, failure to repatriate cultural patrimony to countries generates ongoing harms that are serious and sustained.

Then there is the question of future good will. Countries that have had their requests for repatriation denied might retaliate in ways that would bring archaeology to a grinding halt (or at least significantly reduce the number of archaeological expeditions permitted to be undertaken). Zahi Hawass, for example, has already denied permission to German archaeologists to work in Egypt, and is threatening to deny permission to *any* non-Egyptian archaeologist (Vallely 2003). Assuming that the goal of such endeavors is to recover and more fully appreciate the past, this achievement is more likely to be attained if more, rather than fewer, qualified archaeologists and historians are engaged in the project. If repatriation of patrimonial objects encourages such collaborations, that is reason enough to return them.

A final consequential concern is the worry that allowing cultural artifacts to travel contributes to the looting of archaeological sites that typically destroys, or at least detracts from, the ability to reconstruct the history of a particular culture or era (Atwood 2004; Greenfield 1989: ch. 7; Warren 1989: 6–11). The loss of knowledge is both inestimable and tragic.

Consider, next, autonomy. Autonomy, most broadly construed, is self-governance in terms of carefully considered values in terms of which one chooses to live one's life. Although often thought to apply to individuals, no theoretical argument precludes autonomously chosen value systems from attaching to institutions, communities, or peoples. The point is this: societies often come into being through (or persist in virtue of) sharing a life based on particular values. These value-based cultures are often exemplified by indigenous peoples, who often have explicit requirements and restrictions regarding respect for their values. Consider the Ganalbingu people of the Northern Territory, Australia. In the Ganalbingu culture, images depicting religious or mythic themes or symbols may only be created by clan members explicitly authorized by the clan to do so: "[T]he act of creating [art] honors the beings who gave the clan its territory. Misuse of those images . . . endangers the clan's relationship to the spirits who animate the land" (Brown 2004: 44–5). Reproducing or altering clan art – commonly seen in posters advertising or souvenirs commemorating exhibitions of indigenous art – is expressly forbidden, because doing so is disrespectful of clan values. Had the clans' permission been requested, it would have been denied.

Questions of autonomy also arise in the complicated issue of contracts between source countries and receivers of artifacts. Although many institutions and private collectors have acquired their antiquities legitimately, in many other cases the provenance (i.e., the history of an object's owners, handling, restoration, etc.) is questionable. The ongoing trial of Marion True, the now-dismissed curator of antiquities for the J. Paul Getty Museum in Los Angeles, has brought to light the illegal traffic in cultural artifacts (Povoledo 2007a, 2007b, 2007c). Many private collectors have purchased their artifacts from art dealers who are often less conscientious about the source of these materials than are institutions. The black market in art is lucrative, and many purveyors obtain pieces from looters and "tomb raiders" (Atwood 2004). When these private collectors donate pieces to museums, sometimes for tax benefits, the museums are implicated in this chain of theft and deception. The point is this: the circumstances of acquisition of cultural objects cannot always be documented. As a result, later owners may reasonably believe they have legitimately acquired the objects, having purchased them from reputable art dealers or received them as gifts from persons who did. But the more distant past may be shady, and earlier acquisitions may have been illicit. Artifacts that were seized as spoils of war (as was the case with the Rosetta Stone) might be thought to belong rightfully to the vanquished, rather than the victors. This has been the belief in regard to many of the art objects seized by the Nazis during their reign of terror (Simpson 1997). Victories in war entitle the winners to political authority – which does not extend to looting losing countries of anything and everything of value, a position taken in at least one US court decision (*United States v. McClain* 1979) and by UNESCO (1970: Article 11). In short, many persons believe that *all* ownership outside the country of origin is suspect.

Finally, justice requires the return of artifacts. Although current residents in the countries from which the artifacts were obtained did not create the objects in question, they are nonetheless the rightful owners. According to UNESCO, "property which, on religious or secular grounds, is specifically designated by each State as being of importance for archaeology, prehistory, history, literature, art or science" (Article 1) "forms part of the cultural heritage" of a state (1970, Article 4) if it was "created by the individual or collective genius of nationals of the state concerned" (ibid. at a.) or by persons residing in their territory (ibid.), if it was found in a state's territory (UNESCO 1970: Article 4 at b.), if it was acquired as a result of archaeological or other scientific undertakings (ibid. at c.), or if it was gifted to other(s) or legally purchased (ibid. at d.).

Since the UNESCO Convention issued its findings in 1970, one might think that their resolution does not apply to artifacts that were acquired earlier. While legally this may be true, the moral appeal to justice determines otherwise. If the cultural artifacts are as important to national identity and welfare as UNESCO has indicated, and if they may rightly be claimed under the conditions articulated in Article 4, then no moral reason supports limiting their return to objects acquired after 1970. The criteria that, if met, oblige their return have no such temporal arbitrariness. Justice requires their return.

In conclusion, the appeals to consequences and justice require the return of cultural patrimony. Although autonomy might suggest that contracts support the retention of artifacts by current "owners," the disrespect often entailed by acquisition or exhibition, as well as the uncertain provenance attached to many of these pieces, makes these practices and contracts suspect. The objects must be returned to the countries of origin.

Additional Issues to Consider

Q What, if any, criteria *would morally justify* a country's retaining a cultural artifact from another country?

Q Are individuals or institutions that purchased an artifact in good faith (i.e., believing it to have been consistently honestly acquired) morally permitted to keep those artifacts?

> **Q** Are individuals or institutions that were given an artifact by previous government officials or organizations morally permitted to keep those artifacts?

NOTE

1   On September 14, 2007, the government of Peru and Yale University announced that they had reached an agreement regarding the return of the Machu Picchu artifacts. Upon completion of a new museum at the site, "the museum quality objects will return to Peru along with a portion of the research collection" (para 4).

REFERENCES

Atwood, R. (2004) *Stealing History: Tomb Raiders, Smugglers, and the Looting of the Ancient World*. New York: St Martin's Press.

BBC News (2007) France stops Maori mummy's return (October 25). Available at: http://news.bbc.co.uk/2/hi/europe/7061724.stm (accessed February 2, 2008).

Brown, M. (2004) *Who Owns Native Culture?* Cambridge, MA: Harvard University Press.

Encyclopædia Britannica (2007) Bingham, Hiram. Available at: Encyclopædia Britannica Online: www.britannica.com/eb/article-9079232 (accessed September 3, 2007).

Gayford, M. (2006) Bones of contention. *The Spectator* (May 20). Available at: http://findarticles.com/p/articles/mi_qa3724/is_200605/ai_n16523374/pg_1 (accessed September 6, 2007).

Government of Chile (n.d.) Customs and the protection of cultural patrimony. Available at: www.aduana.cl/p4_principal_eng/antialone.html?page=http://www.aduana.cl/p4 principal_eng/site/arctic/20051129/pags/20051129121706.html (accessed September 4, 2007).

Government of Peru and Yale University (2007) Joint Statement (September 14). Available at: www.yale.edu/opa/newsr/07-09-14-01.all.html (accessed September 17, 2007).

Greenfield, J. (1989) *The Return of Cultural Treasures*. Cambridge: Cambridge University Press.

Handwerk, B. (2006) Egypt's antiquities chief combines passion, clout to protect artifacts. National Geographic News.com (October 24). Available at: http://news.nationalgeographic.com/news/pf/85286600.html (accessed September 6, 2007).

Harman, D. (2005) 90 years later, Peru battles Yale over Incan artifacts. *The Christian Science Monitor* (December 29). Available at: http://www.csmonitor.com/2005/1229/p01s03-woam.html (accessed September 9, 2007).

Hendry, J. (2005) *Reclaiming Culture: Indigenous People and Self-representation*. New York: Palgrave/McMillan.

King, J. (1989) Cultural property and national sovereignty. In P. M. Messenger (ed.), *The Ethics of Collecting Cultural Property: Whose Culture? Whose Property?* Albuquerque, NM: The University of New Mexico Press, pp. 199–208.

Locke, J. (1980 [1690]) *Second Treatise of Government*, ed. C. B. Macpherson. Indianapolis, IN: Hackett.

Lorenzi, R. (2007) Parthenon fragments won't go back home. Discovery Channel News (March 30). Available at: http://dsc.discovery.com/news/2007/03/30/

parthenon_arc.html?category=archaeology&guid=20070330141530&dcitc=w19-502-ak-0000 (accessed September 9, 2007).

Lubow, A. (2007) The possessed. *New York Times* (June 24). Available at: http://query.nytimes.com/gst/fullpage.html?res=9C00E6DA123FF937A15755C0A9619C8B63 (accessed September 9, 2007).

Messenger, P. M. (ed.) (1989) *The Ethics of Collecting Cultural Property: Whose Culture? Whose Property?* Albuquerque, NM: The University of New Mexico Press.

Povoledo, E. (2006) Boston art museum returns works to Italy. *New York Times* (September 29). Available at: http://select.nytimes.com/search/restricted/article?res=F30B1EF83D540C7A8EDDA00894DE404482 (accessed September 9, 2007).

Povoledo, E. (2007a) Antiquities trial fixes on collectors' role. *New York Times* (June 9). Available at: www.nytimes.com/2007/06/09/arts/design/09gett.html?ex=1339041600&en=8a9a9c9536078508&ei=5088&partner=rssnyt&emc=rss (accessed September 9, 2007).

Povoledo, E. (2007b) In a tug of war, ancient statue is symbol of patrimony. *New York Times* (July 4). Available at: http://travel.nytimes.com/2007/07/04/arts/design/04dig.html (accessed September 9, 2007).

Povoledo, E. (2007c) Two marble sculptures to return to Sicily. *New York Times* (September 1). Available at: http://select.nytimes.com/search/restricted/article?res=F50F15F9395B0C728CDDA00894DF404482 (accessed September 9, 2007).

The Rosetta Stone (n.d.(a)) Available at: www.ancientegypt.co.uk/writing/rosetta.html (accessed September 6, 2007).

The Rosetta Stone (n.d.(b)) Available at: www.crystalinks.com/rosetta.html (accessed September 6, 2007).

The Rosetta Stone (2006) Available at: www.rosetta.com/RosettaStone.html (accessed September 6, 2007).

Rothstein, E. (2006) Protection for Indian patrimony that leads to a paradox. *New York Times* (March 29). Available at: http://select.nytimes.com/search/restricted/article?res=FB0C1FF735550C7A8EDDAA0894DE404482 (accessed September 9, 2007).

Simpson, E. (ed.) (1997) *The Spoils of War: World War II and its Aftermath: The Loss, Reappearance, and Recovery of Cultural Property.* New York: Harry N. Abrams, Inc.

UNESCO (United Nations Education, Scientific and Cultural Organization) (1970) Convention on the means of prohibiting and preventing the illicit import, export and transfer of ownership of cultural property: articles. Available at: www.unesco.org/culture/laws/1970/html_eng/page2.shtml (accessed September 9, 2007).

Vallely, P. (2003) Stonewalled. *Independent* (July 24). Available at: http://findarticles.com/p/articles/mi_qn4158/is_20030724/ai_n12701051/pg_3 (accessed August 16, 2008).

Warren, K. (1989) A philosophical perspective on the ethics and resolution of cultural properties issues. In P. M. Messenger (ed.), *The Ethics of Collecting Cultural Property: Whose Culture? Whose Property?* Albuquerque, NM: The University of New Mexico Press, pp. 1–25.

Web Journal on Cultural Patrimony (n.d.) Available at http://en.wikipedia.org/wiki/Web_Journal_on_Cultural_Patrimony (accessed September 4, 2007).

CASE FIVE: FAUX PAWS – THE GENETICALLY ENGINEERED BUNNY

In September of 2000, artist Eduardo Kac unveiled his latest work of art: a live, glow-in-the-dark bunny named Alba. Injected as an embryo with the genes of a phosphorescent jellyfish, Alba emitted a greenish glow when held under ultraviolet light. According to Kac, he collaborated with a team of French geneticists at the National Institute of Agronomic Research in Paris to produce Alba (Young 2000). Denying any interest in genetic research, Kac insisted that his goal was to develop a performance piece, one in which the rabbit would interact with him in a kind of faux living room. "GFP [green fluorescent protein] Bunny" was to consist, not simply in the bunny's interaction with Kac, but also in the bunny's social integration and the public dialogue surrounding it (Kac 2000). Kac described Alba as "merely a new art form for the 21st Century" (Allmendinger 2001). Unfortunately, after public protest, the rabbit was confined to the laboratory until its death two years later (Philipkowski 2002).

As word spread about the glow-in-the-dark bunny, criticism began to emerge. One kind of objection questioned the moral propriety of using biotechnology for artistic purposes. "Ethically, I don't think we should use genetics simply for artistic exhibitionism. I think that is an abuse," said Arthur Caplan, Director of the Center for Bioethics at the University of Pennsylvania (Allmendinger 2001). Even if "GFP Bunny" were not an abuse of genetic technology, as Caplan suggested, some scientists, such as Harvard University's Woodland Hastings, viewed the project as silly and frivolous (ABC News 2006).

Other objections were more specifically concerned with the bunny's moral status as an animal. Some persons believe that animals in general have moral claims – even rights – not to be used as mere means to the enjoyment of others (Singer 1981). Others applied this philosophy to Alba herself: "If he [Kac] is really interested in glowing bunnies, he should stick to Playboy. At least they have a choice," said Bill Neely from People for the Ethical Treatment of Animals (Allmendinger 2001). Still others wondered how we might know if Alba's "condition" caused her any pain (Cook 2000: A01). Finally, some persons argued that there would be no way to determine the consequences to the ecosystem if Alba were to reproduce in the wild (ibid.).

Nonetheless, it is worth noting that genetic engineering has often been put to purposes other than meeting human medical or biological needs. For instance, a kind of genetic engineering is responsible for modern dogs and cats (ibid.). Their sizes and characteristics are not naturally occurring, but rather are the product of deliberate human intervention. The common goldfish represents another example of genetic engineering of sorts, strictly for the purpose of human amusement. The orange hue of the goldfish is, in fact, a result of selective breeding (American Goldfish Association n.d.). Hence, some uses of genetic engineering of animals for the purpose of simple human enjoyment seem uncontroversial. Moreover, other cases of injecting the green fluorescent protein gene (used to make Alba glow) into other kinds of animals have not attracted criticism. For example, the gene has been injected into the tumors of mice so that tumor growth could be studied more easily (*Boston Globe* 2000: F6). Admittedly, in the latter case, there is a significant scientific purpose. However, the fact that it has gone without criticism suggests that there is little moral discomfort with the procedure of injecting the fluorescent protein into animals, as such. Objections seem to arise when there is no scientific justification for the procedure.

Should Alba have been genetically engineered to glow in the dark?

Additional Issues to Consider

Q Is genetically engineering a person, assuming she consents, to glow in the dark morally permissible?

Q Is altering animals in a non-permanent way (e.g., shaving or painting) for artistic purposed morally permissibly?

REFERENCES

ABC News (2006) Glow-in-the-dark pig makes debut (January 12). Available at: http://abcnews.go.com/print?id=1498324 (accessed October 13, 2007).

Allmendinger, U. (2001) One small hop for Alba, one large hop for mankind. *NY Arts Magazine* 6 (6). Available at: http://www.ekac.org/ulli.html (accessed October 13, 2007).

American Goldfish Association (n.d.) Goldfish history. Available at: http://www.golgfishpages.com/History%20Pages.htm (accessed October 14, 2007).

The Boston Globe (2000) Art imitates science (September 24): F6. Available at: www.ekac.org/bosglobed.html (accessed October 10, 2007).

Cook, G. (2000) Cross hare: hop and glow. *The Boston Globe* (September 17): A01.

Kac, E. (2000) GFP bunny. Available at: www.ekac.org/gfpbunny.html#gfpbunnyanchor (accessed October 13, 2007).

Philipkowski, K. (2002) RIP: Alba, the glowing bunny. *Wired* (August 12). Available at: www.wired.com/medtech/health/news/2002/08/54399 (accessed 13 October 2007).

Singer, P. (1981) *The Expanding Circle: Ethics and Sociobiology.* New York: Farrar Straus & Giroux.

Young, E. (2000) Mutant bunny. *New Scientist* (September 22). Available at: www.newscientist.com/article.ns?id=dn16&print=true (accessed October 13, 2007).

4

GREEN ACHERS

Ethical Issues and the Environment

Case Six: All Used Up and Nowhere to Glow – Goshute Nuclear Waste Siting and Native American Sovereignty

Case Seven: Not in My Back Yard – Environmental Injustice and "Cancer Alley"

Case Eight: The Boiled Frog – Global Warming, US Interests, and Vulnerable Nations

Case Nine: A Gorilla on the Grill is Worth Two in the Bush – Wild Meat, Malnutrition, and Biological Conservation

Case Ten: Future Farmers – The Ecology, Economics, and Ethics of Genetically Modified Rice

Case Eleven: Till Rivers Run Dry – Mexican-American Water Politics

Control of the world's limited natural resources is determined not by need, but by economic and political power and the chance circumstances of birth, social status, and geography. We do not yet possess the knowledge or will to utilize the forces of nature without exploiting and depleting them, nor to meet the world's basic needs without creating collateral damage in the form of pollution, toxic waste, perdurable garbage, environmental stress, and vast social inequities. Expanding populations increase the demand and competition for water, land, energy, and food. We are on a collision course between those who want to preserve privileged use of resources and those who desire unfettered access to them. We are depleting the earth of its natural beauty while littering it with the detritus of our extravagance. Continued access by all parties to resources that were freely available in the past cannot be sustained, raising troubling questions about *how* resources will be limited, about *who* will make allocation decisions, and about choosing criteria to resolve both these procedural and substantive decisions.

Who will determine who is to have future access to resources? What are the environmental responsibilities of nations? Of individuals? Are the wealthy morally obligated to bear the cost of their luxurious lifestyles? Are the wealthy ever justified in forcing the pernicious by-products of privilege into poor communities with few resources? Are leaders of nations ever justified in seeking access to scarce resources for their own countries if doing so disadvantages other countries, particularly those with fewer resources or less power? Is it morally justifiable to seek to be an economic superpower?

Moral dilemmas examined in this chapter, "Green Achers: Ethical Issues and the Environment," focus on environmental concerns.

CASE SIX: ALL USED UP AND NOWHERE TO GLOW – GOSHUTE NUCLEAR WASTE SITING AND NATIVE AMERICAN SOVEREIGNTY

The question of Native American sovereignty has been an enduring problem throughout United States history.

In the seminal case, *Cherokee Nation v. Georgia*, the US Supreme Court rejected a Cherokee request to be recognized as a "foreign nation." Instead, and suggestively, the Court defined Indian tribes as "domestic dependent nations" (1831). Chief Justice John Marshall wrote that the Cherokee were a "distinct political society separated from others, capable of managing its own affairs and governing itself" (ibid.). The next year, in *Worcester v. Georgia*, Marshall added that the Cherokee Nation was "a distinct community, occupying its own territory, with boundaries accurately described, in which the laws of Georgia . . . have no force" (1832).

The political implications of the Supreme Court precedent have been profound. The Court recognized the sovereignty of US tribes, and checked state intrusion into tribal operations and control over tribal lands (Coté 2001: 20). For many Native American communities, sovereignty has turned out to be the greatest economic development asset they possess (Cornell and Kalt 1992: 45). To these tribes, sovereignty is survival (Egan 1998).

Yet in describing tribes as "dependent," the Court stipulated that the 554 autonomous "nations" and allied 314 reservations (Egan 1998) cannot exercise powers that conflict with the US government (Coté 2001: 20). All Native American tribes are subordinate to Congress (Egan 1998). Thus, practically speaking, Native American "nations" are really only *semi*-autonomous.

The semi-autonomous status of "domestic dependent nations" is intrinsically ambiguous and has led to complex tensions between Indian tribes and their surrounding political jurisdictions. Such tensions are nowhere more evident than in the plans of the Skull Valley Band of the Goshute, a tiny tribe in the desolate Utah desert, to store highly radioactive waste on its reservation.

Roaming the Great Basin of Nevada and Utah for thousands of years, the Goshutes – whose name means "dry earth" or "ashes" (Christensen 1995) – once numbered 20,000; but by the mid-nineteenth century the tribe had been decimated by disease, violent clashes with settlers of European descent, and encroachment on habitable land by Mormon immigration and development. Goshute leaders signed a treaty in 1863 with the US government (Woolf 1997b), in which that government granted sovereignty of a 17,777-acre reservation in Skull Valley, 50 miles and two mountain ranges southwest of Salt Lake City. (Another separate band of Goshute live near the Utah-Nevada border.) By the end of the twentieth century, the total number of Goshute had dwindled to 600 – the number of Skull Valley Goshute to 120. Diaspora left only a few dozen on the Skull Valley reservation (Wald 1999).

Beautiful to some in its barren sublimity, the valley to most is a wasteland of blistering heat, cold wind, and ashen alkaline dust. In the Goshute community, the windows of houses are broken, roofs sag, pink fiberglass insulation hangs from mobile homes, and cars rust where they quit running (Woolf 1997b) – tangible evidence that economic opportunities on the reservation are scarce.

Like other Native American nations, the Skull Valley Goshute became interested in nuclear waste storage in the late 1980s and early '90s when the US Department of Energy (DOE) began offering Native American tribes grants to study the feasibility of temporary nuclear waste storage (Gowda and Easterling 1998), known by the Nuclear Regulatory Commission (NRC) as "monitored retrievable storage" (2007). In a 1992 report describing the findings of the tribe's investigation into the issue of monitored retrievable storage, Goshute leaders wrote:

> European Americans must re-examine their lifestyles and ask how we can co-exist with the environment. They must understand as Chief Seattle warned over a century ago that man is only a strand in the web of life. The real political question which every American politician is avoiding is: Do Americans really need to conspicuously consume energy to have this standard of living? (Woolf 1992)

Probing further into the issue of nuclear waste storage, the idealistic hope of Goshute leaders to vanquish the paradigm of free-market industrialization seemed to collapse into a desire to work within the paradigm of free-market industrialization. Exploring the economic opportunities of using their forbidding desert reservation for monitored retrievable storage, Goshute leaders visited repositories in Canada, France, Britain, Sweden, and Japan (Woolf 1997b). In 1997, under the controversial leadership of Leon Bear (Israelsen 1999b; Westby 2001), Chairman of the Skull Valley Goshute, the tribe signed a lease with Private Fuel Storage (PFS), a private consortium of electric utility companies (Woolf 1999a). According to the terms of the lease, the Goshute agreed to store high-level radioactive waste for 50 years until a permanent repository opened at Yucca

Mountain, Nevada (Wald 1999). Shortly thereafter, PFS submitted an application to the NRC Safety Licensing Board for a permit to build and operate a repository (Israelsen 1997). In 2000, officials of Tooele (pronounced TO-WIL-AH) County, where Skull Valley is located, also entered into an agreement with PFS (Spangler and Kemp 2000).

According to PFS technical manager, Scott Northgard, the intent of the plan has been to create a "provably safe" (Claiborne 1999), centralized, and economical storage site until the federal government is ready to take possession of the waste (Northgard 2000). The plan calls for encasing 40,000 metric tons of spent uranium in 4,000 stainless steel casks (Maddox 1997). The uranium would be engirdled in cement onsite at nuclear reactors throughout the country, and then shipped by train to Timpe, Utah, a whistle-stop on a main rail line. At Timpe, the casks would either be loaded onto trucks for the final 26-mile trip down a narrow two-lane highway, or transferred to another railway dedicated for the purpose. At the facility, the casks would be placed above-ground in vaults standing on a huge concrete slab, where they would remain until a permanent facility, such as the one contemplated at Yucca Mountain, opened.

The estimated cost of the project exceeds $3 billion (Mims 2000). The amount of the Goshute's remuneration remained confidential until 2007, when it was revealed in court documents that the tribe stood to make $1 million, or more, annually (Winslow 2007). This money, according to Bear, would help the tribe build desperately needed infrastructure, such as a fire station, police station, health clinic, and water and electrical utilities (Claiborne 1999). Tooele County, whose officials endorsed the project early, also expected to benefit fiscally. PFS agreed to pay the county $500,000 a year in lieu of property taxes, and $3,000 for each cask brought to the site, eventually totaling $12 million. Prior to completion of the facility, the county was to receive $5,000 per month for education (Spangler and Kemp 2000).

Predictably, the prospect of storing out-of-state nuclear waste ignited intense criticism from a wide spectrum of Utahans: environmentalists, other Native Americans, and, most crucially, Utah State lawmakers.

For Steve Erickson of Utah Downwinders, an environmental group dedicated to radioactive waste issues, the Goshute-PFS proposal amounted to nothing more than a "shell game" aimed at getting waste out of the neighborhoods of nuclear power plants rather than finding a long-term solution to the problem of nuclear energy production (Woolf 1997c). Referring to the utilities that are eager to get rid of their nuclear waste, Erickson said: "It's time Americans stop operating under the misconception that they can deposit whatever they don't want out in the middle of the American desert" (Scholl 1997).

Perhaps predictably, the proposal divided the Indian community itself. The Skull Valley Band's sister tribe, the Confederated Tribes of the Goshute, voiced strong opposition (Woolf 1997c). Margene Bullcreek, a member of the Skull Valley Band which lives three miles from the proposed site, believes that the repository is inconsistent with traditional Indian respect for the land. "It's about being in harmony with our creator, and showing Him we do not wish to spoil

His gift to us" (Miller 1997). "I'm going to stand up and try to have my people understand that nuclear storage is not an economic salvation when in fact it might be the ruin of our land" (Scholl 1997). To Sammy Blackbear, another resident and vocal critic of Bear, Skull Valley is a holy place and should not serve as a nuclear waste dump (Mims 2000).

Asserting that tribal leaders pushed ahead with plans without properly consulting the tribe, in 1999 more than half of the Skull Valley Goshutes living on the reservation, led by Bullcreek, joined a lawsuit suing the Department of Interior's Bureau of Indian Affairs (BIA) to overturn the lease agreement, claiming that the federal government had failed to look after the well-being of the tribe (Woolf 1999a).

But the greatest impediment to the plan has been opposition by Utah State lawmakers. Hamstrung by Goshute sovereignty and thus unable to prohibit the Goshutes from legally entering into a contract with PFS, Governor Michael Leavitt focused on preventing the waste from getting to the reservation. Buoyed by confirmed reports that casks similar to the PFS design had leaked in Germany (Israelsen 1998), Leavitt emphasized apprehensions regarding the safety of transporting nuclear waste, vowing to dig a jurisdictional "moat" around the Goshute kingdom and controlling traffic with a figurative "drawbridge" (Claiborne 1999).

Joining Leavitt's effort to prohibit transportation of the casks, state Representative Merrill Cook introduced the Hazardous Waste Transportation Act (Maddox 1997). Enacted in 1998, the bill effectively transferred control from the county to the state of the 26-mile highway from Timpe to the reservation (Woolf 1998). PFS officials responded with a proposal to build a railroad from the mainline at Timpe; this proposal was immediately countered with concerns that an earthquake could derail trains transporting the waste (Woolf 1999b).

State opposition to the Goshute-PFS plan has made no difference to Bear, progeny of a legally savvy generation of leaders known for forcefully asserting the rights of Native Americans and promoting economic development in the name of sovereignty. "I don't belong to two nations," Bear said. "I belong to one – the Skull Valley Goshute Nation" (Egan 1998). "[W]e don't feel we're part of Utah. We're a sovereign nation" (Christensen 1995). This feisty and flippant attitude induced Utah politicians to cast aspersions on Native American sovereignty, echoing the sentiment of some members of Congress that tribal autonomy is "un-American" (Egan 1998).

In spite of the best efforts of Utah's political elite to stamp out the Goshute siting, plans continued to move ahead. In Leavitt's opinion, money generated an unstoppable inertia:

> It's pretty clear that utilities are willing to spend billions to move [nuclear waste] out of their back yard and into ours. They were able to satisfy the needs of the Indian tribal nation – with money. They were able to satisfy the needs of . . . private landowners – with money. They were able to satisfy the needs of the county – with money. (Woolf 2000)

By 2000 Leavitt admitted that the state may not have the power to stop the project and appeared resigned to defeat (Kemp 2000). In 2006, nearly nine years after submitting an application, the NRC granted PFS an operating license (Struglinski and Bauman 2006).

But then, as is often the case in political showdowns, a bizarre twist changed the course of the conflict.

Utah Republican lawmakers, who typically have been adversarial to environmental causes, suddenly became advocates of wilderness. Representative Jim V. Hansen, a reliable foe of wilderness designation (Jenkins 2006) had once disparaged national park legislation as unwarranted on the reasoning that "if you've been there once, you don't need to go again" (Smith 1995). Nonetheless, in 1999 Hansen inserted language into legislation proposing that a wilderness study area, which the proposed Timpe-Skull Valley rail spur would transect, become federally protected (Israelsen 1999a).

Building on Hansen's earlier work, Representative Rob Bishop initiated legislation to create the Cedar Mountain Wilderness Area. Utah Senators Orrin Hatch and Bob Bennett help shepherd the bill through Congress in 2005 (Gehrke 2005b). In January 2006 President George W. Bush signed into law (Gehrke 2006) the first federally designated wilderness to be created in Utah in more than two decades (Gehrke 2005a).

As a result of the new wilderness status of the area, the Bureau of Land Management (BLM) was unable to approve construction of the rail line across the federal land (Gehrke et al. 2006). Subsequently, the Department of the Interior, which exercises authority over the BIA, invalidated PFS's lease with the Skull Valley Goshute nation in September 2006 (ibid.).

In the summer of 2007, PFS and the Skull Valley Goshute filed a lawsuit in US District Court in Salt Lake City asking the court to throw out the Department of the Interior's decision, which the plaintiffs characterized as "arbitrary, capricious, an abuse of discretion, not in accordance with law, without observance of procedure required by law, and otherwise fatally flawed" (Fahys 2007). Untoward political pressure by Utah politicians had driven the decision, the suit alleged. Court papers revealed that the tribe was to receive payments from PFS of $200,000 a year until deliveries commenced, $1 million a year after that, and opportunities for "profit sharing" with PFS (Winslow 2007).

Legally, there is no ambiguity over the fact that some degree of sovereignty was given to Native American tribes in general by the Supreme Court in 1831, and to the Goshutes in particular by treaty 32 years later. Native American polities, as "domestic dependent nations," are free from state intercession but subject to congressional control.

Not so clear is the degree to which state lawmakers are justified in exerting their influence in federal policy and procedure regarding Indian affairs. As the Goshute nuclear waste siting demonstrates, the line between sovereignty and subjugation is, more than ever before, fuzzy.

Have Utah State political leaders been ethically justified in opposing the Goshute-PFS plan?

Perspective One

Utah State political leaders have been ethically justified in opposing the Goshute-PFS plan.

According to utilitarianism (an appeal to consequences), Utah State leaders are ethically obliged to act for the greatest good of the northern Utah population, independently of claims of Native American sovereignty. The plain truth is that storing a potent concentration of high-level radioactive waste, only 49 miles from downtown Salt Lake City, and close to one million people, is not good public policy.

Leavitt was ethically correct, during his tenure as governor, to raise several kinds of objections. First, Leavitt reasoned that the waste is extremely dangerous, else the utilities would not be so eager to get rid of it. As such, the waste poses a significant threat to the lives, health, and overall welfare of the residents of northern Utah. Although the members of the Goshute tribe would benefit financially, this benefit does not outweigh such dire threats to so many more people.

Second, Utah has no nuclear reactors. The interests of Utahans, albeit citizens of a politically weak state, should not be trounced by the electricity consumers of Alabama, Florida, Georgia, Illinois, Iowa, Kentucky, Michigan, Minnesota, Mississippi, New Jersey, New York, North Dakota, Ohio, Pennsylvania, South Dakota, Tennessee, Virginia, West Virginia, and possibly California (Israelsen 1997), for whom the waste was generated. Referring to the states where the nuclear reactors are located, Leavitt said: "If you create the waste, you take care of it" (Wald 1999). The populations that benefited from the reactors should, on a utilitarian calculation, absorb their burdens.

Third, once the waste is ensconced in Skull Valley, there would be no political incentive for the DOE to follow through with building the permanent site at Yucca Mountain (Woolf 1996). Leavitt's fears that "interim" may become "permanent" were given credence by Arjun Makhijani, President of the Institute for Energy and Environmental Research. The DOE, as Makhijani put it, "never met a repository location it didn't like. Once you take all the trouble of taking the waste to a certain place, I have a sneaking suspicion they will find geological virtues nobody knew existed" and end up burying the waste in Skull Valley (Wald 1999). If such predictions are true, not only are Utahans generally threatened without their autonomous consent; the Goshute themselves would also have their consent – to a *temporary* risk – disrespected.

Hyperbolic assertions of Goshute sovereignty are galling. Representative Cook, whose district bordered Skull Valley, lambasted the Goshute-PFS plan as a repudiation of the will of the majority: "Something is dead wrong when a small group of people can ignore the will of 90% of our state," Cook said. About the political autonomy that made the deal possible, he added, "I don't think this is what the Founding Fathers had in mind. It's just not right, this use of sovereignty. The implications are frightening for us as a nation" (Egan 1998).

Asked about Goshute autonomy, Leavitt responded that he was "more interested in the 2 million people who live nearby" (Miller 1997).

In sum, the appeals to consequences (i.e., the benefit to the majority of Utahans) and respect for autonomy trump any claim of Native American sovereignty.

Perspective Two

Utah State political leaders have not been ethically justified in opposing the Goshute-PFS plan.

According to both deontological and consequential ethical theories, Utah State lawmakers have a duty to honor the legitimate claims of Goshute sovereignty, independently of the particulars of the plan to store radioactive waste in Skull Valley. The issue, as Bear has correctly pointed out, is not just about radioactive waste. The issue is about nothing less than the survival of his tribe. The PFS facility could provide 40 permanent and 500 temporary construction jobs, jobs which could draw displaced Goshute back home and revitalize the community (utility) (Claiborne 1999). The community is clearly in dire straits; the opportunities provided to tribal members could reverse the tribe's march toward extinction.

Furthermore, denying Goshutes the right to pursue financial prosperity is tantamount to denying them the right to self-determination (autonomy). The right to control the use or disposition of one's property is well established, legally and morally. This right is meaningless if it can be overridden by a utilitarian calculus posited by those who disagree with an owner's decision. To intercede in some rights-based decisions, but not others, violates the right to equal treatment under the law. Or, as Lawrence Bear, the uncle of Leon Bear, who was elected Goshute Chairman in 2006 (Bulkeley 2006), said of the most recent legal action: "The Goshute people are tired of being treated unfairly. This lawsuit was brought to vindicate the rights of the Skull Valley Band to decide how best to use our own land for economic development" (Fahys 2007). The issue of sovereignty for the Skull Valley Goshute remained fundamental.

In sum, appeals to consequences, autonomy, rights to self-determination and property disposition, and justice, support denying the Utah State political leaders a voice in this decision.

Perspective Three

The answer is not simple. Above and beyond utilitarian concerns about the effects of radioactive waste on human health, and environmental concerns about the effect of radioactive waste on Great Basin ecosystems, the political question must be asked: have the Goshute been treated fairly?

Step 1: Information-gathering

Implications

- If the Goshute-PFS plan goes through, what are the possible environmental dangers of the presence of the radioactive waste siting?
- If the Goshute-PFS plan goes through, what are the possible public policy precedents set by the development?
- If the Goshute-PFS plan does not go through, what are the alternative opportunities for tribal economic development?
- If the Goshute-PFS plan does not go through, what are the possible public policy precedents set by Utah State's opposition to the plan?

History

- What is the environmental history of Tooele County? In particular, what is the history of the development of hazardous waste siting in the region, and what has been the Utah State position on such development?
- What is the history of the development of hazardous waste siting throughout the US, and what has been the nation's position on such development?

Legal/policy information

- In addition to Supreme Court rulings, what are the laws, both at the state and federal levels, regarding the transportation and storage of radioactive waste?

Economic considerations

- What is the potential for economic development in Skull Valley besides radioactive waste storage?

Cultural and psychological information

- Have the Goshutes been disenfranchised and marginalized?
- What possible psychological effects could such political forces have on tribal members?

Step 2: Creative problem-solving

Any creative solution to this dilemma must *simultaneously* prevent the risk of harm to residents of northern Utah while respecting the self-determination of the Goshutes. However, unless the Goshutes can be persuaded to change their minds (perhaps in virtue of being offered an equally appealing and less risky economic opportunity), the two sides will remain at an impasse.

Step 3: Listing pros and cons

Options	Pros	Cons
Goshute-PFS plan goes through.	1. Populous states with nuclear reactors get rid of their waste (C-U) 2. Dangerous materials are concentrated in one area rather than being spread out over scores of sites in numerous states (C-U) 3. Goshutes benefit from economic development (C-B, C-U) 4. Goshutes' right of self-determination is respected (A, R) 5. Utah leaders remain consistent in their position on hazardous waste siting in Tooele County (V-integrity, J-E)	6. High-level radioactive waste stored near large human population is potentially deleterious (C-NM, C-U) 7. Accidental discharge of radiation could damage ecological systems (C-NM, C-U) 8. Siting could set precedent for future radioactive waste siting (C-NM, C-U, J-E) 9. Danger that "temporary" siting could become permanent (C-NM, C-U, A)
Goshute-PFS plan does not go through.	10. Utahans are not saddled with the radioactive waste of others (C-NM, E) 11. No threat of high-level radioactive waste (C-B, C-U) 12. No precedent for other plans for high-level radioactive waste siting (C-B, C-U)	13. Goshutes lose best opportunity for economic development (C-B) 14. Temporary siting for Yucca Mountain-bound waste prevented (C-U) 15. Cost-effective management of radioactive waste for PFS consortium not realized (C-B, C-U) 16. Community self-esteem damaged (C-NM, C-U) again by disenfranchisement and marginalization (A, J-E)

Step 4: Analysis

Factual assumptions

- High-level radioactive waste is dangerous.
- The Skull Valley Band of the Goshutes have no other viable opportunities for economic development.

Value assumptions

- No one should be exposed to high-level radioactive waste near where they live because such materials are detrimental to living beings.
- A community's right to self-determination should be respected.
- Communities' legitimate economic development projects should not be interfered with.

Step 5: Justification

This is a complex case involving ecology, sociology, economics, politics, the law, and history. Utilitarianism and deontology are directly relevant to this case (as noted in the first two perspectives). In addition to utilitarian and deontological considerations, the Goshute case warrants examination in terms of justice as fairness. Finally, this case must also take account of a broader historical context of the environmental history of Tooele County.

Prima facie, Utah political leaders have been right to oppose the Goshute-PFS plan on utilitarian grounds (i.e., the environmental and human threats of radioactive waste). However, taken in the broad context of the history of hazardous waste-siting in Tooele County, and the Utah Sate political establishment's full endorsement and support of that development, recent opposition to the Goshute-PFS plan is hypocritical.

If one analyzes the case from the perspective of justice, Goshutes have been treated both unfairly and unequally by Utah State leaders. In fact, the Goshute had been virtually ignored by both Utah leaders and the Utah citizenry until the PFS plan surfaced.

Independently of intra- and inter-tribal dissension, the nuclear storage site proposal is entirely congruous with the environmental history of the area (Ishiyama 2003). After World War II, Tooele County became home to some of the most notoriously poisonous agents, such as deadly sarin and VX nerve gas (Riebsame et al. 1997), in what sociologist Valerie Kuletz (1998) has referred to as "national sacrifice zones" created by the federal government. The result has taken its toll on the environment. On March 13, 1968, a military jet inadvertently released 20 pounds of VX nerve agent. This toxic substance settled in Skull Valley, killing wildlife and more than 6,000 sheep (Ward 1999: 102).

Utah State leaders consented to siting the hazardous waste facilities of the US military, and later actively welcomed the hazardous waste facilities of private industry. This conglomeration of governmental and private facilities has made Tooele County one of most concentrated areas of pernicious waste in the nation. Just to the east of the proposed Goshute-PFS siting, over the Stansbury Mountains, sits the Tooele Army (Deseret Chemical) Depot, home to the nation's largest stockpile of chemical weapons; Dugway Proving Ground, a biological weapons testing and storage site, is southwest; EngerySolutions (formerly Envirocare), a low-level radioactive waste dump, the Grassy Mountain hazardous waste site, and several toxic waste incinerators all lay to the northwest of the proposed site. The infamous Magnesium Corporation of America, which has emitted enough chlorine and sulfur dioxide to earn it the title of the worst air polluter in the nation (Spangler and Spangler 2001), according to the Environmental Protection Agency's Toxics Release Inventory (2001), is situated to the north. Together, these sites make Tooele County, in the words of historian Mike Davis, "the nation's greatest concentration of hyper-hazardous and ultra-deadly materials" (1998: 35). Thus the plan has the virtue of concentrating dangerous waste in one remote location in a region already used for similar purposes, rather than leaving it in many densely populated locations (Reasons ##1, 2).

Taken in context, therefore, the Goshute-PFS plan is consonant with public policy precedent set by Utah lawmakers themselves. It was consequently surprising to many Utahans that the greatest opposition to the plan has came from the upper echelon of Utah State political leadership, who suddenly exhibited interest and vigor in denouncing hazardous waste in Tooele County.

The opposition was led by Governor Leavitt whose stance, is outlined in Perspective One (Reasons ##6, 7, 8, 9). Leavitt grew up in southern Utah in the shadow of mid-twentieth-century open-air nuclear testing. Explaining his opposition to the Goshute-PFS plan, he recounted: "I've seen pink clouds of radiation float over my grandmother's house. I had childhood friends who died of leukemia and cancer and neighbors who lost entire sheep herds overnight from radioactive fallout" (Claiborne 1999). In light of these experiences, Leavitt vowed, when nascent signs of a Goshute-PFS deal began to emerge in 1993, that the repository would only be built "over my dead body" (Mims 2000). In 1997, Leavitt formed a special taskforce – the High Level Nuclear Waste Storage Opposition office – with the sole goal of identifying "everything possible" to kill the Goshute-PFS project (Woolf 1997a) (Reasons ##10, 11, 12).

But Utah State officials themselves had earlier concluded that the transportation and storage of spent nuclear fuel is safe and, therefore, legal. In 1996 officials concluded, to use their own words, that "from a technical standpoint, spent fuel can be safely stored. However, a significant issue exist [sic] in public perception and acceptance of such storage" (Woolf 1997c). Consequently there is good reason to believe assertions by PFS officials that worries about the dangers of the plan are uninformed and irrational. Northgard argued that state officials in fact have contradicted themselves. "People's perceptions have been skewed," Northgard has maintained. "There's a lot of fear-mongering going on out there. This storage facility will be safe, environmentally sound and benign" (Scholl 1997) (Reasons ##14, 15). As he contended: "Each train will be followed by an emergency-response team prepared to arrive and take charge of any incident within minutes. Thanks to the robust design of the transportation casks, there is less risk in spent-fuel transportation than in transporting chemicals and other hazardous materials" (Northgard 2000). The PFS system is designed the withstand the most adverse conditions, Northgard claimed, including fire, flood, and earthquake, adding – apparently in response to fears that an Air Force fighter jet flying over a nearby bombing range could crash into a cask (Wald 1999) – "impacts" (Northgard 2000).

Numerous observers of the controversy noted the apparent incoherence of Utah lawmakers on the Goshute-PFS plan (Reason #5). Brigham D. Madsen, a Professor of History at Brigham Young University, who opposed the plan, said:

> When the Mormon settlers moved in, the hills were covered with wheat grass, one of the main sources of food for the Indians. . . . When the pioneers moved in, they brought their cattle herds and destroyed these grasslands. Now you have Skull Valley and it looks like a desert. . . . Why can't the federal and state government help them out in other ways? After all, we took their homeland from them. (Claiborne 1999) (Reason #3)

Similarly, David R. Keller, a Professor of Philosophy and Environmental Studies at Utah Valley University, whose campus is a scant 56 miles from the proposed site, wrote:

> [A]ttempts by Utah political leaders to derail the Goshute-PFS plan are simply the latest chapter in a long story of injustices to Native Americans. Unless taxpayers are willing to provide economic support, the Goshute are legally and morally justified in pursuing the right to self-determination in overcoming the marginalization they have long suffered. (2002)

Far from being "un-American," as politicians have contended, Keller held that the Goshute's plan to receive the noxious dross of industrial civilization for profit is in fact "very-American" (ibid.) (Reason #4).

In his role as Chairman, Bear was most pointed in his criticism of state officials. Bear accused Leavitt of "selective discrimination, which is hypocritical and unfair" (1998). "People talk about environmental justice, but in Skull Valley we talk about environmental injustice. The impact [from the repository] will be a lot less than all the hazardous sites we already have around us" (Mims 2000) (Reasons ##3, 4).

At the very least, the position of the Utah politicians would treat those residing within their borders unequally (i.e., unjustly). If former exposure to toxins was morally permissible, either because the dangers were minimal or because they provided useful economic opportunities to Utahans, then the current proposal is equally morally permissible. At the least, a cynic might suspect that the objections stem not from dangers posed by the project, but by the fact that the economic benefits will redound to the Goshutes rather than the state of Utah. But no reason exists to suggest that the Goshutes are not equally deserving of prosperity.

Worse than hypocrisy, Bear alleged that the opposition of Utah politicians has been "blatantly racist" (Claiborne 1999):

Before Utah was even a state, in 1863, my people signed a treaty with the federal government. We were granted a small reservation in Skull Valley – a piece of land no one wanted. We were placed out of sight and out of mind. During the past 50 years, the Utah and US governments have built many hazardous-waste facilities and disposal sites near our reservation, even burying sheep killed by nerve gas on our tribal lands. Did either government ask for our permission? Of course not. (Bear 1997)

"The federal government once tried to isolate us from the rest of the world when they put us on this remote reservation land which no one else wanted," Bear wrote. "Now when we see some prosperity, Utah's governor wants to again isolate us" (1998).

Harsh as they are, Bear's criticisms carry weight. Utah State officials had a hand in approving every single hazardous waste facility encircling the Skull Valley reservation and making Tooele County a sprawling toxic waste dump (Claiborne 1999). "Only when the tribe wants to do it they suddenly have endless objections," Northgard cynically observed (ibid.). Therefore supporting the development of numerous waste sites by both the military and private corporations over decades and then suddenly opposing the Goshute-PFS plan, which is squarely in line with the environmental history of the region, is arbitrary and capricious. As arbitrary and capricious, the actions of Utah State lawmakers violate the basic ethical principle of equality. Disparate treatment of the Goshute nation on the one hand and the industrial-military complex on the other is inequitable and hence unjust.

If the aspirations of the Goshute are once again crushed, their self-esteem as individuals and as a community could be detrimental in ways that cannot be predicted (Reason #16).

If Utah State officials are concerned about justice, as well as the environmental health of northern Utah, they must provide economic development opportunities meeting or exceeding the economic opportunities offered by PFS. Otherwise, they have no choice, ethically speaking, but to remain consistent with their previous decisions regarding land use in Tooele County and allow the Goshute-PFS plan to proceed. Justice demands equal treatment under the law.

Additional Issues to Consider

Other possible moral dilemmas arising within this case:

Q Under what conditions *would* communities be morally justified in interfering with risky behavior by their neighbors?

Q Would Utah State officials be justified in rejecting the Goshute plan if the tribe were wealthy? If the tribe were economically stable but members were living only slightly above the federal poverty line?

Q Would Utah State officials be justified in interfering if a different neighbor (say, Idaho, which is not a sovereign nation) had agreed to house the nuclear waste?

REFERENCES

Bear, L. D. (1997) Goshute Indians have right to business opportunities. Opinion-editorial. *Salt Lake Tribune* (July 6): AA4.

Bear, L. D. (1998) Utah perpetuates persecution of Skull Valley Goshutes. Opinion-editorial. *Salt Lake Tribune* (February 22): AA7.

Bulkeley, D. (2006) Goshute leader backs N-storage. *Deseret News* (October 26): B6.

Christensen, J. (1995) Surprises of sovereignty. *High Country News* 27 (April 3).

Claiborne, W. (1999) Utah resisting tribe's nuclear dump: On a reservation ringed by hazards, Indians see jobs, money in radioactive rods. *Washington Post* (March 2): A3.

Cornell, S., and Kalt, J. P. (1992) Reloading the dice: Improving the chances for economic development on American Indian reservations. In S. Cornell and J. P. Kalt (eds.), *What Can Tribes Do? Strategies and Institutions in American Indian Economic Development*. American Indian Manual and Handbook Series No. 4. Los Angeles, CA: UCLA American Indian Studies Center, pp. 2–51.

Coté, C. (2001) Historical foundations of Indian sovereignty in Canada and the United States: A brief overview. *American Review of Canadian Studies* 31 (1–2): 15–23.

Davis, M. (1998) Utah's toxic heaven. *Capitalism, Nature, Socialism: A Journal of Socialist Ecology* 9 (2): 35–9.

Egan, T. (1998) New prosperity brings new conflict to Indian country. *New York Times* (March 8): A1.

Environmental Protection Agency (United States) (2001) Toxics release inventory: Utah. Available at: http://www.epa.gov/tri/tridata/tri01/state/Utah.pdf (accessed July 21, 2007).

Fahys, J. (2007) Goshute nuclear storage allies sue Interior Department. *Salt Lake Tribune* (July 18): B1.

Gehrke, R. (2005a) Utah scores in nuke-dump fight. *Salt Lake Tribune* (December 17): A1.

Gehrke, R. (2005b) Plan passes to hinder Skull Valley N-storage. *Salt Lake Tribune* (December 20): B2.

Gehrke, R. (2006) Bush approves nuke-blocking wilderness area. *Salt Lake Tribune* (January 7): A4.

Gehrke, R., Fahys, J., and Burr, T. (2006) Interior dumps N-waste plan. *Salt Lake Tribune* (September 8).

Gowda, M. V. R., and Easterling, D. (1998) Nuclear waste and Native America: The MRS siting exercise. *Risk: Health, Safety & Environment* 229 (Summer): 229–58.

Ishiyama, N. (2003) Environmental justice and American Indian tribal sovereignty: Case study of a land-use conflict in Skull Valley, Utah. *Antipode* 345 (1): 119–39.

Israelsen, B. (1997) Nuclear agency accepts waste-site application. *Salt Lake Tribune* (July 26): D3.

Israelsen, B. (1998) Goshutes and downwinders promote opposing views. *Salt Lake Tribune* (June 2): B2.

Israelsen, B. (1999a) Anti-nuclear waste effort makes strange bedfellows. *Salt Lake Tribune* (February 9): B2.

Israelsen, B. (1999b) Goshute accused of offering bribes in waste dispute. *Salt Lake Tribune* (August 27): A1.

Jenkins, M. (2006) Wilderness: The new anti-nuclear weapon. *High Country News* (March 6).

Keller, D. R. (2002) The Goshute nuclear waste repository: Un-American or very American? Opinion-editorial. *Salt Lake Tribune* (December 29): AA5.

Kemp, D. (2000) N-dump moving closer to reality. *Deseret News* (June 17).

Kuletz, V. L. (1998) *The Tainted Desert: Environmental Ruin in the American West.* New York: Routledge.

Maddox, L. S. (1997) Leavitt, Cook battle Goshute waste storage. *Salt Lake Tribune* (June 27): A10.

Miller, P. (1997) Goshutes protest tribe's nuclear-waste proposal. *Salt Lake Tribune* (June 1): B1.

Mims, B. (2000) For the Goshutes, a test of tradition. *Salt Lake Tribune* (July 17): D1.

Northgard, S. D. (2000) Nuclear storage would benefit Utah. *Salt Lake Tribune* (August 27): AA6.

Nuclear Regulatory Commission (United States) (2007) Code of Federal Regulations. Title 10 sec.72.2 (June 29). Available at: http://www.nrc.gov/reading-rm/doc-collections/cfr/part072/part072-0002.html (accessed July 23, 2007).

Riebsame, W., Robb, J., Gosnell, H., et al. (eds.) (Center of the American West) (1997) *Atlas of the New West: Portrait of a Changing Region.* New York: W. W. Norton & Company.

Scholl, B. (1997) A nuclear dump proposal rouses Utah. *High Country News* 29 (September 1).

Smith, C. (1995) Great Basin Park doing fine despite Hansen's remarks: Number of visitors continue to grow. *Salt Lake Tribune* (May 14): B3.

Spangler, J. D., and Kemp, D. (2000) Tooele inks deal on N-storage. *Deseret News* (May 24).

Spangler, J. D., and Spangler, D. K. (2001) Toxic Utah: mending toxic Utah: environmental laws score hits – and misses. *Deseret News* (February 18).

Struglinski, S., and Bauman, J. (2006) PFS gets a draft license. *Deseret News* (February 14): B1.

United States Supreme Court (1831) *Cherokee Nation v. State of Georgia.* 30 U.S. 1 (Pet.). Available at: http://caselaw.lp.findlaw.com/scripts/getcase.pl?court=US&vol=30&invol=1 (accessed July 20, 2007).

United States Supreme Court (1832) *Worcester v. Georgia.* 31 U.S. 515 (Pet.). Available at: http://caselaw.lp.findlaw.com/scripts/getcase.pl?court=US&vol=31&invol=515 (accessed July 20, 2007).

Wald, M. L. (1999) Tribe in Utah fights for nuclear waste dump. *New York Times* (April 18): A16.

Ward, C. (1999) *Canaries on the Rim: Living Downwind in the West.* New York: Verso.

Westby, T. (2001) Nuclear storage site splinters Goshutes. *High Country News* (November 19).

Winslow, B. (2007) Goshutes, PFS sue Interior. *Deseret News* (July 18): B1.

Woolf, J. (1992) N-waste facility in western Utah? Goshutes take no stand. *Salt Lake Tribune* (September 16): B1.

Woolf, J. (1996) Utah's not aglow over Goshute deal to store N-waste. *Salt Lake Tribune* (December 25): A1.

Woolf, J. (1997a) Utah tribe won't dump plan for its N-facility. *Salt Lake Tribune* (April 16): A1.

Woolf, J. (1997b) Nuclear $torage: Goshute defends band's right to riches. *Salt Lake Tribune* (October 5): A1.

Woolf, J. (1997c) Utah politicians oppose N-dump. *Salt Lake Tribune* (December 3): D1.

Woolf, J. (1998) Panel OKs Skull Valley road-transfer bill. *Salt Lake Tribune* (February 20): B1.

Woolf, J. (1999a) More than half of Goshutes sue tribe over waste plan. *Salt Lake Tribune* (March 13): D4.

Woolf, J. (1999b) Quake could derail trains, geologist warns. *Salt Lake Tribune* (April 30): B1.

Woolf, J. (2000) Nuclear waste battle a lost cause? *Salt Lake Tribune* (May 26): B1.

CASE SEVEN: NOT IN MY BACK YARD – ENVIRONMENTAL INJUSTICE AND "CANCER ALLEY"

Environmental injustice is the inequitable exposure to deleterious pollution based on socioeconomic status (Keller 2005). In the United States, sources of pollution, such as manufacturing plants, toxic waste dumps, incinerators, and other industrial facilities, are typically located in low-income neighborhoods, whose residents are often African American, Latino, and Native American. Environmental injustice often entails a racial component, expressed by the common phrase "environmental racism" (ibid.).

Environmental injustice is a complex issue involving demography, geography, epidemiology, economics, and politics. Factors that cause or aggravate environmental injustice include zoning policies that permit residential and industrial areas in close proximity (Richardson 1997), the intentional targeting by corporations of minority communities as sites for hazardous materials facilities (Pellow 2004: 523), and the political weakness of minority communities to resist exploitation (Pastor et al. 2001). For example, in a report to the California Waste Management Board by a private consulting firm, the consultants observe: "All socioeconomic groupings tend to resent the nearby siting of major [toxic waste] facilities, but middle and upper socioeconomic strata possess better resources to effectuate their opposition. Middle and higher socioeconomic strata neighborhoods should not fall within the one-mile and five-mile radius of the proposed site" (Cerrell Associates 1984). Even the effectiveness of the use of bribery and corruption has been identified as considerations in hazardous waste-siting (Pellow 2004: 521).

As a consequence, noxious facility siting often occurs in low-income and minority areas (Bullard 1994). In Chicago, 92 percent of the city's approximately one million African Americans live in racially segregated areas. One segregated area, the Altgeld Gardens housing project in southeast Chicago, is 70 percent African American and 11 percent Hispanic (ibid.: 13). Altgeld Gardens is encircled by municipal and hazardous waste landfills, sewage treatment plants, toxic waste incinerators, smelters, steel mills, chemical plants, and a paint factory. The co-location of Altgeld Gardens and industry can be traced to racist zoning decisions dating back to the 1920s, in which homes preceded the construction of hazardous waste facilities (Grossman 1991). Collectively, the industrial facilities around Altgeld Gardens emit pollutants that are deleterious to health, particularly respiratory health (Summerhays and Croke 1987). Across the US, asthma is more prevalent within minority groups, such as Hispanics and Blacks; area of residence has been identified by public health researchers as a factor in this difference (Litonjua et al. 1999).

Between the 1920s and the 1970s, the city of Houston placed all its landfills and six of its eight incinerators in African American neighborhoods (Bullard 1983). The zip-code 90058, known as the nation's most polluted, lies in the middle of Los Angeles's largest African American and Hispanic neighborhood. In the one-square mile community, huge toxic-waste incinerators and dumps expose employees and neighbors to asbestos, lead, pesticides, polychlorinated biphenyl (PCB), and other hazardous materials (*Orange County Register* 1991).

Significantly, in the United States, awareness of environmental injustice as a serious ethical concern has its origins in the civil rights, rather than the mainstream environmental, movement. In 1982, in the spirit of grassroots activism, the largely African American community of Warren County, the poorest county of North Carolina, fought a PCB disposal site (McGurty 2007). This event differed dramatically from the mainstream environmental movement, which has traditionally focused on wilderness legislation (Keller 2005). Gradually, mainstream environmentalists became cognizant of the incidents of environmental racism and found common ground with civil rights activists, as evidenced by the 1993 roundtable discussion on environmental injustice organized by the Sierra Club. This cooperation between mainstream environmental and civil rights groups has taken the forms of technical advice, expert testimony, financial assistance, research, fundraising, and legal advice. For a growing number of both groups of activists, in order to take the issue of civil rights seriously, the problem of environmental racism cannot be overlooked (Keller 2005).

The role of race in environmental injustice was highlighted in a landmark report by the United Church of Christ Commission for Racial Justice (1987). The study revealed that the most significant variable associated with the location of hazardous waste sites was race, and that the greatest number of hazardous waste sites were located in minority communities. During the 1990s, the Environmental Protection Agency (EPA) began investigating allegations of environmental discrimination under the Civil Rights Act of 1964 (Bullard 1994: 15). In 1991, Delegates to the First National People of Color Environmental Leadership Summit drafted 17 "Principles of Environmental Justice." In 1992 an influential legal analysis found that race, not income, was the determining factor in EPA enforcement of federal environmental law (Lavelle and Coyle 1992). According to the analysis, penalties levied against industries for violating environmental laws were 46 percent higher in white communities than in minority communities, and that abandoned toxic waste sites in minority areas took 20 percent longer to be placed on the Superfund clean-up priority list than those in white areas (ibid.).[1]

Title VI of the Civil Rights Act states: "No person in the Untied States shall, on the ground of race, color, or national origin, be excluded from participation in, be denied the benefits of, or be subjected to discrimination under any program or activity receiving Federal financial assistance." Building on that Act, in 1993 Congress passed the Environmental Justice Act (EJA), the Environmental Equal Rights Act, and the Environmental Health Equity Information Act. In 1994, President Clinton signed an executive order specifically aimed at addressing environmental injustice (Office of the President of the United States 1994).

All these conceptual currents converge along an 85-mile stretch of the Mississippi River from Baton Rouge to New Orleans. Officially known as the Industrial Corridor, this stretch is disparagingly referred to as "cancer alley" (*Advocate* 1999). This "toxic gumbo," as locals call it (Richardson 1997), is a heavily industrialized area consisting of numerous oil refineries, scores of petrochemical plants, and hundreds of factories. According to the EPA's Toxic Release Inventory (TRI), tons of pernicious chemicals are released into the environment along the Industrial Corridor, many of them known carcinogens (McQuaid 2000).

The people who live in the towns and parishes that dot this stretch of the river are mostly poor and black. Not surprisingly, the area is heavily polluted and illustrates demographic differentials inherent to environmental injustice. Each year, 7 pounds of pollutants per person are released into the air in the US. The state of Louisiana averages 21 pounds per person, while some counties in Louisiana, such as St James Parish around the town of Convent in the center of the Industrial Corridor, reach 2,277 pounds per person (Jackson and Bullard 1998). Out of the approximately 185 million pounds of toxic substances that are emitted into the environment each year in the state of Louisiana, 132 million pounds are emitted in this corridor (ibid.).

Anecdotal evidence suggests that noxious waste facilities along the Industrial Corridor cause numerous significant diseases, including cancer. A Baton Rouge physician has claimed that many of his asthma patients had not experienced respiratory ailments until they moved to the area, and symptoms disappeared when they moved away and reappeared when they returned (Koeppel 1999: 17). An oncologist who began practicing in Baton Rouge in the early 1990s said he saw far more cancer than he expected (ibid.). Florence Robinson, a biology professor at Southern University who lives near Baton Rouge, has had four dogs die of cancer, noting that no other dogs from the same litters developed cancer – nor lived in Louisiana (ibid.: 16).

To Robinson, the inordinate incidence of cancer is informative. In March 1997, a barge capsized on the Mississippi River, sending a plume of toluene and benzene fumes over the Southern University campus. Both chemicals are flammable and carcinogenic. After the incident, one student, Catherine Anthony, developed a red rash on her face and said that her health has been failing since the accident. "It seems like my future has ended," Anthony lamented (Kern 2001).

The Shintech-Convent plant controversy is a case in point. The Houston-based company is the wholly owned US subsidiary of Tokyo-based Shin-Etsu Chemical Company, the world's largest manufacturer of polyvinyl chloride (PVC), a common plastic pipe material. In 1996, Shintech investigated the possibility of building a chemical plant on a former sugar-cane plantation near the town of Convent in St James Parish, which has been consistently ranked as one of the most polluted counties in the nation. The parish is also home to the IMC-Agrico fertilizer plant which discharges 174 million pounds of toxic chemicals into the Mississippi River every year, earning it the distinction of being the most toxic plant in the US until it was shut down in 1994 (Cockburn 1997).

Shintech was charged by the Tulane Law Clinic with environmental racism under the EJA of 1994, which makes illegal any "disproportionate distribution of environmental hazards" in low-income communities. Shintech was open to such charges, as about 40 percent of Convent residents had incomes at or below the federal poverty line. Rather than fight the charges in court, Shintech canceled plans to build the plant and eventually decided instead to build a $1 billion plant in Plaquemine, Louisiana, which has markedly less poverty than the Convent area and thus makes it less susceptible to the legal ramifications of the EJA. There is, however, another side to this controversy, as LSU economist Loren Scott argued: without the Shintech plant, it would be even harder to find jobs in St James Parish, where they are desperately needed (McConnaughey 1999). Economists and politicians argue that meddling with market forces hurts, rather than helps, poor people who need economic development the most (Payne 1998).

Given this background, have communities of the Baton Rouge-New Orleans Industrial Corridor been unfairly targeted for the development of hazardous facilities?

Perspective One

Allegations of environmental racism along the Baton Rouge-New Orleans Industrial Corridor are unfounded. Charges of corporate wrongdoing are premised on a causal connection between pre-existing poverty and the targeting of poor communities for the siting of industrial development involving hazardous materials. No such connection exists.

Allegations of environmental injustice raise the classical causal conundrum: given the co-occurrence of two events, what is the connection between the two? Is one event the causal antecedent of the other, or the other way around? Or is there any causal connection at all, aside from the two events being simple symptoms of some larger phenomenon? In terms of environmental injustice, are hazardous waste facilities located where they are because those communities have been singled out on account of their relative political weakness, or do lower-income people migrate to areas that just happen to be home to industry?

Sociological research on the causality between low-income residence and industrialization has been mixed. Studies have found the primary demographic factors of areas with hazardous waste facilities are low-income, minority residents, and a preponderance of rental property (Pastor et al. 2001: 15). Even so, some scholars have refrained from identifying low-income residence as a causal antecedent to industrialization. Land amenable to industrial activity might be less desirable for residential purposes, so the two phenomena – lower-income populations and industrialization – might be externally related to a third factor: the area itself (Mennis and Jordan 2005: 266). For instance, a swampy area may be amenable to industrial development because of the accessibility of barge and rail traffic, and unattractive to middle-class and high-income families because of the humidity and mosquitoes. Hence some studies state that there is no clear temporal ordering of either minority settlement with hazardous waste-facility siting, or hazardous waste-facility siting with minority settlement (ibid.).

According to Elizabeth "Terry" Fontham, Dean of Louisiana State University (LSU) School of Public Health, the elevated cancer rates in the Baton Rouge-New Orleans Industrial Corridor might be due to lifestyle, not pollution. Residents along the river tend to eat a Cajun diet laden with fat and sparse on fruits and vegetables, and also tend to smoke tobacco earlier and more during their lifetimes (Koeppel 1999: 17). This complication is enough for some epidemiologists to remain skeptical about any definitive link between industrial pollution and cancer (Pope 2004), or to dismiss environmental factors outright (McQuaid 2000).

A study funded by a state office, the Louisiana Tumor Registry (LTR), found that, taken as a whole, the cancer rates along the Industrial Corridor were normal: "Incidence rates for the Industrial Corridor are either similar to, or statistically significantly lower than, the combined [national] rates for most of the common cancers (prostate, breast, colon, and rectum) as well as for rare tumors such as brain and leukemias" (Chen et al. 1998: 165).

Therefore, according to the Principle of Utility, industrialization creates the greatest good for the greatest number of people, even after factoring in the costs of pollution. This holds even if poor communities had been targeted for the development of hazardous waste facilities (or what activists inaccurately refer to as "environmental injustice"). Since no causal connection is evident, industrialization along the Baton Rouge-New Orleans Mississippi River corridor is a forteriori ethical.

Perspective Two

Environmental racism along the Industrial Corridor is real and substantiated by evidence.

According to deontology (the theoretical foundation for the principles of autonomy and rights), persons living along the Industrial Corridor have been used as means to the end of profit-making for others. Therefore their intrinsic value as human beings has been ignored and their rights violated.

Demographic research has discerned a causal connection between minority populations and hazardous waste-facility siting: the disproportionate siting of hazardous waste facilities in minority areas is much greater than disproportionate minority relocation to areas of pre-existing hazardous waste siting (Pastor et al. 2001: 1). In other words, minorities attract hazardous waste facilities, but hazardous waste facilities do not generally attract minorities (ibid.: 18).

Some studies suggest a higher incidence of cancer linked to environmental pollution on the Industrial Corridor. A study of 20 parishes in southern Louisiana found a statistically significant connection between drinking Mississippi River water and rectal cancer (Gottlieb et al. 1981). Another study found that people not employed by the petrochemical industry but living within one mile of a plant were four times more likely to die of lung cancer than people not employed by the petrochemical industry and living two to four miles away (Ferstel 1998).

St Bernard Parish of metropolitan New Orleans has high cancer rates, particularly for lung cancer, according to LSU Public Health School Dean Terry Fontham (Pope 2004). Specifically, the cancer death rate in 1997 was 18 percent above the Louisiana's average and 22 percent above the national average (Correa et al. 2004).

Naysayers dismiss research that does not draw connections between industrialization and cancer as severely flawed science. "It tells me they don't know what they're doing or they're trying to distort the truth," said Robinson (McQuaid 2000). The glaring defect of the LTR studies is that they dilute clusters of cancers in vast pools of populations and include non-industrialized areas and vast tracts of uninhibited swamp in statistical analyses (Koeppel 1999: 18).

The LTR studies would be more epidemiologically sound if they focused on the swath of the Industrial Corridor rather than entire parishes, as LTR studies do (McQuaid 2000). For example, in 1995, three boys from Ascension Parish were diagnosed with rhabdomyosarcoma, a very rare and extremely malignant tumor of soft tissue (Ferstel 1998). Sheila Moore, a physician from Baton Rouge, felt that further study of this cancer cluster was warranted, but the state Office of Public Health decided that three cases were too few to justify the effort (ibid.).

This is scientifically myopic, since clusters of cancer are exactly where the focus should be, according to Patricia Williams, a physician and director of the Occupational Toxicology Outreach Program at LSU Medical Center (Koeppel 1999: 17–18). In 1993, responding to an alleged cluster of cancers around the Denham Springs/Walker dumpsite, a facility used by numerous companies to dispose of noxious waste, the state identified only a few cases of cancer and concluded that exposure was too minimal to cause harmful health effects by using numbers from the LTR. Williams, however, studied the same case for plaintiffs suing the companies that used the dump, using, instead, numbers gleaned from fieldwork. Contrary to the state's finding, she found many more cases than the state acknowledged, and observed a striking connection between exposure to toxins and contraction of cancer. The companies settled for $131 million in 1997 (ibid.: 19).

Therefore, according to the principles of nonmaleficence (namely, refraining from causing harm by toxic waste emissions), rights (namely, the right of all persons to live in a healthy environment), and equality (equitable treatment of persons across racial and socioeconomic classes), intensive industrialization along the Baton Rouge-New Orleans Industrial Corridor is unethical.

Perspective Three

The answer is not simple. The fact that environmental injustice is part of the environmental history of the Industrial Corridor between Baton Rouge and New Orleans does not entail the conclusion that *all* industrial development meets the description of environmental injustice, nor that industrial development in some forms cannot be morally justified. The challenge is to identify criteria by which to distinguish ethically acceptable industrial development from that which is not. The ethical status of development depends on the public policy process through which the siting takes place, who is benefited, who is exploited, the balance between implementing pollution-reducing technologies at the expense of profit, and, most importantly – at least in an open, democratic society – whose voices are included in the discourse.

Step 1: information-gathering

Medical information

- How reliable are the findings of epidemiological research?

Public heath officials admit that they have been reluctant to study small clusters of cancer which, they say, points to limitations of the structure of epidemiology itself, not their studies. Epidemiologists typically work on large scales, trying to discern patterns within groups of tens of thousands to millions. If the sample size is a community neighborhood next to a hazardous waste facility, small numbers can have large statistical impacts. For example, one more case of cancer could double a rate, said Vivien Chen, director of the LTR (McQuaid 2000). The large sample sizes needed for epidemiological research make it an imprecise science. Therefore, the direct causal connection between industrialization along the river corridor and deleterious health amongst the local population cannot be decisively determined.

Implications
What would be the effect of restricting industrial development along the Mississippi River?

- If no industrial development takes place in the communities along the Mississippi River from Baton Rouge to New Orleans, economic opportunities will be significantly reduced and poverty may persist, albeit in a cleaner environment.
- If industrial development continues to take place in the communities along the Mississippi River from Baton Rouge to New Orleans in an unrestrained manner, the possibility of economic prosperity for those communities exists, albeit with the threat of pollution and deleterious ecological and pubic health consequences.
- If industrial development continues to take place in the communities along the Mississippi River from Baton Rouge to New Orleans in an undemocratic manner, then the possibility exists that the costs of development may be foisted on those communities without any meaningful benefit.
- If industrial development continues to take place in the communities along the Mississippi River from Baton Rouge to New Orleans in a democratic

manner and based on reliable epidemiological information, then the costs of toxic waste emissions may be compensated for by increased standards of living of local community members.

History

■ What is the environmental history, particularly the history of land-use development, along the Mississippi River between Baton Rouge and New Orleans?

Legal/policy information

■ Do environmental regulations exist which would protect the rights of residents of the Industrial Corridor against untoward hazardous pollution at both state and federal levels, and, if so, are those regulations enforced?

Economic considerations

■ What will be the economic future of communities along the Mississippi River between Baton Rouge and New Orleans if industrial activities cease?
■ What will be the economic future of communities along the Mississippi River between Baton Rouge and New Orleans if industrialization continues?
■ What are the unique attributes of the region in terms of economic development?

Cultural and psychological information

■ Are local people, even if they are aware that their communities are being targeted for hazardous facility siting, motivated to engage in political processes to resist exploitation by special interests?

The region has a history, noted above, of marginalization, disenfranchisement, and exploitation of local communities by commercial and political interests. Monique Harden, co-director of Advocates for Environmental Human Rights, a nonprofit public interest law firm, has described the demography of the region: "Louisiana has only known two forms of economic development: slave plantations and heavy industry" (Greenberg 2006), both exploitative of African Americans. According to Harden, during the decades in which industrial facilities were beginning to be built along the Industrial Corridor (from the 1930s to the 1950s), African Americans did not have the right to vote and residents had no say in the location or operation of industrial installations (ibid.: 35).

Step 2: Creative problem-solving

Ironically, careful consideration suggests that the market forces that have caused environmental injustice are also the very same forces that could mitigate socioeconomic inequity. The challenge is balancing the benefits of industrial development against its costs, which is to say, generating corporate profit while at the same time not violating the right of locals to the basic necessity of a clean environment. Political leaders have a duty to ensure that basic rights of their constituents are not violated.

Step 3: Listing pros and cons

Options	Pros	Cons
Allow continued industrialization along Mississippi River between Baton Rouge and New Orleans.	1. In the absence of industrialization, persons no longer exposed to deleterious toxins (C-NM) 2. Industrial pollution dissipates; ecosystems begin to recover (C-B, C-U) 3. General population health benefits in terms of reduced exposure to toxins (C-U) 4. Citizens empowered at local political levels to make decisions without intrusion by outside interests (A) 5. Individuals' rights to clean environment not compromised by corporate hegemony (R) 6. Epidemiologists and environmental regulators not pressured to compromise professional integrity (V) 7. Poor blacks not treated differently from affluent whites in terms of exposure to hazardous waste (J-E)	8. No potential for locals to benefit economically from unique geographical feature of the region (i.e., to benefit industrially from industrialization of river corridor) (C-U)
Allow continued industrialization along Mississippi River between Baton Rouge and New Orleans.	9. Locals have possibility to benefit financially and to enjoy increased standard of living (C-B) 10. Community as a whole has possibility of benefitting financially; improved infrastructure (roads, utilities, public facilities) and services (police, fires, schools) (C-U) 11. Inclusive, transparent decisional approach gives local citizens potential to	13. Some persons will be exposed to industrial toxins (C-NM) 14. Select few possibly benefit financially at expense of majority (C-U) 15. Corruption may distort political processes and disenfranchise those most affected (A)

	have a voice in own self-determination (A) 12. If policies equally value voices of individuals of lower socioeconomic status, progress made toward equality (J-E)	16. Persons not free to live in a relatively toxin-free environment (R) 17. Extreme political pressure may cause regulators to compromise professional integrity (V) 18. Corruption may render epidemiological data unreliable (C-U) 19. Environmental injustice continues (J-E)

Step 4: Analysis

Factual assumptions

- Industrial processes cause some level of hazardous pollution.
- Hazardous pollution has deleterious health effects.
- Industrial development provides for the possibility of economic growth.

Value assumptions

- All other things being equal, health is more important than wealth; persons cannot enjoy material possessions when sick or dead.
- Political self-determination of communities is good.

Step 5: Justification

The first step is to obtain epidemiological data that are as reliable as possible. Such data are a necessary condition for informed public policy decision-making. The subjects of human epidemiology – human populations – are diverse, complex, and mobile. As a result, epidemiological conclusions are imprecise and approximate. Because of the intrinsic imprecision of epidemiological science, the corrupting influences of money and political power must be eliminated to the greatest extent within a public policy framework.

However, environmental justice activists complain that epidemiology, at least as practiced in Louisiana, is contaminated by the corrupting influences of money and power, making its findings more political than scientific (Reason #17). Environmental Health Network and the National Toxics Campaign Fund, two nonprofit environmental organizations, reported that federally funded studies are designed to be inconclusive in order to reassure the public of safety and not cause alarm (Russell et al. 1992). Federally funded studies use statistical methods that are ill-equipped to deal with small and mobile populations living around hazardous waste sites. The report also makes the claim that researchers known to hold a bias against correlating public health and industrial waste are chosen to run the studies (ibid.). For this reason, Tulane University law professor, Oliver Houck, is dubious about any research paid for by government or industry. Of epidemiological studies, he says, "You have to ask the primary question, 'Who paid for the research[?]'" (Ferstel 1998).

In Louisiana, industries give enormous gifts to medical schools and universities which, together with the State Health Department, run the cancer studies (Reason #18). Freeport-McMoRan, one of the world's largest manufacturers of fertilizers and historically one of the biggest polluters of Louisiana waterways, donated $1 million to the LSU cancer center and $1.6 million to the University of New Orleans Center for Environmental Modeling. Oil tycoon C. B. Pennington gave LSU $125 million to build a Bio-Medical Research Center; and Lod Cook, chairman of Arco, paid for most of LSU's alumni center. Texaco leased Tulane a building at no cost for its Public Health School, and Tidewater Industries, a company that services oil rigs, gave the university a 24-story building for its medical programs (Koeppel 1999: 19–20). Finding large petrochemical corporations that have not donated generously to public health programs is a greater challenge than finding those that have.

Allegations of reprisals have been made by researchers who do not play the industry-government political game (Reason #17). Paul Templet, a professor at LSU and former head of the state's Department of Environmental Quality (DEQ), claimed that his salary at LSU was cut by $10,000 after he questioned industry practices while serving at the DEQ (Koeppel 1999: 22). After Marise Gottlieb, a physician and former medical researcher at Tulane, published research findings linking ill-health and pollution, she lost her funding at the university (ibid.). "We were making progress," Gottlieb said. "You have to ask why it stopped. My surmise is that I was doing the 'wrong' kind of work. Had I said there was no relation, everybody would have been happy" (Ferstel 1998). And Williams, whose conclusions have differed pointedly from those of state health officials, was allotted $1.1 million by the legislature to open a clinic to treat patients exposed to toxic chemicals. However, the funds were blocked by Governor Mike Foster and Mervin Trail, the Chancellor of LSU's Medical Center, and the clinic never opened (Koeppel 1999: 22).

The dynamics of money and politics also influence environmental regulation. At a 2001 town hall meeting in New Orleans, attorneys, environmentalists, scientists, and citizens testified that state officials are lax in environmental law-enforcement (Swerczek 2001). According to Templet, the close alliance between the chemical industry and political establishment automatically hampers enforcement of environmental regulations (ibid.). Former governor and millionaire businessman Mike Foster, for example, has earned up to $200,000 a year in royalties from Exxon for drilling on his land (Koeppel 1999: 20). Jim Porter, who was director of the state's Department of Natural Resources from 1984 to 1988, took a top job at the Mid-Continent Oil and Gas Association after employment with the state (ibid.). Some Louisiana officials are even employed simultaneously by government and industry (ibid.).

In the Shintech–Convent plant controversy, Governor Foster approached Shintech with inducements of $120 million in property-tax reductions and tax credits in return for the prospect of creating 165 permanent new jobs (ibid.). Local community activists expressed perplexity at the rationale of creating new jobs, since the parish was already home to 11 chemical plants. "If these industrial plants are so great," one activist asked, "why does our community still have 62% unemployment? It's about profit and greed, not jobs and justice" (ibid.).

Given the area's poverty, high cancer rates, and largely minority population, the Tulane University Environmental Law Clinic sued to have the plans stopped on behalf of local opposition led by the St James Citizens for Jobs and the Environment under the auspices of President Bill Clinton's 1994 Executive Order (ibid.) (Reasons ##16, 18).

Tulane's legal action provoked outrage from Governor Foster. At a May 1997 meeting of the New Orleans Business Council, Foster assailed those affiliated with the clinic as "a bunch of modern day vigilantes who are just making up reasons to run businesses out of the state" (ibid.). Foster threatened to revoke the tax exempt status of Tulane, which – at 7,000 employees – has the largest workforce in the state (ibid.).

Therefore the issue of environmental injustice along the Mississippi River Industrial Corridor involves money and politics as much as epidemiology. Templet has likened Louisiana to a developing country where a few industries and their political allies profit handsomely, while the masses languish (Koeppel 1999: 24) (Reason #14). In 1998, for example, the petrochemical industry accounted for nearly a quarter of the State of Louisiana's total gross state revenue (ibid.: 19). At the same time, some of the state's worst polluters donated generously to potential candidates – and even environmental groups (Reason #15). Freeport-McMoRan donated $5 million to the Audubon Institute and $350,000 to the Nature Conservancy; and Shell gave $5 million to the National Fish and Wildlife Foundation (ibid.: 19–20).

Given the history of environmental injustice in the region, there is less reason to believe that the problem lies in the lack of inadequate environmental regulations on the books than inadequate enforcement of existing regulations.

The arguments against industrialization which center around the corrupting influence of corporate money on democratic political processes (Reasons ##14–19) can be dismissed if the political process is made transparent. The solution to political interference in both the practice of epidemiological science and the enforcement of environmental regulation is to prohibit, as a matter of public policy, contributions of corporations and political parties to research universities, and of corporations to politicians and their campaign funds (Reasons ##6, 17). If the political process can be made transparent, the previously disenfranchised communities along the Industrial Corridor from Baton Rouge to New Orleans may regain faith in political engagement (Reasons ##11, 12). As it stands now, these communities suffer from a history of marginalization, disenfranchisement, and exploitation (Reason #15).

But forcing out industrial installations may harm, rather than benefit, local communities (Reasons ##9, 10). Other economic opportunities are few. The fertility of the soil has been severely depleted by intensive large-scale cotton farming; consequently, agricultural opportunities – the most logical economic alternative to industry – are limited. Thus, paradoxically, while industrialization and free-market economics are the root of environmental injustice,[2] industrialization is also the most obvious remedy. Even if industries have unfairly targeted certain communities with past, untoward environmental practices, forcing industry out will only worsen socioeconomic inequities and erode quality of life, rather than improve it (Payne 1998).

That some persons will be exposed to deleterious toxins if industrialization continues (Reason #13) is trumped by the considerations that continued industrialization stands to benefit the affected communities overall (Reason #10) – that is, if development occurs in a democratic and transparent manner (Reasons ##11, 12). That the arguments against are weakened by arguments in favor flows from the fact that exposure to hazardous emissions is not the only health threat faced by residents of the Industrial Corridor. Another looming threat persists: poverty. As Loren Scott has put it: "Poverty kills a lot more people than the environment does" (McConnaughey 1999). Industrial processes involve the use of solvents, fuels, lubricants, compounds from combustion, residual by-products from manufacturing processes, and other synthetic compounds (Reason #15). These processes create profit, but they also pollute. Since poverty also results in grave health effects related to lack of access to medical care, poor diet, and other lifestyle habits, the wealth created by industry could, in theory, improve public health by increasing the overall standard of living of a community.

Research suggests that the two types of communities with the lowest levels of pollution are poor communities with little economic activity and affluent communities that derive income from non-industrial sources (Daniels and Friedman 1999). If this is true, cynics of environmental justice legislation argue convincingly that blocking new industry through claims of environmental injustice may be exactly the wrong tack to take in improving the lives of poor minorities: "The final determination of the best public policy depends on how much weight is given to the benefits of jobs as against the cost of pollution to the area" (Couch et al. 2003: 244). While persons have been exposed to deleterious pollution because of their communities' low socioeconomic status and weak political power, resulting in environmental injustice, banning the development of facilities that produce hazardous waste may, ironically, worsen the quality of life in those communities, rather than improve it (Reason #8).

The region of southern Louisiana is bisected by the Mississippi River, providing it with a unique geographical feature that has value in a global industrial economy (Reason #8). The region must utilize its unique features to the benefit of local communities.

The solution is measured industrial development (Reason #7). Industrial development along the Industrial Corridor is not justified, however, if the local people are harmed – without compensating benefits – from the operations of industrial plants (Reason #14). If corporations merely provide a token number of low-skill, low-wage jobs, the presence of those facilities has not been justified. Individuals of communities along the corridor generally are neither highly skilled nor highly educated. To ensure that these residents can compete for higher-paying jobs that demand workers with higher skills, public community colleges and vocational-technical colleges must be expanded to provide the training necessary for skilled labor. Since the industrial facilities will themselves benefit from a skilled local labor pool, property taxes must go directly into public education, and not be siphoned off by governmental bureaucracies. Corporations should absolutely not be given tax breaks by politicians, as this will limit monies available for public education, as well as public health services.

Proponents of the EJA accurately claim that the old argument about environmental regulation damaging the economy and driving away jobs is just plain false. "The economy has probably quadrupled since the National Environmental Policy Act was passed in 1970," Ken Cook of the Clearinghouse on Environmental Advocacy and Research, a nonprofit organization, has pointed out. "I don't think anybody . . . is going to object to a factory that's going to produce clean products in a clean way. But if you don't set that bar up, any old factory can produce any old way" (McConnaughey 1999).

Templet thinks that Louisiana will continue to entice big petrochemical corporations, even with tightened regulations: "They have everything they need here – the gas and oil, water transport and pipelines. And chemical firms spend just 1 percent or less of their total revenues on pollution controls" (Koeppel 1999: 24).

EJA legislation turns out to be a double-edged sword: it may help mitigate the problem of environmental injustice, but at the same time it creates obstacles for surmounting socioeconomic injustice. Industrial development is justified along the Baton Rouge-New Orleans Industrial Corridor if it occurs within a democratic and transparent decision-making framework. To be acceptable, this framework must be determined by epidemiological research uncontaminated by the influences of corporate power. Corporations must only be given the opportunity to benefit from the region's unique geographical features if their facilities are equipped with safeguards that secure locals' rights to a healthy environment.

If corporations claim that they cannot compete within such a framework, industrialization does not meet the minimum standard – simultaneously avoiding harm to and benefiting local Louisianans – and is therefore not ethically justifiable. If the standards set by the public policy framework can be met, industrialization is ethically acceptable.

In summary, modern land use in southern Louisiana has been driven by market forces, with politics close in tow, that conflict with the ideals of open society. Industrialization is not inherently bad; what are bad are political processes by which industrialization leads to environmental injustice. As long as political processes are transparent and democratic, the outcomes of those processes, industrialization included, are ethically justified.

Additional Issues to Consider

Other possible moral dilemmas arising within this case:

Q Are "dirty" industries morally justified in opening new facilities at previously uncontaminated sites in Southern Louisiana along the river if local populations consent?

Q Would "dirty" industries be morally justified in continuing to operate contaminated sites if adjacent populations were largely Caucasian and middle class?

Q Are states that are adjacent to Louisiana, and that might be contaminated by water flowing by their boundaries, morally justified in obstructing further industrial development along the river?

NOTES

1   Issues of environmental injustice are not limited to issues of race, but also include socioeconomic status. In Bhopal, India, a leak at a Union Carbide plant killed 4,000 people in 1984. The only plant in the US that produces methyl isocyanate, the deadly gas that caused the Bhopal tragedy, was produced at Union Carbide's plant in Kanawha Valley, West Virginia (Murphy 1984), whose residents are typically of lower socioeconomic status. Local residents protested that Union Carbide and EPA officials were unduly sluggish in addressing community health concerns (Oder 1985). The area is predominantly Caucasian, indicating that environmental injustice is not just an issue of race but also of socioeconomic status.
2   Industrialization in communistic economies can also result in environmental injustice, such as seen in the Soviet Union (see Komarov 1980).

REFERENCES

Advocate (Baton Rouge) (1999) Louisiana's petrochemical corridor: a river runs through it. (September 12): 49–50K.

Bullard, R. D. (1983) Solid waste sites and the Black Houston community. *Sociological Inquiry* 53 (2–3): 273–88.

Bullard, R. D. (1994) Overcoming racism in environmental decision-making. *Environment* 36 (4): 10–44.

Cerrell Associates (1984) Political difficulties facing waste-to-energy conversion plant siting. Prepared for the California Waste Management Board. Los Angeles: Cerrell Associates.

Chen, V. W., Andrews, A., Wu, X. C., et al. (1998) Cancer incidence in the industrial corridor: an update. *Journal of the Louisiana Medical Society* 150 (April): 158–67.

Cockburn, A. (1997) Environmental justice is put to the test: Federal policy can show its teeth by stopping a plant in Louisiana's "Cancer Alley." *Los Angeles Times* (August 28): 9.

Correa C. N., Wu, X. C., Andrews, A., et al. (2004) Parish profiles, 1988–2000. *Cancer in Louisiana* 18. Louisiana Tumor Registry. Available at: http://publichealth. lsuhsc.edu/tumorregistry/PDF/Profiles/S.pdf#page=2 (accessed June 18, 2007).

Couch, J. F., Williams, A., Halvorson, J., et al. (2003) Of racism and rubbish: The geography of race and pollution in Mississippi. *Independent Review* 8 (2): 235–47.

Daniels, G., and Friedman, S. (1999) Spatial inequality and the distribution of industrial toxic releases: Evidence from the 1990 TRI. *Social Science Quarterly* 80 (2): 244–62.

Delegates to the First National People of Color Environmental Leadership Summit (1991) Principles of environmental justice (October 24–27). Available at: www.ejnet.org/ ej/principles.html (accessed June 17, 2007).

Ferstel, V. (1998) Studies make no concrete cancer-pollution link. *Advocate* (Baton Rouge) (June 24): 1A.

Gottlieb, M., Carr, J. K., Morriess, D., et al. (1981) Cancer and drinking water in Louisiana: Colon and rectum. *International Journal of Epidemiology* 10 (2): 117–25.

Greenberg, B. (2006) Katrina hits cancer alley: Interview with environmental justice activist Monique Harden. *Dollars & Sense* (March/April): 34–51.

Grossman, K. (1991) Environmental racism. *Crisis* 98 (April): 14–17, 31–2.

Jackson, B. P., and Bullard, R. D. (1998) From plantations to plants: Report of the Emergency National Commission on Environmental and Economic Justice in St James Parish, Louisiana (September 15). Cleveland, OH: United Church of Christ Commission for Racial Justice.

Keller, D. R. (2005) Environmental racism. *International Global Studies Encyclopedia*, ed. I. I. Mazour, A. N. Chumakov, and W. C. Gay. Amherst, NY: Prometheus Books, pp. 133–5.

Kern, E. (2001) Pollution spotlight: Greenpeace brings tour of "cancer alley" to Baton Rouge, Plaquemine. *Advocate* (Baton Rouge) (June 10): 1B.

Koeppel, B. (1999) Cancer Alley, Louisiana. *The Nation* (November 8): 16–24.

Komarov, B. (1980) *The Destruction of Nature in the Soviet Union*. Foreword by Marshall I. Goldman. White Plains, NY: M. E. Sharpe.

Lavelle, M., and Coyle, M. A. (1992) Unequal protection: The racial divide in environmental law, a special investigation. *National Law Journal* 21 (September): 1–16.

Litonjua, A., Carey, V. J., Weiss, S. T., et al. (1999) Race, socioeconomic factors, and area of residence are associated with asthma prevalence. *Pediatric Pulmonology* 28 (6): 394–401.

McConnaughey, J. (1999) Environmental racism cases hurt industry. *Advocate* (Baton Rouge) (January 1): 1B.

McGurty, E. M. (2007) *Transforming Environmentalism: Warren County, PCBs, and the Origins of Environmental Justice*. Brunswick, NJ: New Rutgers University Press.

McQuaid, J. (2000) "Cancer Alley": myth or fact? *Times-Picayune* (May 24): A9.

Mennis, J. L., and Jordan, L. (2005) The distribution of environmental equity: Exploring spatial nonstationarity in multivariate models of air toxic releases. *Annals of the Association of American Geographers* 95 (2): 249–68.

Murphy, J. (1984) Could it happen in West Virginia? *Time* (December 17).

Oder, N. (1985) Changes after Bhopal evident, but are they enough? *Charleston Gazette* (West Virginia) (November 28): 1A.

Office of the President of the United States (1994) Executive Order 12898: Federal Actions to Address Environmental Justice in Minority Populations and Low-Income Populations (February 11). Washington, DC. Available at: www.epa.gov/history/ topics/justice/02.htm (accessed June 20, 2007).

Orange County Register (1991) Minority-area dumps called toxic racism: Southern California districts contain larger share of emissions, paper says. (April 8): A3. (A news brief on "Fighting toxic racism: L.A.'s minority neighborhood is the 'dirtiest' in the state.") *San Francisco Examiner* (April 7): A1.

Pastor, M., Jr., Sadd, J., and Hipp, J. (2001) Which came first? Toxic facilities, minority move-in, and environmental justice. *Journal of Urban Affairs* 23 (1): 1–21.

Payne, H. (1998) Green redlining: how rules against "environmental racism" hurt poor communities most of all. *Reason Magazine* (October). Available at: www.reason.com/news/show/30762.html (accessed June 18, 2007).

Pellow, D. N. (2004) The politics of illegal dumping: an environmental justice framework. *Qualitative Sociology* 27 (4): 511–25.

Pope, J. (2004) St Bernard cancer figures raise eyebrows: rates higher than normal, study finds. *Times-Picayune* (August 23): 1.

Richardson, S. A. (1997) It takes a movement to secure environmental justice. *Austin American Statesman* (July 24): A15.

Russell, D., Lewis, S., and Keating, B. (1992) Inconclusive by design: waste, fraud and abuse in federal environmental health research. Environmental Health Network and the National Toxics Campaign Fund.

Sierra Club (1993) A place at the table: A Sierra roundtable on race, justice, and the environment. *Sierra* 78 (3): 51–8, 90–1.

Summerhays, J., and Croke, H. (1987) *Air Toxics Emissions Inventory for the Southeast Chicago Area.* Washington, DC: US Environmental Protection Agency.

Swerczek, M. (2001) Greenpeace visits chemical corridor: celebrity activists see plants, neighbors. *Times-Picayune* (June 10): 1.

United Church of Christ Commission for Racial Justice (1987) *Toxic Waste and Race in the United States: A National Report on the Racial and Socioeconomic Characteristics of Communities with Hazardous Wastes Sites.* New York: Public Access.

United States Congress (1964) Title VI of the Civil Rights Act of 1964, 42 USC. §2000d et seq. Washington, DC. Available at: www.usdoj.gov/crt/cor/coord/titlevi.htm (accessed September 27, 2007).

United States Congress (1993a) Environmental Equal Rights Act (HR 1924). Washington, DC.

United States Congress (1993b) Environmental Health Equity Information Act (HR 1925). Washington, DC.

United States Congress (1993c) Environmental Justice Act (HR 2105). Washington, DC.

CASE EIGHT: THE BOILED FROG – GLOBAL WARMING, US INTERESTS, AND VULNERABLE NATIONS

The allegory of the boiled frog states that if you put a frog into a pot of boiling water, it will leap out immediately to escape the danger. But if you put a frog into water that is cool and pleasant and then gradually heat the water to boiling, the frog will not become aware of the threat until it is too late, and will get boiled.

Environmentalists have equated the allegory of the boiled frog to global climate change. Despite persistent skepticism, there is growing consensus that the Earth is warming. Scientific studies show that for each decade of the past 30 years, global surface temperature has increased approximately .2°C, consistent with initial rates predicted by 1980s climatological modeling (Hansen et al. 2006). An additional increase of 2–3°C would make the Earth as warm as it was 3 million years ago, when the sea level was about 80 feet higher than it is today (ibid.).

The phenomenon of global warming is multifactorial, but is attributed largely to human activity. In terms of geologic time, the Earth's climate oscillates naturally between hot spells and ice ages (Zachos et al. 2001). Scientists explain these regular oscillations in terms of variations in the amount of solar radiation the atmosphere receives. The amount of radiation the Earth's atmosphere receives depends on its eccentricity, tilt, and precession (wobble) as it travels in its orbit around the sun. The convergence of these regular and predicable cycles, called the Milankovitch Cycles, accounts for oscillations in climate between hothouse conditions and ice ages (*Science News* 1985). Taken by themselves, such cycles should not cause undue alarm, as they are part of the natural rhythm of biospherical processes, as numerous commentators on global climate change have pointed out. However, extrapolated onto human history, we should currently be experiencing cooling and entry into the next ice age (Goldsmith 2007). But climatological data indicate the opposite, revealing the human hand in global climate change (Ruddiman 2005).

The engine of the modern industrial economy is powered by the combustion of fossil fuels that emit carbon dioxide (CO^2) and other gases into the atmosphere. Solar energy re-radiating from the Earth's surface, which would normally dissipate into space, is deflected back down to Earth by these gases, creating a "greenhouse effect." As industrialization has expanded, so has the release of "greenhouse gases" into the atmosphere. According to a recent United Nations report, the emission of heat-trapping gases increased 70 percent between 1970 and 2004 (Barker et al. 2007: 3).

Receding ice is a visible manifestation of global warming. In the Antarctic, satellite data show that unusually warm air masses have begun pushing southward to within 300 miles of the South Pole, remaining long enough to melt snow across expanses the size of California (Revkin 2007d).

In the Arctic during the summer of 2005, a 41-square-mile sheath of ice, which had jutted into the Arctic Ocean for 3,000 years, broke off and drifted out to sea (Revkin 2006b). During the winter of 2005–6, sea ice failed to re-form for the second year in a row (Connor 2006). According to specialists, sea ice is at its lowest point since satellite monitoring began in 1979, probably a sign that the Arctic is responding to global warming (ibid.). The rapidity of sea ice disappearance is evidence of a positive environmental feedback loop wherein sunlight that would normally be reflected by the ice is instead absorbed by dark blue seawater, speeding up the warming and melting processes (ibid.). Even with modest increases in greenhouse gas emission, summer sea ice is expected to vanish by the end of the century (Revkin 2005b).

Because floating ice displaces water in the same manner as a ship, melting sea ice does not cause ocean levels to rise, but melting glaciers do. New dynamics of glacial melting provide the most startling adumbration of the likelihood of rising sea levels due to global warming. The vast Greenland Ice Sheet, a two-mile-thick slab of ice made up of about the same volume of water as the Gulf of Mexico, contains enough water to push up the sea level by 20 feet worldwide (Revkin 2005a). In southern Greenland, the amount of glacial ice flowing into the ocean has doubled in the past 10 years (Rignot and Kanagaratnam 2006). As melting spreads north, that rate is likely to accelerate, indicating that previous estimates of sea-level rises are too conservative (Dowdeswell 2006).

Changes in the Earth's climate at the poles are only the tip of the iceberg (Kanter and Revkin 2007). The latest comprehensive report on the impact of climate change on the biosphere, prepared by more than 200 scientists and endorsed by more than 120 countries, including the United States, makes the dramatic claim that global warming is anthropogenic (human-generated) and well under way (Daley 2007). Effects associated with anthropogenic climate change will challenge the resiliency of ecosystems from the equator to poles, resulting in a significantly altered biosphere (Adger et al. 2007: 5).

Beginning in the 1980s, American politician Al Gore (2007) famously made the issue of global warming and greenhouse gas emissions a political issue, both domestically and internationally. Growing awareness of the potential dangers of anthropogenic climate change during the 1980s and 1990s laid the groundwork for the United Nations Framework Convention on Global Warming (1992) and the Kyoto Protocol (1998).

During his two-term presidency, George W. Bush maintained a robust skepticism about the scientific legitimacy of global warming. He consistently highlighted "the incomplete state of scientific knowledge" (Regalado 2001) and its anthropogenic underpinnings, an uncertainty echoed by the editorial board of the *Wall Street Journal*, which upheld the president's position: "There is no scientific consensus that greenhouse gases cause the world's modest global warming trend, much less whether that warming will do more harm than good, or whether we can even do anything about it" (*Wall Street Journal* 2003).

To President Bush, basing public policy on scientific uncertainty is reckless. In the case of climate change, curtailing greenhouse gas emissions would damage the domestic economy and, given the uncertainty of global climate change, it would be irresponsible for the US to foist regulations on industry. It would be much better, the president maintained, to ask industry to reduce emissions voluntarily while researching technological solutions to greenhouse gas emissions without restricting economic productivity.

Environmental economists, backing the Bush strategy of measured action, have argued that developing technologies for reducing greenhouse gas emissions over the next several decades would be better than taking drastic action now. For one thing, drastic action would force coal-fired power plants to shut down before they reach the end of their operational lives and, hence, be a waste of useful industrial capital (Hilsenrath 2001).

President Bush adjusted course slightly in 2007 when, in his State of the Union address, he acknowledged the need to "confront the serious challenge of global climate change" and the promise of science and technology to do it. At the meeting of the powerful Group of 8 (G-8) industrialized nations five months later, President Bush stated: "In recent years, science has deepened our understanding of climate change and opened new possibilities for confronting it" (Stolberg 2007).

Although President Bush's position on the role of the human hand in global warming did change, his position on mandatory caps for greenhouse gas emissions did not. The United Nations Framework Convention on Global Warming was signed by his father, President George Herbert Walker Bush, and laid the groundwork for the Kyoto Protocol. This treaty was negotiated in Japan in 1997 and was endorsed by President Bill Clinton and the leaders of more than 100 other nations (Revkin 2001). All G-8 nations, with the exception of the US (Canada, France, Germany, Italy, Japan, Russia, and the UK), as per guidelines of the protocol, agreed to bring their emissions down to 1990 levels by 2012 (Eilperin 2005).

In March 2001, President Bush notoriously rescinded the US commitment to the protocol (Drozdiak and Pianin 2001), explaining that he opposed the treaty because it would hurt the US economy and because it exempted developing industrialized countries, most notably China and India, from committing to reductions on emissions (Revkin 2001). It was unfair to expect the US to restrict its industrial activity without demanding that developing nations do the same, President Bush explained.[1]

Independently of the political and economic ramifications of global warming in the industrialized West, the prospect of climate change poses very tangible threats to small and politically weak developing nations. The worlds' wealthiest nations, which have contributed by far the most to global warming, stand to suffer the least. G-8 members are located in temperate climates where the capricious effects of atmospheric change might be mitigated, and they are already spending billions of dollars to limit the repercussions of rising tides and drought (Revkin 2007a).

The world's poorest nations, often located in tropical coastal regions, face the gravest risk (Barker et al. 2007). Less industrialized nations have not reaped the benefits from the wealth generated by the economic activity that appears to have precipitated global warming, but will bear the brunt of its consequences. For this reason, Eskimos, or Inuit, have cast the issue of global warming as a human-rights issue (Revkin 2004b).

Small island nations are particularly vulnerable. Fear of flooding is already discouraging foreign investment (Lewis 1992). But there is a much greater, much more catastrophic, fear: advancing tides could – quite literally – wipe them off the map. A study by the National Oceanic and Atmospheric Administration identifies the Marshall Islands as one such "innocent victim" of global warming (ibid.). There, residents are running out of places to live. An unprecedented storm surge washed over the island of Kili in 1996, poisoning the soil, killing crops, and demolishing homes. But the residents could not move back to their original home, the island of Bikini, because it is still severely polluted by radioactive waste left from US nuclear testing during the 1950s. The best option is the island of Marjuro. But moving to Marjuro is not without worry: a mere 3-foot rise in the sea level would flood 80 percent of the island. All this points to the unthinkable for Marshall Islanders: they may have to abandon their homeland entirely (Fialka 1997).

In the Maldives, a nation in the Indian Ocean consisting of more than 1,000 low-lying reefs where the highest point in the entire archipelago is only eight feet, rising seawater could drown the entire nation within 100 years (Crossette 1990). Of course, all nations with coastal areas are vulnerable to rising sea levels, but most do not face the total obliteration that small island nations face.

Given the current state of knowledge about global climate change, the possible repercussions that restrictions on greenhouse gas emissions could have on the domestic US economy, and the impact of rising sea levels on island nations, was the Bush administration policy ethically sound?

Perspective One

According to deontological theory (the source of the principles of autonomy, respect for persons, and rights), President Bush qua president had a moral duty to the citizens of the US to act for the welfare of the nation.

The maxim "President Bush ought to act to promote the welfare of US citizens above and beyond considerations of non-US citizens" can easily be universalized as "all leaders of sovereign nations ought to promote the welfare of their citizens above and beyond considerations of citizens outside of their boundaries."

President Bush's position was squarely in line with free-market principles and was deservedly praised. Philip Stott, Emeritus Professor of Biogeography at the University of London, derided climate change as a "myth" foisted on the public by "authoritarian greens." According to Stott (2001):

> "Global warming" was invented in 1988, when it replaced two earlier myths of an imminent plunge into another Ice Age and the threat of a nuclear winter. The new myth was seen to encapsulate a whole range of other myths and attitudes that had developed in the 1960s and 1970s, including "limits to growth," sustainability, neo-Malthusian fears of a population time bomb, pollution, anticorporate anti-Americanism, and an Al Gore-like analysis of human greed disturbing the ecological harmony and balance of the earth.

According to S. Fred Singer, atmospheric physicist at George Mason University, "Allowing for uncertainties in the data and for imperfect models, there is only one valid conclusion from the failure of greenhouse theory to explain the observations: The human contribution to global warming appears to be quite small and natural climate factors are dominant" (2006).

Given all the unanswered questions about global warming, President Bush would have been remiss in his duty to act rashly and cap greenhouse gas emissions.

Perspective Two

According to deontological theory, President Bush qua president had a moral duty to the citizens of the US to act for the welfare of the nation above and beyond special interest groups.

President Bush consistently framed public policy for the benefit of fossil-fuel-based corporations. The most obvious transgression of President Bush's duty *as president* has been the politicization of climatological science.

In the White House, economic and political aims have overridden scientific claims; the Bush administration actively suppressed empirical evidence in order to align the science of climatology with the politics of the fossil-fueled economy. National Aeronautics and Space Administration (NASA) scientist James E. Hansen, who publicly criticized the White House for inaction (Revkin 2004a), has alleged that the Bush administration tried to prevent him from speaking out (Revkin 2006a). Hansen claims that he received explicit orders from NASA head-quarters to submit all public communications to public affairs staff for review (ibid.). One public affairs officer is reported to have said that, as a White House appointee, his job was "to make the president look good," which required him to vet Hansen's work (ibid.).

The politicization of global warming science by the White House is corrob-orated in a survey by the Union of Concerned Scientists of climatologists at seven federal agencies. Of 279 respondents, 43 percent "perceived or personally experi-enced changes or edits during review that changed the meaning of scientific findings," and 46 percent "perceived or personally experienced new or unusual administrative requirements that impair climate-related work" (Donaghy et al. 2007: 2).

Political interference with the process of climatological research is evinced in White House alterations to scientific reports before publication of the final versions. The White House rewrote Environmental Protection Agency (EPA) reports to impart the impression that the status of global warming evidence was extremely tentative (Jackson 2003), and in 2002 and 2003, Philip A. Cooney, a former lobbyist for the American Petroleum Institute who led the fight against limits on greenhouse gas emissions, adjusted and removed descriptions of clim-ate research in order to amplify suggestions of uncertainty and the dubiousness of anthropogenic causation (Revkin 2005a). In another report, he crossed out a paragraph on glacial melting and wrote in the margin, "straying from research strategy into speculative findings/musings" (ibid.).

Representative Henry Waxman, chair of the House Oversight and Govern-ment Reform Committee, characterized the Cooney scandal as an "orchestrated campaign to mislead the public about climate change" (Neikirk 2007). In 2005, *the Houston Chronicle* cynically observed in a descriptively titled editorial, "Blinded Science: The Bush Administration's Solution to Global Warming is a Good Copy Editor": "In the Bush White House, it seems, certain energy companies are allowed to pick and choose which scientific theories best fit their business plan." White House interference with the scientific method has drawn comparisons to the Catholic Church's suppression of heliocentrism (*Houston Chronicle* 2005), and Soviet party commissars revising science to meet the demands of USSR communism (Goldsborough 2004).

Public policy analysts have discerned credible evidence for anthropogenic global warming for decades. In the words of one DuPont corporate official, refer-ring to the importance of reducing CO^2 emissions: "We saw sufficient science emerging to warrant what in our judgment was prudent action back in 1991"

(Revkin 2001). But the Bush administration remained unconvinced about the reality of global climate change and its anthropogenic origins, maintaining steadfastly, year after year, the need for further study before substantive action is taken (Nesmith 2002). Eventually, however, evidence swamped recalcitrant skepticism, forcing President Bush to admit to the connection between industrialization and global warming (Stolberg 2007).

Not unfairly, environmentalists have ridiculed President Bush for being a pawn of big energy corporations, ignoring the facts, and living in denial. Larry Schweiger, President and CEO of the National Wildlife Federation, claimed that the president's unwillingness to show leadership in breaking the US economy's addiction to oil discouraged the innovation of alternative energy technologies: "Instead of paving the way to such an energy future, the Bush administration clings to the past" (Schweiger 2005). As continuing evidence of President Bush's intransigence on global warming, the EPA, acting under the direction of the Bush administration, issued a license in September 2007 for a coal-fired power plant to be built in Utah with no restrictions whatsoever on greenhouse gas emissions, leaving environmentalists stunned and scientists astounded (Fahys 2007).

Global warming may have local roots, but it is global in reach. Bush administration policy ignored, almost myopically, the extent of the problem. A Maldivian government spokesman warned wealthy nations: "Our message to the US is as simple as this: sea level rise is not just a phenomenon which is just going to engulf the Maldives and then stop. If it affects us tomorrow, it will affect you the day after" (Kristof 2006). US coastal areas will not be immune to rising tides.

Perspective Three

The answer is not simple. Because the climatology of global warming is incredibly complex, the danger exists that rash public policy decisions could unnecessarily damage the economy. And because global warming is, by definition, a global issue, foreign policy set from the model of disconnected sovereign nation-states will no longer suffice. The ethical trick is achieving a delicate balance in the midst of meteorological flux and market forces.

Step 1: Information-gathering

Implications

- If anthropogenic climate warming is real and the US does not take any action to curb domestic greenhouse gas emissions, will the US be morally culpable for the effects of rising sea levels?
- If anthropogenic climate warming is not real and the US does not take any action to curb domestic greenhouse gas emissions, is moral culpability regarding rising sea levels moot?

- If anthropogenic climate warming is real and the US takes action to curb domestic greenhouse gas emissions, would US actions be morally praiseworthy within the context of global politics?
- If anthropogenic climate warming is not real and the US takes action to curb domestic greenhouse gas emissions, will the US suffer from a damaged economy unnecessarily?

History

- Assuming anthropogenic global climate change actually exists, what is the history of its known causation?
- How might warming have been initiated, and what kinds of actions could be taken, given the history of global warming, to slow it?

Legal/policy information

- Because the issue of greenhouse gas emissions occurs within the interstices of international politics, and because contemporary international politics are based on the paradigm of nation-states as autonomous independent polities, do any binding legal mandates exist?
- Or are all obligations regarding greenhouse gas emissions voluntary and negotiated between sovereign nation-states?

Economic considerations

- At what threshold should evidence be acted upon?
- What effects could caps on greenhouse gas emissions have on the domestic US economy?
- What effects could continued US reliance on fossil fuels have if the global economy develops in a non-fossil-fuel direction?

Cultural and psychological information

- Given the fact that American culture is built in large part around a fossil-fuel-based economy, what is the likelihood that Americans are mentally prepared to adopt lifestyles that restrict the consumption of large amounts of energy derived from fossil fuel sources?

Step 2: Creative problem-solving

The ethical challenge is to weigh greenhouse gas reductions (assuming industrialization could in fact cause sea levels to rise and devastate vulnerable island nations) against restrictions that would unduly damage the US domestic economy (especially in light of the fact that factors beyond our control or knowledge could arise and halt, slow, or reverse global warming).

Step 3: Listing pros and cons

Options	Pros	Cons
US does not accept caps on greenhouse gas emissions.	1. Domestic economy is not damaged; national interests maintained (C-U) 2. US avoids unfair situation where US shoulders burden of restricting greenhouse gas emissions while rapidly developing nations such as China and India do not (J-E) 3. US doesn't over-react if it turns out that climatology of global climate change is not anthropogenic (C-U) 4. Possibility that, taken as a whole, global warming turns out to be beneficial (C-U)	5. Global warming continues; sea levels rise, vulnerable nations flooded (C-NM, C-U) 6. US seen as renegade in global politics; US interests suffer (C-U) 7. US policy not based in ecological reality; US interests suffer (C-U) 8. US economy damaged in the long run by failure to develop alternative energy sources (C-U)
US accepts caps on greenhouse gas emissions.	9. Global warming attenuated; threat of rising seal levels assuaged (C-NM, C-B, C-U) 10. US works cooperatively with world community and is seen to be a good global citizen; US interests benefit (C-B, C-U, A, R, J-E) 11. Social incentives to develop alternative energy move US away from fossil fuel-based economy (C-U) 12. Incentives at individual level to conserve; develop personal habits that are ecological (V)	13. Fossil fuel-based economy suffers; corporate earnings plummet (C-NM, C-U) 14. US national interests suffer by becoming less competitive on a global marketplace (C-U) 15. Severely polluting nations like China and India escape restrictions (J-E) 16. US acts unnecessarily when climatology of global warming is not anthropogenic (C-NM, C-U)

Step 4: Analysis

Factual assumptions

- Global warming is well under way. While the free market faithful question the anthropogenic underpinnings of global warming, a preponderance of evidence indicates that human activity, most obviously industrialization, is a major factor.
- Human modification of ecological systems is inherently risky. Given the complexity of the structure and function of natural systems, tampering with ecological systems is a risk (Commoner 1972). While human modification of the biosphere may not be bad, radical alternation of ecological systems is poor common sense without overwhelmingly good reasons for doing so.
- Global warming will not prove to be a blessing (Reason #4). All things considered, there is no evidence that global warming *will* be a blessing.

Value assumptions

- Policy change should be embraced when a preponderance of evidence suggests the change would maximize human welfare.
- Leaders should place the welfare of their citizens above that of themselves or their friends. OR
- Leaders should place the welfare of the world at large above that of their own citizens.

Step 5: Justification

Global climate change is the quintessential multinational political problem. Taking the scope of moral consideration to be the six billion human beings currently in existence, according to the Principle of Utility informed by ecological science, the US must adopt some measures to reduce greenhouse gas emissions to secure the greatest happiness for the greatest number of people.[2]

First, the climatological history of global warming suggests anthropogenic causation. Charles David Keeling, a Scripps Institution of Oceanography scientist, began measuring atmospheric carbon dioxide (CO_2) concentration atop the Hawaiian volcano, Mauna Loa, in 1958. Factoring in seasonal changes in global plant respiration, Keeling and others (2005) demonstrated that global atmospheric carbon dioxide concentration is on the rise. This geometrical increase, known as the Keeling Curve, is based on data referred to by climatologists as the Mauna Loa Record. One logical explanation of the Keeling Curve is that (1) the burning of fossil fuels since the advent of the Industrial Revolution has been incrementally and inexorably increasing the level of atmospheric carbon dioxide; and (2) deforestation intensifies atmospheric carbon dioxide buildup.

A recent UN report claims that, given the solid body of scientific evidence, the threshold enjoining action has been reached; excuses for hesitancy and delay cane no longer be justified (Barker et al. 2007). Industrialized nations must commit to binding limits, such as those set forth in the Kyoto Protocol. Alluding to the failed Bush strategy, one author said: "We can no longer make the excuse that we need to wait for more science, or the excuse that we need to wait for more technologies and policy knowledge" (Revkin 2007c).

Second, economic reasons support enacting restrictions on greenhouse gas emissions as being in the US's best interest (Reasons ##8, 10, 11). Journalist and economist Anatole Kaletsky (2007) has argued that the Bush strategy of cautious gradualism might actually damage the economy (Reasons ##13, 14) rather than protect it (Reason #1), by prolonging unsustainable reliance on fossil fuels.

Third, given the reciprocity of relations between nations, it is not favorable for the US that President Bush has provoked such outrage from the international community (Reasons ##6, 10). "History will not judge George Bush kindly," a London newspaper predicted, and mocked the back-pedaling from agreements made by his father and President Clinton as "not even isolationism, it is in-your-face truculence" (*Independent* 2001). An editorial published the same day in another English daily characterized the US under President Bush as "the ultimate rogue state" (*Guardian* 2001). Animosity from the UK, one of the US's most important allies, does not bode well for American interests.

Fourth, in an era of globalization, US foreign policy based on the model of absolute national sovereignty is no longer apt (Reason #7). The reasons that the Bush administration wrongly used to resist caps on greenhouse gas emissions (Reasons ##5, 6, 7, 8) are the same reasons about which President Bush rightly complained that China and India should not be exempt from restrictions (Reason #2). Pollution from a developing county is no less damaging to the biosphere than pollution from a developed country.

These issues indicate the obsolescence of the sovereign nation-state model upon which the Bush policy has been built. Political boundaries rarely correspond to ecological boundaries. The most obvious examples are political boundaries determined by high, mountainous ridgelines, which divide watersheds and inhibit species migration, such as the borders between the Himalayas demarcating India and Nepal from China, or the Alps which separate Switzerland from Italy.

In the main, however, political boundaries are arbitrary lines determined by stealth politics, brute war, or simple geometry. In the first example, modern Iraq was formed in 1916 by secret negotiations, called the Sykes-Picot Agreement, by British and French diplomats standing around a table, looking at a map, and drawing lines – figuratively and literally – in the sand. In the second instance, the Mexican-American War of 1846–8 ended with the Treaty of Guadalupe Hidalgo, which ceded vast tracts of land to the United States (in essence, all the southwestern states). In the third example, many boundaries follow latitudinal lines, as does a large portion of the US–Canadian border, which traces the 49th degree northern parallel.

Ecologically, framing foreign policy in terms of arbitrary mathematical boundaries is absurd, because such boundaries do not correspond to topography. In terms of international politics, boundaries circumscribe 190 independent, sovereign nation-states which negotiate with each other through diplomacy, treaties, embargoes, tariffs, war, and so on. This model has its origins in the Treaty of Westphalia (1648). The treaty is founded on the premise that nation-states are absolutely autonomous, and that interference in internal affairs by other nations is forbidden. From the mid-seventeenth century on, the international political order has been structured in terms of such discrete, sovereign nation-states (Gross 1948: 20).

While the model of sovereignty may have been an improvement over the provincial tribalism and deference to ecclesiastical authority it displaced, the Westphalian model is no longer sufficient in the age of globalization. Why? Ecological systems do not respect political boundaries. In terms of global climate change, the few ecological boundaries which do conform reasonably well with political boundaries, (e.g., high mountain ridgelines) are utterly irrelevant. Therefore, while the Westphalian model of sovereign, discrete nation-states worked relatively well for centuries, it does not provide an adequate framework for the ecological issues of global political economy.

Most worrisome is the fact that President Bush's stance on global warming indicates an ignorance, rather than an awareness, of the need for ecologically informed foreign policy. The Bush administration's intransigence on ecological internationalism emerged from a disdain for diplomacy and multilateralism (Halper and Clarke 2004: 11, 256), a desire for a weakened United Nations (Gerson 1996: 165–74), and a vision of the US as a "unipolar" power – or, as Irving Kristol puts it, an autonomous sovereign state flexing its military muscle in a display of outright "global unilateralism" (Nordlinger 1995: 18). These approaches are exactly opposite of those for which the US government should be aiming, in light of the myriad ecological challenges that confront the world at the beginning of the twenty-first century, global warming being among the most pressing.

Briefly stated, in the age of globalization, political borders are little more than artificial human constructs devoid of ecological marrow. Ecology calls for global cooperation, not Westphalian nationalism and selfish unilateralism.

Fifth, changes in behavior on the societal level will require changes in behavior on the personal level. Living within the constraints of the biosphere in a way that one's action do not harm others – both present and future generations – is a mark of virtuous character (Newton 2003). Americans' willingness to buy and drive hybrid cars (Carty 2004) hints at a flexibility in consumer behavior that is surprising in light of the motoring public's infatuation with large sport utility vehicles (Higgins 2005). This suggests that changes in cultural attitudes and consumer behavior patterns are possible – a possibility that signals the promise of environmental virtues with regard to reducing greenhouse gas emissions (Reason #12).

These five reasons all point to the need for the US voluntarily to adopt caps in greenhouse gas emissions. The reasons for doing so swamp the reasons against doing so. To do so is for our own national interest in the long run, as well as the interests of peoples of other nations (Reasons ##9, 10). Wealthy nations such as the US have an ethical responsibility to help mitigate the consequences of a problem they probably instigated. In the view of Peter Gleick, co-founder and President of the Pacific Institute for Studies in Development, Environment, and

Security: "We have an obligation to help countries prepare for the climate changes that we are largely responsible for" (Revkin 2007b).

Additional Issues to Consider

Other possible moral dilemmas arising within this case:

Q Are *developing* countries morally justified in refusing to voluntarily adopt caps in greenhouse gas emissions?

Q Do *developed* countries have a moral obligation to help clean up the effects on developing countries of their past polluting practices?

NOTES

1 In June 2007, when this case study was written, China was poised to pass the US in greenhouse gas emissions within the year (Oster 2007).
2 The same line of reasoning could be strengthened by including people of future generations.

REFERENCES

Adger, N., Aggarwal, P., Agrawala, S., et al. (2007) *Climate Change 2007: Impacts, Adaptation and Vulnerability. Summary for Policymakers.* Working Group II Contribution to the Intergovernmental Panel on Climate Change. Fourth Assessment Report. New York: United Nations.

Barker, T., Bashmakov, I., Bernstein, L., et al. (2007) *Climate Change 2007: Mitigation of Climate Change.* Summary for Policymakers. Working Group III Contribution to the Intergovernmental Panel on Climate Change. Fourth Assessment Report. New York: United Nations.

Bush, G. W. (2007) State of the Union address (January 23). Available at: www.white-house.gov/news/releases/2007/01/20070123-2.html (accessed June 12, 2007).

Carty, S. S. (2004) Hybrids could hit 20% of car market by 2010, study says. *Wall Street Journal* (October 14): D3.

Commoner, B. (1972) *The Closing Circle: Nature, Man, and Technology.* New York: Alfred A. Knopf.

Connor, S. (2006) Climate change "irreversible" as arctic sea ice fails to re-form. *Independent* (London) (March 14): 7.

Crossette, B. (1990) Male journal: 1,190 islands in danger: sea could drown them. *New York Times* (November 26): A4.

Daley, B. (2007) A climate change warning: panel says humans are probably causing shifts around the world. *Boston Globe* (April 7): A1.

Donaghy, T., Freeman, J., Grifo, F., et al. (2007) *Atmosphere of Pressure: Political Interference in Federal Climate Science.* A Report of the Union of Concerned

Scientists and the Government Accountability Project. Cambridge, MA: UCS Publications.

Dowdeswell, J. A. (2006) The Greenland ice sheet and global sea-level rise. *Science* 311 (5763): 963–4.

Drozdiak, W., and Pianin, E. (2001) US angers allies over climate pact; Europeans will ask Bush to reconsider. *Washington Post* (March 29): A1.

Eilperin, J. (2005) US pressure weakens G-8 climate plan; global-warming science assailed. *Washington Post* (June 17): A1.

Fahys, J. (2007) Coal plant may hurl Utah into CO^2 fight. *Salt Lake Tribune* (September 4): A1.

Fialka, J. J. (1997) From dots in the Pacific, envoys bring fear, fury to global-warming talks. *Wall Street Journal* (October 31): 1.

Gerson, M. (1996) *The Neoconservative Vision: From the Cold War the Culture Wars.* New York: Madison Books.

Goldsborough, J. O. (2004) The White House war against science. Opinion-editorial. *San Diego Union-Tribune* (October 25): B7.

Goldsmith, D. (2007) Ice cycles. *Natural History* 116 (March): 14–18.

Gore, A. (2007) *An Inconvenient Truth: The Crisis of Global Warming.* Revised edn. New York: Viking.

Gross, L. (1948) The peace of Westphalia, 1648–1948. *The American Journal of International Law* 42 (1): 20–41.

Guardian (Manchester, UK) (2001) A dirty business: Mr Bush has put US credibility on the line. Editorial (March 30): 21.

Halper, S., and Clarke, J. (2004) *America Alone: The Neo-Conservatives and the Global Order.* New York: Cambridge University Press.

Hansen, J., Sato, M., Ruedy, R., et al. (2006) Global temperature change. *Proceedings of the National Academy of Sciences* 103 (39): 14288–93.

Higgins, M. (2005) What's big, guzzles gas and is getting faster? Answer: the latest crop of SUVs, as makers add horsepower to many models. *Wall Street Journal* (March 24): D1.

Hilsenrath, J. E. (2001) Eco-economists back Bush on Kyoto pact: Obscure group says accord contains serious flaws, slower course favored. *Wall Street Journal* (August): A2.

Houston Chronicle (2005) Blinded science: the Bush administration's solution to global warming is a good copy editor. Editorial (June 10): 10.

Independent (London) (2001) Kyoto treaty: A cynical man, a catastrophic error (March 30): 1.

Jackson, D. Z. (2003) Bush fries climate change. Opinion-editorial. *Boston Globe* (June 20): A15.

Kaletsky, A. (2007) Right problem, George. But wrong solution. Comment/opinion. *The Times* (London) (January 25): 17.

Kanter, J., and Revkin, A. C. (2007) Scientists detail climate changes, poles to tropics. *New York Times* (April 7): A1.

Keeling, C. D., Piper, S. C., Bacastow, R. B., et al. (2005) Atmospheric CO^2 and $^{13}CO^2$ exchange with the terrestrial biosphere and oceans from 1978 to 2000: observations and carbon cycle implications. In J. R. Ehleringer, T. E. Cerling, and M. D. Dearing (eds.), *A History of Atmospheric CO^2 and Its Effects on Plants, Animals, and Ecosystems.* New York: Springer-Verlag, pp. 83–113.

Kristof, N. (2006) A paradise drowning. *New York Times* (January 8): A15.

Kyoto Protocol to the United Nations Framework Convention on Climate Change (1998) New York: United Nations.

Lewis, P. (1992) Danger of floods worries islanders. *New York Times* (May 13): A8.

Neikirk, W. (2007) Warming data allegedly manipulated. *Chicago Tribune* (January 31): 3.

Nesmith, J. (2002) Federal climate study blasted global warming demands action, critics complain. *Atlanta Journal-Constitution* (December 4): A6.

Newton, L. H. (2003) *Ethics and Sustainability: Sustainable Development and the Moral Life*. Upper Saddle River, NJ: Pearson Education.

Nordlinger, E. (1995) *Isolationism Reconfigured*. Princeton, NJ: Princeton University Press.

Oster, S. (2007) China seems poised to pass US as top greenhouse-gas emitter. *Wall Street Journal* (April 24): A6.

Regalado, A. (2001) Weighing the evidence of global warming: MIT study calculates odds of higher temperatures, indicates need for action. *Wall Street Journal* (March 22): B1.

Revkin, A. C. (2001) Bush's shift could doom air pact, some say. *New York Times* (March 17): A7.

Revkin, A. C. (2004a) NASA expert criticizes Bush on global warming policy. *New York Times* (October 26): A22.

Revkin, A. C. (2004b) Eskimos seek to recast global warming as a rights issue. *New York Times* (December 15): A3.

Revkin, A. C. (2005a) Bush aide edited climate reports. *New York Times* (June 8): A1.

Revkin, A. C. (2005b) No escape: thaw gains momentum. *New York Times* (October 25): F1.

Revkin, A. C. (2006a) Climate expert says NASA tried to silence him. *New York Times* (January 29): A1.

Revkin, A. C. (2006b) After 3,000 years, arctic ice shelf broke off Canadian island, scientists find. *New York Times* (December 30): A9.

Revkin, A. C. (2007a) Poorest nations will bear brunt as world warms. *New York Times* (April 1): A1.

Revkin, A. C. (2007b) Wealth and poverty, drought and flood: reports from 4 fronts in the war on warming. *New York Times* (April 3): F4.

Revkin, A. C. (2007c) Climate panel reaches consensus on the need to reduce harmful emissions. *New York Times* (May 4): A8.

Revkin, A. C. (2007d) Analysis finds large Antarctic area has melted. *New York Times* (May 16): A15.

Rignot, E., and Kanagaratnam, P. (2006) Changes in the velocity structure of the Greenland ice sheet. *Science* 311 (5763): 986–90.

Ruddiman, W. E. (2005) How did humans first alter global climate? *Scientific American* 292 (3): 46–53.

Schweiger, L. (2005) The administration's rhetoric presents a false choice between the environment and the economy. Opinion-editorial. *Chicago Sun-Times* (July 7): 41.

Science News (1985) The climate, it is achanging. 128 (16): 251.

Singer, S. F. (2006) Earth's climate is always warming or cooling. *Wall Street Journal* (June 20): A21

Stolberg, S. G. (2007) Bush proposes goal to reduce greenhouse gas. *New York Times* (June 1): A1.

Stott, P. (2001) Hot air + flawed science = dangerous emissions. Opinion-editorial. *Wall Street Journal* (April 2): A22.

Treaty of Westphalia: 1648 (2007) British Foreign Office (trans.) Münster, Germany. Available at: www.yale.edu/lawweb/avalon/westphal.htm (accessed September 27, 2007).

United Nations Framework Convention on Global Warming (1992) New York: United Nations.

Walker, M., and McKinnon, J. D. (2007) G-8 aims for 2009 climate accord; Bush unwilling to endorse targets Germany proposed; race to shape global talks. *Wall Street Journal* (June 8): A6.

Wall Street Journal (2003) A Republican Kyoto. Editorial. (April 8): A14.

Zachos, J., Pagani, M., Sloan, L., et al. (2001) Trends, rhythms, and aberrations in global climate 65 ma to present. *Science* 292 (5517): 686–94.

CASE NINE: A GORILLA ON THE GRILL IS WORTH TWO IN THE BUSH – WILD MEAT, MALNUTRITION, AND BIOLOGICAL CONSERVATION

In the Congo Basin, people have been hunting wildlife for 40,000 years (Bahuchert 1993). Meat from wildlife – *bushmeat* – is an important source of protein for the people who live in forest border regions (Bennett and Robinson 2000). Today, the diet of 80 percent of central Africans includes bushmeat (Pearce 2005).

African bushmeat includes ungulates, such as forest antelope, known as duiker (Robinson and Bennett 2000); reptiles and large-bodied birds (Hennessey 1995); smaller-bodied mammals, such as porcupines and cane rat (Fa et al. 1995); and primates. In west and central Africa, bushmeat primates include monkey and chimpanzee (Willcox and Nambu 2007), baboon and colobus (Chapman et al. 2006), and even the majestic and endangered mountain gorilla (Grevengoed 2001). Taken together, primates account for between a tenth and a quarter of all bushmeat harvested in the region (Bowen-Jones and Pendry 1999).

Primates are particularly desirable bushmeat prey. Compared with other bushmeat taxa, primates are relatively large-bodied, diurnal, and live in groups – making them fairly conspicuous and easy to kill in number (Chapman et al. 2006). And they are considered exceptionally tasty (Struhsaker 1999).

Bushmeat hunting remained sustainable for generations (Goodall 2004; Cowlishaw et al. 2005b). Recently, however, as human populations have grown and trade in bushmeat has increased, the harvest of wildlife has become unsustainable. In the Congo Basin, the equivalent of four million cattle in bushmeat is killed per year (Bennett et al. 2002), six times the replacement rate (Bennett 2002). According to zoologists, bushmeat hunting has resulted in a precipitous drop in the number of apes (Walsh et al. 2003). If continued unchecked, bushmeat hunting is likely to lead to the extinction of many species (Bowen-Jones et al. 2003).

Primates are especially vulnerable because they tend not to be widely distributed. Most are restricted to forested regions of west and central Africa (Cowlishaw and Dunbar 2000). These areas are undergoing rapid economic development.

Newly cut logging roads, for example, have accelerated bushmeat hunting by providing access to previously isolated forest reaches (Wilkie and Carpenter 1999).

Primates are integral elements of tropical forest ecosystems (Chapman et al. 2006). They are primary frugivores and crucial seed dispersers (Chapman 1995). For example, a tree common in South American lowland forests, the Icecream Bean (*Inga ingoides*), depends on spider monkeys to disperse seeds through feces (Moore 2001). Ecological interconnections, such as seed dispersion and food webs, cause conservationists to worry about bushmeat hunting and to make dire predictions about extinction and "empty forest syndrome" – a forest devoid of large animals (Bennett et al. 2002). The ecology of an empty forest has yet to be investigated and understood. Either the forest might appear intact but lack the richness and wonder of faunal life, or the absence of large animals could catalyze an ecological cascade of unpredictable outcomes (Redford 1992).

Conservation biologists have focused on the importance of cutting off supply. One obvious course of achieving this goal is setting aside protected areas, such as preserves and parks, as the Okapi Wildlife Reserve and Garamba, Kahuzi-Biega, Nouabalendoki, Salonga, and Virunga National Parks. Another option is to ban trafficking through legislation. Since the 1970s, for example, the Convention on International Trade in Endangered Species of Wild Fauna and Flora (CITES) has prohibited international trafficking of the products of threatened species.

Yet legislation and litigation are not enough to regulate bushmeat trade. Laws are ignored, due to weak enforcement in both Ghana (Mendelson et al. 2003) and the Democratic Republic of Congo (Rowcliffe et al. 2004). Thus some conservationists argue that strengthening governance capabilities of political structures must complement legislation (Davies 2002).

Other conservationists emphasize the need for economic development. It will be virtually impossible, they argue, to stop bushmeat hunting and trade when no other viable economic alternatives exist for impoverished forest inhabitants (Dresden 2004: 39). A hungry and undernourished African is not about to forgo a bushmeat meal today for the promise of external aid tomorrow.

Dubious about the efficacy of supply-side curbs, another group of conservationists focuses on psychological strategies, like decreasing demand for bushmeat by increasing acceptance of domestic meat (Wilkie and Carpenter 1999).

Given the ecological, economic, and ethnic complexities of the bushmeat issue, common sense suggests to most conservationists that a variety of interventions is needed. First, forest peoples must have alternative income streams beyond hunting. Second, cultural preference for wild meat must be replaced with preference for domestic meat, through education and advertising. Third, and a prerequisite of the second, affordable alternatives to bushmeat must be available (Willcox and Nambu 2007: 260). Because these three factors seldom intersect in the same way from place to place, solutions must be varied, flexible, and context-dependent (Crookes and Milner-Gulland 2006: 164).

There is no disagreement that bushmeat hunting, trade, and consumption, as currently practiced, are deeply problematic, unsustainable, and portend calamity.

Western conservationists generally concur that the outright termination of bush-meat hunting is not socially or economically feasible.

Disagreement arises about the relative importance of market-based interventions versus behavior modification of consumers – and, perhaps most pointedly, the extent to which Westerners are justified in involving themselves in African affairs.

Given the urgent state of the bushmeat crisis, ought the harvesting of bush-meat be prohibited outright as soon as possible, avoiding the inherent delays of incremental interventions?

Perspective One

Bushmeat harvesting ought to be prohibited outright as soon as possible.

According to the ethical theory of utilitarianism (the theoretical foundation for the appeal to consequences), informed by ecology, the possible negative consequences of empty forest syndrome, extinction, and postponed starvation caused by the unsustainable practice of bushmeat harvest are grave. Thus, this practice must be terminated at once and completely.

Threats to biodiversity and ecological sustainability have led scientists to decry, justifiably, the killing of wild animals (Whitfield 2003). In 1999 the Bushmeat Crisis Task Force was formed to stop the killing of primates for food (Eves 2001), and Western conservationists have repeatedly called for an absolute abolition of bushmeat hunting (Bowen-Jones et al. 2003: 392).

Bushmeat trade is driven by cultural proclivity. Africans favor wild meat over domestic meat for several reasons. On the one hand, bushmeat is traditional African cuisine, and familiarity perpetuates the preference for it (Schenck et al. 2006). Africans also find in bushmeat certain properties that are not found in domes-ticated animals. They claim that ingesting bushmeat, especially primate bushmeat, makes one feel stronger and more vigorous (Dresden 2004: 37).

Africans enjoy eating primate bushmeat because of the animals' similarities to *Homo sapiens*. This difference in worldview between Africans and Westerners is a bone of bitter contention. Primatologist Jane Goodall is right to blame the imperiled future of primates on the African people themselves for failing to develop a taste for domesticated animals (Machan 2000). The exact same reason Africans prefer bushmeat is the reason that consuming primates is ethically offensive (*Population and Development Review* 2006).

Subsistence for some, bushmeat has become a luxury item for others (Bennett 2002). Its consumption in urban areas connotes elevated socioeconomic status (Bowen-Jones et al. 2003: 392). Clandestine commodity chains lead from rain-forests, down logging roads, through small villages, to cities (ibid.), such as Ouésso, Brazzaville, and Kinshasa. These commodity chains are fluid, forming and re-forming during alternating periods of peace and war (de Merode and Cowlishaw 2006). As carcasses pass down these commodity chains, they change hands between hunters, wholesalers, market traders, and restaurant owners who cook and serve

bushmeat in stews (Cowlishaw et al. 2005a: 141). One such eating establish-
ment in Nairobi is descriptively named "The Carnivore" (Dresden 2004: 35).
These commodity chains extend beyond Africa to Europe and the Unites States,
ending up as contraband in the bustling street markets of Paris, Brussels,
London, New York, Montreal, Toronto, Chicago, and Los Angeles (Brown 2006).
In London, African nationals who want to retain connections to their cultural
heritage gladly pay as much for medallions of baboon as for filet mignon (ibid.).
Consumers also include Westerners interested in the novelty of eating bushmeat,
probably thinking of it as an "organic" specialty.

Back in the Congo, driven by poverty and hunger, hunters are decimating
primate populations (*Science* 2006). At current rates, wild meat supply will drop
over 80 percent in less than 50 years (Fa et al. 2003). Unfortunately, this vector
points toward both extinction for vulnerable primate species *and* starvation for the
indigenous peoples who depend on bushmeat for protein (ibid.). Present-day
reliance on bushmeat is likely to precipitate future starvation and suffering.

There are other anthropocentric reasons to worry about bushmeat consumption. The handling and transportation of animal carcasses creates pathways for
zoonotic infections – diseases transmitted to humans from nonhuman animals
– e.g., Lassa Fever (Dresden 2004: 37), Ebola, Severe Acute Respiratory Syndrome (SARS), Human Immunodeficiency Virus (HIV), monkeypox (Bailey 2004)
and retrovirus (Wolfe et al. 2004). Epidemiological evidence suggests that HIV
arose from Simian Immunodeficiency Virus (SIV) through the butchering of
bushmeat (Gao et al. 1999).

Given the facts that (1) much bushmeat trade is based on cultural preference
and that cultural preference can be modified, (2) the bushmeat trade presents
dangers for its human handlers, (3) bushmeat harvest is no long-term solution
to the nutritional crisis of the Congo Basin, and (4) primates contribute to the
stability and integrity of Congo Basin ecological systems, an appeal to consequences demonstrates conclusively that terminating bushmeat hunting, harvest,
and trade – through the most robust legal and legislative process and as soon
as possible – is ethically mandatory. There is no time for delay.

Perspective Two

Bushmeat harvesting ought not be prohibited.

According to the ethical theory of utilitarianism, as informed by anthropology, prohibiting the harvesting of bushmeat would result in the starvation and death of the Congo Basin's poorest and most vulnerable people. To
the extent that hunger is alleviated by the harvest of bushmeat, it is ethically
justified.

Humanitarians correctly point out that bushmeat is an important resource
for staving off hunger in central Africa, where one-third of the population is
undernourished (Food and Agricultural Organization 2006: 33). Here hunting

contributes between 30 and 80 percent of the dietary protein of forest-dwellers (Wilkie and Carpenter 1999). Given this situation, Africans perceive, with good reason, that Western conservationists who protest against bushmeat hunting are misanthropic – valuing animals over humans (Dresden 2004: 39).

For people living in forest borderlands, the problem of malnutrition is exacerbated by inaccessibility to markets and lack of economic development (Bennett 2002), problems partially mitigated by bushmeat resource exploitation. Bushmeat for many hungry Africans is more plentiful and less expensive – actually, free – than meat from domestic animals (Dresden 2004: 37). Those who own domestic animals often keep them for emergencies or ceremonial events, rather than using them as an everyday staple (Bennett 2002). Bushmeat is a commodity that can be bartered for other goods and money.

The greatest hope lies not in the outright termination of bushmeat harvest but rather in the type of sustainable bushmeat hunting that occurred for hundreds or thousands of years (Bennett et al. 2007), before the socioeconomic changes of the twentieth century radically reconfigured the dynamics of human-animal interactions.

As sad as it is to see a gorilla on the grill, the palliation of human suffering – in the forms of malnutrition and starvation – and the preservation of human life take precedence over animal rights.

Additional Issues to Consider

Other possible moral dilemmas arising within this case:

Q Are more affluent nations morally required to provide alternatives to bushmeat for Africans who require it for sustenance?

Q Are more affluent nations morally required to provide education about the threat to bushmeat populations to Africans who require it for sustenance?

Q Are more affluent nations or cities morally required to (enforce a) ban on importing and serving bushmeat to more affluent populations?

Q Are coercive efforts to prevent the consumption of bushmeat *ever* morally justified?

REFERENCES

Bahuchert, S. (1993) History of the inhabitants of the central African rain forest: Perspectives from comparative linguistics. In C. M. Hladik, A. Hladik, O. F. Linares, et al. (eds.), *Tropical Forests, People and Food: Biocultural Interactions and Applications to Development*. Pearl River, NY: Parthenon Publishing Group, pp. 37–54.

Bailey, N. (2004) Bushmeat, health and conservation impacts. *Bushmeat Quarterly* 11 (Spring/Summer): 4–5.

Bennett, E. L. (2002) Is there a link between wild meat and food security? *Conservation Biology* 16 (3): 590–2.

Bennett, E. L., and Robinson, J. G. (2000) *Hunting of Wildlife in Tropical Forests: Implications for Biodiversity and Forest Peoples*. Washington, DC: International Bank for Reconstruction/The World Bank.

Bennett, E. L., Blencowe, E., Brandon, K., et al. (2007) Hunting for consensus: Reconciling bushmeat harvest, conservation, and development policy in west and central Africa. *Conservation Biology* 21 (3): 884–7.

Bennett, E. L., Robinson, J. G., Wilkie, D., et al. (2002) Why is eating bushmeat a biodiversity crisis? *Conservation in Practice* 3 (2): 28–9.

Bowen-Jones, E., and Pendry, S. (1999) The threat to primates and other mammals from the bushmeat trade in Africa. *Oryx* 33 (3): 233–46.

Bowen-Jones, E., Brown, D., and Robinson, E. J. Z. (2003) Economic commodity or environmental crisis? An interdisciplinary approach to analysing the bushmeat trade in central and west Africa. *Area* 35 (4): 390–402.

Brown, S. (2006) West develops a taste for primates. *New Scientist* 191 (2559): 8.

Chapman, C. A. (1995) Primate seed dispersal: coevolution and conservation implications. *Evolutionary Anthropology* 4 (3): 74–82.

Chapman, C. A., Lawes, M. J., and Eeley, H. A. C. (2006) What hope for African primate diversity? *African Journal of Ecology* 44 (2): 116–33.

Convention on International Trade in Endangered Species of Wild Fauna and Flora (1973) Available at: www.cites.org/eng/disc/text.shtml#texttop (accessed July 17, 2007).

Cowlishaw, G., and Dunbar, R. I. M. (2000) *Primate Conservation Biology*. Chicago, IL: University of Chicago Press.

Cowlishaw, G., Mendelson, S., and Rowcliffe, J. M. (2005a) Structure and operation of a bushmeat commodity chain in southwestern Ghana. *Conservation Biology* 19 (1): 139–49.

Cowlishaw, G., Mendelson, S., and Rowcliffe, J. M. (2005b) Evidence for post-depletion sustainability in a mature bushmeat market. *Journal of Applied Ecology* 42 (3): 460–8.

Crookes, D. J., and Milner-Gulland, E. J. (2006) Wildlife and economic policies affecting the bushmeat trade: a framework for analysis. *South African Journal of Wildlife Research* 32 (2): 159–65.

Davies, G. (2002) Bushmeat and international development. *Conservation Biology* 16 (3): 587–9.

de Merode, E., and Cowlishaw, G. (2006) Species protection, the changing informal economy, and the politics of access to the bushmeat trade in the Democratic Republic of Congo. *Conservation Biology* 20 (4): 1261–71.

Dresden, E. (2004) The bushmeat trade: personal reflections within a context of human–animal interactions. *ReVision* 27 (2): 33–41.

Eves, H. E. (2001) The bushmeat crisis task force. In: *The Apes: Challenges for the 21st Century*. Conference Proceedings, Brookfield Zoo, May 10–13, 2000. Brookfield, IL: Chicago Zoological Society, pp. 230–1.

Fa, J. E., Currie, D., and Meeuwig, J. (2003) Bushmeat and food security in the Congo basin: linkages between wildlife and people's future. *Environmental Conservation* 30 (1): 71–8.

Fa, J. E., Juste, J., Del Val, J., et al. (1995) Impact of market hunting on mammal species in equatorial Guinea. *Conservation Biology* 9 (1): 1107–15.

Food and Agricultural Organization (2006) *The State of Food Insecurity in the World 2006.* United Nations, Rome, Italy. Available at: ftp://ftp.fao.org/docrep/fao/009/a0750e/a0750e00.pdf (accessed July 17, 2007).

Gao, F., Bailes, E., Robertson, D. L., et al. (1999) Origin of HIV-1 in the chimpanzee *Pan troglodytes troglodytes. Nature* 397 (February): 436–40.

Goodall, J. (2004) When primates become bushmeat. *World Watch* 17 (4): 20.

Grevengoed, S. (2001) Mountain gorilla killed and eaten in Rwanda. Press release (June 6). African Wildlife Foundation, Washington, DC. Available at: www.bushmeat.org/html/crisismtgorillajune01.htm (accessed June 18, 2007).

Hennessey, A. B. (1995) *A study of the meat trade in Ouésso, Republic of Congo.* Wildlife Conservation Society: New York.

Machan, D. (2000) The bushmeat crisis. *Forbes* 166 (13): 130–2.

Mendelson, S., Cowlishaw, G., and Rowcliffe, J. M. (2003) Anatomy of a bushmeat commodity chain in Takoradi, Ghana. *Journal of Peasant Studies* 31 (1): 73–100.

Moore, P. D. (2001) The rising cost of bushmeat. *Nature* 409 (6822): 775–6.

Pearce, F. (2005) The protein gap. *Conservation in Practice* 6 (3): 117–23.

Population and Development Review (2006) On the survival of great apes and their habitat. June, 393–6.

Redford, K. H. (1992) The empty forest. *BioScience* 42 (6): 412–23.

Robinson, J. G., and Bennett, E. L. (2000) Carrying capacity limits to sustainable hunting in tropical forests. In J. G. Robinson and E. L. Bennett (eds.), *Hunting for Sustainability in Tropical Forests.* New York: Columbia University Press, pp. 13–30.

Rowcliffe, J. M., de Merode, E., and Cowlishaw, G. (2004) Do wildlife laws work? Species protection and the application of a prey-choice model to poaching decisions. *Proceedings of the Royal Society of London.* Series B: *Biological Sciences,* 271: 2631–6. Also available at: www.zoo.cam.ac.uk/ioz/people/Publications/2004%20ProcRoySocB%20271%202631-2636.pdf (accessed March 18, 2008).

Schenck, M., Effa, E. N., Starkey, M., et al. (2006) Why people eat bushmeat: Results from two-choice, taste tests in Gabon, Central Africa. *Human Ecology* 34 (3): 433–45.

Science (2006) Mapping bushmeat threats. 311 (5758): 153.

Struhsaker, T. T. (1999) Primate communities in Africa: the consequences of long-term evolution or the artifact of recent hunting. In J. G. Fleagle, C. H. Janson, and K. E. Reed (eds.), *Primate Communities.* New York: Cambridge University Press, pp. 289–94.

Walsh, P. D., Abernethy, K. A., Bermejo, M., et al. (2003) Catastrophic ape decline in western equatorial Africa. *Nature* 422: 611–14.

Whitfield, J. (2003) Bushmeat: The law of the jungle. *Nature* 421: 8–9.

Wilkie, D. S., and Carpenter, J. F. (1999) Bushmeat hunting in the Congo Basin: an assessment of impacts and options for mitigation. *Biodiversity and Conservation* 8 (7): 927–55.

Willcox, A. S., and Nambu, D. M. (2007) Wildlife hunting practices and bushmeat dynamics of the Banyangi and Mbo people of southwestern Cameroon. *Biological Conservation* 134 (2): 251–61.

Wolfe, N. D., Switzer, W. M., Carr, J. K., et al. (2004) Naturally acquired simian retroviral infections in central African hunters. *Lancet* 363 (9413): 932–7.

CASE TEN: FUTURE FARMERS – THE ECOLOGY, ECONOMICS, AND ETHICS OF GENETICALLY MODIFIED RICE

Plant breeding, the science of crop production, has traditionally developed – in the spirit of Gregor Mendel (1965) and his peas – new cultivars (i.e., non-naturally occurring varieties of plants that arise as a result of cultivation) through selective breeding. Plant breeders hybridize (that is, crossbreed) plants that have been selected for some desired trait. By hybridizing plants with desirable traits, desirable alleles – and combinations of alleles – are concentrated, thereby improving the fitness of the offspring. Plant breeders then test the new geno-types in different environments in order to compare the fitness of offspring against that of their parents, in the hope of improving the progeny's performance across a greater range of environmental conditions.

Now, with the advent of sophisticated genetic technology, plant improvement often involves the direct manipulation of the genetic code of plants by activat-ing or deactivating genes, or by inserting genes from other organisms.

The list of genetically modified organisms (GMOs) developed for agriculture is sizable and growing. Roundup-Ready® soybean is genetically engineered to withstand glyphosate, an inexpensive herbicide trademarked as Roundup® which allows farmers to kill "weeds," but not their genetically modified crops (Stokstad 2004). Both corn and cotton contain desoxyribonucleic acid (DNA) from a common soil bacteria (*Bacillus thuringiensis*) which produces an endo-toxin repellent to the European corn borer and cotton bollworm (Linacre and Thompson 2004), obviating the need for pesticide (Brody 2000). Genetically modified papaya resists ringspot virus (Gonsalves 1998); snippets of bacterial genes inserted into potatoes repel the voracious colorado potato beetle (*New York Times* 1995); and genetically modified strawberries tolerate frost much better than their natural counterparts (Houde et al. 2004).

The idea to manipulate the genetic code of a common strain of rice (*Oryza sativa*) arose from a determination to solve an acute nutritional problem. The World Health Organization (2007) estimates that between a quarter and a half million children go blind each year due to Vitamin A Deficiency (VAD) syndrome. Half of these children die. When adults are included, the annual VAD death toll exceeds one million (Baggott 2006: 28). The unnerving fact for humanitarian activists is that VAD is completely preventable; better nutrition is all that is needed.

Upwards of three billion people depend on rice as their main staple. Beta-carotene, a natural plant pigment, provides the chemical precursor for the body to produce Vitamin A. For this reason beta-carotene is also called provitamin A. In rice, beta-carotene is present only in the outer grain layers. Unfortunately, in order to keep the grain from rotting, these layers are removed during milling and polishing. The kernel that most people eat – the starchy interior called the endosperm – does not contain beta-carotene. Since no species in the entire Oryza family produces beta-carotene in its endosperm, hybridization of Oryza lines – the traditional crop improvement approach – is not considered feasible.

Because normal plant breeding techniques were unpromising, Gary Toenniessen, Director of Food Security of the Rockefeller Foundation, looked elsewhere. If genetic technology could produce a rice that contained provitamin A in the part of the plant that people eat, VAD might be vanquished and human suffering greatly alleviated (Nash and Robinson 2000). With the support of Toenniessen and a Rockefeller Foundation grant, Ingo Potrykus, Professor of Plant Science at the Swiss Institute of Technology, began collaborating with Peter Beyer, Professor at the Department of Cell Biology at the University of Freiberg, an expert on the beta-carotene pathway in daffodils, on the genetic modification of rice.

Potrykus (2001) has been adamant about the humanitarian origin of this project. It began at public institutions with public funding and independent of industry influence. The hope, Potrykus said, was that the technology would be transferred to other major human food staples such as banana, cassava, grain, legumes, sweet potato, and wheat (ibid.).

The outcome of their research was "Golden Rice," so-called because the endosperm contains three genes (ibid.) which produce beta-carotene, giving it a yellowish, rather than whitish, color (Schaub et al. 2005). This triumph of genetic engineering was accomplished by splicing DNA from common soil bacterium (*Erwinia uredovora*) and wild daffodil (*Narcissus pseudonarcissus*) into *Oryza sativa* (Al-Babili and Beyer 2005). These genetic modifications created provitamin A pathways in the endosperm of the rice (Beyer et al. 2002).

This extraordinary scientific achievement did not mark a victory for the eradication of VAD, but instead encountered a series of stumbling blocks in getting the rice to the people for whom it was intended. The first unforeseen obstacle was intellectual property rights: the genes and technology used by Potrykus and Beyer to transfer DNA from bacteria and daffodils to rice were encumbered by 70 patents (Potrykus 2001).

Intellectual property rights automatically brought corporations into the mix. Greenovation, a German company specializing in orchestrating academic discoveries within the biotechnology industry, brokered a deal between the professors and Zeneca Agrichemicals, which held crucial patents (Christensen 2000). Through a corporate merger, Zeneca became Syngenta in 2000 (ibid.). St Louis-based Monsanto, the largest agricultural biotechnology company in the world and a darling of investors because of aggressive research and development (Stewart 2005), also held key patents.

With huge multinational corporations now involved, Potrykus and Beyer quickly realized they needed a partner with the expertise to deal with the legal and commercial dimensions that they, as academics, were ill-equipped to handle. The partners they found were in the private sector (Potrykus 2001). With legal advice, the number of patents impeding distribution was brought from 70 down to 12 (ibid.). Zeneca agreed to support the project on the basis of its humanitarian intent by allowing the remaining patents to be used if the profits accrued by its use did not exceed $10,000 per year, a cap well above the income of poor farmers (Christensen 2000). In a similar gesture of good-will, Hendrick Verfaillie, President and Chief Executive of Monsanto, proclaimed "The purpose of golden rice is to bring Vitamin A where people suffer" (Marquis 2000), and waived all fees associated with patents on Golden Rice technology (*Wall Street Journal* 2000). Surmounting these obstacles cleared the way for shipment of Golden Rice to the International Rice Research Institute (IRRI) in Los Banos, Philippines, for greenhouse research (Schiermeier 2001). As the US is one of the few countries with clearly delineated regulations for growing genetically modified plants (History of the Golden Rice Programme), Golden Rice was harvested for the first time outdoors in Louisiana four years later (Treadway 2005).

But another, more imposing obstacle loomed: adverse public opinion. Americans are customarily more trusting of governmental oversight than Europeans (Baggott 2006: 29), and the most intense reproach of Golden Rice has come from Europe, driven by environmental groups, most notably, Greenpeace. Greenpeace has dismissed Golden Rice as "fool's gold" (Connor 2001) and condemned it as unecological and unjust. As the controversy was heating up in 2001, Charlie Kronick, Chief Policy Adviser for Greenpeace, wrote:

> We oppose GM crops because the technology is unpredictable, imprecise and irretrievable. The fundamental environmental safety issues remain unresolved for "golden rice" just as for any other GM organism. We and others also oppose it for specific reasons: nutritionists say that it won't solve Vitamin A deficiency because the absence of fat in diet of the poor won't allow the uptake of pro-Vitamin A in the rice. We believe it is based on unsound nutritional science – a genetic engineer's approach to hunger. The only function that GM crops such as golden rice can be guaranteed to perform is to divert attention and resources from the challenge of creating a genuinely sustainable future for agriculture in both the developed and developing worlds. A technical "fix" to economic and social problems such as poverty is no solution. (Kronick 2001)

The health benefits initially touted by biotechnology proponents were dismissed as overrated (Schnapp and Schiermeier 2001). The rice consumption of an average Asian adult would provide only 8 percent of the needed daily intake of Vitamin A. The average adult would need to consume nearly 20 pounds of uncooked rice – twice that amount for pregnant women – to meet daily Vitamin A requirements (Brown 2001). This prompted Kronick to claim: "It is clear that the GM industry has been making false claims about golden rice" (ibid.).

Other unanswered nutritional questions arose. Some claimed that elevated levels of beta-carotene did not necessarily improve health, because in order to absorb beta-carotene the body must be fairly fit. People suffering from poor nutrition have trouble absorbing beta-carotene in the first place. The scourge of malnutrition, nutritionists maintain, is complex and cannot be solved by simply inventing a new strain of rice. The real problem is the whole diet, particularly the lack of green vegetables (Cavendish 2004).

Others have raised psychological issues regarding culture blindness, suspicious that European men in white lab coats had not considered cultural factors. Asians, for example, prefer white rice to brown rice even though brown rice is known to be more nutritive. An American writer wondered whether Asians even *wanted* to eat yellow rice (Pollan 2001).

For untold numbers of people, messing around with the genetic infrastructure of the human foodstuffs defies common sense. Justifiable anxiety exists over unwittingly subjecting people to allergens. Transferred genes (transgenes) contain information for making proteins, and some proteins – such as those in peanuts – can cause death (Nash and Robinson 2000).

Apprehension extends from diet to ecology: worries about "genetic pollution" or "contamination" cascading through ecosystems, "the consequence of dumping genes into genomes" (Cavendish 2004). Biologists emphasize that gene flow is a natural property of ecological systems. Genetically modified wind-pollinated cultivars spread transgenes through ecosystems. A furor flared up when farmers in England, France, Germany, and Sweden unknowingly planted genetically modified canola from Canada which interbred with non-genetically modified canola in adjacent fields, consequently "contaminating" the natural stock (Nash and Robinson 2000). Ecologists point out that the immanent implementation of Golden Rice will invariably disseminate modified genes to nearby wild populations. These ecological effects are uncertain and call for further study (Lu and Snow 2005).

In light of all this ecological uncertainty, European Union public policy-makers have adopted a "precautionary principle" which holds that if the consequences of some action, like using GMOs in food production, are undetermined and potentially dangerous, implementation ought to be avoided (Baggott 2006: 29). Given current knowledge, this principle weighs against use of GMOs as cultivars.

For proponents of Golden Rice, it is time to quit quibbling about the pluses and minuses of GMOs and get on to improving the human condition. Attention must shift from debate to implementation (Al-Babili and Beyer 2005: 571). A US Department of Agriculture research geneticist exhorted, "The current resistance to acceptance of this novel technology should be assessed and overcome so that its full potential in crop improvement can be realized" (Jauhar 2006: 1841).

Whatever else may be true, two things are certain. One is that genetically modified cultivars are and will continue to be part of human foodstuffs. The other is that malnutrition will persist and genetic technology could have some role in successfully addressing this humanitarian crisis. The open question is the extent of biotechnology's future role in confronting chronic malnutrition, and the guiding principles that will direct strategies.

From an ethical point of view, should the development of GMOs, such as Golden Rice, be encouraged?

Perspective One

The development of GMOs should not be encouraged. According to the ethical theory of utilitarianism, the possible negative consequences of GMOs do not outweigh their potential benefits. Too many ecological, nutritional, and cultural uncertainties exist to justify the development of GMOs.

The reasons to oppose Golden Rice are reasons to oppose GMOs in general. Lingering suspicions of the altruistic intentions of big corporations have rightly induced many to worry that acceptance of Golden Rice may lead down a slippery slope to the acceptance of other GMOs with less noble purposes, a "dangerous domino" in a larger agricultural game (Baggott 2006: 30).

It would be irrational not to be suspicious that the seemingly humanitarian, utilitarian arguments given by the proponents of Golden Rice are merely ruses to generate profits for a very small number of people – namely, agribusiness stockholders. The conspicuous emphasis on the humanitarian potential of Golden Rice by biotechnology acolytes, in spite of seemingly obvious economic evidence against its continued promotion, is cause for distrust. Possibly, Golden Rice has been used as a public relations stunt to win widespread acceptance for GMO use in agriculture. Critics have aptly snubbed Golden Rice as a "Trojan horse" (Pollack 2001a) whose true purpose is to bolster biotechnology profits, which had been failing to meet the rosy expectations of investors (Stewart 2005).

Therefore the veracity of the biotechnology industry's claims of good intentions are doubtful. American journalist Michael Pollan posed a rhetorical question after an ordinary observation: "Granted, it would be immoral for finicky Americans to thwart a technology that could rescue malnourished children. But wouldn't it also be immoral for an industry to use those children's suffering in order to rescue itself?" (Pollan 2001). This worry seemed to be echoed in the comments of Rockefeller Foundation President Gordon Conway, who judged that "the public relations uses of golden rice have gone too far" (Brown 2001).

Anti-globalization activists sensibly fear that the outcome of GMO agriculture could be the loss of local autonomy (Pearce 2001) and subsequent corporate control of the world's food market (Pollack 2001b). In the words of English journalist Camilla Cavendish (2004):

> GM crops will not solve world hunger. In fact they could worsen it, by enabling a few giant conglomerates to monopolise the food chain. These companies are patenting seeds, the processes that create those seeds and the chemicals that are used on the resulting crops. They can sell seeds that will not reproduce, locking farmers into a dependency that will soon turn from mild exploitation into rampant extortion. [The result will be] the surrender of poor farmers into a new form of slavery.

The bottom line is this: in terms of straightforward economic cost/benefit analysis, the money that has gone into developing and marketing Golden Rice might have yielded better consequences had it been spent on handing out Vitamin A supplements and teaching farmers how to grow green leafy vegetables on the margins of their rice paddies (ibid.).

Perspective Two

The development of GMOs should be encouraged. According to the ethical theory of utilitarianism, the potential benefits of GMOs outweigh any possible negative consequences.

Criticism regarding the initial overblown nutritional advantages of the first generation of Golden Rice (Golden Rice-1) have been blunted with the development of "Golden Rice-2." In 2005, scientists substituted daffodil DNA for maize DNA (Paine et al. 2005). The new rice contained 23 times the beta-carotene of its prototype (Mayer 2005) and, in the minds of some observers, resolved the dispute about provitamin A content (Baggott 2006: 30). This innovation demonstrates that the worst worries of GMO opponents will most likely be assuaged through technological advances, given the chance.

Even those opposed to Golden Rice development have been awakened to its humanitarian potential. Benedikt Haerlin, Genetic Engineering Campaign Coordinator for Greenpeace International, had categorically maintained a "permanent and definite and complete opposition" to GMOs (Taverne 2003) – except in the case of Golden Rice. "I feel that 'golden rice' is a moral challenge to our position," Haerlin conceded. "It is true there is a different moral context, whether you have an insecticidal or pesticide-resistant GM, or whether you have a GM product that serves a good purpose" (Connor 2001).

The palpable frustration of scientists to this discourse is understandable. Many exhibit exasperation that the issue is no longer about helping the impoverished or about sound science, but about anti-technology politics. As Potrykus complained: "It is not so much the concern about the environment, or the health of the consumer, or help for the poor and disadvantaged. It is a radical fight against a technology and for political success" (Pollack 2001a).

To counter politics – which many scientists feel is based more on emotion than agronomy, genetics, and humanitarianism – more than 3,000 scientists, including 25 Nobel Laureates, signed a "Declaration in Support of Agricultural Biotechnology." This Declaration (2005) asserts:

> [R]ecombinant DNA techniques constitute powerful and safe means for the modification of organisms and can contribute substantially in enhancing quality of life by improving agriculture, healthcare, and the environment. The responsible genetic modification of plants is neither new nor dangerous. . . . Through judicious deployment, biotechnology can also address environmental degradation, hunger, and poverty in the developing world by providing improved agricultural productivity and greater nutritional security.

Golden Rice, these scientists convincingly argue, is not a ruse to addict the world's population to a monoculture controlled by multinational corporations. Rather, introgression of Golden Rice into local varieties can occur within two years, thus preserving biodiversity (Mayer 2005). Nor is Golden Rice intended to be the final solution to VAD, but rather an additional arrow in the humanitarian quiver of weapons aimed at mitigating malnutrition (Nash and Robinson 2000). It effectively delivers a beneficial natural trait (beta-carotene) in a standard crop plant (Mayer 2005). Therefore, Golden Rice is meant to complement, not replace, existing strategies (Dawe et al. 2002).

GMOs in general and Golden Rice in particular will secure the greatest happiness for the greatest number of people. In the words of former US President Jimmy Carter, "Responsible biotechnology is not the enemy; starvation is" (Nash and Robinson 2000).

Additional Issues to Consider

Other possible moral dilemmas arising within this case:

Q Under what, if any, conditions is starvation of some populations morally permissible?

Q At what, if any, point do concerns about contamination of ecosystems play a major role in halting development of GMOs?

REFERENCES

Al-Babili, S., and Beyer (2005) Golden rice five years on the road five years to go? *Trends in Plant Science* 10 (12): 565–73.

Baggott, E. (2006) A wealth deferred: the politics and science of golden rice. Commentary. *Harvard International Review* (Fall): 28–30.

Beyer, P., Al-Babili, S., Xudong, Y., et al. (2002) Golden rice: introducing the β-carotene biosynthesis pathway into rice endosperm by genetic engineering to defeat vitamin A deficiency. *Journal of Nutrition* 132 (3): 506S–510S.

Brody, J. E. (2000) Gene altered foods: a case against panic. *New York Times* (December 5): F8.

Brown, P. (2001) GM rice promoters "have gone too far". *Guardian* (Manchester, UK) (February 10): 21.

Cavendish, C. (2004) How to grow a packet of profits from seed. Commentary. *The Times* (London) (March 10): 24.

Christensen, J. (2000) Golden rice in a grenade-proof greenhouse. *New York Times* (November 21): F1.

Connor, S. (2001) Greenpeace promises not to halt trials of GM vitamin rice. *Independent* (London) (February 10): 4.

Dawe, D., Robertson, R., and Unnevehr, L. (2002) Golden rice: what role could it play in alleviation of vitamin A deficiency? *Food Policy* 27 (5/6): 541–61.

Declaration in Support of Agricultural Biotechnology (2005) Available at: www.agbioworld.org/declaration/petition/petition.php (accessed October 2, 2007).

Gonsalves, D. (1998) Control of papaya ringspot virus in papaya: a case study. *Annual Review of Phytopathology* 36 (1): 415–37.

History of the Golden Rice Programme (n.d.) Available at: www.goldenrice.org/ Content1-Who/who2_history.html (accessed October 2, 2007).

Houde, M., Dallaire, S., N'Dong, D., et al. (2004) Overexpression of the acidic dehydrin WCOR410 improves freezing tolerance in transgenic strawberry leaves. *Plant Biotechnology Journal* 2 (5): 381–7.

Jauhar, P. (2006) Modern biotechnology as an integral supplement to conventional plant breeding: the prospects and challenges. *Crop Science* 46 (5): 1841–59.

Kronick, C. (2001) The Greenpeace line on golden rice. Opinion-editorial. *Guardian* (Manchester, UK) (April 18): 9.

Linacre, N. A., and Thompson, C. J. (2004) Dynamics of insect resistance in Bt-corn. *Ecological Modelling* 171 (3): 271–9.

Lu, B.-R., and Snow, A. A. (2005) Gene flow from genetically modified rice and its environmental consequences. *BioScience* 55 (8): 669–78.

Marquis, C. (2000) Monsanto plans to offer rights to its altered-rice technology. *New York Times* (August 4): A11.

Mayer, J. (2005) The golden rice controversy: useless science or unfounded criticism? *BioScience* 55 (9): 726–7.

Mendel, G. (1965) *Experiments in Plant Hybridisation*, trans. Fisher, R. A. Edinburgh: Oliver & Boyd.

Nash, M. J., and Robinson, S. (2000) Grains of hope. *Time* 156 (5): 38ff.

New York Times (1995) Monsanto's potato approved by US regulators (May 6): A45.

Paine, J. A., Shipton, C. A., Chagger, S., et al. (2005) Improving the nutritional value of golden rice through increased pro-vitamin A content. *Nature Biotechnology* 23 (March): 482–7.

Pearce, F. (2001) Protests take the shine off golden rice. *New Scientist* 169 (2284): 15.

Pollack, A. (2001a) A food fight for high stakes. Commentary. *New York Times* (February 4): A14.

Pollack, A. (2001b) The green revolution yields to the bottom line. *New York Times* (May 15): F1.

Pollan, M. (2001) The great yellow hype. Commentary. *New York Times Magazine* (March 4): 15–16.

Potrykus, I. (2001) Harvest of hope or fear? Opinion-editorial. *Guardian* (Manchester, UK) (April 18): 8.

Schaub, P., Al-Babili, S., Drake, R., et al. (2005) Why is golden rice golden (yellow) instead of red? *Plant Physiology* 138 (1): 441–50.

Schiermeier, Q. (2001) Designer rice to combat diet deficiencies makes its debut. *Nature* 409 (6820): 551.

Schnapp, N., and Schiermeier, Q. (2001) Critics claim "sight-saving" rice is over-rated. *Nature* 410 (6828): 503.

Stewart, J. B. (2005) Monsanto's crops and financials contain promise. *Wall Street Journal* (December 7): D3.

Stokstad, E. (2004) A new tack on herbicide resistance. *Science* 304 (5674): 1089.

Taverne, D. (2003) When crops burn, the truth goes up in smoke. Opinion-editorial. *The Times* (London) (November 18): 22.

Treadway, J. (2005) Rice may be "golden" to world's poor: genetically altered grain grown by LSU. *Times-Picayune* (New Orleans) (January 17): 1.

Wall Street Journal (2000) Foreign-aid bill boosts spending for biotechnology (November 27): A32.

World Health Organization (2007) Micronutrient deficiencies: vitamin A deficiency. Available at: www.who.int/nutrition/topics/vad/en/ (accessed October 2, 2007).

CASE ELEVEN: TILL RIVERS RUN DRY
– MEXICAN-AMERICAN WATER POLITICS

Water politics is a function of two variables: supply and demand. Supply is determined by climate. Demand is determined by population size and the thirst of that population. Of these variables, demographers forecast increased global population growth and use of water, while meteorologists forecast, in many parts of the world, drought.

The western United States, particularly the southwest, is the fastest growing region of the nation (Roberts and Dougherty 2006). The region is also in the throes of an extended multi-year drought, which scientists caution may be the norm rather than the exception. For example, the current drought pales in comparison to the drought of 900–1300 CE, suggesting cycles of aridity are a normal feature of the region's climate (Cook et al. 2004). Convergence of climate models indicate that the transition to a more arid climate, reminiscence of the Dust Bowl of the 1930s, is already taking place and will become the new climate for the west within a matter of years or decades (Seager et al. 2007).

These precautions stand in stark contrast to the relatively wet twentieth century, when water policy was set. For example, the Colorado River Compact of 1922, which adjudicates allotment of water to the seven basin states, was negotiated on data from unusually wet years dating back to the 1890s. The faulty assumptions of the compact consequently make it inherently problematic (Dean 2007). The year the compact was signed, American ecologist Aldo Leopold canoed through the Colorado River delta estuary with his brother and discovered a lush oasis teeming with life:

> A verdant wall of mesquite and willow separated the channel from the thorny desert beyond. At each bend we saw egrets standing in the pools ahead, each white statue matched by its white reflection. Fleets of cormorants drove their black prows in quest of skittering mullets; avocets, willets, and yellow-legs dozed one-legged on the bars; mallards, widgeons, and teal sprang skyward in alarm. As the birds took to the air, they accumulated in a small cloud ahead, there to settle, or to break back to our rear. When a troop of egrets settled on a far green willow, they looked like a premature snowstorm. All this wealth of fowl and fish was not for our delectation alone. Often we came upon a bobcat, flattened to some half-immersed driftwood log, paw poised for mullet. Families of raccoons waded the shallows, munching water beetles. Coyotes watched us from inland knolls, waiting to resume their breakfasts of mesquite beans, varied, I suppose, by an occasional crippled shore bird, duck, or quail. At every shallow ford were tracks of burro dear. We always examined their deer trails, hoping to find signs of the despot of the Delta, the great jaguar, *el tigre*. (1960: 142–3)

Now the Colorado flowing into the Gulf of California is nothing more than a briny trickle (Alexander 1998), and the ecosystem that astonished Leopold has been totally decimated. The Rio Grande has met the same fate; the river once described as "mighty" has become so weak it peters out even before reaching the Gulf of Mexico (Yardley 2002).

The Colorado River and Rio Grande symbolize the complex ecological and economic co-dependence of the US and Mexico. Ecologically, the estuaries of both rivers have been obliterated. In Big Bend National Park, Texas, the loss of instream flows from the Rio Conchos, the largest tributary of the Rio Grande, has threatened floral and faunal populations (United States Geological Survey 2007). The research of Randy Blankinship, a Texas wildlife biologist, has shown that innumerable species, including the white shrimp and mullet, have been deleteriously affected by the reduced outflow of the Rio Grande. Water hyacinth and hydrilla, which would normally be flushed away by currents, have choked some sections of the river (Yardley 2002). Economically, the future of agriculture in the Imperial and Rio Grande valleys depends on the supply of water, as do the growing industrial centers, spawned by the North American Free Trade Agreement (NAFTA), which dot the length of the international border.

Water policy between the two neighbors was set in 1944 by the Treaty Regarding Utilization of the Waters of the Colorado and Tijuana Rivers and of the Rio Grande, known colloquially as the US-Mexican 1944 Water Treaty (Senate of the United States America 1944). The treaty stipulates that the US allow 1.5 million acre feet of Colorado River water (about 486 billion gallons) to flow from the US into Mexico, and that Mexico allow 350,000 acre feet (114 billion gallons) of Rio Conchos water to flow from Mexico into the Rio Grande at the US border. The treaty releases Mexico from meeting its obligations in case of "extraordinary drought or serious accident to the hydraulic systems on the measure Mexican tributaries" (ibid.: 11).

The California side of the Imperial Valley relies on water from the Colorado River to produce $1 billion worth of food annually. Much of this water is delivered through the 82-mile All American Canal running just north of the border, which leaks so much water that Mexican farmers have been pumping aquifers and using it for irrigation since the 1940s. A proposal to line the canal and prevent leakage has triggered Mexicans to protest loudly, claiming that it will end farming in the Mexican side of the border (Rohter 1989). "How can they take away the farmers' water after all these years?" asked a Mexicali merchant. "Americans always want more, but we are used to this" (Archibold 2006). Mexicans warn that the proposal will force farmers to cross the border, illegally if need be, to find work on the American side (ibid.). Environmentalists have argued that if desertification occurs through the deterioration of Mexican farmlands and wetlands, air pollution would result and endangered species of birds and lizards would be threatened (ibid.). Americans point out that lining the earthen canal with concrete is not forbidden by the 1944 treaty, and that Mexico already gets its allocation of water as promised (Kravets 2006).

In Texas, border tension over water is no less acute than in California. The politics of water are much more pointed and pressing today than in 1944 when the Rio Grande Valley had only 1 percent of the current population (Weiner 2002). By 2002 Mexico had fallen 456 billion gallons in arrears on its treaty obligations (ibid.). Drought exempted Mexico from delivering the water, in compliance with the terms of the treaty, Mexican authorities claimed. "No water treaty can demand a country to deliver water that doesn't exist," one official said (Yardley 2002).

Texans have not been so sure, their suspicions heightened by the dire consequences of drought on both sides of the border. Rumors have circulated about satellite imagery showing water in Mexican reservoirs (Yardley 2002). US farmers contended that Mexican crops thrived while US crops withered (Montgomery 2005). During the twelve years that Mexico owed the US water, an estimated one-hundred-thousand acres of farmland was permanently lost when farmers sold land they were unable to irrigate (Vindell 2005). Culinary water became so expensive in some places that poorer Texans could not pay water bills and had their service shut off (Stroud 2006).

Oddly, Texas water woes have not necessarily encouraged conservation, as officials were not eager to prove that Mexican water could be done without. In the words of one top Texas water manager: "Do you plan for water that you should have during a drought of record based on full implementation of the treaty? Or do you throw in the towel and plan for a supply of something less than what the treaty says – and thus admit that you can get by without that water?" (Stroud 2006).

The dispute has abated, in part due to forgiveness by the US of 154,846 acre feet of water (Montgomery 2005). The main factor, however, was not diplomacy but weather: several years of heavy rainfall have replenished water supplies, which allowed Mexico to send more water down the Rio Conchos (Kraul 2005).

One thing is clear: in the politics of water, ripples flow upstream. In a time of drought, the city of Brownsville sued farmers when water never made it down the Rio Grande (Stroud 2006). In Texas and the Mexican state of Tamaulipas, farmers downstream blame farmers upstream in Chihuahua of hoarding water (Weiner 2002).

In the equation of water politics, demand will assuredly increase and supply will possibly decrease as a result of global climate change. Some have looked to divine intervention or luck to increase supply. One Mexican sorghum farmer prays to San Isidro, a patron saint, for rain (Weiner 2002). Others doubt that prayer is the best solution, however. "For the longest period of time, the Rio Grande Valley has had a water policy in which we hope and pray for a moderate-sized hurricane every 8 to 10 years that would bypass the Valley, land in the watershed and dump in the reservoir," the highest elected official of Cameron County, Texas, said. "That isn't a water policy" (Yardley 2002).

Most public policy planners feel solutions will have to be political and involve conservation. Part of the problem will be mitigated by lower use per capita as land is converted to residential from agricultural use. The 2007 Texas State Water Plan predicts that while the population of the eight-county Rio Grande Valley region will triple by 2060, water use will increase only 13 percent (Stroud 2006). Yet officials concede there will still not be enough water. Referring to residents of the Rio Grande Valley, one San Antonia water consultant said: "They can convert all the irrigation water rights down there and they still won't have enough" (ibid.). While conservation can help slake the thirst of burgeoning populations, politicians – and the constituents they represent – may come to the harsh realization that in naturally arid areas there may be limits to growth.

Rivers disrespect political boundaries. They will continue to flow from one political jurisdiction to another, straining relations between neighbors. As the governor of the state of Coahjuila speculated at the dawn of the twenty-first century: "I think the struggle for water will be the gravest problem of this century" (Weiner 2002).

As thirst grows worldwide, more squabbles – and wars – over water are certain to erupt. As such, how should water fights be addressed? Should upstream users take as much as they need, independently of the concerns of downstream users, or must everyone make do with less water, with concession and compromise as the key-log of unjamming water disputes?

REFERENCES

Alexander, B. (1998) Between two west coast cities, a duel to the last drop. *New York Times* (December 8): G9.

Archibold, R. C. (2006) A border dispute that focuses on water, not immigration. *New York Times* (July 7): A13.

Cook, E. R., Woodhouse, C. A., Eakin, M. S., et al. (2004) Long-term aridity changes in the western United States. *Science* 306 (5698): 1015–18.

Dean, C. (2007) That "drought" in Southwest may be normal, report says. *New York Times* (February 22): A16.

Kraul, C. (2005) US and Mexico water dispute settled, Rice says. *Los Angeles Times* (March 11): A7.

Kravets, D. (2006) US, Mexico water interests at issue in canal case. *Daily Breeze* (Torrance, California) (December 5): A8.

Leopold, A. (1960) *A Sand County Almanac and Sketches Here and There*. New York: Oxford University Press.

Montgomery, D. (2005) US, Mexico reach settlement on longstanding water dispute. *Fort Worth Star-Telegram* (March 11): 1.

Roberts, S., and Dougherty, J. (2006) Arizona displaces Nevada as fastest-growing state. *New York Times* (December 22): A16.

Rohter, L. (1989) Canal project sets off US-Mexico clash over water for border regions. *New York Times* (October 1): A1.

Seager, R., Ting, M., Held, I., et al. (2007) Model projections of an imminent transition to a more arid climate in southwestern North America. *Science* 316 (5828): 1181–4.

Senate of the United States America (1944) *Treaty Regarding Utilization of the Waters of the Colorado and Tijuana Rivers and of the Rio Grande*, 59 Stat 1219 (February 3. Treaty Entered into Force November 8, 1945.)

States of Arizona, California, Colorado, Nevada, New Mexico, Utah, and Wyoming (1922) Colorado River Compact. Signed November 24.

Stroud, J. S. (2006) Valley water woes grow. *San Antonio Express-News* (August 18): 1A.

United States Geological Survey (2007) Baseline assessment of instream and riparian
    zone biological resources and the establishment of benchmark stations on the Rio
    Grande in Big Bend National Park, Texas. Available at: http://tx.usgs.gov/bigbend/
    index.html (accessed October 2, 2007).
Vindell, T. (2005) Texas officials plan talks on Mexico's water debt. *Valley Morning Star*
    (Harlingen, Texas) (April 6): 1.
Weiner, T. (2002) Water crisis grows into a test of US–Mexico relations. *New York Times*
    (May 24): A3.
Yardley, J. (2002) Water rights war rages on faltering Rio Grande. *New York Times* (April
    17): A16.

5

PLAYS WELL WITH OTHERS?
Ethical Issues in Intra-social Conflicts

Case Twelve: Am I My Brother's Keeper? – What Are Friends For?

Case Thirteen: Give Us Your Tired, Your Poor, Your Healthcare Professionals – Recruiting Nurses from Developing Nations

Case Fourteen: Deadly Secrets – Releasing Confidential Medical Records to Law-Enforcement Officers

Case Fifteen: Perish the Thought! – Academic Affairs and "Community Values"

Case Sixteen: The Sound and the Fury – Noises and Neighbors

Case Seventeen: Shoot to Thrill – Gun Schools in the United States

Each human life is intimately entangled with the lives of others, and is necessarily affected by their choices and behaviors, and by the negative or positive outcomes their actions produce. Differences in cultures, customs, laws, traditions, perspectives, values, and goals create the rich tapestry of human meaning and human interaction. This same diversity also gives rise to misunderstanding and conflict when competing interests and values clash. Our personal wishes and goals are often at odds with the desires and rights of others, both individually and collectively, raising questions regarding our relationships with others and our roles within our multiple social communities.

How do we negotiate the tension between responsibility to self and to others, balancing self-actualization and altruism? Are standards of moral behavior immutable, or does morally justifiable behavior change over time, from one value system to another, or with proximity, scale, and circumstance? Does accommodating diversity change moral values, or does it change the perception of what constitutes morally justifiable behavior? These and other moral challenges of pluralism are examined in the cases presented in this chapter, "Plays Well With Others? Ethical Issues in Intra-social Conflicts."

CASE TWELVE: AM I MY BROTHER'S KEEPER?
– WHAT ARE FRIENDS FOR?

Bob and Ted are good friends who attend the same university. Early one Saturday morning Bob arrives at the door of Ted's dormitory room. Bob is obviously distraught. He asks Ted if he can talk to him in strictest confidence. Ted, barely awake, mumbles, "Sure. What are friends for?"

Bob then confesses that he has gonorrhea. He was diagnosed yesterday at the Student Health Center, given an antibiotic, and told not to have sexual intercourse until he had taken the drug for at least 72 hours. Unfortunately, last night he met this great girl at a local bar. They really hit it off! One thing led to another and – both of them having had too much to drink – they had unprotected sexual intercourse. Now he does not know what to do. She gave him her name and phone number, but he is too embarrassed to call and tell her about the problem. He tells Ted the girl's name and – OMIGOD!!! – it's Ted's good friend Carol.

Ted tells Bob that Carol is also a good friend of his – just as good a friend as Bob is, in fact. He insists that Carol has a right to know that she has been exposed to – indeed, has probably been infected with – a sexually-transmitted disease. In fact, Ted states that if Bob will not tell Carol she has been exposed to gonorrhea, he believes that he (Ted) should tell her. Bob begs Ted not to tell Carol, reminding Ted that he promised to hold Bob's remarks "in strictest confidence."

Should Ted tell Carol she has been exposed to gonorrhea?

Perspective One

Of course Ted should tell Carol she has been exposed to gonorrhea! What, indeed, are friends for, if not to protect each other from avoidable harms?

The consequences for Carol of not telling her about this exposure are uniformly negative: she may suffer the symptoms of this disease, such as painful urination and vaginal discharge (CDC 2008; Mayo Clinic Staff 2007). Even worse, since most women do not experience the symptoms of acute gonorrheal infection, she is at significant risk of serious, long-term complications without knowing why (e.g., infertility). In addition, she may unwittingly transmit the disease to others. True, Bob will be embarrassed when Carol learns he has exposed her to a sexually transmitted disease; but his embarrassment is a small price to pay for protecting her from serious threats to her acute and long-term health.

Also, Carol has a right to be informed of known risks to her health; Ted has such information and he can easily convey it to Carol. Furthermore, as her friend, Ted is obligated to provide this information to Carol. Friendship implies a commitment to the welfare of the friend; the virtue of the integrity of this relationship requires that Ted tell Carol of her exposure.

Perspective Two

Ted should not tell Carol she has been exposed to gonorrhea! She got herself into this mess and he has no obligation to extricate her from it.

When she had sex with a stranger, Carol implicitly consented to the risks to which she exposed herself. As a college student, Carol is presumably an intelligent, educated person who understands the risks of casual and unprotected sex. Thus, she cannot claim that she did not know what she was getting into. Moreover, nothing in the case suggests that she was coerced into having sex with Bob. Rather, the sex appears to have been mutually consensual. Thus, Carol autonomously assumed the risks of casual sex (though, no doubt, hoping to be spared them).

As a friend, Ted is obligated to protect Bob's right of confidentiality. Further, friendship implies a willingness to be a confidant to the friend who needs to share personal or distressing information, often as a means to sorting out difficult problems; the integrity of this relationship requires that Ted keep Bob's secret. Furthermore, Ted had promised to keep Bob's secret. Promises lose their force if they are abrogated whenever keeping them becomes difficult. So, the virtues of fidelity and integrity require Ted to keep mum.

Perspective Three

Should Ted tell Carol that Bob has exposed her to gonorrhea? Before Ted decides, he should gather relevant information. To wit:

Step 1: Information-gathering

Medical information

- How likely is it that Carol has contracted gonorrhea?
- How likely is it that Carol has contracted some other/additional sexually transmitted disease (e.g., HIV) from Bob?

- If Carol gets gonorrhea, how likely is it that she will know she has the disease?
- If Carol has the disease and is not treated, what effects will it have on her health?

Historical information

- Has Carol had unprotected sex with anyone other than Bob?
- What are Carol's sexual habits (e.g., is she likely to have past or future casual or unprotected sex with others)?

Psychological information

- Is Bob likely to tell Carol (perhaps after a day or two has passed)?
- If Ted tells Carol, will Bob survive the embarrassment?
- How is Carol likely to react to this news if Ted tells her? If Bob tells her?

Sociocultural

- Does gender play a role in this case? For example, would your response differ if Carol had exposed Bob to gonorrhea?

Implications

- If Ted tells, what will be the effects on his friendship with Bob? With Carol?
- If Ted doesn't tell, what will be the effects on his friendship with Bob? With Carol?

Economic

- What will treatment cost if Carol is treated now?
- What will treatment cost if Carol delays treatment?

Step 2: Creative problem-solving

It is worth noting that Ted has a third option that will eliminate the dilemma: convincing Bob to tell Carol himself. If Bob can gather up his courage to face Carol (perhaps with Ted in attendance for psychological support), the moral conflict vanishes: negative consequences to Carol's health are avoided and her right to be informed of the risks to her health is respected. Further, by promoting the welfare of both Carol and Bob, Ted respects the integrity of his friendship with both parties. And, of course, if Bob fesses up, Ted doesn't have to break his promise to Bob not to tell.

But assume that Bob remains adamant about not telling Carol. Ted's next step should be to consider the moral pros and cons of his options.

Step 3: Listing pros and cons

Options	Pros	Cons
Ted tells Carol she has been exposed to gonorrhea.	1. Carol is treated before she gets complications (C-B) 2. Ted respects Carol's right to be informed of threats to her welfare (R) 3. Ted respects Carol's autonomy (A)	6. Ted causes embarrassment, shame for Bob (C-NM) 7. Bob has a right not to be harmed (R) 8. Ted promised he would not tell (V-fidelity) 9. Ted violates the integrity of his friendship with Bob (V-integrity)
Ted does not tell Carol she has been exposed to gonorrhea.	4. Carol freely chose to risk her health (A) 5. Ted protects Bob's right to confidentiality (R)	10. Carol infects others with the disease (C-NM, C-U) 11. Ted violates the integrity of his friendship with Carol (V-integrity) 12. Carol suffers serious, long-term reproductive disabilities (C-B)

Step 4: Analysis

Factual assumptions

- Carol was exposed to gonorrhea by Bob.
- Carol does have gonorrhea.
- If informed of her exposure, Carol will seek medical treatment.
- Medical treatment will successfully treat Carol's gonorrhea.
- Bob will be embarrassed, but will get over it.
- Carol's decision to have sex with Bob was *not* autonomous.

Value assumptions

- Sexually transmitted diseases should be treated promptly (to minimize adverse outcomes).
- People should not suffer harsh consequences for their non-autonomous choices.

- Persons' secrets should not be revealed without their express consent.
- Friends should act to protect each other's welfare.

Step 5: Justification

Clearly good moral reasons exist for both of Ted's options. Which of those reasons are stronger?

Ted should tell Carol that she has been exposed to gonorrhea. The appeals to consequences and the virtue of integrity support this course of action.

Beginning with a comparison of the anticipated consequences, Ted identifies good reasons to weigh the negative consequences to Carol's health more heavily than Bob's embarrassment. Because gonorrhea is highly contagious (Mayo Clinic Staff 2007: para 1), Ted can reasonably assume that Carol has been infected.

Because most infected women (unlike most men) do not experience obvious symptoms (ibid.: para 8), Carol is unlikely to realize on her own that she has the disease. Even if she eventually does have noticeable symptoms, treating her before these appear avoids pain and suffering on her part (Reason #1). If the disease goes untreated, Carol could develop pelvic inflammatory disease (PID). According to the CDC (2008):

> Women with PID do not necessarily have symptoms. When symptoms are present, they can be very severe and can include abdominal pain and fever. PID can lead to internal abscesses (pus-filled "pockets" that are hard to cure) and long-lasting, chronic pelvic pain. PID can damage the fallopian tubes enough to cause infertility or increase the risk of ectopic pregnancy. Ectopic pregnancy is a life-threatening condition in which a fertilized egg grows outside the uterus, usually in a fallopian tube. Women themselves can also develop later-onset generalized infection throughout the blood stream. (See also Mayo Clinic Staff 2007)

In short, if untreated, Carol is likely to develop long-term health conditions that can cause significant reproductive disabilities. If, like many young adults, she hopes to have children, the possibility of infertility could be particularly devastating to her future happiness (Reason #12). These concerns, coupled with the possibility that Bob passed on to Carol diseases in addition to gonorrhea, support the argument that she should be told.

Moreover, other persons are at risk if Carol's gonorrhea goes untreated. If Carol gives birth to a child while still infected, she could infect the baby. Perinatal infection of infants can cause blindness, joint infections, and life-threatening general blood infections (CDC 2008). And, of course, she could infect future sexual partners (Reason #10). Although Carol may not be sexually promiscuous, Ted knows that she has engaged in casual, unprotected sex on at least one occasion – last night with Bob. So he should at least consider the possibility of her passing on the infection to other sexual partners. Given the highly contagious nature of gonorrhea, Ted can reasonably assume that Carol's future partners would be infected.

The critic will cite the negative consequences to Bob: his shame and embarrassment (Reason #6). Admittedly, Bob will be ashamed and embarrassed, and both these feelings may be intense. However, in most persons these powerful emotions are short-lived (although some guilt and psychological discomfort may persist for quite some time). Conversely, the threats to Carol's health may be both persistent and severe. Moreover, because gonorrhea is so contagious, some threats to her health are quite likely. While we are less certain about the health effects to others – because we are uncertain about the extent of Carol's promiscuity – the fact that Carol did engage in casual and unprotected sex with a stranger should raise this possibility. If Carol is sexually engaged with other partners, her likely (even if unknowing) transmission of this highly contagious sexually transmitted disease will spread disease and distress to others (Reason #10), which is surely a negative outcome.

Because the negative consequences to Carol are both actually and potentially much more serious and longer lasting than the negative consequences to Bob, the appeal to consequences (here, utility) favors telling Carol. This consequential appeal is further supported by the possibility of Carol's spreading gonorrhea to other partners.

What about autonomy? Didn't Carol, in choosing to engage in unprotected sex, assume responsibility for the consequences of that choice, including the possibility of acquiring a sexually transmitted disease? Isn't she thereby responsible for monitoring her sexual health?

A choice is autonomous when made by a competent chooser (White 1994: 154–83) who is informed, understands the relevant information, and is uncoerced (Faden and Beauchamp 1986: chs. 8–10). Because persons who choose autonomously cannot avail themselves of the conditions that typically excuse behavior – incompetence, ignorance, or coercion – they are held responsible for the outcomes of their actions. If Carol's choice to engage in unprotected sex with a stranger was an autonomous choice (Reason #4), the obligation to seek healthcare – for diagnosis and treatment – is hers alone.

But was her decision autonomous? Since she had been drinking, we might question her competence to make such a decision. She might have been unable, at the time she actually decided to engage in sex, rationally to weigh (or even contemplate) the risks against the benefits of her behavior. She might have been coerced (or at least powerfully motivated) by strong biological forces (e.g., sexual desire). Or she might have been unable to persuade Bob to wear a condom (words failed her). Or perhaps neither had a condom. Thus, although Carol apparently was a willing (voluntary) participant in the sexual encounter, good reasons exist to question whether her decision to participate was truly autonomous. As a result, some doubt exists about whether she is fully responsible for her actions and should be held fully accountable for their noxious effects. Put another way, she may not deserve a full measure of blame or a full measure of burdens. (Of course, Carol might have autonomously chosen earlier in the evening not to drink enough to impair her decision-making ability and then acted accordingly, but that is water under the bridge at this point.)

So, the appeal to autonomous choice does not provide a very strong argument for withholding information from Carol.

Nonetheless, a fuller analysis of autonomy per se is helpful because it reminds us that autonomous *choice* is a mechanism by which autonomous *persons* are respected. A deontological (specifically, Kantian) theory values persons as the grounds for and source of moral obligations; its first obligation is that persons not be used as mere means to the goals of others. Under good conditions, autonomous persons are given choices – and information relevant to those choices – and the freedom to decide for themselves what to do. When persons are temporarily incapable of autonomous choice (for example, when they are inebriated), others have the obligation not to harm them (perhaps even to protect them from harm) until their autonomy is restored. To take advantage of one whose autonomy is temporarily impaired is to disrespect that person (Brody 1982). In the case at hand, Bob should not have taken advantage of Carol's diminished cognitive abilities to use her as a means toward his sexual fulfillment.

We might suspect that Bob's behavior was itself not autonomously chosen (after all, he, too, had been drinking). Even so, his poor judgment last night does not justify withholding important information from Carol this morning, when he is fully capable of autonomous choice. We are assuming that information about her exposure to gonorrhea is material to Carol; that is, she will behave differently if she has this information than if she does not. Specifically, we are assuming that Carol will seek to determine if she does have gonorrhea and, if she does, will seek treatment. So this morning, Bob cannot keep Carol uninformed; doing so uses her as a mere means to avoid the harms of shame and embarrassment (Reason #6). Rather, he must respect her as an autonomous person and give her (or allow Ted to give her) the information to make an autonomous choice (Reasons ##3, 11).

The appeal to rights identifies two relevant rights that are in conflict here: the right (here, of Carol) to be informed of threats to one's life or health (Reason #2) and the right (here, of Bob) to confidentiality (Reason #5). A third right, Bob's right to not be harmed (in this case, shamed or embarrassed) is also relevant (Reason #7). Is any one of these rights stronger than the others? To answer this question, we should consider the logic of rights (Brody 1988: 22–32). A right is, by definition, a claim on everyone else to not obstruct and, sometimes, to provide whatever the right specifies. For example, a right to be informed of threats to one's life or health is a claim on others who possess important information about such threats to share that information with the right-holder (here, Carol). A right to confidentiality is a right to not have one's personal information disseminated without one's express consent (here, Bob).

Contrary to popular belief, rights are *not inalienable*:

1   They can be waived ("alienated") by the right-holder. For example, Bob could waive his right of confidentiality by saying, "Oh, go ahead; tell Carol."
2   Nor are rights absolutely binding. Persons can lose their rights as a result of immoral behavior – e.g., those convicted of capital crimes lose the right to life (in some states).
3   Rights can be overridden if respecting them leads to catastrophe. A man steals a car from a neighbor who refuses to let him borrow it (and because the

neighbor owns the car, he has a right to withhold its use) to rush his chok-
ing child to the emergency room (preventing the catastrophe of her death)
(Brody 1988: 22–32).

Comparing Bob's right of confidentiality with Carol's right to know of threats
to her welfare, we discover the following:

1   Neither Carol nor Bob has waived the right in question; in fact, Bob is insist-
    ing that his right be respected. Since Carol does not know she has been exposed
    to a health threat, she cannot possibly have waived her right to know about
    that threat.
2   Has either person lost the right through immoral behavior? Both behaved
    foolishly, but only Bob behaved immorally: he knowingly (though we might
    suspect that he, like Carol, did not choose autonomously to behave badly)
    exposed Carol to a disease. (Note that had Carol autonomously – that is,
    knowingly – consented to this exposure, she would have waived her right to
    not be threatened with a harm. But, as noted above, we have good reasons
    to think that her consent to the risk was not autonomous. Certainly she had
    not been informed about Bob's gonorrhea.)
3   Finally, does some potential catastrophe warrant overriding Carol's right
    to be informed of threats to her health? The only candidate is Bob's embar-
    rassment. Perhaps Bob is so unusually sensitive that his shame and embar-
    rassment could reach catastrophic proportions (e.g., driving him to suicide,
    or some such disastrous outcome), but – given what we know about typical
    feelings of shame and embarrassment – this is unlikely. Rather, we assume
    he will get over his psychological distress. Since Bob is a friend, our predic-
    tions of his psychological responses are likely to be reasonably accurate.

Conversely, does some possible future catastrophe warrant overriding Bob's
right of confidentiality? The potentially negative health outcomes for Carol are
not genuinely catastrophic, so overriding Bob's right to confidentiality is not clearly
justified. Still, as these outcomes are uniformly negative and some are potentially quite serious (e.g., the possibility of infertility), they provide some support
for overriding Bob's right. The possibility of Carol's infertility is quite likely
material (i.e., determinative). Certainly, these outcomes seem to warrant greater
moral concern than Bob's embarrassment.
    In sum, the appeal to rights provides more support for telling Carol than for
keeping Bob's secret.
    We come now to what many would see as the heart of the matter: being
a good friend. We might think of friendship as a role we assume. Like other
established or familiar roles (e.g., the role of being a parent, the role of being
a physician), the role of friend carries certain expectations. Just as the physician
demonstrates the virtue of professional integrity when she puts her patients' interests ahead of the interests of others, so the friend demonstrates the virtue
of personal integrity when he puts his friends' interests ahead of others. The problem here is that Ted's personal integrity requires him to violate the interests of

one friend to promote the interests of the other: protecting Carol's interests (Reason #11) requires disrespecting Bob's interests (Reason #9), and vice versa. Whatever Ted does, he cannot avoid behaving unvirtuously. Does Ted have any means of comparing the interests at stake?

Interests come in varying degrees of importance. Carol's interests – preserving/ restoring her health and future reproductive capacity – just do seem more significant than Bob's interest in avoiding embarrassment. (Again, we are assuming that Bob is not unusually psychologically fragile.) That is, Carol's welfare is more severely threatened than is Bob's. If this assumption is correct, the virtue of the integrity of friendship gives Ted a good reason for promoting Carol's interests over Bob's: Carol's interests in this case are weightier than Bob's. That is, the virtue of integrity of friendship indicates that Ted should tell Carol she has been exposed to gonorrhea.

But what about Ted's promise to Bob to keep his comments in confidence (Reason #8)? The virtue of fidelity (doing what one has promised) supports keeping Bob's secret. But this appeal may be weak, given the circumstances in which the promise was made: Ted was barely awake and made the promise without thinking or without any idea of what was at stake. Had he any inkling of what Bob planned to tell him, he might not have made the promise. In short, this promise does not seem to be especially weighty (even though the topic surely is). Finally, if Ted reveals Bob's confidence, he can "make it up to" Bob. He can spend extra time with Bob, promote Bob's other interests, help Bob overcome his shame, convince Bob of the wisdom of telling Carol, etc. Ted cannot, however, behave similarly with Carol: if he fails to provide her with the only and very specific help she needs, he cannot compensate in other ways, as he can with Bob. Thus the virtue of fidelity seems fairly weak here. (Note, though, that Ted need not tell Carol that Bob was the source of her exposure. After all, he only assumes that to be the case; Carol could have been exposed by someone else.)

In sum, the appeal to consequences demonstrates that worse outcomes will result from keeping Bob's secret. The appeal to autonomy is stronger than it may initially appear: failure to reveal her exposure uses Carol as a means merely to prevent Bob's psychological distress, failing to respect her as an autonomous person. Carol's right to be informed outweighs Bob's right to confidentiality. Finally, the virtue of personal integrity demonstrates that Carol's welfare is more binding on her friend, Ted, than is Bob's.

Ted should tell Carol that she has been exposed to gonorrhea.

Additional Issues to Consider

Other possible moral dilemmas arising within this case:

Q Do persons who engage in unprotected sex forfeit their moral claims on their partners (e.g., right to know about threats to their own health)?

Q Do persons whose level of inebriation leads to poor decisions forfeit their moral claims on others (e.g., right to be aided)?

Q Are good friends morally obligated to help get their friends out of trouble?

REFERENCES

Brody, B. A. (1982) Towards a theory of respect for persons. In O. H. Green (ed.), *Respect for Persons: Tulane Studies in Philosophy* 31. New Orleans, LA: Tulane University Press, pp. 61–76.

Brody, B. A. (1988) *Life and Death Decision Making*. New York: Oxford University Press.

CDC (2008) Gonorrhea – CDC fact sheet. Department of Health and Human Services. Centers for Disease Control and Prevention. Available at: www.cdc.gov/std/Health Comm/fact_sheets.htm (accessed June 16, 2008).

Faden, R. R., and Beauchamp, T. L. (1986) *A History and Theory of Informed Consent*. New York: Oxford University Press.

Mayo Clinic Staff (2007) Gonorrhea (January 12, 2007). Available at: www.mayoclinic.com/health/gonorrhea/DS00180 (accessed October 5, 2007).

White, B. C. (1994) *Competence to Consent*. Washington, DC: Georgetown University Press.

CASE THIRTEEN: GIVE US YOUR TIRED, YOUR POOR, YOUR HEALTHCARE PROFESSIONALS – RECRUITING NURSES FROM DEVELOPING NATIONS

Australia, Canada, the United Kingdom (UK), and the United States (US) are facing an increasing shortage of professional nurses. Australia's nursing shortage is anticipated to reach 12–13,000 by 2010 (Productivity Commission 2005: 12). The Canadian Nursing Association projects that Canada will be short by roughly 78,000 nurses by 2011 (CNA 2002). The UK needs 35,000 more nurses by 2008 (Buchan 2004: S1:11); and in the US the deficit is expected to reach 275,000 nurses by 2010 and 800,000 nurses by 2020 (Brush et al. 2004: 78).

As populations grow older in developed countries, more nurses are needed to manage the increasing morbidity typically associated with aging. Older patients more frequently face chronic illnesses and the complications thereof, which benefit from more healthcare interventions and oversight. Further, with a move away from extended hospitalization, patients in hospitals are sicker (requiring more nursing attention) and, upon discharge, often require more home healthcare than in times past. All these factors contribute to an increased need for nurses: "Projections from the [US] Bureau of Labor Statistics through 2006 show that positions for RNs will experience faster than average employment growth, with job opportunities increasing by 21 percent in nursing, versus 14 percent for all occupations. Government projections indicate that demand for RNs will out-strip supply by 2010" (Duke University Health System 2003: para 17).

The importance of registered nurses in generating positive and avoiding neg-ative health outcomes is well documented (ANA 2000; McKenna 1998; Stanton 2004). Patients who receive their care from a registered nurse (RN) are less likely to experience urinary tract infections, pneumonia, shock, or cardiac arrest. RN care also shortens lengths of hospital stay. But as job opportunities for women expand, fewer enter nursing (although 92 percent of nurses are still women).

Additional reasons for the declining number of nurses are many (Aiken et al. 2004: 71; Buchan 2004: S1:14; ICN 2001: table 1; Stone et al. 2003). Nurses are perceived to have limited professional autonomy and restricted input into healthcare decisions and policies (Hardill and Macdonald 2000: 682–3); many nurses object to the transformation of hospitals into businesses, where the focus on the "bottom line" is manifested by ruthless cost-control measures, prema-ture patient discharges, and drastic understaffing – all of which make proper professional performance difficult and sometimes virtually impossible (Berliner and Ginsberg 2002: 2744). Such onerous working conditions contribute to increased and earlier burnout, accelerating the retirement of nursing professionals (ibid.: 2742). Further, although nursing is one of the most psychologically and physically demanding of professions, wages are comparatively low and have declined in terms of inflation-adjusted purchasing power. Age also plays a factor, with the average age of nurses rising as the average age of the general population rises. Finally, even if more persons desired to enter nursing, a paucity of nursing schools and declining numbers of qualified professors of nursing virtually insure a wor-sening shortage (Buerhaus et al. 2003: 196; Goodin 2003: 336–7; Press release 2003: 2).

In an attempt to alleviate this shortage, many healthcare institutions in devel-oped nations recruit foreign-born and foreign-educated nurses, particularly from developing nations. According to the US Census Bureau, of the 2.4 million US-registered nurses, 3.5 percent received their education outside the country (HRSA 2004: 14). Further: "From the mid-1990s through 2001, employment among foreign-born RNs increased 6 percent a year, faster than for domestic RNs generally. . . . In 2002, employment of foreign-born RNs increased 13.8 per-cent" (Press release 2003: 2). In the UK, 8 percent of the 645,000 nurses are foreign-born, as are approximately 7 percent of Canadian nurses. In 2002 the UK saw more foreign-trained than native-trained nurses enter its workforce (Aiken et al. 2004: 73; Batata 2005: 1). In addition to recruitment to meet general demands for RNs, countries with significant immigrant populations often target RNs from those same populations; for example, US states with large Latino populations recruit heavily from Mexico, hoping to acquire RNs who can both communicate with and understand the cultural particulars of Latino patients. Great Britain employs a disproportionate number of Indian RNs, especially in urban areas with large Indian populations.

Nurses emigrate for many reasons: to attain better educational and professional development opportunities; to avail themselves of better working conditions; and to escape adverse environments or unsafe working conditions in their home countries (Bach 2003: 2, 7; Buchan et al. 2003: 2; Buchan and Calman 2005:

10–11; Kingma 2006: 13–36 and ch. 2; ICN 2001: 5–6; Kline 2003: 108). Economic advancement is a particularly compelling motivation for emigrating from an underdeveloped to an industrialized country (Martineau et al. 2004: 2).

While the needs of developed countries and the attractions for emigration can be appreciated, developing countries desperately need their nurses. The "brain drain" of nurses from developing nations has significant noxious implications for their native countries (Kingma 2006: ch. 6). Without nurses, healthcare access and quality suffer immensely, and underserved populations are unlikely to receive much (if any) healthcare at all. Sub-Saharan African countries will need 620,000 nurses by 2010 to meet the profound health crises that disproportionately affect their impoverished populations (Buchan and Calman 2005: 4). The World Health Organization (WHO) notes that the flight of healthcare professionals from Africa severely compromises that continent's ability to respond to its HIV/AIDS epidemic (BBC News 2007), and to deal with its widespread endemic infectious diseases, such as tuberculosis and malaria (Batata 2005; Buchan and Calman 2005: 4; WHO 2006: 11).

Finally, developing countries, which heavily subsidize nursing education, lose the return on their intellectual investments when their nurses – educated at public expense – emigrate. The United Nations has estimated that each migrant African health professional (of whom nurses are one example) represents a loss of $184,000 (Brush et al. 2004: 82). Their departures leave nurses' home countries facing their own serious labor deficits (Batata 2005; Martineau 2004).

Is the recruitment, by developed nations, of RNs from developing countries morally permissible?

Perspective One

Recruiting RNs from developing countries is morally permissible.

The consequences of recruiting nurses from developing countries are many and positive. First, benefits will accrue to the patients in developed countries, whose morbidity and mortality rates will be reduced. Since morbidity can reduce – in some cases, significantly – the quality of a patient's life, a healthcare workforce that reduces that morbidity contributes positively to that quality of life. Of course, mortality by definition makes a good life impossible and for that reason alone, other things being equal, is to be avoided whenever possible.

As indicated in the case itself, data suggest that these benefits to life and health will not be achieved without importing nurses. Developed countries all face an increasing shortage of nurses, and good reasons suggest that this shortage will continue. First, consider age. The average age of nurses in developed countries is increasing: the typical nurse in the US is nearly 47 years old (HRSA 2004: 5). In the UK approximately 27 percent of nurses (approximately 100,000) are over the age of 55 (RCN 2005: 47; Batata 2005); in Canada, the average age of nurses is almost 45 years old (Canadian Institute for Health Education 2006: 3); and in Australia 38 percent of nurses are over 45 years of age (CDEST 2001). Not surprisingly, as the average age of nurses increases, death and retirement exact a proportionally larger decline in the nursing workforce (Buerhaus et al. 2003: 196). Moreover, the average age of nursing students in developed countries continues to rise (HRSA 2004: 11; RCN 2005: 46), implying fewer years of professional contribution per graduate. And, according to the American Association of Colleges of Nursing, entry-level BSN (Bachelor of Science in Nursing degree) enrollment fell 4.6 percent in fall 1999, dropping for the fifth year in a row (Duke University Health System 2003: para 14). If the increasing health-care needs of increasingly aging populations are to be successfully addressed, nurses will need to be imported (Martineau et al. 2004: 4–5).

Further, nurses who emigrate to developed nations will benefit from the better working conditions they will find there (Batata 2005). Nurses in developing countries often practice in desperately unhealthy environs; for example, lack of running water makes providing a clean (let alone a sterile) environment difficult, if not impossible (Buchan and Sochalski 2004: 591–2; Martineau et al. 2004: 6–8; WHO 2006: xxii). In such circumstances, achieving professional goals becomes a pipe dream and the frustration of these ubiquitous, insurmountable barriers to professional excellence is demoralizing. This is a recipe for burnout, and countries that do not correct or ameliorate these wretched working conditions should not be surprised by a mass exodus of nurses from jobs in such surroundings – if not from the profession itself. If, however, nurses migrate to developed nations where working conditions are better, they are more likely to enjoy – and continue practicing within – the profession.

Nor is the profession itself the only victim of unsanitary conditions. Nurses themselves are at risk for contracting the infectious diseases that are endemic in their own countries. In South Africa, an estimated 15 percent of health workers are HIV-positive (Ehlers 2006: 660). In sub-Saharan Africa and in India, tuberculosis is endemic. No one should have to practice in conditions that endanger their own health. Providing nurses with employment options that enable them to escape exposure to these life- and health-threatening infectious diseases would be beneficent.

Further, nurses who relocate to developed countries have far more extensive and diverse opportunities for professional growth and advanced education (Buchan 2006: 458). As many developing nations are unable to provide post-baccalaureate opportunities, RNs in these countries are stymied in their attempts to gain further qualifications. Relocating to a developed country allows them to pursue higher education up to Master's level, become nurse practitioners, and train as nurse midwives. As many nurses do eventually return to their countries of origin, they not only enrich their own lives, but those of their fellow citizens as well, by bringing advanced skills back to their home countries.

Immigrating nurses will further benefit by receiving better wages. In the Philippines, for example, the typical hospital nurse's *annual* salary is $2,000–$2,400 (Brush et al. 2004: 81) – roughly equal to the *monthly* salary of a nurse working in the UK. An RN working in a Mexican hospital makes $4,200 per year – compared to an average salary of $57,784 in the US (HRSA 2004: 9). Admittedly, the cost of living in developed countries is greater than the cost of living in developing countries. Nonetheless, nursing salaries in developed countries enable them to live comfortable middle-class lives – which is not the case in many of their native countries.

Finally, the emigration of nurses from developing countries benefits their families and native countries, because many of these nurses are able to send significant amounts of money back home. Many families rely heavily on this money – not for luxuries, but to meet basic subsistence needs. Countries also rely on the infusion of monies from emigrant citizens. Filipinos living abroad, for example, return more than $800 million dollars each year to their families and home country, funds that constitute a significant contribution to the Filipino economy (Kline 2003: 109).

In sum, the consequences to patients in developed countries and to emigrating nurses, their native countries, and their families are uniformly positive.

The appeal to consequences provides striking moral support for recruiting nurses from developing countries. But if this appeal is not sufficient in and of itself, it can be bolstered by an appeal to self-determination (autonomy): the nurses are *choosing* to leave their home countries to work in recruiting nations. Given the choice between staying and leaving, tens of thousands of nurses choose to leave. Since freedom of movement and association are not only necessary conditions for operationalizing autonomous choice but are also basic human rights (ICN 2001: 1), these choices must be respected. Obstructing emigration of nurses would obstruct the most basic of human rights – freedom to live one's life as one sees fit – and would be tantamount to slavery.

In conclusion, the appeals to consequences – to nurses themselves and to their patients, families, and source countries – and to autonomy and to basic human rights provide strong moral support for recruiting RNs from developing countries.

Perspective Two

Recruiting RNs from developing countries is not morally permissible. The negative consequences of recruiting RNs from developing nations are many and serious.

First, nurses provide the vast majority of healthcare in developing nations (WHO 2001: 11–15). In many countries, nurses, midwives, and allied health personnel are the main providers of healthcare, particularly in rural and remote areas where the most vulnerable populations reside:

> [I]n Chile 92% of child health visits are by nurses; in Colombia more than 75% of consultations for expectant mothers are by nurses; in Kiribati nurses are the only health workers in the rural and remote areas; in Samoa 99.5% of all healthcare is provided by nurses; and in Indonesia the use of community midwives increased antenatal coverage from 74% to 88%. (Ibid.: 14)

In developing nations nursing care is critical to reducing maternal and infant mortality.

Take, for example, prenatal care. The single greatest factor in giving birth to a healthy newborn is to have that baby born at term (as opposed to being born prematurely). The single greatest factor in full-term birth is access to prenatal care, during which the health of the pregnant woman and, derivatively, of the fetus are maximized by regular visits to assess health status and to provide prompt attention to complications of pregnancy (e.g., anemia, urinary tract infection). Just limiting this analysis to the countries cited immediately above, we can infer that a loss of nurses in Columbia and Indonesia would jeopardize the health of pregnant women and significantly decrease the probability of the birth of healthy babies in those countries. According to the WHO, a country should, at minimum, provide prenatal care to 80 percent of its pregnant women. Using this baseline, Africa will need to increase its healthcare professionals (doctors, nurses and midwives) by 139 percent, while the Americas need only a 40 percent increase. Europe already meets this standard (WHO 2006: 13).

Consider, second, the immense problem of infectious diseases in sub-Saharan Africa. The administration of vaccines against tuberculosis and of complicated pharmaceutical regimens needed to control HIV disease is currently directly dependent on the presence of nurses – nurses who increasingly leave their countries seeking better working conditions.

Clearly, the health and welfare of the population in developing countries depends heavily – often exclusively – on nurses. Yet Zimbabwe (for example) lost roughly 30 percent of its 2001 class of graduating nurses to the UK. In 2000 twice as many nurses left Ghana as graduated that year from Ghanian nursing schools (Brush et al. 2004: 78). Chad needs to increase its workforce by 300 percent, and the United Republic of Tanzania has only 60 percent of the health professionals it needs (WHO 2006: 11).

In sum, further loss of nurses from developing countries will have devastating health effects on the populations of those countries, populations that already are disproportionately burdened by avoidable morbidities and early mortality.

Furthermore, emigration raises questions of justice. Most of these nurses are indebted to the governments in their home countries for their education (Buchan and Sochalski 2004: 588). Had their governments not funded nursing programs, the nurses would have no recruit-worthy skills. But governments fund educational programs to promote the health and welfare of their own citizens, not citizens of other countries. In accepting an education, be it in nursing or some other profession, the recipient of this benefit receives an *undeserved benefit*, in virtue of which he or she incurs a debt of gratitude. Put a bit differently, nurses educated at their countries' expense owe their countries something in return for resources expended on their behalf. Failure to repay this debt is not only selfish, but may be thought to constitute theft of communal resources.

Several moral norms are at stake here. First (and assuming a zero-sum game), this theft harms one's community by usurping resources that could have been used so as actually to promote the general welfare. So the moral obligation of nonmaleficence is violated. Second, the nurses themselves have received an *undeserved benefit* or, more accurately, a benefit that they cannot deserve except *post facto*: only after they repay their debts can they be said to (have) deserve(d) the investment made in their education. Failure to repay the debt then becomes an unjust allocation of scarce community resources, that is, a failure of justice that afflicts all parties. Nurses who abscond with their undeserved educations deny their fellow citizens relief of their undeserved health burdens. So the principle of justice (understood as fairness) is violated as well.

In conclusion, the appeals to consequences, both individual and collective, and to justice (fairness) argue against nurse recruitment from developing countries.

Perspective Three

Is recruiting RNs from developing countries morally permissible? At its most basic level this question represents a conflict between the consequences to patients in developing countries versus the consequences to patients in developed countries, both of whom need (more) nurses to maximize their health status. To determine the morally preferable answer, further information is needed.

Step 1: Information-gathering

Implications

- What are the health outcomes on patients if *developing* countries have too few nurses?
- What are the health outcomes on patients if *developed* countries have too few nurses?
- What are the workplace outcomes for *developing* countries if nurses emigrate?
- What are the workplace outcomes for *developed* countries if nurses immigrate?

Legal/policy information

- Are immigration laws relevant here?
- Do codes of ethics give any guidance about nurse recruitment?
- Do codes of ethics give any guidance about nurse emigration, particularly from countries that subsidize nursing education?

Psychological information

- What are the likely psychological effects of restricting recruitment?
- What are the likely psychological effects of permitting recruitment?
- What are the likely psychological effects on emigrating nurses?
- Do developed countries believe that they have some claim on resources (here, nurses) from developing countries?

History

- Is the long tradition of usurping the resources of developing countries at work here?
- Has the commercialization of healthcare in the US contributed to its nursing shortage?

Economics

- What are the likely economic effects of permitting recruitment?
- What are the likely economic effects of not permitting recruitment?

Step 2: Creative problem-solving

The case as written suggests a conflict between promoting good outcomes for patients in developed countries and promoting good outcomes for patients in developing countries. Dramatically increasing the number of nurses in all countries would enable both populations to be adequately cared for, but – for reasons addressed in the case (particularly, the shortages of nursing schools and faculty) – this seems unlikely in the foreseeable future. So the conflict persists.

Since a creative solution is unavailable, we consider the pros and cons of the original options.

Step 3: Listing pros and cons

Options	Pros	Cons
Nurse recruitment should be allowed.	1. Improves health outcomes for patients in developed countries (C-B, C-U) 2. Immigrant nurses have better educational opportunities (C-B, C-U) 3. Immigrant nurses are more economically secure (C-B) 4. Immigrant nurses' families are more economically secure (C-U) 5. Emigrant nurses' home countries benefit economically (C-U) 6. Protects nurses' autonomy (A) 7. Respects liberty rights (R)	8. Constitutes theft of scarce resources from developing countries (C-NM, C-U) 9. Entices migrating nurses to unjustly usurp undeserved scarce resources from developing countries (J-F) 10. Risks noxious and inequitable treatment of emigrating nurses (C-NM, J-E)
Nurse recruitment should not be allowed.	11. Thwarts improved health outcomes of patients in developing countries (C-NM, C-U) 12. Thwarts improved working conditions in both developing and developed nations (C-U) 13. Unfairly burdens patients in developing countries (J-F) 14. May prompt commitment of more resources to fund schools of nursing and training of nursing faculty (C-U)	

Step 4: Analysis

Factual assumptions

- Persons in developed and in developing countries all suffer from too few registered nurses.
- Populations in developing countries have greater *lifetime* morbidity and earlier mortality than populations in developed countries.
- Registered nurses working in developing countries will decrease morbidity and mortality of the populations they serve.
- Populations in developing countries often have access to no other healthcare professionals than registered nurses.
- Improved financial conditions for emigrating nurses and their families is less impressive than is often believed.
- Developed countries have other/more options for increasing their supplies of registered nurses than do developing countries.

Value assumptions

- Persons should have a reasonable probability of achieving a species-typical lifespan.
- Respect for persons requires that no one should be treated differently based on their country of origin.
- Countries should not usurp valuable resources of other countries.
- Registered nurses in developing countries should repay the resources their countries have invested in their education.

Step 5: Justification

Developed nations should not actively recruit registered nurses from developing countries. Appeals to the moral principles of consequences and justice support this position.

A quick glance at the pros and cons chart indicates that, in keeping with the foci of earlier perspectives, this dilemma is one of competing consequences for patients in developed and developing countries (Reasons ##1, 11). This same *quick* look suggests that two populations are in *equal* need of a scarce resource – nursing care – and that the position that provides nursing care to one population *and* is bolstered by further positive states of affairs will be most morally defensible. This suggestion of equality is, however, illusory. The World Health Organization notes:

> Countries with the lowest relative need have the highest numbers of health workers, while those with the greatest burden of disease must make do with a much smaller health workforce. . . . The Region of the Americas, which includes Canada

and the United States, contains only 10% of the global burden of disease, yet almost 37% of the world's health workers. . . . In contrast, the African Region suffers more than 24% of the global burden of disease but has access to only 3% of the health workers. (WHO 2006)

Consider, first, nurse/patient ratios (NPRs) (see, generally, Buchan and Calman 2005). The ratio of nurses to patients in the UK is 5.9:1,000; that is, 590 nurses for every 100,000 patients (RCN 2005: 14). In Australia, Canada, and the US, the NPRs are 830:100,000, 897:100,000, and 972:100,000 respectively (Kline 2003: 109). Compare these ratios with those in China (99:100,000), India (45:100,000), and Pakistan (34:100,000) (ibid.), or Uganda: 6:100,000 (Buchan 2006: 457). The unexamined claim – that developed and developing nations are *equally* in need of professional nurses – dramatically misrepresents reality. In fact, patients in developing nations are woefully underserved *even if they retain all their registered nurses*. Yet, "In 2005 . . . 44 nurses graduated in Malawi while 86 left the country" (BBC News 2007: 8).

This patient–professional disparity in itself contributes to significant extant differences in health status. For example, in 2001, the average lifespan in the US was 77.1 years. However, "life expectancy in Zimbabwe plummeted from 56 years in 1970–5 to just 33.1 today. Zambia went from 49.7 years to 32.4 in the same period, Lesotho from 49.5 to 35.1, and Botswana from 56.1 to 39.7" (*Christian Science Monitor* 2004: para 10). The under-5 mortality rate in the UK is 6/1,000 live births, while in Botswana that rate is 124/1,000 – up from 58 in 1990 (UNICEF 2007: 56–7). In Botswana, an estimated 270/1,000 persons are living with HIV (UNICEF n.d.(b)); in Australia the rate of infection is 16/1,000 (UNICEF n.d.(a)). In Canada, tuberculosis is infrequently seen, while in India this disease is endemic. Even more shocking is that lifespans in many of the sub-Saharan countries, as noted just above, have *decreased* over the last decade.

Perhaps the most morally significant difference is what nursing care achieves in developing and developed nations. Increasingly, healthcare problems in developed nations involve the management of older adults afflicted with a chronic illness or the complications thereof (e.g., diabetics with renal disease). Conversely, many patients whom a nurse will encounter in a developing nation are children who are victims of an acute (i.e., immediate) life- or health-threatening illness. In these environs, nurses will often be lifesavers – for example, providing the fluid replacement that saves the lives of children with rotovirus; vaccinating populations against myriad infectious diseases which can be fatal in a country lacking healthcare facilities; providing, explaining, and administering the medication regime that will control HIV disease. In developing countries, nurses provide the prenatal care that reduces premature birth, with its attendant and often life-long impairments; they deliver the babies and manage the complications encountered by the mother and infant in the perinatal period. The greater the number of nurses, the greater the amount of prenatal care received by women (WHO 2006: 11ff).

Why are these disparate population characteristics and health outcomes morally relevant? The basic argument is articulated by Norman Daniels (1985, 1988). If self-interested, rational persons are given the (hypothetical) choice of healthcare that will give them a good shot at a life that approximates a normal lifespan *or, instead*, healthcare that extends one's lifespan after they have already achieved old age, they will choose the former. That is, if healthcare must be rationed, disinterested persons sensibly will choose care that gives them many healthy years rather than healthcare that will extend their later (and often unhealthy) life over a few months (or even years). By extension, rational, self-interested persons will allocate nursing resources in ways that will contribute to a longer, healthier life from birth on, rather than a longer life from old age to death. This, according to Daniels, is only fair – everyone deserves an equal chance to achieve a species-typical lifespan. Put differently, no one deserves to be burdened with an early death or a lifetime of disability when these could have been prevented. Moreover, the burden of knowing that early deaths and disabilities could have been prevented magnifies pain and suffering. To provide extra care for the elderly who are fortunate enough to reside in developed countries rather than providing even basic care to unfortunate youth in developing countries is unjust (Reasons ##10, 13), an undeserved burden (or, in the case of getting care, an undeserved benefit).

In sum, the extent and magnitude of the negative consequences to developing countries that will accompany emigration of their nurses cannot be exaggerated. Further, respecting persons in developing countries requires not depriving them of a service that is crucial for their achieving a species-typical lifespan. Doing so saddles them with particularly heinous and undeserved burdens – early mortality and life-long morbidity. Although patients in developed countries will also suffer greater morbidity and earlier mortality, the extent and the timing of these will be less striking: they will lose fewer life years than residents in developing countries.

Achieving the health benefits that will enable residents of developing countries to achieve a normal lifespan will, however, require keeping a sufficient number of nurses in these countries. The toll on healthcare providers of too many patients cared for by too few nurses is well documented (McKenna 1998: 1403). As more and more people die or become chronically unhealthy, and as hope of reversing these trends fades or is altogether obliterated, nurses are more likely to quit their jobs (or even their profession). One effect of the loss of nurses is that even more people die and, as a result, even more nurses leave, *ad indefinitum*. This vicious cycle can only be broken with enough nurses in place to make a difference in health outcomes (ibid.).

Brief mention must be made of the cluster of beneficial consequences that are projected for emigrating nurses and their families (Reasons ##2, 3, 4, 5). While emigrating nurses often will have enhanced educational opportunities, their economic status may not be enhanced. True, the salaries they make in developed countries would increase their purchasing power *if they made those salaries in their own countries*; but the cost of living in the countries in which they are employed often minimizes the hoped-for economic advantage. Furthermore, immigrant nurses are often paid less than their native-born colleagues (Buchan 2004: S1:15). These realities make sending money home to needy families more difficult than anticipated. Moreover, immigrants commonly are assigned the least desirable working conditions, such as night shifts, inner city or rural clinics, etc. (Martineau et al. 2004: 3–4); indeed, many nurses are assigned non-nursing duties and paid commensurately lower wages (ICN 1999; Bosely 2005: para 10).

Beyond the short-term health outcomes of particular individuals is the need for a long-term solution to the shortage of professional nurses (Reason #12). Recruiting foreign nurses is, at best, a stop-gap measure that does nothing to address – and thus, to eradicate – the conditions that have led to the nursing shortage in developed countries (Reason #14) (Chaguturu and Vallabhaneni 2005; DeRaeve 2003; Goodin 2003; Mullen 2003; Wickett et al. 2003). Consider the reasons most nurses in developed countries give for working only part-time, for quitting, or for retiring early:

- no respect, at least in part because nursing is denigrated as "woman's work" (Buchan 2006: 458; Goodin 2003: 338, 340; Hardill and Macdonald 2000: 682–3);
- no autonomy in planning patient care or controlling working conditions (Sochalski 2002: 161);
- no flexibility in working schedule (ibid.: 159);
- low pay: in the past 15 years nursing has, at best, kept up with inflation (Bergmann 2006; Sochalski 2002: 161); further, nurses with 20 years' experience earned only 10 percent more than new graduates just beginning their careers (Sochalski 2002: 162);
- horrendous working conditions, including but not limited to too few nurses, making providing high quality patient care difficult, if not impossible (WHO 2006: xxii; ANA 2001).

Not surprisingly, these factors commonly and quickly lead to burnout and resignation or early retirement (Sochalski 2002: 161), thereby contributing to the nursing shortage.

The foreign-born nurse may, in comparing these noxious conditions to those in her own country, wonder why her colleagues are complaining. After all, things could be (and, in her own country, usually are) so much worse. But given the nurse/patient ratios that patients in developed countries have come to expect, importing nurses will never be enough to meet the nursing need. Developed countries simply must take steps to make nurses' working conditions sufficiently positive to recruit *and retain* far greater numbers of professional nurses (Reason #14) (Buerhaus et al. 2003: 196–7).

In sum, an all-things-considered appeal to consequences (i.e., an appeal to utility) demonstrates that the morally defensible outcome is achieved through non-recruitment. True, recruitment would likely draw more nurses to developed nations. Also true, this immigration would, in the short term, ameliorate (though not eliminate) the nursing shortage in the receiving countries. And, yes, patients in developed countries would profit – temporarily – from the influx of professional nurses. But the advantages are only temporary; and the disadvantages to the populations of contributing countries are profoundly noxious, ongoing, and – as mortality statistics document – worsening. Again, respect for persons in developing countries requires not depriving them of a species-typical lifespan or encumbering them with the undeserved burdens of early mortality and lifelong morbidity (Reasons ##10, 13). The extent and magnitude of the negative, disrespectful, and unfair outcomes for residents of developing countries that will accompany emigration of their nurses are profound. Although patients in developed countries will also suffer greater morbidity and earlier mortality, they will lose fewer life years than patients in developing countries.

The critic will charge that nurses from developing countries, like all humans, must be free to travel where they choose (Reason #6); indeed, they have a right to this freedom (Reason #7). To restrict their emigration would violate one of their most basic human rights – liberty. But the question before us here is not about blocking emigration, but about the moral propriety of encouraging it. Certainly, nurses who choose to leave their countries should be allowed to do so; but enticing their departure, in the face of so great a need for their services in their home countries, is a horse of a different color. The negative liberty right of freedom of movement does not translate into a positive right to be provided with (nor a duty to provide nurses with, or even inform them about) circumstances that they might find more to their liking. In fact, providing such information might be seen as tempting nurses to abandon their duties to the societies that have educated them and enabled them to enjoy professional opportunities at all (Reason #9).

This concern, of course, has justice at its heart. Most countries (the US being the notable exception) finance the professional education of their healthcare professionals (Aiken et al. 2004: 76). Their motives for doing so are not – or at least not wholly – altruistic. True, the students get a good education without direct costs to themselves; and, as a result of this education, the students become professionals with a markedly expanded arena of job opportunities that will enable them to achieve a better lifestyle than they would face without this education. All this benefits the students/nurses. But governments' primary motivation is the welfare of their societies, considered collectively – and by that we do not mean merely the improved health outcomes for a group of *individuals* but, rather, a holistic well-being. Because citizens live better lives individually, they contribute to the improvement of the collective welfare. The educated professional can participate fruitfully in public life; through her better wages, she is a positive influence on the economy; she provides services that her neighbors need; etc. Thus, government-funded education is, at least in part, a quid pro quo: we will educate you so that you will be able to help make the country a better place to live. Although such agreements may not be formally (i.e., contractually) stipulated, they are widely understood to be in force. Thus, the person who emigrates fails to hold up her end of the bargain (Reason #9). To entice persons to ignore their civic duties, especially if such temptation is successful, counts as theft of a valuable social resource (Reason #8).

In sum, while the consequences to patients in developed countries are improved by immigrant nurses, the consequences to the nurses themselves are mixed. Moreover, the consequences to patients in developing countries are uniformly and significantly noxious. So, at best, an appeal to consequences is a "tie" – a tie that an appeal to justice breaks. The negative outcomes to residents of developing countries are undeserved. A just system gives persons a fair shot at a decent life over an average lifespan only if resources are abundant. Thus, only after a decent average lifespan is achieved for all should nurses from developing countries be imported.

Therefore, recruiting nurses from developing countries is morally wrong: it is maleficent, disrespectful, and unjust.

Additional Issues to Consider

Other possible moral dilemmas arising within this case:

Q Is emigrating (in the absence of active recruitment) from developing countries to nurse in developed countries morally permissible?

Q Which, if any, moral rights are in conflict here; and why?

Q What role, if any, does justice play in deciding appropriate actions of nurse recruiters?

Q Are developing countries morally responsible for alleviating the conditions in their own countries that contribute to their nursing shortage?

REFERENCES

Aiken, L. H., Buchan, J., Sochalski, J., et al. (2004) Trends in international nurse migration. *Health Affairs* 23 (3): 69–77.
Aiken, L. H., Clarke, S. P., Sloan, D. M., et al. (2002) Hospital nurse staffing and patient mortality, nurse burnout, and job satisfaction. *JAMA: Journal of the American Medical Association* 288 (16): 1987–93.
ANA (American Nurses Association) (1999) Principles for nurse staffing. Available at: http://nursingworld.org/MainMenuCategories/HealthcareandPolicyIssues/Reports/ANAPrinciples/NurseStaffing/PrincipleswithBibliography.aspx (accessed June 16, 2008).
ANA (American Nurses Association) (2000) Executive summary. Nurse staffing and patient outcomes in the inpatient hospital setting. *Nursing World* (March). Available at: http://nursingworld.org/FunctionalMenuCategories/MediaResources/PressReleases/2000/NurseStaffing.aspx (accessed June 16, 2008).
ANA (American Nurses Association) (2001) Press release: Nurses concerned over working conditions, decline in quality of care, ANA survey reveals. *Nursing World*

(February 6). Available at: www.nursingworld.org/FunctionalMenuCategories/
MediaResources/PressReleases/2001/ANAPressRelease.aspx (accessed June 16, 2008).

Bach, S. (2003) International migration of health workers: labour and social issues (working paper). International Labour Office, Geneva. Available at: www.ilo.org/public/english/dialogue/sector/papers/health/wp209.pdf (accessed October 6, 2007).

Batata, A. S. (2005) International nurse recruitment and NHS vacancies: a cross-sectional analysis. *Globalization and Health* 1 (7). Available at: www.globalizationandhealth.com/content/1/1/7 (accessed October 6, 2007).

BBC News (2007) Lack of nurses "killing Africans" (May 24). Available at: http://news.bbc.co.uk/2/hi/africa/6689255.stm (accessed October 6, 2007).

Bergmann, B. R. (2006) Curing the nursing shortage: the role of compensation. *New England Journal of Medicine* 354 (15): 1648–9.

Berliner, H. S., and Ginsberg, E. (2002) Why this hospital nursing shortage is different. *JAMA: Journal of the American Medical Association* 288 (21): 2742–4.

Bosely, S. (2005) UK agencies still hiring poorest nations' nurses. *Guardian Unlimited* (UK) (December 20). Available at: www.guardian.co.uk/frontpage/story/0,,1671243,00.html (accessed 6 October 2007).

Brush, B., Sochalski, J., and Berger, A. M. (2004) Imported care: recruiting foreign nurses to US health care facilities. *Health Affairs* 23 (3): 78–87.

Buchan, J. (2004) International rescue? The dynamics and policy implications of the international recruitment of nurses to the UK. *Journal of Health Services Research & Policy* 9 (suppl. 1 to issue 1): S1:10–16.

Buchan, J. (2006) Evidence of nursing shortages or a shortage of evidence? *Journal of Advanced Nursing* 47 (5): 457–8.

Buchan, J., and Calman, L. (2005) *The Global Shortage of Registered Nurses: An Overview of Issues and Actions: Summary.* International Council of Nurses, Geneva, Switzerland. Available at: www.icn.ch/global/summary.pdf (accessed October 6, 2007).

Buchan, J., and Sochalski, J. (2004) The migration of nurses: trends and policies. *Bulletin of the World Health Organization* 82 (8): 587–94.

Buchan, J., Parkin, T., and Sochalski, J. (2003) International nurse mobility: trends and policy implications. Geneva, Switzerland: World Health Organization.

Buerhaus, P., Staiger, D., and Auerbach, D. (2003) Is the current shortage of hospital nurses ending? *Health Affairs* 22 (6): 191–8.

Canadian Institute for Health Education (2006) *Highlights from the Regulated Nursing Workforce in Canada, 2005.* Author, Ottowa, Ontario. Available at: http://secure.cihi.ca/cihiweb/products/ndb_workforce_highlights_regulated_nursing_canada_2005_e.pdf (accessed October6, 2007).

CDEST (Commonwealth [Australia] Department of Education, Science, and Training) (2001) Job growth and replacement needs in nursing occupations. Available at: www.dest.gov.au/archive/highered/eippubs/eip01_18/4.htm (accessed October 6, 2007).

Chaguturu, S., and Vallabhaneni, S. (2005) Aiding and abetting: Nursing crises at home and abroad. *New England Journal of Medicine* 353 (17): 1761–3.

Christian Science Monitor (2004) In some nations, the rise of "shortgevity" (November 4). Available at: www.religiousconsultation.org/News_Tracker/in_some_nations_the_rise_in_shortgevity.htm (accessed October 6, 2007).

CNA (Canadian Nurses Association) (2002) *Planning for the Future: Nursing Human Resources Projections.* Ottawa, Canada: CNA.

Daniels, N. (1988) *Am I My Parents' Keeper? An Essay on Justice Between the Young and the Old*. New York: Oxford University Press.

Daniels, N. (1985) *Just Healthcare*. Cambridge: Cambridge University Press.

DeRaeve, P. (2003) The nursing shortage in the United States of America: an integrative review of the literature. Commentary: A European perspective. *Journal of Advanced Nursing* 43 (4): 348–50.

Duke University Health System (2003) What's the scoop on the nursing shortage? Available at: www2.mc.duke.edu/9200bmt/shortage.htm (accessed March 11, 2007).

Ehlers, V. J. (2006) Challenges nurses face in coping with the HIV/AIDS pandemic in Africa. *International Journal of Nursing Studies* 43: 657–62.

Goodin, H. (2003) The nursing shortage in the United States of America: an integrative review of the literature. *Journal of Advanced Nursing* 43 (4): 335–50.

Hardill, I., and Macdonald, S. (2000) Skilled international migration: the experience of nurses in the UK. *Regional Studies* 34 (7): 681–92.

HRSA (Health Resources and Service Administration) (2004) *The Registered Nurse Population: National Sample Survey of Registered Nurses: Preliminary Findings*. Washington, DC: HRSA. Available at: http://bhpr.hrsa.gov/healthworkforce/reports/rnpopulation/preliminaryfindings.htm (accessed October 6, 2007).

ICN (International Council of Nurses) (1999) *Position Statement: Nurse Retention, Transfer and Migration*. Geneva, Switzerland. Available at: www.icn.ch/psretention.htm (accessed March 3, 2007).

ICN (International Council of Nurses) (2001) *Position Statement: Ethical Nurse Recruitment*. Geneva, Switzerland. Available at: www.icn.ch/psrecruit01.htm (accessed October 6, 2007).

Kingma, M. (2006) *Nurses on the Move: Migration and the Global Healthcare Economy*. Ithaca, NY: Cornell University Press.

Kline, D. (2003) Push and pull factors in international nurse migration. *Journal of Nursing Scholarship* 35 (2): 107–11.

Martineau, T., Decker, K., and Bundred, P. (2004) "Brain drain" of health professionals: from rhetoric to responsible action. *Health Policy* 70 (1): 1–10.

McKenna, H. (1998) The "professional cleansing" of nurses: the systematic downgrading of nurses damages patient care. *British Medical Journal* 317 (7170): 1403–4.

Mullen, C. (2003) The nursing shortage in the United States of America: an integrative review of the literature. Commentary: An English perspective. *Journal of Advanced Nursing* 43 (4): 345–8.

Press release (2003) Influx of older and foreign-born workers slows five-year hospital nursing shortage. *Health Affairs* (November 12, 2003). Available at: www.healthaffairs.org/press/novdec0301.htm (accessed October 6, 2007).

Productivity Commission (2005) *Australia's Health Workforce*. Research Report, Canberra. Available at: www.pc.gov.au/__data/assets/pdf_file/0003/9480/health workforce.pdf (accessed June 16, 2008).

RCN (Royal College of Nurses) (2005) *Past Trends, Future Imperfect? A Review of the UK Nursing Labour Market in 2004/2005*. London: RCN. Available at: www.rcn.org.uk/publications/pdf/past.trends.future.imperfect.a.review.of.the.UK.nursing.labour.market.2004-5.pdf (accessed October 6, 2007).

Sochalski, J. (2002) Nursing shortage redux: turning the corner on an enduring problem. *Health Affairs* 21 (5): 157–64.

Stanton, M. (2004) Hospital nurse staffing and quality of care. *Agency for Healthcare Research and Quality: Research in Action*. Available at: www.ahrq.gov/research/nursestaffing/nursestaff.htm (accessed October 6, 2007).

Stone, P., Tourangeau, A., Duffield, C., et al. (2003) Evidence of nurse working conditions: a global perspective. *Policy, Politics, & Nursing Practice* 4 (2): 120–30.

UNICEF (United Nations International Children's Emergency Fund) (n.d.(a)) Information by Country: Australia: Statistics: HIV AIDS. Available at: www.unicef.org/infobycountry/australia_statistics.html (accessed June 16, 2008).

UNICEF (United Nations International Children's Emergency Fund) (n.d.(b)) Information by Country: Botswana: Statistics: HIV AIDS. Available at: www.unicef.org/infobycountry/botswana_statistics.html (accessed June 16, 2008).

UNICEF (United Nations International Children's Emergency Fund) (2007) *Progress for Children: A World Fit for Children: Statistical Review* 6 (December). Available at: www.childinfo.org/files/progress_for_children.pdf (accessed June 16, 2008).

WHO (World Health Organization) (2001) *Strengthening Nursing and Midwifery: Progress and Future Directions: Summary Document: 1996–2000.* Geneva, Switzerland: WHO.

WHO (World Health Organization) (2006) *Working Together for Health: The World Health Report 2006.* Geneva, Switzerland: WHO.

Wickett, D., McCutcheon, H., and Long, L. (2003) The nursing shortage in the United States of America: an integrative review of the literature. Commentary: an Australian perspective. *Journal of Advanced Nursing* 43 (4): 343–5.

CASE FOURTEEN: DEADLY SECRETS – RELEASING CONFIDENTIAL MEDICAL RECORDS TO LAW-ENFORCEMENT OFFICERS

On May 30, 2002, workers at the Harold Rowley Recycling Center in Storm Lake, Iowa, found the body of a baby boy estimated to have been born 24–48 hours previously. Because the center's machinery had shredded the baby's body, sheriff's investigators were unable to identify the baby or determine the cause of his death, bringing the investigation into the newborn's death to a standstill.

Officials, believing access to medical records might help them discover the identity of the woman who gave birth to the baby, issued subpoenas to all area hospitals and clinics for the records of all women who tested positive for pregnancy between August 15, 2001, and May 30, 2002.

Planned Parenthood (PP), which guarantees in writing that medical records will be kept confidential, refused to release the records of women who sought their services. Jill June, director of PP of Greater Iowa, cited the professional obligation of healthcare providers to preserve the confidentiality of medical records. Although Storm Lake is a small community of approximately 10,000 residents, PP performed more than 1,000 pregnancy tests in the time period covered by the subpoenas. Ms June asked people to imagine the invasion of privacy and loss of confidentiality that would result, were the sheriff's deputies to knock on the doors of more than 1,000 women and demand documentation of a live birth, a spontaneous miscarriage, or a pregnancy termination.

Preserving confidentiality is notoriously difficult in small towns. (Sue Thayer, manager of Storm Lake's PP clinic, noted that the body had been found by her brother-in-law.) In such close confines, a visit by the sheriff's deputies is likely to be noticed and to set tongues wagging, raising speculation about why a woman had sought obstetrical or gynecological care – especially if she has neither an expanding belly nor a baby. Women who had kept information about contraception or pregnancy (the Storm Lake clinic does not perform abortions) from family members, partners, or friends could be "outed" – sometimes with profoundly negative consequences.

PP has cooperated with law-enforcement officials in the past, working with a particular suspect and her lawyer to agree on release of records. However, no suspect had been identified in the case in question, and no evidence existed that the woman who gave birth to the baby was ever a patient at the clinic. PP officials indicated their willingness to cooperate in the investigation if they could do so without violating the confidentiality of hundreds of women, all but one (if even one) of whom have nothing to do with the case.

Philip E. Havens, the County Attorney, argued that the records constituted the only hope of identifying a suspect, and that identifying the baby's mother and determining the cause of death (e.g., determining whether the infant died as a result of foul play) would be necessary to bring the perpetrator to justice. He claimed that the right to confidentiality (and privacy) is not absolute, and that the obligation of justice is stronger than the right of women to keep their medical information confidential. Responding to concerns expressed about the burdens that would be caused by opening the records, Havens replied: "I'm sorry for that. I apologize. But a human being was thrown into the garbage and shredded and I think that crime was important enough to society to at least attempt to find out who did it" (Larsen 2005).

Ms June countered that the clinic's records may not help: women in socially conservative Storm Lake who receive PP services often give false names. Further, the mother may not be from the area, may never have been tested, or may not have sought medical care.

Following her refusal to comply voluntarily with the subpoena, a district court judge ordered Ms June to turn over the records. She again refused.

From a moral point of view, should PP turn over patients' records to the sheriff's office?

Perspective One

PP should turn over their records to the sheriff. An innocent and helpless infant has been killed and tossed away – literally – like so much garbage. Such a heinous crime should not go unpunished, and any actions that might bring the perpe-trator(s) to justice are morally required.

Justice requires that the perpetrator pay for this crime, but this can only hap-pen if the perpetrator is identified – which is unlikely unless the baby's mother (and, through her, other possible perpetrators, if any) can be questioned. Since available evidence has led nowhere, new evidence – the identity of the mother – is essential for justice to be served.

Failure to identify the perpetrator(s) means that not only will this grizzly crime go unpunished but, as a result, citizens may lose trust in their law-enforcement agencies' abilities to keep the community secure. Individuals or institutions that accept the benefits that society offers implicitly agree to assume at least some social burdens as well. Thus, the virtue of fidelity requires that residents and institutions not merely abide by the laws, but assist law-enforcement officials in keeping the community safe.

Since the only way to bring the perpetrator(s) to justice and to reassure community residents is to identify the mother, and the only way to identify the mother is through medical records, PP should release the records.

Perspective Two

PP should not turn over their records to the sheriff.

First, releasing the records would give rise to a plethora of noxious conse-quences: (1) women who seek healthcare under a guarantee of confidentiality may lose trust not only in PP, but in the healthcare community more broadly; and (2) if doctors, nurses, clinics, and hospitals release confidential medical informa-tion, countless patients will feel much more insecure about seeking care. They may forgo needed care entirely, or fail to disclose important health information to care providers. Without full and accurate information, the ability of health-care professionals accurately to diagnose and prescribe appropriate therapies would be diminished; patients might receive improper interventions and fail to get well – or even get worse.

Second, patients have a right to confidentiality. Because persons in general and patients in particular properly have the right to control access to personal information, and because PP explicitly guaranteed the confidentiality of medical information, this right should not be violated. In fact, because PP guaranteed confidentiality, they have an obligation of fidelity (promise-keeping) to secure the women's medical records.

Finally, release of the records would be unjust. All but one (if even one) of the women who sought care from PP have done nothing to deserve legal scrutiny or the harms it would bring. Any negative effects suffered by women who, because of the investigation, lose control of confidential reproductive information are both undeserved and unconsented-to; that is, the women will suffer unwarranted harms or burdens.

Therefore, PP should continue to refuse to turn over the records.

Perspective Three

Should PP turn over the medical records requested by the sheriff's office? This question represents a conflict between consequences for women who used PP's services and for the greater population; and between justice and the right to confidentiality. Before PP can determine its moral obligation, they should gather relevant information.

Step 1: Information-gathering

Implications

- If PP releases records, will the birth mother be identified?
- If PP releases records, what will be the effects on their patients? on all patients?
- If PP doesn't release records, what will be the effects on the community, including its general sense of security?

Legal/policy information

- What are Iowa's laws regarding confidentiality of medical records?
- Do any federal laws govern confidentiality of medical records?
- Does PP's policy of confidentiality specify any exceptions?

Psychological information

- Are PP patients likely to consent to release of their records?
- Will PP's refusal to release records affect the community's sense of security?

Step 2: Creative problem-solving

It is worth noting that PP has a third option: contacting women who tested positive for pregnancy between August 15, 2001, and May 30, 2002, and requesting permission to release their records. If all patients consented, the sheriff's office would acquire the desired information and, because patients consented to release of their records, PP would not have violated their confidentiality. However, for the reasons Ms June cites (e.g., use of pseudonyms), this approach is unlikely to garner universal permission. Thus the sheriff's office would still lack access to some women. So PP's next step should be to consider the moral pros and cons of their options.

Step 3: Listing pros and cons

Options	Pros	Cons
PP provides the records to the sheriff.	1. Birth mother and/or perpetrator is identified (C-B) 2. Perpetrator is punished (J-F) 3. Legal institutions do their job and residents feel secure (C-U)	7. Undeserved burdens on PP patients (C-NM, J-F) 8. Loss of trust in Planned Parenthood (C-U) 9. Loss of trust in healthcare providers/institutions generally (C-U) 10. Diminished efficacy of healthcare encounters (C-U) 11. Gender-based discrimination (J-E)
PP does not provide the records to the sheriff.	4. Respects patients' right to confidentiality (R) 5. Respects patient autonomy (A) 6. Keeps promise to patients (V-F, V-I)	12. Fails to honor general societal obligation to aid community (V-F)

Step 4: Analysis

Factual assumptions

- The probability that the birth mother will be identified if the records are opened is extremely low.
- Release of PP records to the authorities will deter women from seeking reproductive healthcare.
- Release of PP records will subject women to harassment, embarrassment, and other noxious outcomes.

Value assumptions

- Reproductive health decisions should belong to the women involved, and only to them.
- Women's medical records should be as strictly guarded as the medical records of men.

Step 5: Justification

This dilemma appears, most prominently, to represent a conflict between negative consequences (maleficence) to individual women versus bringing a killer to justice. Which of those reasons is stronger?

Beginning with a comparison of the anticipated consequences, good reasons (Reasons ##7, 8, 9) support weighing the negative consequences to patients more heavily than positive consequences to the community (Reasons ##1, 3). First, people keep information confidential for a variety of reasons, many of which include avoiding untoward outcomes. Persons are often treated differently when their secrets are made public – and this treatment is not necessarily better. For example, when Stan discovers that Stu beats his wife, Stan's regard for and treatment of Stu is likely to be cooler or more guarded than before Stan had this information. For this reason, most societies have general rules about, and often quite stringent protections regarding, sharing secrets (Bok 1984: chs. 9 and 14).

Information on reproductive choices is especially emotionally charged and especially likely – if known – to evoke disparate treatment. Decisions about whether and when to have children and, conversely, whether, when, and how to avoid conception are among the most personal a woman (or man) can make. While family and friends often have strongly held opinions on family planning, women and their partners may not welcome those opinions, preferring to keep this part of their lives quite private. However, in the circumstances described in the case, the arrival of the sheriff's deputies at one's door would constitute clear evidence of a previous visit to PP for family planning, counseling, or treatment – and would be certain to evoke questions from partners, family, and friends. While women can refuse to answer such questions, if their PP visits were undertaken *without* input from partners or spouses, the deputies' visit will likely evoke unpleasant challenges to these women. Women whose reproductive choices are at odds with those that significant others would make are, again, likely to suffer, through word or deed, for those choices (Reason #7).

Moreover, given the public nature of the investigation, one cannot assume that violations of confidentiality will themselves be kept confidential. The arrival of deputies at one's front door will clearly signal to patients that their confidentiality has been violated. A subsequent loss of trust in the healthcare system generally, and healthcare providers in particular, should be anticipated – with further negative results (Jackson 2001; Pellegrino et al. 1991). This outcome is particularly worrisome because trust is critical to successful patient–professional encounters. Consider, for example, a teenage girl who needs advice on contraception. She may be deeply concerned that her parents not learn that she is, or is contemplating becoming, sexually active. If she believes her healthcare providers are unlikely to protect her secret, she may eschew medical consultation altogether and engage in unprotected sex – with untoward outcomes for herself, her partner(s), and her (presently undesired) future offspring (Reason #7). In fact, in July 2002 – the month after the county attorney subpoenaed PP's records – the number of women seeking pregnancy tests at Storm Lake PP clinic declined by at least 70 percent (Reason #8) (ACLU 2002), suggesting that such fears regarding loss of trust and failure to acquire reproductive advice or medications/devices are warranted.

Further, breach of confidentiality is likely to curtail the willingness of patients who do consult healthcare providers to divulge especially sensitive information (Reason #9). The same teenager may not admit to smoking – relevant information to selecting a contraceptive agent – if she thinks this information, too, might fall into the hands of her parents. Patients who are concerned about private information becoming public are less likely to share such information and, as a result, are at greater risk of inaccurate diagnoses and inappropriate interventions (Reason #10) (ibid.). Good care depends on a provider's being able to diagnose reliably both healthcare needs and the risks and benefits of various interventions and, based on these analyses, to select appropriate treatment. In sum, confidentiality is a necessary condition for good healthcare – by all providers, not just those at PP (Kottow 1986; cf Siegler 1982), and is threatened by release of records.

What about autonomy (Reason #5)? A choice is autonomous when made by a competent chooser who is informed, possesses and understands the *relevant* information, and is not coerced (Faden and Beauchamp 1986: 238). Ms June notes: "It is explicitly stated to women when they come in for services that information from pregnancy test results is only disclosed when they file their written authorization" (Basu 2002: paras 12, 14). PP's *explicit* guarantee of confidentiality suggests that this protection had greater-than-average relevance for women choosing to seek care and, as such, was factored into their analyses of the burdens and benefits of particular treatments. In fact, in the weeks following the subpoena of their records, PP reported "a flood of calls" from patients, "begging" the clinic not to release their records (Kaiser Family Foundation 2002), suggesting that the promise of secrecy constituted an important factor in decisions to receive care, and that women might have made different choices or forgone care in the absence of this promise. Thus, an appeal to autonomy supports keeping the records confidential.

The commitment to confidentiality is sufficiently strong that the American Medical Association (AMA) and the American Nursing Association (ANA) both explicitly promise, in their codes of ethics, to respect patients' right to confidentiality (Reason #4) and keep patient information secret. As a result, the virtues of fidelity and professional integrity (Reason #6) support not releasing the records.

Finally, the possibility of gender-based injustice deserves some mention. Have the subpoenas been deemed appropriate because all those whose confidentiality will be violated are women (Reason #11)? Consider the following. Imagine that an unmarked medicine bottle containing Viagra is discovered by the body of a victim of homicide. After laboratory tests reveal that the victim was *not himself* taking Viagra, would the records of healthcare professionals and institutions be subpoenaed so that investigators could identify everyone for whom the drug has been prescribed and, thus, identify possible suspects? Perhaps, although this seems unlikely. Or, consider a victim who, according to the medical examiner, has injuries so violently inflicted that she suspects the perpetrator was psychotic. Would psychiatrists be expected to open up their records so that the sheriff's office could identify patients with violent psychoses or a history of violent behavior? Since judges typically reject assaults on confidential information in mental health records, why would the records of those providing reproductive care to women be considered fair game? Such unequal treatment would require some explanation, especially given the longstanding, pervasive societal discrimination against women. Equal treatment appears to require leaving the medical records untouched.

Although the critic has her own appeal to the negative consequences of *not* releasing the records, this appeal is less compelling. Assuming that Storm Lake's local law-enforcement agencies typically secure the peace of the community, a single unsolved case, however heinous, is unlikely to generate loss of trust in those agencies (Reason #3). This is particularly true given the uncommon circumstances in this situation: finding a dead newborn in the dump seems unlikely to recur and, thus, failure to solve the case seems unlikely to evoke loss of trust in law-enforcement officers or institutions.

The most compelling reason for releasing the record is that this action seems to provide the only possibility of identifying the infant's birth mother and, through her, punishing those responsible for the death (or at least the desecration of the corpse) (Reasons ##1, 2). However, the probability that the birth mother will be identified is very, very low. First, as Ms June noted, many women give false information to further obscure their own identities. Second, according to Priscilla Smith, an attorney at the Center for Reproductive Law and Policy, "Somebody who went to a physician and was obtaining prenatal care is the least likely to have this sort of outcome. . . . In the typical cases, mothers who have abandoned newborns have denied to themselves that they were pregnant, sought no care and delivered the infant without assistance" (Basu 2002: para 17). Put another way, even were PP to release its records this action would be unlikely to aid the investigation.

So the appeal to consequences provides a stronger argument for not releasing the records than for sharing them.

The critic might also note that the AMA qualifies its commitment to patient autonomy/confidentiality: "A physician shall . . . safeguard patient confidences . . . within the constraints of the law" (AMA 2001: Principle IV). If the law permits public officials to survey patient records, physicians must turn them over. But whether the sheriff's subpoena would count as an overriding "constraint," justifying the release of records, is unclear.

The ANA obligation is also qualified: "Duties of confidentiality . . . are not absolute and may need to be modified in order to protect the patient, other innocent parties and in circumstances of mandatory for public health reasons" (ANA 2001: sec. 3.2). So, a *general* appeal to the virtue of professional integrity does not unambiguously support either option. However:

> Federal laws protect the privacy of medical records and Iowa statutes guarantee
> doctor-patient confidentiality and the state of Iowa supports confidentiality with

especially stringent statutes. In fact, Iowa privacy laws are so stringent that an investigator cannot obtain information about which videos or library books a suspect in a particular case checked out of a library or rental store without the suspect's permission or without convincing a judge of a probable link to a crime. (Basu 2002: para 14)

In sum, healthcare professionals' codes of ethics give advice that – in this case – can be conflicting: do what is best for patients *and* comply with legal require-ments. Which mandate has the greater moral force? The ANA commitment to confidentiality would hold in this case, as none of the specified exceptions is met: releasing the records would not protect patients or other third parties (the child is, after all, already dead), and is not required to protect public health. Thus nurses – facing the conflict of which of their ethical requirements should be respected – get reasonably clear advice from their code of ethics. Physicians, how-ever, face greater ambiguity. Since they are required without exception to do no harm *and* comply with the law, physicians suffer an assault on professional integrity with either choice. Their only recourse is to examine even more fundamental professional principles. If the purpose of medicine – promoting *patient* welfare – requires protecting patient confidentiality in the case at hand, then professional integrity requires such protection. While the welfare of particular patients can be compromised if doing so will prevent catastrophic harm, violating confiden-tiality will not here avoid further untoward outcomes: the catastrophic harm (to the infant) has already occurred. Thus, the virtues of professional integrity and fidelity to patients support physicians' refusal to release records.

Perhaps the strongest argument supporting releasing the records is that they may hold the key to the identity of the baby's killer (Reason #1) and enable the law to bring the killer to justice (Reason #2). (We should note in passing that the infant may have been stillborn, that is, that no one killed him.) Unless the killer is identified, he or she will not be punished for this heinous crime (Reason #2). While this is surely true, one must question whether access to PP's med-ical records will reveal the killer's identity. As noted above, because many women give false names and addresses, many of the records will lead investigators nowhere. Further, no evidence has demonstrated that the baby's mother sought medical care or had a pregnancy test at PP – or even in Storm Lake. As a result, finding the woman whose DNA matches the baby's is hardly guaranteed. Perhaps if a match were virtually assured, the moral obligation to identify and punish a murderer would outweigh the undeserved harms to hundreds of women; but the improbability of such a match weakens the appeal to justice as supporting the release of records, while the probability of women suffering undeserved harms is significant. So justice also speaks against releasing the records.

In sum, the appeal to consequences demonstrates that worse outcomes will result from violating confidentiality. The appeals to autonomy and virtues, when considered within a patient–professional context, support maintaining patient confidentiality. Finally, the appeal to justice demonstrates that undeserved burdens to hundreds of women are not outweighed by an appeal to deserved punishment, the realization of which cannot be predicted, but is reasonably deemed to be remote.

PP should not release their records.

Additional Issues to Consider

Other possible moral dilemmas arising within this case:

Q Would PP be morally required to release their records if the law-enforcement community had more information about the baby (say, a DNA profile)?

Q Would PP be morally required to release their records if the law-enforcement community could guarantee privacy and confidentiality of the women to be questioned?

REFERENCES

ACLU (American Civil Liberties Union) (2002) ACLU asks Iowa Supreme Court to protect confidentiality of patients' medical records (September 30). Available at: www.aclu.org/reproductiverights/medical/12682prs20020930.html (accessed October 5, 2007).

AMA (American Medical Association) (2001) *Principles of Medical Ethics.* Available at: www.ama-assn.org/ama/pub/category/2512.html (accessed October 5, 2007).

ANA (American Nurses Association) (2001) *Code of Ethics for Nurses with Interpretive Statements.* Washington, DC: ANA.

Basu, R. (2002) Iowa D. A. seeks data on 100s of prenatal patients. *Women's eNews* (2 July). Available at: http://womensenews.org/article.cfm/dyn/aid/965/ (accessed October 5, 2007).

Bok, S. (1984) *Secrets: On the Ethics of Concealment and Revelation.* New York: Vintage Books.

Faden, R. R., and Beauchamp, T. L. (1986) *A History and Theory of Informed Consent.* New York: Oxford University Press.

Kottow, M. H. (1986) Medical confidentiality: An intransigent and absolute obligation. *Journal of Medical Ethics* 12 (3): 117–22.

Jackson, J. (2001) *Truth, Trust and Medicine.* London: Routledge.

Kaiser Family Foundation (2002) Kaiser daily reproductive health report. Available at: www.kaisernetwork.org/daily_reports/rep_repro.cfm (accessed October 5, 2007).

Larsen, D. (2005) Baby's death divides small Iowa town. *USA Today.* Available at: www.usatoday.com (accessed July 23, 2005).

Pellegrino, E., Veatch, R. M., and Langan, J. P. (1991) *Ethics, Trust, and the Professions: Philosophical and Cultural Aspects.* Washington, DC: Georgetown University Press.

Siegler, M. (1982) Confidentiality in medicine: a decrepit concept. *New England Journal of Medicine* 307 (24): 1518–21.

CASE FIFTEEN: PERISH THE THOUGHT! – ACADEMIC AFFAIRS AND "COMMUNITY VALUES"

The mere appearance of a disheveled filmmaker, invited by student leaders, sent shock waves across a college campus, even jostling academic affairs.

The controversy began to rage during fall semester, 2004. The Associated Students of Utah Valley State College (ASUVSC) announced plans to bring Bush-bashing filmmaker, Michael Moore, to the campus just two weeks before the presidential election. Previous speakers invited by ASUVSC, such as Alan Keyes and Barbara Bush (Vogel 2004), elicited lackluster student response. This year, student leaders wanted to bring a speaker to campus who would energize the student body and "put UVSC on the map" (Vogel 2006: 16).

They succeeded. Outraged locals, who prided themselves as being residents of one of the most conservative areas in the country, called upon college President William A. Sederburg –newly arrived from Michigan – to cancel the event (Gravois 2004). The imbroglio over Moore, documented in the film *This Divided State* (Minority Films 2005), can only be understood in historical context. UVSC is a public, state-supported institution and part of the Utah System of Higher Education. Tension between the college and community has incrementally intensified over recent decades as UVSC's mission and makeup has rapidly and radically changed. UVSC originated in the 1930s as a vocational-technical school which, after several name changes, became Utah Technical College at Provo in 1967, and Utah Valley Community College in 1987. Six years later, the school began offering a small number of baccalaureate degrees and was renamed UVSC. The number of baccalaureate programs the school offered exceeded five dozen in 2007, when the Utah State legislature changed UVSC's name and charter to Utah Valley University (UVU), which became effective on July 1, 2008.

UVSC's history also includes its shifting relationship with the only other institution of higher education in Utah County, Brigham Young University (BYU), which is owned and operated by the Church of Jesus Christ of Latter-Day Saints (LDS, or Mormon, Church). UVSC is located in Orem; BYU is situated in adjacent Provo. In the past, if a Utah Valley high school student, regardless of religious affiliation, wanted a traditional baccalaureate liberal arts education, BYU was the place to go. Students who wanted vocational training went to UVSC. Since the early 1990s BYU has implemented increasingly rigid expectations of obedience to ecclesiastical authority, which resulted in censure for violations of academic freedom by the American Association of University Professors,[1] making the university attractive to select LDS faithful.

Increasingly, Utah Valley residents seeking a secular baccalaureate education began to look to UVSC. In spite of its history as a vocational-technical institute and a community college, changes at BYU and other demographic trends had resulted in increasing expectations that UVSC should also provide a solid liberal education – that is, an education which frees, or "liberates," one from ignorance, dogma, and prejudice for the duties and responsibilities of engaged citizenship required by democracy.

Unfortunately, many area taxpayers see this vector from vocational to liberal education as undesirable. Many Utahans believe that one goes to church for moral guidance and to UVSC for job training.

For these area taxpayers, the Moore issue was evidence that UVSC had run afoul of its original and intended mission. Many expressed consternation at the apparent lack of authoritative oversight of student government by the college administration. These community members felt that the administration should have prevented the student leadership from extending the invitation in the first place, and now should intervene and cancel the event. Some faculty, however, pointed out that student government is by definition the exercise of self-governance by students for educational purposes; student government ought not be a puppet regime of the executive office, and the administration should refrain from meddling unless some overriding legal or public safety concern is involved. Moore's visit, for the defenders of student government, clearly did not rise to that standard (Keller 2004).

Numerous critics said that Moore should be barred from campus simply on the basis of his "lies and propaganda" (Kirkby 2004). Margaret Dayton, an Orem legislator known for staunch right-wing politics, derided Moore as a "grandstanding demagogue" (Decker 2004). Parents and faculty worried that impressionable young minds would be corrupted. The words of one incensed parent sounded paranoid to some: "If you continue to expose my children to evil they will become evil" (Vogel 2006: 55). ASUVSC President Jim Bassi and Vice-President for Academics Joe Vogel received scores of inflammatory emails and voice mails excoriating their invitation to Moore. One caller threatened to "come after" Vogel and make his life "a living hell" (ibid.: 26). In an email that found its way into a local newspaper, the sender claimed that Vogel should be "tarred, feathered and run out of the state on a rail" (Randall 2004). The legitimacy of Bassi and Vogel's standing as Mormons was questioned, one person denouncing Vogel as "evil" and a spawn of Satan (Vogel 2006: 26).

As these barbs flew, it became clear that the ASUVSC was achieving the other part of their goal – namely, energizing a usually apathetic student population. Students were organizing protests, marching up and down the hallways of the student center with placards for Moore and against Moore, voicing opinions at demonstrations, instigating petition drives, writing letters, and criticizing or defending their own student government for using student fees on such a notorious speaker. Several faculty remarked that UVSC suddenly felt like a *real* college campus.

In the spirit of open dialogue, UVSC's Center for the Study of Ethics organized a public panel discussion in late September on the Moore controversy and the role of pubic institutions of higher education in the democratic process. The panel included Pierre Lamarche (Philosophy Faculty), Bob Rasmussen (Assistant Vice-President for Student Life and Dean of Students), William A. Sederburg (President), and Joseph Vogel (ASUVSC Vice-President of Academics). Under the watchful eye of police, 300 people crammed into a space with seating for 160; the atmosphere was charged with anticipatory electricity.

Some parents, who did not admire Moore or his work, nonetheless supported his visit. In the words of a mother of three UVSC students – one who had spent a year in Iraq – "I disagree with Moore's ideas, but I'm glad he's coming. Try not to go in there with all these preconceived ideas. Go in there with an open mind" (Jensen 2004b).

Sitting impassively in the audience was Kay Anderson, a neighbor and outspoken critic of UVSC who was incensed that the college issued a concert permit for rap artist Nelly, whose offensive lyrics Anderson had been able to hear from his porch. Shutters clicking and red lights on camcorders glowing, Anderson held up a cashier's check for $25,000 and vowed to hand it over to President Sederburg on the spot if the administration rescinded Moore's invitation, explaining: "I should not have to send my children to a private university [that is, BYU] to get a conservative education when I live in a conservative community and have a state college in my back yard that is paid for by conservative taxpayers and donors. A balanced education does not require we teach our children to be so open-minded that their brains fall out" (ibid.).

Clearly for Anderson, Utah Valley and environs are analogous to a pristine park whose integrity must be actively preserved. As invasive, non-endemic species and development threaten the ecological integrity of wilderness, inviting Moore to campus threatens the moral fabric of the community. As he explained: "[T]he most liberal of the leftist liberals . . . are the people that we in Utah County . . . were trying to keep out of here" (Eddington 2004a).

In response a student chimed in (to applause): "It's important that we as a state remember that this state was founded by people that were chased out of town" (Jensen 2004b), alluding to the persecution of the Mormons in Illinois and Ohio in the nineteenth century.

Virulent opponents of UVSC's invitation to Moore remained unfazed and undeterred. The school received bomb threats (Gravois 2004). Salt Lake County resident Bill McGregor issued an ultimatum to organize a protest of tens of thousands of drivers aimed at clogging all traffic routes and shutting down the interstate highway unless Sederburg called off the event (Nokkentved and Andrus 2004). Student Sean Vreeland, a supporter of the invasion of Iraq and a Bush admirer, raised enough money to post a billboard on the interstate highway near UVSC that read: "Michael Moore – High in Cholesterol, Low in Truth" (Vogel 2006: 128).

More consequentially, Vreeland instigated a petition drive in an effort not only to force the UVSC administration to cancel the Moore event, but also to have Bassi and Vogel impeached (Hyde 2004a; Warner 2004a). When that effort foundered, Vreeland filed a grievance with the Student Services Judiciary Committee, which was dismissed (Vogel 2006: 125). Meanwhile, another Republican lawmaker, Howard Stephenson, drafted legislation that would limit the autonomy of student governments by restricting uses of student fees – such as prohibiting invitations to objectionable speakers to campuses of the Utah System of Higher Education (Decker 2004).

In a final effort to repulse Moore, Anderson enlisted another pro-war student, Dan Garcia, to file a lawsuit in the student body's behalf, *Anderson and Garcia v. ASUVSC Student Council*, in Utah State Fourth Judicial District Court (Vogel 2006: 145), claiming procedural violations of school policy (Warner 2004b). Vindicating punitive action, Anderson said: "If you stand for something and speak your mind, people will try to shut you down" (Eddington 2004b) which was met with charges of outrageous hypocrisy.

Garcia's motivations for supporting legal action against UVSC were presaged by earlier sentiments about anti-war protesters in the pages of the student newspaper:

> This country was born in bloodshed, the use of realized or projected violence is what keeps America stable, free and allows small cowards . . . to hide behind bigger men who have the courage to do what is right[.] We honor, venerate, and relish the strong warrior in our culture: we love football and pro wrestling, sports and entertainment where one contestant exerts dominace [*sic*] over the other through pure use of brute, violent force. Americans are HE-Men, we by and large don't like or want pacifist, small minded, sissies . . . in our country. (Garcia 2003)

Or in our county. Apparently for Garcia, Moore was a "sissy" not welcome in his neighborhood.

Anderson specifically set the faculty in his crosshairs. He claimed that taxpayers like himself, who intend to inculcate conservative values in their children, should not be paying the salaries of "liberal" professors who undermine the very values they attempt to instill in their children (Eddington 2004b; Hyde 2004b).

John L. Valentine, a Republican legislator from Orem and President of the Utah State Senate, went for the whole institution. On a campus visit, he issued a stern warning:

> What we need to have happen is not a repeat of what happened at this institution in the last couple of years. This institution reflects the values of the community in which it resides. And if we have continual efforts to try and move this institution away from the values of this community we are going to have some problems up at the state capital. (Ditzler 2005b)

Valentine was alluding to a constellation of activities that local citizens felt offended their particular "community values," and explained Utah State political leadership's decision to delay funding of UVSC's new library (Ditzler 2005a).

Public recriminations of the whole college were also leveled by Norman Nielsen, a former Republican state representative. Nielsen complained that UVSC exhibited a "disturbing drift to the left" illustrated not only by Moore's visit but also by a literature course on Queer Theory, student and faculty productions of Eve Ensler's *Vagina Monologues*, and a student activity night themed on "mock gambling" (Ditzler 2005a). Nielsen (2005a, 2005b) called for "balance" of liberal and conservative viewpoints in the UVSC curriculum.

To this external criticism, some UVSC faculty argued that much of the controversy had been based on an outright misunderstanding of the fundamental differences in the missions of private-sectarian institutions on one hand and public-secular institutions on the other. In the case at hand, BYU's central mission (as a private ecclesiastical institution) is the exploration of reason within the framework of faith, while UVSC's central mission (as a public institution) is the straightforward exploration of reason – and faith, if relevant, only within the framework of reason. Unfortunately, the condemnation of UVSC's invitation to Moore was seriously misguided insofar as it failed properly to understand the purpose of public education (Keller 2005a).

Some faculty defended the college by defending the students. Professors pointed out that although a majority of UVSC students reported that they planned on voting for Bush, they wanted to see Moore, and that they were offended that a self-appointed protectorate of the youth would see the need to shield them from corrosive ideas (Keller 2007). In the words of philosophy professor Pierre Lamarche (2004), the notion that the youth need to be insulated and isolated "is both offensive and patently absurd. It is offensive in that it implies that the UVSC student body is populated by so many naive, idiot children, who are incapable of independently evaluating Mr Moore's remarks."

Faculty turned the rhetoric of the community interventionists back on themselves. Through abuse of the liberal/conservative dichotomy, detractors of UVSC such as Nielsen (2006) reflexively aligned their "conservative" position with "true" American ideals, and "liberalism" with anti-Americanism. Against this equivocation, faculty retorted that, in the parlance of American political discourse, UVSC's mission was in fact exceedingly traditional and hence "conservative" in upholding the ideals upon which the nation was founded: pluralism, democracy, civility, open discourse, freedom of expression, and freedom of association (Keller 2005b).

Most jolting for academic affairs, faculty began attacking faculty. Some professors condemned their colleagues for supporting the students' decision. An anonymously authored memo, surreptitiously placed in "liberal" faculty boxes, argued that all faculty should boycott the event, and made the threat that faculty who did not boycott Moore's talk would be duly noted. This hostility lingered long after Moore's limousine had departed for the Salt Lake International Airport. Faculty known for endorsing the ideals of liberal education, free speech, and pluralism, found an anonymous memo dated January 1, 2006, in their boxes – presumably placed there by another faculty member, since school doors were locked on that day – stating: "Eventually, people with a strong Left-wing orientation . . . will leave UVSC because the community will not abide them. They will realize that they cannot be happy here. And like it or not, the community – especially this one – calls the shots."

Clearly, the controversy over Moore was much more than an issue about bringing a divisive celebrity to campus. Moore was merely a symbol of a threatening, invading force penetrating the heart of a placid, traditionalist homeland settled by Mormon pioneers. The incident was really about the larger issue of the role of a secular public institution of higher education in a homogenous community (Keller 2005c). On one side of the debate were those who held that institutions of higher education are forums for the origination of novel and often controversial ideas, and that these institutions must enjoy significant ideological autonomy from political interference (Keller and Sederburg 2005a). On the other side of the debate were those who held that institutions of higher education should be accountable to the particular – if peculiar – mores of the communities within which they are embedded, as a student and daughter of Nielsen publicly contended (Anderson 2006).

So, in terms of ethics, was the political intervention of individuals external to UVSC (now UVU) into the internal affairs of the institution sound public policy? Should academics be held accountable to "community values" advocacy groups?

Perspective One

Academics should be held accountable to "community values" advocacy groups.

According to the consequentialist ethical theory of utilitarianism, the common good is promoted when UVU academic affairs are overseen by those who represent community values. As a *Salt Lake Tribune* reporter astutely observed, UVU is "one of the most conservative campuses in one of the most conservative counties in one of the most conservative states in the country" (Jensen 2004a). The academic program of UVU ought to reflect this local character, else the university fails, for several reasons, in its mission to serve the community it purports to serve.

First, in Utah Valley one goes to church for moral education and to public school for job training. Religion provides the only moral compass students need. The faculty member who complained in a 1999 campus-wide email of the "abuse of . . . students' values" was justified in worrying that exposure to an untold miscellany of ideas in the General Education humanities course (gay rights, capital punishment, gun control, immigration policy, feminism, public policy on the environment, biodiversity, the connection or disconnection between ethics and religion, global warming, militarism, property-owners' rights, the separation of church and state) is damaging to the integrity of the community. The community has collectively issued its edict on all of these positions, and there is no point in discussing them in college courses.

Parents, faculty, citizens, and political leaders continue rightly to assert that alternative positions on some of these issues are incompatible with community values and unbecoming of UVU curricula. Liberal education involves questioning, and constant questioning eats at the glue that binds the community together.

Second, Kay Anderson was absolutely right to assert that: "If we've got a conservative community here that is paying for this college and sending our children here . . . we have a right to expect the college to reflect the values of the community" (Ditzler 2004). Since many students who would like to attend BYU are not admitted, they turn to UVU. As such, UVU's proper identity is a publicly accessible satellite of BYU.

There is no good reason why Utah Valley citizens – the most faithful Bush supporters in the nation (Egan 2006) – must endure Moore's anti-Bush diatribe on campus just two weeks prior to a presidential election. There is no good reason why taxpayers should pay professors to lecture on Marx, Nietzsche, Freud, Beauvoir, Sartre, Cixous, Dawkins, or Hitchens, when the ideas of these thinkers run counter to the worldviews of a significant number of people surrounding the school. There is no good reason why a course on Queer Theory should be offered. There is no good reason why the college should be a venue of *The Vagina Monologues*. There is no good reason why Student Services should host a social activity themed on "mock gambling." Local taxpayers, who support the school, should not have to tolerate advocacy in the classroom, or in extra-curricular activities, of events and ideologies that are incommensurable with community values.

Third, as Nielsen (2006) presciently observes, UVU has the opportunity to chart a new, revolutionary course through the black stagnant waters of academe by setting high normative standards – based on shared community values – in its programming. To this end, UVU ought to prohibit any discussion of seditious topics (e.g., abortion rights, feminism, international law and world government, and criticism of free-market capitalism) which have become all too common at other college and universities controlled by dangerous liberal professors (ibid.). The academic program of morally praiseworthy colleges and universities ought to be framed by shared values which bond morally praiseworthy communities. The foundation of a good curriculum involves identifying a morally good community and then promoting the shared values of that community. Utah Valley is one such community and those shared values include Christianity, capitalism, and commitment to military action – simply put, the political principles of the Republican Party which dominate Utah Valley politics almost in totality.

Therefore UVU's proper role is *not* as a forum for discussion of controversial public policy issues and critiques of normativity, but an affirmation and celebration of shared community values.

Perspective Two

Academics should not be held accountable to "community values" advocacy groups.

According to the ethical theory of utilitarianism, the common good is furthered by securing academic freedom at UVU. Intervention by political forces outside the Academy into its internal affairs is morally impermissible, and for several reasons.

First, the project of conjuring "community values" as a font of normativity fails before it even begins. Whether a "community" is defined in terms of geography, religion, language, vocation, or race, the definition is always subject to exception and stipulation. Even relatively cohesive religious communities do not

enjoy consensus on primary values. In Afghanistan, for example, former Taliban
soldiers argue that educating females is un-Islamic (Rohde 2002). Other
Muslims argue that such education furthers the common good, citing that fact
that Muhammad's first wife, Khadijah, was an educated and highly successful
businesswoman, and that the prophet advocated the education of his daughters,
most notably Fatima. Among LDS faithful, there is disagreement on core
political values. Most Utah Mormons unthinkingly assume that to be a good
Mormon one must vote Republican. However, Mormons on the East Coast tend
to vote Democrat because helping the downtrodden through social programs is
considered authentically Christian. So even within the LDS community, there is
no consensus on which a political party platform might stand.

"Community values" exist nowhere but in the minds of their political beholders.
Since the sum of individuals living together in a particular location at a particular time will never universally share the same values, the notion of a community based on shared values is an artifice based on exclusion. The "community"
is not a self-sufficient entity, but precipitates out of a plane of multiplicity (Keller
2002). When Anderson and Nielsen and others claim to speak for "the community," suspicions rightly arise as to whether they are really speaking for others
or merely propping up their own political agenda.

Second, using a "community values" standard for curricular content would
result in a grossly imbalanced academic program so wobbly it would topple over
on its own accord and shatter to pieces. Consider natural science. If it were
somehow determined that a majority of "morally good" members of a religiously
homogenous community consider teaching evolution by natural selection an
odious threat to "community values," then educators would be compelled to
omit the Modern Synthesis of Darwinism and genetics from biology courses. At
minimum, educators would be compelled to include in biology syllabuses supernaturalistic hypotheses such as "intelligent design theory" – as Utah lawmaker
Chris Buttars has proposed (Nardi 2005).

Or take geology. If the majority of members of a community believe that the
age of the Earth is several thousand years, then the formation of sedimentary
rock, the physics of plate tectonics, and isostatic uplift ought not be taught
in geology courses. Required reading would not be based on peer-reviewed
scientific methodology, but might be creationist George McCready Price's *The
New Geology* (1923) and texts of the same genre, with fossils in the lower reaches
of the Grand Canyon explained in class as the handiwork of Satan aimed at
leading the righteous astray like the melody of the Pied Piper.

Obviously, then, basing curriculum on "community values" would result in
the antithesis of education (that is, liberation from ignorance). No such institution would likely receive accreditation from agencies such as the Northwest
Commission on Colleges and Universities, UVU's sanctioning body.

The absurdity of using "community values" as a normative standard for academic affairs extends to invited speakers. UVU has hosted a long list of speakers
whom most citizens would identify as "conservative" (Church of Jesus Christ
of Latter-Day Saints President Gordon B. Hinckley, Senators Robert Bennett and
Orrin Hatch, Utah State Representative Chris Cannon, author and business

leader Stephen R. Covey, Utah Eagle Forum President Gayle Ruzicka, former US State Department official Alan Keyes, former First Lady Barbara Bush, and Fox media personality Sean Hannity, to name a few). Meanwhile, the list of overtly "liberal" speakers is short (Ralph Nader, if he can be consider "liberal," and Moore).

Taken at face value, what Utah Valley interventionists' describe as "balance" (Nielsen 2005a, 2005b) would constitute a mandate for more "liberal" speakers and events. But this is certainly not what the community interventionists have in mind. For them, one "liberal" event in Utah Valley is one too many, rendering their cries for "balance" utterly meaningless.

Third, and most importantly, all US public institutions of higher education must fulfill their indispensable function in open society. American society is, and always has been, composed of citizens of different ethnic, racial, religious, and political backgrounds. Public institutions have a responsibility to reflect and celebrate this diversity. As Thomas Jefferson repeatedly emphasized, public education is essential for democracy (see, for example, Jefferson 1944: 642–9). Democracy, in turn, depends upon voicing a multiplicity of perspectives in a respectful and civil manner. The fabric of American society is woven from the warp of freedom and the weft of mutual respect (Keller and Sederburg 2005b). In this way, UVU merely aims to fulfill the democratic directive given to it by the people of the State of Utah.

In order to create a healthy learning atmosphere, universities must acknowledge and respect the cultural values of the students they serve. Yet at the same time these institutions of higher learning must not be held hostage by parochial idiosyncrasies of various communities. Achieving equipoise is hard, especially for college and universities in relatively homogenous, traditionalist communities where tolerance has limits. But it can be done.

Fourth, colleges and universities have a duty to students to provide an education that will serve them well in achieving their life goals. To be recognized as an authentic institution of higher education, institutions like UVU must adhere to national academic standards so that a degree from the school is acknowledged as legitimate from Alaska to California and from Hawaii to Florida. A degree from an institution where the academic program was based on "community values" would be disregarded outright. UVU could do no greater disservice to students than to offer curricula and hire faculty based on "community values."

Globalism requires that students be able to relate with persons of many different worldviews in both the personal and professional dimensions of their lives. The group up to the task of determining what kind of education serves students best within the framework of democracy consists of professional educators. Outside interference can only frustrate this laudable goal.

Colleges and universities are citadels for introspection and interlocution. New ideas flower from thinking and sharing ideas with others. It is upon ideas – not the blind obedience of theocracy or fear of totalitarianism – that democracy grows and flourishes. Intervention and interference into these citadels by outside political forces kills many new ideas, retards the growth of others, and stunts democracy.

Additional Issues to Consider

Other possible moral dilemmas arising within this case:

Q Should academics adhere "unofficially" to "community values"?

Q What is the appropriate role of taxpayers in setting curriculum at institutions of higher learning?

Q What would have been an appropriate moral response on the part of faculty?

Q What, if any, rights are in conflict with the right of free speech?

NOTE

1 The American Association of University Professors (AAUP) is the professional association of the professoriate founded by esteemed scholars Arthur O. Lovejoy and John Dewey. Censure by the AAUP is considered within American academia as an indictment of illegitimacy of the worst order.

REFERENCES

Anderson, K. N. (2006) Letter to the editor. *College Times* (September 23).
Decker, M. (2004) Invitation to Moore irks GOP legislators. *Deseret News* (September 18): A1.
Ditzler, J. (2004) Defining UVSC. *College Times* (October 3).
Ditzler, J. (2005a) DLC is DO.A, state closes the book on new library. *College Times* (February 13).
Ditzler, J. (2005b) State senator puts stipulations on UVSC's university status. *College Times* (November 20): A3.
Eddington, M. (2004a) Moore foes press on with UVSC suit. *Salt Lake Tribune* (December 1): C5.
Eddington, M. (2004b) Moore than enough? The man behind UVSC lawsuit. *Salt Lake Tribune* (December 9): A1.
Egan, T. (2006) All polls aside, Utah is keeping faith in Bush. *New York Times* (June 4): A1.
Garcia, D. (2003) Letter to the editor. *College Times* (March 5).
Gravois, J. (2004) The making of a political "circus." *The Chronicle of Higher Education* 51 (9): A48.
Hyde, J. (2004a) Moore invitation a UVSC violation? *Deseret News* (October 5): A1.
Hyde, J. (2004b) Suit over Moore visit dropped. *Deseret News* (December 11): B1.
Jefferson, T. (1944) *The Life and Selected Writings of Thomas Jefferson*, ed. A. Koch and W. Peden. New York: The Modern Library.
Jensen, D. P. (2004a) "Fahrenheit 9/11" director steaming up Utah county. *Salt Lake Tribune* (September 15): A1.
Jensen, D. P. (2004b) "Fahrenheit UVSC," it's hot. *Salt Lake Tribune* (September 29): A1.

Keller, D. R. (2002) The perils of communitarianism for teaching ethics across the curriculum. *Teaching Ethics* 3 (1): 67–76.

Keller, D. R. (2004) From the campus, lessons learned from Moore flap at UVSC. Opinion-editorial. *Salt Lake Tribune* (October 10): AA8.

Keller, D. R. (2005a) UVSC serves a vital role as a public, secular institution. Opinion-editorial. *Salt Lake Tribune* (January 9): AA5.

Keller, D. R. (2005b) UVSC is not shifting to the left. Opinion-editorial. *Daily Herald* (June 27): A5.

Keller, D. R. (2005c) Homogeneity and free Speech in Utah. *Academe* 91 (5): 31–2.

Keller, D. R. (2007) Academic freedom vs. community values? *Academe* 93 (5).

Keller, D. R., and Sederburg, W. A. (2005a) UVSC stays true to its core values. Opinion-editorial. *Salt Lake Tribune* (February 13): AA4.

Keller, D. R., and Sederburg, W. A. (2005b) UVSC complements LDS values. Opinion-editorial. *Deseret News* (March 2): A12.

Kirkby, B. (2004) Letter to the editor. *College Times* (September 26).

Lamarche, P. (2004) UVSC student body not a bunch of naive, idiot children. Opinion-editorial. *Salt Lake Tribune* (September 25): AA1.

Minority Films (2005) *This Divided State* (DVD). Orem, UT: Minority Films.

Nardi, E. (2005) Buttars drafts bill on origins teaching. *Salt Lake Tribune* (December 24): B1.

Nielsen, N. L. (2005a) Find a measured, balanced course at UVSC. Opinion-editorial. *Daily Herald* (June 6): A5.

Nielsen, N. L. (2005b) Public must demand balance at UVSC. Opinion-editorial. *Daily Herald* (July 10): A5.

Nielsen, N. L. (2006) UVSC has opportunity to shine in academia. Opinion-editorial. *Daily Herald* (April 24): A5.

Nokkentved, N. S., and E. Andrus (2004) Much ado about Moore. *Daily Herald* (October 9): A1.

Price, G. M. (1923) *The New Geology, A Textbook for Colleges, Normal Schools, and Training Schools, and for the General Reader*. Mountain View, CA: Pacific Press.

Randall, D. (2004) Moore visit sparking controversy. *Daily Herald* (September 16): C1.

Rohde, D. (2002) Attacks on schools for girls hint at lingering split in Afghanistan. *New York Times* (October 31): A1.

Vogel, J. (2004) Why Michael Moore? *College Times* (September 19).

Vogel, J. (2006) *Free Speech 101, The Utah Valley Uproar Over Michael Moore*. Silverton, ID: Wind River Publishing.

Warner, L. (2004a) Anti-Moore petition is circulating at UVSC. *Deseret News* (September 21): A1.

Warner, L. (2004b) Lawsuit targets Moore contract. *Deseret News* (October 20): B1.

CASE SIXTEEN: THE SOUND AND THE FURY – NOISES AND NEIGHBORS

The sounds and smells of Ted's family farm marred the city slickers' image of their idyllic pastoral retreat. Auditory and olfactory disappointments notwithstanding, more urban refugees followed. As suburban sprawl crept closer to farmland, zoning battles increased as residents from encroaching suburbs litigated to remove perceived nuisances from their experience. Despite "Right to Farm" policies that required residents and visitors to accept aesthetically challenging sights and smells, slow-moving vehicles, dust, chemicals, noise, and other necessary agricultural inconveniences, challenges were time-consuming and stressful. The irritating complaints became music to Ted's ears when a developer made a lucrative offer for his land. Ted retired with no regrets from the uncertainties and arduous work of farming. Hoping to find their own peace and quiet, Ted and his wife moved permanently to their renovated family summer lake "cottage" on Don Jean Bay and watched the local land and water battles with interest and bemusement.

Ted is no stranger to land-use disputes. He grew up listening to stories of generations of conflict between his farming family and ranchers, the government, hunters, environmentalists, big business, and developers. His great-grandfather aroused the ire of cattle ranchers by closing off the open range to protect his crops from free-wandering cattle. His grandfather was involved in range wars fought over access to water siphoned off by new upstream irrigation systems. His father disputed with energy companies that viewed the land as an impediment between them and the coal beneath its surface, and whose demand for water depleted aquifers and increased the concentration of chemical run-off to a level toxic to the land and the rivers running through it.

Ted is also interested in global land-use issues. He is sympathetic both to the Kenyan farmers who want to protect the lands their families have farmed for more than a century, and to the desperate Masai herdsmen who graze their animals on nearly barren land and seek the return of their lush ancestral grazing lands, leased under force to the British government before Kenyan independence. The half million members of the Masai tribe claim the land was leased to the settlers for 100 years: the 38 landowners claim the lease agreement was for 999 years (Faris 2004). Ted has little sympathy for the 3.5 percent of Brazilian landowners who claim 60 percent of the best agricultural land, and no sympathy at all for the lumber companies that force Brazilian farmers and their families from their land and into camps, sometimes resorting to murder to do so (Frayssinet 2007). He is fascinated by Indonesia's refusal to allow shipments of sand to Singapore to feed its building frenzy, and amazed that so much sand and gravel has been removed from some uninhabited Indonesian islands that they have disappeared under water – threatening Indonesia's right to claim the waters around them (Parry 2007). Although Ted is intrigued by the never-ending attempts of competing groups worldwide to dictate land- and water-use policies that monopolize use and accommodate no interests other than their own, his main interest in such disputes is closer to home.

At the LaGrange (Wisconsin) Town meeting on September 12, 2005, the Lake Management District Report noted that a small group of Don Jean Bay residents had requested that the Lauderdale Aqua Skiers be prohibited from using the lake for practice and shows (LaGrange 2005).

The Lauderdale Aqua Skiers have practiced and performed on Don Jean Bay since the 1970s. The water-ski team practice maneuvers about nine hours each week, sometimes to loud music, to prepare for their Saturday shows. About 80 skiers from approximately 55 lake families participate on the ski team, which works year round: practicing and performing in summer and making costumes, fundraising, and planning for the next season during the winter. Family and friends who don't perform often pitch in to help. Some team members are fourth-generation Lauderdale Aqua Skiers. The ski show is a longstanding Don Jean Bay family and community tradition (Black 2006).

New families who have purchased vacation homes on Don Jean Bay in the past few years are not enthusiastic about the tradition. The Lauderdale Aqua Skiers disrupt the quiet the newcomers envisioned when they bought their lake retreats. Among other complaints, newcomers cite noise, safety concerns, violations of Wisconsin Department of Natural Resources and National Show Ski Association (NSSA) rules, lack of medical oversight, environmental damage, lack of unrestricted access to the lake, and damage to property (NSSA 2006).

Until 1999, the team launched from the shore of Don Jean Bay on privately owned land. When the owner sold the land, the team moved to nearby Elkhorn Lake for practice, but continued to perform on Don Jean Bay and practice there on a more limited basis. In 2000, the Lauderdale Lakes Lake Management District Board purchased the original site on Don Jean Bay. The team continued to split its practices and performances between the two lakes. In 2003, the Elkhorn Lake Council passed an ordinance prohibiting powerboats, and by 2004 the team was again using Don Jean Bay exclusively.

When the team began solely using Don Jean Bay again, a Chicago-area lawyer who had purchased a home on the lake in 1998 requested that the Lake Management District withdraw the team's permit to launch from their site. He alleged that the land was designated as a conservation area, and that the team was violating environmental laws by using the shore as a launch site. The Lake Management District, a strong supporter of the team and its traditions, ruled that the Lauderdale Aqua Skiers were using the land as the zoning ordinances intended. It expressed concern that a small number of newcomers were trying to undermine the community's values and established traditions. The LaGrange Town Board also denied petitions to restrict the ski team's use of the lake, citing strong community support for the skiers (Black 2006: 32). When opponents of the ski shows filed a complaint with the NSSA alleging that the skiers were violating the national association's rules, the NSSA, instead of siding with opponents of the team, came to the skiers' defense (NSSA 2006).

Thwarted by the local and national authorities, the team's opponents appealed to Walworth County. In the spring of 2007 Walworth County ruled that the team was violating environmental regulations by launching from designated wetlands, and ordered the Lauderdale Aqua Skiers to find a different launch site. However, it also ruled that the team would be able to use the Lake Management District wetlands site permanently if they could prove they had used the site every year since 1974, the year before the wetlands zoning ordinance was approved. In the interim, the skiers are permitted to launch from a pontoon (Heine 2007).

Ted is hopeful that the conflict will be resolved in a way that will restore harmony to the community and accommodate everyone's needs. He admits that at times he was a little disgruntled when music blaring over the lake disturbed his afternoon snooze in the hammock. That now seems to him to be a small price to pay to live in a community where young people work together to provide entertainment for the lake-dwellers and visitors, take pride in being healthy, and are involved in wholesome activities. Ted thinks it's unfair for a lawyer to spend years trying to prevent a group of young people from continuing their summer tradition. He is somewhat amused at himself that his irritation with the adults seems to have increased his enjoyment of the kids' music.

The attempt to eliminate the ski team tradition is not unique to Don Jean Bay. Paul Miller's family spent summers at their cottage on Wisconsin's Moose Lake, where his children participated on the ski team. Young people coming to the lake for the first time were always invited to join the team. The kids practiced together, played together, shared meals, and were in and out of their neighbors' homes on a daily basis. Families knew each other, and parents didn't worry about their children getting into trouble because everyone did everything together. In recent years, however, the lake community changed. Newcomers were more likely to be retirees or older couples escaping for the weekend from the noise of the city. Their complaints to officials forced the young people to discontinue the ski shows at Moose Lake. With the loss of the lake community's common tradition, the former friendly welcome, invitations to group activities, frequent intergenerational game nights and beach barbeques, and the camaraderie of a close-knit summer lake community have all but disappeared. Dr Miller believes this to be a great loss to the entire community, but especially to the young people (P. Miller, Personal conversation, 2007). Others, however, are thoroughly enjoying their new-found peace and quiet.

Ted settles into his hammock with the newspaper, bemused by how the issues of his little lake community are a microcosm that reflect the conflicting interests of stakeholders on a global scale.

From a moral point of view, should the Lauderdale Aqua Skiers continue to use the lake for practice and shows?

Additional Issues to Consider

Other possible moral dilemmas arising within this case:

Q What rights are in conflict here? Which is/are stronger, and why?

Q When, if ever, should community traditions have priority over concern for the environment?

Q When, if ever, should concern for the environment have priority over community traditions?

Q Is the preservation of colonial rights and privileged access to resources anachronistic in today's world, or will undermining these rights and privileges destabilize communities or entire regions of a country?

Q Disputes over access and use of land and water are prevalent worldwide. From a moral perspective, what are the similarities and differences in these issues between the Lauderdale Aqua Skiers and newcomers to Don Jean Bay, and the Kenyan farmers and the Masai? What are the similarities and differences in these issues between the dispute between Brazilian landowners and timber companies against small farmers, and the dispute over sand between Indonesia and Singapore?

Q Are mere aesthetic preferences (e.g., not wanting to listen to raucous music) morally compelling?

Q Loud sound can create high levels of stress. The US government used loud music as a weapon when it besieged Manuel Noriega in Panama and the Branch Davidian compound in Waco, Texas. Is it morally justifiable to force on others loud music that they find stressful?

REFERENCES

Black, L. (2006) The battle of Don Jean Bay. *Chicago Tribune* (30 June): 1, 32.
Faris, S. (2004) The land is ours. *Time Europe* 164 (12). Available at: www.time.com/time/magazine/article/0,9171,699336,00.html (accessed October 2, 2007).
Frayssinet, F. (2007) Dorothy Stang sentence – more than symbolic? *Inter Press Service News Agency.* Available at: http://ipsnews.net/news.asp?idnews=37757 (accessed October 2, 2007).
Heine, M. (2007) Battle for the bay reaches settlement: Lauderdale skiers will move performances. *The Week* (3 May). Available at: www.walworthcountydining.com/news/0507/050307skiers.html (accessed October 2, 2007).
LaGrange, Wisconsin Minutes of regular town board meeting (September 12, 2005). Available at: www.lagrangetalkofthetown.com/viewminutes (accessed May 30, 2007).
NSSA (National Show Ski Association) (2006) Minutes of the board of directors meeting. (March 3, 2006). Available at: http://usawaterski.com/pages/divisions/showski/2006SpringNSSABoardMinutes.pdf (accessed May 30, 2007).
Parry, R. L. (2007) Singapore accused of land grab as islands disappear by boatload. *The Times* (UK edition) (March 17, 2007). Available at: www.timesonline.co.uk/tol/news/world/asia/article1527751.ece (accessed October 2, 2007).

CASE SEVENTEEN: SHOOT TO THRILL – GUN SCHOOLS IN THE UNITED STATES

The Minnesota National Guard Camp Riley's shoothouse has an apartment, a retail store, and office cubicles (Horwich 2003). The Protection Technology Los Alamos (PTLA) shoothouse is made up of modular components that can be arranged into a variety of room, doorway, and hallway configurations for live-ammunition training (Paris-Chitanvis 2003: 8). Blackwell USA offers "RU Ready High," a shoothouse designed in the aftermath of the Columbine High School massacre to train law-enforcement officers to handle school hostage-taking and shootings (Hemingway 2007: 20). The front and cockpit of the jumbo jet at Colorado's Valhalla Training Center feature training for hijacking scenarios (Valhalla Trainign Center 2004).

Shoothouses simulate urban and indoor environments where much military combat and community violence now occur. Shoothouse training prepares trainees to respond successfully under pressure to a worst-case scenario where multiple players interact in realistic settings. Live-ammunition training prepares law-enforcement officers, government agents, military personnel, Special Forces, and private security personnel to handle violent and chaotic situations, before they are confronted with them in real life. With urban combat and house-to-house fighting becoming a necessary skill for most members of the armed services, and with law-enforcement personnel increasingly called on to handle deadly situations in crowded areas (school shootings, hostage-taking in public buildings, drug houses in densely populated neighborhoods), demand for shoothouse training has expanded.

Law-enforcement agencies, the military, government agencies, and private security firms rely more and more on private combat training organizations to provide expertise and facilities to ensure their personnel receive the most skilled, productive, and cost-effective training. Law-enforcement officers have multiple responsibilities: very little of their training time is spent on hostage negotiation or violent confrontation in a crowded public space. Few law-enforcement agencies have the resources to build and equip shoothouses, develop intensive training programs, and retain experienced trainers, particularly as these skills may be called upon only infrequently. The military is also faced with limitations. In the 1990–1 Gulf War, there were 60 military personnel for every private contractor; in the Iraq war, the low number of military recruits has resulted in a ratio of one to one (Hemingway 2007: 15). Despite its size and resources, the US military is encumbered by a bureaucracy that does not allow for rapid response (ibid.: 16). The US military uses simulated combat environments at schools such as the Valhalla Training Center to prepare thousands of armed service personnel for combat in the Middle East.

A new industry emerged following 9/11: private businesses and clubs that offer shoothouses and other tactical training for civilians. The demand for defense and combat training has risen among private individuals. Thriving in a time of war and terrorism, enrollment at Arizona's Gunsite Academy has doubled since the terrorist attacks of 2001 (Fahrenthold 2006: A3). Students enroll in these programs for a variety of reasons: personal safety, career advancement, survival training, recreation, and to maintain military or law-enforcement skills. Students want to learn how to defend themselves against home intruders, muggers, and other real-life threats. Thunder Ranch in Mountain Home, Texas, holds special classes to train women to repel or escape from attackers. Gun-owners who don't feel comfortable with the firearm they bought for self-defense take classes to increase self-confidence and gun-handling proficiency. Some students seek employment as bodyguards, or in executive protection or private security services. Some enroll for personal improvement. Other clients enjoy the adrenalin rush of close-quarters fighting with live ammunition. Active duty and retired military and law-enforcement personnel enroll in courses to retain or hone their combat skills.

The growing popularity of private schools that teach combat techniques has raised concern. Little regulation encumbers these private programs, called gun schools, military schools, spy schools, or commando schools. The Bureau of Alcohol, Tobacco, Firearms, and Explosives licenses gun-dealers, but no federal or state oversight exists to regulate privately run gun schools. A few of these schools are highly restricted, providing specialized training to Special Forces of the US military. Some are less restrictive, limited to law-enforcement, military personnel, or agents of the US government and its allies. Several schools partner with colleges or universities, often offering college credit. Membership at the private Valhalla Shooting Club and Training Center is limited to 50 corporate members and 550 individual members, with individual memberships starting at $52,000 (Valhalla Training Center 2004). Other gun schools are open to the public, but enforce enrollment requirements such as criminal background checks and gun permits. Some, however, have no restrictions on who may enroll.

What might persons who decide to enroll in one of these private schools expect to learn? In addition to military training, Valhalla provides combat training and entertainment for civilian members in its luxurious environment. Broadway set designers created Valhalla Training Center's shoothouse. The Scenario House features a fully furnished house, front section and cockpit of a jumbo jet, night club, offices, subway station, warehouse, and a convenience store, and other environments where serious fighters can train, or where "serious Walter Mittys" (Spy Schools n.d.) can be entertained by participating in a mock shooting with training guns that shoot wax-tipped plastic bullets (Fahrenthold 2006: A3). A glance at other schools advertised on the Internet shows that students can study lock-picking, methods of entry, explosive entry, surveillance, electronic surveillance, electronic security, eavesdropping, bugging, escape and evasion driving, protection tactics, terrorism defense, explosives, demolition, bombs (for purposes of counterterrorism), exotic martial arts, lethal force (for self-defense), unconventional warfare, interrogation methods, covert operations, covert devices, use of deadly force "useful to civilians," street survival, rifle use for urban self-defense, use of chemical agents, raids and ambushes, stalking, techniques for breaking bones and tearing muscles, military weaponry, improvised weapons, shooting, urban shootouts, ballistics, night-firing, urban mercenary tactics, sniper-training, assault weapons, knife combat, crossbow, shuriken (Japanese metal throwing spikes), and stick combat with a kubotan (a metal or plastic cylinder, five and a half inches long, used on pressure points or as a club).

Supporters of private combat schools that enroll students who are not in professions that require combat-ready skills point to the US Constitution (Amendment II) and its encouragement for citizen preparedness: "A well regulated militia, being necessary to the security of a free state, the right of the people to keep and bear arms, shall not be infringed." In shoothouse simulations, students learn what to do in a life-threatening situation. Gaining proficiency and confidence through training, they are less likely to make mistakes when danger threatens, and are better prepared to survive and help others to survive as well. Professor Liviu Librescu died in the April 2007 shooting spree at Virginia Tech, but not before he barred the door with his body and instructed his students to flee the room. His experiences of survival during the Holocaust and under Romanian dictator Nicolae Ceausescu's repressive regime enabled him to realize the danger in time to save his students (Moynihan 2007: A20). Practice on a firing range by itself is not sufficient preparation for dealing with the uncertainties, chaos, and stress of a situation of real danger (Meyer 2007).

Those who oppose commando schools charge that these enterprises teach few skills that are practical or applicable to everyday life. After all, how many citizens need to know anything about the use of chemical agents, raids and ambushes, stalking, techniques for breaking bones and tearing muscles, military weaponry, urban mercenary tactics, sniper-training, assault weapons, or a crossbow? Furthermore, live ammunition training, particularly in close quarters, is very dangerous. Shoothouses must be bulletproofed to protect those on the outside, but inside the schoolhouses' ricocheting bullets, self-inflicted wounds, and blind sightlines present grave dangers to both students and trainers. Some shoothouses allow trainers to observe students from catwalks and, while this is a good vantage point for teaching, it exposes the trainers to stray bullets. Frangible bullets pulverize on contact, but hollowpoint bullets can shatter bones, which then become projectiles that can inflict even further damage on the body. Even experienced trainers are surprised by the reactions of students under stress. The uncertainty of not knowing what people will do makes the scenario more realistic, but it also significantly increases the danger. Perhaps the biggest danger is that once the live ammunition drill begins, there is no way out (Meyer 2007). Adrenaline causes physical responses that can affect behavior: tunnel vision, auditory distortion, loss of fine-motor coordination, and physical and mental paralysis.

Opponents of recreational shoothouses fear that weapons training will make students more aggressive. They criticize the lack of regulation of both enrollment and program content, which allows unstable individuals access to lethal-skills training. A group of men who received training in a Pennsylvania program were linked to the terrorist group that bombed the World Trade Center in 1993 (Fahrenthold 2006: A3). Gun-school supporters counter by saying that they teach students to avoid confrontation, and to fight only as a last resort.

If live ammunition shoothouses do not provide enough challenge, there is always the option of an urban grenade house (BTI 2007).

From a moral perspective, should private gun schools be permitted to teach advanced combat tactics to the general public?

Additional Issues to Consider

Other possible moral dilemmas arising within this case:

Q From a moral perspective, should shoothouses, where fantasies of lethal fighting are played out, be prohibited entirely?

Q Are either state or federal governments morally required to oversee gun schools?

Q From a moral point of view, should gun-school use be restricted to adults?

Q Can a moral justification be made that citizens should be free to learn chemical warfare, urban mercenary tactics, sniper-training, or the use of assault weapons or crossbows?

REFERENCES

Ballistics Technology International (2007) Available at: www.ballisticstech.com/products/grenadehouse.htm (accessed October 11, 2007).

Fahrenthold, D. A. (2006) Schools teach combat skills to civilians: Lack of regulation of private training troubles some. *Washington Post* (28 May): A3.

Hemingway, M. (2007) Warriors for hire. *Portland Police Association Rap Sheet* 38 (1): 20, 15–17.

Horwich, J. (2003) Fighting "house to house, room to room." *Minnesota Public Radio* (radio broadcast) (26 February). Available at: http://news.minnesota.publicradio.org/features/2003/02/27_horwichj_livefire/ (accessed October 11, 2007).

Meyer, J. T. (2007) Shoot house instructor development. European Police training Conference (8 March), Nurnberg, Germany. Available at: www.eptk2007.de/policetrainerconference/Bulletin%202007.html (accessed October 11, 2007).

Moynihan, C. (2007) Massacre in Virginia: Professor's violent death came where he sought peace. *New York Times* (April 19): A20.

Paris-Chitanvis, J. (2003) PTLA shows its stuff. *Los Alamos National Laboratory Newsletter* 4 (9): 8.

Spy schools (n.d.) Available at: www.textfiles.com/survival/sschools.txt (accessed October 11, 2007).

United States Constitution, Amendment II (1789) Available at: http://memory.loc.gov/cgi-bin/ampage?collId=llsl&fileName=001/llsl001.db&recNum=144 (accessed October 11, 2007).

Valhalla Training Center (2004) Available at http://valhallashootingclub.com (accessed October 11, 2007).

6

HEALTHY, WEALTHY, AND WHYS

Ethical Issues in Healthcare

Moral dilemmas in healthcare go to the very heart of what it means to be human, encompassing concepts of identity, autonomy, physical and psychological integrity, spiritual and cultural values, and human dignity. They intricately intertwine diametrically opposing concerns: life and death, humanness and technology, the highly intimate and the impersonally bureaucratic. They raise ethical concerns involving the ancient and immediate fundamental issues of life: its beginning, its quality, and its end – how to define these and how to evaluate their quality and meaning. Moral dilemmas in healthcare challenge our expectations that medicine is a compassionate and altruistic calling, that we can trust those who provide care when we are most vulnerable, and that decisions will be in our best interests and for our optimal benefit. In this arena of life and death, tensions arise between professional obligation and individual choice. Conflicts emerge among personal, cultural, religious, economic, and social values, raising questions that define our understanding of human worth and dignity.

Is dehumanization the inevitable consequence of the onslaught of technology in medicine? Who should have and who should determine access to limited health-care resources? Does professional duty or the patient's autonomy carry greater moral authority in conflicts over healthcare decisions? Are all anatomical and physiological variations *medical* anomalies, or do they reflect a natural and diverse range of human characteristics and abilities? Is medical intervention ever morally justifiable when its purpose is not to improve health, but only to accommodate societal preferences? Should cultural values ever drive medical decisions? In "Healthy, Wealthy, and Whys: Ethical Issues in Healthcare," we examine these and others moral dilemmas related to health and healthcare delivery.

CASE EIGHTEEN: WHOSE LIFE IS IT ANYWAY? – COLLISIONS BETWEEN PERSONAL CONSCIENCE AND PROFESSIONAL OBLIGATIONS

In June 2005, Luke Vander Bleek, an Illinois pharmacist, filed a suit challenging the state requirement that pharmacists make Plan B (also known as the morning-after pill) available "without delay."[1] Like other chemical contraceptives, Plan B prevents ovulation. Vander Bleek, however, believes that the morning-after pill, unlike other contraceptives, prevents uterine implantation of a fertilized ovum and is the moral equivalent of abortion. As a Roman Catholic, Vander Bleek believes that full moral status begins at conception; thus, emergency contraception (EC), as he understands its functional mechanism, is morally impermissible (MSNBC 2005).[2]

Vander Bleek's action is not uncommon (Borrego et al. 2006; Chuang and Shank 2006; Curlin et al. 2007). Across the US, pharmacists are appealing to so-called "conscience clauses" (which initially became germane for pharmacists when some Oregon practitioners wished to refuse to fill prescriptions written for the purpose of physician-assisted suicide (Ginty 2005)), to justify their decisions not to dispense EC (Pugh 2007). Moreover, pharmacists have taken their appeals beyond their sites of employment: as of March 2007, 27 states had considered legislation "which gives pharmacists the right to refuse to perform certain services based on a violation of personal beliefs or values" (National Conference of State Legislatures 2007; see also Charo 2005). Some states have passed laws that explicitly allow pharmacists the right of conscientious objection; others state laws require pharmacists to comply with legitimate requests for medications (National Conference of State Legislatures 2007; Guttmacher Institute 2007).

Pharmacists who refuse to dispense certain medications ground their case in moral appeals to autonomy and *personal* integrity (Wicclair 2006): No one should be forced to embrace another's values or abandon his own when he goes to work.

Many persons, some pharmacists included, have deeply held beliefs regarding when human life – and the right to life – begin. Those who believe that human life and full human rights begin at conception are morally obligated to refuse to participate in any activity that destroys a zygote (conceptus). Many express the additional worry that easily available EC will promote irresponsible sexual behavior, particularly among younger women and teens who may be less able to weigh burdens and benefits associated with taking EC, especially repeatedly.

Opponents of conscientious refusals argue that those who invoke them violate the autonomy, and often the consciences, of others. If pharmacists justify their behavior in terms of their own personal values, they are logically required to recognize the importance of the personal values of others. This implies that women who value reproductive autonomy – or, more specifically, who disvalue parenthood – are justified in acting in concert with that value. Moreover, reproductive autonomy is critically important to women. An unwanted pregnancy can wreak havoc with a woman's life and she should be free to prevent it.

From a moral point of view, should pharmacists be allowed to opt out of filling requests for emergency contraception?

Perspective One

Pharmacists who believe life begins at conception should be allowed to refuse to fill EC requests. The state must not compel them to engage in acts that violate their consciences.

This claim is supported by the appeal to autonomy. Autonomy, also known as self-determination, recognizes the importance of a person's freedom to choose for himself the values in terms of which to structure and measure the worth of his own life. In times past, persons typically inherited, without much conversation, the values of their families or communities. As communities have become more pluralistic, persons have attained greater information and freedom about the values they will embrace. Pluralistic societies, by definition, lack a single set of values shared by all their members; rather, they comprise multiple smaller communities that embrace disparate – and at times competing – value systems. As individuals mingle with members of various communities, they may revisit and revise their values, ultimately compiling a constellation of values that is unique to themselves. Autonomy protects the freedom of individuals to do just that and to live in terms of their own value systems. (Of course, individuals whose values directly threaten to harm others may be restricted by the larger society and resisted by individuals, should the occasion arise.)

Residents of pluralistic societies may align themselves with individuals who share many of their values. They may join formal organizations (churches, clubs, service societies) or merely spend time with like-minded others. Some associations have minimal behavioral requirements for their members, while others are quite demanding. Rigidly structured behavior is not, however, a violation of autonomy as long as persons freely and knowingly accept these restrictions, and as long as they are free to dissociate from the group at any time (Engelhardt 1996: 74–84).

Once a set of autonomously chosen values is in place, the virtue of (personal) integrity comes into play. If stating one's values is defined as "talking the talk," integrity may be defined as "walking the walk." Integrity requires a person to act in concert with his espoused values on (nearly) every occasion: what would it mean (to take the case at hand) to claim to value human life from the moment of conception, yet fail – when one has the opportunity – to act to protect a conceptus? Filling requests for emergency contraceptives involves – albeit indirectly – a pharmacist who holds this belief in the destruction of a zygote whose life, on his value system, must be respected and preserved.

In sum, the appeals to autonomy and the virtue of personal integrity support allowing pharmacists to follow their consciences and refuse to dispense EC.

Perspective Two

Pharmacists should not be allowed to refuse to fill requests for EC. This claim is supported by an appeal to autonomy. Autonomy protects an individual's freedom to choose both her own personal values and actions that reify those values. Protection of autonomy is the foundational value in pluralistic societies where citizens are free to choose and live according to their own values. In a pluralistic society the (nonmaleficent) values and beliefs of all persons must be protected, with a person's most central and self-defining values commanding the most stringent respect.

Reproductive values are profoundly important to most persons, given their life-changing, long-term effects. Since the advent of reliable contraception in the 1960s, women have achieved decisional authority regarding reproduction that had previously eluded them. Parenting has such profound implications for one's range of opportunities that it should not be undertaken lightly. Moreover, one's personal identity is substantially altered by choices about parenting. For example, a woman who values the pursuit of a demanding profession with lengthy educational requirements may opt to delay child-bearing or omit parenting entirely. Should she (even if temporarily) define herself in terms of a profession, an unwanted child may – quite literally – devastate her sense of self. Thus, a woman's reproductive autonomy must be insured.

Once a person has embraced a set of values, the virtue of personal integrity requires a life in accordance with them. In fact, the integration of a person's identity with her values implies that actions by others that thwart choices in terms of these values constitute not only a disrespect of autonomy, but also an assault on personal identity.

The moral values of autonomy and personal integrity require that others respect and permit contraceptive (and other) choices and actions by women who value reproductive freedom. Interference with reproductive freedom violates the woman's autonomy. Respect for women as persons and for their autonomous choices requires that pharmacists fill requests for ECs.

Pharmacists should *not* be allowed to follow their consciences and refuse to dispense EC.

Perspective Three

Should pharmacists be allowed – for reasons of conscience – to refuse to fill legitimate requests for EC? This dilemma arises because protecting and respecting the autonomy and personal integrity of pharmacists can only be achieved by disrespecting the autonomy and personal integrity of women, and vice versa. To determine the morally preferable answer, further information is needed.

Step 1: Information-gathering

Medical information

- What is the mechanism by which EC works? Is it a contraceptive or an abortifacient?
- Does EC pose health risks to women? If so, how do these risks compare with the risks of pregnancy or of surgical abortion?

Legal/policy information

- What do state and federal laws permit or require?
- What do the pharmacist's code of ethics and standards of practice specify about dispensing EC?

Psychological information

- What are the likely psychological effects on women if access to EC can be denied?
- What are the likely psychological effects on pharmacists if access to EC is mandated?

Implications

- If pharmacists are permitted to opt out, will the number of unwanted pregnancies increase?

- If pharmacists are permitted to opt out, will the number of abortions increase?
- If pharmacists are permitted to opt out, will the number of *unsafe* abortions by unlicensed providers increase?
- If pharmacists are not permitted to opt out, will pharmacists exit the profession?
- If pharmacists are not permitted to opt out, will the number of unprotected sexual encounters increase?

History

- Is the long tradition of oppression of women at work here?
- How have the health professions typically/previously addressed concerns of conscience?

Step 2: Creative problem-solving

It is worth noting that three approaches could eliminate this dilemma: (1) making EC drugs available *without restriction* over the counter (i.e., not requiring pharmacists to dispense them); (2) making the drugs available to physicians to give to patients who come to their offices/clinics; and (3) *requiring* refusing pharmacists *to refer* the client to a colleague or a different pharmacy.

1 Giving the drugs *unrestricted* OTC status would eliminate the need to involve pharmacists at all, but fails to comply with the FDA's recommendations.
2 Allowing physicians to provide EC drugs would also let pharmacists off the hook, but not all women have timely access to a physician: "More than 40% of the women received emergency contraception services from pharmacies during evenings, weekends, or holidays" (Downing 2000: iv), that is, when physicians are less likely to be available. And women whose physicians themselves invoke a conscience clause will still be unable to exercise reproductive freedom.
3 Finally, referrals themselves are often contested on moral or pragmatic grounds: pharmacists who refer patients with EC needs to colleagues are (the argument goes) still morally complicit in the death of an innocent; furthermore, referrals may be impossible (e.g., small towns with only one pharmacy or pharmacist). Even where possible, referrals may delay a woman's access to EC, thereby diminishing its efficacy.

Since no creative solution is immediately forthcoming, we need to consider pros and cons of the original options.

Step 3: Listing pros and cons

Options	Pros	Cons
Allow pharmacist to refuse to dispense EC.	1. Respects pharmacist's choice (A) 2. Respects pharmacist's liberty rights (R) 3. Respects pharmacist's *personal* integrity (V-I) 4. Other HCPs are allowed to exercise conscience clause (J-E)	5. Risks woman's reproductive health (C-NM) 6. Forces woman to risk an unwanted pregnancy (C-NM, A) 7. Trust between pharmacist and client violated (C-NM, V-F) 8. Pharmacists promised to uphold code of ethics (A, V-F) 9. Violates woman's right of self-determination (R) 10. Denies reproductive freedom to woman (R-liberty) 11. Professional promise to put client's well-being first (V-F) 12. Discriminates against women (J-E) 13. Other HCPs must provide services in emergencies (J-E) 14. Discrimination expands (C-U, RFP, A, R, J-E, J-F)
Require pharmacist to fill	15. Unwanted pregnancies avoided (C-B, C-U) 16. Reduces number of abortions (C-B, C-U) 17. Respects patient's values (A, RFP) 18. Respect patient's choice (A) 19. Separation of public and private morality (A, R, J-E) 20. Monopoly on drugs restrictive (R-liberty) 21. Pharmacist has other options (R-liberty) 22. Compassion for woman (V) 23. Cost-effective (J-CE)	24. Crisis of conscience for pharmacist (C-NM) 25. Causes anxiety among pharmacists (C-NM) 26. Fails to respect pharmacist's values (C-NM, A) 27. May kill a zygote (C-NM? R-life?)

Step 4: Analysis

Factual assumptions

- Pregnancy does not begin until the zygote implants in the uterine wall.
- A woman forced to bear an unchosen child is at significant risk of facing limited personal, educational, economic, and professional opportunities throughout her life.
- Some women whose access to EC is delayed or denied will sustain an unwanted pregnancy.
- Some women whose access to EC is delayed or denied will undergo an unwanted abortion.
- Gender injustice does contribute to this dilemma.

Value assumptions

- In pluralistic environments, no one should deny or obstruct a (non-maleficent) autonomous choice of another person.
- In pluralistic environments, no one should deny or obstruct the (non-maleficent) integrity of another person.
- In pluralistic environments, human zygotes and embryos should not be treated *legally* as moral equals of adults.
- In pluralistic environments, personal integrity should trump professional integrity.

Step 5: Justification

Clearly good moral reasons exist for both options. Which of those reasons are stronger?

Although autonomy is most often discussed in the context of particular decisions (e.g., to forgo life-sustaining treatment), it actually plays a much broader role in shaping one's life. As persons move through life, they encounter many values: they embrace some, reject others, and ignore the rest. The values that persons embrace and reject collectively constitute their autonomously developed value structures (ADVS), and form the basis of their identity (White 1994; Engelhardt 1996). Acts that express one's ADVS give evidence of one's values and commitment thereto; to act in concert with/to protect one's autonomously chosen values is to act with integrity.

Admittedly, constructing an ADVS is a messy and often poorly articulated process. Moreover, it is always a work in progress. Children inherit values from parents, spiritual leaders, peers, teachers, coaches, the media, etc. As they age and experience the world more extensively, they choose to discard some of these values and to retain and adopt others. Nonetheless, at any given time most adults could specify their core values and use them to explain their behavior. For example, a deep and abiding commitment to Catholicism can explain becoming a nun, regularly confessing to one's priest, or eschewing birth control. A commitment to economic security or a desire not to parent can explain limiting the size of one's family (to adults only).

Respect for autonomy requires that one not impede another's choices and actions that are manifestations of that other's ADVS – especially when those values are central to a person's sense of self and definition of a good life. This obligation of respect is, however, limited: One need not tolerate – indeed, one may act to prevent – autonomous actions that directly and unavoidably (attempt to) harm others. While one is free to define and live a uniquely personalized good life, one is *not* free to harm others or use them as means to one's own ends. (Jake is not, for example, morally required to respect John's autonomous decision to kill Jim.)

One particular type of act that may be resisted is persons' attempts to *impose* their own ADVS on others. Since all persons capable of autonomy are equally worthy of respect, all are free to reject others' constellations of values and the behavioral guides and rules to which they give rise. Persons whose values are rejected cannot – from a moral point of view – bully or coerce others into living by those values. That is, no one can deny or obstruct the (nonmaleficent) autonomy or integrity of another as a means to proselytizing or protecting her own values or integrity. This requirement has particular force in pluralistic environments; that is, in arenas in which persons of disparate values come into contact. While one may rightly attempt to enforce *shared* values – for example, a good Catholic may strongly criticize and even attempt to prevent an abortion by another good Catholic – a good Catholic may not interfere with the abortion of a non-Catholic who does not share the Catholic conception of fetal personhood. To do so is to fail to respect the values of – and, derivatively, actions in concert with those values – an autonomous person equally deserving of respect and of behavioral freedom. One may attempt to dissuade persons – that is, persuade them to make a different *autonomous* choice; but one may not coerce another to follow her own values.

These restrictions have implications for pharmacists refusing to fill requests for EC: Decisions to have children are among the most central in developing and defining persons' values, identities, and obligations, and in determining their behavior (Reasons ##17, 18). As profoundly important as family-planning choices are to both women and men, they are particularly crucial for women, who continue to bear most of the day-to-day child-rearing responsibilities. The 24/7 obligations of caring for a child not surprisingly limit a woman's opportunity to engage in other activities that she may value (e.g., continuing her education, pursuing a career). As a result, "being able to determine whether and when to bear children is one of the most basic aspects of self-determination [autonomy], and it has become a prerequisite for women's full participation in modern life" (Gold 2006: 2) (Reasons ##6, 9, 10, 11, 15). A woman forced to bear an *unchosen* child is at risk for *unchosen and limited* personal, educational, economic, and professional opportunities throughout her life. In short, restricting access to emergency contraception fails to respect the woman's values and autonomous choices, and uses the woman as a mere means to promulgating one's own values.

Furthermore, restricting access to EC perpetuates age-old gender-based injustice (Reason #23). In societies with patriarchal traditions, the disparate reproductive capacities of men and women have historically oppressed women. Each year, 3.5 *million* unintended pregnancies occur in the US (Raine 2005: 54) (Reason #6). Men whose sexual behavior unintentionally contributes to a pregnancy often see themselves as free to ignore their role in that outcome. Women find such pregnancies much more burdensome; they must terminate the pregnancy or carry the child to term and either surrender it for adoption or raise it. All three options have both physical and psychological costs, particularly the option of raising the child. As Rebekah E. Gee notes (2006: 4): "[Limiting access to contraception] sets women back decades, threatening their right to achieve equally in society by robbing them of options for planning their childbearing" (Reason #23).

Justice – understood as equal opportunity – demands that women who do not desire to parent must be free to remain childless. Currently, two medical options are available to women choosing not to parent: prevent a pregnancy or terminate a pregnancy that has been established. EC, in virtue of not taking a human life (even if one deems that life not to have full – or any – moral status), seems morally preferable (Reasons ##16, 27), if only because prevention avoids the riskier – to a woman's physical and psychological health – procedure of abortion. In fact, women without healthcare insurance may resort to more affordable but untrained, unlicensed abortion providers in which the risk of adverse health outcomes increases Reasons ##5, 15). Until and unless "sperm donors" see themselves as morally obligated to become responsible parents, equality requires that women – like men – be allowed to opt out of unwanted, unplanned pregnancies.

Beyond unjustly failing to respect women's autonomous choices, pharmacists' refusals to provide EC can directly harm the women involved (Hepler 2005) (Reasons ##5, 6). EC is most effective when administered in a timely fashion. Plan B is 95 percent effective in pregnancy prevention if taken within 24 hours of intercourse, 85 percent effective in 25–48 hours, 59 percent effective in 49–72 hours, and ineffective after 72 hours (Task Force 1998; Litt 2005). In the least worrisome scenario a pharmacist is forcing a woman (who is presumably already under stress) to go in search of another pharmacist, whom she may not find in a timely fashion. In the most worrisome scenario – for example, where a pharmacist is the only provider available to women in geographically isolated, rural communities; or where a woman's economic status or insurance plan requires her to use a particular pharmacy – women may be unable to get EC *at all* and must suffer weeks of worrying about a possible unwanted pregnancy (Reason #6), or must get an unwanted abortion (Reason #16), or must carry an unwanted pregnancy to term and surrender for adoption or raise an unwanted child – any of which may compromise her own values, forcing *her* to act without integrity and disrespecting her autonomous choice (Reasons ##17, 18). That is, women whose access to EC is delayed or denied may be *forced to sustain a pregnancy valued by the pharmacist but disvalued by the woman herself, or undergo an abortion that they both disvalue.* Again, while such coercion may be morally permissible in closed communities whose members share values, it is morally impermissible in pluralistic, typically secular, environments – such as business environments – in which values are quite likely to diverge.

These possibilities, of course, might be quite appealing to the *pharmacist's personal* sense of autonomy and integrity (Reasons ##1, 3). If a pharmacist's ADVS incorporates the beliefs that moral considerability begins at conception, that a conceptus has a right to life (Reason #27), and that she (the pharmacist) has an obligation to protect that life, shouldn't those values also command respect? Why should the pharmacist be required to set aside her own values for those of the woman requesting EC? Forcing pharmacists to act against their core values is not only disrespectful (Reason #26), but can cause physical and psychological harms to the pharmacist (Reasons ##24, 25).

At this point it is clear that appealing to autonomy and *personal* integrity is a moral standoff. After all, since personal integrity requires persons to live by their autonomously chosen values, morality supports both pharmacists who refuse and women who request and use EC. Moreover, just as refusal causes anxiety in women (or their partners), forcing pharmacists to dispense EC precipitates a crisis of conscience for them (Reason #24). Note, however, that pharmacists have choices that allow them to preserve their personal integrity: pharmacists who object to contraception in general or EC in particular are free to work in environs in which the conflict does not occur – nursing homes or Neonatal Intensive Care Units, for example – or they can change professions (Reason #21). Even if pharmacists would prefer to work in community pharmacies, other professional options remain. The fact that conscience-protecting choices are less appealing does not mean that such choices do not exist. Conversely, many women seeking EC have no other autonomy- and integrity-protecting choices.

This lack of choices is more generally problematic. In the US (though not in most European countries), access to many drugs is legally limited, raising the question of *professional* integrity (Reasons ##8, 11). The only way women can obtain non-emergency chemical contraceptives is by presenting their requests for these drugs to a pharmacist *licensed by the state to practice*. States license healthcare professionals (HCPs) as a means of providing healthcare to their populations and of protecting residents against unqualified practitioners. In accepting these licenses to practice, *providers accept the responsibility to provide these services* (Reason #8): "By granting a monopoly, [states] turn the profession into a kind of public utility, obligated to provide service to all who seek it. Claiming an unfettered right to personal autonomy while holding monopolistic control over a public good constitutes an abuse of the public trust" (Charo 2005: 2473) (Reasons ##8, 20). This same argument applies to all restricted access, such as pharmacists who are the designated by the FDA as legal "guardians" of EC (so as to insure the drugs do not fall into the hands of minors). Analogous to public utilities, pharmacists who are the only available suppliers of EC "are obliged to render their services impartially to all potential customers within the geographical area over which the monopoly holds sway" (Fenton and Lomasky 2005: 586) (Reason #20). In a monopolistic public distribution system, consumers face a single distributor. If the system is regulated by the government – which (in the absence of justified legislation to the contrary) is bound to make the goods or services being distributed equally available – private purveyors have no authority to distribute goods or services according to their idiosyncratic preferences or values (Reason #19). Personal values might legitimately play a role in a system with multiple outlets that make goods easily available to consumers. But in the US, EC is typically only available from pharmacists (Pugh 2007). Lacking other options, clients must get EC drugs from these professionals; lacking special dispensation (no pun intended) to the contrary, pharmacists must provide them.

Professional integrity is relevant in a second way. When one enters a profession, one commits to the values and behaviors that define the profession in question (Reason #8). These values and behaviors are typically specified in professional codes of ethics. In the case of pharmacists, professional integrity requires filling patients' legitimate requests for drugs. According to the American Pharmaceutical Association: "APhA advocates and will facilitate pharmacists' participation in . . . patient care . . . in order to optimize *desired therapeutic outcomes*" (APhA 2004, emphasis added). This obligation is amplified in the APhA Code of Ethics for Pharmacists (APhA 2005; emphases added):

I.   A pharmacist respects the covenantal relationship between the patient and pharmacist.
      Considering the patient–pharmacist relationship as a covenant means that a pharmacist has moral obligations in response to the gift of trust received from society. In return for this gift, a pharmacist promises to help individuals achieve optimum benefit from their medications, *to be committed to their welfare*, and to maintain their trust.
II.   A pharmacist promotes the good of every patient in a caring, compassionate, and confidential manner.
      A pharmacist places concern for the well-being of the patient at the center of professional practice. In doing so, *a pharmacist considers needs stated by the patient* as well as those defined by health science. . . .
III. A pharmacist respects the autonomy and dignity of each patient.
      A pharmacist promotes the right of self-determination [autonomy] and recognizes individual self-worth by *encouraging patients to participate in decisions about their health.* . . . In all cases, *a pharmacist respects personal and cultural differences* among patients.

As the Code specifies, the professional obligations of the pharmacist include not violating the trust placed in the profession, of which the individual practitioner is a representative (Reason #7), recognizing the *primacy of the patient's welfare* (Reason #9) in a compassionate and caring fashion (Reason #22), and meeting patients' needs as a means of respecting their dignity and autonomy (Reasons ##17, 18). None of the Code's requirements is unique or counterintuitive. All *professions* (as opposed to jobs) are fiduciary in nature: recognizing the (typically tax-supported) educational advantage that accompanies the long and specialized training typical of professions, and the psychological distress that frequently accompanies a consultation, practitioners promise to put the welfare of their clients first. Codes of ethics are a sign of this promise by a profession to the public. If keeping the promise in particular instances causes a crisis of conscience, the professional may refer the patient to a colleague, if one is available. But when her back is against the wall, the professional's values must take second place: "[I]n a profession that is bound by fiduciary obligations and strives to respect and care for patients, it is unacceptable to leave patients to fend for themselves" (Cantor and Baum 2004: 2011).

Note, further, that the APhA is not in principle opposed to EC. A special continuing education report on EC states: "At its 2000 Annual Meeting, the . . . APhA adopted a policy supporting the voluntary involvement of pharmacists . . . in emergency contraception programs that include patient evaluation, patient education, and direct provision of emergency contraceptive medications" (APhA 2000: 10). The report also specifies: "Because emergency contraceptives *act before implantation and cannot disrupt an established pregnancy, they are not considered to be abortifacients*" (ibid.: 3, emphasis added); and "The efficacy of emergency contraception is greatest when treatment is initiated soon after unprotected intercourse; . . ." (ibid.: 4). In sum, APhA's *educational efforts directed at its members* rebut the claim that EC is equivalent to abortion and advise prompt direct provision of EC. Of course, pharmacists who believe – for religious reasons – that moral worth begins at conception will not find this reassuring; but scientific data strongly suggest that EC precludes ovulation, that it does *not* inhibit implantation but prevents the appearance of an implantable object (Davidoff and Trussel 2006: 1776; see also Sulmasy 2006 for a limited defense, grounded in Catholic theory, of why Catholic institutions may and should provide EC in cases of rape).

True, the APhA's 1998 Pharmacist Conscience Clause recognizes "the individual pharmacist's right to exercise conscientious refusal and supports the establishment of systems *to ensure patients' access to legally prescribed therapy* without compromising the pharmacist's conscientious right of refusal" (APhA 2005: 1, emphasis added) (Reasons ##1, 2, 3). Note, however, that this right is to be located within systems that "ensure patients' access;" it does not recognize an *unfettered* right, the result of which is an unmedicated patient (Hepler 2005), that is, "patients left to fend for themselves."

Thus, the critic is misguided: autonomy and the virtue of *professional* integrity favor the patient.

One further value assumption should be addressed: human zygotes and embryos should not be treated as moral equals of adults. Those who believe that human life is sacred from the moment of conception believe that EC, like abortion, constitutes murder. If one is not morally justified in acting to prevent a murder, something is dreadfully wrong (Reason #27).

While one can sympathize with the pharmacist who believes in the moral status of a zygote (conceptus) and must dispense EC, we must remember that the moral standing of a conceptus is broadly contested – and has been so for centuries, if not millennia. As strongly as some persons believe the conceptus to be the moral equal of an adult, just as strongly do other persons believe the fetus has no moral standing at all. The true metaphysical status of the moral standing of a conceptus is currently unknown. To allow an individual or group to resolve this vexed question by fiat is capricious and, thus, morally un-justifiable. In particular, "[r]eligious grounds must be considered private and subjective: because different people differ in their religious views, and no impartial method exists for selecting between them, no particular set of religious views can form a legitimate basis of legislation in a pluralist society" (Jollimore 2006: 141) (Reason #19). Groups or individuals are, of course, free to grant moral status to a conceptus within their own communities; but, and again, *in pluralistic environments* no group can demand allegiance of any other to contested values.

In sum, autonomy, justice, and professional integrity (as well as metaphysical neutrality) morally support requiring pharmacists to fill requests for EC. If possible, a dissenting pharmacist may refer a woman to a colleague; but if no colleague is *immediately* present, the pharmacist is morally required to provide the drug to the adult who requests it.

Additional Issues to Consider

Other possible moral dilemmas arising within this case:

Q If pharmacists are morally permitted to opt out, does that permissibility extend (perhaps through an appeal to equality) to other parties? For example, can a bus driver refuse to drop off a passenger in front of an abortion clinic? Can a check-out clerk refuse to ring up and bag a package of (emergency) contraceptives? of condoms?

Q Should professional codes of ethics be allowed to include opt-out clauses if their expressed primary commitment is to their clients?

Q Can service providers be morally *required* to attend *particular programs* in continuing education if they give evidence of relying on mistaken or outdated information in making professional decisions? If so, can they be suspended from practice until they demonstrate competency?

Q Should legislative bodies legislate questions of conscience?

NOTES

1 On August 24, 2006, the Federal Drug Administration announced that Plan B would be available over the counter – that is, without prescription – to women of 18 years of age and older. However, "Plan B will be stocked by pharmacies behind the counter because it cannot be dispensed without a prescription or proof of age" (FDA 2006: para 5). Consequently, access can still be obstructed by pharmacists. In fact, a survey of customers in Canada following similar legislation in 2005 revealed that

women's privacy was violated by pharmacists asking them to reveal personal information (Shuchman and Redelmeier 2006: 1338). Further studies reveal that a year after
the FDA's decision, access to EC is not everywhere available (Pugh 2007). In
short, this case is not mooted by the FDA's granting over-the-counter (OTC) status
to EC.
2 Some possibility exists that EC acts to prevent the implantation of a fertilized ovum.
   However, data have increasingly failed to demonstrate this as the mechanism by which
   EC prevents pregnancy (Davidoff 2006: 21; Davidoff and Trussel 2006: 1776–7;
   Croxatto et al. 2001: 111–21).

REFERENCES

APhA (American Pharmaceutical Association) (1994) Code of Ethics for Pharmacists.
    Available at: http://students.washington.edu/prepharm/articles/codeofethics.pdf
    (accessed 6 October 2007).
APhA (American Pharmaceutical Association) (2000) APhA Special Report: A continu-
    ing education program for pharmacists: emergency contraception: the pharmacist's
    role. Available at: www.pharmacist.com/pdf/emer_contra.pdf (accessed July 23,
    2007).
APhA (American Pharmaceutical Association) (2004) House of Delegates. Report of the
    policy review committee: ethics. Available at: www.aphanet.org/ (accessed July 23,
    2007).
APhA (American Pharmaceutical Association) (2005) Memorandum to Delegates to the
    APhA 2005 House of Delegates. Available at: www.aphanet.org/AM/Template.
    cfm?Section=Search&section=About_APhA1&template=/CM/ContentDisplay.cfm&C
    ontentFileID=663 (accessed July 23, 2007).
Borrego, M. E., Short, J., House, N., et al. (2006) New Mexico pharmacists' know-
    ledge, attitudes, and beliefs toward prescribing oral emergency contraception.
    Journal of the American Pharmacists Association 46 (1): 33–43.
Cantor, J., and Baum, K. (2004) The limits of conscientious objection – may pharma-
    cists refuse to fill prescriptions for emergency contraception? *New England Journal
    of Medicine* 351 (19): 2008–2012.
Charo, R. A. (2005) The celestial fire of conscience – refusing to deliver medical care.
    New England Journal of Medicine 352 (24): 2471–3.
Chuang, D., and Shank, L. (2006) Availability of emergency contraception at rural and
    urban pharmacies in Pennsylvania. *Contraception* 73 (4): 382–5.
Croxatto, H. B., Devotob, L., Durand, M., et al. (2001) Mechanism of action of hor-
    monal preparations used for emergency contraception: a review of the literature.
    Contraception 63 (3): 111–21.
Curlin, F., Lawrence, R., Chin, M., et al. (2007) Religion, conscience, and controver-
    sial clinical practices. *New England Journal of Medicine* 356 (6): 593–600.
Davidoff, F. (2006) Sex, politics, and morality at the FDA: reflections on the Plan B
    decision. *Hastings Center Report* 36 (2): 20–5.
Davidoff, F., and Trussel, J. (2006) Plan B and the politics of doubt. *JAMA: Journal of
    the American Medical Association* 296 (14): 1775–8.
Downing, D. (2000) Pharmacist prescribing of emergency contraception: the Wash-
    ington state experience. *American Pharmaceutical Association Special Report 2000:*
    i–iv. Available at: www.aphanet.org/ (accessed July 30, 2005).

Engelhardt, H. T., Jr. (1996) *The Foundations of Biomedical Ethics*, 2nd edn. New York: Oxford University Press.

FDA (Federal Drug Administration) (2006) FDA approves over-the-counter access for Plan B for women 18 and older. FDA News (August 24). Available at: www.fda.gov/bbs/topics/NEWS/2006/NEW01436.html (accessed January 19, 2007).

Fenton, E., and Lomasky, L. (2005) Dispensing with liberty: Conscientious refusal and the "morning-after" pill. *Journal of Medicine and Philosophy* 30 (6): 579–92.

Gee, R. E. (2006) Plan B, reproductive rights, and physician activism. *New England Journal of Medicine* 355 (1): 4–5.

Ginty, M. (2005) Pharmacists dispense anti-choice activism. Women's eNews. Available at: www.womensenews.org/article.cfm/dyn/aid/2278 (accessed July 27, 2005).

Gold, R. (2006) Rekindling efforts to prevent unplanned pregnancy: a matter of "equity and common sense." *Guttmacher Policy Review* 9 (3): 2–7.

Grimes, D., Raymond, E., and Jones, B. (2001) Emergency contraception over-the-counter: the medical and legal imperatives. *Obstetrics and Gynecology* 98 (1): 151–5.

Guttmacher Institute (2007) State policies in brief: emergency contraception. Available at: www.guttmacher.org/statecenter/spibs/spib_EC.pdf (accessed January 19, 2007).

Hepler, C. (2005) Balancing pharmacists' conscientious objections with their duty to serve. *Journal of the American Pharmacists Association* 45 (4): 434–6.

Jollimore, T. (2006) Societal obligations and pharmacists' rights. *Teaching Ethics* 7 (1): 139–42.

Litt, I. (2005) Placing emergency contraception in the hands of women. *JAMA: Journal of the American Medical Association* 293 (1): 98–9.

MacLean, L. (2005) Freedom of conscience for small pharmacies: testimony of the American Pharmacists Association before the Small Business Committee, United States House of Representatives, July 25. Available at: www.aphanet.org/AM/Template.cfm?Section=Search&section=July6&template=/CM/ContentDisplay.cfm&ContentFileID=640 (accessed January 29, 2007).

MSNBC (2005) Pharmacist sues over "morning after pill". Available at: http://msnbc.msn.com/id/8172573 (accessed July 29, 2005).

National Conference of State Legislatures (2007) Pharmacist conscience clauses: laws and legislation (November). Available at: www.ncsl.org/programs/health/conscienceclauses.htm (accessed March 14, 2008).

Pugh, T. (2007) A year after Plan B change, access still hit-or-miss. McClatchey Newspapers. Available at: www.mcclatchydc.com/staff/tony_pugh/story/16153.html (accessed March 3, 2008).

Raine, T. et al. (2005) Direct access to emergency contraception through pharmacies and effect on unintended pregnancy and STIs. *JAMA: Journal of the American Medical Association* 293 (1): 54–62.

Shuchman, M., and Redelmeier, D. (2006) Politics and independence – the collapse of the Canadian Medical Association Journal. *New England Journal of Medicine* 354 (13): 1337–9.

Sulmasy, D. (2006) Emergency contraception for women who have been raped: must Catholics test for ovulation, or is testing for pregnancy morally sufficient? *Kennedy Institute of Ethics Journal* 16 (4): 305–31.

Task Force on Postovulatory Methods of Fertility Regulation (1998) Randomized controlled trial of levonorgestrel versus the Yuzpe regimen of combined oral contraceptives for emergency contraception. *The Lancet* 352 (9126): 428–33.

White, B. C. (1994) *Competence to Consent*. Washington, DC: Georgetown University Press, pp. 13–27.

Wicclair, M. (2006) Pharmacies, pharmacists, and conscientious objection. *Kennedy Institute of Ethics Journal* 16 (4): 225–50.

CASE NINETEEN: CONGRATULATIONS! DID YOU HAVE A BOY OR A GIRL? – SURGICAL INTERVENTIONS ON INFANTS WITH DISORDERS OF SEX DEVELOPMENT

According to rough estimates, one in every one to two thousand infants born each year has ambiguous genitalia (Dreger 1998; Preves 2003: 2; ISNA(2) n.d.). These intersex infants display "a range of anatomical conditions in which an individual's anatomy mixes key masculine anatomy with key feminine anatomy" (Dreger 1998: 26), or have "congenital conditions in which development of chromosomal, gonadal, or anatomic sex is atypical" (Lee et al. 2006: e488; see also ISNA(3) n.d., and Green 2006.). This is to say that intersex persons have various combinations of both female and male external and internal genitalia (e.g., an enlarged clitoris with only a rudimentary vaginal opening or undescended testes (external), or an XY genotype with an inability to respond to masculinizing hormones (internal)).

Historically, the position of the American Academy of Pediatrics (AAP) was that "[t]he birth of a child with ambiguous genitalia constitutes a *social emergency*" (AAP 2000: 138, emphasis added). The AAP advised:

> The infant should be referred to as "your baby" – not "he," or "she." It is helpful to examine the child in the presence of the parents to demonstrate the precise abnormalities of genital development . . . and [to emphasize] that the abnormal appearance can be corrected and the child raised as a boy or a girl as appropriate. Parents should be encouraged not to name the child or register the birth, if possible, until the sex of rearing is established. (Ibid.)

However, in 2006, noting improved diagnosis and treatment modalities and the "place of patient advocacy" (Lee et al. 2006: e488), participants in the International Consensus Conference on Intersex (ICCI) published new suggestions (including designating such infants as having "disorders of sex development (DSD)," rather than "intersex" for the treatment of infants with ambiguous genitalia).[1] Their recommendations include:

> Optimal clinical management of individuals with DSD should comprise the following:
> (1) gender assignment must be avoided before expert evaluation in newborns;
> (2) evaluation and long-term management must be performed at a center with an

experienced multidisciplinary team; (3) all individuals should receive a gender assignment; (4) open communication with patients and families is essential, and participation in decision-making is encouraged; and (5) patient and family concerns should be respected and addressed in strict confidence.

The initial contact with the parents of a child with a DSD is important, because first impressions from these encounters often persist. A key point to emphasize is that the child with a DSD has the potential to become a well-adjusted, functional member of society. Although privacy needs to be respected, a DSD is not shameful. It should be explained to the parents that the best course of action may not be clear initially, but the healthcare team will work with the family to reach the best possible set of decisions in the circumstances. (Ibid.: e490)

Both the AAP and the ICCI recognize that diagnosis and treatment of an infant born with DSD will be complicated and ongoing. They also note that initial gender assignments may be mistaken: an infant who is diagnosed and/or socialized as one gender may come to identify with the other. The ICCI recommends: "Optimal care for children with DSD requires an experienced multidisciplinary team that is generally found in tertiary care centers. Ideally, the team includes pediatric subspecialists in endocrinology, surgery and/or urology, psychology/psychiatry, gynecology, genetics, neonatology, and, if available, social work, nursing, and medical ethics" (Lee 2004).

Parents giving birth to infants with DSD are, understandably, distraught. The first question asked of new parents is: "Did you have a boy or a girl?" Being unable to answer this question is not only anxiety-producing for new parents, but also for family and friends who are eager to welcome the newborn into their circle. Given the centrality of sex and gender for structuring a child's social interactions and developing a sense of self, some decision about the child's sex and gender must be made and, by some estimates, be made as soon as possible. Both the ambiguity of the child's sex and gender and the parents' (and others') reactions to that ambiguity will have significant implications for the child's long-term well-being (Preves 2003). Parenthetically, this ambiguity poses legal questions as well; for example, what sex will be designated on the child's birth certificate and, later, on passports and marriage certificates.

Typically, evaluations are undertaken to determine both the infant's genetic sex (i.e., whether the child's chromosomal pattern is XX, XY, or some other variant) and the cause of the sexual ambiguity. Additional pediatric, urological, endocrinological, and gynecological evaluations are undertaken to determine potential fertility, the capacity for normal sexual function, the estimated functional efficacy of various hormones, and the child's predicted phenotype (whether the child is more likely to have a masculine or feminine outward appearance). Once these complex, interdigitating factors are understood, a sex and gender can be assigned and the parents can answer the common question. One further issue remains: whether to undertake surgical interventions to revise the infant's genitalia to conform cosmetically to the selected sex and gender.

Surgical reconstruction is rarely a medical urgency/emergency (Preves 2003; Dreger 1998; Dreger 1999; Lee et al. 2006). Nonetheless, parents, other family members, and members of society generally will interact differently with boys and girls; until the child's sex and gender are established, interactions are likely to be stilted, stunted, aberrant, confusing, or discomfited. In addition to the distress of the parents and others, the child whose genital appearance is uncommon may experience ostracism and isolation, and suffer from confused self-identity and self-understanding. The child who does not know whether to join the boy or girl scouts, or whether to line up with boys or girls for physical education, is at a distinct social disadvantage. Many parents imagine a lifetime of exclusion for their children with DSD, seeing them as unable to attend sleep-overs, swimming parties, or any typical childhood activity in which nudity, however brief, is a possibility. In the presence of the ongoing public, polarized, and judgmental discussions of the morality of sex and gender orientation, the negative impact on self-esteem and sexual identity for a child with DSD could be enormous. For a pre-teen or teenager with DSD, trying to determine her/his sexuality must be even more frightening and confusing than for a teen without any such anatomical variation. At these ages, the angst can be almost unbearable. With these concerns in their minds, parents might understandably hope that surgery will make the child's external genitalia "normal," even if internal ambiguity persists.

Nonetheless, the propriety of early surgical correction has come under increasing challenge. Some pediatricians, neonatologists, and other healthcare professionals, as well as some medical ethicists, argue that unless DSD is demonstrably threatening to life or health, the surgery should be postponed until the person who will be most affected – the individual with DSD – can give autonomous consent (or, in the case of younger children, at least can assent – that is, the younger child can agree with some, albeit incomplete, level of understanding) to the surgery. The risk of post-operative compromise in the function of and sensation to the sexual organs, as well as of gender confusion, is significant: the child could face a lifetime deprived of sexual satisfaction or the trauma of gender confusion at a later age. Because these risks are of great magnitude and not uncommonly realized, they should not (the argument goes) be accepted by anyone other than the person who will experience them (i.e., the person with DSD). In fact, some argue that children as young as seven years of age should be part of the decisional process (Dreger 1998; Frader et al. 2004); although incapable of legal or autonomous consent, these children could give or withhold their assent. Regardless of who consents to or refuses the procedures, a full explanation of their burdens and benefits, as well as those of delaying reconstructive surgery, must be provided – a particularly difficult task as the precise nature and extent of these burdens have yet to be determined (Kipnis and Diamond 1999). Almost no controlled research (see Perspective Three, *infra*, for a description and discussion of this issue) has been done on the long-term outcomes of surgeries to cosmetically reconstruct external genitalia (Lee et al. 2006; Migeon et al. 2002a; Migeon et al. 2002b), although retrospective and narrative reviews have recently been undertaken (Kipnis and Diamond 1999). The crucial point is that, to date, the particulars of the long-term physiological or psychosocial sequelae of these interventions remain largely unknown. Healthcare professionals simply cannot reliably determine whether early surgical treatment is always – or ever – in the child's best interests.

In the last decade, adults with DSD have begun to come forward to report various harmful effects of early surgical intervention. First-person accounts testify to the pain and loss of trust that arise upon learning that parents and physicians have deceived persons with DSD about the nature of their bodies and their earlier surgeries. This loss of trust is often accompanied by a assumption that the deceit stems from embarrassment or from seeing the child with DSD as a "freak" (Preves 1999). This perception of "freakishness" is usually amplified by the fact that most reconstructive surgeries are performed in academic medical centers – replete with cadres of medical and nursing students, interns, residents, fellows, and the like – all trooping through the child's room and staring at her/his genitals, usually without asking permission or offering any explanation or apology for the embarrassing intrusion (Frader et al. 2004). Since many of these reconstructions must be revised as the child grows, these mortifying experiences are repeated again and again and again. Finally, surgery that involves revising a penis or clitoris often results in loss or diminution of sensation and of orgasmic capacity. Not surprisingly, many post-operative children become adults who deeply regret these losses. Or, as one young adult, who had 16 surgeries on his genitalia, rued: "[F]rom the point of view of the physicians, I am a competent male. From my point of view, I wish they would have left me alone" (Preves 2003: 31). As a result Lee (among others) has recommended that the care of patients with DSD must include explicit concern for "(3) excessive exposure during medical examinations . . . and (5) the challenge to defer surgery until the child is 'old enough' to give consent" (2004: 133).

Although treatment approaches have become both more sophisticated and more compassionate, parental anxieties persist. One must wonder, from a moral point of view, what should be the appropriate response of healthcare professionals to parents who request immediate surgical reconstructions on their newborns with DSD for *merely cosmetic* reasons?

Perspective One

The parents' request for immediate surgery on their infant with DSD should be honored. This position is supported by an appeal to consequences and an appeal to the virtue of integrity, particular of the integrity of parents in their role of caring for and protecting the interests of their minor children.

Considering consequences first, we note that children who appear different from their peers are, at all ages, ridiculed. Being labeled as "weird" or "funny looking" or "a freak" can be devastating for a child. Such children typically suffer ostracism: either their peers refuse to socialize with them (for fear of "getting cooties" or of being themselves ostracized for "hanging out with the weirdos"), or the DSD children ostracize themselves as a defense mechanism ("I don't like them anyway") or to protect themselves from harsh teasing and derogatory remarks, or from fear of having their "secret" discovered. This social isolation can make difficult – perhaps impossible – the normal psychosocial relationships that are important in developing one's identity, and in providing a support group from which to make experiential forays into the world. In particular, the child is likely to (be forced, by his parents, to) avoid social opportunities of which nakedness is a natural component: sleepovers, swimming parties, and so forth. Physical education class, with its public showers, will be a nightmare. Children with DSD will be forced to become, and will come to see themselves as, loners, outcasts, unlikable (worse: unlovable), as outsiders who have nothing to offer the group. Their self-esteem will suffer and these children are likely to experience chronic or recurring depression or rage.

As children with DSD enter their pre-teen or teenage years, when sexuality becomes a more prominent focus of peer interactions, their genital differences will assume greater importance. Fear of (further) rejection can impair a teen's ability to develop bonds of intimacy and to enjoy the pleasures that attend sexual expression within an intimate relationship. As sexual growth and practice are a critical aspect of a life well lived, the teen is at further risk for the problems that attach to social isolation. Although an optimist might argue that, upon reaching adulthood and personal independence, the unreconstructed child can leave an unhappy childhood behind, this is unlikely. Personality is formed in childhood and often follows the person throughout life.

In sum, the severely negative, persistent, probably life-long consequences for the child argue against leaving her/him in the "natural" state of birth.

And who is better placed to predict and evaluate these effects than the parents? Although all parents make unwise choices on some occasions, they are nonetheless recognized – legally and morally – as the parties responsible for choosing for their children until they reach the age of – and acquire the capacities associated with – adulthood (Blizzard 2002: 619). The rationale for assigning decisional authority to a child's parents is the quite reasonable assumption that no one will be more interested in protecting and promoting the child's well-being. Parents (nearly always) love their children deeply and are powerfully motivated to see that no harm comes to them; indeed, that the child experiences as many good things as the parents can provide. If anyone is keen to work on the child's behalf, year after year and in the face of frustrating difficulties and setbacks, it will be a child's parents.

Parents, so long as they are capable of autonomous choice, retain decisional authority for their children unless clear evidence indicates that their decisions avoidably cause their children serious harm. Parents retain this authority even when their espoused values – and their espousal to inculcate those values in their children – diverge from mainstream values. So, for example, parents are allowed to raise their children in non-mainstream religious traditions, to be vegetarians, to perpetuate their own biases (e.g., to be sexist). Here the rationale is that democracies in general and non-theocratic societies in particular will, by definition, make room for a plethora of values, beliefs, and practices. Because children are, at least for many years, incapable of examining and rationally reflecting on competing values and making decisions based on complex experiences, their parents are free to transmit their own values to their offspring (which the children, when adults, may reject if they choose – and are able – to do so).

The result of combining parental responsibility with value diversity is the not-so-surprising fact that different parents will choose different therapeutic interventions for their children, even when those children have identical diagnoses. As long as providers continue to disagree about the advisability of different therapeutic approaches, parents are free to choose in concert with their own values, beliefs, and concerns – without facing charges of failing to promote a particular child's welfare. Thus, if some parents determine that surgery to reconstruct a child's ambiguous genitalia and assign a gender is in the best interests of their child, that decision should be respected.

The appeals to consequences, autonomy, and the virtue of parental integrity support honoring the parents' wishes for cosmetic surgical reconstruction of their children's ambiguous genitalia.

Perspective Two

The parents' request for immediate surgery to reconstruct the ambiguous genitalia of and assign a gender to their infant with DSD should not be honored. This position is supported by an appeal to consequences and an appeal to the virtue of professional integrity, particularly the integrity of the primary professional promise of physicians, typically stated as "First, do no harm."

The published outcomes of surgery to reconstruct a child's ambiguous genitalia and assign a gender have been widely reported to be noxious (Blizzard 2002; Chase 1999; Crouch 1999; Dreger 1998; Dreger 1999; Frader et al. 2004; Preves 2003). First-person accounts of the post-operative sequelae are chilling. Adults who had surgical modifications as children report that many of their school breaks were not spent vacationing or playing with their peers, but having yet another revision of their genitalia to correct earlier problems or to revise structures that had not kept up with normal childhood growth. Because their parents usually refused to discuss their conditions or divulge the nature of the "illness" for which surgery had been performed, the children often assumed that something was terribly wrong with them. As a result they experienced both shame and fear – shame that whatever was wrong with them was too awful to be mentioned out loud, and fear that the repeated surgeries implied a terminal illness. As a result, their childhoods were neither happy nor carefree.

Nor did their situations improve. Adolescents whose gender was incorrectly reassigned early in life are often sexually attracted to members of their assigned gender: perceived homosexual advances can result in ostracism and worse. Something as fundamental as urination can become problematic when the student is forced to urinate in a semi-public place, such as a school bathroom. John/Joan, the subject of John Colapinto's groundbreaking report on the consequences of sex reassignment surgery, detailed the ridicule he received when, as Joan, he urinated standing up (easier and more natural for him) in the girls' bathroom, and the threats he received when he subsequently tried to use the boys' bathroom, resulting in his refusal to attend school (Colapinto 1997). Additionally, adults with DSD report that one of the costs of earlier surgeries was loss or diminution of sensation in their clitoris or penis. Because surgeries had often damaged or destroyed the nerves enervating their sexual organs, they were unable to achieve sexual satisfaction or, sometimes, any physical pleasure at all. As a result, their relations with intimates were often strained or unfulfilling, for both them and their partners. As sexuality is a vital component of a full and rewarding life, these adults have suffered a grievous loss.

Further, because of the secrecy surrounding their conditions, their relationships with their parents were strained and, upon learning the truth, sometimes irreparably damaged (Chase 1999; Hedley 2006; Preves 2003). In cases where parents had explicitly lied to their children, loss of trust was a common result; not uncommonly this loss bled over into an inability to trust other persons (Hedley 2006). In particular, many lost trust in their healthcare providers, an especially regrettable result given their ongoing need for surgery, hormone treatments, and counseling (Blizzard 2002; Frader et al. 2004; Lee et al. 2006).

Clearly, the consequences for the persons with DSD of early surgical cosmetic reconstruction of ambiguous genitalia are egregiously negative.

An additional consideration, given the untoward outcomes, is the obligation of healthcare professionals to avoid harming their patients. Of course, some harms (e.g., pain) are always associated with surgery; but commonly these are justified as being offset by much greater benefits. The person who has an emergency appendectomy has pain, yes; but the pain is greatly outweighed by the fact that the patient's life has been spared from the deadly threat of a ruptured appendix with widespread infection. These compensating benefits are not present with surgical reconstructions of genitalia. In addition to the risks inherent in any surgery, there is increased risk of morbidities such as blood clots, hypertension, and cystic acne due to the extended use of hormones required to complete the sexual transition (Spack 2005: 2). Furthermore, the deceit that commonly accompanies these surgical interventions itself causes harms of great magnitude (as noted earlier). Add to these harms the mortification of having one's genitals stared at repeatedly by curious strangers, some of whom even handle the genitalia. The acute chagrin is overwhelming to children, as is the chronic shame it generates. Moreover, the psychological damage seems never-ending, following the child into adulthood.

Knowing, as they do, both the common occurrence and persistence of these harms, as well as the documented lack of compensating benefits, healthcare professionals cannot in good conscience be party to such harms; certainly they should not be their cause. Their professional promise to do no harm requires that they politely but firmly refuse to perform these surgeries. Of course their refusal should be explained fully and, if necessary, repeatedly to the infant's parents. But their professional integrity requires their refusal to perform genital reconstructive surgeries, as long as the life or health of the child is not immediately threatened.

In conclusion, the appeals to consequences and professional integrity require the healthcare professionals to refuses parents' requests for cosmetic surgery to reconstruct a child's ambiguous genitalia and assign a gender.

Perspective Three

From a moral point of view, should healthcare professionals (HCPs) honor parents' requests for surgical reconstructions of their newborn infants with DSD?

Step 1: Information-gathering

Medical

- Are early surgical reconstruction/gender assignments necessary for the child's health and welfare?
- What are the usual outcomes – physical and psychological – of this type of surgery?
- Will surgical procedures and, hence, their usual outcomes improve over time?
- What effect does surgery have on the overall health of the child?
- How would having surgery effect puberty? How would not having surgery effect puberty?
- What psychological or physiological complications might a child face if surgery is not done? If it is performed?
- What, if any, non-surgical treatments are available?

Psychosocial

- What is motivating the parents' request?
- Are the parents capable of autonomous decision making about early surgery?
- What are the implications for parent-child bonding with and without the surgery?
- What are the likely psychological effects on the children who have the surgery?
- What are the likely psychological effects on parents whose children have the surgery?
- What are the likely psychological effects on the children who do not have the surgery?
- What are the likely psychological effects on parents whose children do not have surgery?

- What are the implications for adolescent and adult intimacy?
- What are the implications for adolescent ego development and self-identity?
- Do genetic studies reliably predict gender?
- How important is gender to psychosocial well-being, self-esteem, and self-identity?
- Which approach will better minimize stigmatization, isolation, and shame of DSD child?

Cultural

- Do professional codes of ethics give any guidance?
- How likely is social stigmatization of the untreated child?
- What are the cultural conceptions of sexuality, and how do they structure interactions with persons whose sexuality is uncommon?
- What are the cultural conceptions of gender, and how do they structure interactions with persons whose gender is ambiguous?
- To what extent are variations in the cultural conceptions of sexuality and gender tolerated?
- What effects will the cultural conceptions of sexuality and gender have on children with DSD, with and without reconstructive surgery?
- What are the cultural conceptions of parental obligations regarding non-emergency surgeries generally? Regarding gender- or sexuality-based conditions?

Legal

- Who has legal decisional authority about surgery?
- Under what, if any, conditions may legal decisional authority be overridden?
- Are reliable, double-blind studies of the short- and long-term effects of gender-reassignment surgery possible?

History

- What is the history of treatment of persons with DSD?

Step 2: Creative problem-solving

Perhaps the surgeons (or other healthcare professionals) could convince the parents to delay the surgery for a few years, at least until the child begins to demonstrate some gendered behavior (e.g., plays with trucks rather than dolls, is more aggressive than a typical female toddler, etc.). Such behavior might give at least some indication of the child's gender tendencies and more accurately forecast future gender preferences. However, as such behavior is only imperfectly predictive of adult gender preferences, we need to consider an immediate response to the parents.

Step 3: Listing pros and cons

Options	Pros	Cons
Honor parents' request for surgery.	1. Decreases parental stress, anxiety, and guilt (C-B) 2. Makes parenting easier (C-U) 3. Improves parent-child bond (C-U) 4. Improves social interactions for the child/teen/adult with DSD (C-B) 5. Diminishes gender ambiguity (C-B) 6. Improves child's self-esteem (C-B) 7. Decreases child's psychosexual anxiety (C-B) 8. Decreases child's and parents' cognitive dissonance (C-B, C-U)	9. Exposes child to shame, embarrassment (C-NM) 10. Exposes child to fear of death (C-NM) 11. Gender assignments sometimes mistaken (C-NM) 12. Surgery cannot be undone if gender misassigned (C-NM) 13 Children have a right to know about their bodies (R) 14. Parents should accept , love their children "as is" (V-I) 15. Child deceived (V-H) 16. Requires HCPs to violate promise to do no harm (V-F, V-I) 17. DSD is no different than other physical differences (J-E). 18. Constitutes genital mutilation, which is widely condemned (C-NM, J-E)
Do not honor parents' request for surgery.	19. No post-operative loss of or diminished sexual sensation or responsivity (C-B) 20. Surgery causes uncompensated pain/suffering for patient (C-U, V-I) 21. Prevent compromised or eliminated fertility (C-B) 22. Surgery uses infant as means to parents' peace of mind (RFP) 23. Inhibits development of self-image (C-NM, RFP) 24. Preserves patient choice about her/his body (A) 25. Parental acceptance provides greater psychological benefits (C-B, V-I: parents)	26. Parents recognized decisional authorities for their children (A, R) 27. Parents obligated to protect their children according to their best estimates (V-I) 28. Parents of children with DSD are no different from parents of other children with impairments, who are allowed to opt for surgical intervention under less than ideal circumstances (J-E)

Step 4: Analysis

Factual assumptions

- Children without surgical reconstruction will be teased, but no more so than any child whose physical characteristics are atypical, including (perhaps) the child who has a cosmetic reconstruction of her/his genitalia.
- A more normal appearance will not guarantee less teasing.
- Psychological health does not depend on normal-appearing genitalia.
- Children are not born gender-neutral.
- Following the initial reconstructive surgery, the child will have to undergo further surgical interventions.
- The child will suffer significant and detrimental embarrassment and assaults on his self-image and psychological well-being on each surgical occasion.
- Surgical outcomes will continue to improve over time.
- Deception is a key requirement for the success of gender assignment.
- Many children with surgical reconstruction will come to wish the surgery had not been done.
- Genetic or hormonal testing do not always accurately predict gender preference.
- Gender is critically important in a person's well-being and identity.
- Reconstructive surgery plays a minimal (if any) role in forming a child's gender.
- Most parents will bond satisfactorily with their unreconstructed DSD children.
- Cosmetic surgery does not guarantee parent–child bonding.
- Loss or serious diminution of the capacity for sexual pleasure is considered to be a grave harm by most persons.

Value assumptions

- Persons should not be exposed to risks of serious harm without their autonomous consent or the potential for serious compensating benefits.
- Loss or serious diminution of the capacity for sexual pleasure should not be entertained without serious – perhaps life- or health-saving – compensating benefits; that is, should not be entertained for mere cosmetic purposes.
- Healthcare professionals should not expose their patients to risk of serious harm without good evidence that it will be accompanied by a compensatory benefit.
- Parents and healthcare professionals should not deceive their children/ patients about the need for or nature of their surgical reconstructions.
- Parents should love their children in spite of any physical anomalies.

Step 5: Justification

The parents' request for immediate surgery to *cosmetically* reconstruct the ambiguous genitalia of their infant with DSD should not be honored. This position is supported by the moral appeals to consequences, and the virtues of professional integrity (particularly the integrity of healthcare professionals who have promised to do no harm) and of parental integrity (particularly the parental obligation to promote the welfare of their children).

Three important sets of *negative consequences* support not acceding to parental requests for cosmetic reconstructive surgery:

1 Life-long *physical* harms to the child/future adult without commensurate compensating benefits (Reasons ##19, 20, 21).
2 Life-long *psychological* harms to the child/future adult without commensurate compensating benefits (Reasons ##9, 10, 11, 12).
3 Life-long psychological harms to the parents (Reason #25).

The possibility of improving outcomes for the larger community of persons with DSD also warrants consideration.

Only infrequently is genital reconstruction required for preservation of life or health (Dreger 1998; Frader et al. 2004). In those cases, it should certainly be performed. When no threat to life or health exists – that is, when surgical reconstruction is undertaken for primarily cosmetic reasons – the procedures commonly generate more harms than benefits. Some would claim these surgeries generate no benefits at all.

The list of physical harms suffered by children undergoing reconstructing surgery is long and weighty. First-person accounts of harms include the pain associated with the surgeries themselves (Reason #20) or with the aftermath (Reasons ##9, 10, 11, 12, 19, 20, 21, 23) of those surgeries (Aspinall 2006; Blizzard 2002; Crouch 1999; Dreger 1998; Frader et al. 2004; Preves 2003): recurrent infections (Dreger 1998), urinary incontinence (Chase 1999), and diminished or absent sexual responsiveness (Chase 1999; Dreger 1998; Dreger 1999; Frader et al. 2004). Frequently reconstructions must be repeated (Blizzard 2002; Chase 1999; Frader et al. 2004; Preves 1999), subjecting the child to multiple hospitalizations for minimal and merely temporary improvement.

Consider, next, psychological harms (Reasons ##9, 10, 23), starting with the critical role played by sex and gender. According to Sharon Preves:

> The sex and gendering of babies at birth as either female or male is one of the most rudimentary demarcations of North American culture. . . . When an infant is not "sexable" because of genital . . . obscurity, its entrance into the social world may be halted until the child is sexed and gendered. Because sex and gender provide expectations for a majority of our social interactions, the inability to sex and gender an individual is extremely problematic socially. Clarity of sex and gender grants an individual "personhood"; an ability to be considered human rather than monster or subhuman. (Preves 1999: 52)

The further role of gender in successful socialization, mating, and intimacy is also well documented: "Gender as a social category is of central importance within society; indeed, in the West, if one is neither man nor woman, then one has no social place or state to occupy" (Crouch 1999: 35; see also Dreger 1998 and

Fausto-Sterling 1993). These places and states are found in the most quotidian aspects of life: "Most of us check off the 'M' or the 'F' box and choose the corresponding clothing, hair removal routines, rest rooms, careers, urination positions, intimate partners, and underarm deodorants" (Kipnis and Diamond 1999: 182). In short, the ungendered person will have difficulty functioning in society.

A critic will argue that sexual and gender identity are so important to self-identity and social success that taking unusual and, even, extreme measures to insure it is permissible – even morally mandatory (Reasons ##3, 4, 5, 6, 7, 8).

While understanding one's sexual identity is critical to understanding one's larger personal identity, this importance does not, in and of itself, require early operative interventions. Genetic determination and accurate diagnoses of the pathophysiology involved should always precede surgery, but the data gained from these studies only give imprecise guidance as to which gender the child is likely to embrace as puberty approaches (Blizzard 2002; Dreger 1998; Dreger 1999; Frader et al. 2004; ISNA(1) n.d.; Preves 2003). Further, gender is not as malleable as once believed (ibid.), and gender development is only partially (if at all) a function of physical appearance (Reason #11). Some evidence suggests that intrauterine hormonal environments play a larger role than has been previously appreciated (Blizzard 2002; Crouch 1999). Moreover, gender development is an ongoing process, one that premature surgical interventions may complicate needlessly (Ahmed et al. 2004; Frader et al. 2004). The problem for post-operative patients is that "[s]urgically constructed genitals are extremely difficult if not impossible to 'undo,' and children altered at birth or in infancy are largely stuck with what doctors give them" (Herndon 2006). In short, surgical mistakes are forever (Reason #12). Even after surgery, the appearance of the child's genitalia may, at best, be less atypical; their appearance will not necessarily be normal (Asch 2006; Chase 1999). Moreover, the permanency of early surgeries may be aggravated by the irreversible effects of cross-gender hormone treatments (Spack 2005: 2). Finally, mistaken gender designations are not uncommon (Reason #11); a person can change socially to the alternative, but this is less difficult if surgical intervention has not complicated the choice (Frader et al. 2004).

Gender identification is closely linked to, but not identical with, sexual identity: "*Gender* represents the individual's psychological and emotional identification as either male or female" (Wilson and Reiner 1999: 121). Usually, sex (a cluster of physical manifestations) and gender match: an individual with female sexual anatomy identifies herself as a girl, while an individual with typical male anatomical structures most often sees himself as a boy. Sex–gender matching can be difficult for individuals with DSD. The psychosocial challenges faced by the estimated 10 percent of the human population whose sexes and genders are at odds with cultural expectations (i.e., homosexuals) demonstrate how important this issue is for both broadly social and narrowly intimate relationships.

Professionals who care for patients with DSD are aware of the potential for distress and seek to minimize it by withholding information likely to elicit its occurrence (Reasons ##15, 16):

Since the overarching rule . . . is "avoid psychological confusion about the patient's gender identity," doctors often do not tell intersexuals and their parents all that the doctors know, lest information about intersexuality confuse or complicate the family's understanding of gender [Reasons ##5, 7, 8]. All of the professional energy is aimed at producing a physically "right" girl or boy who, presumably, the parents will then be able to raise in an unambiguous way. (Dreger 1999: 12)

To minimize noxious outcomes, parents are advised to say nothing about the condition to the child with DSD; in fact, if questions arise, the parents are advised to avoid answering or, if an answer must be given, to lie (Wilson and Reiner 1999: 124). In considering the argument for secrecy and deception, Carl Elliott observes the importance of

an internal therapeutic logic to this deception. According to this logic . . . deception is thought to be a necessary part of the treatment. To *be* (for example) a female the child must really *believe* she is a female. If she doesn't unquestioningly believe she is a female she may not grow to identify herself as female; and if she does not identify herself as female then she is not a female. (Or at least not *simply* a female.) The same kind of logic goes for the practice of deceiving parents, and for undertaking the treatment as early as possible, before the child is able to give consent. Sexual identity is largely determined by socialization and anatomical appearance, this line of reason goes, so if parents do not unquestioningly believe that the child is female, their doubts will become apparent to the child. [Reasons ##2, 3, 6] The child will then have doubts herself, and consequently her own identity will come into question. (Elliott 1998: 38; emphases in original)

The argument, in a nutshell, is that one's social, sexual, and personal successes are deemed to require an unambiguous conception of one's gender. This conception can only be achieved if everyone – the child and those she meets – see her as a female (or him as a male). But these perceptions require that *no one* – not the child, not the parents – ever have the faintest doubt about the child's gender/sex. Thus, keeping all parties in the dark is required in the name of beneficence.

The weakness of this argument lies in the probability of the deception succeeding. As Shakespeare's Launcelot noted: "Truth will out." Given the complexity of and life-long necessity for treatment, confusion, ambiguity, and curiosity are virtually certain to arise. First-person accounts relate the tragedies associated with discovery (Reasons ##9, 15). Some discover the truth about their DSD as adults when, for a variety of reasons, they gain access to their medical records. Others, however, discover their diagnoses when, during their teen years, they fail to achieve puberty. Some are started on hormones to achieve secondary sex characteristics, but secretly stop taking the medications; as a result, they retain their child-like characteristics or develop secondary sex characteristics that conflict with their surgically assigned genders (Morris 2006). Still others learn the truth when their bodies compensate for the reconstruction, as did Kira Triea when she began to menstruate through the penis created for her when she was assigned a male gender at the age of 2 (Colapinto 1997).

The fact is that the harms of deception are clearly the greater of two evils (Reason #25). Data show that secrecy is far more psychologically damaging than truth (Dreger 1999; Preves 1999; Wilson and Reiner 1999; Morris 2006). As a result of discovering the deception foisted upon her, Sherri Morris (2006) avoided seeing a physician for 18 years. Other post-operative adults with DSD report that the discoveries of deception resulted in a devastating loss of trust in their parents and healthcare providers (Frader et al. 2004; Preves 1999). Why? Because the lies they had been told were not inconsequential, but struck at the very core of their identities. These persons discovered that they were, quite literally, not who they thought they were. That their parents and the healthcare professionals upon whom they had relied for so long and in regard to issues of such importance had repeatedly and systematically lied to them not only destroyed their ability to trust others – a critical capability for developing the intimate relationships that are central to a fulfilling life – but is simply horrific.

The greatest psychological damage, however, comes as a result of the explicit message sent by surgical reconstruction (Reason #9): shame (Chase 1999; Herndon 2006; Lee et al. 2006; Preves 2003; Wilson and Reiner 1999). "The primary source of harm described by former patients is not surgery per se, but the underlying attitude that intersexuality is so shameful that it must be erased. . . . Early surgery is one means by which that message is conveyed to parents and to intersexed children" (Chase 1999: 147). This shame is amplified by the all-too-common occurrence of medical rounds, during which numerous strangers stare at and murmur about the child's genitalia, to the child's mortification (Frader et al. 2004; Lee et al. 2006; Morris 2006).

The pervasiveness of shame gives rise to even more noxious psychological sequelae, particularly the damage to one's sense of self. Persons with DSD attest to having come to see themselves as freaks, or monsters, or something worse – something so awful it could not even be described. As one adult DSD survivor noted: "What I knew myself to be was too horrible . . ." (Preves 1999: 57). In another's words: "[The geneticist] said . . . 'I'm obliged to tell you that certain details of your condition have not been divulged to you, but I cannot tell you what they are because they would upset you too much.' So she's telling us we don't know everything, but she can't tell us what it is because it's too horrible" (ibid.). Many children come to see themselves as so grotesque as to be/have been unlovable (Asch 2006; Chase 1999; Dreger 2006; Hedley 2006; Wilson and Reiner 1999).

Some post-operative DSD patients knew that they had undergone surgery, but had been deceived about the reason for the surgery. For example, children with androgen insensitivity syndrome (genetic males whose bodies do not respond to testosterone and who therefore appear female) often have undescended testes. Because after puberty the testes may become malignant, they are often removed surgically. Children who inquire about the surgery are often told that their ovaries were "twisted" or cancerous and had to be removed to prevent malignancies (Reason #10). Sherri Morris recounts the fear precipitated by this lie: "I was worried that my 'ovaries' were not removed as a prophylactic measure to prevent cancer, but that I instead actually had cancer and that my parents just weren't telling me the truth" (Morris 2006: 4; see also Preves 1999).

The list of psychological harms goes on, including violation of privacy (Dreger 1999; Frader et al. 2004; Morris 2006), discrimination due to difference – which often persists after surgery, if the genitalia still appear unusual (Frader et al. 2004) – and frustrating relationships (not limited to loss of trust) with healthcare professionals and parents (Morris 2006; Preves 1999). Frader et al. describe this last problem: "Some patients have experienced humiliation at the hand of physicians (violations of privacy and dignity) and endured secrecy and confusion in and disruption of their relationships, especially with parents – who have themselves suffered in the web of deception – and healthcare professionals" (2004: 427). This observation gives rise to the second set of harms – those afflicting the parents of persons with DSD.

One can easily sympathize with parents who, expecting a "normal" child, are suddenly faced with a child of indeterminate sex whose genitalia look "odd" (Dreger 2006). The birth of a child with anomalies "will precipitate what feels like a crisis to the parents" (Aspinall 2006: 22). This may be especially true if the anomalies involve the sexual organs. Faced with genital anomalies, most parents' first impulse is, understandably, to "fix" the child, to make the child "normal" – if only in appearance (Asch 2006; Aspinall 2006; Hedley 2006; Preves 1999). A child with a normal outward appearance will (the thinking goes) not be subject to ridicule by peers, caused discomfort by adults, or stared at by everyone (Reasons ##1, 2, 3, 8). Parents – and often healthcare providers – worry that children with DSD will suffer embarrassment, shame, and teasing; become depressed; be ostracized because of their different appearance; and experience difficulty with dating and developing intimate relationships, etc. (Preves 2003). Eva Kittay (2006) argues that many, probably most, persons equate normality with desirability. If Kittay is correct, being not normal equates with being not desirable – particularly problematic in matters of sexuality. Of course the responsible parent will want to take measures to avoid these states of affairs (Reason #27). Nonetheless, responsible parents should not succumb to the temptation to "fix" their child merely as a means to reducing their own angst (Reason #22).

Moreover, parents get many and powerful signals that encourage early reconstructive surgery: (1) the general belief that *good* parents ease their children's burdens. In societies where appearance is given undue weight, this message can be particularly strong; (2) that social burdens (e.g., shaming) should be avoided insofar as is possible; (3) that the anomaly is somehow the parents' fault and, thus, that they are required to make it right; and (4) the parents' feeling that they (as well as their children) don't deserve this "burden" and should be able to rid themselves of it (Dreger 1998; Elliott 1998; Frader et al. 2004; Preves 2003). These concerns, if coupled with persistent advice from healthcare professionals to opt for a surgical intervention, can be very difficult to resist (Feder 2006).

The data on parental effects are mixed, at best. First, surgery often fails to improve the lives of parents (Asch 2006; Frader et al. 2004), not least because of the stress that attends living a life of deception. Equally important is that

parents need to be aided so that they can come to love their children, regardless of any disparities, disabilities, or differences they display (Reason #14) (Asch
2006; Dreger 2006; Harmon-Smith 2006). After the initial shock wears off, the
parents can see the infant as *their* child, and incorporate the baby into their lives
(nearly) as easily as they would a "normal" child (Dreger 2006; Hedley 2006;
Kittay 2006). The message implied by this common human response is that
parents typically love and bond with their children, regardless of any unusual
physical configurations. Given the documented pitfalls of cosmetic reconstruction, devoted parents, in virtue of parental obligations to secure their children's
well-being, should adopt a wait-and-see approach – especially since postulated
harms regarding parent–child bonding have been challenged (Reason #27).

A different set of harms – rejection of parents by their adult children –
further supports the wait-and-see approach. Adult children learning of their DSD
status frequently find themselves quite angry with their parents over the decades
of deception. As noted earlier, when persons discover their true diagnoses, their
recognition of a life-long deception often lays waste to the relationships with
their parents (Feder 2006; Preves 2003): "[T]he realization that I had been told
lies by those from whom I had a right to expect the truth – my parents – left
me sad and angry in equal measure" (Morris 2006: 7). Many adult children,
upon discovering the deception, are sufficiently angry to sever ties with their parents, believing that such deception makes their parents unworthy of respect or
devotion. The effects of this deception on the ability to trust others, or to form
close relationships that require trust, are well documented. As the perceived cause
of these effects, parents may be shunned completely by their adult children.

The data on effects on children born with DSD, however, are considerably
less ambiguous. Although recent studies have identified some adults who are
satisfied with early surgical repairs of anomalies associated with DSD (Migeon
et al. 2002a; Migeon et al. 2002b; Wilson and Reiner 1999), most research gives
evidence of extensive and enduring distress – physical and psychosocial. One might
hope this issue could be definitively decided by further research; but this is unlikely
for at least two reasons. First, scientifically suitable research requires both a study
population and a control population. Since many effects are not fully appreciated for years, even decades, after the medical intervention, control populations
could be deprived of potentially useful treatment for long periods of time (Weil
2006). Second, because effects are only fully appreciated once the treated child
becomes an adult, data would be unavailable for years, and probably not be available to interim populations – making therapeutic suggestions during that interim
uneducated guesses, at best. To date, these guesses have proven misguided.
Moreover, the argument that surgical techniques have improved/are improving
makes an even stronger case for waiting – perhaps until the surgical techniques
have been *perfected*.

But more to the point, a plethora of non-surgical therapies are now available.
As Lee et al. (2006) note, treatment of children and their parents *must* include counselors who can help all concerned address the psychosocial aspects of
DSD and the obstacles that attend this diagnosis (Dreger 1999; Frader et al.
2004; Weil 2006). Eva Kittay notes that after the birth of her developmentally

disabled daughter, she and her husband took care to surround themselves with friends and family who would love, encourage, and support their child – rather than with those who would discourage or reject her. Lisa Hedley (2006) recounts similar efforts to insure that her child's playmates would come to realize that everyone looks different, albeit in different ways. Given the extensive social component that attends a diagnosis of DSD, one might sensibly look to social solutions – as these parents have (Feder 2006). After all, parents of children with many impairments come to grips with and learn effectively to manage their children's differences; no in-principle reason suggests DSD parents would not be equally successful (Reason #17).

The significant harms that devolve from deception require further explicit discussion: Many parents, like their DSD children, suffer significant trauma entailed by ongoing deception (Reason #15). Traditionally, healthcare professionals have recommended deceiving children about their diagnoses and the nature and purpose of any surgical or medical (e.g., hormonal) therapies. It is worth re-emphasizing that these deceptions go on for years and years until, usually after achieving adulthood, the DSD patients discover the true nature of their medical histories. Living a lie is never easy, and this is a lie that pervades multiple arenas of interaction. Parents must not only deceive their children, but also the children's siblings, other family members, friends, their children's peers, and other adults who interact with their children (e.g., teachers, school nurses, swimming coaches, etc.). The particular untruths that are related about the child will be, no doubt, difficult to remember, so missteps and conflicting statements are quite likely. Previous untruths may require revision when, for example, their children and their children's peers age and their knowledge bases change.

Perhaps all these harms to children and their parents could be justified were the physiological and psychological outcomes overwhelmingly beneficial; but they are not (Reason #25). No data support the claim that surgery generates any positive psychological effects on the parents or improves parent–child relationships (Frader et al. 2004; Lee et al. 2006: e491; Wilson and Reiner 1999: 124). Then, too, parents face a paradox: if they elect for cosmetic reconstruction, are they rejecting their children? "[Surgery] seems to negate the idea of accepting your child just as she is. After all, how are you supposed to pull off 'I love you, now change'?" (Dreger 2006: 254) (Reason #14). Also, and also paradoxically: "How is it that parents who will insist that they love their children for who they are in their uniqueness, so ardently want the same children to be no different than other children . . . ?" (Kittay 2006: 107). Perhaps parental ambiguity about cosmetic surgery in such cases is unavoidable and, again, the surgery might be morally justified if the children really were better off post-operatively. But, as noted above, they are not. In the last consequential analysis, the constellation of noxious outcomes argues against genital reconstruction for cosmetic purposes only.

This is not to say that cosmetic surgery is never indicated. Should the person who will undergo the surgery desire and consent to it, then reconstructions are morally permissible. This is to say that cosmetic reconstructions require *the patient's* autonomous choice (Reason #24). The problem here is that genuine autonomous choice is thought to be impossible in children below a certain age (typically, 14). Nonetheless, many parents and healthcare providers testify to the ability of children as young as 7 years of age to understand at least some of the implications of surgery and to give assent. True, their agreements may be comparatively uninformed, at least to the extent that they fail to appreciate the meaning of abstract concepts or deeply appreciate the implications of effects that may arise in the distant future. Nonetheless, professionals, parents, and previous patients alike argue for including the child in the decision-making process (Asch 2006; Dreger 1998; Derger 1999; Frader et al. 2004; Lee et al. 2006). If, for whatever reason, surgery seems advisable for the pre-adult, the child's feelings and preferences must be incorporated into the consent process. After all, the child will live most intimately with the results and, the argument goes, must have a say in what happens to his/her body (Reason #13).

The virtue of professional integrity (Reason #16) also speaks to this collection of harms (Frader et al. 2004). The healthcare professional often explicitly expresses – and is understood by the public to have – a commitment to "Do no harm." Of course healthcare professionals often harm their patients. Think of the harms – pain, nausea, altered appearance, etc. – that are suffered by the patient undergoing chemotherapy. The justification for such harms is their being outweighed by the potential compensating benefits, specifically, life saved and health restored. But no such unequivocal compensating benefits attach to cosmetic reconstructive surgeries of persons with DSD. Or, if benefits do exist, their degree and predictability are currently unknown. Thus, healthcare professionals have an obligation, in virtue of their professional promise, to forgo these interventions until and unless patients can autonomously determine that they will achieve compensating benefits. This is unlikely to be the case until self-identity and gender preferences have been developed (if not fully, at least extensively). But this development is unlikely to be achieved before (young) adulthood. This moral principle, thus, provides another reason to forgo surgical reconstruction for any but life- or health-threatening reasons.

Finally, the virtue of honesty (Reason #15) demands that the option of cosmetic surgery for children with DSD be reconsidered. Once the standard of care for children born with DSD, advocacy of prompt surgery was based on false information about the malleability of gender. The mistaken understanding was widely accepted because it was advocated by one of the world's (then) most respected and pre-eminent sex and gender identity researchers, John Money. In a ground-breaking story in the December 11, 1997, *Rolling Stone* magazine, that earned author John Colapinto the 1998 National Magazine Award, Colapinto revealed the deceptions and falsifications that led to the adoption of gender assignment surgery as the standard of care for infants with DSD. At the time of publication, it was estimated that at least 15,000 sex reassignment surgeries performed each year were based on erroneous data and fabricated outcomes. Although many in the medical establishment are resistant to acknowledging that, for decades, the standard of care inflicted egregious harm on particularly vulnerable patients and their parents, new information testifying to such harms must be part of the information given to – indeed, stressed for – parents prior to undertaking cosmetic surgeries.

The moral appeals of nonmaleficence, autonomy, and the virtues of parental and professional integrity and of honesty make a compelling case for avoiding merely cosmetic reconstruction of the genitals of infants and children with DSD. One final note chillingly confirms this analysis: clitorectomy "has come to be considered sexual mutilation and a violation of women's human rights" (Chase 1999: 151), and its being performed by a surgeon makes the harm no less egregious than its being performed by an African mother or shaman (ibid.: 152). If this procedure deserves condemnation in developing countries (as it does), the appeal to equality demands its condemnation in developed nations as well (Reason #18): genital mutilation by any other name (e.g., cosmetic reconstructive surgery) should be forbidden for the harm that it does. This takes such surgery out of the realm of congenital anomalies over which parents are thought to have legitimate say regarding their repair (Reasons ##17, 26).

In conclusion, the principles of nonmaleficence, autonomy, the virtues of parental and professional integrity and of honesty, and justice argue that merely cosmetic genital reconstruction of newborns should not be performed.

Additional Issues to Consider

Other possible moral dilemmas arising within this case:

Q Should surgery be forgone generally in favor of public education on the flexibility of sexuality and gender?

Q Should a guardian *ad litem* be appointed to protect the infant's interests in such cases?

Q Should a legal age be stipulated, prior to which merely cosmetic reconstruction cannot be performed?

Q Should surgeons refer parents of children with DSD to colleagues who may be less reluctant to operate?

NOTE

1 In keeping with this recommendation, we will use "DSD" rather than "intersex."

REFERENCES

AAP (American Academy of Pediatrics) (2000) Policy statement. Evaluation of the newborn with developmental anomalies of the external genitalia. *Pediatrics* 106 (1): 138–42.

Ahmed, S. F., Morrison, S., and Hughes, J. A. (2004) Intersex and gender assignment: the third way? *Archives of Disease in Childhood* 89 (9): 847–50. Available at: http://adc.bmj.com/cgi/reprint/89/9/847 (accessed March 20, 2008).

Asch, A. (2006) Appearance-altering surgery, children's sense of self, and parental love. In E. Parens (ed.), *Surgically Shaping Children: Technology, Ethics, and the Pursuit of Normality.* Baltimore, MD: The Johns Hopkins University Press, pp. 227–52.

Aspinall, C. (2006) Do I make you uncomfortable? Reflections on using surgery to reduce the distress of others. In E. Parens (ed.), *Surgically Shaping Children: Technology, Ethics, and the Pursuit of Normality.* Baltimore, MD: The Johns Hopkins University Press, pp. 13–28.

Blizzard, R. M. (2002) Intersex issues: a series of continuing conundrums. *Pediatrics* 110 (3): 616–21. Available at: http://pediatrics.aappublications.org/cgi/reprint/110/3/616.pdf (accessed October 8, 2007).

Chase, C. (1999) Surgical progress is not the answer to intersexuality. In A. Dreger (ed.), *Intersex in the Age of Ethics.* Hagerstown, MD: University Publishing Group, pp. 146–59.

Colapinto, J. (1997) The true story of John/Joan. *Rolling Stone* 774 (December 11): 54–97.

Crouch, R. A. (1999) Betwixt and between: the past and future of intersexuality. In A. Dreger (ed.), *Intersex in the Age of Ethics.* Hagerstown, MD: University Publishing Group, pp. 29–49.

Dreger, A. (n.d.) Shifting the paradigm of intersex treatment (prepared for the Intersex Society of North America). Available at: www.isna.org/compare (accessed October 8, 2007).

Dreger, A. D. (1998) "Ambiguous sex" – or ambivalent medicine? Ethical issues in the treatment of intersexuality. *The Hastings Center Report* 28 (3): 24–35.

Dreger, A. D. (1999) A history of intersex: from the age of gonads to the age of consent. In A. Dreger (ed.), *Intersex in the Age of Ethics.* Hagerstown, MD: University Publishing Group, pp. 4–22.

Dreger, A. (2006) What to expect when you have the child you weren't expecting. In E. Parens (ed.), *Surgically Shaping Children: Technology, Ethics, and the Pursuit of Normality.* Baltimore, MD: The Johns Hopkins University Press, pp. 253–66.

Elliott, C. (1998) Why can't we go on as three? *The Hastings Center Report* 28 (3): 36–9.

Fausto-Sterling, A. (1993) The five sexes: why male and female are not enough. *The Sciences* (March–April): 20–5.

Feder E. (2006) "In their best interests": parents' experience of atypical genitalia. In E. Parens (ed.), *Surgically Shaping Children: Technology, Ethics, and the Pursuit of Normality.* Baltimore, MD: The Johns Hopkins University Press, pp. 189–210.

Frader, J., Alderson, P., Asch, A., et al. (2004) Healthcare professionals and intersex conditions. *Archives of Pediatrics & Adolescent Medicine* 158 (5): 426–8.

Greene, A. (2006) MedlinePlus Medical Encyclopedia: Intersex. Available at: www.nlm.nih.gov/medlineplus/ency/article/001669.htm (accessed March 3, 2008).

Harmon-Smith, H. (1999) A mother's 10 commandments to medical professionals: treating intersex in the newborn. In A. Dreger (ed.), *Intersex in the Age of Ethics.* Hagerstown, MD: University Publishing Group, pp. 195–6.

Hedley, L. (2006) The seduction of the surgical fix. In E. Parens (ed.), *Surgically Shaping Children: Technology, Ethics, and the Pursuit of Normality.* Baltimore, MD: The Johns Hopkins University Press, pp. 43–50.

Herndon, A. (2006) Why doesn't ISNA want to eradicate gender? Available at: www.isna.org/faq/not_eradicating_gender (accessed October 8, 2007).

ISNA(1) (Intersex Society of North America) (n.d.) How can you assign a gender (boy or girl) without surgery? Available at: www.isna.org/faq/gender_assignment (accessed October 8, 2007).

ISNA(2) (Intersex Society of North America) (n.d.) How common is intersex? Available at: www.isna.org/faq/frequency (accessed October 8, 2007).

ISNA(3) (Intersex Society of North America) (n.d.) What is intersex? Available at: www.isna.org/faq/what_is_intersex (accessed October 8, 2007).

Kipnis, K., and Diamond, M. (1999) Pediatric ethics and the surgical assignment of sex. In A. Dreger (ed.), *Intersex in the Age of Ethics*. Hagerstown, MD: University Publishing Group, pp. 172–93; orig. pub. in *The Journal of Clinical Ethics* 9 (4) (1998): 398–410.

Kittay, E. F. (2006) Thoughts on the desire for normality. In E. Parens (ed.), *Surgically Shaping Children: Technology, Ethics, and the Pursuit of Normality*. Baltimore, MD: The Johns Hopkins University Press, pp. 90–110.

Lee, P. A. (2004) A perspective on the approach to the intersex child born with genital ambiguity. *Journal of Pediatric Endocrinology & Metabolism* 17 (2): 133–40.

Lee, P. A., Houk, C. P., Ahmed, S. F., et al. (2006) Consensus statement on management of intersex disorders. *Pediatrics* 118 (2): e488–e500. Available at: www.pediatrics.org (accessed 8 October 8, 2007).

Migeon, C., Wisniewski, A. B., Gearhart, J. P., et al. (2002a) Ambiguous genitalia with perineoscrotal hypospadias in 46, XY individuals: long-term medical, surgical, and psychosexual outcome. *Pediatrics* 110 (3): e31. Available at: http://pediatrics.aappublications.org/cgi/search?andorexactfulltext=and&resourcetype=1&disp_type=&sort-spec=relevance&fulltext=%22genitalia+with+perineoscrotal+hypospadias+in+46%2C%22&submit.x=0&submit.y=0&submit=send (accessed March 20, 2008).

Migeon, C., Wisniewski, A. B., Brown, T. R., et al. (2002b) 46 XY individuals: phenotypic and etiologic classification, knowledge of condition, and satisfaction with knowledge in adulthood. *Pediatrics* 110 (3): e32. Available at: http://pediatrics.aappublications.org/cgi/content/full/110/3/e32?maxtoshow=&HITS=10&hits=10&RESULTFORMAT=&fulltext=%22genitalia+with+perineoscrotal+hypospadias+in+46%2C%22&andorexactfulltext=and&searchid (accessed March 20, 2008).

Morris, S. E. (2006) Twisted lies: my journey in an imperfect body. In E. Parens (ed.), *Surgically Shaping Children: Technology, Ethics, and the Pursuit of Normality*. Baltimore, MD: The Johns Hopkins University Press, pp. 3–12.

Preves, S. E. (1999) For the sake of the children: destigmatizing intersexuality. In A. Dreger (ed.), *Intersex in the Age of Ethics*. Hagerstown, MD: University Publishing Group, pp. 50–65.

Preves, S. E. (2003) *Intersex and Identity: The Contested Self*. New Brunswick, NJ: Rutgers University Press.

Spack, N. (2005) Transgenderism. *Medical Ethics* 12 (3): 1–2, 12.

Weil, E. (2006) What if it's (sort of) a boy and (sort of) a girl? *New York Times Magazine* (September 4, 2006). Available at: www.nytimes.com/2006/09/24/magazine/24intersexkids.html?ex=1188878400&en=952e7132b1c7e0ba&ei=5070 (accessed September 9, 2007).

Wilson, B. E., and Reiner, W. G. (1999) Management of intersex: a shifting paradigm. In A. Dreger (ed.), *Intersex in the Age of Ethics*. Hagerstown, MD: University Publishing Group, pp. 119–35.

CASE TWENTY: THE HEART OF THE MATTER – WHO DECIDES WHEN THE PATIENT IS DEAD?

So full of life and laughter only 48 hours ago, Mr Ahmed now lay in the ICU (intensive care unit) of the local community hospital after suffering a massive heart attack. While CPR was successful in securing a heartbeat, Mr Ahmed now has marginal brain activity and is currently breathing with the assistance of a ventilator. The well-liked, energetic patriarch of a large Shiite Muslim Arab-American family, Mr Ahmed was known as a generous family man and a community leader. Indeed, while several of Mr Ahmed's adult children were flying in from out-of-state, friends came to the hospital to lend emotional support to the family.

Mrs Ahmed remained silent as her son spoke with the doctor, Linda Hopkins, MD. Dr Hopkins's suggestion that the family begin to think about withdrawing ventilator support was not well received by Mr Ahmed's son, Jamshid. Even though Dr Hopkins explained that Mr Ahmed would never regain consciousness, Jamshid insisted that every effort should be made to keep his father alive. When Mr Ahmed's other children arrived at the hospital, Jamshid filled them in on his conversation with Dr Hopkins. Meanwhile, Mr Ahmed's nurse, Janet Simpson, RN, attempted to talk with Mrs Ahmed about what she thinks her husband would have wanted. Mrs Ahmed felt uncomfortable speculating, since they never spoke of such things. Concerned that his mother was too distressed to talk, Jamshid broke into the discussion. He reiterated that the family wanted everything done to save their father.

Anxious to diffuse the emotionally charged situation, Nurse Simpson recommended that the family sit in a conference room to talk with Dr Hopkins and the staff Imam from pastoral care. While they were waiting for Dr Hopkins and the Imam, Janet listened to the family talk about Mr Ahmed and their family. Jamshid used to help his father with the family business, a neighborhood grocery store. However, he and his father often disagreed about business decisions. For instance, Jamshid was always critical of the amount of money that was spent sponsoring local youth athletic teams (e.g., providing uniforms, snacks, refreshments, and trophies). These differences of business philosophy led Jamshid to take a job out of state several years ago. The daughters, however, still live close to Mr and Mrs Ahmed and still help keep the books for the store. In fact, the youngest daughter, Naja, was at the store with her children decorating the store window for the holidays when Mr Ahmed suffered his heart attack.

Dr Hopkins arrived, and the Imam shortly after. The Imam explained to Dr Hopkins and Nurse Simpson that, for many Shiite Muslims, brain death is not considered death. Instead, they believe that death occurs only upon cessation of cardiac function. After a long pause in the conversation, Nurse Simpson asked the family to imagine what Mr Ahmed might say if he were sitting among them. "He would say that we should keep trying," said Naja. Other family members nodded.

Hours passed and brain activity waned until Mr Ahmed was brain dead. Dr Hopkins spoke with the family about his condition. "We're sorry that there isn't anything more we can do. We think that we should turn off the ventilator and let nature take its course." Jamshid appeared shocked at Dr Hopkins's suggestion and responded angrily: "How can you say that you've done everything you could? I'm not going to let you give up on him as long as he's still alive." Later, Nurse Simpson reminded Dr Hopkins about what the Imam had said regarding the Shiite beliefs about death. "That's fine," she said, "but by 'death' *we* mean brain death, and that's the law in this state."

After a day and a half, Dr Hopkins was growing impatient. She felt that allowing a brain-dead patient to remain on a ventilator was permissible for a brief period if doing so would allow out-of-town family time to get to the hospital to say goodbye. However, Mr Ahmed's family had been present for more than a day and was still insisting that Mr Ahmed was alive and that the healthcare professionals do everything to keep him alive.

From a moral point of view, should Dr Hopkins accommodate Mr Ahmed's family's request to keep him on the ventilator?

Perspective One

Dr Hopkins ought *not* to accommodate Mr Ahmed's family's request to keep him on the ventilator. According to the Uniform Determination of Death Act (UDDA): "An individual who has sustained either (1) irreversible cessation of circulatory and respiratory functions, or (2) irreversible cessation of all functions of the entire brain, including the brain stem, is dead" (National Conference of Commissioners on Uniform State Laws 1980; Garrett et al. 2001: 258). Supported by the UDDA, most states, including that in which Mr Ahmed is being treated, have chosen to define death as the irreversible cessation of brain function. Hence, according to criterion #2 of the UDDA, Mr Ahmed is dead; the fact that his heart is still beating does not change that fact. Mechanical ventilation, along with any other kind of medical intervention, is only for the living. In fact, given Mr Ahmed's brain death, his circulatory and respiratory functions would be non-existent if the ventilator were removed.

Definition aside, medicine, like all professions, is built upon a set of core values to which physicians commit themselves when they freely choose to enter the profession. Among other things, physicians must promote the good of, and avoid harming, the patient (Veach 2003: 47–57). Physicians have an obligation to offer only treatments that are medically appropriate for a patient's condition. Indeed, most hospitals have policies that reflect this. Whether the policy refers to "futile treatment" or "non-beneficial treatment," most healthcare institutions formally recognize a physician's authority to withhold treatment that he or she believes is not medically indicated (i.e., futile or non-beneficial). The American Medical Association states: "Physicians are not ethically obligated to deliver care that, in their best professional judgment, will not have a reasonable chance of benefitting their patient. Patients should not be given treatments simply because they demand them" (AMA 2005).

No healthcare professional should be required to act contrary to the moral standards of the profession and contrary to her own professional judgment. As a member of the medical profession and as a matter of professional integrity, Dr Hopkins is ethically bound to offer treatments that, in her professional judgment, are medically appropriate for Mr Ahmed (Brody 2001: 346–8). And certainly, if Mr Ahmed *is* dead, allowing any treatment *at all* would be medically futile.

Finally, healthcare institutions have an obligation to allocate resources fairly, that is, in a responsible manner. According, again, to the American Medical Association: "Decisions regarding the allocation of limited medical resources among patients should consider only ethically appropriate criteria relating to medical need. These criteria include likelihood of benefit, urgency of need, change in quality of life, duration of benefit, and, in some cases, the amount of resources required for successful treatment" (AMA 1994). As Mr Ahmed will not (because dead) benefit or experience any improvement in his quality of life, and because the duration of ventilation could last for a very long time without providing any benefit, allowing him to remain on a ventilator is an irresponsible waste of an expensive resource.

As the appeals to consequences and the virtue of professional integrity demonstrate, the ventilator should be discontinued.

Perspective Two

Dr Hopkins ought to accommodate the Ahmed family's request to keep Mr Ahmed on the ventilator. Mr Ahmed is considered dead only because in the past 25 years the definition of death shifted from the absence of a heart beat to the absence of brain activity. As reflected in its laws, society decided that a person should be categorized as dead when there is no brain activity. Society could have decided to continue to define death solely in terms of the cessation of cardiac activity. Hence, it is not a *fact* that Mr Ahmed is "dead" as much as it is a philosophical choice about how to define death. Cultures (including religious traditions) may choose to define death differently, and sensitivity to cultural differences will require sensitivity to different definitions of death. If the Ahmeds' Islamic beliefs lead them to define death differently from the predominant definition in the US, then their beliefs should be respected and their request accommodated. Respecting such choices, both about values and about individual healthcare choices, is what is meant by respecting persons and their autonomy.

Further, the morally and legally accepted method of decision-making for incompetent patients who were formerly competent (the so-called "substituted judgment" standard) is to make the decision that the patient would have made were he competent (Veach 2003: 107). Healthcare professionals turn to family members, since they are the ones best situated to know what the patient would have chosen. In the case of Mr Ahmed, Nurse Simpson rightly asked the family what he would choose if he were competent and able to communicate. To this, his daughter, who presumably knows him well, stated that "he would say to that we should keep trying."

What is more, any judgment stating that continued mechanical ventilation on Mr Ahmed is "futile" is a *value* judgment, not a *medical* judgment, and therefore beyond the expertise of Dr Hopkins, Nurse Simpson, and the other professionals involved in Mr Ahmed's care (Rubin 1998: 88–114; Gampel 2006). Keeping Mr Ahmed on the ventilator is obviously not futile to the Ahmed family. Treatments are given to achieve some goal; in this case, the goal is sustaining Mr Ahmed's heartbeat and, thus, his life. Judgment that a treatment is medically futile only means that a physician believes that there is an unacceptable probability that a treatment will achieve the goal of benefiting the patient. However, what should count as "benefit," and what should count as an "acceptable probability"? These decisions also are clearly value judgments. Some patients or families, either because of their own personal value commitments or because of cultural influence, believe that human life should always be preserved. Viewed in this way, keeping a person alive in *any* condition counts as benefit. Also, how one defines "acceptable probability" will vary from one person to the next. For some people, a 3 percent chance that a treatment will produce a certain benefit is unacceptably low. For others, a 3 percent chance of benefit is more than enough to initiate or continue treatment. For the Ahmed family, keeping Mr Ahmed's heart beating is enough benefit to justify continuing treatment. And if they *were* hoping for Mr Ahmed somehow to regain some brain activity, the remotest of possibilities may be enough for them. In short, for the Ahmed family, the consequences of maintaining mechanical ventilation are significantly positive.

Given the support of the principles of autonomy and beneficence, the family's wishes should be honored.

Perspective Three

Dr Hopkins finds herself in a difficult position. She wants to be sensitive to the cultural values of the Ahmed family. However, as a physician, she has an obligation only to offer treatments that she believes are medically appropriate. Should she accommodate Mr Ahmed's family's request to keep him on the ventilator? Additional information would be helpful.

Step 1: Information-gathering

Medical Information

- How certain is Dr Hopkins regarding Mr Ahmed's neurological status?
- How long will Mr Ahmed's heart likely remain beating on the ventilator after his brain has ceased functioning?

Sociocultural information

- Is there room in the Islamic faith to withdraw life support from a patient whose brain is no longer functioning?

Implications

- If Mr Ahmed is removed from the ventilator, and this becomes the manner in which all similar cases are handled, will this have a negative effect on the hospital's relationship with the local Muslim community?
- If the hospital made a policy of accommodating the wishes of Muslim families when their family member is brain-dead, what will the consequences be on hospital resources?

Legal Information

- What is the legal precedent on cases in which families have challenged the brain death criterion?

Step 2: Creative problem-solving

There does not appear to be any creative way to resolve the conflict regarding whether or not Mr Ahmed is dead. Dr Hopkins believes that he is dead and the Ahmed family believes that he is alive. Nevertheless, short of either turning off the ventilator or allowing Mr Ahmed to remain on it indefinitely, the Ahmeds can be given some additional time to come to terms with the decision to turn off the ventilator. Many families have great difficulty accepting news that nothing can be done for their loved one when their loved one's decline comes on very suddenly. There is often an understandable knee-jerk reaction to insist on continued treatment. For this reason, healthcare professionals should maintain good, clear, and ongoing communication with patients and families in cases where a patient's prognosis is poor. While inappropriate treatments ought not to be offered (or continued if they have been initiated), there could be circumstances, like in the case of Mr Ahmed, under which it may be permissible to allow additional time, with the understanding that if certain benchmark improvements are not achieved within a week, then ventilator support will be withdrawn. Granted, if the Ahmed family's position is that Mr Ahmed is alive, and that no further improvement is necessary to justify keeping him on the ventilator, they will certainly resist this compromise. Nonetheless, it will allow them more time to process and come to terms with the tragic situation.

Step 3: Listing pros and cons

Options	Pros	Cons
Allow Mr Ahmed to remain on the ventilator.	1. Respects family's wish (A) 2. Respects Mr Ahmed's autonomy (assuming he would choose, if he could, to remain on the ventilator) (A, Right to self determination) 3. Respects religious beliefs (A) 4. Benefits Mr Ahmed's (from family's point of view) (C-PPB)	5. Violates Dr Hopkins's professional integrity (V-I) 6. Provides futile (i.e., non beneficial) treatment (C-NM) 7. Misuse of scarce, costly hospital resources (C-NM, U, J)
Remove Mr Ahmed from the ventilator against the family's wishes.	8. Preserves Dr Hopkins's professional integrity (V-I) 9. Conserves valuable resources (e.g., ventilator, ICU bed) (J, C-PU)	10. Overrides family wishes (A) 11. Could breed mistrust among the local Muslim community (C-PU)

Step 4: Analysis

Factual assumptions

- Mr Ahmed is dead.
- Resources spent on Mr Ahmed are futile.
- The insurance company will not cover the costs of Mr Ahmed's care.
- The Ahmed family cannot afford to pay for his care themselves.

Value assumptions

- Brain-dead patients should not be given medical "treatments."
- The healthcare professionals should have the final say in whether a patient is dead.

Step 5: Justification

Disagreements between families and healthcare professionals in end-of-life care, such as that between Dr Hopkins and the Ahmed family, often reflect mistrust on the part of the family. Families, especially those from different cultures, may have difficulty trusting the judgments of healthcare professionals. They may fear that their status as cultural outsiders means that they might not receive the same level or quality of care as others. In such cases, it is often helpful to try to incorporate into the treatment team people whom the family is likely to trust. In the case of Mr Ahmed, Dr Hopkins and Nurse Simpson were wise to solicit the help of the Imam from pastoral care, and perhaps should seek the assistance of an Arab or Muslim physician in the hospital. There may be more room in their religion for withdrawal of treatment than the Ahmeds realize.

Of course, a central point of dispute in this case has to do with whether Mr Ahmed is dead. Admittedly, there are different ways to define death. Islam, along with certain other faith traditions (e.g., Orthodox Judaism) adheres to a cardiac definition of death (Silbani 1998: 85–6). Nonetheless, the law (the Uniform Determination of Death Act) allows death according to a whole brain criterion, and Mr Ahmed shows no brain activity. So it is, at the very least, *legally* permissible for Dr Hopkins to discontinue ventilation on Mr Ahmed.

A consideration of consequences does not appear to lend decisive support to accommodating the Ahmed family's wish to continue ventilation on their father. From the hospital's point of view, allowing Mr Ahmed to remain on the ventilator in his condition will not result in any real benefit (Reason #6). It will not bring him back to being the person that the family knew, nor will it even lead to any neurological improvement. However, from the Ahmed family's point of view, keeping Mr Ahmed's heart beating does, in fact, represent real benefit (Reason #4). Granted, one might point out that claims about benefit and likelihood of benefit reflect value judgments rather than medical judgments. This is certainly true. What is more, there does not seem to be any compelling sense in which Mr Ahmed himself is being harmed. So any suggestion that he is being harmed by continued ventilation is misguided. Certainly the consequences to his family are positive; they have him with them longer and they do not feel as if their values are being ignored.

Nonetheless, the hospital and Dr Hopkins also have their own conceptions of benefit and acceptable probability of benefit. There is no reason why the Dr Hopkins's understanding of reasonable benefit should necessarily have to take a back seat to that of the Ahmed family. And even if there is no identifiable harm to Mr Ahmed, there are other consequences to consider. A hospital practice of allowing patients to remain on a ventilator after they are brain-dead would become costly to the hospital (Reason #7). Certainly, no insurance company is going to pay for continued treatment on someone who is, according to the accepted legal definition, dead. Admittedly, as mentioned above, a brain-dead patient does not *typically* survive more than few days on a ventilator before the rest of the organs shut down. However, this still represents a considerable expense, one which families could not likely pay if the insurance company denies the request for payment. The hospital would simply have to absorb the financial loss and, in the end, pass it on to others.

Certainly, attention to consequences should also consider the possible impact that such cases might have on the relationship between the hospital and the local Muslim community. If the local Muslim community develops the impression that the hospital is insensitive to its religious values, this could lead to reluctance on the part of the community to use the hospital (Reason #11). However, while this deserves serious attention, and the hospital should make efforts to build a dialogue with the Muslim community and identify ways in which situations like Mr Ahmed's could best be handled, the hospital and its professional staff should not be forced to provide treatments that are inconsistent with what the medical profession holds to be medically appropriate (Reason #7).

So the appeal to consequence gives no clear answer. However the last point, that of offering only treatments that are medically appropriate, is also an appeal to the virtue of professional *integrity* (Reasons ##5, 8). Healthcare professionals have a commitment to providing treatment that they believe will offer benefit and, more to the point here, to *not* providing non-beneficial treatment. Professional integrity consists in being true to this commitment (Brody 2001: 346–8). In Dr Hopkins's professional judgment, continued ventilation of Mr Ahmed is not medically appropriate (i.e., is futile). Although this judgment reflects a value commitment that is at odds with the beliefs and values of the patient/family, for a physician simply to acquiesce to the demands of patients, whether they are medically appropriate or not, is to reduce the physician–patient relationship to a commercial arrangement in which "the customer is always right." Surely a physician should not give in to a patient's demands for a prescription of birth control pills to cure his sinus infection or bypass surgery to cure his arthritis. To endorse this would be to misunderstand the important social role of medicine. Health is a foundational good for all members of society. Physicians and other healthcare professionals undergo years of education and training in order to acquire the knowledge and skills necessary to provide this good. When someone seeks out the help of a physician, that person must trust that the physician will use her knowledge and skill with integrity for the good of the patient. That is, because of the vast disparity in knowledge and skill between the physician and the patient, the patient must place significant trust in the physician. This leaves the physician with an enormous amount power, which requires, as a safeguard, a correspondingly high obligation to act only for the good of the patient.

Hence, the appeal to the virtue of professional integrity gives Dr Hopkins a good reason not to accommodate the wishes of the Ahmed family.

This brings us to a consideration of the place of autonomy and rights in our analysis. Mr Ahmed's autonomy could be reflected through a substituted judgment standard (Reason #2). However, respect for a patient's autonomy does not, without good reason, override a physician's professional autonomy. Just as patients value their autonomy, so too do physicians. Indeed, one of the hallmarks of a profession is autonomy of practice (Davis 2001: 4, 8–11). This means that medical professionals have autonomy in the judgments they make and the treatments they recommend. Presumably no physician would autonomously choose to provide a non-beneficial treatment; indeed, they would autonomously choose *not* to do so. Thus, they should not be forced to provide treatments that they do not believe are medically appropriate (Schneiderman and Capron 2000: 529). So a consideration of Dr Hopkins's professional autonomy would justify her refusal to follow the wishes of the Ahmed family. But respect for Mr Ahmed's autonomy would counter this refusal. So the appeal to autonomy gives no help here.

Sometimes claims regarding respect for autonomy are expressed in terms of rights. A patient has a right to decisional authority, or self-determination. However, what does such a right imply? What does it require of those who must respect a right to autonomy? A patient's right to decisional authority may be interpreted in two different ways. On the one hand, it may be seen as a so-called negative right (or liberty right), a right that requires others to refrain from interfering with the patient. On the other hand, it may be understood as a positive right (or welfare right), a right requiring others to provide some service or meet some need (Veach 2003: 73–4).

Traditionally, a patient's right to self-determination is strongest when it is understood as a negative right, which is usually expressed as a refusal of treatment. A patient's right to refuse treatment (so long as the patient is competent and informed) typically trumps all other considerations. A positive right to autonomy is a much weaker right, and is reflected in requests for treatment. Physician's have an obligation to accommodate medically reasonable requests for treatment. However, given the above discussion of professional integrity and medical futility, a patient's positive right to autonomy has limitations. It cannot require a physician to violate her professional integrity. Therefore, an appeal to rights does not support allowing Mr Ahmed to remain on the ventilator.

Finally, what would justice require in this case? That is, what would a responsible management of resources imply? In the case of Mr Ahmed, the use of resources such as pastoral care and social work seem appropriate. However, as suggested above, allocating expensive resources to maintain the heartbeat of a brain-dead patient is using a scarce and expensive resource for which the insurance company is unlikely to reimburse the hospital. Further, the family is unlikely to be able to afford these resources. As a result, the hospital faces a large bill for which it will not be compensated. The hospital likely will pass these costs on to patients who are insured, or to the taxpayers. However, insured patients and taxpayers do not deserve to bear the financial burdens of Mr Ahmed's futile care. Moreover, as most hospitals have a limited number of ventilators, Mr Ahmed's use thereof makes it unavailable to other patients, at least some of whom could likely benefit from it. So, an appeal to justice argues against continuing the ventilator.

In sum, although a consideration of consequences and autonomy are unhelpful in this case, the appeals to rights, the virtue of professional integrity, and justice ethically support removing Mr Ahmed from the ventilator.

None of this is to say that Mr Ahmed should be removed from the ventilator without allowing time for the patient's family to say goodbye. It may take a day or so for out-of-town family to make travel arrangements. Hence, while Dr Hopkins ought not to allow Mr Ahmed to remain on the ventilator for any extended length of time, compassion for the family and allowing them some control (autonomy) justifies permitting him to remain as he is for a few days so that family members can say their goodbyes and begin to adjust to their loss.

Additional Issues to Consider

Other possible moral dilemmas arising within this case:

Q Should Dr Hopkins transfer the care of Mr Ahmed to a physician who shares the family's conception of death?

Q Should Dr Hopkins transfer the care of Mr Ahmed to a hospital or extended care facility that either shares the family's conception of death or at least does not object to providing life-support?

REFERENCES

AMA (American Medical Association) (1994) Opinion E-2.03: Allocation of Limited Medical Resources. Available at: www.ama-assn.org/ama/pub/category/8388.html (accessed October 4, 2007).

AMA (American Medical Association) (2005) Opinion E-2.035: Futile Care. Available at: www.ama-assn.org/ama/pub/category/8389.html (accessed October 4, 2007).

Brody, H. (2001) The physician's role in determining futility. In T. Mappes and D. DeGrazia (eds.), *Biomedical Ethics*, 5th edn. New York: McGraw-Hill, pp. 345–50. Orig. pub. in *Journal of the American Geriatrics Society* 42 (8) (1994): 875–8.

Davis, M. (2001) Introduction. In M. Davis and A. Stark (eds.), *Conflict of Interest in the Professions*. Bloomington, IN: Indiana University Press, pp. 3–19.

Gampel, E. (2006) Does professional autonomy protect medical futility judgments? *Bioethics* 20 (2): 92–104.

Garrett, T., Baillie, H., and Garrett, R. (2001) *Healthcare Ethics: Principles and Problems*, 4th edn. Upper Saddle River, NJ: Prentice-Hall.

National Conference of Commissioners on Uniform State Laws (1980) Uniform determination of death act. Available at: www.law.upenn.edu/bll/archives/ulc/fnact99/1980s/udda80.htm (accessed March 20, 2008).

Rubin, S. (1998) *When Doctors Say No: The Battleground of Medical Futility*. Bloomington, IN: Indiana University Press.

Schneiderman, L., and Capron, L. (2000) How can hospital futility policies contribute to establishing standards of practice? *Cambridge Quarterly of Healthcare Ethics* 9 (4): 524–31.

Silbani, M. (1998) *Islam: The Muslim Patient*. Dearborn, MI: Oasis Health and Educational Services, Inc.

Veach, R. (2003) *The Basics of Bioethics*, 2nd edn. Upper Saddle River, NJ: Prentice Hall.

CASE TWENTY-ONE: LIP SERVICE – COSMETIC USE OF CADAVER TISSUE

"Want luscious, pouty, kissable lips?" the lush-lipped model in the ad purred.

"Who doesn't?" thought Jenna, as she dialed Alexa's cell phone. Alexa, her best friend, was going to be her maid of honor in two months. More importantly, Alexa was her support in times of tribulations, such as when she got her tattoos. Lip-enhancement sounded like it would hurt and, if it did, she could count on Alexa for moral support and sympathy. Besides, Alexa was really smart, and thought about things Jenna didn't. Alexa liked doing Internet searches to get information, something Jenna found tedious – unless she was looking at wedding sites.

Alexa got on the Internet right away. She entered "lip-enhancement" in the search box and hit "enter." Links to more than a million websites immediately popped up.

It was a good thing Jenna called Alexa. Jenna hadn't thought about the different materials and methods used in lip-enhancement, but Alexa was all over it. Silicon oil was one option, but the breasts of some of their friends' moms had been ruined by silicon implants. They got hard and lumpy, and who wants hard, lumpy lips? Eeaauuu! Something natural seemed better. Another method used bovine collagen, and although they knew collagen was used in a lot of beauty products and cows were natural, they were nervous about the bovine part. Could you get Mad Cow Disease from lip injections? At first, permanent enhancement seemed like the best idea, but as Alexa read more she learned that if a problem such as granuloma or necrosis occurred (she wasn't sure what they were, but they sounded ghastly!), the problem could be permanent. Jenna finally decided to have injections made from human fascia, a fibrous tissue containing collagen that is found throughout the body (Dorland 1994), and often used for lipenhancement. Although the effects would last only about four months, Jenna would have perfectly luscious, pouty, kissable lips for her wedding day.

While Jenna was thinking about plump, juicy lips, Marcia and Ben Carlson could barely think at all, let alone about the serious decision they faced. Stretching to catch a fly ball, their 14-year old son Randy lost his balance and fell from the stands. Randy snapped his neck and suffered severe brain trauma. Maureen Fletcher, a bereavement counselor for the local organ-procurement organization (OPO), was alerted by the hospital of an imminent death and reached the hospital shortly after Randy arrived. After the physician had discussed the unlikelihood of Randy's survival with his parents, and the viability of his organs for transplantation had been assessed, a life-support system kept him alive while Ms Fletcher approached the Carlsons to discuss donating Randy's organs and skin. (Skin is actually an organ, but for the purposes of donation it's considered a tissue. Most countries forbid the sale of human organs, but the prohibition does not apply to human tissue.) As Randy's parents discussed whether or not to donate his organs, Maureen was comforting and knowledgeable. She assured them that a donation would give another person, perhaps a boy like Randy, the gift of life. If Randy were fighting for life because he had been badly burned, they would be deeply and eternally grateful that grafts from donor skin could allow him to heal. They knew that time was important, but it was agonizing to think what would happen to Randy's body if they agreed to donate. In the end, the Carlsons knew that as difficult as their loss was to bear, in the months and years to come, they would regret their decision if they failed to give another person the chance to live that Randy no longer had. As time passed, and the pain of Randy's loss was less intense, they knew they had done the right thing. They took comfort in knowing that, in a way, Randy lived on in the gifts he had given others.

Marcia and Ben Carlson would have been devastated had they known that Randy's donation had not helped to save a life, but instead had given Jenna luscious, pouty, kissable lips.

Sometimes Maureen Fletcher had niggling qualms about the way she did her job, and she couldn't figure out how to assuage her discomfort. She believed her work was noble and that it provided untold benefits, not just for those suffering as they waited for organs, but for all the people who loved them. She felt somewhat uncomfortable because she knew that by deliberately omitting information about the potential commercial use of donated tissue, she was not being completely truthful. On the other hand, she didn't know how to reconcile the great good she was doing with the tiny deceit she felt was necessary to persuade people to agree to donate.

Maureen had assured the Carlsons that their son's organs and skin would be used to save the lives of others, giving special meaning to Randy's short life. Even as she said the words, she knew this was not a certainty. So few organs are available and so many people are waiting for them, hoping desperately the call will come before it is too late. It would be wonderful if all donations ended up being transplanted, but that isn't possible. Once removed from the body or life support, organs are fragile. A heart or lung is viable for only about 4 hours; a pancreas or intestines, up to 8 hours; a liver may be preserved for 18 hours; and a kidney, up to 48 hours (NYODN 2007). Sometimes, despite everyone's best efforts, organs do not arrive on time. Sometimes, the time it takes to make a decision compromises the viability of the organs and tissue. Sometimes, the intended recipients die waiting for a transplant. Sometimes, the final safety testing identifies a problem with the donation that was not initially apparent, such as a positive viral test or other evidence of infectious disease.

Maureen's thoughts turned again to the Carlsons. She understood the anguish that Marcia and Ben felt as they imagined what procuring organs and skin would do to Randy's beautiful body. She believed absolutely that donation was one of the greatest gifts anyone could give or receive, but was afraid that the Carlsons would not agree to donate Randy's organs if they knew that the organs might not be used for transplantation. The cost of organ-procurement was enormous, as were all the costs associated with preserving organ viability and transporting organs to the recipients. Organizations like the one she worked for were essential to the process, but they also were costly to run. Maureen saw the necessity of securing resources to cover expenses. She understood the need for research to increase the success of transplantation and improve longevity and quality of life for organ recipients. She knew that organs that were no longer viable were sold to laboratories to be used in research, and to commercial businesses, where they might be processed for use in non-life-threatening, medically indicated surgeries such as breast reconstruction following cancer surgery, joint-replacement, dental implants – or for purely elective cosmetic surgeries such as face-lifts and penis-enlargement. Maureen believed these commercial sales were justifiable as they insured the survival of organizations that make transplantation possible.

Were Maureen Fletcher and Randy's physician morally justified in withholding information from Marcia and Ben Carlson about the possible uses of Randy's donated organs and tissues?

Perspective One

Maureen Fletcher (acting for the doctor) and the doctor were morally justified in withholding from the Carlsons information that would emotionally bias their decision to donate Randy's organs and skin. This position is supported by the moral concepts of good consequences, autonomy, and virtue.

To increase the supply of organs and tissues, the National Organ and Tissue Donation Initiative was launched in 1997 by Vice-President Al Gore. This initiative required hospitals to inform organ-procurement organizations about every death or imminent death. As soon as the OPO is notified, a bereavement counselor is sent to meet with the family. If the patient has not previously consented to be a donor, and the family doesn't mention donation, the OPO representative will encourage the family to consider it as a possibility. The need for organs is great, as are the benefits they confer. In the United States alone, 90,000 individuals are waiting for organs, and each year 6,500 die waiting for an organ (Korobkin 2005, M5). Because of organ and tissue donation, the blind are able to see, burn victims can heal with far less pain and scarring than in the past, donated biological material prevents limb amputation for cancer victims, and people can move easily after joint-replacement. Maureen was aware of the potential for so much good to come from Randy's donation, and was motivated, in part, by beneficence.

Maureen also knew that although commercial interests might profit from Randy's donation, that profit also provides social benefit, honoring the moral principle of utility. Medical care advances as research on donated tissues and organs makes more effective treatments possible.

When people are under great stress it is more difficult for them to understand a large amount of information. Consent is compromised when too much information is given in a short period of time to emotionally distressed decision-makers. Recognizing the problem of information overload, healthcare workers do not explain in exacting detail the procedures that will be used to try to save a patient's life. Necessary medical procedures can seem gruesome, and consent does not require a complete set of mental images to be valid. Likewise, transplant professionals do not burden family members with vivid details of organ- and tissue-procurement.

When Maureen Fletcher met with the Carlsons, they were in a state of shock and grief over their son. Nonetheless, and in spite of their extreme duress, the Carlsons would have to give consent before Randy's organs and tissue could be removed. For that consent to be morally binding (autonomous), the Carlsons would have to be informed about and understand what organ transplantation involves, and would have to consent freely to the use of their son's organs and tissue. Maureen's decision to withhold information was driven by her belief that graphic information about procurement procedures and detailed use of donated organs and tissue would unnecessarily burden the Carlsons. She was trying to protect their autonomy by helping them make the choice she believed they would make under less stressful circumstances.

Maureen was further motivated by the virtue of compassion. Imagining images of the procurement procedures, perhaps being haunted by memories of them, was unnecessary to the informed consent process and would likely only bring psychological unease to families. As a result, Maureen chose to withhold some information that she believed, in her professional judgment, was unnecessary and would upset the Carlsons.

In conclusion, there is a critical shortage of organ and tissue donors. Nonprofit tissue banks and organ-procurement programs are concerned that full disclosure of information at an extremely emotional time will discourage potential donations, donations that a decision-maker would consent to when calmer and thinking more clearly. The passage of time, however, might render the organs and tissue unusable, denying scores of potential beneficiaries the gift of better health. Therefore, the appeals to consequences, autonomy, and virtue morally justify the omission of some upsetting information.

Perspective Two

Either Maureen Fletcher or Randy's doctor was morally obligated to provide the Carlsons with all information relevant to their decision to donate their son's organs and skin, even if it meant the Carlsons would decide against the donation. This position is support by the moral concepts of good consequences, autonomy, the virtue of professional integrity, and equality of respect (justice).

Imagine your horror if you learned that parts of the body of your deceased loved one had been removed and used for commercial purposes. Imagine how much greater your outrage and sense of betrayal would be if you subsequently learned that the physician who encouraged you to discontinue life support, and convinced you to agree to the donation, benefited financially from the transaction.

If physicians and transplant specialists withhold or misrepresent information about the uses of donated organs and tissue, the consequences to organ-donation

programs and for the health outcomes of persons with end-stage organ failure
are likely to be severe. The public will be reluctant to donate organs and tissue
if they learn that donation programs employ deceit. Consequently, the shortage
of available organs will become even more acute; morbidity and mortality will
increase.

An added danger is that the public will lose trust in the medical profession if
they know that doctors withhold information that might lead patients to make
decisions based on their own values, rather than the doctor's preferences. Trust
is essential in the practice of medicine. If patients lose confidence in physicians'
honesty and professional duty to protect them from harm, the fundamental values
of medicine are compromised. Failure to disclose the possible commercial use
of donated organs and tissue is a deceit that exploits patients and their families
when they are most vulnerable, and has the potential to cause irreparable emotional harm if families discover the truth. The moral principle of consequences
forbids deception.

Deliberately withholding information to insure that people make a decision
they would not make were they fully informed denies their autonomy. In choosing not to discuss the possibility of cosmetic or commercial use with the
Carlsons, or insure that the discussion Maureen Fletcher had with Marcia and
Ben Carlson was comprehensive, Randy's physician failed to honor the Carlson's
autonomy. Maureen Fletcher's failure to disclose the possible uses of donated
organs and tissue, substituting her own goals for the (unknown) goals of the
Carlsons regarding their son, and justifying this deceit by offering a counter-
vailing need for donation, disregarded the principle of autonomy. Both Maureen
Fletcher and the doctor failed Randy and his parents.

The American Medical Association (AMA) *Code of Medical Ethics* requires
physicians to insure that patients, or those responsible for making medical
decisions on their behalf, have voluntarily consented to allow specific treatment
to be undertaken or refused. Consent is valid only after decision-makers have
received – and thoroughly discussed and understood – complete information about
the recommendations and alternatives (AMA 2000–1: section 8.08). AMA
guidelines for informed consent specifically for organ and tissue donation are
discussed separately (sections 2.15–2.167). Section 2.16(3) mandates full and
informed disclosure to both organ donors and recipients, or to their legitimate surrogate decision-makers. The guidelines recommend that full disclosure
include information on the importance and success of organ transplantation
(section 2.155); they caution that the physician's scientific interest in organ donation may not override the patient's interest (section 2.16[3]).

Still another section (2.08) of the AMA *Code of Medical Ethics* (2000–1) is
written for physicians who participate in the profitable body business themselves.
Section 2.08 addresses the issue of informed consent and disclosure in cases where
the physician stands to benefit financially from the commercial use of human
tissue. The code requires the doctor to inform the patient, prior to donation,
that the physician may profit from the patient's donated tissue, and directs the
physician specifically to obtain the patient's informed consent to use that tissue
for commercial purposes. (Although the code requires the disclosure of the
physician's potential commercial gain from tissue donation, it is silent on the

physician's obligation to disclose that others may profit from the downstream commercialization of donated tissue, even if the attending physician does not. This is an omission the authors believe should be rectified.) The AMA *Code of Medical Ethics* also articulates the professional expectation that physicians will provide decision-makers with full and relevant information, especially the sorts of information that may lead to outcomes the professionals would not choose for the patient. Failure to honor the code of ethics demonstrates a lack of professional integrity. Thus virtue requires that Maureen Fletcher or the physician provide the Carlsons with all information relevant to their decision.

It is inevitable that the availability of scarce resources, whether financial or otherwise, drive decisions about medical care. To insure fairness to all parties concerned, just policies governing the allocation of scarce resources, such as organs and tissue, must involve transparent and participatory public discourse (Sharpe and Faden 1998: 131–2). How would the public react if they knew the truth?

The greatest beneficiaries of the National Organ and Tissue Donation Initiative are commercial tissue banks, while the shortage of organs for transplant persists (Josefson 2000: 658). Organ and tissue donation is portrayed to potential donors and the public as an altruistic act, when in fact it frequently feeds a multi-billion dollar commercial industry. While federal law regulates organ transplantation, the tissue retrieval and processing business is largely unregulated. Organ-processing organizations, biotechnology companies, surgical centers, hospitals, and physicians all profit from donations (Holland 2001: 265–6). By weight, the value of human tissue approximates diamonds, and the market value of a human body, sold piece by piece, is nearly a quarter of a million dollars (Katches et al. 2000).

Skin for burn victims is often unavailable, as commercial tissue banks give priority to customers who pay a premium. Cosmetic surgeons charge more than burn specialists and are willing to pay more for products (Heisel et al. 2000). Many organ-procuring organizations have exclusive contracts with commercial firms, such as cosmetics companies, to ensure a constant supply of the donated biological materials required by the industry (Katches et al. 2000).

Those who benefit from organ and tissue donation argue that disclosing to potential donors that human *materia medica* may be sold downstream for profit will result in a decrease in the number of donations. This, however, is a compelling reason for disclosure. When those in a position of power, by virtue of trust and professional responsibility, deliberately withhold material information, their acts constitute selfish and unconscionable behavior that uses human beings as mere means to their own ends. Randy and his parents were so used. Equality of respect does not allow people to be used as means to an end, nor does it allow human beings to be treated as commodities. When healthcare providers deliberately withhold relevant information, deceiving those with less knowledge and power who must rely on them precisely because of that disparity, justice is compromised. By their failure to discuss the possible uses of Randy's organs and tissues, Randy's physician and Maureen Fletcher disregarded the ethical principle of equality (justice).

Although the United States and many other countries forbid the sale of human organs or tissue, US companies may charge reasonable expenses to cover their operational costs. Public Law 98-507 (1984) allows "reasonable payments associated with the removal, transportation, implantation, processing, preservation, quality control, and storage of a human organ" (Title 111, Section 301 (c)(2)). Companies are allowed to charge reasonable fees to cover their costs. What reasonable fees include is undefined, leaving it up to the enterprise to determine whether both laboratory equipment and golf outings to St Andrews constitute reasonable expenses.

A combination of factors makes the requirement of informed consent more urgent than ever. The proliferation of biotechnology companies and the enormous profits they realize have greatly increased the demand and competition for human tissue donation. Biomedical science has a history of deliberately failing to inform patients of options and consequences (Josefson 2000: 658). The National Organ and Donor Initiative requires hospitals to notify an organ-procuring organization when a death is imminent so that the OPO can encourage families to consent to donate organs and tissue. The AMA acknowledges that some of their physicians participate in commercialization of human tissue. Deliberate deceit in organ donation cannot be allowed to continue.

In conclusion, either Maureen Fletcher or Randy's physician is morally required to give the Carlsons full information about the potential uses of their son's organs. This position is supported by the moral concepts of good consequences, autonomy, professional integrity, and equality. Without disclosing all the information that the Carlsons need to make an informed decision, the medical profession and organ-procurement organizations contribute to the combination of chilling factors that has the potential to turn the practice of medicine into the business of spare parts.

Additional Issues to Consider

Other possible moral dilemmas arising within this case:

Q Would healthcare professionals be obligated to inform families if donor organs or tissue were *given* (i.e., not sold) to companies or research institutions?

Q Would healthcare professionals be obligated to inform families if donor organs or tissue were *given or sold*, but only to research institutions?

Q Is selling donor organs or tissues *ever* morally justifiable?

REFERENCES

AMA (American Medical Association Council on Ethical and Judicial Affairs) (2000–1 edn.) *Code of Medical Ethics: Current Opinions with Annotations*. Chicago: American Medical Association.

Dorland, W. A. N. (1994) *Dorland's Illustrated Medical Dictionary*, 29th edn. Philadelphia, PA: W. B. Saunders.

Heisel, W., Katches, M., and Kowalczyk, L. (2000) The body brokers: Part 2 – Skin merchants. *The Orange County Register* (April 17). Available at: www.ocregister.com/health_fitness/features/body/tissue00119cci.shtml (accessed May 24, 2007).

Holland, S. (2001) Contested commodities at both ends of life: buying and selling gametes, embryos, and body tissues. *Kennedy Institute of Ethics Journal* 11 (3): 263–84.

Josefson, D. (2000) US hospitals to ask patients for right to sell their tissue. *British Medical Journal* 321 (7262): 658.

Katches, M., Heisel, W., and Campbell, R. (2000) The body brokers: Part 1 – Assembly line: donors don't realize they are fueling a lucrative business. *The Orange County Register* (April 16). Available at: www.ocregister.com/health-fitness/features/body/index.shtml (accessed May 24, 2007).

Korobkin, R. (2005) Compensation for donations? It's one way to help those on transplant waiting lists. *Los Angeles Times* (October 30): M5.

Public Law 98-507 (1984) To provide for the establishment of the Task Force on Organ Transplantation and the Organ Procurement and Transplantation Network, TITLE 111, Section 301 (c)(2).

NOTDA (1997) National Organ and Tissue Donation Initiative. Available at: www.hhs.gov/news/press/1999pres/990519.html (accessed June 20, 2008).

NYODN (New York Organ Donor Network) (2007) Organ donation process. Available at: www.nyodn.org/organ/o_donationfacts_process.html (accessed October 11, 2007).

Sharpe, V. A., and Faden, A. I. (1998) *Medical Harm: Historical, Conceptual and Ethical Dimensions of Iatrogenic Illness.* Cambridge: Cambridge University Press.

CASE TWENTY-TWO: DRUG OF CHOICE – PATIENTS' ACCESS TO EXPERIMENTAL DRUGS

Most people who suffer from some kind of illness can make an appointment with a physician and receive a course of treatment that will cure or manage that illness. When the physician prescribes a medication in the US, she selects one from the many kinds of drugs approved by the Food and Drug Administration (FDA). The FDA is a government agency whose main purpose is to protect the American public by regulating the production and sales of food and drugs. When prescription drugs are developed, they must be given FDA approval before physicians can prescribe them to patients. However, a lengthy process precedes this. A drug developer who believes that a particular drug may hold promise for treating a certain disease first conducts laboratory and animal testing to identify the active compound of a drug and study the way in which the compound is metabolized (Martinez 2002). After an institutional review board (typically consisting of scientists, physicians, ethicists, and others with relevant expertise) has reviewed the protocol for human testing, the developer must submit an Investigational New Drug application to the FDA. This application details the plan for the study of the drug, indicates any findings from preliminary animal testing, and names the principal investigators (often research physicians affiliated to university medical centers) who are directing the study. The plan will also list inclusion and exclusion criteria – that is, criteria that specify what characteristics a person would have to fulfill in order to be considered for the study and what characteristics would disqualify a person from the study. For instance, a drug being studied to determine its effectiveness on advanced colon cancer may exclude subjects who are in the early stages of the disease or who suffer from a different form of cancer altogether. Similarly, a study looking at a possible treatment for high blood pressure might exclude subjects who are pregnant or who suffer from some advanced disease.

If the FDA and the IRB approve the protocol, a drug is then subjected to a four-tiered trial process in which the effects of a drug on voluntary subjects is studied (ClinicalTrials.gov 2007a). Specifically:

> Clinical trials are conducted in phases. The trials at each phase have a different purpose and help scientists answer different questions:
>
> In Phase I trials, researchers test an experimental drug or treatment in a small group of people (20–80) for the first time to evaluate its safety, determine a safe dosage range, and identify side effects.
>
> In Phase II trials, the experimental study drug or treatment is given to a larger group of people (100–300) to see if it is effective and to further evaluate its safety.
>
> In Phase III trials, the experimental study drug or treatment is given to large groups of people (1,000–3,000) to confirm its effectiveness, monitor side effects, compare it to commonly used treatments, and collect information that will allow the experimental drug or treatment to be used safely.
>
> In Phase IV trials, post-marketing studies delineate additional information including the drug's risks, benefits, and optimal use. (ClinicalTrials.gov 2007b)

If a drug proves safe and effective, it may be approved by the FDA. If, however, it turns out to be unsafe or ineffective, it will not be approved. Ordinarily, if a drug has not been approved, it will not be available by prescription. However, for patients who have not responded to any of the FDA-approved drugs (in particular, patients with terminal illnesses), the only hope may be a drug that has not been approved.

In December 2007, the FDA proposed allowing greater access to unproven drugs, in particular for terminally ill patients who have not benefited or who are no longer benefiting from approved medications (FDA 2006). This proposal was likely influenced by a ruling by the US Court of Appeals for the District of Columbia on a suit filed by a patient advocacy group, the Abigail Alliance (Goozner 2007: 10; for details, see the Abigail Alliance website at www.abigail-alliance.org/). The court ruled "that terminally ill patients . . . have a constitutional right to unapproved drugs as long as the potential benefit exceeds the risk" (ibid.).

The court's ruling seems to support the autonomy of terminally ill or otherwise dying patients. After all, if standard or approved drugs have failed, and death is predicted to be inevitable in the near future, where is the harm? At least dying patients have some chance of a cure, however slight. However, not everyone views greater access to unproven drugs as a step in the right direction. Some worry that greater access to unproven drugs – drugs that have not advanced much beyond a Phase I clinical trial – will simply weaken the ability of the FDA to protect the public (ibid.). The fact that a patient is terminally ill does not lessen a physician's obligation to prevent harm to that patient (Gesme 2007). Moreover, while drugs that pass Phase I testing have been found to be safe (so should, in theory, not make the patient worse off), over 90 percent of the drugs in Phase I trials will be found to be ineffective in later phases (i.e., fail to improve the patient's condition) (ibid.). Even those drugs that make it through all four phases and receive FDA approval will likely only offer modest benefit (ibid.). Only rarely are genuinely life-saving, one-of-a-kind, "miraculous" drugs discovered. For these reasons, one could argue that the quality of the dying patient's life is much more likely to be improved by identifying interventions that would reduce noxious symptoms – physical and psychological – than by ingesting unproven drugs that are unlikely to alter the ultimate outcome. Finally, greater access to unapproved drugs could undermine the whole process of clinical trials designed to study the safety and efficacy of drugs (Rubin 2007). Greater access to unproven drugs may make it more difficult to recruit subjects into research populations. That is, what incentive would there be for patients to subject themselves to the restrictions of a particular study when they can gain access to a drug without those restrictions? In short, access to unapproved drugs could interfere with the development of experimental drugs that will ultimately be found to have some therapeutic potential.

Despite these concerns, many view greater access to unapproved drugs as a way of providing hope to patients who would otherwise succumb to despair. Given the desperate situations of many terminally ill patients – patients for whom death may be imminent, how could taking an unproven medication cause them more harm than the disease process itself – or the loss of hope? (But see Howe 2003; Ruddick 1999.) Even if one were to grant that there is a serious risk of harm, should not the patient have a right to determine if it is an *acceptable* risk (Freireich 2007)? Even the FDA and the National Cancer Institute have at times allowed the "compassionate use" of an unapproved drug (ibid.).

From a moral point of view, should terminally ill patients have access to drugs that are not approved by the FDA?

Additional Issues to Consider

Other possible moral dilemmas arising within this case:

Q Should terminally ill patients be enrolled in Phase II and Phase III studies?

Q Should healthcare professionals take care to insure that patients are given neither information nor opportunity to take Phase I drugs?

Q Should patients for whom all standard treatments have failed be automatically enrolled in a hospice program?

REFERENCES

ClinicalTrials.gov (2007a) An introduction to clinical trials. Available at: http://clinical-trials.gov/ct/info/whatis (accessed October 20, 2007).

ClinicalTrials.gov (2007b) What are the different types of clinical trials? Available at: http://clinicaltrials.gov/ct/info/whatis#types (accessed October 20, 2007).

FDA (Food and Drug Administration) (2006) Proposed rules for charging for investigational drugs and expanded access to investigational drugs for treatment use. Available at: www.fda.gov/cder/regulatory/applications/IND_PR.htm (accessed October 19, 2007).

Freireich, E. (2007) Should terminally ill patients have the right to take drugs that pass Phase I testing? Yes. *British Medical Journal* 335 (7618): 478. Available at: www.bmj.com/cgi/content/full/335/7618/478 (accessed October 19, 2007).

Gesme, D. (2007) Should terminally ill patients have the right to take drugs that pass Phase I testing? No. *British Medical Journal* 335 (7618): 479. Available at: www.bmj.com/cgi/content/full/335/7618/479 (accessed October 19, 2007).

Goozner, M. (2007) Patient access to experimental drugs could cause more problems than it solves. *Bay Area Oncology News* (February): 10. Available at: www.baoncologynews.com/news/2007/02/patient_access_to_experimental.shtml (accessed October 20, 2007).

Howe, E. G. (2003) Hope or truth: commentary on the case of Mr T. *Journal of Clinical Ethics* 14 (3): 208–19.

Martinez, L. (2002) An overview of the drug approval process – FDA Overview. *Research Initiative/Treatment Action!* (Summer). Available at: http://findarticles.com/p/articles/mi_m0EXV/is_1_8/ai_90100882 (accessed March 3, 2008).

Rubin, R. (2007) Unapproved drugs spark life and death debate. *USA Today* (April 4). Available at: http://usatoday.com/news/nation/2007-04-02-unapproved-drugs_n.htm (accessed October 19, 2007).

Ruddick, W. M. (1999) Hope and deception. *Bioethics* 13 (3/4): 343–57.

CASE TWENTY-THREE: A FEVERED HAND ON A COOLING BROW – THE NURSE'S ROLE IN AID-IN-DYING

Discussions of aid-in-dying (AID) have been seen increasingly in public venues since Oregon passed its Death with Dignity Act in 1997. This law "allows terminally-ill Oregonians to end their lives through the voluntary self-administration of lethal medications, expressly prescribed by a physician for that purpose" (Death with Dignity Act n.d.). The legitimacy of physician-prescribing activities covered by this Act has been the subject of much debate. In particular, opponents have contested that prescribing lethal medications for the purpose of suicide violates the Controlled Substances Act (CSA 1994/1996), which authorizes the use of such drugs only for "legitimate medical purposes" (ibid.). In 2001 then-Attorney General, John Ashcroft, announced that assisted suicide did not count as a legitimate medical purpose and threatened to revoke the licenses to prescribe controlled substances of physicians who were determined to have aided their patients' suicides (Ashcroft 2001). In 2002, the US District Court for the District of Oregon found that Attorney General Ashcroft had exceeded the authority of the CSA, and issued an injunction against revoking the licenses of participating physicians. The legitimacy of physicians' ability to prescribe drugs to assist in suicide was upheld, in 2004, by the US Court of Appeals for the Ninth District.

Although the legal and public discussions of aid-in-dying have been couched almost exclusively in terms of its moral implications for physicians, this narrow focus overlooks the role of nursing in the dying process (De Beer et al. 2004). Nurses are often asked: "How long do I have?" They are also questioned regarding which drugs could cause death, how to insure death, what diseases portend – particularly in terms of pain and suffering – and how to discuss AID with families, friends, etc. (Hall 1996). Nurses also devote their professional expertise to "listening to and interpreting the patient's request, reporting and explaining the request to other nurses and physicians, and lending support to the patient and the patient's family" (De Beer et al. 2004: 497). Furthermore, a survey of physicians found that those who agreed to patients' requests for euthanasia (although euthanasia remains illegal almost everywhere) asked nurses to administer the lethal agent in approximately one-third of the cases (Meier et al. 1996). As the public discussion of the moral propriety of AID continues, nurses must determine whether participating, as professionals, in AID is ethical (Davis et al. 1995; Kopala and Kennedy 1998; De Beer et al. 2004).

The International Council of Nurses (ICN) acknowledges that assisted suicide "is a real problem in Switzerland and also in other countries such as the US" (WHO n.d.: 5). But although the Council recognizes the presence of ethical issues surrounding euthanasia, it has no formal policy on aid-in-dying (ICN 2006). In the Netherlands, the only country in which euthanasia is legal, the National Nurses Association has established guidelines for the role of nurses in this process: "One of the guidelines states that the involvement of nurses in decision-making is desirable because of the nurses' specific skill and everyday involvement in patient care. The administration of the euthanaticum, however, is an action that is reserved for physicians" (De Beer et al. 2004: 495). Great Britain's Royal College of Nursing remains officially opposed, though 60 percent of their membership favored aid-in-dying (Joffe 2006).

The American Nurses' Association gives four moral objections to assisted suicide by nurses:

(1) The profession of nursing is built on the Hippocratic tradition 'do no harm' and an ethic of moral opposition to killing another human being;

(2) Nursing has a social contract with society that is based on trust and therefore patients must be able to trust that nurses will not actively take human
life;

(3) In order to preserve the moral mandates of the profession and the integrity
of the individual nurse, nurses are not obligated to comply with all patient
and family requests; and

(4) There is high potential for abuse . . . particularly with vulnerable patients such
as the elderly, poor, and disabled. (ANA 1996: 84)

Although these objections suggest that professional integrity requires practitioners
to stay clear of assisted death, they bear closer scrutiny before their prohibition
of AID can be definitively ascertained.

Do no harm. The implications of the claim that nurses should do no harm are
not straightforward. Nurses regularly harm patients (e.g., administering toxic
chemotherapy that damages normal cells; causing pain during rehabilitative
efforts), but the harms are typically thought to be morally justified because they
contribute to a projected greater benefit – saving life, minimizing disease or
disability, restoring health, or preventing even greater pain and suffering.

Most persons believe (albeit almost always unreflectively) that death is the worst
possible outcome one can suffer. If this belief is correct, then death always harms
patients. But this belief is not obviously true. The common-sense belief that death
may not be a (or the greatest) harm is acknowledged when persons speak of "a
fate worse than death." If "harm" is "thwarting, defeating, or setting back the
[person's] interests" (Beauchamp and Childress 1994: 193), patients (particularly those with terminal illnesses in which death is imminent) can have legitimate interests in avoiding uncompensated pain and suffering (i.e., pain and
suffering which achieve no positive physical or psychological outcomes). If the
only way to end one's misery is through death, then death may not be harmful. If death is not always harmful, it cannot justify a universal ban on AID as
intrinsically maleficent.

In keeping with these suspicions, support for AID in the US is roughly
65 percent (Emmanuel 2002); 76 percent in Australia (Gargett n.d.); and 80
percent in the UK (Joffe 2006). Public surveys typically show that persons are
more afraid of being kept alive in misery than of dying (Blendon et al. 1992;
Harris et al. 2006), and that they believe that AID can sometimes be in their
best interests.

Trust. Nursing exists as a profession to promote patients' interests. At the least,
patients should be able to trust nurses not to hurt them; certainly (the argument goes) patients should be able to trust nurses not to kill them. Many patients
who interact with nurses are vulnerable: in pain, fearful, worried, and – as a result
of these states – are not at the top of their cognitive game; being able to trust
their nurses is key to achieving their interests, health and otherwise.

Whether patients even think about the possibility of their nurses killing them
is unknown. One might quite reasonably assume that, were patients to consider

this possibility, they would hope their lives did not lie in their nurses' hands. But if one really wants to know the public's feelings about AID by nurses, the public should be queried about this issue. Surveys show that legalizing AID would do little, if anything, to undermine public trust in physicians who perform it. Moreover, repeated surveys demonstrate that support for AID continues to rise. In 1996, 41.6 percent of patients and 32.8 percent of the general public thought patient–physician conversations that explicitly addressed AID would increase – not decrease – trust in the physician (Emmanuel et al. 1996: 1808). By 2004 public support for AID had risen to 82 percent in the UK among the general population, and to 80 percent among persons with disabilities (Branthwaite 2005). Whether this trust would extend to nurses is uncertain, but, again, one should assume neither that the public would trust nurses who engage in AID nor that AID would destroy public trust in the nursing profession. Presumably, most people assume that nurses' duties include preventing premature, unwanted death; promoting, preserving, and restoring health; and minimizing pain and suffering. But patients for whom all these options have been foreclosed might support (even hope for) AID by nurses.

Professional integrity. Integrity is "having a reasonably coherent and relatively stable set of cherished values and principles" (Benjamin 1990: 51), and expressing those values and principles in words and actions. One clearly articulated nursing value is "an ethic of moral opposition to killing another human being" and, more particularly, that "patients must be able to trust that nurses will not actively take human life." As clear and unambiguous as these statements are, we should remember that "reasonably coherent" or "relatively stable" values can – and do – evolve. The Hippocratic Oath forbade abortion and surgery, yet both are now important for patient well-being and are regularly provided by healthcare professionals as means to their patients' best interests.

What professional practice requires will change as social and professional environments change. The Hippocratic tradition began in an era where life was much more fragile. Ancient cures were rare and ancient Greek physicians who failed to cure serious maladies often saw their patients die. Conversely, when contemporary practitioners fail to cure, their patients may survive in a state worse than death. The ancient professional who saved a life was much less likely to harm the patient than her twentieth-century counterpart (MacIntyre 1975).

In addition, saving life is only one of several cherished professional values. Nurses are also committed to relieving pain and suffering. To acknowledge other values does not denigrate life nor deny that saving life – under most circumstances – is crucial to professional integrity. Nonetheless, acknowledging a plurality of values raises the possibility of moral conflict among professional commitments. For some patients, life cannot be saved, health cannot be promoted and disease cannot be prevented or cured. But relief of pain and suffering is still within the nurse's power. When patients elect early death and the only professional value that still can be promoted is relief of pain or suffering, AID is compatible with professional integrity (White 1999). Of course, many nurses (like many physicians) might personally believe that nurses should have nothing to do with actively participating in ending a patient's life. This possibility raises the question of whether, given the professional commitment to relief of pain and suffering, they are morally obligated to aid patients in dying if those patients are competent and request such assistance. Presumably an "opt out" clause – such as those permitting physicians to opt out of performing abortions – would permit morally opposed nurses from participation in aid-in-dying.

Abuse. Critics worry that AID might be "overused" in many Western societies, in those who are undervalued (i.e., the elderly, minorities, the poor, and persons with impairments) and whose vulnerability makes them less able to protect their own interests. Such groups may be at risk if AID is permitted because they lack resources – cognitive, emotional, physical, or financial – to protect their own interests, and society is not motivated to protect these interests for them. Such worries are legitimate. Elderly and black populations, although overall in favor of euthanasia, were less supportive than younger, white populations (Hall et al. 2005). The question of abuse per se arises because of the worry that nurses (or other persons) might erroneously assume the lives of vulnerable patients are not worth living and, based on these inaccurate assumptions, provide unrequested and unwanted AID to these patients.

The data on the extent – or even the existence – of such vulnerability is contested (Death with Dignity Act n.d.; Branthwaite 2005; Quill 2007; Thorns 2007). But even if such risks are real, they can be managed procedurally or professionally. Procedural management demands criteria for providing AID. Strictly limiting AID to patients who meet carefully specified criteria should protect the vulnerable. The law is no stranger to statutes enacted to protect the vulnerable and we have no reason to think statutes could not be constructed to protect against unwanted AID. Indeed, the criteria embraced by Oregon and the data collected following legalization there of physician AID suggest that AID is used infrequently and, typically, by the least vulnerable populations (Death with Dignity Act n.d.).

Given the professional commitment to saving life, the risk of abuse is likely to be small. Persons are at greatest risk for abuse or neglect if they are poorly understood and undervalued. Nurses are unlikely to assist in early, unwanted death because, in virtue of their intimate, ongoing interactions with patients, nurses are more likely to appreciate a patient's own values and be governed by those interests. This point may be put more pragmatically: if AID is legalized, vulnerable populations are more likely to be protected if nurses are involved. So even if nursing continues officially to oppose AID by nurses, patients may be better protected when nurses are involved in these discussions.

However, nurses who practice in institutions are less likely to know their patients' social and personal backgrounds than are their physicians (although in this age of specialization and referral, many physicians may know little about their patients beyond their medical particulars). But patients may have a greater tendency to trust the role of the physician than that of the nurse. Still:

[F]or the nurse, intensive care may actually mean spending an intensive amount of time with the patient and the family. They may see and hear first-hand of the patient's pain and suffering as the patients are being turned, bathed, medicated, and generally taken care of. It is likely that the nurse may be the first one to appreciate the patient's level of continuous discomfort, and also may be first to recognize an endless cycle of pain and suffering coupled with a dim hope for any meaningful recovery. As a result, nurses, often rightly so, feel that they have a greater and earlier insight into a patient's wishes concerning these difficult issues.

Therefore, at one time or another in their nursing careers, one out of five of those nurses who responded to the [Asch 1996] survey questionnaire were put in a position where a patient desperate for relief was paired with a physician unable to recognize the situation, and the nurse took matters into her own hands. But saying that one of five nurses has participated in hastening the death of a patient is not saying that the practice happens 20% of the time. . . . In fact, the survey reported that 65% of those nurses who had "hastened death" did so three times or less, and about 93% of those were based on repeated requests by the patient or family. (Miller 1996)

A profession that is responsible to the community must consider community opinions when formulating practice guidelines. Throughout the world, the public perspective is changing to support AID. In recognition of these evolving attitudes, nursing must revisit its position as a means of insuring its policies and practices truly are designed to promote the welfare of patients.

In addition, the perspective of the wider professional community is evolving. The National Association of Social Workers (2000) supports all self-determined choices, including AID. Social workers polled in South Carolina echoed this approval (Manetta and Wells 2001). While the American Medical Association (AMA) remains opposed to AID (AMA 1992, 1996), many physicians disagree (O'Reilly 2005; Lee et al. 1996; Preston 1994; Reisner and Damato 1995; Bachman et al. 1996; and Emanuel et al. 1996). And, as the American Medical Student Association favors physician-assisted suicide as a last resort (n.d.), the AMA's official position may change as students become practicing professionals. But these other professionals have distinctly different relationships with patients than do nurses. The 24/7 intimacy between nurses and patients often lends itself to brutally honest discussions of fears, hopes, anxieties, and so forth. Should AID endanger these conversations, it would likely remove a great source of comfort to patients and a great source of information to nurses that is requisite to good patient care.

Ultimately, however, death is irreversible. An unwanted or premature death deprives a person of her entire future, the particulars of which are always to some extent unknown, and the value of which may be unknown or may be revised. With aid-in-dying, mistakes are permanent.

In any case, were nurses to become actively involved in aid-in-dying, their designation as "angels of mercy" would certainly take on expanded meaning.

Should nurses be morally permitted to aid their patients in dying?

Additional Issues to Consider

Other possible moral dilemmas arising within this case:

Q Should aid-in-dying remain illegal, but with the understanding that nurses who engage in that practice will not be prosecuted?

Q Should nurses who are morally opposed to aid-in-dying be permitted to refuse to participate, in the event that AID is legalized?

REFERENCES

AMA (American Medical Association Council on Ethical and Judicial Affairs) (1992) Decisions near the end of life. *JAMA* 267 (16): 2229–33.
AMA (American Medical Association Council on Scientific Affairs) (1996) Good care of the dying patient. *JAMA* 275 (6): 474–8.
American Medical Student Association (n.d.) Principles regarding physician-assisted suicide. Available at: www.amsa.org/about/ppp/pas.cfm (accessed March 1, 2008).
ANA (American Nurses Association) (1996) Position statement on assisted suicide. *Compendium of ANA Position Statements.* Washington, DC: ANA, p. 84.
Asch, D. A. (1996) The role of critical care nurses in euthanasia and assisted suicide. *New England Journal of Medicine* 334 (21): 1374–9.
Asch, D. A., and DeKay, M. L. (1997) Euthanasia among US critical care nurses: practices, attitudes, and social and professional correlates. *Medical Care* 35 (9): 890–900.
Ashcroft, J. (2001) Memo: Office of the Attorney General: dispensing of controlled substances to assist suicide. Available at: http://news.findlaw.com/legalnews/documents/archive_d.html (accessed October 223, 2007).
Bachman, J. G., Alcser, K. H., Doukas, D. J., et al. (1996) Attitudes of Michigan physicians and the public toward legalizing physician-assisted suicide and voluntary euthanasia. *New England Journal of Medicine* 334 (5): 303–9.
Benjamin, M. (1990) *Splitting the Difference.* Lawrence, KS: University Press of Kansas.
Beauchamp, T. L., and Childress, J. F. (1994) *Principles of Biomedical Ethics*, 4th edn. New York: Oxford University Press.
Berghs, M., Dierckx de Casterle, B., and Gastmans, C. (2005) The complexity of nurses' attitudes toward euthanasia: A review of the literature. *Journal of Medical Ethics* 31 (8): 441–6. Available at: http://jme.bmj.com/cgi/content/full/31/8/441 (accessed March 3, 2008).
Blendon, R. J., Szalay, U. S., and Knox, R. A. (1992) Should physicians aid their patients in dying? The public perspective. *JAMA* 267 (19): 2658–62.
Branthwaite, M. A. (2005) Taking the final step: changing the law on euthanasia and physician assisted suicide. *British Medical Journal* 331 (7518): 681–3.
British Medical Journal (2007) Press release (September 29): Vulnerable groups are not at higher risk of physician assisted death. Available at: www.bmj.com/content/vol335/issue7621/press_release.dtl (accessed October 22, 2007).
Cotton, P. (1995) Medicine's position is both pivotal and precarious in assisted-suicide debate. *JAMA* 273 (5): 363–64.

CSA (Controlled Substance Act) (1994/1996) USC sections 801–971.

Davis, A. J., Phillips, L., Drought, T. S., et al. (1995) Nurses' attitudes toward euthanasia. *Nursing Outlook* 43 (4): 174–9.

Death with Dignity Act (n.d.) Summary of Oregon's death with dignity act – 2006. Available at: http://egov.oregon.gov/DHS/ph/pas/ (accessed October 20, 2007).

De Beer, T., Gastmans, C., and Dierckx de Casterlé, B. (2004) Involvement of nurses in euthanasia: a review of the literature. *Journal of Medical Ethics* 30 (5): 494–8.

Emmanuel, E. J. (2002) Euthanasia and physician-assisted suicide: A review of the empirical data from the United States. *Archives of Internal Medicine* 162 (2): 142–52.

Emanuel, E. J., Fairclough, D. L., Daniels, E. R., et al. (1996) Euthanasia and physician-assisted suicide: attitudes and experiences of oncology patients, oncologists, and the public. *Lancet* 347 (9018): 1805–10.

Gargett, E. (n.d.) Grasping the nettle. Available at: www.saves.asn.au/resources/archive/issues/grasping_the_nettle.pdf (accessed March 3, 2007).

Hall, J. K. (1996) Assisted suicide: nurse practitioners as providers? *Nurse Practitioner* 21 (10): 63–71.

Hall, M., Trachtenberg, F., and Dugan, E. (2005) The impact on public trust of physician aid in dying. *Journal of Medical Ethics* 31 (10): 693–7.

Harris, D., Richard, B., and Khanna, P. (2006) Assisted dying: the ongoing debate. *Postgraduate Medical Journal* 82 (970): 479–82.

ICN (International Council of Nurses) (2006) Nurses' role in providing care to dying patients and their families: ICN Position Statement. Available at: www.icn.ch/pscare00.htm (accessed March 14, 2008).

Joffe, Lord (2006) The case for a dignified death in the United Kingdom. Presented at Challenge in Choice: World Federation of Right to Die Societies: 16th Biennial Conference. September 7–10. Toronto, Canada. Available at: http://dyingwithdignity.ca/new_and_noteworthy/worldconference06/Challenge_in_Choice_2006_Conference_Summary.pdf (accessed October 22, 2007).

Kopala, B., and Kennedy, S. L. (1998) Requests for assisted suicide: a nursing issue. *Nursing Ethics* 5 (1): 16–26.

Lee, M. A., Nelson, H. D., Tilden, V. P., et al. (1996) Legalizing assisted suicide – view of physicians in Oregon. *New England Journal of Medicine* 334 (5): 310–15.

MacIntyre, A. (1975) How virtues become vices: values, medicine and social context. In H. T. Engelhardt, Jr., and S. F. Spicker (eds.), *Evaluation and Explanation in the Biomedical Sciences*. Dordrecht, Holland: D. Reidel Publishing Company, pp. 97–111.

Manetta, A. A., and Wells, J. G. (2001) Ethical issues in the social worker's role in physician-assisted suicide. *Health & Social Work* 26 (3): 160–6. Available at: http://mantis.csuchico.edu:3095/ehost/pdf?vid=3&hid=105&sid=5b3f81b7-bb43-4275-9ae6-b92db5d9d487%40sessionmgr102 (accessed October 18, 2007).

Meier, D. E., Emmons, C., Wallenstein, S., et al. (1998) A national survey of physician-assisted suicide and euthanasia in the United States. *New England Journal of Medicine* 338 (17): 1196.

Miller, S. (1996) Much ado about nothing. Ethics Roundtable: Do nurses participate in euthanasia and assisted suicide? (Would it be a bad thing?). *Community Ethics* 3 (4). Available at: www.pitt.edu/~cep/34roundtable.html (accessed October 20, 2007).

National Association of Social Workers (2000) Client self-determination in end of life decisions. In *Social Work Speaks: NASW Policy Statements 2000–2003*. Washington, DC: NASW Press.

O'Reilly, K. B. (2005) Doctors favor assisted-suicide less than patients do. *AmedNews. com* (November 21). Available at: http://compassionandchoices.org/documents/20051121suicidepolls.pdf (accessed October 22, 2007).

Preston, T. A. (1994) Professional norms and physician attitudes toward euthanasia. *Journal of Law, Medicine & Ethics* 22 (1): 36–40.

Quill, T. W. (2007) Editorial: Physician assisted death in vulnerable populations. *British Medical Journal* 335 (7621): 625–6.

Reisner, M., and Damato, A. N. (1995) Attitudes of physicians regarding physician-assisted suicide. *New Jersey Medicine* 92 (10): 663–6.

Sommerville, A. (2005) Taking the final step: changing the law on euthanasia and physician assisted *suicide*. *British Medical Journal* 331 (7522): 686–8.

Thorns, A. (2007) Rapid Responses for Quill (1 October): there is more to vulnerability. *British Medical Journal* 335 (7621): 625–6.

White, B. C. (1999) Assisted suicide and nursing: possibly compatible? *Journal of Professional Nursing* 15 (3): 151–9.

WHO (World Health Organization) (n.d.) Collated background briefing: Topics and issues suggested by participants for discussion at Inaugural Triad meeting. Available at: www.icn.ch/triad/inaugural/Topics_Issues.pdf (accessed March 14, 2008).

7

BUSINESS AS USUAL

Ethical Issues in the Marketplace

Case Twenty-four: Sale of a Lifetime – Ovum "Donation"

Case Twenty-five: Only God Can Make a Tree – Patenting Indigenous Plants

Case Twenty-six: Body Shop – International Trafficking in Human Organs

Case Twenty-seven: Straits of Strife – Japanese Whaling, Cultural Relativism, and International Politics

Case Twenty-eight: Big Pharma Wants You – Direct-to-consumer Advertising

Case Twenty-nine: This Gun's For Hire – ExxonMobil and the Indonesian Military

The world runs on the exchange of goods and services for a price. Ideally, to be successful, businesses should operate on principles of ethical behavior: dependability, concern for consumer safety, fair dealings, honesty, and trust. But commercial enterprises too often gain a competitive advantage by disregarding collateral damage to the environment and consumers; compromising future welfare for short-term gain; withholding information or releasing deceptive information; and using economic, legal, or other kinds of power to maintain a privileged market position.

While globalization has increased both opportunity and competition for resources and markets, it has also created moral quandaries resulting from pluralistic cultures whose systems of values and laws differ; competing claims over resources of land, the oceans, and space; and conflicting concepts of ownership of cultural and intellectual heritage. Scientific and medical advances have created explosive new business opportunities, but the sale of human ova, international trafficking in human organs, and proprietary control of indigenous genetic resources by foreign interests are morally repugnant to many. These and other ethical concerns raise questions about moral issues in business practices and the marketplace.

Can everything be owned, or are there reasonable limits to what should be commercialized? Should some things not be for sale? Does the development, commercialization, and control of products derived from the human body compromise human dignity? Do individuals or their heirs have a moral right to share in the financial gains from products developed with their genetic material, tissues, or organs? Is the preservation of endangered natural resources a morally legitimate rationale for their expropriation, or against their expropriation? Does business have an ethical responsibility to those who will never use their products, and to future generations, or only to their shareholders?

Regardless of the categories into which the cases in this book were placed – and many cases could comfortably fit into more than one category – two common themes emerge in business environments. First, at the deepest level, so many moral dilemmas in the arts, environmental issues, government, society, healthcare, and education arise from the inevitable competition for limited resources. A second source of moral tension stems from mutually exclusive responsibilities to multiple stakeholders. As we will see in "Business as Usual – Ethical Issues in the Marketplace," business is not exempt from ethical conundrums.

CASE TWENTY-FOUR: SALE OF A LIFETIME – OVUM "DONATION"

Despite their hectic schedules, childhood friends Beth, Zoe, and Kate meet at least every other month for dinner. A frequent topic over the past few years has been Zoe's continued difficulty in getting pregnant. Neither Beth nor Kate was comfortable raising the subject, knowing it was a painful topic for Zoe, and knowing also that Zoe would mention it when she was ready. They didn't have long to wait.

"Matt and I are going to try in vitro fertilization," Zoe announced after they were seated. "I start getting the hormone shots next week."

"Doesn't in vitro fertilization happen in a Petri dish? Isn't it for women who have problems with their reproductive systems? I thought the difficulty for you and Matt was low sperm count. How will your getting shots increase Matt's sperm count?" asked Kate.

"True, in vitro does happen in a Petri dish – not very romantic, is it? Dr. Foster suggested we try in vitro because it sometimes works with low sperm count. The hormone injections cause 10–20 or more eggs to ripen and be released at the same time, instead of the single ovum that usually matures during ovulation. There are that many more chances that the sperm will successfully fertilize at least one ovum, and it's a sprint, rather than a long-distance swim! Sperm can be directly injected into the ovum, almost guaranteeing fertilization."

"What happens if more than one egg is fertilized? What if 15 of them get fertilized?"

"The risk of harm to the baby increases with multiple births. At this point, we're just praying for one healthy baby. If more than one egg is fertilized, we'll have two embryos implanted, just to be on the safe side. If there are more than two embryos, we'll freeze the others so we can try again if we need to. It's so expensive to go through the process, and it has cost so much already to get to this point. Also, Dr Foster told me that the process is pretty painful and emotional, and there are health risks, so I don't want to go through it again if I don't have to."

Beth had been silent, but now spoke up: "Since it's so expensive, have you talked to your doctor about a fee reduction if you give extra embryos to other women who are trying to get pregnant?"

"Dr Foster asked us if we wanted to donate extra embryos to other women or to research. We never seriously entertained the idea, even if it would make the treatments more affordable. If the first time, or the second or third doesn't work, we want to be able to keep trying. Besides, Matt and I wouldn't want someone else raising our child. What if they wanted a child for the wrong reason and didn't really love the baby?"

"What do you mean, 'the wrong reason'? Why would you try to have a baby if you didn't really love it?" Beth asked.

"Maybe you don't want a baby to love, maybe you want someone to love you. Or maybe you want someone to take care of you when you get old, or to carry on the family name, or the family business."

Kate chimed in. "Maybe to be the concert pianist or brain surgeon or pro ball player you never were. Who knows? But I can think of a lot of people I'm glad aren't my parents!"

Zoe added, "I've done so much reading about fertility. Lori Andrews mentions a lot of frightening cases in her book, *The Clone Age*. One egg donor failed to get pregnant, while the woman to whom she donated conceived and delivered a child. I don't think I could live with myself, knowing someone else was raising the child we desperately wanted but couldn't have because we gave away that embryo."

At that point, Beth grabbed Zoe's hand and burst into tears. "Oh, Zoe. I just know this time you'll have your baby! You call me right away if you need anything, or just want someone to hold your hand or talk to during the next few weeks."

What Beth didn't tell her two best friends was that she was an egg donor. Tall, beautiful, an excellent athlete, a gifted musician, and a Stanford University graduate, Beth's eggs were in demand. When Beth had seen the advertisement recruiting "high-end" egg donors, she thought of what having a child meant to Zoe. Beth was happy to help someone as sweet and loving as her friend to become a mother. She was also relieved to be able to begin repaying the tens of thousands of dollars in school loans after three cycles of donation. Beth was still emotionally fragile because of the high levels of hormones in her system from her most recent donation. Until that evening she hadn't thought about the kind of life her children might have, or the possibility that the high fees she received for donating eggs contributed to the expensive costs of fertility treatments for people desperately trying to conceive a baby – like her dear friends Zoe and Matt.

Is paying women for oocyte donation morally justifiable?

Before considering perspectives on compensating egg donors, clarification is needed on the definition of "donation." Although typically the word "donation" denotes a gift, in egg-donation the word refers both to eggs given altruistically and for compensation. Don't get distracted by the imprecise use of language; focus on the moral dilemmas.

Perspective One

It is morally justifiable to pay women for donating ova.

Looking first at the consequences, we note that paying egg donors will lead more women to donate ova and, as a result, to more likelihood of pregnancies for infertile women who want to have children. This would be an enormously positive outcome for persons wishing to become parents. Although a few women willingly donate without compensation, they usually donate to family members or close friends. Most women, however, donate to strangers and are unwilling to go through the arduous process of egg-donation if they are not compensated. After Britain, which previously compensated egg donors, reduced payments to comply with European Union guidelines, the decline in the number of donors created a severe shortage of ova (Green 2005: B7). As a result, Britain is considering reversing its reduction of payment to egg donors. This evidence suggests that failure to compensate results in a scarcity of donated ova. If society values assisted reproduction (and research), which depend on donated ova, the principle of utility directs compensating donors.

Critics worry that compensating egg donors will lead to one particularly negative consequence: the commodification of women – treating women as "things" or "objects" that may be bought, sold, or "rented" at the behest of others. But women are not commodified when they are compensated for the effort, time, risk, pain, lost wages, and inconvenience of egg-donation; they are only commodified when their bodies are used as a means to benefit others. Commodification occurs not when financial value is attributed to the products and labor women provide, but when women are expected to act altruistically while others benefit. Failure to compensate egg donors commodifies women by failing to respect their labor in producing something of value for which they should, as independent contractors, be fairly compensated.

The question of commodification raises, further, the moral principle of autonomy. Autonomy requires that a woman be allowed to make decisions about her own body, including the use and disposition of her ova. As long as women are given full information about the process and its burdens, risks, and benefits, they are capable of and have a right to determine what is in their own best interests. Critics worry that paying egg donors will make women (especially poor women) vulnerable to exploitation; that is, that payment will constitute a coercive offer that undermines autonomy. But extreme poverty itself de facto limits autonomy and increases the likelihood of exploitation and coercion. Moreover, people are allowed to engage in all sorts of risky behavior; respecting autonomy requires that individuals decide for themselves what counts as excessively risky behavior, regardless of economic status. Poor women do not differ from their more affluent counterparts in this regard; they, too, are capable of burden-benefit analyses. Finally, why should one assume that women who are compensated are coerced into donating, and women who receive no payment are not?

The final moral principle supporting paying ova donors is justice, first in the sense of equality. Unless an egg and a sperm are united, neither can develop into a human; both are equally necessary for creating a zygote. Paying for sperm has long been accepted by society. (Interestingly, compensation also pays an important role in attracting sperm donors. A Canadian study showed that only about 2 percent of willing sperm donors would donate without compensation (ASRM/CFAS 2005).) There is no moral distinction between ova and sperm, which suggests that paying female gamete donors should be morally equivalent to paying male donors.

Moreover, ova donors are the only participants in technologically assisted reproduction who are not compensated handsomely. Physicians who specialize in infertility are among the highest-paid medical specialists (Andrews 1999: 48). Lawyers are well compensated for their part in legal transactions involving egg-donation. Researchers stand to make fortunes through the development of treatments derived from embryonic stem cells (the existence of which depends on both ova and sperm). Yet research subjects are expected to be altruistic, while patents protect lucrative commercial interests for other participants. Ironically, the researchers who own patents resist sharing profits with the research subjects whose biological material make their profits possible, insisting that payment for reproductive material, though not their own mechanical manipulations, diminishes the dignity of human life (Knowles 1999: 40). Perhaps neither is morally permissible, but to argue that one's own contribution to research is morally permissible while another's contribution is not is disingenuous. Clinics, laboratories, biotechnology companies, and universities all profit from egg-donation. Society sees nothing morally wrong with businesses, physicians, scientists, lawyers, and their staffs being paid handsomely for their work in assisted reproduction and embryonic stem cell research – work that is not possible without egg donors. Uncompensated donors suffer all the risks and receive none of the benefits enjoyed by others who profit from using the donors' eggs. Justice is not respected when women are expected to give their eggs to others who stand to make large profits from their use. Equality demands that women who undertake the burdens associated with providing ova for medical treatment and research also share in the benefits. Non-compensation perpetuates discrimination against women.

In fact, strong reasons, based on fairness, support compensating female gamete donors more than male donors. Unlike sperm, which are constantly regenerated, a woman has a finite number of ova. A woman produces about 7 million ova by the twentieth week of gestation. Only 300,000 remain by puberty, and donation reduces that number. Moreover, a woman who donates ova runs some risk of irreparable damage to her ovaries, with subsequent infertility, while donating sperm is essentially risk-free. Egg-donation involves weeks of both psychological and physical pain and risk, whereas sperm-donation involves a few minutes of pleasure (Coombes 2004: 1206; Andrews 1999: 13, 96).

The strongest argument against donor compensation, that paying for eggs devalues human life, is specious. The unfertilized egg is a cell that alone, like the millions of other eggs the woman produced, is incapable of creating or sustaining life. Only when a sperm fertilizes the egg does an embryo become capable of life. Yet the egg donor is the only person in the process who is not compensated. If life is devalued when compensation is involved, then it's wrong for everyone who profits in the process of egg-donation, and no one engaged in assisted reproduction or stem cell research should receive compensation. This is unrealistic: were such compensation denied, assisted reproduction and stem cell research would screech to a halt. It is because the good of these technologies outweighs their evil that they are supported. Refusing to pay egg donors creates the perception of preserving the dignity of embryonic life. In reality, it shifts all of society's qualms of conscience and moral responsibility to the women who provide the biological material essential for assisted reproduction and stem cell research. This suggests that something wrong is going on, but that the only person to blame is the ova donor. If, however, the benefits outweigh the burdens – that is, if ova-donation is not intrinsically wrong, and the benefits of parenthood and anticipated benefits of stem cell research are morally compelling – the better approach would be to make that case publicly.

In conclusion, appeals to consequences, autonomy, and justice as both equality and fairness, support paying women for donating ova.

Perspective Two

Paying women for donating ova is not morally justifiable.

Consider, first, the consequences associated with egg-donation. The fertility industry is lucrative and secretive, with poor oversight and accountability (Andrews 1999: 48). There is little incentive for infertility specialists to provide follow-up investigation of egg donors to determine long-term health effects of donation, as negative outcomes could result in diminished donation, reduced earnings, or even legal action. Known risks from egg-retrieval and the drugs used in superovulation are many, and include infection, sterility, and death. Suspected risks, suggested by anecdotal accounts, have not been assessed definitively in clinical trials. The full nature and extent of long-term risks are unknown. Consequently, few research data are available to allow donors to fully understand the potential consequences.

History provides many cautionary tales about drugs whose risks were identified only decades after their use. Diethylstilbestrol (DES), a synthetic estrogen, is one example. In the 1950s, DES was prescribed routinely to pregnant women to prevent miscarriage. In the 1970s, DES was demonstrated to have caused a host of problems in daughters of women who received the drug, including reproductive cancers, hormonal abnormalities, pregnancy complications, and infertility. Yet when it was first introduced, DES was widely praised as a wonder drug and quickly became a standard treatment. Researchers who questioned its risks were ignored or discredited (Van Dyck 1995: 97).

The threat of harm in egg-donation is additionally problematic: the donor, who does not have a medical problem, undergoes a rigorous course of treatment using powerful hormones the full nature and extent of whose risks are unknown; the courses of drugs are followed by potentially harmful medical procedures. Moreover, the donor may not receive adequate follow-up care in the event of adverse outcomes. Offering payment for young women to engage in activities that risk known and unknown harms to them and their offspring, with no benefits, violates the principle of nonmaleficence. The potential harms are not only physical, but can be emotional as well. Donors may regret their decisions later, particularly if their own fertility was compromised by the donation.

The principle of respect for autonomy requires truth-telling, self-determination, and informed consent. Payment is an incentive for women to donate ova, and offering payment to egg donors threatens all three aspects of autonomy. Websites and brochures recruiting donors are deceptive. Risks are downplayed, if they are mentioned at all. Advertisements promise many incentives beyond financial compensation, such as massages and letters and gifts from recipients. The large, especially lucrative payments mentioned in advertisements are not offered to all potential donors, only those deemed "high-end" donors – those with the most desirable traits and accomplishments. Once face-to-face with the egg broker, the donor may be asked to consider a significantly reduced fee (Hamilton 2000: 57). It is not only the donors who are subject to deceptive advertising; egg brokers also market to prospective parents. The prospective parents may not realize that a donor with ideal characteristics might not pass on those genes to the baby; as a result, the child could face a lifetime of unreasonable expectations and the parents may face long-term disappointment. Donors are not always screened for genetic diseases, so those traits may be passed on (Andrews 1999: 82). Hamilton likens the glossy brochures and websites created by egg brokers to seed catalogs that praise the characteristics of their varietals (2000: 55). Advertising for egg donors and marketing them to prospective parents compromises informed consent in failing to inform all parties adequately.

Payment for ova promotes coercion and undermines voluntary participation. Monetary incentives may unduly influence the decision to donate, leading women to underestimate the risks. Some researchers and physicians actually facilitate women's underestimation of the risks, as they feel no obligation to discuss suspected or unknown risks with potential donors, but address only those that have been scientifically documented. Donors become merely a means to achieve the goals of the "real" patients, who "just want us to make them pregnant" (Andrews 1999: 49). Doctors are willing to accommodate the wishes of women trying to become pregnant, even if it means glossing over the risks when they discuss the process with donors.

The patient's or subject's informed consent is required prior to any medical or research procedure. Egg-donation requires that donors freely consent to the process only after being fully informed of – and understanding – the procedures and all common, serious, or material risks and consequences. Because the risks to egg donors are unknown, women are being used as de facto experimental research subjects. And since most procedures take place in private practices or clinics, there is no oversight of the experimental aspects of treatment. Donors are not protected by federal regulations safeguarding research subjects, particularly the assessment of risks and benefits, the use of new or evolving procedures, and the oversight of the process of informed consent (BBC News 2005; Andrews 1999: 33).

The moral authority of society to curtail a right of individual liberty is legitimate when that power is exercised to prevent harm to others. The right to reproduce is not absolute. Incest, polygamy, and sex with minors are forbidden in most cultures. Although reproductive decisions are typically protected by a right of privacy, the potential harms that attach to technologically assisted reproduction make these procedures a legitimate matter of public concern and, as such, justify societal regulation of egg-donation (ESHRE 2002: 1407). Society has a vested interest in the health and welfare of the mother, child, and egg donor, and bears some responsibility to prevent their exploitation. The right to be a parent must be weighed against the actual and potential harms to the donor and the child. The overall benefit to individual women, measured against the unknown consequences for donors and the children conceived from their ova, is not morally supportable and justifies society's limitation of individual liberty of both donor and recipient.

Physicians who treat both the donor and recipient incur an inherent conflict of interest by putting a healthy patient, who will receive no health benefit, at risk for the benefit of a paying patient. This violates the virtue of professional integrity (i.e., the professional promise to do no harm, unless justified by the patient's autonomous decision that the burden is outweighed by a compensating benefit).

Calling egg-donation altruistic is disingenuous; egg-donation is a business in which a higher value is placed on a woman's eggs than on her health. The health and welfare of women is of little concern in biotechnological research that uses the female body or tissues (Spar 2007: 1290–1). Reproductive technology renders egg donors invisible: they are the means to an end (Morgan and Michaels 1999: 4). The Kantian principle of respect forbids using people this way.

Egg donors are often young, and often impoverished or saddled with debt. Fertility treatments are costly and rarely covered by insurance, and women who attempt pregnancy with donor eggs are relatively affluent. A single donor may produce eggs that go to multiple recipients, who each pays full price for reproductive services. One woman who had agreed to donate ova to a particular couple was contacted several months after the baby was born and asked to donate again so the baby would have a natural half-sibling. Nineteen eggs had been harvested from the donor, and apparently none were left (Andrews 1999: 97). Because of confidentiality concerns and the secrecy that surrounds donation, it is difficult to determine how pervasive this practice of selling ova without the donor's consent is. The principle of fairness is denied when women are cheated out of the full market payment for their services. As more countries pass laws restricting egg-donation, women from wealthy countries travel to other countries with less restrictive laws to obtain ova. Reproductive tourism supports a thriving black market that exploits impoverished women for donations of human ova. This combination of factors encourages exploitation that violates justice by the disparity in power between recipient and donor, and allows the bodies of poor women to be exploited as a means to satisfy the desire of wealthy women for children.

In conclusion, appeals to consequences – in particular, nonmaleficence, autonomy (as truth-telling, self-determination, and informed consent), liberty rights, the virtues of honesty and professional integrity, and justice as equality of respect and of treatment – forbid paying women for donating ova.

Perspective Three

Advances in reproductive technologies and stem cell research will continue to accelerate the business of infertility treatment and egg-donation (Hamilton 2000: 54). Stem cell research and the treatment of infertility using donated ova create a moral tension in the balance between harms to healthy young women, who provide the ova, and benefits to infertile women and researchers, who utilize donated ova. The potential benefit from scientific discoveries made possible through donated ova also play a role. Paying egg donors presents an intriguing ethical conundrum where moral appeals to consequences, autonomy, and equality support both champions and opponents of the practice. We are faced with a troubling moral dilemma if women are paid to donate ova: we are faced with an equally troubling moral dilemma if they are not. A number of questions must be considered before a course of action can be recommended.

Step 1: Information-gathering

Medical information

- Does the process of egg-donation involve medical risks for the donor? Does it confer any benefits?
- Does the process of egg-donation involve medical risks for the recipient?
- Are any long-term health risks associated with egg-donation?
- Does egg-donation carry health risks for any child conceived using this method?

History

- Is there sufficient history to understand the medical, social, moral, and technological risks of egg-donation?
- Has the demand for ova for fertility treatment increased?
- Has the demand for ova for research increased?
- What events shaped perspectives surrounding egg-donation?
- What role is played by the history of discrimination against women?

Law and policies

- What laws regulate egg-donation?
- Has legislation that prohibits compensation to egg donors adversely affected the supply of ova needed for treatment and research in countries other than the UK?
- Are there professional guidelines for egg-donation?

Economic

- Can many women afford fertility treatment? What are characteristics of those who can?
- How many women will donate ova if payment is offered? What are the characteristics of these women?
- How many women will donate ova without an economic incentive?
- Does paying egg donors significantly increase the cost of infertility treatment?
- Who benefits financially from egg-donation, and who pays?
- Is there a sufficient supply of ova to meet demands for research and treatment?

Psychological information

- Do donors face psychological risks associated with egg-donation?
- Does egg-donation pose psychological risks for the recipient or the child?

Cultural information

- Do emerging technologies shape social mores?
- How do different countries view the moral and commercial aspects of egg-donation?
- What degree of consensus exists on the moral justification of paying egg donors?

Step 2: Creative problem-solving

A creative solution must offer a way for infertile women to obtain donated ova, while safeguarding the health and autonomy of donors. One possible option is to allow friends and family to be ova donors without compensation, until such time as national and international guidelines for egg-donation are adopted (such as those for live organ and blood donors), and the infertility industry is strengthened by greater oversight and regulation. Although allowing donation under any circumstance poses risk to donors, removing payment, and thus removing an incentive that may compromise autonomy, may lessen coercion. But this solution raises the specter of encouraging a black market in ova. With that risk looming, we return to a deeper analysis of the original case.

Step 3: Listing pros and cons

Options	Pros	Cons
Allow egg donors to receive payment.	1. Allows infertile women to become pregnant (C-B) 2. Ensures adequate supply of ova for medical procedures and research (C-B, C-U) 3. Offers a source of income for poor women (C-B) 4. Respects donors' right to make decisions about their bodies (A) 5. Sperm donors paid (J-E) 6. Others in infertility business (physicians, lawyers, researchers) all profit (J-E)	7. Money may persuade donors to underestimate risks (C-NM, A) 8. Unknown risk to offspring from fertility drugs (C-NM) 9. Doctors compromise one patient's health for another patient's pregnancy (V-I) 10. May cause emotional harms to donor (guilt, regret) or child (lost trust, questioned identity, rejection) (C-NM) 11. Commodifies donors by treating them as means to an end (J-E) 12. Poor women exploited as a means to give wealthy women children (J-E) 13. Potential invasion of donor's privacy (Rights) 14. Potential for familial disharmony (C-M, C-U)
Do not allow payment to egg donors.	15. Donors protected from medical harms associated with superovulation and ova extraction (C-B) 16. Coercive incentives compromise voluntary participation (A) 17. Encourages altruism and promotes compassion, generosity (V) 18. Avoids extra health risks to newborns (C-B) 19. Avoids loss of trust in healthcare profession (C-U)	20. Scarcity of embryos for infertility treatment, research (C-U) 21. Women are commodified when they are not paid for their efforts (J-E, C-NM)

Step 4: Analysis

Factual assumptions

- Women will rarely donate ova if they are not compensated for doing so.
- Using donated ova offers the best chance for some infertile women to become pregnant.

- Egg-donation carries physical and emotional risks.
- Paying egg donors increases availability of ova, but increases the cost of assisted reproduction.
- The development of embryonic stem cell research will continue to increase demand – and competition – for donated ova.

Value assumptions

- People should not be allowed to pursue all options to become parents.
- Human ova should not be considered morally legitimate commodities.
- The medical specialty of infertility treatment should have greater oversight and be more strictly regulated.
- Reporting of success rates for infertility treatments should be standardized.
- If it is morally justifiable for professionals who provide services for assisted reproduction with the use of donated eggs to profit, it should be morally justifiable for egg donors to profit from their services as well.

Step 5: Justification

Women who donate ova should not be paid.

For the sake of discussion, we presuppose that the use of donor oocytes to further progress in the treatment of devastating diseases and to allow the childless to become parents is a good thing, and therefore morally justifiable. Societies that seek to alleviate physical and emotional suffering demonstrate benevolence and the virtue of compassion (Reason #1). Donated eggs are in demand for both fertility treatment and research. Although women may receive compensation for ova donated for fertility treatments, under guidelines suggested by the National Academies of Science, compensation for ova used in research is not allowed (NAS 2005: 87). The following analyses do not focus on whether payment should be allowed for eggs used in fertility treatments and not for research, but whether compensation should be allowed at all. The analyses assume that if it is not morally objectionable for women to sell their eggs for treatments to help others conceive a child, neither is it morally objectionable for women to sell their eggs for research to find treatments for other medical conditions. As the process and risks are the same for the donor whether eggs are used for treatment of infertility or for research, the moral dimensions are not appreciably affected.

Developing technologies carry the potential for great benefit – and great harm. The prodigious commercial expectations promised by emerging technologies can quickly erode ethical misgivings and downplay possible harms. When sufficient data are not yet available to determine the full panoply of consequences of technologies, the potential for harm for those directly involved, for progeny, and for the larger society, allows interventions that would not be morally justifiable were the risks known (Sherlock and Morrey 2002: 33). Compensation for egg donors is a situation appropriate for intervention. Egg-donation is fraught with medical, social, and emotional risks, many of which are as yet unknown.

The ethical issues surrounding compensation for oocyte-donation are complex and compelling. The issue of compensating egg donors involves multiple ethical dilemmas to which there are currently no satisfactory solutions. Politics and economics desensitize us to the ethical issues surrounding payment for and use of donated oocytes, such that we have not seriously examined the moral dimensions or the consequences, but "are only fighting about the price" (Spar 2007, p. 1291).

Jose Van Dyck (1995) traced the history of the development of assisted reproduction, and the intertwined evolution of technological advances and shifting moral perspectives. In 1978, Louise Brown, the first child conceived through in vitro fertilization, was born (Van Dyck 1995: 62). Despite reactions of outrage from religious leaders and the public at what was initially perceived as an affront to nature, assisted reproduction quickly became hailed as an almost miraculous treatment for infertility caused by damaged fallopian tubes. Within a few years, doctors regularly implanted a fertilized embryo in an infertile woman who could not conceive, but who could sustain a pregnancy. Technological advances soon allowed harvested eggs to be screened for genetic conditions, and embryos selected for implantation that did not carry the flawed genes. In vitro fertilization became a widespread treatment for all types of infertility, including low sperm count, even though the patient undergoing medical treatment in this case is not the person with the medical problem (ibid.: 82).

Thousands of babies (nearly 6,000 in 2003, according to the Centers for Disease Control and Prevention) are born each year in the United States to infertile couples – births made possible through egg-donations (Spar 2007: 1289). As reproductive and genetic technologies advanced, human embryonic stem cells derived from fertilized oocytes showed potential for organ replacement, as well as treatment of neural degeneration or injury, coronary disease, type 1 diabetes, and other diseases (Giudice et al. 2007: 1). Increasing demands for treatment of infertility and a mushrooming environment of medical and stem cell research that demands hundreds of thousands of ova a year require a constant supply of harvested oocytes. The demand falls far short of supply (Reasons ##1, 2).

Ethical concerns emerged along with technology. Leon Kass charged that in vitro fertilization turns "procreation into manufacture" (1997: 23). Many countries ban payment for organ-donations to prevent exploitation and commodification – that is, turning humans into mere objects to be used for material gain (Reasons ##11, 12, 21). Holland argues that the harm of commodification that results from buying and selling human gametes, organs, and tissue diminishes the dignity not only of individuals, but of society as well. The callousness of commodification creates a society that no longer values humanity and that is insensitive to social responsibility (Holland 2001: 277). Other critics of compensation for egg-donation compare the treatment of egg donors to that of prize-breeding animals, with premiums paid for the best stock. Some suggest that egg-donation for research is too much like cloning. Others emphatically hold that embryos should not be used for research (Spar 2007: 1290).

Ethical concerns about egg-donation were heightened when a leading South Korean researcher, Dr Woo Suk Hwang, used egg donors who were employed as members of his research team, were paid for their ova, and were accompanied by researchers during the extraction process (Johnston 2006: 29) (Reason #4). These conditions were deemed morally problematic because payment, the unequal balance of power in a relationship between employer and employee, and the presence during the procedure of a representative of the employer are factors that often undermine autonomy (Reason #16). Any one of those factors would be a concern; all three together suggest a situation of extreme coercion.

In its 2005 guidelines, the National Academies of Sciences strongly recommended that egg donors not be paid, but stated that its position is meant to encourage discussion of the issues surrounding donor compensation. The Academies intend to review and reconsider their recommendations regularly, and revise them appropriately as technology evolves and experience grows (NAS 2005: 87).

The demand for human eggs is increasing, outpacing the available supply (Dickenson 2004: 167). In Canada (SSCSAST 2004), Great Britain (Spar 2007: 1291), and the United States (Green 2005: B7), it has become apparent that, unless the recipient is a family member or friend, women are rarely willing to donate eggs for either research or fertility treatments without compensation for the time, effort, and pain the process entails (Reasons ##2, 20). The main impediment to stem cell research is the lack of human eggs (Check 2006: 26).

Sperm-donation, a low-tech process, has been practiced for over a century. Egg-donation, by contrast, is a highly technical process that has only been practiced since the 1980s (Mastroianni 2001: 28). In vitro fertilization (fertilization that takes place outside the body) has become a standard treatment for many types of infertility (Grinnell 2003: B13). In addition to treatments for women with infertility problems, in vitro fertilization is sometimes used when conception is difficult because of low sperm count (Van Dyke 1995: 82). Some women do not produce healthy oocytes, and using a donor's eggs often offers the best hope for conception of a genetically related child to individuals with reproductive limitations.

Natural ovulation usually involves maturation and release of a single egg from one of a woman's two ovaries. Occasionally, more than one egg is released; fertilization of more than one ovum results in fraternal twins, triplets, or other multiple conceptions. Superovulation uses fertility drugs to stimulate 10–20 or more eggs to mature and be released in a single cycle (Giudice et al. 2007: 2). The process carries a high risk of harm. Ovarian overstimulation can cause 70 or more eggs to ripen at one time, but can also cause donor death (Dickenson 2004: 167) (Reason #15). Egg-donation is a grueling and painful process that takes about three weeks, with the donor spending about 56 hours in the clinic during that time (ASRM 2000: 219). The donor is screened for physical and, occasionally, psychological problems. A pituitary suppressor (a hormone such as Lupron, Cetrotide, or Antagon) is injected to suppress the donor's ovarian function. If the recipient is known, hormone injections can be timed to synchronize the cycles of the donor and recipient. Later, the donor is given daily shots of other potent hormones to cause multiple eggs to ripen (superovulation) and prevent their premature release (Hamilton 2000, p.54). Clinic visits are required daily, or at least every other day, for ultrasound and blood tests to monitor egg-production, reduce the possibility of overstimulation, and determine when eggs are mature. When the ova are ready for harvesting, the patient is put under anesthesia or conscious sedation. The ova are extracted during a 25–40-minute outpatient process. Most often, a 15-inch needle is inserted through the vaginal wall and into the ovary to extract the ova. The eggs are inseminated in a Petri dish in the clinic or laboratory, and fertilization usually occurs within 24 hours. Within two to five days, the embryos are transferred to the recipient (Andrews 1999: 96; Braude and Rowell 2003: 852–3).

As many as 20 percent of women undergoing superovulation experience adverse reactions that are mild to moderate, and 1 percent experience life-threatening symptoms (BBC News 2005). Adverse effects may take months to resolve. Risks include nausea and vomiting, bloating, increased concentration of red blood cells, enlarged ovaries, rupture of ovarian cysts, respiratory distress, liver problems, kidney dysfunction, heart failure, blood clots, extreme mood swings, hair loss, digestive upset, headaches, edema, urinary dysfunction, abdominal distention, pain requiring hospitalization, and severe cases of Ovarian Hyperstimulation Syndrome (OHSS). OHSS can be fatal as a result of liver or kidney failure, circulatory collapse or heart failure, stroke, or excessive bleeding (Andrews 1999: 96; Giudice et al. 2007: 17–20). Superovulation is stopped about 10 percent of the time because of OHSS or other problems in ovarian stimulation (Braude and Rowell 2003: 852) (Reasons ##8, 9).

Egg-donation is medically and surgically invasive (Coombes 2004: 1206). Egg-retrieval surgery can cause bleeding, ovarian trauma, and infection (Giudice et al. 2007: 33). Puncture of the ovaries during retrieval, infection (Abrams 2006), and superovulation may lead to oocyte donors' subsequent sterility or difficulty conceiving their own children (ASRM 2000: 217). Donated oocytes can spread sexually transmitted diseases that might not be evident for some time after exposure; even if the donor has been tested, these diseases can be transmitted to the recipient and baby (ASRM 2002: S7; Andrews 1999: 214). The donor may pass on undetected genetic conditions to the baby. Because women experience many OHSS symptoms as part of their regular cycle, complaints are often dismissed and problems are not reported, so there are insufficient data to indicate the true degree of risk (Reasons ##8, 9).

The moral mandate of nonmaleficence – avoiding harm – is problematic because many adverse effects, beyond those currently documented, are suspected but not yet well studied. As a result, the full nature and extent of risks remain unknown. The use of ovarian stimulant drugs began fairly recently: superovulation has been practiced extensively for only about a decade. It is too early to assess long-term risks for women who may not experience consequences until later in life (Pearson 2006: 608). Long-term effects of drugs used for superovulation on either egg donor or child have not been determined (Chandrareddy 2004: 1206). A small number of babies conceived through superovulation either are born with breasts and/or pubic hair, or develop them within a few months of birth. Studies following these children as they grow older are not yet complete, and the effects of precocious puberty on their normal development and fertility remain to be discovered (Reason #8). Other adverse results of in vitro fertilization include low birth weight, and higher risk of retinoblastoma (Rojas-Martin et al. 2005: 190). There is increased risk of congenital malformation, a risk that is even greater when the egg is fertilized by sperm donated by men with genetically based infertility problems (Braude and Rowell 2003: 855). Despite data demonstrating risks to children born through in vitro fertilization, there is no registry that documents adverse effects and follows these children, or collects data for research (Andrews 1999: 55). Limited research has neither established nor refuted a link between superovulation and breast or ovarian cancers, but studies indicate that ovarian stimulation may increase the risk of uterine cancer (Giudice et al. 2007: 26). Standard of care in infertility treatment, such as recommended limitations on the number of times a women can safely donate eggs, has yet to be determined (Hamilton 2000: 58).

Soliciting egg donors for research is premature, according to Dr Stephen Minger, researcher and stem cell expert at King's College London. Research with human oocytes is still in its preliminary stages, and the risks are not known (BBC News 2007) (Reasons ##8, 9). The American Society for Reproductive Medicine recognizes the need for further study to determine risks, yet compliance with its guidelines for egg-donation is voluntary; to the extent that such compliance reduces profit or stretches inadequate research budgets, we have good reason to expect that it will be limited.

Because several donor eggs are often simultaneously implanted to increase the probability of a pregnancy, multiple births are not uncommon. In 2004, 36,760 in vitro deliveries resulted in 49,458 live births (CDC 2006: 13). The rate for multiple births experienced by women undergoing fertility treatments is about 10 times higher than the rate of natural multiple births. Multiple births carry a significant risk of harm to the infants, risks that the fertility specialists, not being part of neonatal care, do not have to address (Reason #18). Babies are at increased risks for cerebral palsy, intracranial hemorrhage, inadequate lung development, premature birth, and the creation of chimeras, caused when embryos fuse to each other (Andrews 1999: 52–4, 58). Mothers carrying multiple fetuses are at increased risk for gestational diabetes, high blood pressure, preeclampsia, anemia, and caesarean section (Sack 2006). Although a number of countries have enacted laws restricting the number of embryos that doctors may transfer (Andrews 1999: 56), the egg-donation industry is unregulated in the United States (Hamilton 2000: 52).

Many factors impact the success rate of technologically assisted pregnancies, including age of the recipient, quality of egg and sperm, genetics, health of the donor and recipient, and the skill of the specialist (CDC 2006: 71–2, 81). There is no consistency in the reporting of pregnancy rates. Some clinics measure pregnancy by biochemical changes in a woman's body, others by detection of a gestational sac and fetal heartbeat, and still others by a live birth (Braude and Rowell 2003: 854). These are clearly imprecise standards. The inconsistencies make it difficult for a patient to compare the success rates of clinics, and can be used to mislead women desperate not merely for a successful *pregnancy*, but for a *child who will become part of her family*. On the other hand, a requirement to standardize reporting of success rates may result in clinics turning away women who have particularly problematic cases. While this is not a policy issue specific to donor-compensation, the hesitancy to standardize reporting and the secrecy surrounding outcomes in fertility treatment protects a lucrative industry while misleading would-be parents and disregarding the risks to donor, recipient, and child (Reasons ##8, 15).

Egg-donation involves emotional as well as medical risks. A young woman, whether motivated by altruism or compensation, may not anticipate or may underestimate the power of psychological risks (Reason #10). Regret over donation, concerns about the welfare of her genetic child, or other emotional responses may haunt her later. Egg donors face three periods of psychological risk: during screening, if emotional or medical problems interfere with the donation; during the process of superovulation and harvesting, when donors may experience extreme emotional volatility and physical discomfort; and following the donation, if donors become concerned about their future health risks, develop regrets, or face concerns about their genetic progeny (Giudice et al. 2007: 41–7). The emotional extremes caused by the hormone injections can be so severe that some refer to the behavior resulting from superovulation as the Hitler-Bambi Syndrome (Andrews 1999: 96) (Reason #10).

Britain has legislated the right of children to learn the identity of their genetic parents, regardless of the wishes of the donor or the parents raising the child. The rights of donor and child may be in direct conflict (ESHRE 2002: 1407; Craft and Thornhill 2005: 301). While the donor – and parents – may wish for privacy and confidentiality, some ethicists and lawmakers believe the child should have the right to information about the biological parent, particularly in cases of medical need. Revealing her identity can create emotional distress not only for the donor, but also for the child and the parents who raised the child. Children who find out they were created by donation may experience major psychological trauma, compounded by discomfort with their families, grief, confusion, and loss of trust (Idreos Education Trust 2006: 31). The loss of privacy might be emotionally difficult for the egg donor, and, if this results in a meeting with the child, the results can be devastating guilt or regret (Reasons ##10, 13). Some women keep the donation hidden, even from their spouses (Barnett and Smith 2006). In such cases, its revelation could damage or destroy the relationship, particularly if the donation resulted in infertility (ESHRE 2002: 1407) (Reasons ##10, 14). With donations made to family members or friends, conflicts may arise over disclosure as well as over raising the child, visitation, discipline, or any number of issues (ESHRE 2002: 1407) (Reason #14).

Because of the high cost of infertility treatments, some women agree to share their eggs with other infertile women in return for reduced fees. Many clinics prefer using their own patients who are already undergoing superovulation for their own infertility as donors for other women, frequently offering reduced fees as an incentive to donate extra eggs to other patients (Reason #3). It may seem counterintuitive for a doctor to use the ova of a fertility-challenged donor for another patient, particularly as the donor is also a patient who is trying to get pregnant. Besides offering a way for women to access treatments they otherwise could not afford, using a patient avoids the necessity of going through an egg broker, and has the added advantage that the doctor knows the donor, is aware of her health, and may be more comfortable using her eggs, rather than a stranger's, for other patients.

There are, however, serious ethical concerns about egg-sharing. Sharing harvested ova reduces the chances that the donor will conceive (Craft and Thornhill 2005: 301; Spar 2007: 1291) (Reasons ##7, 11, 12). Women who share their eggs have fewer embryos available for future attempts; and it is emotionally devastating if the recipient becomes pregnant, while the donor remains childless (Andrews 1999: 98). Further, patient donors who themselves are trying to get pregnant may be coerced by the perception – or the fact – that continued access to costly infertility treatments depends upon continued egg-sharing (Reason #16). Egg-sharing may have long-term psychological implications for the donor that she may disregard at the time of donation because of financial or emotional duress (Reasons ##7, 9, 10, 16). Professional duty is compromised when doctors encourage patients whose own fertility is challenged to share their eggs with other patients who can afford to pay more (Reason #9).

A particular ethical concern arises when the same doctor cares for the egg donor and the recipient. Healthy egg donors, who are not trying to become pregnant themselves, are placed at risk for no medical reason other than to benefit another patient. Hamilton reports that some specialists consider donors to be just an instrument to be used to help their "real" patients conceive (2000: 58) (Reasons ##9, 11). To achieve pregnancy, the doctor may be tempted to increase the number of eggs produced or encourage additional cycles of stimulation. The egg recipient usually pays the doctor for the cost of procedures both for herself and the donor, as insurance rarely covers infertility treatments (Johnson 1999: 1913, 1916). Despite their acknowledged professional duty to *all* patients, it may be almost impossible for doctors not to promote the welfare of their recipient (paying) patients over that of their donor patients.

Some health risks to donor, recipient, and child are known, but the extent of other adverse effects and long-term consequences are not. Egg-donation is a relatively new field, and longitudinal studies have not been completed (Reason #8). Secrecy enshrouds the highly profitable fertility industry, and oversight is a patchwork of limited state and federal regulations, professional guidelines, and institutional policies. Trust, as a function of utility, is confidence that individuals, or professionals, will conduct themselves in an acceptable way. Utility is undermined by loss of trust in the medical profession when doctors profit handsomely while endangering the health of their patients by downplaying risks and withholding information patients need to make informed choices (Hamilton 2000: 55) (Reason #19).

Autonomy is a concern, as solicitations, such as advertisements in college newspapers, target women as young as 18. About 75 percent of egg donors in the United States are college-aged women. Living away from parental guidance and often concerned about paying for expenses or repaying college loans, these women may be lured by *seemingly* easy and lucrative compensation with little explanation of the risks involved (Kaledin 2006) (Reasons ##7, 16).

Lack of information about many aspects of infertility treatment is a concern, both for understanding the balance of benefit and harm, and ensuring that decisions about donation are fully autonomous (Reasons ##15, 16). The Centers for Disease Control and the American Society for Reproductive Medicine warn that published success rates are unreliable. There is no consistency in reporting or measuring outcomes, with some centers counting pregnancies, others counting deliveries, and others counting live births (Reason #7). If a woman is implanted with three embryos that all develop to term, is that one or three successful pregnancies? Autonomy rests on informed consent. To assure legitimate informed consent, decisions must be based on sufficient information and free from pressure or coercion. The inconsistent standards for measuring pregnancy and success rates of donor-assisted conception severely compromise informed consent. Women cannot assess the likelihood of *taking home a child* without a standard definition of what constitutes success in technologically assisted reproduction, nor can they weigh acceptable risks against potential benefits without uniformly measurable outcomes.

Women choose fertility specialists based on their success rates – success rates that often are based on implanting multiple embryos, in the hope that at least one will be carried to term. Doctors have economic incentives to help their patients conceive, and patients who spend tens of thousands of dollars on treatments, usually without insurance coverage, are often willing to do whatever it takes to get pregnant. This is not to suggest that doctors are motivated by profit, but that the financial benefit to them may bias their objectivity in weighing the potential harms and benefits for both patients (egg donor and recipient). Neither is this to suggest that women are not capable of assessing risk, but that they too may be swayed by the overwhelming desire for a child.

While some ethicists consider the prohibition against women receiving compensation for eggs a threat to autonomy (Andrews 1999; Green 2005: B7) (Reason #4), Johnson considers financial barriers to treatment so compromising that autonomous consent is only an illusion (1999: 1914) (Reason #16). Anecdotal evidence indicates that egg-sharing, whether donors are paid or compensated only by fee reduction, is the last resort for women who cannot afford fertility treatments, and so is highly coercive. Because benefit to the donor cannot be assured and, in fact, the donor may remain childless while the recipient becomes pregnant, egg-sharers clearly are unwittingly used as a means to an end (Reason #11). Not only is such use morally reprehensible in and of itself; it strongly suggests that consent is not freely given (Johnson 1999: 1913).

While a donor may be willing to help another women conceive, she may not want her eggs used for research. The right of autonomy protects subjects from forced participation in research, but the legal rights of patients and research subjects to make decisions about the use of their excised tissue are almost non-existent (Charo 2006: 1518). Once permission has been given for a medical procedure, with a few exceptions (e.g., disposition of cord blood) the right to decide if and for what kind of research their tissue may be used is limited. New "owners," with custodial rights to "their" eggs, may use excess ova in research – a use which donors would have refused had they been informed. Informed consent requires the disclosure of all potential dispositions of donated oocytes, including medical treatment, research, genetic modification, patenting, designer babies, and/or destruction. Multiple embryos implanted to ensure pregnancy might be reduced if more than one is viable, and pregnancies may be terminated because of fetal abnormalities (Reason #16). In what Dickenson refers to as the "Enclosure Movement," biotechnology corporations, university laboratories, researchers, and governments are claiming (that is, enclosing) property rights to biological materials – including DNA, organs, and tissue. Once removed, the biological materials become tangible commodities available for commercial exploitation by the new owners (Dickenson 2006: 43–4). Donors should be informed of choices prospective parents, doctors, and researchers have regarding use and disposition of embryos.

The high cost of assisted reproduction, driven in part by fees paid to egg donors, can create unrealistic expectations in parents. After paying thousands of dollars – a six-figure payment is not unheard of – and carefully interviewing and selecting a donor with desired traits and accomplishments, parents may count on a "perfect" child. If the child fails to meet expectations, the parents may feel as if they have been cheated, and the child may feel the parents' disappointment in having a "defective product" that cannot be returned. Despite widespread opposition to eugenics, little concern has been raised about recruitment of egg donors with specific traits and accomplishments (Hamilton 2000: 55) (Reason #10).

In addition to fueling great expectations about "the quality of the product" by purchasing genetically desirable ova, the economics of egg-donation raise other moral concerns. As treatments are not generally covered by insurance, most patients undergoing fertility treatments have financial resources. Paying egg donors further increases the cost of treatment, pricing it out of reach for most women (Johnston 2006: 30) (Reason #12). But, as noted above, donors are more likely to be women of limited means who can ill-afford unsuspected medical costs. Because insurance policies in the United States rarely cover infertility treatments or research-related injury, the donor must be informed of treatment options if she suffers harm because of the donation, what these treatments would cost, and whether the costs of her injuries will be covered by the recipient or the medical practitioners/facilities – neither of which is common. The Committee on Guidelines for Human Embryonic Stem Cell Research notes that compensation for injuries is unusual (NAS 2005: 87). Without this information, donors who suffer harms – including serious threats to health – may have no financial redress. The principle of autonomy requires that the information on economic risks, as well as medical risks, be provided (Reason #16).

Egg-donation is a growth industry. Although scientists may want tighter regulation of human tissue, most specialists in the lucrative practice of reproductive medicine do not. Fertility is a multi-billion-dollar-a-year business in the United States. As clinics compete for wealthy clients, fertility specialists are now among the highest-paid medical practitioners. While many women are offered several thousand dollars to donate their eggs, those with particularly desirable characteristics may be tempted by offers of tens of thousands of dollars. Many clinics allow four or more cycles of donations, which can earn highly desirable donors compensation in the six figures. Payment is not made per egg, but per donation cycle, so excess eggs can be very profitable to the clinic. As most insurance plans don't cover fertility treatments, patients usually pay around $40,000 out-of-pocket for fertility treatments, and some may pay over $200,000 by the time an actual pregnancy is achieved (Andrews 1999: 95, 48). Patients pay cash up front, and they pay whether or not they achieve a pregnancy (Hamilton 2000: 58). The infertility business, like any other business, is demand driven (Reason #12).

In addition to physicians, egg donors, and researchers, countless attorneys, agencies, laboratories, and fertility clinics are involved in the egg-donation business, mediating transactions between the parties (Hamilton 2000: 55). Some argue that if it is morally justifiable for these individuals to receive ample compensation for their services, the principle of justice requires that donors also should be paid (Reasons ##6, 21).

Profits from technologies and treatments derived from oocytes promise to be extremely lucrative, and researchers stand to make fortunes. More than 2,000 patents for stem cells and more than 500 patents for embryonic stem cell technologies were filed as of October 2001 (Van Overwalle 2002: 23) (Reason #6). Women pay hundreds of millions of dollars for fertility drug prescriptions each year, a profitable market for the pharmaceutical industry (Andrews 1999: 51) (Reason #6).

The American Society for Reproductive Medicine determined minimum compensation for egg donors, based on compensation to sperm donors. Assuming sperm donors were paid $60–$75 and the process took an hour, at the same rate the 56 hours that the women spend in the clinic would amount to compensation of $3,360–$4,200. However, this figure does not include compensation for the time required for injections and other treatments given at home, travel time, or additional economic losses due to having to miss work as a result of pain or other symptoms associated with the medications or retrieval procedures (ASRM 2000: 219). Nonetheless, equality requires that sperm and egg donors either both receive compensation, or that neither does (Reason #5).

While infertility treatment is a highly private matter, the issues surrounding egg-donation have social implications. If women are implanted with embryos from eggs donated by women from the same community – especially ova from women who make multiple donations, half-sisters and half-brothers might unknowingly become sexually involved with each other, increasing the risk of genetic maladies in their children (Chandrareddy 2004: 1206). Establishing lineage may also be a concern. In Conservative Judaism, Jewish heritage is passed through the mother. The status of the child has not been established in the case of egg-donation, particularly if neither donor nor recipient is Jewish (Hamilton 2000: 58) (Reason #8). Children who learn they were conceived with a donated egg may experience anger, distrust, and feelings of alienation from their family and rejection by their biological mothers. It may be difficult for the child and donor, as well as for the child's family, if identities are revealed. When the donor and recipient know each other as, for example, when a donor gives eggs to a sister or friend, tension may arise over child-rearing practices (Reasons ##10, 14). The specter of eugenics hangs over the selection of egg donors. Trait selection poses a risk of commodification of human life when superficial traits command exorbitant prices and potential donors who do not meet standards of beauty are dismissed.

Feminists are divided on the issue of reproductive technology. Some raise concerns about the unknown risks to women's health or the commodification of women (Spar 2007: 1290) (Reasons ##8, 15). Some feminists view reproductive technologies, controlled primarily by male scientists and physicians, as unavoidably coercive and a threat to women's reproductive autonomy. Maria Mies, for example, accuses reproductive specialists, be they men or women, of exploiting women for commercial purposes. Women both provide and consume the commodities, and enable the technologies. Both commodities and technologies have high commercial value, providing lucrative returns for reproductive specialists – but *not* for the women who make these practices possible (Reason #6). Others argue that reproductive technologies provide greater reproductive freedom for women (Reason #4). Naomi Pfeffer accuses opponents of reproductive technologies of failing to acknowledge the needs and rights of women, and the potential benefits technologies offer them. Both sides, however, agree that their foremost concerns are the protection of women's health and reproductive rights (Van Dyck 1995: 89, 99) – goals that, as noted earlier, cannot be reliably predicted, let alone assured (Reasons ##4, 15).

Social mores evolve as perceptions of need and technological, economic, and social environments change. Traditional opposition in Canada to the sale of reproductive material challenges the efforts of infertile women to bear children (Reason #20). In 2004, as the demand for eggs for infertility treatment was intensified by the competing demand for eggs for stem cell research, the Committee on Social Affairs, Science and Technology of the Canadian Parliament recommended initiating a public relations campaign to inform people of the shortage of donor eggs, overcome opposition to egg-donation, and encourage women to donate ova (SSCSAST 2004) (Reason #17).

Trafficking in human oocytes, shared stem cell lines (Hall 2005: A-11), reproductive tourism (Sauer 2005: 431), and other concerns that cross international boundaries make payment for egg-donation a global issue. Regulations vary widely from country to country, and the current status of regulations is a moving target. Many scientists would welcome international guidelines on the derivation and use of human tissue and genetic materials (Check 2006: 26). Under the Human Fertilization and Embryology Act of 1990, Great Britain set limits on compensation to sperm and egg donors. After it became apparent that prohibiting payment for ova-donations resulted in a severe shortage of gamete donations (Reason #20), the country revised the Act to allow significantly greater compensation for egg-donation, and has pledged to contribute financially to the campaign to increase gamete-donations (Idreos Education Trust 2006: 38–9) (Reason #1). Effective from April 7, 2006, however, EU Directive 2004/23/EC prohibited member states from compensating egg donors beyond reasonable expenses (Coombes 2004: 1206). As a result of the ban, Britain had to reduce compensation rates, and fertility programs are now struggling to secure a sufficient number of donations (ibid.). Although there is still modest compensation, there is two-year wait for donated eggs, and the wait is growing (Reason #20). Britain's recent law removing the right to donor-anonymity has further reduced donations (Craft and Thornhill 2005: 301). As competition from researchers seeking embryonic stem cells increases, it has become more difficult for infertile women to secure donated eggs in Britain, and many turn to reproductive tourism, seeking eggs abroad (Sauer 2005: 431) (Reason #12).

To bypass European Union Directive 2004/23/EC, some clinics in Britain and other EU countries do a thriving business in infertility services that includes sending infertile women to countries outside the European Union for embryo implantation. A well-established black market exists, primarily in East European countries, where reproductive treatments are often an unsavory and unregulated underground industry. These countries have no oversight systems to protect women from reproductive and research predators. Their exploitation is exacerbated by the unlikelihood that the donors will benefit from the technologies they enable (Dickenson, 2002: 55). The black market in ova is supported by foreign women of means, who yearn to have a child and have no qualms about exploiting poor women from impoverished countries to satisfy that longing. Coercive practices, such as payment per egg harvested (rather than payment per cycle), lead to the injection of extremely high, unsafe levels of hormones into the donors to produce as many eggs as possible, and pressure to donate several times a year. Egg-donation, in effect, becomes a job for these women that places them increasingly at risk for serious harm and infertility. If they do suffer harm, they will likely receive substandard follow-up care, if any care is provided at all. The principle of justice is violated as the black market thrives on the desperation of poor women, who risk their lives for the couple of hundred dollars they receive, while wealthy people and wealthy countries disregard their own countries' legal constraints, as well as the exploitation of impoverished young women and the risk to their health and lives (Barnett and Smith 2006). The payment, in being so scanty, is unfair compensation for the burdens assumed. (Reasons ##7, 8, 9, 11, 12).

Justice cannot require that all needs be met, but that competing needs be considered and resources distributed so all members of society benefit, regardless of social class or economic status. If egg-donation is a question of respect, we have reasons to reject it even if the women do autonomously consent, or so say the feminists who argue that the only reason we tolerate this is because women have been and continue to be unworthy of the same degree of respect – especially with regard to not inflicting harm – that we routinely tender to men. Consider this example: you might autonomously consent to be my slave, but if I did enslave you – even with your autonomous consent – I would fail to respect you as a person, because I would take away your freedom to engage in many worthwhile activities of your own choosing. This seems to be analogous to the poor women: even if they do – say they do, just for the sake of argument – autonomously consent, by imposing these harms on them we deny that they are worthy of respect, in particular that we should not harm them in these ways (Reason #11).

Paying egg donors challenges justice, as it does not ensure shared benefit of scarce resources; rather, it denies poor women equal access to fertility treatment. Reproductive technology does not benefit all classes of people equally. Most treatments are available only to a relatively few patients who are wealthy or whose insurance covers treatment; consequently, most fertility patients are middle- to upper-socioeconomic class Caucasian women (Giudice et al. 2007:

54). Although costs vary widely, access to low-cost treatments is limited to both patients and doctors. Women with limited financial resources may have no option of becoming pregnant except by donating ova to women with greater financial means, thereby decreasing their own chances of conceiving. Justice fails as poor women provide children for the rich (Johnson 1999: 1913) (Reason #12).

Israel and Denmark have policies discouraging the use of paid egg donors and instead promote egg-sharing, as do Australia, Spain, and Greece (Reason #17). Meanwhile, Britain's practices are both highly regulated and highly permissive; Germany has banned embryo research; and Japan is more concerned with the technology of organ transplantation than of embryo research (Franklin 1999, pp. 70–1). Japan, Norway, and Germany prohibit egg-donation because of the risks to women's health (Coombes 2004: 1206) (Reason #15); Sweden prohibits payment to donors (Check 2006: 26) (Reason #17); Singapore allows only compensation for expenses (Spar 2007: 1291); Canada encourages altruistic dona-tions, and prohibits payment to egg donors, but is concerned about gamete short-ages (SSCSAST 2004) (Reason #17, #20). Although Korea formerly allowed donor compensation (Woo Suk Hwang's Korean research team was able to secure enough eggs only after offering to pay donors), payment was banned in 2005 following controversies raised by Dr Hwang's research. (Korean women have essentially nullified the law by offering to donate eggs gratis to Dr Hwang's research (Johnston 2006: 30–1)) (Reasons ##4, 17). Russia, Bulgaria, Romania, Ukraine, Georgia, and Croatia allow the sale of gametes (Dickenson 2004). The many different ways that countries prohibit, regulate, promote, or ignore over-sight and regulation of egg-donation indicate the multiplicity of moral values and perspectives surrounding this issue.

In the United States, reproductive treatments and technologies – even experi-mental technologies – are poorly regulated (Kaledin 2006). The few regulations that exist do not always apply to private practice or research (Charo 2006: 1519). The American Society for Reproductive Medicine established guidelines for gamete donation in 2002, but compliance is voluntary. The guidelines allow fees to be charged for transferring embryos and payments to donors for expenses, including "the time, inconvenience, and physical and emotional demands and risks associated with oocyte donation" (ASRM 2002: S8 IX, B), but ban the sale of eggs. The ASRM cautions that compensation should not be so large as to give the impression that payment is for the eggs and not expenses. Although the ASRM states numerous times in its guidelines that egg donors should not be paid, it does not offer reasons for its position.

California's Proposition 71 funded a £3 billion program for stem cell research (Charo 2006: 1518). Although dependent on oocytes for stem cell research, California and Massachusetts forbid paying donors, counting on altruism to provide the necessary eggs (Spar 2007: 1290) (Reason #17).

The laws of reproductive medicine are still being established, causing emotional turmoil for all involved. Three "parents" in Ohio, Texas, and Pennsylvania, fought for two and a half years over custody of triplets conceived with the father's sperm, a donor's eggs, and carried to term by a surrogate mother. After their birth in

2003, the birth mother refused to relinquish the babies to the father, as stipulated by their contract; she took them home from the hospital and raised them herself for eight months. In addition to the $20,000 she had already received from the father to carry the pregnancy, the birth mother sued him for monthly child support. The father eventually won custody after nearly three years of court battles, and the boys were moved from the surrogate mother's home to the father's home (Fields 2007) (Reason #10). Such cases demonstrate the morally complex concerns of commercialization of reproduction – and the potentially difficult circumstances for all involved (Reasons ##10, 14).

Yet, the other horn of the dilemma is the fact that if compensation to egg donors is not allowed, it is unlikely that sufficient oocytes will be available for either fertility treatments or research. As Britain and Canada have discovered, limiting compensation has resulted in a severe shortage of eggs. The shortage of oocytes causes delays of more than two years for fertility treatment, further compromising the ability of an infertile woman to become pregnant (Reasons ##2, 20).

Up to $100,000 has been offered for a donor with the right combination of desired traits (Hamilton 2000: 53). Paying donors raises the cost of fertility treatments, putting them out of reach for most people. Altruistic donation will only work if physicians and researchers also agree to provide services altruistically. Lower profits are likely to deter many from specializing in reproductive technologies and research, however, leaving even more women childless (Reasons ##2, 12, 17).

The longing to have a child is instinctive, natural, and often profound. Infertility is not a life-threatening medical condition, yet it causes enormous emotional duress. The benefit that reproductive technologies provide by allowing infertile women to bear children, and the joy this brings, can hardly be overestimated. Other medical conditions are life-threatening, and wreak havoc on those inflicted and those who care about them. Embryonic stem cell research shows tremendous potential for medical treatments that may benefit millions. The burdens imposed and the benefits lost because of illness and injury, the tremendous resources required for healthcare, and the diminished capacity for happiness that affliction causes require that virtuous societies seek ways to alleviate suffering and promote health. Oocyte donation is a virtuous act of compassion and kindness – even if the donor receives compensation – that allows infertile women to carry a pregnancy, and embryos to be created for medical research (Reasons ##1, 17).

There are many compelling reasons to pay women for donating ova, and many reasons not to pay them. The medical treatment of infertility requires ova. Some of the most promising advances in the treatment of disease are likely to involve research on human embryonic stem cells. Infertility treatments and stem cell research depend on a large supply of ova. It has been demonstrated that, without payment, women are not willing to donate eggs. However, because of the lack of reliable data on the risks of egg-donation, and the lack of transparency in the medical treatment of infertility, paying egg donors cannot be morally justified unequivocally. The present system of procurement must be changed to address issues of harm, autonomy, professional duty (including oversight and accountability), and equality.

Some fertility specialists have proposed harvesting the eggs from aborted fetuses and maturing them in a laboratory to use as a source of oocytes (Andrews 1999: 213). Although the National Academy of Sciences guidelines prohibit donor compensation, they note that cadaveric fetal tissue offers "remarkable scientific and therapeutic possibilities" (NAS 2005: 17). Britain prohibits the use of eggs harvested from the aborted fetuses of cadavers. However, resistance to this prohibition is weakening (Johnson 1999: 1913). With skyrocketing demands for ova and common law that regards excised tissue as medical waste over which the patient has no rights, it's not inconceivable that oocytes might be harvested from aborted fetuses, organ donors, or patients undergoing oophorectomies. Perhaps this alternative can provide ova until the preceding concerns can be addressed.

Assuming that future research can adequately identify the nature and probability of significant risk to donors, recipients, and children conceived with technological assistance, several additional recommendations should be considered as ways to lower health risk for egg donors (including several that create greater accountability on the part of professionals). These include mandating insurance coverage for donors; establishing national guidelines, similar to those in place for live organ and blood donors, to inform women of the risks involved in egg-donation – including the fact that many cannot be reliably identified at present, and ensuring that donors' consents are given without manipulation or exploitation (Spar 2007: 1291); and regulating the process to reduce risk in such ways as monitoring the number of eggs being released to avoid complication of OHSS (Giudice et al. 2007: 57). Johnson proposes that counselors, rather than physicians or their staff, advise women on the risks of donation, to avoid conflict of interest and bias (1999: 1913), as well as mandating a cooling off period before consent is finalized to protect autonomy (ibid.: 1917). Johnson also suggests the establishment of standard sliding-scale fees and egg-sharing through professional associations (ibid.: 1914), and requiring that a percentage of excess eggs be donated to a bank, making treatment more widely accessible and addressing issues of justice (ibid.: 1915). Andrews recommends the creation of a registry to monitor the long-term health effects on donors and children created from superovulation, that would protect confidentiality but maintain records in case of the child's medical need (1999: 55). Recommendations also include scientific studies on the long-term health effects of superovulation, with rigorous analyses of factors contributing to complications (Spar 2007: 1290), and the use of mammal eggs to perfect technologies before continuing to use them on humans (BBC News 2007).

In conclusion, egg donors should not be paid at this time. A moratorium on all egg-donations should be enforced until scientifically sound research clearly identifies the risks of superovulation to donors and children created from their eggs. An exception could be granted for women who donate ova to family or friends, or women undergoing in vitro fertilization using their own eggs. Although the procedure does pose medical and physical risk, by removing the option of payment, the threat to autonomy by coercive incentive is removed. At the same time, the principle of autonomy is upheld by allowing a woman to make informed decisions about her body, even when those decisions could result in harm. Once practices that control risk are integrated into standard medical care, egg-donations for research and to fertility clinics, and the moral inquiry into compensation to donors, could resume.

Technology, when coupled with enormous commercial potential, too often blinds participants to ethical concerns. Until the short- and long-term risks are assessed, ova donors should not be compensated. The appeals to consequences – specifically beneficence, nonmaleficence, and utility – autonomy – as truth-telling, self-determination, and informed consent – virtue, and equality of respect as justice all lead us to determine that paying ova donors is morally impermissible. This position could be reconsidered in the light of greater oversight and accountability to address concerns of risk and autonomy. Only then, and with careful re-examination of the ethical issues, can the practice of compensation to egg donors be justified.

Additional Issues to Consider

Other possible moral dilemmas arising within this case:

Q Is egg-donation, whether compensated or not, morally justifiable?

Q Is there a moral difference between egg-donation and organ-donation?

Q Assuming payment for ova-donation can be justified, should standard rates of payment be established for egg-donation, or should donors be free to negotiate fees based on the demand for their traits such as accomplishments, beauty, intelligence, and talents?

Q Should preference be given to the use of cryopreserved embryos that will not be used in treatment, and if not used will be destroyed, for reproduction over research?

Q Should women who are past the age of ovulation, but are still able to carry a baby with the use of donor eggs, be allowed to undergo in vitro fertilization, although increased risks such are well documented?

Q Should the reason for infertility make a difference? For example, should the use of donor eggs be allowed if a woman is seeking a last chance at pregnancy after years of fertility treatment, carrying a child for her daughter, trying to replace an only child who has been killed, or has delayed pregnancy to further her career?

Q Should older parents be allowed to use in vitro fertilization if their life expectancy (according to standard actuarial tables) would indicate they are unlikely to live until their children have reached the age of emancipation?

REFERENCES

Abrams, F. (2006) The misery behind the baby trade. *Daily Mail* (July 17). Available at: www.dailymail.co.uk/pages/live/femail/article.html?in_article_id=396220andin_page_id=1879 (accessed October 12, 2007).

Andrews, L. B. (1999) *The Clone Age: Adventures in the New World of Reproductive Technology*, Owl Book edn. New York: Henry Holt and Company.

ASRM (American Society for Reproductive Medicine) (2002) 2002 guidelines for gamete and embryo donation. *Fertility and Sterility* 77 (6): Suppl. 5.

ASRM (American Society for Reproductive Medicine) (2000) Financial incentives in recruitment of oocyte donors. *Fertility and Sterility* 74 (2): 216–20.

ASRM/CFAS (American Society for Reproductive Medicine/The Canadian Fertility and Andrology Society) Highlights from the Conjoint Meeting (2005) Press Release: Requiring identification and lowering compensation may make gamete donation more difficult (October 19).

Barnett, A., and Smith, H. (2006) Cruel cost of the human egg trade. *Observer UK News*. Available at: http://observer.guardian.co.uk/uk_news/story/0,,1764680,00.html (April 30) (accessed October 12, 2007).

BBC News (2007) Altruistic egg-donation "allowed." (February 21). Available at: http://news.bbc.co.uk/2/hi/health/6379827.stm (accessed October 12, 2007).

BBC News (2005) Safety of egg-donation "unclear." (June 30). Available at: http://news.bbc.co.uk/2/hi/health/4634625.stm (accessed October 13, 2007).

Braude, P., and Rowell, P. (2003) ABC of subfertility: Assisted conception. II: In vitro fertilisation and intracytoplasmic sperm injection. *British Medical Journal* 327 (7419): 852–5.

Centers for Disease Control and Prevention, and the American Society For Reproductive Medicine (2006) *2004 Assisted Reproduction Technology Success Rates: National Summaries and Fertility Clinic Reports*. Atlanta, GA: US Department of Health and Human Services Centers for Disease Control and Prevention.

Chandrareddy, A. (2004) Paying for egg-donation: Buying and selling eggs (November 23 response to Coombes). *British Medical Journal* 329 (7476): 1206.

Charo, R. A. (2006) Body of research: Ownership and use of human tissue. *New England Journal of Medicine* 355 (15): 1517–19.

Check, E. (2006) Ethicists and biologists ponder the price of eggs. *Nature* 443 (7107): 26.

Code of Federal Regulations (2002) 21 CFR 50.25 (6).

Coombes, R. (2004) Authority consults public on paying women £1,000 to donate eggs. *British Medical Journal* 329 (7476): 1206.

Craft, I., and Thornhill, A. (2005) Would "all-inclusive" compensation attract more gamete donors to balance their loss of anonymity? *Reproductive BioMedicine Online* 10 (3): 301–6. Available at: www.rbmonline.com/4DCGI/Article/Detail?38%091%09=%201687%09 (accessed March 21, 2008).

Dickenson, D. L. (2002) Commodification of human tissue: implications for feminist and development ethics. *Developing World Bioethics* 2 (1): 55–63.

Dickenson, D. L. (2004) The threatened trade in human ova. *Nature Reviews Genetics* 5 (3): 167.

Dickenson, D. L. (2006) The lady vanishes: what's missing from the stem cell debate. *Journal of Bioethical Inquiry* 3 (1–2; Special Issue on Stem Cell Research): 43–54.

Directive 2004/23/EC of the European Parliament and of the Council of March 31, 2004 on setting standards of quality and safety for the donation, procurement, testing, processing, preservation, storage and distribution of human tissues and cells. *Official Journal of the European Union* (2004), L. 102: 48–59.

ESHRE (European Society of Human Reproduction and Embryology) Task Force on Ethics and Law (2002) Gamete and embryo donation. *Human Reproduction* 17 (5): 1407–8.

Fields, R. (2007) Ohio Supreme Court: surrogate mothers have no right to child if egg isn't theirs. *Cleveland Plain Dealer* (December 21) Available at: www.cleveland.com/news/plaindealer/index.ssf?/base/news/119822958348330.ml&coll=2 (accessed June 20, 2008).

Franklin, S. (1999) Dead embryos: feminism in suspension. In L. M. Morgan and M. W. Michaels (eds.), *Fetal Subjects, Feminists Positions*. Philadelphia, PA: University of Pennsylvania Press, pp. 61–82.

Giudice, L., Santa, E., and Pool, R. (eds.) (2007) *Assessing the Medical Risks of Human Oocyte Donation for Stem Cell Research: Workshop Report*. Committee on Assessing the Medical Risks of Human Oocyte Donation for Stem Cell Research. Washington, DC: National Academies Press.

Green, R. M. (2005) It's right to pay women who give their eggs for research. *San Francisco Chronicle* (July 19): B7.

Grinnell, F. (2003) Defining embryo death would permit important research. *Chronicle of Higher Education* 49 (36): B13.

Hall, C. T. (2005) "Stem cell hub" cloning network project folding: US organizer cites "misrepresentations" by plan's collaborators in South Korea. *San Francisco Chronicle* (November 15): A-11.

Hamilton, J. O. C. (2000) What are the costs? *Stanford Magazine* 28 (6): 52–8.

Holland, S. (2001) Contested commodities at both ends of life: Buying and selling gametes. embryos, and body tissues. *Kennedy Institute of Ethics Journal* 11 (3): 263–84.

Idreos Education Trust (2006) *Who Am I? Experiences of Donor Conception*. London: Idreos Education Trust.

Johnson, M. H. (1999) The medical ethics of paid egg sharing in the UK. *Human Reproduction* 14 (7): 1912–18.

Johnston, J. (2006) Paying egg donors: exploring the arguments. *Hastings Center Report* 36 (1): 28–31.

Kaledin, E. (2006) Inside the business of egg-donation: the "right" DNA can fetch $35,000, but women may not consider emotional risks. *CBS Evening News* (May 17). Available at: www.cbsnews.com/stories/2006/05/17/eveningnews/main1626874.shtml (accessed October 13, 2007).

Kass, L. R. (1997) The wisdom of repugnance: Why we should ban cloning of human beings. *The New Republic* 216 (22): 17–26.

Knowles, L. P. (1999) Property, progeny, and patents. *Hastings Center Report* 29 (2): 38–40.

Mastroianni, L. (2001) Risk evaluation and informed consent for ovum donation: a clinical perspective. *American Journal of Bioethics* 1 (4): 28–9.

Morgan, L. M., and Michaels, M. W. (eds.) (1999) *Fetal Subjects, Feminists Positions*. Philadelphia, PA: University of Pennsylvania Press.

NAS (National Academy of Science) (2005) *Guidelines for Human Embryonic Stem Cell Research*. Washington, DC: National Academies Press.

Pearson, H. (2006) Health effects of egg-donation may take decades to emerge. *Nature Digest* 3 (9): 607–8.

Rojas-Marcos, P. M., David, R., and Kohn, B. (2005) Hormonal effects in infants conceived by assisted reproductive technology. *Pediatrics* 116 (1): 190–4.

Sack, K. (2006) Procedures often result in risky preterm births. *Los Angeles Times* 30 (October 30). Available at: www.latimes.com/news/nationworld/nation/la-na-surrogacyside30oct30,0,6333272.story (accessed October 13, 2007).

Sauer, M. V. (2005) Further HFEA restrictions on egg-donation in the UK: two strikes and you're out! *Reproductive BioMedicine Online* 10 (4): 431–3. Available at: www.rbmonline.com/4DCGI/Article/2005/1738/RB1738%20Sauer.pdf (accessed March 21, 2008).

Sherlock, R., and Morrey, J. D. (eds.) (2002) Fundamental issues of ethics and biotechnology. In *Ethical issues in Biotechnology*. Lanham, MD: Rowman & Littlefield, pp. 31–95.

Spar, D. (2007) The egg trade – making sense of the market for human oocytes. *New England Journal of Medicine* 356 (13): 1289–91.

SSCSAST (Standing Senate Committee on Social Affairs, Science and Technology) The Parliament of Canada. (2004) 2nd report on Bill C-6, An Act Respecting Assisted Human Reproduction and Related Research (March 9, 2004) Available at: www.parl.gc.ca/37/3/parlbus/commbus/senate/com-e/soci-e/rep-e/rep02mar04-e.htm (accessed October 13, 2007).

Van Dyck, J. (1995) *Manufacturing Babies and Public Consent: Debating the New Reproductive Technologies*. New York: New York University Press.

Van Overwalle, G. (2002) *Study on the Patenting of Inventions Related to Human Stem Cell Research*. Luxembourg: Office for Official Publications of the European Communities.

CASE TWENTY-FIVE: ONLY GOD CAN MAKE A TREE – PATENTING INDIGENOUS PLANTS

From the time she was a little girl, Mallory O'Brian was fascinated by early explorers' accounts of their travels through primeval jungles and rainforests. Their descriptions of lush foliage, huge vines, enormous trees, exuberant flowers, gaudy plumes, and exotic fruits generated an insatiable hunger to visit these places. In elementary school, Mallory collected aluminum cans and donated the deposits to campaigns to save the rainforest, afraid it would disappear before she was old enough or could afford to travel there. In high school biology, she discovered that encroaching development, clear-cutting, burning, ranching, subsistence farming, mining, logging, and access roads crisscrossing the jungle divided and destroyed delicately balanced ecosystems. In the course of her university studies, Mallory became intrigued with the potential of rainforest plants for medicinal purposes: in a warm, moist environment that is a perfect medium for fungal and bacterial growth, jungle plants have developed remarkable immune systems over millennia that enable them to resist disease while coexisting with harmful microorganisms. The same chemical compounds that protect plants also offer the potential to prevent or treat human diseases.

The more she learned, the more Mallory's appreciation grew for indigenous people's knowledge, built up over centuries, of the healing properties of native plants. At the same time she became increasingly concerned with the predominant perspective at her university: a view of the jungle as a green mine to be exploited for commercial gain, even as exploitation threatened the survival of these fragile and bountiful areas. Few among her colleagues and professors valued the indigenous perspective of the jungle as a life source providing food, shelter, medicine, fuel, clothing, tools, and a way of life that has been sustained over tens of thousands of years. Lucrative contracts with pharmaceutical, chemical, and agri-business corporations, with the goal of patenting indigenous compounds and germ lines, held more persuasive and immediate significance for them.

Although a degree in ethnobotany was not offered at that time, Mallory minored in anthropology and attended seminars on ethnobotany during her doctoral studies in pharmacognosy. After earning her degree, Dr O'Brian spent several months with three Amazonian tribes, patiently gaining their trust and learning the traditional medicinal uses of indigenous plants. Shadowing the tribal shaman as they gathered plants and prepared potions, Mallory collected samples and recorded preparations and uses. Sometimes she would ask to be shown what was used for a specific malady, to fill in gaps in her training. At other times she would visit villages that were large enough to have a market. Making her way to the herb-seller, she would ask how plants she was unfamiliar with were used.

After collecting samples and identifying their medicinal uses, Mallory returned home to begin laboratory analyses. In addition to rigorous scientific testing of the effectiveness of indigenous plant products against disease, she attempted to synthesize the active compounds found in the plants. Because so much of the rainforest and so many rainforest species are threatened, synthesizing compounds (it is hoped) preserves potential treatments in the event the plants from which the compounds were derived became extinct. The first step in the laboratory was extracting and isolating the particular compounds that were thought to work against the particular diseases that the shaman treated with the plant products. After the compounds were isolated, each was tested to determine its effectiveness against disease, and to gauge whether it was curative, preventive, merely masked the symptoms, or had no apparent effect against the disease. The laboratory personnel then attempted to synthesize compounds that demonstrated the potential for medicinal efficacy.

After two years in the laboratory, Dr O'Brian returned to the tribes with good news. Two of the compounds extracted from indigenous plants showed promising effects, and had been successfully synthesized. She was committed to ensuring that tribal members would profit from their knowledge, have the means to preserve traditional healing practices in the face of attempts to exploit them, and benefit from expanded opportunities that sharing in the profits derived from their knowledge would allow. She wanted to help develop ways to preserve and pass on indigenous knowledge within the tribes, hoping to establish a modest laboratory where young people could employ the less complex scientific methodologies to isolate and test compounds. She also wanted to help tribal members learn to negotiate offers for patents on compounds that would inevitably come to them.

Dr O'Brian was stunned to see the changes two years had brought. Tribal members sported Western-style clothing, jewelry, and haircuts. They listened to generator- and battery-operated CD players and radios. They sang pop songs and danced to pop music, preferred by the younger members of the tribes to their traditional songs and dances. More disturbing to Mallory was evidence of Western diseases, canned food, and alcohol and marijuana. Bows and arrows had been traded for guns.

Mallory discussed with the shaman and tribal leaders how the tribes could share in profits from any drugs brought to market that were derived from their indigenous plants and knowledge. She was distressed to learn that in exchange for Western material goods, the tribes had entered into a contract with a biotechnology company to allow the company exclusive rights to patent medicinal, chemical, and agricultural products developed from tribal knowledge of indigenous plants. The tribes would not share in the profits from any drugs, chemical products, or genetically modified crop seeds the company developed. Members of the tribes would receive free drugs, insecticides, and herbicides developed from their native plants, relieving them of some of the work of preparing the products themselves, of harvesting plants and preparing them for medicinal and other uses. However, they would have to purchase genetically modified seeds, although they could continue freely to use the unmodified seeds.

When she returned home, Mallory met with a former classmate, Tony, who worked for the biotechnology company that had secured the rights to patent the tribes' plant products. Tony told her that his company was deeply concerned about the destruction of the rainforest and the loss of human habitat, knowledge, and culture. Recognizing that the loss of traditional knowledge meant that potential disease treatments, agricultural germ lines, and applications for industrial products could be lost forever, Tony worked to preserve germ lines of plants used by traditional healers and farmers. For strategic reasons, both for the company and for the country, he believed it was unwise to rely on plant sources from other countries, particularly those in fragile or endangered environments. Tony believed in particular that the scientists who searched to discover new drugs to treat emerging diseases, as well as diseases that have plagued people throughout human history, were in a desperate race against time and the loss of irreplaceable biological resources.

"Mallory, we're on the same side," Tony told her. "I have tremendous respect for you and your work and values, but I worry that you are tilting at windmills. The biotechnology companies are the least of the problems indigenous people face. Timber, mining, ranching, and expanding agricultural tracts are much bigger threats to the survival of the rainforest and the people who live there. We don't destroy native cultures and habitats: we would like nothing better than to preserve them."

"Tony, I don't know how your company justifies exploiting the tribes' knowledge without sharing the benefits with them. I realize that you gave them some goods in exchange for their knowledge and plant materials, but the goods are mere trinkets compared with the potential profits you stand to make," Mallory replied. "The tribes' contributions are invaluable. There are more than 350,000 plant species in the rainforest. Without the benefit of the tribes' knowledge, you'd have no idea which of the thousands of species in their region might be useful, or what to use them for!"

"Only a minuscule percentage of compounds turn out to be useful in developing new products, and even when an effective new compound is discovered, it takes years to bring a new product to market," Tony explained. "Research and testing are extremely costly, difficult, and time-consuming. As much as the company would like to preserve habitat and cultural infrastructure, it is not a social service agency and it simply cannot afford to invest heavily where the likelihood of profit is minimal. The tribes do not have the knowledge or resources to synthesize drugs and bring them to market, or quickly develop new genetic varieties of agricultural products, or create derivatives from plants that can replace environmentally damaging petroleum products. There is a real danger that the knowledge and the biological sources of that knowledge will be lost forever. We didn't steal anything: we traded the potential for useful knowledge in the future for material goods and conveniences that the tribes want today. We don't know if we'll even discover any useful products, let alone make a profit."

"Tony, when was the last time you visited the tribes? Do you realize the young people prefer Western clothes and music, and are losing their cultural identity along with their traditional knowledge?" asked Mallory.

"Mallory, maybe you've romanticized traditional values to some extent. Why should it bother you if the kids prefer jeans to breechcloths, or dancing to the radio to dancing to tribal chants? They have options and these are choices they've made, just as you've made choices about your options. Bottom line, Mallory: if destruction of the rainforest and the indigenous way of life is inevitable, we want to make sure that knowledge isn't destroyed as well."

From a moral point of view, is Tony's company obligated to share profits from sales of products, derived from indigenous plants and knowledge, with the tribes that provided knowledge of the plants and their uses?

Perspective One

Tony's company is under no obligation to share profits from sales of products derived from indigenous plants and knowledge with the tribes that provided knowledge of the plants and their uses. Indigenous plants are in danger of extinction because of numerous threats to the ecosystem, a situation in which a majority of biotechnology companies played no part.

The preservation of endangered plant germplasm and compounds derived from rainforest plants, as well as the knowledge of their applications and uses, provide a benefit to humanity. The costs of research are borne by companies such as Tony's, with no guarantee that their enormous investment will ever return a profit. The quest for the discovery of new drugs and nutritionally enhanced food products is an honorable undertaking that serves the ethical principle of utility by contributing to improved health and nutrition for the global community. The overall welfare of the billions of people who inhabit the earth is of greater consequence and moral significance than maximized profit-sharing for the tribes whose knowledge provided a shortcut to the discovery of useful products.

The tribes made a decision to exchange their knowledge, which does not diminish by being shared, in exchange for material goods they desired. They exercised autonomy in agreeing to the terms of their contract with the biotechnology company.

The tribes also exercised their rights to determine the use of their property in their agreement with the biotechnology company. The knowledge developed by tribal members over the centuries is their intellectual property: the tribes have the right to share it, sell it, barter it, or refuse to reveal it. Tony's company did not compromise the tribes' property rights through their agreement.

The company has ethical obligations to its shareholders to generate a return on their investments and run the company in a financially sound manner. The company is obligated neither to disclose nor to agree to terms that are maximally beneficial to the tribes, but has a professional obligation to negotiate terms that are in its own best interests and those of its investors.

The moral concepts of utility, autonomy, property rights, and the virtue of professional (business) integrity support the position of Tony's company to refrain from sharing with the tribes profits derived from products developed from their traditional knowledge.

Perspective Two

Tony's company is morally obligated to share profits from sales of products, derived from indigenous plants and knowledge, with those who provided access to the plants and knowledge of their uses. This knowledge has been developed by the tribes over hundreds – perhaps thousands – of years, and is part of the tribes' cultural and economic heritage. Monopolizing this knowledge for commercial gain, without compensating the tribes, is little more than robbery.

If the rainforests and the unique biomaterials they hold are destroyed, the sources for potential drugs and other products derived from this ecosystem will also be destroyed. The consequences of failing to develop a trusting relationship between Tony's company and the tribes could irreparably damage future cooperation. Even though the tribes have agreed to exchange knowledge for material goods, if they come to believe they have been exploited, they are unlikely to be willing to continue to share their knowledge, and it may be lost forever. Causing the loss of future access to plants from which even more useful drugs and food stuffs could be developed is maleficent and a failure to maximize utility, possibilities the company certainly should have considered.

The principle of autonomy is predicated on self-determination, truth-telling, and informed consent. It would be hard to imagine that the representatives of Tony's company who negotiated the exchange with the tribes fully disclosed the potential profits that could be earned from the successful introduction of new drugs. More likely, they convinced tribal members that they should relinquish any claim to share in the profits so the company would receive all the benefits (if, indeed, they mentioned the possibility of profit-sharing at all). It might be safe to assume that the tribes were given only selective information that led them to make the decision of greatest benefit to the company. Although the company's representatives might have assumed that the indigenous peoples would never learn of this deception, the tribe's enthusiasm for modern electronics suggests that, sooner or later, they will acquire computers, television sets, and other means of communication that will put them even more extensively in touch with the outside world. When this happens, they will likely learn they have been deceived.

The knowledge the tribes shared with Tony's company is their cultural and economic heritage, a heritage essential to sustaining their way of living. Depriving them of a share in the economic benefits derived from their traditional intellectual property deprives them of their essential right to benefit from the fruits of their labor. It disregards the justifiable claim of the tribes to protect their cultural and economic interests.

Failure to share profits with the tribes demonstrates the vices of dishonesty, untrustworthiness and manipulation. It is conceivable that the vice of greed played a part in the negotiations as well.

International trademark and intellectual property law is greatly skewed in favor of developed countries in Europe, the United States, and Japan. International patent law allows economic exploitation of indigenous knowledge without compensation by using values, conditions of ownership, and legal statutes and processes that are unfamiliar and (at least to date) largely inaccessible to the creators and keepers of traditional knowledge. Intellectual property rules are made and enforced by entities with power and wealth, and imposed on those with negligible bargaining power (Hansen and Van Fleet 2003: 4–5). The moral principle of justice, specifically the fairness of earned benefits, is compromised by the company's decision not to share profits.

Therefore, the moral principles of consequences, autonomy, rights, virtue, and justice require Tony's company to share profits with the tribes.

Perspective Three

The dilemma before us exemplifies a conflict between the moral appeal to utility and the moral appeal to justice (understood as fair consideration). Our position is that justice is the stronger appeal; thus, Tony's company is morally obligated to share profits from sales of products derived from indigenous plants and knowledge with the tribes that provided knowledge of the plants and their uses. Moreover, his company and other pharmaceutical companies that seek drug candidates based on the intellectual and biological resources of indigenous peoples are morally obligated to contribute to efforts to conserve the traditional cultures and knowledge of those whose resources the seek to commercialize.

Participants at the 2006 United Nations Convention on Biological Diversity in Spain suggested that until agreement can be reached on benefit-sharing, there should be a moratorium on foreign bioprospecting (Ngandwe 2006). Dr Doel

Soejarto, a researcher from the University of Illinois at Chicago, collected specimens from a tree in Borneo, which he discovered, in laboratory testing, to be
effective against the HIV virus. When Dr Soejarto returned to Borneo to collect
additional samples, no remaining trees could be found (Plotkin 1993: 9).

Some chemical components change as the plant dies, so significant amounts
(about two pounds) of plant material are necessary for chemical analysis. Few
pharmaceutical companies are as interested in conserving plant resources as they
are in extracting compounds with commercial application. They appear to be little
concerned if the species becomes extinct, as long as the active therapeutic agent
is known and can be synthesized (ibid.: 9–11). The *Prunus africana* tree grew
in Cameroon, where its bark had been used for medicine for centuries. After a
European company learned it was useful in treating prostate swelling, it applied
for a patent. In one year's time, in 1985, 424 tons of bark were harvested from
the trees, stripping them bare. The trees died, and Cameroon lost one of its
important cultural and economic resources (Bequette 1997: 44).

What can be done to prevent similar losses? How can conservation and access
to endangered biological resources be ensured, while guaranteeing equitable benefits
for the traditional communities who developed and preserved the knowledge of
their healing powers?

The issue is clearly larger than the question of Tony's company compensating
the members of one tribe for their contributions to developing commercial products. Nonetheless, let's examine what moral justification supports the choice of
Tony's company not to share profits with the tribes that provided plant samples
and instructions on their medicinal uses, and what moral justification supports
Mallory's contention that Tony's company is morally obligated to share profits
with the tribes. Which perspective carries greater moral authority?

Step 1: Information-gathering

Implications

- How serious is the threat of the loss of biodiversity?
- What are the consequences of proprietary ownership of plant germplasm?
- If Tony's company does not share profits with the tribes, are they fueling
  an international system of exploitation of indigenous peoples by powerful
  corporations and nations, or are they conserving threatened biological resources within a system that awards intellectual property rights to encourage
  innovation?
- If Tony's company shares profits with the tribes, will that encourage other
  tribes to withhold knowledge that has tremendous potential beneficial to benefit
  humanity – even as that knowledge is threatened with extinction – to ensure
  that they share in financial benefits?
- If Tony's company does not share profits with the tribes, will they be
  likely to withhold knowledge in the future, or knowingly give inaccurate
  information?

- Do other tribes who have also used these plants for centuries have any right to benefit, or is excluding them because of geographic luck of the draw justifiable?
- Does the alarming rate of rainforest destruction and the resultant extinction of plant species justify, or even demand, saving germplasm by whatever means possible?
- Do we miss drugs that haven't been discovered? Or put another way, are we harmed by potential loss of what we never had?

History

- Is the source of disputed value indigenous knowledge or laboratory innovation?
- Have biological materials traditionally been shared among nations as the heritage of humankind, or have they been claimed by individuals?

Legal/policy information

- What is the purpose of intellectual property protection?
- How does international patent law recognize and reward indigenous knowledge?
- What laws govern international intellectual property rights?

Economic considerations

- What are the costs associated with bringing a new drug to market?
- How important are products derived from indigenous germplasm to the economic development of a country?
- How are financial benefits from profitable drugs developed from indigenous knowledge now shared?

Cultural and psychological information

- What is indigenous (or traditional) knowledge? What is its role in the welfare of the populations who possess it?
- What are the likely consequences of failing to protect indigenous knowledge?

Step 2: Creative problem-solving

A creative resolution to the moral tension between utility and justice must ensure the pharmaceutical benefits of continued drug development in the fight against disease and, at the same time, guarantee just treatment of indigenous peoples. The goal of enhancing indigenous genetic resources should be to provide food and medicine for the world, and to do so in a just and equitable way that rewards both indigenous communities for conserving and developing bioresources and knowledge of their use, and researchers for developing innovative and useful products. Can these interests, often seen to be competing, be mutually served by a creative solution? If not, our original moral dilemma persists.

Step 3: Listing pros and cons

Options	Pros	Cons
Biotechnology companies do not share profits.	1. Company preserves bioresources from extinction (C-B, C-U) 2. Company recovers the cost of drug discovery, so stays in business (C-U, V-I) 3. Company returns dividends to investors (V-I, trust)	4. Deprive tribes of economic benefits (C-NM, C-U) 5. Current laws to stop plunder limit access, impede discovery (C-NM, C-U) 6. Knowledge becomes extinct (C-NM, C-U) 7. Tribes manipulated when full disclosure withheld (A) 8. Monopoly deprives tribes of use and benefits of their own resources (R-property) 9. Company acts with greed, insensitivity, manipulation, ingratitude, untrustworthiness (V, C-U) 10. Tribes, tribal knowledge not respected, treated as means to end (RFP, J-F)
Biotechnology companies do share profits.	11. Increases future collaboration, likelihood of more new drug discoveries (C-B, C-U) 12. Company acts with good faith, integrity, generosity, honesty, trustworthiness (V) 13. Company acknowledges value of tribal culture and traditional wisdom (RFP, J-E, J-F)	14. Increases costs of new drug discovery (C-NM, C-U) 15. May encourage other tribes to withhold knowledge (C-U) 16. Establishing proper ownership of traditional knowledge may be impossible (A, R) 17. Diminishes profits (V-I)

Step 4: Analysis

Factual assumptions

- Indigenous peoples, their knowledge and language, and their richly biodiverse habitats are threatened with extinction.
- Ways of knowing and interacting with the natural world vary among cultures.
- Developing countries of the southern hemisphere are home to most of the world's biodiversity (Fecteau 2001: 72).

- Removing small samples of endangered plants causes negligible ecological harm, and is a way to save from extinction germplasm that has the potential to benefit humanity through medical or agricultural products.
- Intellectual property claims based on indigenous knowledge are not afforded the same legal protection as patentable knowledge as defined by Western concepts.
- Opponents of profit sharing from drug discovery insist that the innovative and useful value of medicinal plants is added not by pointing out a plant that is used for a specific medicinal purpose, but through laboratory analysis and development of novel drugs. Supporters of profit-sharing claim that the innovative and Herculean effort of drug discovery occurs over millennia as knowledge of medicinal uses of plants is acquired and refined. Does evidence support either perspective?
- Compared with the indigenous tribes whose knowledge they commercialize, biotechnology companies have abundant financial resources.

Value assumptions

- Multiple types of knowledge should have legitimacy and validity as useful and innovative.
- Each country should have the right to control its biological resources.
- We should conserve as much of the world's biodiversity as possible for future generations.
- Biotechnology companies act immorally by omission if they fail to use some of their resources to help the tribes maintain their way of life, even if the companies do not realize a profit on the bioresources they take from them, and even though the companies may not be directly responsible for loss of sustainable habitat.
- Pharmaceutical corporations bear some responsibility for the survival of the way of life of the indigenous peoples whose biological resources they seek.
- A just international law that governs intellectual property rights should be universally accepted.

Step 5: Justification

Tony's company should share benefits with the tribes from which they received biological materials and knowledge of their medicinal uses.

Those who argue that indigenous peoples should be compensated for their knowledge appeal to four moral failings of current practices:

1 Inequity and unfairness in failing to share financial benefits (Reasons ##4, 8, 9).
2 Disregard of the right of communities to control and use the intellectual property rights of their native resources, including germplasm (Reasons ##7, 8)
3 Failure to respect cultural values regarding plants considered sacred (Reasons ##9, 10, 13).

4   Denial that traditional uses of plants constitute prior art or existing know-
    ledge if their use has not been documented in peer-reviewed journals
    (Reasons ##8, 13, 10). (Kohls 2007: 111–12)

Indigenous (traditional) knowledge is collective intelligence about local animal and plant resources, traditionally shared by a community, and transmitted
through specific – often sacred or secret – processes or practitioners. It includes
both intangible and tangible repositories of knowledge, practices, technologies,
and belief systems concerning well-being and the natural world. Because cultural
identity and survival depend on traditional knowledge, many indigenous societies
consider traditional knowledge to be communal wealth. The concept of individual ownership of this knowledge for personal economic benefit is incompatible with cultural values of many traditional communities (Hansen and Van Fleet
2003: 3–4).

More than 400,000 seed plant species, and thousands more non-seed species,
such as mosses and ferns, exist in the world (Govaerts 2001: 1085). Over one
and three quarter million biological species have been scientifically catalogued
(Ahmed 2003: 23). Only 1–10 percent (somewhere between 3 and 100 million) of the half-billion plant and animal species estimated to have existed during the last 600 million years still survive. Loss of species is a natural part of the
Earth's evolution, but the current estimated rate of up to 1,000 species lost each
year far exceeds the natural process of extinction. It is estimated that during the
past three decades tens of thousands of species have disappeared. If this rate is
unchecked, more than 25 percent of the Earth's extant species will disappear by
the middle of this century. This is a conservative estimate, however, as at least
50 percent of the earth's biological species exist in the equatorial rainforests where
the rate of loss is accelerating. The rainforests are threatened by overpopulation
by settlers usurping indigenous land (the world's population more than doubled
between 1950 and 2000, from 2.5 billion to 6 billion people); encroaching farms,
plantations, and cattle ranches; ecosystem degradation as the result of human
intervention due to water diversion, poor land management, logging, human-
caused fires, and deforestation for fuel or logging; invasive plant species, pests,
and pathogens; unsustainable use of natural resources, principally by wealthy nations;
climate change; pollution and chemical contamination of the environment by
toxic pesticides, insecticides, herbicides, and industrial waste. At the current rate
of loss, the world's equatorial rainforests may disappear by the end of the century (Ahmed 2003: 23, 64, 68, 75).

Along with biodiversity, traditional knowledge and the material and spiritual
way of life, indeed survival itself, for the 150 million indigenous people who live
in the tropical rainforests are threatened (Ahmed 2003: 75). The importance of
the loss of knowledge of bioresources may be subtler to discern, as its effect
exists only as a nullity. Nonetheless, the permanent and irretrievable privation of
knowledge of potential medical treatments and agricultural cultivators poses a
significant harm to humanity.

Thinking of a particular example may help to illustrate what is at risk with the
loss of rainforest habitat. Until Alexander Fleming's discovery of penicillin in

1928, people frequently died of infection from simple cuts and diseases that we now have little fear of or even seriously regard. Although new antibiotics have been discovered in the past several decades, their chemical structures are fairly similar to each other. Microbial pathogens are notoriously adept at mutating. They have become increasingly resistant to the arsenal of known antibiotics, whose chemical makeup has remained a stable target for their counteraction (Rosamond and Allsop 2000: 1973). Many common antibiotics were developed from rainforest products (Ahmed 2003: 71). Imagine scraped knees and paper cuts again becoming life-threatening events because of the potential therapeutic agents lost with the depletion of biodiversity.

Or consider another example: cinchona. Malaria is the world's most virulent disease in terms of the number of victims it has claimed. For centuries, South American natives have used the bark of the cinchona tree to cure malaria. Cinchona contains the alkaloid quinine, the agent that destroys the malaria parasite. Synthetic quinine has been made for nearly half a century, but while strains of the malaria parasite have developed resistance to the synthetic drug, the naturally occurring quinine retains its efficacy. A single rainforest species is one of the few treatments against the world's deadliest disease (Plotkin 1993: 6–7).

Some cultures use art or handicrafts, such as woven rugs or baskets to preserve and transmit traditional knowledge. When the collection, preparation, and administration of healing agents are intricately interwoven with a ceremonial process, the transmission of ideas may take the form of ritual developed over centuries. Just as ritual developed slowly over millennia, domestication of plants occurred over eras. Until recently, it was commonly believed that the domestication of plants happened rather quickly in the grand scheme of human life on Earth: over a period of 200 years or less. New data reported in *Science* magazine indicate that the process of carefully identifying and cultivating useful plants, with deliberate human selection for specific traits, actually occurred over thousands of years (Balter 2007: 1830–1). Traditional healers have honed their knowledge over centuries to understand whether to use the root, stem, spore, bark, seed, fruit, leaves, or flowers; when to harvest the plant; and how to prepare it (UNEP 2001). It takes many generations to understand the healing properties of a flower that blooms only a few days a year (Plotkin 1993: 280–281). Without the benefit of traditional knowledge, trial and error experimentation on the worlds' hundreds of thousands of plant species could take another few thousand years (ibid.: 7–9).

What would happen if a few wealthy nations and their powerful companies controlled the world's germplasm? Consider this question in the context of the history of food. Most centers of agricultural origin, most botanical genetic diversity, and most varieties of food are indigenous to developing tropical and subtropical regions of the world (Gepts 2004: 1298–300). Harvard ethnobotanist, Mark Plotkin, points out that international and intercontinental exchange of agricultural plant varieties has been responsible for people in the United States being able to enjoy eating more than the eight agricultural products indigenous to the US: four types of berries, three types of nuts, and the Jerusalem artichoke (1993: 17). What would life be like without potatoes? They are nutritious, tasty, inexpensive, easily stored, and adaptable to many environments and altitudes. According to archaeologist Winifred Creamer, several thousand varieties of potatoes have been developed from plants indigenous to the South American Andes region, making the potato a worldwide food staple (W. Creamer, personal communication 2007). Without free-flowing international trade in agricultural and medicinal plant products, countries could be extorted for food and medicine.

Natural heritage, while under the dominion of the state in which it exists, is the common heritage of humanity, and so obligates all countries to assist in its protection. The ability of poorer nations to protect their natural heritage is compromised by lack of financial, scientific, and technological resources. As of July 2007, 186 countries were signatories to the Convention Concerning the Protection of the World Cultural and Natural Heritage, including the United States, Japan, and almost all European countries (UNESCO 1972: Introduction, Articles 4, 6). With rare exception, until the 1970s biological materials were considered to be the common heritage of humankind, and their ownership, use, and development a non-exclusive right (Gepts 2004: 1295). In the past four decades, however, proprietary ownership has been granted for thousands of naturally occurring biological products. The patenting of biological materials dramatically increased following the 1980 United States Supreme Court decision that allowed patenting of living biological organisms (*Diamond v. Chakrobarty* 1980: 303). Despite the provisions of the UNESCO Convention, indigenous peoples are harmed by the inequities in their position when forced to negotiate their heritage with powerful organizations with dissimilar – often diametrically opposing – values, and legal, social, and economic systems, of which they have limited, if any, knowledge.

Intellectual property rights are protected to encourage and reward the creation of knowledge, and ensure that the creators of knowledge and its useful products benefit from their work (Reasons ##2, 3). A patent gives exclusive control to its holder over the use, development, production, sale, and financial gain of an invention or innovation. A patent is granted based on three criteria: the innovation or invention must be novel, that is, not based on "prior art" or an existing knowledge base; it must be non-obvious, that is, it must involve some degree of enhancement not obvious to others familiar with the product or process; and it must demonstrate industrial application, that is, commercial value (Hansen and Van Fleet 2003: 9).

Current international patenting practice legalizes the monopolization of indigenous genetic resources by technologically advanced nations and organizations, with little or no compensation to countries where the plants were grown, or to individuals or communities that developed the knowledge of the plants and their uses (Reason #4) (Kohls 2007: 109). Technologically advanced countries and corporations hold 99 percent of all patents awarded (Gonzalez-Arnal 2004: 139). The United States Patent and Trademark Office (USPTO) recognizes that traditional knowledge exists. Unlike traditional knowledge or invention known to have been used within the United States, however, the USPTO does not accept foreign traditional knowledge or its products as intellectual property – even when they meet the criterion of demonstrating prior art, novelty, or usefulness – if they have not been previously "patented or described in a printed publication" (35 USC §102e 1972/2002). This interpretation of law codifies and imposes on other cultures a Western value that acknowledges discovery, regardless of how sophisticated and refined, as legitimate only after it has been published. This condescension is contrary to the values of many cultures that honor knowledge as a communal heritage that is to be shared and not monopolized for profit, or that perceive traditional knowledge as a sacred and dangerous power that must therefore be limited to initiated practitioners (Gonzalez-Arnal 2004: 148; Fecteau 2001: 70). Indigenous knowledge holders are treated as a mere means to others' ends when the value of traditional knowledge and use is not extended patent protection, and property rights to those resources are granted to outsiders without requisite benefit-sharing (Reasons ##4, 10). This economic and cultural imperialism withholds legitimate benefits from traditional societies, while it imposes pecuniary and legal burdens on them, with neither their knowledge nor the likelihood of their (autonomous) consent.

Intellectual property rights as legally defined in terms of Western values and which, some charge, promote economic exploitation of indigenous knowledge, are gaining global traction as the predominant rule of law. Prevailing legal practice gives primacy to individual rather than communal property rights, creates prohibitive financial and logistical barriers to register intellectual property claims and defend challenges to them for those with limited financial resources, and awards intellectual property rights based on publication or patents that disregard prior creation and oral transmission of traditional knowledge. Defending or challenging a claim to intellectual property rights is cost-prohibitive to indigenous communities, particularly in developing countries, and is adjudicated in a legal system that is unfamiliar in terms of both processes and values. Developing countries are being pressured to revise their laws to conform to these standards, but fear even greater exploitation if they do so, as current international law does not recognize traditional use as prior knowledge (Hansen and Van Fleet 2003: 4–5). These cultures are truly on the horns of a dilemma: if they comply with international law, they risk losing control of their biological resources; if they ignore international law, they risk being denied access to technology to develop their resources and markets to sell their products. The current system of international patent law allows corporations and individuals from developed countries (in particular Europe, Japan, and the United States) to appropriate indigenous knowledge, and the financial benefits derived from it, without recognizing or compensating its creators. Patent-holders may bring legal action against developing countries that try to commercialize their own indigenous biological resources, if commercialization infringes on patent rights awarded to foreign patent-holders (Chalmers 2004: 3). International patent law has been imposed on developing countries without their consent or the participation of their citizens or leaders in the decision-making process (Gonzales-Arnal 2004: 147).

The two most important international agreements on protection of intellectual property rights are the 1992 Convention on Biological Diversity, and the

Trade-Related Aspects of Intellectual Property Rights – or TRIPS (Makinde 2004: 122). The Convention on Biological Diversity is an agreement among nations to protect the world's biodiversity and genetic resources, promote sustainable use of bioresources, and share equitably in their financial and other benefits. Currently, 189 countries are partners to the Convention on Biological Diversity; noticeably missing is the United States (UNCBD 1992). In 2002, at the Sixth Conference of the Parties to the Convention on Biological Diversity held at The Hague (The Netherlands), US Deputy Assistant Secretary of State Jeffry Burnam addressed the assembly, stating that although the US believed the Convention to be important for discussions on biodiversity, it had not ratified its support (US Department of State 2002).

Why would the United States hesitate to be a party to the Convention? A report prepared for Congress in May 1995 by the Congressional Research Service listed several issues of concern for the United States: the government of each partner country has the right to determine who will have access to that country's germplasm; access to another country's genetic material requires prior informed consent; and results of research, and benefits from commercialization of indigenous genetic materials, are to be shared equitably with the country of origin (Fletcher 1995). US policy, in contrast, suggests that the chance geographic distribution of germplasm does not bestow upon a country the right to withhold its potential benefits from the rest of the world.

The World Trade Organization (WTO) claims that the value of pharmaceuticals comes not from the plants from which they were derived, but from the innovative research that transforms the low-technology plant into a high-technology medicine. Those who create such products have the right to prevent others from using their products or processes (WTO 1994a).

TRIPS is a WTO agreement that is automatically binding on all WTO member states (Kohls 2007: 135). Article 27.3(b) of the TRIPS agreement mandates that innovations in all fields of technology be patented, including innovations derived from micro-organisms or through biogenetic processes. In other words, TRIPS *requires* that pharmaceutical products be patented (Makinde 2004: 122; Kohls 2007: 132; Nicol 2004: 156).

Mandating that developing countries patent their innovations is both inequitable and unrealistic (Reason #13). It is disrespectful of indigenous value systems and the persons who hold them; most developing nations can afford neither to file patent applications nor challenge patent infringement. Failure to challenge patent infringement is a serious matter, as it may result in the loss of the patent. Many indigenous peoples do not consider plant traits that have been developed and processes that have been handed down for thousands of years – and have therefore been in the public domain for centuries – to be novel. Moreover, most would be unlikely to be able to "prove ownership" or to articulate who, exactly, discovered the knowledge or traits that patents protect (Reason #16). From their perspective, international patent law that allows ownership of these resources to be awarded to foreigners because the outsiders' ignorance and inexperience led them to believe the innovations to be novel and original is ludicrous. Further, Western countries hold a bias against publishing and patenting knowledge that has not been distilled within the limitations of the scientific method, disrespecting traditional beliefs and different traditions about the transmission and sharing of knowledge. Even scientists in countries with limited resources do not have the means to access scholarly publications (Asfaw et al. 2007: 1850). The requirement to publish unfairly disadvantages those whose limited financial resources – and different traditions of sharing knowledge – do not allow either print or electronic access. Consequently, even when indigenous knowledge has been written down, it is considered inferior and not acceptable for intellectual property protection, unless published in a peer-reviewed journal or other scholarly format. It is little wonder that many developing countries equate patenting with plundering (Gonzalez-Arnal 2004: 140, 142).

The TRIPS document states that the accord was necessary because inconsistent global standards and principles regarding intellectual property rights created international tensions (WTO 1994b). However, others charge that TRIPS itself has increased tensions. Developing countries strongly oppose the regulations, which devalue traditional knowledge and do little to stop developed countries from seizing biological samples from bio-rich countries and patenting them (Fecteau 2001: 69–71). Many participants in the 2001 WTO meeting in Doha (Qatar) raised concerns that TRIPS was a tool of developed countries to protect the interests of biotechnology corporations – in particular (Reason #17), to prevent countries from commercializing their own indigenous genetic resources in violation of patent rights already awarded to wealthy Western corporations (Reasons ##4, 8, 17). Advocates of profit-sharing charge that while TRIPS protects these corporations' monopoly over germplasm, it imposes Western values on indigenous cultures and offers little reciprocal protection to them from biopiracy (Nicol 2004: 167).

In response to aggressive patenting by Western corporations, Brazil and other countries have enacted restrictive laws to prevent the removal of indigenous plants and the sale of traditional knowledge without tribal consent (Reason #15). Brazil's bio-piracy laws also prohibit research to exploit traditional knowledge for commercial purposes. Unfortunately, the laws also curtail the research of Brazilian scientists, which is particularly harmful as so much of the country's biodiversity is rapidly being destroyed (Reason #5) (Kohls 2007: 123–4). Proprietary imperialism has resulted in the subversion of utility. Even when developing countries enact laws to protect their resources from external exploitation, powerful foreign countries and corporations, intent on monopolizing the commercial value of indigenous resources, ignore the laws countries have enacted to require benefit-sharing and protect their bioresources (McGown 2006: i). In the face of such struggles, tribes may be reluctant to share any information and plants may become extinct before their characteristics or powers are understood (Reason #6).

Although Europe has been criticized, along with the United States, for its imposition of Western legal and cultural values in the matter of commercialization of indigenous resources, at least one significant difference exists between patent laws of the United States and those of the European Patent Office (EPO). The EPO recognizes unwritten knowledge and practice as prior art, demonstrating respect for traditional knowledge and recognition of its potential commercial value, while the United States does not (Kohls 2007: 137). In theory, this means that the EPO is less likely to grant patents on traditional knowledge to non-indigenous applicants, although it doesn't always seem to work that way in practice. The world's ten largest pharmaceutical giants are located in four European countries and the United States (Gepts 2004: 1299–300).

Differences in perception of ownership of knowledge are not limited to developing countries in the southern hemisphere. For example, China has come under heavy criticism for failing to enforce and protect international patent law. In China's traditional value system, knowledge is shared as a communal resource and cannot be owned. Enforcing rights to intellectual property makes no sense in the context of Chinese culture (Gonzalez-Arnal 2004: 145).

Acquiring indigenous biological materials and traditional knowledge can be dangerous and difficult. Procuring specimens from the jungle canopy hundreds of feet in the air is treacherous work (Fadiman 1987: 15). Commercial medicines have been derived from only about 100 of 400,000 known plant species (Plotkin 1993: 7). Yet, between one-quarter and one-third of all medicines are derived from botanical products (Gepts 2004: 1299).

Global sales of plant-based drug products exceed $40 billion a year (Ahmed 2003: 71). Developing a single new drug takes almost a decade, however and carries a price tag exceeding $800 million. Of new drugs, 90 percent fail in safety testing, and of the 10 percent that are successfully brought to market, only 30 percent are profitable (Kohls 2007: 112, 124; Nicol 2004: 155). Pharmaceutical researchers defend their reluctance to share profits because of the enormous cost of research that offers no guarantee of a marketable product (Reasons ##2, 3).

Patentable knowledge is significantly lucrative enough that it can change the economic status of a country. Many developing countries are rich in patentable bioresources, backed by centuries of knowledge of their use. Yet only 1 percent of the world's patents go to developing countries (Gonzalez-Arnal 2004: 139). Rarely have patent holders of blockbuster drugs developed from indigenous knowledge and bioresources shared any profits with the countries that provided the plant materials and information on their uses. Pharmaceutical corporations argue that the tribes do benefit from access to new drugs. However, others disagree, claiming that monopolies on drug products and the high cost of proprietary drugs restrict availability and access in developing countries (Ngandwe 2006). Let's look at some examples of alleged expropriation of indigenous knowledge.

1   Arcabose, a drug for the treatment of diabetes, earns about $380 million a year in profits. Bayer, the pharmaceutical corporation that developed the drug, does not share any profits with Kenya, although the bacterium from which the drug was developed came from Kenyan waters (Dalton 2006: 569).
2   For centuries, Ethiopians have used *Hagenia abyssinica* to treat cancer. In 2004, disregarding protests from Ethiopia, the United States Patent and Trademarks Office awarded a patent for *Hagenia abyssinica* as a cancer treatment

to a Tennessee researcher, despite the fact that the proposed uses were neither specific nor novel (Kohls 2007: 114).

3   Phytopharm, a pharmaceutical company located in the Untied Kingdom, stated in its patent application that it was requesting a patent for the Libyan *Artemisia judaica* plant, used by traditional healers and doctors in Libya to treat diabetes. Despite its prior acknowledged use for the same purpose, a patent was granted to Phytopharm (McGown 2006: 2).

4   In 1986 Lauren Miller was granted a patent for his proposal to use the ayahuasca vine, which he obtained from a domestic garden in an Amazonian village, to develop cancer and psychotherapeutic treatments. Ayahuasca has been used in the Amazon region as a medicine and in religious ceremonies for centuries. The patent was annulled in 1999, after it was determined to be neither new nor distinct. It was noted in a five-year legal appeal by the Coordinating Body of Indigenous Organizations of the Amazon Basin that the Chicago Field Museum of Natural History included samples of the plant in its herbarium and the plant had been illustrated and described in scientific literature that predated Miller's application. Although the patent was reinstated barely a year later when two botanists testified that Miller's specimen was different, the patent expired soon after. Miller never discovered a novel use for his patented plant (Kohls 2007: 117–18; Fecteau 2001: 69, 86).

5   The rosy periwinkle's use by native healers in Madagascar piqued the interest of pharmaceutical companies. Researchers discovered more than 70 alkaloids contained in the plant, 6 of which proved effective against cancerous tumors. Although sales of just two drugs derived from the rosy periwinkle exceed $100 million annually, not a penny was returned to Madagascar (Plotkin 1993: 15–16).

6   Costa Rica had a seemingly equitable arrangement with foreign bioprospectors when it established the National Biodiversity Institute (INBio) in 1989. INBio combined traditional values, conservation, and modern technology, and was seen as a model for other countries that hoped simultaneously to conserve and profit from their biological resources. INBio enlisted excellent and motivated native scientists, attracted generous grant support, and experienced small-scale successes. Despite these advantages, no products of significance were developed.

   What happened? Costa Rica, although rich in natural resources and with a well-educated and motivated population, has limited financial resources. A requirement imposed by foreign grant-funding institutions was that any promising biological materials would be sent to INBio's foreign corporate and university partners for further research. This seemed to be a reasonable provision, as Costa Rica's technology resources were limited and more sophisticate studies could be conducted elsewhere. However, once compounds left Costa Rica, the partners veiled their work in proprietary secrecy. The fate of more than 200 compounds sent out of the country is unknown. Indeed, it is not known if the drug companies even pursued any research on the compounds (Reason #7). For Costa Rica, the result was minuscule return on two

decades of work, and the loss of potentially promising bioresources and products (Dalton 2006: 467–9).

Patented drugs are generally too expensive to be accessible to developing
countries, even when they were developed from their own biological resources.
The catastrophic destruction of HIV/AIDS in sub-Saharan Africa is exacerbated
by the unavailability of appropriate drugs: the cost of the least expensive anti-
retroviral is approximately 10 times the average annual per person expenditure
on healthcare. The world's poorest countries simply do not have the resources
either to make or purchase pharmaceuticals (Nicol 2004: 156, 158). The countries in most desperate need of financial resources are those most likely to have
their biological resources – one of their most significant means of economic
development – expropriated and commercialized by corporations of wealthier
countries (Reason #4).

Despite the richness of ancient wisdom in understanding the natural world
and its plant and animal life, indigenous knowledge is rarely recognized as valid
intellectual labor for protection of intellectual property rights. The patent law
requirement to demonstrate novelty in drug development is frequently interpreted
in practice to mean documentation of a purportedly therapeutic biochemical compound at the molecular level that shows its unexpected (that is, non-obvious)
properties. Few indigenous communities have either the necessity or the means
to describe the biochemical structure of plant products at the molecular level.
Thousands of years of observation and trial and error experimentation have developed shamans' skill in identifying the specific parts of particular plants needed
to treat disease, and the processes to create medicine from the components.
Laboratory analysis is superfluous for their needs, as effective treatments are readily available to them. Nor do most traditional communities have the resources
to conduct laboratory experiments that would satisfy either the publishers of peer-
reviewed publications or patent offices. Because traditional medicines are not
described on a molecular level through laboratory analysis, they are considered
obvious and not patentable. Indigenous peoples are prevented from claiming the
patent rights on their innovations: patents are awarded to foreign bioprospectors who create molecular models of plants' chemical compounds (Reason #4)
(Fecteau 2001: 76).

Not only is traditional wisdom dismissed as unworthy of proprietary protection, but indigenous tribes are under pressure to transform their way of knowing into one that is compatible with international standards for intellectual property
– specifically, to reorganize their communities as corporations to protect or exploit
their commercially valuable knowledge. In many traditional societies, the concept of private ownership of communal knowledge is incompatible with belief
systems, as is profiting individually from its commercialization. The pressure to
align traditional ways of perceiving and transmitting knowledge with the scientific,
legal, and individualistic approaches used by developed nations places traditional
values intrinsic to cultural identity in direct opposition to corporate values: communal consensus vs. administrative decision-making, equal status vs. hierarchical
power, collaborative vs. competitive knowledge, and shared reciprocal benefits vs.

benefit distribution and accumulation of wealth according to rank. To counteract this loss of cultural identity and values, the Global Coalition for Bio-Cultural Diversity advocates multiple systems of recognizing ownership of intellectual property that accommodate cultural differences (Gonzales-Arnal 2004: 146–8).

Failure to respect and reward traditional knowledge has consequences. If traditional practitioners feel exploited or forced under threat to reveal their knowledge, they may protect their formulations by providing inaccurate information, as did Ethiopian shaman when the government required them to submit their knowledge to a national database as a condition for permitting them to continue practicing (Reason #15) (Kohls 2007: 125).

Many native tribes believe that it is sacrilegious to grant patent protection to foreigners to commercialize indigenous plants that, like the ayahuasca vine, are considered sacred. Traditional communities also fear losing control over the plants. According to Maria Jiménez, a journalist with Toronto's *National Post*, both narco-traffickers and representatives of the US government have been discovered harvesting the ayahuasca vine for research. There is particular concern that the plant's careful use for sacred purposes may be exploited and used to develop lucrative and dangerous drugs for recreational users (Jiménez, 2001).

Although traditionally the judicial system has not upheld patents claims that offend morality, this practice has not been extended to denying patents that offend the moral values of indigenous tribes by commercializing their sacred plants and knowledge (Fecteau 2001: 102). This disregard for cultural beliefs and mores that results in inequitable treatment undermines the principle of justice in terms of equal consideration, respect, and fairness (Reason #10).

Indigenous tribes are being exploited for their traditional knowledge, and this exploitation contributes to the disintegration of cultural heritage, social structures, and economic sustainability. Indeed, the exploitation of indigenous tribes' traditional knowledge compromises their very way of life. Yet, the failure to act to preserve and replicate the compounds found in rapidly vanishing species will result in permanent loss of the opportunity ever to do so. There remain sharply divided opinions over who has the right to access and control biological resources, whether sharing benefits with indigenous people in exchange for the use of their resources is required, and, if so, how this can be accomplished.

Despite lack of consensus on the issue of sharing resources with indigenous communities, biotechnology companies are morally obligated to share profits from commercialization of indigenous plants with the tribes who provided resources and knowledge in the successful quest for drug discovery. Moreover, companies in the biotechnology industry are uniquely positioned to advocate for creative solutions to this global problem, and more importantly, to implement them.

Several creative models and solutions that support a more equitable benefit-sharing for the commercialization of indigenous knowledge have been suggested.

1   Together with the South American tribes he worked with, Dr Mark Plotkin developed the Shaman's Apprentice Program, in which Plotkin's notes are translated back into the native language and used to teach younger tribal

members the knowledge of the aging shamans (Plotkin 1993: 18). Word of the program's success spread, reaching the Bribri Indians of Costa Rica, who adopted the program to preserve their own tribal traditions. Using the Shaman's Apprentice Program, the tribe rediscovered their cultural heritage, initiated young shaman apprentices, built a traditional meeting house (the first to be built in a generation), and resurrected the traditional dances. Hearing of the Bribri program, the Guyami Indians of Panama walked over mountains and through jungles to visit the Bribri and decide for themselves if they wanted to return to some of the traditional ways. Following the visit, the Guyami initiated a Shaman's Apprentice Program (ibid.: 18, 288–9). Traditional culture and knowledge were preserved, and the relationships between Dr. Plotkin and tribal shaman led to long and productive collaborations (Reasons ##11, 12, 13).

2   Dr Nigist Asfaw, an Ethiopian chemist, developed gentler methods for extracting essential oils from Ethiopia's traditional medicinal plants. These environmentally sustainable methods took advantage of Ethiopia's abundant sunlight and readily cultivated bioresources. They were sufficiently transferable that the paper Dr Asfaw delivered at a 2004 European Union Green Chemistry conference was adopted for teaching outside Africa. Despite Dr Asfaw's success with innovative use of available resources, Addis Ababa University lacked equipment and training opportunities for young scientists. With international cooperation, Dr Asfaw was able to obtain equipment from the US Environmental Protection Agency, and a research training position at the University of Nottingham (UK) for one of her doctoral students, who is slated to become Ethiopia's first crystallographer. Even this small degree of cooperation provides the means for Ethiopia to control and develop its bioresources, nurture its innovative young scientists, create environmentally sustainable industry, and participate as an international economic partner (Reasons ##11, 13) (Asfaw et al. 2007: 1849–50).

3   Costa Rica has emerged from its initial disappointments with INBio as a stronger negotiator in establishing partnerships. A comprehensive indigenous plant database is being compiled, and the data will be publicly available – even data that are generally considered proprietary, such as responses to pathogens. INBio will continue to work with select drug companies, but under an arrangement that requires further negotiation for the drug company to continue investigating promising compounds if their initial testing suggests viable drug candidates (Reasons ##11, 12, 13) (Dalton 2006: 467–9).

Fecteau and others recommend amending TRIPS to reflect the protections of the Biodiversity Convention: recognizing the prior art of traditional knowledge, allowing communal intellectual property to be protected under international patent law, and prohibiting patent claims that offend the morality and values of traditional knowledge (Reasons ##12, 13) (Fecteau 2001: 102–3).

Those who oppose sharing profits with indigenous communities point to the role that pharmaceutical companies play in preserving rapidly disappearing botanical species. Far from exploiting the inhabitants of the rainforest, they argue, drug companies are one of the few entities engaged in rainforest activities that do not contribute to its destruction, providing instead one of the few opportunities for germplasm protection. Without their efforts, germplasm of potential drug candidates and their potential to benefit all humanity would be lost forever (Reason #1).

While all this may be true, opponents of profit-sharing should consider that some countries, Brazil for example, that have been denied a share of the profits from products based on their biological resources, have elected to block legal access to these resources entirely (Reason #13). Thus, while it cannot be guaranteed that results or profits will be significant if the profits are shared or the communities receive up-front harvesting fees, it is increasingly likely that progress and profits will not occur otherwise.

Corporations contend that their fiduciary responsibility to their organizations and shareholders require them to operate in a financially sound manner to realize maximum return on investment. Distributing profits to communities of origin increases the costs of operation, decreases dividends paid to shareholders, and violates the trust shareholders place in the company (Reasons ##14, 17). As a rule, acting as a social welfare organization is not part of a corporation's mission (Reasons ##2, 3). Advocates for the right of indigenous communities to claim a share in profits reply that profit-sharing is not charity, but a legitimate cost of business: the exchange of payment for valuable materials, knowledge, and services (Reason #10).

Even if companies plan to share benefits with indigenous users, how are they to identify the proper owners of bioresources for purposes of consent and benefit distribution? When so many communities within an ecosystem or region use the same plants for the same purposes, who is authorized to give permission for removing biological materials and doing research on them (Reason #16)? Some medicinal plants are widely distributed. When Uganda charged that SR Pharma's patent for a treatment for HIV/AIDS was based on an indigenous bacterium, the pharmaceutical company countered that the bacterium is found throughout the world (Ngandwe 2006). It is unclear who should arbitrate disagreements among competing tribes over ownership, access, or distribution rights (Reasons ##5, 8). If companies wait until these issues are resolved before obtaining drug candidates, many species will become extinct before their germplasm can be preserved (Reason #6). Yet, if the company compensates some communities for their contributions, other communities may refuse to share resources or misrepresent information without payment up front, and with no guarantee that a drug will be successfully brought to market (Reason #15).

Opponents of benefit-sharing argue that it takes relatively little effort to point to a plant and say, "We use that to treat a sore throat," compared with the decade of research that may be required to bring a drug to market. Supporters of benefit-sharing counter that this perspective disregards the thousands of years of observation, trial and error, and refinement that have gone into identifying what parts of particular plants are effective against specific diseases (Reasons ##8, 10). It is estimated that just one in ten thousand plants may be appropriate for use in medicines (Kohls 2007: 128). Without the shamans' knowledge it would be extremely unlikely that foreign researchers would be able to identify likely plant candidates and their uses, which would add enormous cost and time to research and diminish the likelihood of success (Reasons ##14, 15, 17).

In summary, biotechnical companies and the pharmaceutical industry are obligated by the moral principles of consequences, respect for autonomy, rights, virtues, and justice to share profits from commercialization of indigenous intellectual and biological resources with the communities whose traditional knowledge and practices contribute to their success. Traditional knowledge is essential and invaluable for drug discovery.

Additional Issues to Consider

Other possible moral dilemmas arising within this case:

Q Do biotechnical companies have a moral obligation not to introduce goods, values, or practices from their developed nations into native societies?

Q Are patent offices morally obligated to refuse to issue patents on products or processes developed from native plants or culturally based knowledge if the applicant is not a member of the culture or geographic community from which the knowledge originated?

Q Is the requirement that knowledge be published to count as a discovery morally justifiable?

Q Is the position that only information gained through the scientific method counts as *genuine* knowledge (as opposed to belief or tradition) morally justifiable?

REFERENCES

Ahmed, A. K. (2003) *Environmental Protection, Public Health and Human Rights: An Integrated Assessment.* Report prepared for Science and Human Rights Program. Washington, DC: American Association for the Advancement of Science.

Asfaw, N., Licence, P., Engida, T., et al. (2007) Collaborations: empowering green chemists in Ethiopia. *Science* 316 (5833): 1849–50.

Balter, M. (2007) Plant science: seeking agriculture's ancient roots. *Science* 316 (5833): 1830–5.

Bequette, F. (1997) People and plants. *UNESCO Courier* (January): 42–4.

Chalmers, D. (2004) Commercialization and benefit sharing of biotechnology: cross-cultural concerns? In M. C. Brannigan (ed.), *Cross-Cultural Biotechnology.* Lanham, MD: Rowan and Littlefield Publishers, pp. 3–14.

Dalton, R. (2006) Cashing in on the rich coast. *Nature* 442 (7093): 567–9.

Diamond v. Chakrobarty (1980) 447 US 303, 309.

Fadiman, A. (1987) Dr. Plotkin's jungle pharmacy: an ethnobotanist goes native for science. *Life* 10 (3): 15.

Fecteau, L. (2001) The Ayahuasca patent revocation: raising questions about current US patent policy. *Boston College Third World Law Journal* 21 (69): 69–104.

Fletcher, S. R. (1995) Biological diversity: issues related to the convention on biodiversity. *Congressional Research Service Reports*. Available at: www.digital.library.unt.edu/govdocs/crs/permalink/meta-crs-235 (accessed July 12, 2007).

Gepts, P. (2004) Who owns biodiversity, and how should the owners be compensated? *Plant Physiology* 134 (4): 1295–307.

Gonzalez-Arnal, S. (2004) Indigenous knowledge, patenting, and the biotechnology industry. In M. C. Brannigan (ed.), *Cross-Cultural Biotechnology*. Lanham, MD: Rowan and Littlefield Publishers, pp. 139–51.

Govaerts, R. (2001) How many species of seed plants are there? *Taxon* 50 (4): 1085–90.

Hansen, S., and Van Fleet, J. (2003) *Traditional Knowledge and Intellectual Property: A Handbook on Issues and Options for Traditional Knowledge Holders in Protecting their Intellectual Property and Maintaining Biological Diversity*. Washington, DC: American Association for the Advancement of Science.

Jiménez, M. (2001) Saving the "vine of the soul." *National Post* (June 9) Available at: www.biopark.org/peru/save-vine.html (accessed September 30, 2007).

Kohls, M. (2007) Blackbeard or Albert Schweitzer: Reconciling biopiracy. *Chicago-Kent Journal of Intellectual Property* 6 (2): 108–37.

Makinde, M. O. (2004) Agricultural biotechnology in African countries. In M. C. Brannigan (ed.), *Cross-Cultural Biotechnology*. Lanham, MD: Rowan and Littlefield Publishers, pp. 115–26.

McGown, J. (2006) *Out of Africa: Mysteries of Access and Benefit Sharing*. A report for the Edmonds Institute in cooperation with the African Centre for Biosafety. Edmonds, WA: Edmonds Institute.

Ngandwe, T. (2006) African "biopiracy" debate heats up. *Africa News Service* (February 2). Available at: www.csir.co.za/websource/ptl0002/pdf_files/news/2006/33_African_biopiracy.pdf (accessed July 11, 2007).

Nicol, D. (2004) Cross-cultural issues in balancing patent rights and consumer access to biotechnological and pharmaceutical inventions. In M. C. Brannigan (ed.), *Cross-Cultural Biotechnology*. Lanham, MD: Rowan and Littlefield Publishers, pp. 155–64.

Plotkin, M. J. (1993) *Tales of a Shaman's Apprentice*. New York: Viking.

Rosamond, J., and Allsop, A. (2000) Harnessing the power of the genome in the search for new antibiotics. *Science* 287 (5460): 1973–6.

35 USC §102 (1972/2002) Conditions for patentability; novelty and loss of right to patent (section e revised in 2002).

UNCBD (United Nations Convention on Biological Diversity) (1992) (June 5). Available at: www.opbw.org/int_inst/env_docs/CBD-TEXT.pdf (accessed September 30, 2007).

UNEP (United Nations Environment Programme) (2001) Globalization threat to world's cultural, linguistic and biological diversity. News release (February 8) Available at: www.unep.org/Documents.Multilingual/Default.asp?DocumentID=192andArticleID=2765 (accessed September 30, 2007).

UNESCO (United Nations Educational, Scientific and Cultural Organization) (1972) UNESCO convention concerning the protection of the world cultural and natural heritage. Available at: www.unesco.org/whc/world_he.htm (accessed July 11, 2007).

US Department of State (2002) Statement to the Ministerial Roundtable, Sixth Conference of the Parties to the Convention on Biological Diversity. Press release (April 17).

Available at: www.state.gov/g/oes/rls/rm/2002/9577.htm (accessed September 30, 2007).

WTO (World Trade Organization) (1994a) Intellectual property: protection and enforcement. Available at: www.wto.org/english/thewto_e/whatis_e/tif_e/agrm7_e.htm (accessed September 30, 2007).

WTO (World Trade Organization) (1994b) TRIPS agreement on trade related aspects of intellectual property rights, including trade in counterfeit goods. Available at: www.wto.org/English/docs_e/legal_e/27-trips.pdf (accessed September 30, 2007).

CASE TWENTY-SIX: BODY SHOP – INTERNATIONAL TRAFFICKING IN HUMAN ORGANS

Consider the following:

> On a warm afternoon in Recife, a city on Brazil's northeastern coast, Hernani Gomes da Silva sits alone in the Bar Egipcio, quietly nursing a drink, ruminating about his predicament. He is 32 years old and still lives in his mother's two-room house. Rain comes in through the roof, and cockroaches and rats scuttle across the cement floor. He has three kids, a wife who loathes him, and a mistress twenty years his senior. He is unemployed with no money, no skills, and a criminal record. The future is bleak.
>
> Suddenly the words "we pay people $6,000" leap out at him from behind. . . .
>
> "I don't mean to eavesdrop," he says. . . . "Were you talking about earning money from transplants?" . . .
>
> "Yes," says the man. (McLaughlin et al. 2004: paras 4–7)

Mr da Silva is not unique, nor even particularly uncommon (Kumar 2005; Rahman 2007). Because selling human organs is illegal throughout the world, the number of organs sold each year is undetermined, but is believed to be on the rise (WHO 2004b: para 3). Fueled by burgeoning demand for, but a stable or decreasing supply of, donated organs, persons who are both desperately ill with end-stage organ failure and desperate not to die are increasingly turning to organ brokers who purchase organs on a black market. Typical buyers are affluent, white men; typical sellers are – like Mr da Silva – dreadfully poor persons of color (although, unlike Mr da Silva, most are women). Transplants usually occur in Asian or African countries (India, China, South Africa), but brokers can be found in countries as diverse as Brazil, Canada, Israel, and Iraq.

Organ-trafficking, – the unregulated sale of body parts by one individual to another (or to an entrepreneurial middleman) – is illegal. Nonetheless, its occurrence is neither uncommon nor secret. In 1999, a would-be seller offered a kidney on the Internet auction site, eBay. Before eBay removed the offer (citing their own policy and federal laws prohibiting sale of human organs), the highest bidder had offered *$5.7 million*. At least one Internet site announces that transplants can be provided to patients in as few as ten days. These surgeries cannot be undertaken in European or American countries, but citizens of those nations who are willing to travel to other countries are welcome to apply for bone marrow ($100,000 or less), kidney ($35–85,000) and liver ($150–250,000) transplants (Kidney, Liver Transplant n.d.: paras 3, 11).

Proponents of organ-trafficking argue that persons are free to do what they want with their bodies – including selling parts of them. So long as sellers freely and knowledgeably consent to part with an organ, no one is harmed. Indeed, people who are very poor get more money than most would see in a decade: the average going price for a kidney is $5,000 (WHO 2004b: para 3). This money affords sellers (the argument goes) egress from desperate poverty; and since donors rarely die, they are – overall – much better off. And a person with end-stage organ failure lives. Everyone wins!

Opponents of organ-trafficking counter that donors' consents are rarely, if ever, fully informed or genuinely free (i.e., autonomous). The desperate poverty of the sellers is itself, according to opponents, a coercive influence on decisions to sell organs. Further, while donors do usually live, studies demonstrate that they suffer impaired health and, in fact, rarely recover from the poverty that motivated their decisions. Further, organ sales make transplants – and life itself – disproportionately available to the wealthy, raising questions of just allocation of scarce organs.

From a moral point of view, should organ-trafficking be allowed?

Perspective One

Organ-trafficking should be allowed. This claim is supported by appeals to consequences, autonomy, and justice.

We begin with an appeal to consequences. All participants in organ transplantations would benefit from legalized organ sales. Many people would sell their organs and, as a result, more organ recipients would get their lives and health back; and their families and friends would have them around longer. Saving lives and restoring health are significant benefits, as anyone with end-stage organ failure can attest.

Healthcare professionals and institutions would also benefit from the legal sale of organs: They would have more opportunities to help patients to whom they are committed, and they would reap financial benefits from practicing their craft.

The greater community would also see benefits: fewer citizens would be seriously incapacitated and, thus, would be more productive (whether productivity is measured in social or economic terms). Patients who received kidney transplants would no longer need expensive dialysis, thereby freeing tax dollars (or private insurance company resources) that their governments (or private insurers) can redirect to other goods or services.

In fact, legal organ sales would permit donors to benefit not only psychologically (as they – or their families – do under the current system), but also financially. If healthcare professionals and institutions are not morally tainted by profiting from participation in organ transplants, why should one assume that organ-sellers will become (or are) morally tarnished? In fact, excluding organ donors from making money seems unfair, given that all other individual and institutional participants realize a profit (Erin and Harris 2003: 137; Gill and Sade 2002: 19).

Finally, living organ donors rarely die (ECTS 2005: S53). The UK reports one in every 3,000 donors dies (UKNKF 2001: para 4); the US reports three in every 10,000 donors die (Ingelfinger 2005: 448). Thus, fatal outcomes are sufficiently rare enough to be offset by the plethora of advantages.

In short, the principle of utility (i.e., negative outcomes for a few being outweighed by positive consequences realized by all parties) argues in favor of organ-selling.

The appeal to consequences is buttressed by an appeal to autonomy. Autonomy protects the free and informed choices of persons about how to live their lives, including how to use their bodies. People are free to use their bodies in physically demanding jobs or hobbies, to bear children, and even to donate organs altruistically to, say, friends and family members. Autonomous choices do require that donors are informed about risks and benefits of, and freely consent to, the activities in which they participate and, in the case of transplants, of procedures they will undergo. Yes, kidney donors face risk of future poor health – and even death; but these risks are only infrequently realized (ECTS 2005). The risks of complications vary between transplant centers and surgeons, but these comparative data are available and could – and should – be given to potential donors. As the practice of informed consent – a standard and required process for anyone undergoing any surgery – will be in place, potential donors – armed with relevant information – will be able to choose autonomously whether the selling price is worth the risks.

Nor are risky ventures uncommon: people can and do take chances throughout their lives. They invest retirement funds in the stock market, marry, adopt children, quit their jobs, undergo surgery for non-life-threatening reasons (e.g., cosmetic procedures), and participate in extreme sports. Such ventures are not illegal, and consistency and equality (justice) require that willing donors be allowed to take commensurate risks (Savulescu 2003: 138–9). In fact, living persons are currently allowed to donate paired (kidneys) or regenerative (liver) organs; they are just not allowed to donate for compensation. If the risks of donating an organ are morally acceptable for an altruist, they must equally be acceptable for a commercial donor (Gill and Sade 2002: 21–2).

A capitalist economy allows people to sell all manner of goods and services, including the use of their bodies. Professional athletes subject their bodies to risks of injury weekly – some of which are life- or health-threatening and many of which are often realized. Willing persons sell their time and abilities to employers, and sell the products of their labor to customers. The law doesn't criminalize accepting positions with mean-spirited or low-paying employers. Nor is selling one's products at or below market value illegal. Such decisions are left to buyer and seller to negotiate. Does selling one's body in the service of a draconian employer or an unhealthy work environment (e.g., coal mining) – thereby risking poor health – differ from selling one's organ(s) (Veatch 2003: 27; Gill and Sade 2002: 35–6)? If one can autonomously choose a health-threatening job, one can equally autonomously choose health-threatening organ-donation.

In fact, the general freedom to sell one's resources raises a question of equality (justice). Persons are free to sell their blood, sperm, and ova (Rothman et al. 1997: 2741). While selling sperm has no discernible health risks, and selling blood raises minimal cause for concern, selling ova is accompanied by significant and infrequent (but not rare) risks of infertility, stroke, heart attack, and even death. But, as noted above, women are allowed autonomously to assume these risks for financial remuneration. Equality demands that willing persons be allowed to assume the health risks of donating paired or regenerative organs.

Appeals to widespread positive consequences, respect for personal autonomy, and equality between risk-takers (i.e., justice) morally support legalizing the sale of organs.

Perspective Two

Trafficking in human organs is wrong; appeals to consequences, autonomy, and justice support this evaluation.

Looking first at consequences, we find that, even if recipients and others benefit, donors are almost always worse off. Because many lack access to good health-care after surgery, they end up in worse health than they were pre-operatively. Many report serious decline in health (McLaughlin et al. 2004). In one study, 50 out of 150 – fully one third of – donors who described their pre-operative health as excellent described their postoperative health as poor (Goyal et al. 2002). Further, although 96 percent reported selling a kidney to pay off debts, a year after the transplant the average income of donor families had declined by a third, 17 percent *more* donor families were living below the poverty line, and 75 percent were still in debt (Goyal et al. 2002; McLaughlin et al. 2004). Finally, according to Javaad Zargooshi, Department of Urology, Kermanshah University of Medical Sciences, Iran, who interviewed 300 kidney sellers six months to eleven years post-donation:

Some 65 percent of interviewed donors reported that the kidney sale had led to negative effects on employment. Thirty eight percent, representing largely uninsured manual labourers, had lost their jobs because they were unable to continue working at the same job after the transplant. Many donors were also frightened to go back to work for fear of injuring their remaining kidney. Ninety percent of the vendors complained of impaired physical ability and ill health. Complaints included palpitation, tremors, chest-pain, backache, nervousness and fatigue. Seventy percent of the donors suffered from post-operative depression and 60 percent from anxiety. Several donors said they had attempted suicide and spoke of donors who had killed themselves. Seventy percent of donors said that they felt worthless after the operation and 85 percent stated that if given the chance to go back in time, they would not donate their kidney and would also advise others against donating their kidneys. A large number of donors spoke of social ostracisation and increased marital conflict following the kidney sale. (Ram 2002: para 9)

In short, donors were worse off financially, physically, and psychologically.

Even data that demonstrate fewer harms do report harms (ECTS 2005). Moreover, organ donors do die. Stories abound of donors who consented to donate one particular organ, only to have surgeons harvest others – sometimes with fatal results – *on the operating table!* Reliable evidence attests to the fact that the Chinese government is executing prisoners to provide organs for wealthy foreigners (Parmly 2001; Rothman et al. 1997: 2742–3).

Finally, organ-sellers typically do not reap the compensating advantages achieved by directed donors (who donate to a specific, known individual – typically a family member or friend). While altruistic donors often participate in the recuperation and support system of the recipient, non-directed donors (those who donate to a middleman or a stranger) often lack their own psychological support systems. These organ-sellers, if burdened by physical, psychological, or financial post-operative complications, are on their own (Adams et al. 2002).

In sum, while consequences for some organ-sellers are positive, those for many others are typically and significantly negative.

The appeal to autonomy also supports banning organ-selling. Although in theory donors can be informed about the risks of deteriorating health and death – including the fact that they are more likely than is commonly claimed to experience negative outcomes, coercion of sellers is virtually guaranteed. As analyses of research done in developing countries have demonstrated, offers of reimbursement constitute coercive offers for profoundly poor sellers who are, for that reason, at heightened risk for exploitation (London 2005; Rothman et al. 1997: 2742). An offer of $1,410 to a person whose annual income is $660 (Goyal et al. 2002), or $6,000 to an unskilled, unemployed Brazilian is psychologically overwhelming: only a fool or a madman would refuse. Blinded by so much money, impoverished sellers cannot but consent. But only another fool or another madman – or a greedy exploiter – would label that consent autonomous. And while being a fool or a madman is not unethical, exploitation is.

Finally, consider justice. Selling organs allows the wealthy to jump the queue, which constitutes unfair distribution of scarce medical resources. Organ transplantation programs, as currently constructed, require that organs be allotted on the basis of medical urgency and the patient's place on the list of potential recipients. A potential recipient's ability to pay does not justify preferential organ allocation – especially when needier patients are passed over. And needier patients are more likely to be the poorer patients, given the relationship of poverty to increased morbidity and mortality (Henry J. Kaiser Family Foundation 2006, Rothman et al. 1997: 2741). As the poor are generally not responsible for their poverty, and as the rich already profit from economic and social inequities, the poor may be more deserving of an organ than the rich; certainly they are at least equally so.

In sum, negative outcomes for donors, serious challenges to donors' abilities to make autonomous choices, and unequal burdens on the poor require forbidding trafficking in organs.

Perspective Three

Is organ-trafficking morally permissible? No. Purchased organs do give patients with end-stage organ disease a new – and typically good – chance at a longer life. And sellers do get funds that are usually much-needed. Still, organ-trafficking means that organs will go to those with more financial resources; that is, distribution will be inequitable with the poor (once again) losing out when resources are allocated.

Step 1: Information-gathering

Medical information

- How likely are donors to die (mortality rate)?
- How likely are donors to experience negative health outcomes (morbidity rate)?
- How likely are organ recipients to die (mortality rate)?
- How likely are recipients to experience negative health outcomes (morbidity rate)?
- How many negative health outcomes of donors or recipients will be long-term or serious?

Legal/policy information

- What laws currently govern organ-selling?
- Are these laws effective?
- What motivated these laws?
- What advice is given by codes of ethics of healthcare providers?

Psychological information

- Are sellers capable of autonomous consent?
- Are healthcare providers psychologically able to provide care for sellers *and* buyers of organs?

Economic

- What are the financial ramifications for sellers?
- What are the financial ramifications for buyers?
- What are the financial ramifications for healthcare professionals?
- What are the financial ramifications for healthcare institutions?
- What are the financial ramifications for governments?
- Who pays for the healthcare of a seller who experiences adverse health outcomes?

Implications

- What will be the sociocultural effects of organ-selling on vulnerable populations? On healthcare providers? On the community? On organ transplant programs?

History

- Is class discrimination evident in this practice?
- Is race discrimination evident in this practice?
- Is gender discrimination evident in this practice?

Step 2: Creative problem-solving

Any creative solution would have to increase organ-donation without disadvantaging vulnerable populations. Perhaps policies that carefully regulate the selling and buying of organs (e.g., prohibit direct sales between donors and recipients, and prohibit recipients from jumping the queue) could do so. (See Erin and Harris (2003) and Bagheri (2006) for a list of criteria that morally appropriate organ sales must meet.) However, the absence of international cooperation on developing *and* enforcing just and nonmaleficent organ sales makes protection of vulnerable sellers unlikely. So the next step should be to consider the moral pros and cons of both options.

Step 3: Listing pros and cons

Options	Pros	Cons
Legalize trafficking in human organs.	1. Saves recipients' lives (C-B) 2. Improves lives of recipients' family, friends (C-U) 3. Community healthier (C-U) 4. Improves financial status of sellers/families (C-B, C-U) 5. Respects autonomy of buyers and sellers (A) 6. Right to control one's own body (R-privacy) 7. Relieves misery (V-Compassion) 8. Professionals able to help more patients (V-I, V-F) 9. No different than selling blood, ova or sperm (J-E) 10. All other participants are paid (J-E)	11. Expensive (C-NM) 12. Subsequent morbidity of donors (C-NM) 13. Subsequent morbidity of recipients (C-NM) 14. Takes advantage of desperate persons (A) (RFP) 15. Allocates scarce medical resources on basis of ability to pay (J-E) 16. Unfairly burdens poor or vulnerable populations (J-E, J-F) 17. Unequally burdens women (J-E, J-F) 18. Unequally burdens nonwhites (J-E, J-F)
Do not legalize trafficking in human organs.	19. Maintains trust in organ transplant system (C-U) 20. Human life should not be commodified (C-U, RFP) 21. Respects cultural and religious taboos regarding body integrity (A, J-E) 22. Preserves social nature of social services (J-E)	23. Extends burden on family caregivers (C-NM) 24. Desperate patients must resort to illegal activities (V-I, C-NM, C-U)

Clearly good moral reasons exist for both options. Which reasons are stronger? (The following remarks will be confined to selling kidneys, which are the most commonly sold organ – sellers have two and, hence, one to spare.)

Step 4: Analysis

Factual assumptions

- Number of organ donors would increase.
- More lives would be saved.
- Health outcomes for recipients are mixed.
- Health outcomes for donors are poor.

- Financial outcomes for donors are poor.
- Autonomous choice of donors and recipients is possible, but often unlikely.
- The rich would receive organs preferentially.
- The poor would donate organs more frequently than the rich or middle class.

Value assumptions

- Scarce medical resources should not be allocated on the basis of ability to pay.
- Vulnerable populations should not be exploited for the welfare of others.
- Known or very likely harms should not be perpetrated on others without their autonomous consent.

Step 5: Justification

Before beginning with a comparison of the anticipated consequences, we should note that most countries carefully regulate organ transplants. In the United States:

> United Network for Organ Sharing (UNOS) is a non-profit, scientific and educational organization that administers the Organ Procurement and Transplantation Network (OPTN), established by the U.S. Congress in 1984. Through the OPTN, we [UNOS] collect and manage data about every transplant event occurring in the United States; facilitate the organ matching and placement process using UNOS-developed data technology and the UNOS Organ Center; [and] bring together medical professionals, transplant recipients and donor families to develop organ transplantation policy. (UNOS n.d.: para 1)

The same functions are served, internationally, by the World Health Organization (WHO 1991, 2003, 2004), as well as UNOS-like organizations in other individual countries.

As of 6.59 p.m., March 14, 2008, there were 98,389 candidates on the waiting list for an organ-donation in the United States; 79,160 were hoping for a kidney (UNOS 2008). Between January and December 2007, about 29 percent of those waiting – 28,354 people – received organs. Of the donors, 8,087 were deceased and 6,308 were living donors (UNOS 2008). In Europe the situation is equally bleak:

> There are currently 120,000 patients on chronic dialysis treatment and nearly 40,000 patients waiting for a kidney transplant in western Europe alone. Some 15% to 30% of patients die on waiting lists, as a result of chronic shortage of organs. The waiting time for transplantation, currently about three years, will reach almost ten years by the year 2010. (Parliamentary Assembly 2003: para 2; European Commission n.d.)

Clearly the need for organs is great. Persons on the waiting list are sick, sometimes dreadfully so, and will get better only if they receive new, healthy organs. Presumably, allowing organ sales would increase the number of organs available, as many people are motivated to do things for money (Gill and Sade 2002: 19). So an appeal to beneficence for so many persons stands to be a very powerful appeal indeed, and people often assume that the life saved outweighs the harm of pain, temporary inconvenience, etc., to the donor (Rivera-Lopez 2006: 42).

Nonetheless, consequences of selling organs are mixed (Reasons ##1, 2, 3, 4, 11, 12, 13). Some outcomes are positive (Reason #1). The one-year survival rate for a kidney transplant from a living donor in the US is 95 percent; the average five-year survival rate is just over 80 percent (UNOS 2006). Most survivors experience an improvement in their quality of life. Nonetheless, organ recipients substitute one chronic illness – end-stage organ failure – for another – chronic immunosuppression. All transplant recipients suffer some side effects from the panoply of drugs required post-operatively, and complications that require further treatment or hospitalization are not infrequent (Reason #13). So, although organ recipients are noticeably healthier, they are not healthy.

Moreover, post-transplant patients face significant financial burdens (Reason #11), particularly the costs of laboratory tests and drugs. At least one study documented that 50 percent of post-transplant patients have trouble meeting pharmaceutical costs, which typically run in excess of $10,000 per year. Further, in 2004 Medicare lowered its reimbursement rate for immunosuppressive drugs from 95 to 85 percent of the average wholesale price (ASTS 2006), so financial difficulties will probably increase.

Nor are burdens limited to patients: families and friends are also encumbered (Reason #23). Since most transplant centers will not put a patient on a waiting list unless he or she demonstrates the availability of post-operative caregivers, family or friends must demonstrate a willingness to help patients manage post-operative courses. Care-giving of post-transplant patients often requires a leave of absence from work, aggravating financial difficulties. And data show that care-givers are themselves likely to suffer negative health effects while caring for the transplant recipient, resulting in their own increased morbidity and mortality (Schulz and Beach 1999).

The point is this: although recipients of organ transplants are likely to live, they will continue to bear health and economic burdens, as will their care-givers. This is to say that negative as well as positive consequences are experienced by those who receive organs as well as by those who care for and about them.

Add to this mixed bag of outcomes the very likely constellation of negative effects (and lack of offsetting positive effects, as noted above) for those who sell organs. Most organ-sellers assume they are buying financial security with few, or no, off-setting long-term costs to themselves. This assumption is simply false. As noted above, for most donors the payment received not only does not solve their financial woes; it exacerbates them – while reducing their physical and psychological welfare in the process (Reasons ##16, 17, 18).

Finally, the Bellagio Task Force on Securing Bodily Integrity for the Socially Disadvantaged in Transplant Surgery (1994–6) documented the many social abuses that flow from the traffic in organs, including the sale of organs and the use of organs from prisoners executed – at least in part – to provide organs. Follow-up studies have demonstrated a host of noxious psychosocial effects extending beyond donor and recipient to vulnerable populations that societies already under-serve:

1. strong and persistent race, class, and gender *inequalities and injustices* in the acquisition, harvesting and distribution of organs [Reasons ##16, 17, 18];
2. *violation of national laws* prohibiting the sale of organs;
3. the collapse of cultural and religious sanctions against body dismemberment and commercial use in the face of *enormous market pressures* in the transplant industry [Reason #21];
4. the appearance of new forms of traditional debt peonage in which the commodified kidney occupies a critical space [Reason #16];
5. *persistent and flagrant human rights violations* of cadavers in public morgues, with organs and tissues removed *without any consent* for international sale;
6. the spread and persistence of narratives of *terror* concerning the theft and disappearance of bodies and body parts globally. (Organs Watch 1999; emphases added)

These findings do not attach to identifiable individuals as do effects on particular donors. However, societies in which these abuses occur are likely to be riddled with even greater misery and despair for vulnerable members of their population (Reason #22).

In summary, when one looks beyond the recipient and the recipient's family, an appeal to consequences argues strongly against permitting trafficking in human organs.

What about autonomy (Reason #5)? A choice is autonomous when made by a competent chooser who is informed, possesses and *understands* the relevant information, and is *uncoerced* (Faden and Beauchamp 1986: chs. 8–10). Worries that sellers are not fully informed are probably well founded: sellers seem not to understand that their poverty will persist or worsen (Reason #14) (Rothman et al. 1997: 2741). This concern is not new; however, much work remains to be done on both the content of and the procedures necessary to yield an informed consent to donate (ECTS 2004).

There are also concerns about whether adequate information is given to buyers and their families, who also seem not to retain information about the various risks and benefits. The focus is primarily on the likelihood that the recipient's life will be saved. Recipients and their families often forget the burdens of chronic immunosuppression and complications will be glossed over and may never be fully understood or appreciated (Ingelfinger 1972).

Further suspicion that consents are not autonomous is raised by the possibility of coercion. If sellers are likely coerced by the money, buyers are likely coerced by a fear of death. Wealthy patients who fear dying on the waiting list report they feel they have no choice but to buy a kidney from a stranger, and parents routinely indicate they would "do anything" to obtain an organ for a dying child (Reason #14). So organ recipients' decisions may be no more voluntary than those of sellers (McLaughlin et al. 2004).

We turn next to the issue of professional integrity (Reason #8). Healthcare professionals (HCPs) take their primary commitment to be to the welfare of their patients. Not surprisingly, then, HCPs would likely be keen to improve the health of their patients with end-stage renal failure. If money can induce more people to donate, then more patients will get much-need kidneys. Presumably HCPs would be tempted to encourage organ sales as a means of demonstrating the virtue of fidelity to those patients to whom they are already committed.

But organ *recipients* are not the only patients involved in transplantation. Professional integrity requires a broader and more nuanced examination of where physician responsibility lies. The World Medical Association (WMA) makes the following observation: "The *primary obligation* of physicians is to their individual patients, *whether they are potential donors or recipients* of transplanted organs or tissues. Nevertheless, this obligation is not absolute; for example, the physician's responsibility for *the well-being of a patient who needs a transplant does not justify unethical or illegal procurement of organs or tissues*" (2000, para 3; emphases added).

Note that the WMA considers physicians to be *equally* obligated to the welfare of recipients (with whom they often have a pre-existing relationship) and of donors (who may be strangers). At the very least, this will obligate physicians to provide on-going care to donors – beyond the point where they can walk out of the hospital unassisted (ibid.; ECTS 2004: 492). If physicians cannot insure adequate follow-up care (a real possibility for patients who fly in, have a kidney removed, pocket the money, and fly home; or whose financial situation suggests that their resources for follow-up care will be limited at best), they cannot harvest the donor's organ, no matter how much money might change hands or how devoted they are to their kidney-needing patients.

The WMA also addresses concerns of organs being sold autonomously, acknowledging "a tension between a desire to procure organs for the purpose of providing important medical treatments on the one hand and the preservation of choice and personal liberty on the other" (2000). Concerns about liberty are addressed in no uncertain terms: "In the case of living donors, special efforts should be made to ensure that the choice about donation is free of coercion. Financial incentives for providing or obtaining organs and tissues for transplantation can be coercive and should be prohibited" (ibid.: para 23).

In sum, physicians' *professional integrity requires* refusing to participate in the use of commercially generated organ-donations unless autonomous consent and adequate post-operative care are insured – two conditions that, to date, have often failed to obtain. Until these circumstances change, physicians can advocate for increased organ-donation, but however devoted they are to their patients with end-stage organ disease, physicians cannot transplant sold organs into them.

Finally, justice. Perhaps the strongest argument against selling organs is that, once again, the wealthy will acquire preferential access to a scarce resource at the expense of the poor (Reason #15). This claim, however, is somewhat disingenuous, as the poor already have diminished access to organ transplantation. While poor people who reside in countries with socialized medicine in theory have access to organ transplants, these countries often discriminate: In Israel, for example, preference for organs is given to persons under the age of 18

(McLaughlin et al. 2004). As countries with socialized medicine typically have parallel private systems providing interventions to those with money to jump the queue, the poor are – once again – relatively disadvantaged. In the United States, where medical services are dispensed on a capitalistic system, the poor who are disproportionately among the uninsured, are denied transplants because they cannot afford them. In short, "The practice of soliciting strangers for organ-donation is fundamentally unfair. Those who can pay . . . will have greater access to potential lifesaving transplants" (Caplan 2004: 8).

The WMA denounces organ-trafficking as unjust discrimination on the basis of non-medical factors (Reasons ##8, 15): "Payment for organs and tissues for donation and transplantation should be prohibited. . . . Furthermore, access to needed medical treatment based on ability to pay is inconsistent with the principles of justice. Organs suspected to have been obtained through commercial transaction should not be accepted for transplantation" (WMA 2000: para 30). The American Society of Transplant Surgeons supports directed donation only "as long as the motivation is based in altruism" (2006: para 2.b.2.).

Queue-jumping raises the issue of justice in a further way. If a national allocation system for scarce resources is in place, ought not all who are hoping for the resource defer to this nationwide system (Reason #22)? All countries with government-subsidized healthcare systems ration care, in that process making hard choices about what care to fund *and about who* will receive it. For this reason, both UNOS and WHO recommend allocating organs on the basis of medical urgency, informed by the probability of post-transplant survival. Although OPTN has no authority to obstruct solicitation (e.g., via the Internet) for live organ donors, member institutions are prohibited from participating in transplants unless the organ was truly a gift, that is, the organ was neither purchased outright nor exchanged for some other consideration that has value for the donor (Delmonico and Graham 2006: 39). Unless one is a radical libertarian, one has some commitment – based on social solidarity – for programs that generate the greatest social benefits. Buying oneself out of burdens that must be borne by one's fellow citizens fails to appreciate both the social and natural lotteries, in terms of which many people bear burdens undeservedly (Reasons ##16, 17, 18).

These lotteries introduce the justice-based issue of desert. The idea of "just deserts" is this: one justly receives only the benefits or burdens that one autonomously causes. So, for example, the person who understands the risk of cigarettes and who freely chooses to avoid their use but gets lung cancer anyway does not deserve this affliction. If she gets this disease, the health burden is unjust (i.e., undeserved). Similarly, those who are destitute through no fault of their own do not deserve the poverty that motivates (some would say, coerces) them to suffer the burdens of an organ-donation. Yet, organ-sellers are quite likely to be poor people of color, and buyers are quite likely to be wealthy whites (Reason #17). In South Africa, for example, 95 percent of all organ-buyers are white males (McLaughlin et al. 2004). Because no person can autonomously choose his own race or sex, white men who are lucky enough to be born into societies that economically privilege whiteness and maleness do not deserve the resources that allow them to purchase a replacement organ.

Moreover, the possibility of gender-based injustice is very real (Reason #18). Two women in a study of organ-donations in India told researchers that their husbands forced them to have the transplant (Goyal et al. 2002). International data reveal that "approximately 65% of live kidney donors have been women and approximately 65% of recipients have been men" (ECTS 2005). Thus, selling organs continues longstanding, unjust discrimination against the poor, the non-white, and women. Allowing a practice that aggravates these biases would perpetuate, not ameliorate, injustice – as the WMA explicitly acknowledges: "Physicians have responsibilities to society, which include promoting the fair use of resources, preventing harm and promoting health benefit for all" (2000: para 4). Further, the social support (e.g., funding through taxation) of organ transplant programs – specialized training of transplant professionals, purchase of equipment and facilities, etc. – gives further reason to insure equal sharing of burdens and benefits that attend organ transplantation (Reason #22). Allowing a system that uses these facilities for an end-around-run of social justice is not merely unjust, but ironically so.

The critic will note that many of life's most important decisions – including those that pertain to one's most central values – are made under stressful conditions. Yet autonomy relies on appreciating the effects of a decision, even those reached under adverse circumstances. The worry is often raised that decisions made in the presence of pervasive noxious conditions are ineluctably coerced. Persons who commit to care-giving are surely motivated by significant fears regarding the welfare of their loved ones. Those who sell their homes to pay for medical care would, one might reasonably assume, wish they had other options. For that matter, anyone who consents to life-saving surgery is likely motivated, at least in part, by fear. Yet none of these decisions is decried as being unavoidably inautonomous. The fact is: if need or fear precluded autonomy, most of life's important decisions would be made by those only tangentially affected, if they would be affected at all (Faden and Beauchamp 1986; Veatch 2000).

Nor do the temptations of money inevitably render choices inautonomous. People often take risks for money: they play the stock market, move across country for better-paying jobs, take risky jobs that pay more for that reason, or take thoroughly unappealing jobs with appealing salaries (Savulescu 2003; Gill and Sade 2002: 33–6). Even the armed forces induce, through hazardous duty pay, soldiers, sailors, and marines to serve in combat zones (and, as Gill and Sade note, persons who enlist in the armed services are disproportionately poor). Again, none of these decisions is deemed – in principle – to be coerced.

True, all true. And if organ-sellers were informed and uncoerced, organ-selling would be supported by the appeal to autonomy. However, widespread and recurring reports of uninformed sellers suggest that in the organ bazaars of the world, consent is often coerced by virtue of being inadequately informed. That is, were sellers adequately informed, many would elect *not* to donate. So, even were the significant sums of money non-coercive, choosers who have heard much about benefits and little (if anything) about burdens are *not* choosing autonomously. In short, while autonomy in theory supports organ-trafficking, in practice it is unlikely to do so.

To close: appeals to consequences, professional integrity, and justice all counsel against organ-trafficking. While the appeal to autonomy *in principle* supports allowing the sale of organs, practical problems with adequately informing prospective sellers – and buyers – have been difficult to address. If such issues cannot be resolved, autonomy would also support a ban on (or at least give no moral support to) organ-selling.

Thus, trafficking in human organs is morally impermissible.

Additional Issues to Consider

Other possible moral dilemmas arising within this case:

Q Would organ-selling be morally permissible if sellers were not permitted to cross countries' borders to donate (Savalescu 2003)?

Q Would organ-selling be morally permissible if sellers were guaranteed either a certain amount of money or a certain percent of the sales price (ibid.)?

Q Would organ-selling be morally permissible if organs were sold *only* to organ procurement organizations, rather than to brokers (ibid.)?

Q Is denying an economic opportunity to persons who are very poor and lack employment opportunities morally justifiable, other things being equal?

Q Can one make a *moral* argument to the effect that persons *own* their bodies and, therefore, can do with them what they will?

Q Can persons autonomously consent to be exploited? If they can, is exploiting the morally permissible?

REFERENCES

Adams, P. L., Cohen, D. J., Danovitch, G. M., et al. (2002) The nondirected live-kidney donor: ethical considerations and practice guidelines. *Transplantation* 74 (4): 582–9.

ASTS (American Society of Transplant Surgeons) (2006) Statement on directed donation and solicitation of donor organs (October 23). Available at: www.asts.org/TheSociety/PositionStatements.aspx?content_id=42 (accessed October 7, 2007).

Bagheri, A. (2006) Compensated kidney donation: an ethical review of the Iranian model. *Kennedy Institute of Ethics Journal* 16 (3): 269–82.

Caplan, A. (2004) Organs.com: new commercially brokered organ transfers raise questions. *Hastings Center Report* 34 (6): 8.

Delmonico, F. L., and Graham, W. K. (2006) Direction of the Organ Procurement and Transplantation Network and United Network for Organ Sharing regarding the oversight of live donor transplantation and solicitation for organs. *American Journal of Transplantation* 6 (1): 37–40.

ECTS (Ethics Committee of the Transplantation Society) (2004) The consensus statement of the Amsterdam Forum on the care of the live kidney donor. *Transplantation* 78 (4): 491–2.

ECTS (Ethics Committee of the Transplantation Society) (2005) A report of the Amsterdam Forum on the care of the live kidney donor: data and medical guidelines. *Transplantation* 79 (6 Supp.): S53–S66.

Erin, C. A., and Harris, J. (2003) An ethical market in human organs. *Journal of Medical Ethics* 29 (3): 137–8.

European Commission (n.d.) Boosting organ donation rates. (Scientific Support to Policies (SSP)). Available at: http://ec.europa.eu/research/fp6/ssp/dopki_en.htm (accessed October 7, 2007).

Faden, R. R., and T. L. Beauchamp (1986) *A History and Theory of Informed Consent.* New York: Oxford University Press.

Gill, M. B., and Sade, R. M. (2002) Paying for kidneys: the case against prohibition. *Kennedy Institute of Ethics Journal* 12 (1): 17–45.

Goyal, M., Mehta, R. L., Schneiderman, L. J., et al. (2002) Economic and health consequences of selling a kidney in India. *JAMA: Journal of the American Medical Association* 288 (13): 1589–93.

Ingelfinger, F. J. (1972) Informed (but uneducated) consent. *NEJM: New England Journal of Medicine* 287 (9): 465–6.

Ingelfinger, J. R. (2005) Risks and benefits to the living donor. *NEJM: New England Journal of Medicine* 353 (5): 447–9.

The Henry J. Kaiser Family Foundation (2006) The uninsured and their access to health care. (Kaiser Commission on Medicaid and the Uninsured) (October). Available at: www.kff.org/uninsured/upload/The-Uninsured-and-Their-Access-to-Health-Care-Oct-2004.pdf (accessed October 7, 2007).

Kidney, Liver Transplant, Cirrhosis, Kidney Failure, Liver Failure, Leber Transplantiere, BMT (n.d.) Available at: www.liver4you.org/ (accessed October 7, 2007).

Kumar, S. (2005) Police uncover large scale organ trafficking in Punjab. *British Medical Journal* 326 (7382): 180; also available at www.bmj.com.

London, A. J. (2005) Justice and the human development approach to international research. *Hastings Center Report* 35 (1): 24–37.

McLaughlin, A., Prusher, I. R., and Downie, A. (2004) What is a kidney worth? *Christian Science Monitor* (June 9). Available at: www.csmonitor.com/2004/0609/p01s03-wogi.html (accessed July 23, 2007).

Organs Watch (1999) Social justice, human rights, and organ transplantation. Available at: http://sunsite.berkeley.edu/biotech/organswatch/pages/about2.html (accessed October 7, 2007).

Parliamentary Assembly (2003) Recommendation 1611: trafficking in organs in Europe. Available at: http://assembly.coe.int/Documents/AdoptedText/ta03/EREC1611.htm (accessed October 7, 2007).

Parmly, M. E. (2001) Sale of human organs in China. US Department of State (June 27). Available at: www.state.gov/g/drl/rls/rm/2001/3792.htm (accessed October 7, 2007).

Rahman, S. A. (2007) Business is brisk at "kidney bazaar." *The Toronto Star* (May 27). Available from www.thestar.com/News/article/218071 (accessed October 7, 2007).

Ram, V. (2002) International traffic in human organs. *Frontline* 19 (7). Available at: www.frontlineonnet.com/fl1907/19070730.htm (accessed October 7, 2007).

Rivera-Lopez, R. (2006) Organ sales and moral distress. *Journal of Applied Philosophy* 23 (6): 41–52.

Rothman, D. J., Rose, E., Awaya, T., et al. (1997) The Bellagio task force report on transplantation, bodily integrity, and the international traffic in organs. *Transplantation Proceedings* 29 (6): 2739–45.

Savulescu, J. (2003) Is the sale of body parts wrong? *Journal of Medical Ethics* 29 (3): 138–9.

Scheper-Hughes, N. (1998) Organ trade: the new cannibalism. Organs watch: research and publications: Project publications. Available at: http://sunsite3.berkeley.edu/biotech/organswatch/ (accessed October 7, 2007).

Schulz, R., and Beach, S. R. (1999) Caregiving as a risk factor for mortality: the caregiver health effects study. *JAMA: Journal of the American Medical Association* 282 (23): 2215–60.

Truog, R. D. (2005) The ethics of organ donation by living donors. *New England Journal of Medicine* 353 (5): 444–6.

UKNKF (United Kingdom National Kidney Federation) (2001) What are the practical risks and benefits for both donors and recipients? Donor disadvantages (January 6). Available at: www.kidney.org.uk/living-donor/livdon07.html (accessed October 7, 2007).

UNOS (United Network for Organ Sharing) (n.d.) Who we are. Available at: www.unos.org/whoWeAre/ (accessed October 7, 2007).

UNOS (United Network for Organ Sharing) (2008) Data. Available at: www.unos.org/ (accessed March 15, 2008).

UNOS (United Network for Organ Sharing) (2006) Scientific Registry of Transplant Recipients. OPTN/SRTR Annual Report. One year adjusted graft survival by organ and year of transplant, 1995 to 2004. Available at: www.ustransplant.org/annual_reports/current/111a_dh.htm (access October 7, 2007).

Veatch, R. M. (2000) *Transplantation Ethics.* Washington, DC: Georgetown University Press.

Veatch, R. M. (2003) Why liberals should accept financial incentives for organ procurement. *Kennedy Institute of Ethics Journal* 13 (1): 19–36.

WHO (World Health Organization) (1991) Draft guiding principles on human organ transplantation. Available at: www.who.int/entity/ethics/topics/transplantation_guiding_principles/en/ (accessed October 7, 2007).

WHO (World Health Organization) (2003) Ethics, access, and safety in tissue and organ transplantation: issues of global concern. (October 6–9). Available at: www.who.int/transplantation/en/Madrid_Report.pdf (accessed October 7, 2007).

WHO (World Health Organization) (2004a) Transplantation. Available at: www.who.int/transplantation/en/ (accessed October 7, 2007).

WHO (World Health Organization) (2004b) Organ trafficking and transplantation pose new challenges. *Bulletin of the World Health Organization* 82 (9): 639–718. Available at: www.who.int/bulletin/volumes/82/9/feature0904/en/index.html (accessed October 7, 2007).

WMA (World Medical Association) (2002) World Medical Association statement on human organ and tissue donation and transplantation: justice in access to organs and tissues. Available at: www.wma.net/e/policy/wma.htm (accessed October 7, 2007).

CASE TWENTY-SEVEN: STRAITS OF STRIFE – JAPANESE WHALING, CULTURAL RELATIVISM, AND INTERNATIONAL POLITICS

Whaling began as a modest commercial activity, aimed at obtaining blubber for food and oil for lamps. Over generations, the profession developed a beguiling mystique – part of the enduring allure of Hermann Melville's (1992) tale about Captain Ahab's obsessive and calamitous pursuit of Moby Dick, a mottled sperm whale. The social fabric of seafaring cultures is woven with the yield and yore of whales and whaling.

The strenuous exertions of whaling in Melville's day have given way to diesel-powered factory ships, satellite navigation, sonar, winches, and harpoon guns. The ruthless efficiency of modern whaling devastated whale populations in the twentieth century, pushing some close to extinction (Donlan et al. 2006). Blue whales have declined in number by 96 percent since 1920, and fin whales by 92 percent (Eilperin 2006).

To protect the interests of commercial whaling, the International Convention for the Regulation of Whaling (ICRW) was drafted "to establish a system of international regulation for the whale fisheries to ensure proper and effective . . . conservation of whale stocks and thus make possible the orderly development of the whaling industry" (1946). The International Whaling Commission (IWC) was formed to serve as the decision-making body for the ICRW. Membership in the IWC is voluntary, and commission composition varies depending on which nations decide to attend regular meetings and pay dues (Eilperin 2006).

Article VIII of the ICRW, drafted by Norwegian diplomat and professor of anatomy Birger Bergersen, who served as the first chair of the IWC, exempts any signatory from prohibitions on killing and taking whales as it "thinks fit" for the "purposes of scientific research" (1946), such as vivisection required to describe anatomically a new species (Morell 2007a). Decades later, this seemingly benign stipulation would become a point of bitter contention between Japan and conservationists.

In 1972, the issue of commercial whaling and declining whale populations gained public attention at the United Nations Conference on the Human Environment, when delegates recommended a 10-year ban on commercial whaling (Eilperin 2006).

With many whale populations continuing to decline, in 1982 the IWC ratified a moratorium on commercial whaling which took effect four years later. Because the IWC was originally formed to further the interests of industrial whaling, this ban signaled a sea-change in the commission's focus from commerce to conservation (Rehn 2007). According to Phillip Clapham, a biologist at the Alaska Fisheries' Center for Cetacean Research and Conservation, "The [IWC] moratorium is probably one of the greatest conservation success stories of the 20th century" (Morell 2007a). Thanks to the efforts of environmentalists, most marine biologists agree that certain species of whales have recovered and are even flourishing (Kareiva et al. 2006).

The 1986 moratorium also marked the origination of an intransigent divide within the IWC: those nations in favor of some kind of commercial whaling, and those nations categorically opposed (Jones 2007). The nations most conspicuously against commercial whaling have been Australia, Canada, England, New Zealand, and the United States. The nations most conspicuously in favor of commercial whaling have been Iceland, Japan, Norway, and Russia.

Japan has unabashedly taken a leadership role amongst pro-whaling nations and has continued to hunt whale in spite of international opprobrium. Japan has publicly and forcefully defended its actions in the IWC. Under the auspices of a scientific program launched in 1987, called Japan's Whale Research Program under Special Permit in the Antarctic (JARPA), employees of Japan's Institute of Cetacean Research (ICR) – which receives $10 million per year from the government in subsidies (Jones 2007) – have killed an estimated 6,500 minke whales. By comparison, approximately 2,100 whales were killed worldwide between 1952 and 1986 under the Article VIII stipulation (Morell 2007a). Japan followed JARPA with a similar North Pacific program in 1994 where it targeted Bryde's beaked, minke, sie, and sperm whales, and shocked IWC delegates in 2005 by announcing it would begin killing fin and humpback whales (ibid.). Joji Morishita, chief spokesperson for Japan's Fisheries Agency (JFA) division of international affairs, explained: "We don't see it as endangered" (McNeill 2007). Predictably, Morishita's defense of Japan's decision was vilified in international conservation circles.

Japan's announcement that it would kill 50 humpback whales – a beloved symbol of success in rescuing an imperiled species from extinction – at the IWC's Southern Ocean Whale Sanctuary (Morell 2007a), thousands of miles from port, only exacerbated enmity. In addition to verbal barbs tossed back and forth at IWC meetings between Japan and conservationists, the tension also led to physical confrontation. In 2007, the Japanese whaling vessel, *Kaiko Mar*, and the Sea Shepherd Conservation Society ship, *Robert Hunter*, collided, each blaming the other of ramming (Alford 2007).

While carrying out whaling operations, Japan simultaneously argued for relaxed restrictions in the IWC. Japan has relentlessly called for the revocation of the 1986 ban on commercial whaling. The anti-whaling tide that had been building since the 1970s showed signs of ebbing at an historic IWC meeting in the small Caribbean island-nation of Saint Kitts and Nevis in 2006: pro-whaling nations passed a resolution overturning the 20-year ban on commercial whaling by one vote. The vote was inconsequential in terms of overturning the ban, since a 75 percent majority is needed, but nonetheless carried enormous symbolic weight. It was, in the words of Chris Clark, New Zealand's environmental minister, "the most serious defeat the conservation cause has ever suffered at the IWC" (Eilperin 2006). Akira Nakamae, a Japanese commissioner for the IWC, confidently predicted: "The reversal of history, the turning point is soon to come" (*Seattle Post-Intelligencer* 2006).

This reversal of history has yet to occur. At the next IWC meeting in Anchorage, Alaska, a majority of signatories of the ICRW reaffirmed the 21-year ban on commercial whaling (D'Oro 2007). Angered Japan representatives threatened to pull out of the IWC and unilaterally resume commercial whaling (Ryall 2007), precipitating fears amongst other IWC members of a return to the day when nations acted individually without regard for cetacean biology (Darby 2007).

Japanese authorities deflect reproaches of its whaling policies as "cultural imperialism" by the West (McNeill 2007), due to a lack of understanding of Japanese culture and traditions. "They eat dogs in China and Korea, lambs in Europe and the US," said Yasukazu Hamada, a Japanese lawmaker. "Why shouldn't we eat whales?" (ibid.). Tsukasa Isone, captain of the whaling vessel, *Victory*, mused, "To me it is strange that Americans hunt deer. But I don't tell Americans not to kill deer. Why should they tell us not to eat whale? (Larimer 2000). Shoji said he could not think of a reason: "Why is the whale so special to some people? It's a fishery. What is the difference between a sardine and a whale?" (Jones 2007).

Policy-makers have stated that the lack of cross-cultural understanding is not going to prompt the Japanese to change their habits. As Morishita has put it: "We're not going to stop just because you don't like what we eat" (Dolinsky 2000). Western media hypocritically represent Japan as some kind of villainous rogue nation, "unnecessarily display[ing] flashy pictures full of blood of slaughter work," said Hideki Moronuki, head of the JFA whaling division. "What if we show a scene of . . . cattle being slaughtered to people who eat beef everyday?" Moronuki asked (Ito 2007).

Frustrated with the lack of IWC's punitive powers, the International Fund for Animal Welfare (IFAW) has argued that Japan must be brought to trial in international court for violations of the United Nations Convention on the Law of the Sea and other international law (*Herald Sun* 2007). Other diplomats, such as Turnbull, are hesitant, at least for now, to take such drastic action (Darby 2007).

As negotiators navigate the turbulent straits between the Scylla of conservation and the Charybdis of nationalism, the future of commercial whaling remains uncertain. For those watching from shore, the seemingly straightforward motto "save the whales" is no longer so simple.

Are Japan's continued whaling practices justifiable in light of international opposition and ecological evidence?

Perspective One

According to the ethical theory of deontology, sovereign nations, like persons, have the right to self-determination in principle, independently of the consequences of the exercise of that right.

The Japanese have three good reasons to assert their right to continue their whaling practices:

- the outright resumption of commercial whaling for resource utilization;
- allowance of limited whaling under the umbrella of "community whaling;" and
- whale-hunting and vivisection for the purposes of scientific research.

First, as detailed above, Japan has petitioned without hesitation for the repeal of the 1986 commercial whaling ban. Second, Japan has correctly argued that some whaling should be allowed by the IWC under the umbrella of "community whaling" (*Gold Coast Bulletin* 2007; *Townsville Bulletin* 2007). Exemptions are made for aboriginal peoples, such as the Inuit, who depend on whaling for subsistence and survival. Japanese diplomats argue that their small fishing villages that dot the Pacific coastline, like the isolated hamlet of Wadaura where whaling has been practiced for generations, fall into the same category (*Geelong Advertiser* 2007). Expanded whaling opportunities would, in the words of Nakamae, help assuage "suffering in the villages" (Morell 2007b).

"Some people want to deny us the right to use whales as food," Yoshinori Shoji, of the Japan Small-Type Whaling Association, remarked on a haul of 26 Baird's beaked whales in Wadaura. "The impact of catching this number of coastal whales every year is small and we are only doing as our ancestors did, nothing more. Why are so many people trying to deny us our right?" (Ryall 2007). Shoji and others argue that the limit ought to be upped significantly. "There are about 5,000 of these whales off the coast here during the summer season," he said. "We should be able to take more. There are nine boat licenses in the local whaling association, but because of limits on catches only five are able to operate" (ibid.).

Officials assert that Japan has every right to use natural resources as it sees fit, and not let useful resources such as whales go to waste. "What right does New Zealand have to tell us how to use the global sea commons?" Nakamae complained. "In the high seas, we divide up all resources, so why not whales?" (McNeill 2007)

It is admirable that Japanese officials have taken steps to familiarize Japanese children with lost traditions. Any diminished hankering for whale meat, Morishita has argued, is not the result of changing cultural preference but of interference from the West. The *desire* of Japanese to eat whale meat has not diminished, according to Morishita. "The supply was cut off. The Japanese didn't have a say in the matter" (Onishi 2007). To reintroduce whale meat into the Japanese diet, whale is served in school lunches with ketchup or sweet-and-sour sauce to make the strong-smelling meat, which children generally dislike, more palatable (ibid.).

Third, while working to overturn the ban on commercial whaling within the IWC and arguing for limited community whaling, Japan has justifiably been using the Article VIII stipulation on scientific whaling (Morell 2007a). The Japanese have maintained that whales have recovered from dips in population numbers and are no longer in danger of extinction. In fact, the Japanese contend, whales are "overeating" the world's fish and partially responsible for declining fish stocks (*Seattle Times* 2004). The ICR has estimated that whale consume three to five times the amount of fish caught by the world's fishing fleets (Freeman 2001). Because much of the fish consumed by whales is valuable as human food (Murase et al. 2007), further study – which requires vivisection – is warranted on both scientific and economic grounds (Freeman 2001).

To this end, the ICR kills and cleans more than 1,000 whales annually by "self-awarded" permits (Darby 2007) for scientific purposes (Morell 2007b). Many of these whales are culled from oceans of the southern hemisphere near Antarctica. Dan Goodman, a Canadian fisheries advisor and now a consultant for the Japanese government, has defended Japan's scientific whaling program as an essential component for Antarctic marine resources management (Jones 2007). Norwegian biologist Lars Walløe expressed trust in the Japanese program as "valid science," adding that the Japanese provide useful biopsy samples.

While Japanese whale research is not widely published, Morishita maintains that the Japanese are doing important science: "A lot of non-Japanese scientists are always calling for us to submit our data, and we present our research results every year to the [IWC] Scientific Committee and at other scientific meetings. If they think our data is so useless, I don't think they'd demand it" (Morell 2007a). Morishita believes that Western scientific journals are outwardly biased against Japanese scientific whaling, which accounts for the scant representation of the Japanese in peer-reviewed journals, not because of the lack of quality of Japanese research.

Perspective Two

According to the ethical theory of utilitarianism, the consequences of whaling, whether under the guise of community, commercial, or scientific whaling, are ecologically detrimental and must be stopped. Japanese claims of victimization by the international community are unfounded.

The analogy between Japanese and aboriginal community whaling is bogus (Morell 2007b). George Muller (2007b), a marine biologist from New Zealand, has cynically observed that it "definitely isn't traditional to send an industrial whaling fleet 10,000 km to the other side of the world." In the view of Aleut Indian and Greenpeace spokesperson George Pletnikoff (2007), Alaska Native subsistence whaling has been sustainable for thousands of years, whereas Japanese industrial whaling, despite whatever euphemism it is given, is not sustainable. Pletnikoff is offended by the commodification of whales by the Japanese (Pesznecker 2007).

The contention by Morishita that whaling is needed for domestic consumption is equally bogus. At home, the Japanese appetite for whale meat is meager. Whale consumption declined to 15,000 tons in 1985 from 226,000 tons in 1962 (Onishi 2007). Now only 1 percent of the population regularly eats whale meat (Muller 2007b). "Times have changed," said Mitsuo Matsuzawa, a Tokyo seafood merchant. "Whales used to be an important source of nutrition for generations after [World War II], when we had nothing to eat. Nowadays people buy and eat meat not as a main dish but as a delicacy or out of nostalgia for past dinners" (Ito 2007). In fact, the "cultural traditions" that Japanese officials cite as justification for whaling seem to be products of their own imaginations; according to residents of the Pacific fishing village of Taiji, only people aged 60 and older are enthusiastic about eating whale meat, while people aged 40 and under do not eat whale meat at all (Fackler 2008).

Nor are claims of the legitimacy of scientific whaling any more well grounded. Aside from the issue of whether vivisection is scientifically necessary, the sheer number of whales culled by the Japanese for alleged research raises suspicions about the real aims of the scientific whaling program. Walløe, who has written about Bergersen, said of Article VIII: "It's clear that in his mind he was thinking that the number of whales a country could take for science was less than 10; he didn't intend for hundreds to be killed for this purpose" (Morell 2007a). "Whether or not it is necessary for their study to take so many hundreds of whales every year for science, I cannot comment," Walløe conceded (ibid.).

As many scientists have pointed out, the most interesting and significant questions about whales can be answered through non-lethal methods, such as genetic analysis, satellite tracking, and observation of individual behavior and group dynamics (ibid.; Muller 2007a).

These scientists correctly condemn the Japanese scientific whaling program as a "farce" (*Gold Coast Bulletin* 2007), a shameless sham perpetrated to exploit Article VIII as cover for commercial whaling (Pletnikoff 2007). Australian marine biologist Nick Gale, who has studied Japanese scientific whaling, has claimed that only 34 peer-reviewed research papers have been published after 18 years and 8,300 dead whales (Dyer 2006). The productivity of Japanese researchers is "remarkably low," said Gales; "One would expect a far higher output of papers, certainly of the order several times more papers than they have produced" (ibid.). Muller has complained that "Japan's so-called research has published no worthwhile findings yet" (Muller 2007b), while American marine naturalist, Doug Thompson, has remarked that the Japanese research program has not revealed anything that could not be gleaned from an introductory marine biology textbook (Jones 2007). Less reserved in word-choice is Daniel Pauly, professor of fisheries science at the University of British Columbia. "It's outrageous to call this science; it's a complete charade" (Morell 2007a).

The claims of animal rights activists, who protest that Japanese whaling is cruel, also must be considered. Whales die an agonizing death at the hands of Japanese fishermen. Whales do not die instantly but slowly, bleeding after they are harpooned and drowning as they are winched underwater (*US Newswire* 2006). Morishita has flatly denied charges of cruelty, claiming Japanese whaling technique is done in "the most humane way, it is proved by science" (*Daily Telegraph* 2007).

What is most telling about the charade of the Japanese scientific whaling program is the fact that, though it has not produced much in the way of published findings, it has produced a lot of meat. Japanese officials openly admit that whale meat from the scientific research program ends up in markets and restaurants (*Townsville Bulletin* 2007), an inventory which reached 6,000 tons in 2006 (McNeill 2007). This has led to well-placed skepticism that Japan's scientific whaling program is actually about research. Australia's Federal Minister for Environment and Water Resources, Malcolm Turnbull, has expressed distrust of Japanese leaders and called for honesty on the part of Japan about its scientific whaling program (*Townsville Bulletin* 2007).

Western conservationists and politicians are right to maintain that embargos on whaling are a matter of principle, and exceptions for community and scientific whaling only set the stage for the return of full-scale commercial whaling. In Pletnifkoff's (2007) estimation, "without exception, every time commercial whaling has been tried, it has led to the severe depletion or near-extinction of targeted whale populations." Therein lies the concern. "The minute you open the door to commercial whaling, how do you shut it again?" Turnbull asked rhetorically. "That is the problem" (*Townsville Bulletin* 2007). The concern about repeating past history is confirmed by Toshio Kasuya, a former JFA bureaucrat: "It is common understanding of ours that Japanese coastal whalers [used to take] two or three times the number of sperm whales they actually reported" (Eilperin 2006).

Claims of Japanese cultural exceptionalism cannot hide the truth: under any guise, whaling produces ethically unacceptable results and must end.

Additional Issues to Consider

Other possible moral dilemmas arising within this case:

Q Under what, if any, conditions is moral respect due to the cultural traditions of countries?

Q Is moral respect ever due to aesthetic preferences (e.g., a "taste" for whale meat)?

Q Given Japan's ongoing flouting of the laws against whaling, are other countries that have been/continue to be economically or nutritionally disadvantaged by the whaling ban morally justified in breaking the laws as well?

REFERENCES

Alford, P. (2007) Japanese whalers and Greenies get physical. *The Australian* (February 14): 9.

Daily Telegraph (Australia) (2007) First we beat them in soccer, now it's whales (June 19): 9.

Darby, A. (2007) Japan refuses to back down on humpbacks. *The Age* (Melbourne) (June 2): 3.

Dolinsky, L. (2000) Notes from here and there. *San Francisco Chronicle* (October 20): A16.

Donlan, J. C., Martin, P. S., and Roemer, G. W. (2006) Lessons from land: overture to earth's sixth mass extinction. In J. A. Estes, D. P. DeMaster, D. F. Doak, et al. (eds.), *Whales, Whaling, and Ocean Ecosystems.* Berkeley: University of California Press, pp. 14–26.

D'Oro, R. (2007) Anti-whaling nations gain on final day. *Anchorage Daily News* (June 1): B1.

Dyer, P. (2006) Whaling outrage. *Sunday Times* (Perth, Australia) (January 29): 23.

Eilperin, J. (2006) Pro-hunting nations gain influence in whaling agency. *Seattle Times* (June 3): A7.

Fackler, M. (2008) Mercury taint divides a Japanese whaling town. *New York Times* (June 3): A8.

Freeman, J. (2001) Japanese claim whales eat more fish than humans do in move for full-scale hunting. *Herald* (Glasgow, UK) (June 7): 3.

Geelong Advertiser (Australia) (2007) Double catch heralds whale season (June 22): 27.

Gold Coast Bulletin (Southport, Queensland) (2007) Anti-whaling nations up pressure over hunt farce: Japan in sights as world zeros in (June 1): 11.

Herald Sun (Australia) (2007) Humpback row threatens split (June 2): 4.

ICRW (International Convention for the Regulation of Whaling) (1946) Protocol. Washington DC, December 2. Available at: www.iwcoffice.org/_documents/commission/convention.pdf (accessed October 2, 2007).

Ito, S. (2007) Whaling passions muted in Japan. *Agence France Presse* (English) (June 1).

Jones, N. (2007) Japan's whale of an issue: Commercial interests, conservationists clash on hunt. *Washington Times* (February 16): A17.

Kareiva, P., Yuan-Farrell, C., and O'Connor, C. (2006) Whales are big and it matters. In J. A. Estes, D. P. DeMaster, D. F. Doak, et al. (eds.), *Whales, Whaling, and Ocean Ecosystems.* Berkeley: University of California Press, pp. 379–87.

Larimer, T. (2000) Where harpoons fly. *Time Europe* 156 (15).

McNeill, D. (2007) Japan's whaling chief tackles mission impossible. *South China Morning Post* (June 2): 11.

Melville, H. (1992) *Moby-Dick, or, The Whale.* Penguin, New York (orig. pub. 1851).

Morell, V. (2007a) Killing whales for science? *Science* 316 (5824): 532–4.

Morell, V. (2007b) Whales (mostly) win at whaling commission meeting. *Science* 316 (5830): 1411.

Muller, C. G. (2007a) Whaling talks could backfire on NZ. Opinion-editorial. *New Zealand Herald* (June 12).

Muller, C. G. (2007b) Sustainable whaling: Fishery or a fallacy? Opinion-editorial. *Nelson Mail* (New Zealand) (June 30): 14.

Murase, H., Tamura, T., Kiwada, H., et al. (2007) Prey selection of Common Minke (*Balaenoptera acutorostrata*) and Bryde's (*Balaenoptera edeni*) whales in the western North Pacific in 2000 and 2001. *Fisheries Oceanography* 16 (2): 186–201.

Onishi, N. (2007) Whaling: a Japanese obsession, with American roots. *New York Times* (March 20): A4.

Pesznecker, K. (2007) As delegates gather, Greenpeace forces do too. *Anchorage Daily News* (May 28): A10.

Pletnikoff, G. (2007) Japan's "scientific" whaling a slap in face of conservation. Opinion-editorial. *Anchorage Daily News* (May 15): B4.

Rehn, A. (2007) Oceans of discontent. *Daily Telegraph* (Australia) (June 2): 82.

Ryall, J. (2007) Whalers cry foul over attempts to end slaughter as "research" kill continues. *South China Morning Post* (June 23): 18.

Seattle Post-Intelligencer (2006) Japan tried to dilute whaling ban. Editorial (April 18): B7.

Seattle Times (2004) Japan maneuver fails to undermine ban on whaling (July 20): A6.

Townsville Bulletin (Townsville, Queensland) (2007) Whale talks in stand-off (June 2): 16.

United Nations Convention on the Law of the Sea (1982) (December 10). United Nations, New York. Available at: www.un.org/Depts/los/convention_agreements/texts/unclos/unclos_e.pdf (accessed July 9, 2007).

US Newswire (2006) IFAW: Cruelty of Japanese whale hunt unveiled in new scientific report (June 17): 1.

CASE TWENTY-EIGHT: BIG PHARMA WANTS YOU – DIRECT-TO-CONSUMER ADVERTISING

In 2002 a 59-year-old Florida woman, identified as S.K., sued pharmaceutical giant Eli-Lilly, the drugstore chain Walgreens, and three physicians for improper medical practice, for invading her privacy, and for other violations of the Sunshine State's laws, alleging that Walgreens must have shared a list of antidepressant users with Eli-Lilly (Neergaard 2002). S.K. is one of approximately 150 people who received – unsolicited – a free, one-month supply of a new version of Prozac, *Prozac Weekly*. Michael Grinstead of Palm Beach, who was 16 years old, was another of the recipients (Agovina 2002).

The medication was accompanied by a "Dear Patient" generic letter signed by three local medical doctors, including S.K.'s personal physician, that stated: "We are very excited to be able to offer you a more convenient way to take your antidepressant medication. . . . For your convenience, enclosed you will find a FREE one-month trial of Prozac Weekly. . . . Congratulations on being one step closer to full recovery" (Singer 2002).

S.K., however, had not taken Prozac for years, because she did not tolerate the medication well. Michael, on the other hand, had never been diagnosed with, nor treated for, depression (Liptak 2002b).

As part of an aggressive marketing campaign, sales representatives for Eli-Lilly prepared the letter. The letters and samples of the new, long-acting drug, were delivered to the neighborhood Walgreens drugstore to be mailed in hand-addressed envelopes. Walgreens received reimbursement coupons from Eli-Lilly for the samples; what, if any, compensation prescribing physicians received is unknown (Liptak 2002a).

The increasingly pervasive effects of the pharmaceutical industry on patients, pharmacies, and physicians' prescribing habits are raising vexed questions about the ways in which physicians determine the best medications for their patients (Wazana 2000). Pharmacy–physician relationships typically begin in medical school, with pharmaceutical representatives often providing free food for students.

But bagels and sandwiches come at a price: pharmaceutical representatives have requested that physicians intercede on their behalf by asking hospitals to add their company's drugs to the institution's approved formulary. Continuing medical education opportunities are often sponsored by pharmaceutical companies; physicians attending these events may have travel expenses reimbursed or receive honoraria for presentations in which they laud the companies' products (*New York Times* 2007; Brennan et al. 2006). Companies' drugs are favorably compared with similar products. And in spite of physicians' disclaimers to the contrary, attendance at such events is correlated to increased prescribing of companies' products by physicians (Wazana 2000); presumably physicians are just repaying a favor or rewarding their new "friends."

Although increased prescribing may, in fact, be warranted (e.g., if superior therapeutic products are being under-utilized), the possibility of non-patient-centered motives of prescribing physicians is troubling. To address burgeoning concerns:

> The Pharmaceutical Research and Manufacturers of America (PhRMA) implemented a new code of conduct governing physician–industry relationships among its members in 2002. This code states that the interactions between company representatives and physicians should primarily benefit patients and enhance the practice of medicine. The code also discourages companies from giving physicians tickets to entertainment and recreational events, goods (e.g., golf balls and sporting bags) that do not convey a primary benefit to patients, and token consulting and advisory relationships that are used to reimburse physicians for their time, travel, or out-of-pocket expenses. The American Medical Association [AMA 2005] and the American College of Physicians have also adopted new codes that are similar to that of PhRMA. (Campbell 2007)

In spite of these proscriptions and of piqued interest by the US federal government (Chimonas and Rothman 2005), 83 percent of physicians surveyed continued to receive non-care-related benefits from pharmaceutical companies (Campbell 2007).

But physicians are not the only targets. As shown above, pharmaceutical companies reward major drug-store chains that contact patients and encourage them to either fill prescriptions, change to a different drug, or update to a newer version of a particular medication – all of which can increase profits for local or regional pharmacies and the chains of which they may be an extension. Special services related to particular drugs and/or diseases target patient-consumers by such means as email reminders about medications. Interestingly, the same temptations that seduce physicians also tempt pharmacists, potentially undercutting the patient protections avowed by a second profession (Piascik 2007).

Finally, pharmaceutical companies target patients directly. In 2000, the pharmaceutical industry spent roughly $2.5 billion on direct-to-consumer (DTC) advertising (Jagsi 2007). A survey of oncologists revealed the effects of such efforts: "94% of oncology nurse practitioners had received medication requests prompted by DTC ads and 40% receive one to five such requests per week" (ibid.: 903).

Proponents of DTC advertising (the primary objective of which is increasing sales) claim that – whatever form it takes and whatever the effects on a company's bottom line – DTC advertising provides a public service by fulfilling an educational role (ibid.), although the actual educational value of ads has been contested (Wolfe 2002). The possession of more information, proponents continue, should encourage or enhance physician–patient communications about management of their medical problems, or even encourage poor persons to appreciate their need for and seek healthcare.

On the other hand, DTC advertising is typically skewed. For example, the aimed-at positive effects are displayed and discussed prominently, while noxious, unhoped-for effects are shown in small print or rushed through by an actor. Further, if DTC ads drive patients to physicians – especially needlessly or repeatedly, positive effects on the patient–physician relationship are unlikely. Indeed, the relationships may deteriorate. Further, patients' drug expenses may rise if they replace older generic drugs with newer, patent-protected, more expensive drugs:

> Drugs are the fastest-growing part of the health care bill – which itself is rising at an alarming rate. The increase in drug spending reflects, in almost equal parts, the facts that people are taking a lot more drugs than they used to, that those drugs are more likely to be expensive new ones instead of older, cheaper ones, and that the prices of the most heavily prescribed drugs are routinely jacked up, sometimes several times a year. (Angell 2004)

Given these factors, coupled with the fact that many insurance companies only reimburse for the costs of generic drugs, increased expenses to patients are likely. Whether patients understand or appreciated the extent of these costs is unknown.

Evidence suggests that DTC advertising is effective in improving sales. One public survey discovered that 30 percent of persons who had been exposed to DTC ads discussed an advertised drug with their physicians, and 44 percent received a prescription for the drug (Jagsi 2007). And overhead costs for pharmaceutical companies are high: research, development, and production costs of a single successful drug characteristically climb to hundreds of millions of dollars, while sales profits are realized mostly during the duration of patent protection. Prozac's patent expired in August 2001 and its sales have since plummeted more than 80 percent, as a result both of the substitution of generic drugs for the expensive brand drug form and competition from other brand medications with similar modes of action (Goode 2002).

Should pharmaceutical companies, such as Eli-Lilly, be permitted to market directly to consumers?

Perspective One

Pharmaceutical companies should be allowed to market directly to consumers. Media, mail, and drugstore efforts aimed at introducing medications to patients constitute a valuable educational service. Indeed, DTC advertising may improve patient education, patient–physician communications, and, ultimately, patients' health status. If advertising better informs and empowers patients, healthcare may be better tailored to patients' needs.

Granted, in this particular case, the physicians who signed the letter violated their professional obligation to maintain patient confidentiality. The email should have been sent in such a way that the recipients were not able to see the email addresses of the other recipients. A patient's right to autonomy entails the right to control the amount and type of information available about that person (Beauchamp and Childress 2001: 21; McConnell 1997: 38). This right of control is also reflected in the law. The Health Information Portability and Accountability Act of 1996 requires that patient information be kept confidential unless the patient consents to its disclosure (US Department of Health and Human Services 2003: 4).

However, even though Eli-Lilly's complicity in the disclosure of confidential patient information reflects the above-mentioned violation of patient autonomy, their strategy of marketing directly to consumers should be seen as an effort to promote patient autonomy. Patients – indeed, consumers in general – have a right – based on the appeal to autonomy – to be informed about therapeutic options. Advertising drugs directly to consumers allows them to take greater control of their lives by providing information regarding new drugs and treatments. Hence, patients need not simply choose the treatment prescribed or recommended by their physicians. Rather, DTC marketing allows patients to initiate discussions of treatment alternatives that may have been overlooked or underappreciated. Admittedly, a person may see a drug advertisement and mistakenly be led to believe that the drug would be beneficial for him when it would have no, or even an adverse, effect in his case. However, if a particular drug would not offer benefit to a particular patient, a physician has an opportunity and an obligation to discuss this with the patient. Moreover, a physician can and should refuse to prescribe any drug that she believes to be inappropriate for a particular patient. However, to prohibit pharmaceutical companies, such as Eli-Lilly, from marketing directly to consumers could only be seen as an unjustified violation of the autonomy of patients and consumers.

Perspective Two

Pharmaceutical companies should not be allowed to market directly to consumers. Consideration of treatment alternatives should take place *only* within the physician–patient relationship. Members of the medical profession enjoy a special relationship with society. Society grants considerable power to physicians, power not given to regular citizens, to prescribe medications and perform certain procedures. Because health is such a fundamental good, it cannot be viewed as just any other good or service – legitimately negotiated in the open market. While it is wholly appropriate to advertise and market teeth-whiteners, athletic footwear, and video games, health and healthcare must not be numbered among these kinds of commercial goods. Society allows physicians to wield extraordinary power only under the condition that they adhere to the highest moral standards in protecting the well-being of patients. The physician–patient relationship is intended to provide a sanctuary from those commercial and social forces that may threaten the welfare of patients or physicians' abilities to promote both that welfare and the autonomy of the patient.

Marketing drugs directly to consumers shifts treatment choices from the protective guidance of the physician–patient relationship to the profit-driven open market that has no particular interest in promoting what is best for patients. The subtle forms of manipulation and coercion that society tolerates with the advertising of commercial items, such as those mentioned above (teeth-whitener, athletic footwear, etc.) are morally unacceptable when it comes to healthcare. It is one thing to manipulate a consumer into buying a particular breakfast cereal, but quite another to manipulate a patient into insisting on a particular medication. Health is simply too fundamental a good and patients are simply too vulnerable to be subjected to such forces.

Given all this, the violation of confidentiality that we find in the case should not be surprising. In the commercial realm, where users of products and services are customers, not patients, obligations are much thinner than in healthcare. There is little expectation of confidentiality in the "buyer beware" relationships with businesses. When there is a promise of confidentiality in business dealings, it is usually because the seller of the product or service believes that such a promise will likely enhance profit. However, this kind of justification for confidentiality is importantly distinct from that in healthcare. Healthcare professionals respect confidentiality because it is a necessary condition for meeting a fundament need of vulnerable people. In order for a therapeutic relationship to fulfill its purpose, patients must feel safe enough to speak openly and honestly with healthcare professionals. To this extent, we may identify another key ethical foundation for confidentiality in healthcare (other than the respect for autonomy mentioned in Perspective One): that of the obligation to promote good. Unlike healthcare, business has no intrinsic obligation to promote the good of people.

Our consideration of the violation of confidentiality in the case brings us back to the central point regarding the direct-to-consumer marketing of pharmaceuticals. Healthcare is a good so fundamental to people that it should not be treated like any commodity to be bought and sold. People who are ill and vulnerable to exploitation must be protected from the profit-driven sphere of the open market that has no concern for their well-being. Therefore, pharmaceutical companies should not be allowed to market directly to consumers.

Additional Issues to Consider

Other possible moral dilemmas arising within this case:

Q Should direct advertising to consumers en masse – for example, television, radio, newspaper, and print media ads – be restricted?

Q Should direct advertising to *individual* consumers – for example, direct mailing or door-to-door solicitation – be restricted?

Q Should direct advertising to physicians en masse – for example, television, radio, newspaper, and print media ads – be restricted?

Q Should direct advertising to *individual* physicians – for example, office visits by pharmaceutical representatives – be restricted?

Q Should direct advertising to *individual* pharmacists – for example, on-site visits, provision of free samples – be restricted?

REFERENCES

Agovina, T. (2002) 16-year-old boy gets Prozac in mail. Available at: www.namiscc.org/News/2002/Summer/ProzacMailing.htm (accessed October 19, 2007).

American Medical Association (2005) Ethical guidelines for gifts to physicians from industry. Available at: www.ama-assn.org/ama/pub/category/5689.html (accessed October 22, 2007).

Angell, M. (2004) The truth about the drug companies. *The New York Review of Books* 51 (12). Available at: www.nybooks.com/articles/17244 (accessed October 23, 2007).

Baron, R. B. Debates: Is continuing medical education a drug-promotion tool? NO. *Canadian Family Physician* 53 (10): 1650–3.

Beauchamp, T. L., Childress, J. F. (2007) *Principles of Biomedical Ethics*, 5th edn. New York: Oxford University Press.

Brennan, T. A., Rothman, D. J. Blank, L., et al. (2006) Health industry practices that create conflicts of interest: A policy proposal for academic medical centers. *JAMA: Journal of the American Medical Association* 295 (4): 429–33.

Campbell, E. G. (2007) A national survey of physician–industry relationships. *New England Journal of Medicine* 356 (17): 1742–50.

Chimonas, S., and Rothman, D. J. (2005) New federal guidelines for physician–pharmaceutical industry relations: the politics of policy formation. *Health Affairs* 24 (4): 949–60.

Goode, E. (2002) Antidepressants lift clouds, but lose "miracle drug" label. *New York Times* (June 30) Available at: http://query.nytimes.com/gst/fullpage.html?res=990CE0D81E3EF933A05755C0A9649C8B63 (accessed October 20, 2007).

Jagsi, R. (2007) When the tumor is not the target: conflicts of interest and the physician-patient relationship in the era of direct-to-patient advertising. *Journal of Clinical Oncology* 25 (7): 902–5.

Kahn, J. (2002) Medicine in your junk mail. *CNN.com/Health* (July 9). Available at: http://archives.cnn.com/2002/HEALTH/07/08/ethics.matters/index.html (accessed October 19, 2007).

KRON 4 News (2002) Prozac in the mail. Available at: www.kron4.com/Global/story.asp?S=848714andnav=5D7vA0PG (accessed October 19, 2007).

Liptak, A. (2002a) Free Prozac in the junk mail draws a lawsuit. *New York Times* (July 6). Available at: www.forensic-psych.com/articles/artNYTfreeprozac.html (accessed October 20, 2006).

Liptak, A. (2002b) Prozac mailed unsolicited to a teenager in Florida. *New York Times*, July 21). Available at: http://query.nytimes.com/gst/fullpage.html?res= 9B02E3DB1638F932A15754C0A9649C8B63 (accessed October 19, 2007).

McConnell, T. C. (1996) *Moral Issues in Health Care: An Introduction to Health Care Ethics*, 2nd edn. Wadsworth Publishing Company.

Neergaard, L. (2002) Floridians get Prozac samples in the mail. Available at: www. namiscc.org/News/2002/Summer/ProzacMailing.htm (accessed October 20, 2007).

New York Times (2007) Editorial: Is your doctor tied to drug makers? (July 2). Available at: www.nytimes.com/2007/07/02/opinion/02mon2.html?_r=1andoref= sloginandpagewanted=print (accessed October 22, 2007).

Piascik, P. (2007) Gifts and corporate influence in Doctor of Pharmacy education. *American Journal of Pharmaceutical Education* 71 (4): 1–8.

Singer, G. (2002) Free sample of Prozac triggers privacy lawsuit. Available at: www. namiscc.org/News/2002/Summer/ProzacMailing.htm (accessed 20 October 2007).

Steinman, M. A. (2007) Debates: Is continuing medical education a drug-promotion tool? YES. *Canadian Family Physician* 53 (10): 1650–3.

Wazana, A. (2000) Physicians and the pharmaceutical industry: is a gift ever just a gift? *Journal of the American Medical Association* 283 (3): 373–80.

Wolfe, N. (2002) Direct-to-consumer advertising – education or emotion promotion? *New England Journal of Medicine* 346 (7) (February 14): 524–6.

US Department of Health and Human Services (2003) *Summary of the HIPAA Privacy Rule*. Washington, DC: 4.

CASE TWENTY-NINE: THIS GUN'S FOR HIRE – EXXONMOBIL AND THE INDONESIAN MILITARY

Global economics are bringing multinational corporations and sovereign nations and their armed forces into increasing complex – and problematic – alliances. The relationship of the ExxonMobil Corporation with the Indonesian Military foreshadows ethical difficulties that further globalization is certain to intensify.

The Indonesian archipelago, colonized by the Dutch in the seventeenth century, has a long history of political instability. One of many areas of instability is the Aceh province on the northern tip of the island of Sumatra. The Free Aceh Movement (known by its Indonesian acronym, GAM) was founded in 1976 by the descendant of the last sultan of the Kingdom of Aceh on the principle that the Dutch never legitimately ruled the kingdom. When the Republic of Indonesia was formed in 1949, GAM asserted that Aceh should not have been included and that the sovereignty of Aceh must be restored.

Tensions between the Acehenese people and the Indonesian government have been exacerbated by the perception that the wealth of the province's substantial natural resources has not been fairly shared. The development of ExxonMobil natural gas facilities, for example, displaced many Acehenese from their ancestral homeland. Despite the fact that ExxonMobil earns hundreds of millions of dollars per year in profit from its Aceh operations, no noticeable improvement in the standard of living for most local villagers has resulted. "The poor are getting poorer," one villager said. "The rich are getting richer" (Perlez 2002).

Claiming that ExxonMobil profits rightly belonged to the province of Aceh, GAM insurgents attacked ExxonMobil facilities in 2001, closing down the plant down for four months (ibid.). In order to protect its corporate interests, ExxonMobil increased its security force, comprising members of the Indonesian military and police, to 3,000. The villagers refer to this force as "the ExxonMobil army" (ibid.). Although the Indonesian military is well known for human rights abuses throughout the vast Indonesian archipelago (Banergee 2001), hiring elements of the Indonesian military is not unusual: in Irian Jaya, Louisiana-based Freeport-McMoRan has used Indonesian military patrols to secure its Grasberg mine. To many human rights activists and advocates of the poor, the practice of using the Indonesian military to facilitate the exploitation of local peoples by multinational corporations inflames, rather than mitigates, the atmosphere of antagonism it created in the first place.

In June 2001, the International Labor Rights Fund brought a lawsuit against ExxonMobil on behalf of Acehenese villagers (US District Court 2001). The suit, titled *Doe v. ExxonMobil Corporation*, alleges that ExxonMobil aided and abetted Indonesian soldiers in kidnapping, torture, rape, and murder by providing barracks where the abuses allegedly took place and by providing heavy equipment for digging mass graves (Banergee 2001). ExxonMobil filed a motion to dismiss the case, arguing that honoring the plaintiffs' claims would set a negative precedent for all American companies operating abroad. The US Court of Appeals (2007) denied ExxonMobil's motion.

The legal foundation for *Doe v. ExxonMobil* is the previously dormant Alien Tort Statute (ATS) of the First US Congress, now commonly referred to as the Alien Tort Claims Act (ATCA). The ATCA permits foreign citizens to litigate in US courts alleged violations of international law. These cases may involve foreign litigants who have no direct ties to the United States, but who nonetheless use US courts to try cases of violations of international law – e.g., the 1980 case of a Paraguayan physician successfully suing a former police officer for allegedly torturing and killing the physician's 17-year-old son (Glaberson 2001). The case of ExxonMobil may involve foreign actions of US individuals and/or companies on foreign soil. The suit is but one example of the much larger issue of the moral and legal culpability of private US companies to foreigners; similar lawsuits have been brought against Chevron, Royal Dutch/Shell, and Unocal (Banergee 2001).

The ramification of the ATCA is that US courts might end up carrying the Herculean responsibility of becoming arbiters of international justice. Violations of international law, particularly human rights law, may be treated in US courts, even if those alleged violations occurred in foreign countries. The potential magnitude of such litigation has caused considerable confusion. The US Supreme Court has attempted to clarify the ATCA, but divergence in interpreting the law continues to expand in lower courts. While some courts have construed the ATCA narrowly, limiting the kinds of cases that can be brought to trial, others have interpreted the it broadly, recognizing novel claims and theories of liability (Drimmer 2007). Some argue that if these suits are allowed to proceed, the ATCA could become a powerful tool in increasing corporate accountability. Others worry that the ATCA litigation violates the legal immunity that is traditionally the purview of sovereign nation-states.

The broader interpretation of the ATCA has enormous implications. It raises the question of the liability of rich and powerful multinational corporations that often enter into alliances for practical purposes with governments of dubious human rights records. Perhaps because of the enormity of the possible impact of the ATCA litigation, the Bush administration has split from antecedent executive branch neutrality on such matters (Waldman and Mapes 2002). Contra President Clinton, President Bush has actively sought to dismiss suits brought under the ATCA, instead favoring the big corporations implicated in human rights abuses (Alden 2002), while at the same time categorically denouncing violations of human rights.

President Bush has evoked the rhetoric of unwavering commitment to respect for human life more than any other president in recent memory. In an opinion-editorial published on the anniversary of the September 11 terrorist attacks, President Bush (2002) stated: "We are determined to stand for the values that gave our nation its birth. We believe that freedom and respect for human rights are owed to every human being, in every culture. We believe that the deliberate murder of innocent civilians and the oppression of women are everywhere and always wrong. And we refuse to ignore or appease the aggression and brutality of evil men."

Yet in the same year, top State Department lawyer William Taft (2002) urged the federal judge presiding over the ExxonMobil case to dismiss the lawsuit as the defendants had requested, arguing that allowing it to proceed is antithetical to the best interests of the United States. First, according to Taft, the litigation is likely to be seen by the Indonesian government as an affront to their sovereignty and would damage American–Indonesian relations. Since Indonesia is the world's largest Muslim nation, this could seriously hinder the "ongoing struggle against international terrorism" (ibid.). Second, the litigation is likely to thwart US efforts to work with the Indonesian government to improve business practices, which in the long run would improve Indonesia's human rights record. Third, the litigation is likely to worsen the global economy, a claim backed by a Washington DC think-tank, the Institute for International Economics (IIE): while corporations might face punitive damages of up to $20 billion through the ATCA litigation, the real victim would be the global economy. The IIE argues that the scope of awards under the ATCA would be such that "investment and trade in developing countries will be seriously threatened. The ultimate losers will be millions of impoverished people denied an opportunity to participate in global markets" (Blass 2006).

Critics cite the Bush administration's meddling in the ATCA litigation as an outright betrayal of the very ideals the administration avows to uphold. In the words of the director of the International Labor Rights Fund, who brought the lawsuit against ExxonMobil: "We have an administration that is much closer to corporate interests" (Waldman and Mapes 2002). This perhaps should not be surprising, as ExxonMobil was the second largest campaign contributor in the 2000 election cycle amongst oil and gas companies, with 89 percent of its contributions going to Republicans (ibid.).

Scholars find White House-corporate collusion exceedingly tenuous from a legal standpoint (O'Donnell 2004). Any problems with the implementation of the ATCA in US courts should be addressed and corrected by Congress, which enacted the legislation, not by executive branch fiat (Sebok 2004). It is a violation of presidential powers to intervene in matters of the court.

Seen through the prism of the realties of globalism, the ATCA is either a powerful tool for policing corporate social responsibility or a spanner in the wheels of free trade. As legal scholar Jennifer Elsea notes (2003), the original intention of the First Congress in enacting the ATS will probably never be known. Subsequent congresses will likely confront the task of either clarifying the ATCA's intent or repealing it. Human rights activists are likely to argue that multinational corporations have the freedom and the responsibility to steer clear of forging alliances with objectionable foreign regimes, and if they do forge such alliances, they should not do so outside the purview of international law. Multinational corporations will likely argue that the ATCA legislation unfairly allows human rights activists to use them as proxies to punish those persons or institutions really guilty of human rights violations. If the ATCA legislation succeeds, they will likely assert that the global economy will suffer, as will the poor peoples of the world whom human rights activists are purportedly trying to help.

Yet for the Acehenese who suffered at the hands of ExxonMobil's Indonesian security forces, the ATCA may be the only way to achieve justice and establish standards of multinational corporation accountability.

Was ExxonMobil justified in hiring Indonesian security forces known for violent human rights abuses even though doing so was good for the corporate bottom-line?

Additional Issues to Consider

Other possible moral dilemmas arising within this case:

Q In the era of globalization, should multinational corporations be held to the same ethical standards in foreign operations as in their home countries?

Q Would ExxonMobil be justified in hiring Indonesian security forces if they did not have a history of violent human rights abuses?

REFERENCES

Alden, E. (2002) US tries to halt rights suit against Exxon. *Financial Times* (August 5).
Alien Tort Claims Act. 28 USC §1350.

Banerjee, N. (2001) Lawsuit says Exxon aided rights abuses. *New York Times* (June 21): C1.

Blass, T. (2006) Under the shadow of ATCA. *Foreign Direct Investment Magazine* (June 5). Available at: www.fdimagazine.com/news/printpage.php/aid/1668/Under_the_shadow_of_ATCA.html (accessed June 1, 2007).

Bush, G. W. (2002) Securing freedom's triumph. Opinion-editorial. *New York Times* (September 11): A33.

Drimmer, J. C. (2007) Corporate exposure under the Alien Tort Claims Act. *Corporate Counselor* (June).

Elsea, J. K. (2003) The alien tort statute: Legislative history and executive branch views. *Congressional Research Service* (October 2). Washington DC: The Library of Congress.

Glaberson, W. (2001) US courts become arbiters of global rights and wrongs. *New York Times* (June 21): A1.

O'Donnell, M. J. (2004) A turn for the worse: Foreign relations, corporate human rights abuse, and the courts. *Boston College Third World Law Journal* 24: 223–65.

Perlez, J. (2002) Indonesia's guerrilla war put Exxon under siege. *New York Times* (July 14): A1, A3.

Sebok, A. J. (2004) The Supreme Court confronts the Alien Tort Claims Act: Should the court gut the law, as the administration suggests? *Findlaw* (March 22). Available at: http://writ.news.findlaw.com/sebok/20040322.html (accessed June 1, 2007).

Taft, W. H., IV. (2002) Memo to Louis F. Oberdorfer (July 29).

US Court of Appeals for the District of Columbia Court Circuit (2007) *Doe v. ExxonMobil Corporation*, no. 05-7162 (decided January 12).

US District Court for the District of Columbia (2001) *Doe v. ExxonMobil Corporation*, no. 01-1257 (filed June 11).

Waldman, P., and Mapes, T. (2002) White House sets new hurdles for suits over rights abuses. *Wall Street Journal* (August 7).

8

FREEDOM FROM OR FREEDOM TO?

Ethical Issues in Government

Case Thirty: Battle Scars – Suing the Government for Medical Malpractice

Case Thirty-one: Does the Past Mean Never Having to Say We're Sorry? – Reparations and Apologies

Case Thirty-two: Words Fail – Institutional Responses to Creative Violence

Case Thirty-three: The Idealism of Youth – Civil Disobedience and the BYU Honor Code

Case Thirty-four: Britannia Waives the Rules – Collecting DNA on Arrestees

Case Thirty-five: Land of the Free – The Gun Ban at the University of Utah

We generally accept that we have a responsibility beyond ourselves, and beyond family and friends and our immediate community, to make a positive contribution to the general good. We are taxed in part to provide services to all, but also to create a more equitable balance of benefits and burdens. We do not want limits, restrictions, or forced choices imposed upon us, yet we would have others be restricted in their behavior. Without some constraint on individual freedoms, the preservation of social order and promotion of the general welfare are unlikely to be insured. The often uneasy relationships between individuals and groups give rise to many vexing questions.

How do we balance our personal interests against the common good? Do moral obligations, moral responsibility, or the rules of ethical behavior differ when applied to individuals and to the collection of individuals who comprise a society? When do restrictions on personal freedom demonstrate prudence, and when do they suggest prejudice? When may such restrictions be morally required, and when do they constitute immoral intrusions? When public interest and personal choice cannot both be accommodated, what ethical principles should define the balance between individual freedoms and the welfare of the community?

These and other moral conflicts in defining the responsibilities to and responsibilities of citizens and governments are considered in this chapter, "Freedom From or Freedom To? Ethical Issues in Government."

CASE THIRTY: BATTLE SCARS – SUING THE GOVERNMENT FOR MEDICAL MALPRACTICE

During a complete hysterectomy (removal of the uterus, ovaries, and fallopian tubes) on Dona Perez, the scalpel slipped, slicing a half-inch hole in her bladder. In the months that followed, Mrs Perez suffered continual fever, pain, and loss of bladder control. Repeated visits to the Jacksonville (Florida) Naval Hospital were unsuccessful in identifying the reason for her symptoms, or in alleviating them. More than a year later, Mrs Perez was told that the original surgery had caused an obstructed ureter, which in turn necrotized (caused the death of) one of her kidneys. During a second surgery to remove the dead kidney, the scalpel again slipped, cutting a major artery, resulting in the loss of more than a gallon of blood. Because of complications from the two surgeries, Ms Perez was forced to use a tube to urinate and to endure hormonal imbalances that caused extreme mood swings; she suffered from constant pain and was left with severe scarring. To make matters worse, the original surgery was an inappropriate treatment to alleviate pelvic inflammatory pain, according to both the physician who treated Mrs Perez following her second surgery and the expert witness who testified in the successful malpractice suit filed by Mrs Perez (Pinkham et al. 2006: 1, A6–7).

The swelling and lesions that covered half of Lieutenant Commander Walter Hardin's body were severe enough to require hospitalization. A doctor at the Jacksonville Naval Hospital diagnosed the problem as eczema. By the time the cancer was correctly diagnosed nearly a year later, it had spread so much that it was untreatable. Despite the medical errors and negligence that resulted in Lieutenant Commander Hardin's death, his wife was prohibited from suing the military hospital or its physicians (Pinkham and Lake 2006: A7).

Mrs Perez, a civilian married to a former navy signalman, was able to bring a suit against the naval hospital and its doctors. Had she been an active duty member of the armed services, as was Lieutenant Commander Hardin, she would have been prohibited by the *Feres Doctrine* from suing the military. While even prisoners have the right to sue the government for malpractice or medical negligence, active military personnel are prohibited from suing the United States and its agents (*Estelle v. Gamble* 1976).

The 1950 US Supreme Court case, *Feres v. United States*, greatly expanded the protection offered the US government under the 1946 Federal Tort Claims Act, which prohibits military personnel from suing the government for injuries received in combat. The *Feres Doctrine* prohibits members of the armed services from suing the federal government, or agents of the government, for any injury suffered while in the service, no matter what its cause (*Feres v. United States* 1950).

Malpractice suits at the Jacksonville Naval Hospital, the fourth largest naval hospital in the United States, are significantly more frequent than at comparable hospitals. According to a survey conducted by the *Florida Times-Union News*, malpractice suits were filed against the hospital at five times the regional average in 2002 and 2003 (Ezell 2006). However, this rate may actually reflect only a percentage of the cases of medical error, as active service members are not allowed to file suit against the military, military doctors, or military-contracted physicians – and one in four Jacksonville Naval Hospital patients is on active duty (Pinkham et al. 2006: 1, A6).

The *Feres Doctrine* applies not only to medical malpractice and wrongful death cases, but to any action that would create liability, were the victims civilians. Angela Morse and Stacey Handley were ROTC (Reserve Officers' Training Corps) cadets at the University of Colorado when they became victims of sexual harassment, gender bias, and unwanted sexual advances from several male cadets. When they reported the abuse, they were further victimized by malicious retaliation by superior officers and cadets, including a lawsuit filed against Handley by one of the defendants. The case was dismissed under the *Feres Doctrine*, although the court allowed Morse and Handley to sue the university (*Morse v. West* 1999). Despite the university's claim that it was not responsible for the behavior of participants in the military-sponsored ROTC program, the court decided in favor of Morse and Handley (*Morse v. Regents* 1998). Although the military claims it is doing more to prevent sexual assault, the Associated Press (2007) reported that sexual assault in the military rose 24 percent in 2006. In fact, 78 percent of the women treated for Post-Traumatic Stress Disorder (PTSD) at the Department of Veteran's Affairs Women's Trauma Recovery Program in Palo Alto, California, suffer PTSD as a result of sexual assault by fellow members of the US military (Fratangelo 2007). The Department of Defense does not have a system-wide method to collect data on sexual assault (NOW 2006).

Despite international laws prohibiting experimentation on human subjects without their informed consent, the US military has experimented on hundreds of thousands of non-voluntary military personnel. In the 1994 report to Congress, *Is Military Research Hazardous to Veterans' Health?* (often referred to as the Rockefeller Report, after Senator John Rockefeller, who chaired the committee), a half century of research experiments conducted by the military on non-consenting human subjects was exposed. Members of the armed services were given experimental drugs, exposed to nerve agents, medicated with hallucinogenic drugs, and forced to participate in countless experiments where hazards were known or suspected. For decades, the military denied that the experiments took place, refused to acknowledge or treat veterans who suffered noxious consequences from experimentation, denied research subjects access to their health records, and in many cases threatened punishment or imprisonment if the individual refused to participate or if treatments were discussed with personal physicians after discharge from the service. In spite of these unconsented-to experiments and the resulting harms, many of which are severe, the *Feres Doctrine* precludes the veterans from suing for damages.

Legislators, judges, military personnel, and civilians have repeatedly called for the *Feres Doctrine* to be reconsidered, while the administration and military officers insist its intact preservation is essential to the defense of the country (Greenhouse 1986). Those who support its re-examination maintain that members of the armed services who defend democracy and civil liberties throughout the world should have the same right to redress grievances as those they protect. Opponents contend that allowing service members to sue would undermine the discipline that is essential to an effective military.

From a moral perspective, should the *Feres Doctrine* be safeguarded and should military personnel continue to be prohibited from suing the government?

Perspective One

The *Feres Doctrine* should be preserved intact, and military personnel should be prohibited from suing the government.

Unquestioned authority, the hierarchy of command, and obedience of all lawful orders are necessary to maintain an efficient and disciplined military (Moskop 2004: 3). Obedience, duty, and loyalty are the bases of military discipline (*United States v. Johnson* 1987: 682). Military discipline is essential to an effective fighting or defensive force, and for maximally protecting troops who are in harm's way. If military personnel were allowed to question authority, the chain of command would be compromised to the point of chaos. Questioning military decisions could expose sensitive or strategic information. Strategy and coordination would be impossible, and the military would be crippled. Sound judgment and knowledge are required to make numerous technical, strategic, and command decisions, and to balance necessary compromises between troop safety and military effectiveness (*Boyle* 1988: 511). If military personnel were allowed to sue the military or government, the courts – without the benefit of military experience – would substitute their judgment for those of military leaders. Requiring members of the armed services to testify against superiors or commanding officers would seriously damage loyalty to duty and respect for authority that is essential to military effectiveness. In short, the appeal to the principle of utility entails preserving *Feres Doctrine*.

Entering the military is a morally significant decision (Moskop 2004: 6). Men and women enlist in the military knowing that they may be required to perform duties at odds with their personal values, or cooperate in communal actions that they might prefer to avoid. Parental, spousal, and filial responsibilities may be compromised by military duty. Families often endure emotional and financial hardship, particularly during extended deployment. Multiple obligations create conflicts. Nonetheless, this information is provided to enlistees who, upon joining the armed forces, relinquish their personal autonomy to challenge or avoid these duties or hardships.

Conflicting obligations arise in the practice of military medicine, as they do in any healthcare system where doctors face decisions of resource utilization that limit the extent of care some patients receive. Military doctors are not as free as civilian physicians to make treatment decisions. They do, however, have the same obligations to their patients as non-military physicians do, and are morally obligated to honor the principles of beneficence, non-maleficence, respect for autonomy and patients' rights, and justice.

These obligations, however, may be attenuated by military necessity. Military patients' rights to confidentiality, privacy, and informed consent, as well as to other autonomy-based considerations, are limited. Military physicians may be under orders not to optimize treatment for all patients (Moskop 2004: 1–3). Moreover, military personnel, including physicians, can be reassigned at a moment's notice, compromising patient–physician communication and continuity of care. Increased demands for overseas deployment and a priority for treating deployed troops have created a shortage of healthcare providers in military hospitals (Pinkham and Lake 2006: 7).

The consequences in question – preserving freedom, national security, and order – necessarily take precedence over the rights of individuals. Because the *Feres Doctrine* is needed to achieve these outcomes, its preservation is morally mandated.

Perspective Two

The *Feres Doctrine* should be abandoned, and military personnel should have the same right as private citizens to sue the government.

The *Feres Doctrine* protects military and political leaders, military medical providers, defense and civilian contractors, and civilian military employees who supply products or services to the government from litigation by members of the military.

Although physicians must be licensed to practice medicine in individual states, an exemption is made for military doctors who may practice medicine in every state. Chad Roberts, a lawyer and former member of the navy, accuses the military of protecting negligent doctors by shielding them from personal liability. When the *Florida Times-Union* investigated the licenses of 18 military doctors involved in malpractice claims from 2001 through 2005, it discovered no negative comments or disciplinary actions in their records (Pinkham et al. 2006: A6).

Protection from liability is not only granted to government agencies and personnel, but to civilian contractors as well. Navymen Nollie Costo and Christopher Graham were off-duty when they drowned on a rafting trip run by civilian operators – who were accused of ignoring the river's hazardous conditions. Because Costo and Graham had signed up for the raft excursion through the naval base, the negligence suit brought by their families against the trip operators was dismissed under the *Feres Doctrine*. In a strongly worded dissent in the case, Judge Warren J. Ferguson wrote: "I believe the *Feres Doctrine* violates the equal protection rights of military servicemen and women. I also believe *Feres* violates our constitutional separation of powers" (*Costo v. USA* 2001: 5020).

Judge Ferguson's concern over the separation of powers stems from "judicial legislation," that is, law created by the courts that goes beyond the original intent of Congress. Judicial legislation continues to expand the application of the Federal Tort Claims Act to incidents far removed from its original intent of exemption from liability for combat injuries. This expansion creates egregious inequities and harms to members of the military. The *Feres Doctrine* protects those who cause lasting harm to men and women, sacrificing the personal liberty and rights of those in the service to their country.

Complaints of (unpunished) negligence or harm in the military remain within the chain of command, and even commanding officers may be unaware of incidents. As complaints are not litigated, nor frequently even reported, there is no reliable way of assessing how widespread negligence, abuse, and assault are in the military. Families of victims and survivors are often unaware that they have been victims of negligence, and servicemen and women who need follow-up medical care do not receive it (Turley 2007: 13).

The *Feres Doctrine* should be abolished.

Perspective Three

The dilemma of the *Feres Doctrine* involves several conflicting moral appeals. On the one hand, retaining the *Feres Doctrine* is supported by the moral appeals to utility and to the virtue of professional (military) integrity. On the other hand, abolishing the *Feres Doctrine* is supported by appeals to beneficence and non-maleficence: respect for autonomy, understood as the foundation of informed consent and truth-telling; rights; justice, understood as equal consideration and equal respect; and justice understood as fairness. Although the moral appeals to abolishing the *Feres Doctrine* have great justification, abolishing it could, in fact, undermine discipline and encourage armed service personnel to disrespect their superior officers and shirk from their duties, thereby causing great harm to the military as an institution, as well as to individual members of the armed services. Is there a middle ground that offers a creative solution? If the *Feres Doctrine* were to be revised, what information would need to be considered?

Step 1: Information-gathering

Implications

- Will revising the *Feres Doctrine* undermine the ability of the military to fulfill its mission?
- Will revising the *Feres Doctrine* affect military authority and the chain of command?
- What effects will revising the *Feres Doctrine* have on military discipline?

Medical

- Does the *Feres Doctrine* cause medical harm or allow it to be sustained?
- Will revising the *Feres Doctrine* compromise the ability of scientists to conduct research on immediate dangers to troops?

History

- Do concerns regarding the *Feres Doctrine* reflect a widespread history and practice of deceit and non-accountability in the military, or are they based on a few isolated incidents?

Legal

- Will the scrutiny of the courts in cases involving military personnel jeopardize national security or compromise confidential information?
- Do ethical standards exist that articulate obligatory or prohibited practices in medicine and medical research?
- Do professional standards of practice have their same force in military as in civilian institutions?
- Do professional codes of ethics have their same force in military as in civilian settings?

Economic

- Are disability benefits that military personnel receive for non-combat injuries adequate compensation?
- Will allowing military personnel to sue the government create an unreasonable economic burden for the country?

Psychosocial

- What impact does the *Feres Doctrine* have on morale and trust?

Step 2: Creative problem-solving

A creative solution must allow the military to function efficiently while preserving patient autonomy, preventing human rights abuses, and compensating victims for some types of harms. The *Feres Doctrine* could be revised to define exceptional circumstances under which military personnel could sue government agencies. These would include any activities that *themselves contributed to* a decline in military efficiency. Medical malpractice, harms from non-consensual research experimentation, and sexual assault seem to meet this description. Medical malpractice and experimental interventions expose service personnel to poor medical care and negative health outcomes, limiting their abilities to perform their assigned duties. Sexual assault threatens military efficiency by inflicting physical and emotional harm, destroying trust, and tempting victims to transfer out of positions for which they are qualified (thus reducing efficiency by increasing personnel turnover). In 2002, Senator Patrick Leahy, chair of the Senate Judiciary Committee, expressed this concern with *Feres*:

> In general, our civil justice system forces individuals and organizations to behave with care by punishing negligence. By adopting the FTCA (Federal Tort Claims Act), Congress sought to impose the same discipline on government agencies, while also providing compensation for individuals who had suffered harm. I believe the burden should be on the Executive Branch to show why the *Feres Doctrine* should not be amended or abolished. (Leahy 2002)

Military personnel who protect their country's freedom and citizens' human rights and civil liberties deserve the same right to redress grievances as those whose rights they defend.

Step 3: Listing pros and cons

Options	Pros	Cons
Preserve the *Feres Doctrine in toto*.	1. Preserves military discipline (C-U) 2. Preserves respect for authority (C-U) 3. Promote professional integrity and patriotism (V-I)	4. Lack of accountability for harms sanctions abuse (C-NM, C-U) 5. Loss of trust in government (C-U) 6. Powerful fail in their duty to protect the weak (V-I) 7. Armed services personnel denied rights, benefits they safeguard for others (R, J-E)
Modify the *Feres Doctrine* to allow armed service personnel to bring suit for medical malpractice, unconsented-to research experimentation, and sexual assault.	8. Restitution made for harms (C-B, J-F) 9. Deters negligence and wrongful acts (C-B) 10. Requires truth-telling (A; V-honesty) 11. Protect human and civil rights, liberty (R) 12. Laws applied consistently in both military and civilian society (J-E) 13. Professionals act honorably (V-Integrity) 14. Negligent practitioners would be held accountable (J-F, A)	15. Respect for authority and hierarchy of command may be weakened (C-U) 16. Military discipline may be compromised (C-U) 17. Could result in hundreds of thousands of lawsuits (C-U)

Preserving the *Feres Doctrine* as it is currently interpreted is fraught with moral problems, while modifying it raises other significant concerns. Which alternative carries greater moral justification?

Step 4: Analysis

Factual assumptions

- Military discipline and respect for hierarchy of command are essential for an effective military.
- The military has a history of abuse of human research subjects.
- The major cost of malpractice suits stems from protracted litigation over compensation to victims of preventable harms.
- Failure to adequately compensate victims of negligent or deliberate harm imposes economic and psychological burdens.

Value assumptions

- Persons who have been harmed through negligence or error should be compensated for harms suffered.
- All persons should have the right of access to their medical records.
- Military personnel should have some right to redress grievances, even though it may necessarily be limited.
- The military should comply with the law.
- The military should conduct itself so that it is trusted and respected.
- Persons who have caused harmed through negligence, error, or otherwise inappropriate behavior should be held accountable.

Step 5: Justification

Discipline, obedience, and respect for the hierarchy of command are principles essential to an effective military. Members of a military unit must be able to trust each other with their lives and know that they can depend on others in their units to carry out their duties. Sacrificing autonomy for the common good is necessary to form cohesion and loyalty among comrades and to maximize efficient performance of the group as a unit. Military duty justly requires that some autonomy be relinquished (Reasons ##1, 2, 3). These principles of military service are not absolute. Military personnel are not obliged to obey unlawful orders; in fact, they are required to act autonomously and refuse to follow unlawful commands. Relinquishing autonomy entails mutual duty. Subordinates are required to sacrifice personal choice, in the service of duty, to promote the common goal of an efficient military, which in turn protects the larger society. Superiors also have a duty to subordinates. Legitimate moral authority obligates those with power to protect those who have relinquished their own autonomy to their military superiors. In military service this (obviously) does not mean that commanders must refrain from sending troops into danger; it means that those in authority must accept accountability for their actions and responsibility for the consequences of those actions, and must avoid risking serious harms to troops unless doing so is necessary to achieve military objectives (Reason #3).

In 1946, Congress passed the Federal Tort Claims Act (FTCA) to assure accountability in the actions of the US government and its agencies. The FTCA defined the circumstances under which people could sue the government and its employees for harms caused by negligence, incompetence, or malfeasance. The FTCA allows private parties to sue the government for the actions of an individual who is acting on behalf of the government, if the individual acting on behalf of the government would be liable for those actions as a private person. The FTCA, however, specifically exempts military personnel from the class of persons who are allowed to bring suit against the government. Specifically, armed forces personnel may not sue for "[a]ny claim arising out of the combatant activities of the military or naval forces, or the Coast Guard, during time of war" (FTCA 28 USC sec. 2680{j}). In 1950, the military exemption was greatly expanded, not by Congress but by the United States Supreme Court. The Court ruled in *Feres v. United States* that military personnel, their families, or representatives could not bring suit for harm suffered "incident" to military service (*Feres* 1950: 144–6). Despite advocacy by the public, veterans, members of the judiciary, and members of Congress, the courts have continued to expand the exemption so that even actions that in non-military circumstances would be criminal acts may be exempted from liability.

In 1950, the US Supreme Court ruled in three cases (*Feres*, *Jefferson*, and *Griggs*) that collectively became known as the *Feres Doctrine*. Lieutenant Rudolph J. Feres was 31 years old when he died in a barracks fire. Lieutenant Feres' wife brought suit against the army, charging that it was known that the heating system was defective, that the night guards were derelict in their duty, and that the army had failed in its duty to protect an officer in the service.

While serving in the army, Jefferson required abdominal surgery. Months passed and he still suffered pain. Jefferson underwent a second abdominal surgery eight months later, after he was discharged. During this surgery, a towel measuring 30 by 18 inches, marked "Medical Department U.S. Army," was removed from his stomach (*Feres* 1950). The *Feres* decision prohibited active duty military personnel from suing the government for any injury sustained while in the service, whether combat-related or not (Reason #7).

In upholding the *Feres Doctrine* (albeit by the slimmest majority), the Supreme Court declared:

> [M]ilitary discipline involves not only obedience to orders, but more generally duty and loyalty to one's service and to one's country. Suits brought by service members against the Government for service-related injuries could undermine the commitment essential to effective service and thus have the potential to disrupt military discipline in the broadest sense of the word. (*US v. Johnson* 1987: 691) (Reasons ##1, 2, 3)

At times, military decisions seem to be at odds with moral principles. In the early days of World War II, for example, when antibiotic supplies were limited, priority for antibiotic treatment was given to soldiers with venereal disease rather than to soldiers with infected wounds. Venereal disease, if treated in its early stages, did not prevent soldiers from returning to combat, while serious infection did. While it may seem unfair to favor soldiers who contracted a sexually transmitted disease over those injured in combat, in the face of scarce resources, utility required treating those who could continue to fight.

Under threat of war, many situations arise that require experienced military judgment. Battlefield conditions are not optimal: physicians are often exhausted and lack the supplies and equipment they need. Severe wounds often stretch the doctor's ability. Understandably, mistakes are made under these situations, and protecting doctors from lawsuits is reasonable – and necessary, to keep them focused on the tasks at hand.

Other situations are not morally justifiable. The Rockefeller Report made the chilling observation that the "DOD [Department of Defense] has demonstrated a pattern of misrepresenting the danger of various military exposures that continues today" (Rockefeller 1994: sec. O). Abuses of military personnel in experimental research during and following World War II were documented in the Rockefeller Report. Hundreds of thousands of servicemen and women were used as experimental subjects, without their consent and sometimes without their knowledge. Exact numbers are difficult to determine, as often the military kept no records of the research, the participants, methodologies, results, outcomes, or harms. Sometimes subjects' participation was coerced by threats of dire consequences from their commanding officers (ibid.: note 2). Research subjects were intentionally exposed to radiation, disease-causing organisms, untested vaccines, neurodegenerative agents, psychotropic drugs, and other harmful substances. Sometimes subjects who had agreed to participate in a research project were reassigned, without their consent, to other projects. At other times, subjects were deliberately deceived in order to ensure their participation. In one such incident, thousands of military subjects were promised extra leave time if they would participate in a test of summer clothing. Instead of testing clothing, they were placed in gas chambers and mustard gas was administered. Following the experiments, participants were not given follow-up medical care (ibid.: notes 1, 14). With the perception of increased threat from China and Russia following World War II, and concerns over mind-altering treatments and behavior modification, hundreds of soldiers were unknowing subjects in mind-control research (ibid.: notes 4 and 5). Although the goal to prevent harm and provide effective treatment is admirable, forcing people to participate in research that is known or suspected to be harmful and unlikely to benefit the participant – indeed, is likely to cause unconsented-to harms – is morally wrong (Reasons ##4, 10). Moreover, loss of trust and lack of confidence in the military and in the government is a natural consequence of the abuse of personnel and the secrecy and deceit shrouding the experiments and their aftermath (Reason #5).

The adverse effects of military experimentation and malpractice may be particularly devastating, as they often persist for years, even throughout the victim's lifetime. To receive monthly compensation and medical care at a Veterans Administration facility, veterans must demonstrate that their illnesses or disabilities were due to military service. Veterans who did not know they were subjects in medical research, or who are denied information or access to their records, cannot prove their claim for VA benefits – and so the harms persist and are neither remediated by treatment or rehabilitation nor compensated for. Participation in research experimentation is rarely noted in service records. The Pentagon often persists for decades in denying that experiments occurred (think: mustard gas, radiation, Agent Orange), leaving veterans with life-long disabilities and the financial burden of treatments – burdens that could have been avoided had their commanding officers fulfilled their professional duty to protect their personnel (Reasons ##4, 5, 6).

Often, the only way patients can find out what actually caused the adverse outcomes (e.g., inadequate medical care) is by filing a malpractice suit (Studdert et al. 2006: 2030–1). Understanding what happened is particularly important if the complications require further medical treatment, but this avenue to information is denied to military personnel. During the 1991 Gulf War, soldiers were threatened with imprisonment, even after leaving the service, if they discussed their involvement in forced experimental research with anyone – including spouses or their personal (civilian) doctors from whom they sought treatments for research-related injuries (ibid.: note 15) (Reasons ##6, 9, 10). Several times, over a span of two decades, Representative Barney Frank introduced legislation to allow members of the armed forces to sue military physicians for malpractice. The legislation passed the House, but was blocked each time in the Senate. While Representative Frank agrees that overturning *Feres in toto* could damage the military, he remains a staunch advocate for the right of service personnel to sue in cases of military malpractice (Greenhouse 1986). Equal treatment under the law, and a well-recognized obligation to compensate persons for unconsented-to harms, support this position (Reasons ##8, 12).

Officials of the military, judiciary, and administration argue that revising *Feres* and the Federal Tort Claims Act to allow medical malpractice suits would create a deluge of lawsuits (Reason #17). In addition to possibly undermining military discipline and being incompatible with the bonding that is essential to mutual support and loyalty (Reasons ##15, 16, 17), an onslaught of law suits could swamp the military's legal resources, as well as generate enormous financial outlays. Administrative spokespersons blame the military's reputation for sloppy medical care on a few selected cases (Boffey 1985).

Fears that revising *Feres* would compromise military authority and discipline, and undermine loyalty and duty, have frequently been called into question, including challenges by members of Congress and the Supreme Court. In *United States v. Johnson*, Justice Scalia noted that *Feres* "has long been disputed" (1987: 699). Lieutenant Commander Horton Johnson, a helicopter pilot for the Coast Guard, was killed during a rescue mission. When severe weather rendered visibility to near zero, Johnson called for radar guidance. Air traffic controllers from the Federal Aviation Administration, a civilian agency of the Federal Government, provided incorrect data, and Lieutenant Commander Johnson's

helicopter crashed into a mountainside. In a closely divided Supreme Court decision, Justice Antonin Scalia wrote the dissenting opinion on behalf of Justices
Brennan, Marshall, Stevens, and himself, challenging judicial expansion of *Feres*
and the military's contention that overturning *Feres* would undermine military
discipline: "I do not think the effect upon military discipline is so certain, or so
certainly substantial, that we are justified in holding (if we can ever be justified
in holding) that Congress did not mean what it plainly said in the statute [refer-
ring here to the Federal Tort Claims Act] before us" (*United States v. Johnson*
1987: 699) (Reasons ##5, 11).

In the same dissent, Scalia questioned the negative effects on morale and
loyalty of overturning *Feres*: "After all, the morale of Lieutenant Commander
Johnson's comrades-in-arms will not likely be boosted by news that his widow
and children will receive only a fraction of the amount they might have recovered had he been piloting a commercial helicopter at the time of his death" (ibid.:
700) (Reasons ##5, 8, 12).

Another concern raised in modifying *Feres* is that allowing military personnel
to litigate may expose information critical to national security or defense, given
that civilians may sue the government. Justice Scalia offered a hypothetical example to highlight how insubstantial and unrealistic this contention is. Suppose
a soldier had been asked by his commanding officer to deliver papers to the
courthouse when he drives his daughter there for a class field trip. The military
vehicle had not been maintained, and a wheel broke, causing injury to the soldier,
his daughter, and a US marshal on duty at the courthouse. Neither the soldier
not the marshal could sue the government for the negligence that contributed
to their injuries, although the daughter could. If her father dies, the daughter
may not sue the military for his loss, but she may sue the vehicle's manufacturer.
All three may sue the vehicle's manufacturer for their injuries and losses, and the
manufacturer could in turn sue the military for contributory negligence (ibid.:
701–2). Scalia's point, here, is that such information is no less critical nor at risk
in suits brought by civilians – which are allowed.

Negligence and incompetence affect people outside the military as well.
During the first Gulf War, defense contractors and journalists were given experimental drugs by the military without being told they were research subjects, or
given information about possible adverse outcomes. Several who took the pills
subsequently developed Gulf War syndrome (Rockefeller 1994: note 89).

Disciplinary actions against civilian doctors are required to be reported to
the state medical licensing board, and the records are usually available to the
public so that prospective patients are able to make informed decisions about
selecting a doctor (Reason #14). The Navy Bureau of Medicine and Surgery and
an independent review team examine cases of serious medical error involving
military physicians. The Navy's surgeon-general may report negligent physicians
to state licensing authorities, and to a national, unpublicized malpractice database, but has no obligation to do so, and rarely does (Pinkham et al. 2006: A6).
This enables military physicians to leave the service and enter private practice
with clean records that neither indicate prior malpractice nor provide a record of
negligence or incompetence acquired during their military service. Because no record

of disciplinary action against military physicians usually exists, the public does not have the protection provided by a record of medical error (Reasons ##4, 6, 11, 12, 14).

A strong military that protects individuals and their freedom is good. An abusive military is not (Moskop 2004: 6). Continued justification of the *Feres Doctrine* (in its current, expanded form) sanctions continued abuse of military personnel (Reason #7) and denies them justice (Reasons ##12, 14) through what Justice Scalia refers to as "unauthorized rationalization gone wrong" (*United States v. Johnson* 1987: 702).

For members of the armed services, justice is determined in military tribunals. It is interesting to note that the word "tribunal" is derived from the Latin word "tribunalis," meaning "of a tribute" (Morris 1976: 1369). The Roman tribunal was a special place of privilege where the emperor and his magistrates would watch performances (McCutcheon 2005: 37).

The *Feres Doctrine* has been stretched so far by the courts that members of the military are prohibited from suing for damages from civilian-operated for-profit businesses, such as bowling alleys, bars, gas stations – or rafting operations, such as the one used by Nollie Costo and Christopher Graham – that have contracts with military bases. In addition to the violation of the Fourteenth Amendment right to equal protection cited by Justice Ferguson (*Costo* 2001: 5021), members of the military are denied the First Amendment right to bring grievance against the government when they have been harmed (US Constitution, Amendment XIV, 1) (Reason #7). Almost any injury is exempt under *Feres*, including those caused by non-military personnel (Turley 2007: 13) (Reason #4).

Lower courts have usually, though not always, upheld *Feres*, although they have given differing rationales for this support. The US Supreme Court has consistently upheld *Feres*, although support has been divided (Perlstein 1997: 266, 259). Sometimes the court has been closely split with a five-to-four decision, as in *United States v. Johnson*, with the minority challenging judicial expansion of the *Feres Doctrine*: "*Feres* was wrongly decided and heartily deserves the 'widespread, almost universal criticism' it has received" (1987: 700).

International law prohibits forced medical experimentation. During the 1945–7 Nazi war criminals trials in Nuremberg, Germany, the defendants argued that their medical experiments were little different from American medical experiments, and that no law existed that defined illegal medical experiments on human subjects. American physicians Andrew Ivy, the American Medical Association's expert witness for the prosecution, and Leo Alexander, a psychiatrist who worked with the prosecution, were horrified by the cruel research involving human subjects that took place under the Nazi regime. They drafted six points that proposed criteria for acceptable research (expanded to ten during deliberation), which formed the bases of the verdict. These ten points comprise the Nuremberg Code (Jonsen 1998: 136–6). The Nuremberg Code was written by two Americans working with the prosecution; an American military tribunal conducted the trial; and the United States Counsel for War Crimes rendered the verdict. Many countries have adopted the Nuremberg Code but, ironically, the United States does not include it in its own legal code. The World

Medical Association also adopted principles governing medical research in a document known as the Helsinki Declaration. Despite efforts such as the Nuremburg Code and the Helsinki Declaration to create a universal code of medical ethics, medical ethics are not universal. For example, the Turkish Medical Association does not extend membership to military physicians, as physicians in Turkey's military participate in torture (Moskop 2004: 6).

The United States was not unconcerned with human subject research, however. After the 40-year Tuskegee experiment was exposed (treatment for syphilis was withheld from 600 African American men to observe the effects of the disease as it progressed), the National Commission for the Protection of Research Subjects was formed to balance the interests of scientific research with individual rights and risks of harms. Three doctors, three lawyers, two scientists, a priest, an ethicist, and a member of the public served on the commission; this group was directed to translate ethical principles, such as those articulated in the Nuremberg Code and the Helsinki Declaration, into regulatory language. The specific congressional directive to identify ethical parameters for research using human subjects was addressed at a retreat at the Smithsonian Institution's Belmont House conference center. In 1979, the Belmont Report was published in the Federal Register and became law (Jonsen 1998: 146–8, 99–104).

Because the Department of Defense is federally funded, US law prohibits the military from using human subjects in research without their consent (Rockefeller 1994: note 13). Nonetheless, during the 1991 Gulf War experimental drugs were administered to soldiers deployed in the Middle East, without their knowledge or consent (Moskop 2004: 3). These experiments were conducted, even though federal law prohibits non-consensual experimentation. It is evident, given the documented ethics abuses in medical experimentation during recent wars, that the military exempts itself from accountability either to the law or to the men and women in the armed services (Reasons ##4, 6).

Although injured veterans receive compensation and disability benefits (Boffey 1985), critics argue that these benefits are inadequate. When sponges and a marking device were left in the abdomen of Navywoman Dawn Lambert, the damage they caused and the subsequent surgery to remove them left her infertile at 23 years of age. She receives $66 monthly in disability benefits – compensation far too low to afford in vitro fertilization. The disability benefits granted to a 22-year-old sailor, whose minor surgery left him quadriplegic and brain damaged, are not even enough to cover the daily cost of care or living expenses (Greenhouse 1986).

The failure adequately to compensate victims of medical negligence or incompetence imposes considerable – and unjust – emotional and economic burdens on them and their family. Although *Feres* may be invoked as necessary to avoid crippling costs of litigation, these concerns are overstated, according to a study published in the *New England Journal of Medicine*. The majority of malpractice litigation costs result from legal expenses generated in cases of preventable injury; the recognition of responsibility for injuries and the speedy resolution of meritorious claims would reduce the enormous expenses that plague malpractice litigation (Studdert et al. 2006: 2031) (Reasons ##14, 17).

Dependents of members of the armed forces who die in the service receive less compensation than comparable civilians. Justice Scalia noted: "[B]ecause Johnson devoted his life to serving in his country's Armed Forces, the Court today limits his family to a fraction of the recovery they might otherwise have received" (*United States v. Johnson* 1987: 703). Service men and women harmed by negligence or medical malpractice are not adequately compensated for their losses. Depriving members of the armed services of the same rights afforded other citizens and residents compromises their rights and treats them unfairly and unequally, relegating then to second-class status (Reasons ##7, 12).

A strong military is important for the preservation of freedom and to safeguard human and civil rights. It is an injustice when these rights are denied unnecessarily to those who safeguard them for others (Reason #7). In combat or under threat of war, discipline and obedience are essential. The Federal Tort Claims Act's prohibition denying military personnel the right to sue government agencies under these conditions is reasonable. The expansion of this prohibition to every situation involving active duty personnel is not. The *Feres Doctrine* should be amended to allow military personnel and their families or representatives to sue government agencies, at the very least and initially, for medical malpractice, harms from non-consensual experimental research, and sexual assault – harms whose compensation would not undermine a strong and effective military.

Opponents of modifying the *Feres Doctrine* argue that allowing litigation would erode the trust between superior officers and their subordinates. The opposite may be asserted as well: failing to demand accountability by prohibiting litigation for deliberate or negligent harms undermines the trust between subordinates and their superior officers. Loyalty and patriotism grow from trust, knowing that commanders will not put those in their charge in harm's way unnecessarily (Reason #13). Blind obeisance to arbitrary authority is neither duty nor discipline (Reason #12). Moreover, the public is aware of medical experimentation on members of the military without their knowledge or consent. The public's knowledge of the military's record of coercion, deceit, and cover-ups, and of its history of disregard for law with little accountability or responsibility to those harmed, has already destroyed that trust for many. Government and the military must be truthful and transparent to preserve the public trust. The United States was founded because people no longer trusted their government (Reason #5).

Women, in particular, face enemies on three fronts: foes in battle, sexual assault by their own comrades, and retribution by their confederates and commanders for reporting sexual attacks. Although the military attributes the rise in numbers of sexual assaults to increased reporting rather than increased incidents, these claims are disputed. An investigation by the Associated Press discovered that in 2005 more than 80 recruiters, from all branches of the military, were disciplined for sexually inappropriate behavior with young women who were potential recruits (AP 2007). A survey conducted by the Citadel in spring 2006 revealed that 20 percent of the female cadets surveyed disclosed that they had been the victims of sexual assault, most often by a fellow cadet (NOW 2006). In the military, civil or criminal charges are rarely filed in cases of sexual misconduct: most are handled administratively (CBS/AP 2006).

The military's disregard for the lives and welfare of service members harmed in non-combat situations, even when the actions causing the harms are prohibited by law, has created a system of privileged power without accountability. This abuse of power is particularly dangerous as it involves situations of live and death and harms that can impact on the quality of life forever. Most members of the military are courageous, honorable, and principled. Protecting those who are not and turning a blind eye to those who are victimized by them dishonors those who serve with integrity (Reason #4).

The principle of equality considers the balance of burdens and benefits. Members of the armed services put their lives in danger to protect the civil and human rights of others. While they are protecting others' rights, the *Feres Doctrine* denies members of the military the right to redress grievances, and allows them to be punished for exercising their right of free speech. Unnecessarily denying military personnel civil rights and equal protection violates the moral principles of rights and justice, understood as equal consideration (Reasons ##6, 7).

The *Feres Doctrine* has absolved the military from accountability and responsibility in situations that are far removed from combat. *Feres* protects incompetent and careless doctors from discipline, and does not allow their victims compensation for their injuries. *Feres* protects superiors who knowingly manipulate or coerce subordinates into participation in hazardous experimental research, and allows continued abuse of research subjects by failing to provide treatment or compensation for research-related injuries, or even to acknowledge that the harm occurred. *Feres* protects predators who sexually assault their comrades or subordinates, and further injures victims by failing to stop retaliation against them for reporting the crime. The exploitation and abuse of military personnel, and the deceit and cover-ups all violate moral principles and have eroded the public's trust in the government and military. Continuing to uphold the *Feres Doctrine* as it is currently interpreted causes great harms and is unsupportable.

Modifying the *Feres Doctrine* will enable those harmed by negligence, incompetence, or wrongful acts to be reasonably compensated for their injuries, honoring beneficence. It will make the military accountable for its actions and responsible for their consequences, and serve as a deterrent to future abuse and carelessness, thus satisfying the principle of nonmaleficence. It will require truthfulness and informed consent in human subjects research, demonstrating respect for autonomy. Modifying *Feres* will reinstate constitutional rights to free speech, redress of grievances, and equal protection under the law that are relinquished upon joining the military, even when those rights do not undermine military efficiency, thus addressing the moral principle of rights. Eliminating unnecessary and morally irrelevant discriminatory treatment will create a more equitable balance of burdens and benefits, facilitating equal consideration and respect for the autonomy and rights of those who serve their country.

The military's history of careless medical practice, secret and harmful research, disregard for civil law, and lies and cover-ups demonstrates that, without the right to sue, there is no legal obligation to make whole the individual who has been harmed, and little incentive for moral accountability. US military personnel serve around the world, protecting human and civil rights, yet they have no protection against violation of their own human and civil rights by the actions of their superiors. The *Feres Doctrine* protects a group of powerful individuals from responsibility for their negligence or wrongful acts – even from intentionally harmful or criminal acts – at the expense of the men and women who serve in the armed services. Failure to intervene to prevent abuse and abuse of power sanctions those actions. Protecting those who commit the abuse promotes oppression as a value, and integrates it into the culture of power. Preserving the *Feres Doctrine* perpetuates systemic abuses in a powerful military, and is not morally justifiable.

In conclusion, the principles of beneficence, nonmaleficence, autonomy, rights, and equality argue that the *Feres Doctrine* should be modified to allow members of the military to sue the government and its agents in cases of medical malpractice, unconsented-to experimentation, and sexual assault.

Additional Issues to Consider

Other possible moral dilemmas arising within this case:

Q If the *Feres Doctrine* is not overturned, are similarly situated institutions (e.g., teaching hospitals, publicly funded clinics) morally justified in adopting a no-sue policy?

Q Would moral reasoning support maintaining *Feres Doctrine* in combat situations, but overturning it in other military healthcare facilities?

Q Can sustaining the *Feres Doctrine* be morally supported by the claim that the military justice units would never be able to handle all the resulting suits (i.e., justified by the Principle of Utility)?

REFERENCES

AP (Associated Press) (2007) Military sex assault reports rose in '06 (March 21). Available at: www.msnbc.msn.com/id/17725659 (accessed October 11, 2007).
Boffey, P. M. (1985) Military malpractice law opposed. *New York Times* (July 10). Available at: query.nytimes.com/gst/fullpage.html?sec=health&res=9806E5DF1738F933A25754C 0A963948260 (accessed October 11, 2007).
Boyle v. United Technologies Corp (1988) 487 US 500.
CBS/AP (2006) Sexual abuse by military recruiters – more than 100 women raped or assaulted by recruiters in past year (August 20). Available at: www.cbsnews.com/

stories/2006/08/19/national/main1913849_page2.shtml (accessed October 11, 2007).

Costo v. USA (2001) 248 F.3d 863, 870 (9th Cir.): 5009–31.

Estelle v. Gamble (1976) 429 US 97, 97 S. Ct. 285, 50 L. Ed. 2d 251.

Ezell, W. (2006) Navy hospital story fell short. *Florida Times-Union* (March 11). Available at: www.jacksonville.com/tu-online/stories/031206/ope_21322532.shtml (accessed October 11, 2007).

Federal Tort Claims Act (1946) 28 USC §1346(b1): 2671–80.

Feres v. United States (1950) 340 US 135: 135–47.

Fratangelo, D. (2007) Military sexual trauma – new PTSD: military sexual assaults – and requests for help – are on the rise (May 7). Available at: www.msnbc.msn.com/id/18494197/from/ET (accessed October 11, 2007).

Greenhouse, L. (1986) Washington talk: On allowing soldiers to sue. *New York Times* (December 16). Available at: query.nytimes.com/gst/fullpage.html?sec=health&res=9A0DE3DB123EF935A25751C1A960948260 (accessed October 11, 2007).

Jonsen, A. R. (1998) *The Birth of Bioethics*. New York: Oxford University Press.

Leahy, P. (2002) Senate Judiciary Committee Hearing on the *Feres Doctrine* (October 8).

McCutcheon, M. (2005) *Descriptionary: A Thematic Dictionary*, 3rd edn. New York: Facts On File: Writer's Library.

Morris, W. (ed.) (1976) *American Heritage Dictionary of the English Language*, New College edn. Boston: Houghton Mifflin, p. 1369.

Morse v. Regents of the University of Colorado (1998) 154 F.3d 1124 (10th Cir.).

Morse v. West (1999) 10 Cir 49 172 F.3d 63.

Moskop, J. C. (2004) Ethics and military medicine: new developments and perennial questions. *Ethics & Health Care* 7 (1): 1–6.

NOW (National Organization for Women) (2006) Press release: From the Citadel to military recruiting – sexual harassment in military more pervasive than ever (September 1). Available at: www.now.org/press/09-06/09-01.html (accessed October 11, 2007).

Perlstein, H. C. (1997) TDRL and the *Feres Doctrine*. *The Air Force Law Review* 43: 259–66.

Pinkham, P., and Lake, T. (2006) 55-year-old ruling prevents lawsuits against government. *Florida Times-Union* (5 March): A7.

Pinkham, P., Lake, T., and Piatt, G. (2006) A hospital's deadly problem. *Florida Times-Union* (March 5): A6–7.

Rockefeller, J. D. (chair) (1994) *Is Military Research Hazardous to Veterans' Health? Lessons Spanning Half a Century*. Staff report for the Committee on Veterans Affairs, United States Senate: 103d Congress, 2d Session S. Prt. 103–97, December 8.

Studdert, D. M., Mello, M. M., and Gawande, A. A., et al. (2006) Claims, errors, and compensation payments in medical malpractice litigation. *New England Journal of Medicine* 354 (19): 2024–33.

Turley, J. (2007) What our soldiers really need: Lawyers. *USA Today* (April 12): 13.

United States Constitution. Amendments I, XIV (1789) Available at: http://memory.loc.gov/cgi-bin/ampage?collId=llsl&fileName=001/llsl001.db&recNum=144 (accessed October 11, 2007).

United States v. Johnson (1987) 481 US 681: 681–703.

CASE THIRTY-ONE: DOES THE PAST MEAN NEVER HAVING TO SAY WE'RE SORRY? – REPARATIONS AND APOLOGIES

Beginning in January 1989, Congressman John Conyers (D-Michigan) has annually introduced Bill H.R. 40, the Commission to Study Reparations Proposals for African Americans Act. The bill would acknowledge "the fundamental injustice cruelty, brutality, and inhumanity of slavery in the United States" (GovTrack.us. 2005), and establish a commission to study the institution of slavery in the United States and the subsequent racial and economic discrimination against African Americans. The commission would also study the impact of slavery and subsequent racial discrimination on living African Americans and, finally, make recommendations on how best to redress the harms of slavery and racial discrimination (Martin and Yaquinto 2007: 503–5).

Conyers has found support in both popular and academic literature. In his 2001 book, *The Debt: What America Owes to Blacks*, civil rights activist and Harvard-educated attorney, Randall Robinson, argues that the United States has an obligation to provide reparations to African Americans for slavery and legalized racial discrimination. Robinson notes that the initial proposal by the US government to provide restitution for slavery (i.e., giving each freed slave 40 acres and a mule) failed when it was vetoed by President Andrew Johnson after the Civil War (Robinson 2001: 204). In addition to the losses of well-being brought about through the obvious physical and emotional suffering, Robinson estimates that slaves lost $1.4 trillion in unpaid wages in today's money.

According to Robinson, even after slavery was abolished, legal discrimination, such as Black Codes and Jim Crow laws, extended the debilitating effects of slavery (ibid.: 7–10, 74–80). Education was, for the most part, denied to African Americans. Since people without education cannot compete successfully for jobs, African Americans became trapped in poverty (ibid.: 75–80). Similarly, discriminatory housing practices further interfered with the economic growth of African Americans (ibid.: 227–8). For instance, home-ownership is an important method of building wealth. Robinson claims that discriminatory mortgage policies and redlining – the practice under which real estate brokers only sell property located in certain neighborhoods to Blacks – cost African Americans as much as $90 billion over the years. As a result of such unjust treatment, says Robinson, African Americans have suffered significant economic disadvantage that continues up to the present time.

However, the idea of reparations for slavery (and subsequent discrimination) has met with much criticism and raised some important troubling practical questions. For instance, who, specifically, is entitled to receive reparations? Since not all African Americans are direct descendants of slaves, it may be difficult to argue that they are entitled to reparations. Also, even though reparations advocates propose figures, the critics reject all such proposals as hopelessly speculative and arbitrary.

In his well-known essay, "Ten reasons why reparations is a bad idea for blacks – and racist, too," David Horowitz asserts that in the pre-Civil War period only approximately 20 percent of Whites owned slaves (Horowitz 2000: 127). This would mean that most Caucasian US citizens who fought in the Civil War, a war many believe was fought over the permissibility of slavery, died to free the slaves. It would seem unfair for their descendants to have to pay for reparations when their forefathers sacrificed their lives to end slavery. Indeed, given America's diverse citizenry, many US citizens are descendants of families that came to the US long after the abolition of slavery. Requiring them to contribute to reparations for slavery would be unjust, argues Horowitz (ibid.: 128).

Are African Americans entitled to reparations for slavery and subsequent legalized discrimination?

Perspective One

Reparations should not be given to African Americans. For reparations to make ethical sense, two conditions must obtain: (1) there must be a living party who has been wronged; and (2) there must be a living party guilty of the wrongdoing.

With regard to reparations for slavery, neither of the above conditions can be fulfilled. First, there are no living African Americans who were slaves. Simply because the rights of one's ancestors were violated does not mean that one is entitled to reparations. If a person's great grandfather's car is stolen, that person is not entitled to reparations simply because he is a descendant. One might attempt to argue that the descendant *would have* inherited property from his great grandfather. However, this wrongly assumes that people will always choose to pass along their wealth to their children. People are free to pass along or not pass along wealth as they wish (Waldron 1992: 7–14). Parents are not required to pass along any remaining money or property to their children or their siblings' children. They often choose to do so, but justice does not require it. What is more, even if it is passed along, there is no guarantee that it will not be mismanaged and lost (ibid.). No doubt, African Americans who were enslaved 200 years ago were clearly entitled to significant reparations in one form or another. However, the African Americans alive today are not among them.

Second, the slave-owners who would owe reparations are no longer alive, and descendants of those slave-owners should not be penalized for acts that they did not commit. Hence, African Americans alive today are not entitled to reparations because they themselves were not slaves and, what is more, those from whom reparations would be due are no longer alive. If reparations were to be provided, it would ultimately come out of the pockets of US citizens, many of whom have no connection to slavery, and awarded to individuals who were not themselves victims of the institution of slavery.

There are also a number of practical barriers to reparations. For instance, what would be owed to non-African people of color (e.g., Jamaicans) or to African nationals who recently emigrated to the United States? They are not descendants of slaves. If reparations were to be given to descendants of slaves, what percentage of African blood would qualify one for reparations, and would someone with a lesser percentage than someone else receive less?

In addition to these problems, it is not clear what reparations should strive to achieve? Repairing a harm would seem to require that the parties harmed be restored to the condition and circumstances that they would have been in had the harm never taken place (Sher 1980: 199–205; Waldron 1992: 7–14). This would suggest that African Americans should be returned to the condition and circumstances they would have been in if their ancestors had never been taken from Africa. Since the average African American has an annual income 20–50 times higher than that of an African national (Horowitz 2000: 127), their descendants would be made worse off – clearly not a desired state of affairs. If the ancestors of living African Americans had not been taken from Africa, albeit against their will, modern-day African Americans would be living at a standard of living far below what they now enjoy. Considered from this perspective, a related point emerges: those who truly are descendants of African slaves exist only because of slavery. Children born into slavery were born of slaves, and their parents were brought together only because of slavery. Therefore, descendants of slaves would not have existed were it not for the very acts for which they seek reparations. Certainly, they could not be restored to the state – non-existence – that they would have been in if the harm had never occurred.

The above argument has attempted to establish that reparations for slavery are unjustified. However, the question of whether reparations are due as a result the legalized racial discrimination after slavery still remains. Admittedly, even after the abolition of slavery, Black Codes and Jim Crow laws denied African Americans basic civil rights and liberties. Such legalized racial discrimination continued up into the 1960s (some would argue that it is still ongoing) and represented a serious harm to African Americans. However, affirmative action practices (e.g., hiring practices and university admissions policies), intended to bring about racial equity, have gone a long way toward addressing those wrongs and continue to help create and expand opportunities for African Americans. Yet, affirmative action suffers from many of the same ethical defects as reparations. For instance, like reparations for slavery, affirmative action – to counteract the effects of the racial discrimination after slavery – inevitably ends up unfairly penalizing people, such as non-African American college and employment applicants, who have had no part in any kind of racial discrimination (Cohen 2003: 33–7).

Hence, reparations are warranted neither for slavery nor for the racism that continued after slavery.

Perspective Two

Reparations are owed to African Americans for slavery. It is true that reparations for slavery would only be justified if the parties wronged by slavery and the parties responsible for slavery were still alive. Certainly, if both conditions could not be satisfied, reparations for slavery would not be justified. However, both conditions can, indeed, be satisfied. Slavery was a social institution sanctioned by the US government, and because the US government is still in existence, the party responsible for the wrongdoing exists. The mere fact that no one individual person working for the US government during the time of slavery is still alive is irrelevant (Thompson 2002: 9–14). Like individual persons, governments are entities that make plans and choose courses of action. It follows, then, that, like individual persons, governments may be held responsible for their actions. Therefore, the US government can and should be held responsible for slavery.

Moreover, it is also mistaken to hold that African Americans alive today are not being wronged by the lingering effects of slavery. As Randall Robinson has made clear, the legacy of slavery has had a profoundly negative economic impact on African Americans. They have been denied entry into many of the most important channels for wealth and prosperity, such as real estate and education (Robinson 2001: 75–80, 227–8). Critics of reparations, such as Horowitz, are quick to point out that the economic disparity between African American and Caucasians has decreased significantly in past decades, and that the US African American community enjoys one of the highest annual incomes in the world (Horowitz 2000: 127). However, this view fails to recognize a crucial distinction between *income* and *wealth* (Conley 1999: 25–54). Whereas income refers simply to one's earnings, wealth also includes one's assets, such as property and inheritance, along with one's overall economic power. Most persons accumulate wealth over a lifetime, as the result of gifts from previous generations (Conley 2003: 25). Hence, while there may not be a wide gap in annual income between the average Caucasian family and the average African American family, the average Caucasian family is far wealthier. Since slavery and, later, Jim Crows laws made it difficult for African Americans to acquire valuable properties and other assets, there was little wealth to pass on across generations.

Finally, in response to the view that affirmative action has provided (or may someday provide) adequate reparations, it is important to understand that the purpose of affirmative action is to offset present inequity, not repair past injustices (Thompson 2002: xv–xvi).

Moreover, even if one granted that the goal of affirmative action may be reparative, affirmative action policies and practices across the United States are currently under fire. For instance, in November 2006, Michigan voters came out strongly in favor of Proposal 2, which prohibits public institutions from considering race or gender in admissions or employment practices (Schmidt 2006). Affirmative action met with a similar fate in California and Washington in the 1980s and '90s (ibid.). Therefore, African Americans can hardly rely on affirmative action as a means of reparation.

Hence, reparations are necessary and warranted both for slavery and for the racism that continued after slavery.

Additional Issues to Consider

Other possible moral dilemmas arising within this case:

Q Is the claim that reparations require a living party who has been wronged and a living party guilty of the wrongdoing itself morally justifiable?

Q Can the practical fact that determining *who* is owed would be virtually impossible justify admitting wrong and harm but not making restitution?

Q Is affirmative action morally justifiable?

Q Would a non-monetary form of restitution (e.g., an apology) be morally sufficient?

REFERENCES

Cohen, C. (2003) Why race preference is wrong and bad. In C. Cohen and J. Sterba, *Affirmative Action and Racial Preference: A Debate*. New York: Oxford University Press, pp. 7–188.

Conley, D. (1999) *Being Black in America, Living in the Red: Race, Wealth and Social Policy in America*. Berkeley: University of California Press.

Conley, D. (2003) The cost of slavery. *New York Times* (February 15): 25.

GovTrack.us. HR 40 – 109th Congress (2005) Commission to Study Reparation Proposals for African Americans Act, GovTrack.us (database of federal legislation). Available at: www.govtrack.us/congress/bill.xpd?bill=h109-40 (accessed October 14, 2007).

Horowitz, D. (2000) 10 reasons why reparations for blacks are a bad idea for blacks and racist, too. *FrontPageMagazine.com* (May 31). Available at: www. frontpagemag. com/ Articles/Printable. aspx?GUID={C3832D17-7AA5-4653-8780-DDFEA1E18075} (accessed September 28, 2007). Reprinted in R. Salzburger and M. Turck (eds.), *Reparations for Slavery: A Reader*. Lanham, MD: Rowman and Littlefield, 2004, pp. 127–30. (Page references in text are to this volume.)

Martin, T., and Yaquinto, M. (eds.) (2007) *Redress for Historical Injustices in the United States: On Reparations for Slavery, Jim Crow, and Their Legacies*. Durham, NC: Duke University Press.

Robinson, R. (2001) *The Debt: What America Owes to Blacks*. New York: Plume.

Schmidt, P. (2006) Michigan overwhelmingly adopts ban on affirmative action preferences. *Chronicle of Higher Education* 53 (1). Available at: http://chronicle.com/ subscribe/login?url=/weekly/v53/i13/13a02301.htm (accessed October 14, 2007).

Sher, G. (1980) Ancient wrongs and modern rights. *Philosophy and Public Affairs* 10 (1): 3–17. Reprinted in R. Salzburger and M. Turck (eds.), *Reparations for Slavery:*

A Reader. Lanham, MD: Rowman and Littlefield, 2004, pp. 197–205. (Page references in text are to this volume.)

Thompson, J. (2002) *Taking Responsibility for the Past: Reparations and Historical Justice*. Cambridge: Polity.

Waldron, J. (1992) Superseding historical injustice. *Ethics* 103 (1): 4–28.

CASE THIRTY-TWO: WORDS FAIL – INSTITUTIONAL RESPONSES TO CREATIVE VIOLENCE

The violence and profanity running through an essay written by Illinois high school honor student, Allen Lee, ended in vitriolic criticism of his teacher and the suggestion that her teaching methods could inspire a shooting (Lee 2007). Disturbed by his paper, his creative-writing teacher, Ms Nora Capron, a first-year teacher at Cary-Grove High School, called her department head to discuss her concerns. The department head called Cary-Grove High School principal, Ms Susan Popp. The horror of the prior week's massacre of 32 Virginia Tech students and teachers was very much on school officials' minds. It was widely known that Cho Seung-Hui wrote violent essays in his creative-writing class before launching his killing spree. The previous week, about half the students at Crystal Lake Central High, a neighboring school to Cary-Grove High School, had stayed home for a day in response to threatening graffiti found in the school bathroom. Ms Popp reported her concerns to the Cary police, and filed a criminal complaint against Lee in McHenry County Court (Swedberg and Olson 2007).

The following morning, Cary police arrested Allen Lee as he walked to school. Mr Lee was charged with two counts of disorderly conduct: the first stemmed from the potential threat to the peace posed by his writing (threat to the peace is often the charge for misdemeanors, such as pulling a fire alarm), the second from the perceived threat to Ms Capron (Keilman and Ford 2007: 10). Each charge carried the potential of a 30-day jail sentence and a $1,500 fine. More distressing to Allen Lee was the communication from the Marine Corps canceling his enlistment, returning his acceptance papers, and telling him he would not be attending boot camp as planned in October because of the criminal charges against him. Four weeks away from graduation, Mr Lee was allowed to return to school, but was taught one-on-one for ten days, under constant supervision in a building separate from other students, before being allowed to attend class with other students again (Wang 2007; Swedberg and Olson 2007).

Later in the week, Cary police and McHenry County prosecutors released the parts of Allen Lee's essay that they found most disturbing. Soon after this, Dane Liozzo, Mr Lee's attorney, made the complete essay public (Pallasch et al. 2007: 5). Mr Lee added an author's note clarifying his thinking and identifying the sources of lyrics and characters from popular culture that he had used in the essay. He asked that people judge his intentions after reading both the essay and his remarks in their entirety, rather than reaching a conclusion by reading excerpts out of context (Lee 2007).

Law-enforcement authorities and school administrators, including District 155 Superintendent Jill Hawk, defended the criminal complaint and arrest, and Lee's suspension from regular classes, as the proper responses to potential harm to students and staff, despite the lack of a specific threat against anyone (Rossi 2007: 4). They were concerned not only about the depiction of violence, but the combined and pervasive expressions of brutality, vulgarity, sexual themes, and references to drug-use in Mr Lee's essay. School and local officials acted out of concern for public safety.

Others saw officials' response as overreaction at best, and violations of civil rights and professional trust at worst. Students who knew Mr Lee expressed shock that this smart, quiet, straight-A student athlete was considered a threat. Mr Lee had no disciplinary record and had never been in trouble. Several students organized a petition drive to show support for their classmate and express their dismay at the school's handling of the situation. Some expressed confusion over what school personnel would consider (in)appropriate expression. Allen Lee's essay was written in his creative-writing class, following Ms Capron's instructions to write a stream-of-consciousness essay on whatever came to mind without stopping, revising, or censoring. She assured the students that they would not be judged, and told them that if creativity failed they could even write "I don't know what to write about" over and over again. One student admitted giving a speech the previous month in the same honors English class, imagining himself as a hit man and going so far as to identify students who would be his victims. His expression of violence was not penalized (Swedberg and Olson 2007).

Mr Lee admitted that there was violence in his essay, but maintained that it was taken out of context in the criminal complaint. He insisted that he intended no harm to anyone and was bewildered at being arrested for following his teacher's directions (Rozek 2007: 3). His essay was composed from popular culture sources, pieced together with bits from songs and movies and references to video games (Lee 2007).

Opinions of experts in law, education, and psychology are divided. Some believe the actions of the school and police were justified in light of the inappropriateness of Mr Lee's essay, and defend the right to limit free speech in some circumstances. Others are bewildered at the harshness of officials' response. While acknowledging that Mr Lee's essay showed poor judgment, particularly in the aftermath of the Virginia Tech shootings and the heightened sensitivity to violence in schools following the Columbine tragedy, they raise questions about criminalizing a school assignment and failing to offer counseling or work with the family before having the student arrested (Rozek et al. 2007: 3; Keilman and Ford 2007: 1, 10).

Charges were dropped a month after they were filed. It was determined that Allen Lee did not pose a threat and that Ms Capron did not want the case to proceed (Wang 2007). Yet Lee's life was forever altered.

Allen Lee admits that his essay contained graphic images of sex and violence and references to drugs. Given that he was following specific instructions from his teacher, did the fact that his writing disturbed community and school officials morally justify their response to him? Were the actions of the Cary-Grove High School, Cary police, and McHenry County Court appropriate and morally justifiable?

Perspective One

The actions of the Cary-Grove High School, Cary police, and McHenry County Court were neither appropriate nor morally justifiable. Cary-Grove High School officials, Cary police, and the McHenry County Court overstepped their moral authority in arresting Mr Lee, charging him with a crime, and subjecting him to isolation upon his return to school. These actions by authorities entrusted with promoting the well-being of Allen Lee are untenable according to the moral appeals to utility, rights, the virtue of professional integrity, and equality.

Allen Lee suffered consequences that were disproportionate to his actions. He was publicly humiliated, with judgmental intention, by the publication of his school-work. He was ostracized – separated from his fellow students while continuing to attend school. His acceptance to the Marine Corps was withdrawn, compromising his future plans and limiting his options. He was not acting in defiance when he wrote his essay, but following the explicit directions of his teacher to write whatever came into his mind, without censoring his thoughts or their expression. The enormity of the negative outcomes for Mr Lee of doing as he was instructed is shocking.

The consequences of the actions of school and community officials affect not only Allen Lee, but all other students as well. If students believe that even if they follow directions they risk punishment and severe consequences, they will become fearful of displeasing the teacher; they will stifle their expression; and they will fail to take advantage of opportunities for learning. It is unimaginable that students should fear the noxious consequence of criminal prosecution if teachers find their written work disturbing or offensive.

Adolescence is a time of identity exploration and intensified emotions, as young people practice and pattern the adults they will become. Hyperbolizing angst that is more extreme than the actual experience can be as much a catharsis as it can be a symptom of menace (Keilman and Ford 2007: 10). Writing assignments can offer an intimate look into the mind, interests, and even fears of the writer. It is often impossible to determine whether a student's writing expresses desire, fantasy, intention, imitation, or imagination; or is based on an experience, a dream, visual images, literature, the news, music, or other sources. Teachers often identify troubled students through their writing, and are able to refer them to counselors or other skilled professionals who can help students deal with issues that are both troubling them and troubling to others. But journals and creative-writing assignments can be worrisome for teachers whose students dwell on dark subjects. It is usually not possible to know whether the writing simply mirrors the visually violent and sexually explicit world teens live in, expresses their intentions to wreak havoc or harm others, or just models a favorite writer, such as horror writer Bram Stoker. Writing can be a healthy way to channel aggression. Censoring written expression closes off an avenue for identifying students who are in distress, and who could be helped by appropriately trained counselors or other professionals. When students are discouraged from expressing their anger or misery, or are penalized for doing so, they are unlikely to seek help. Utility, in the sense of the overall welfare of the community, suffers as the actual negative consequences to a particular student may extend, as a ripple effect, through the greater community.

Young people live in a pop culture world of entertainment, music, video, and computer games that is drenched with themes of sex and violence. The pervasiveness of graphic language and imagery desensitizes teens to its power to give offense or be perceived as threatening. Students often do not understand what is and is not appropriate. Further, defining an acceptable level of vulgarity or violence may be difficult, even for experienced teachers. The result is that teachers sometimes give inconsistent guidelines: in an atmosphere of heightened concern about violence and respect, teachers may simultaneously encourage and penalize creativity.

Adolescent psychiatrist Dr Henry Gault was called on to assess a student who had been assigned to write an essay in the style of his favorite author. The teacher found the essay, written in the style of horror author Stephen King, to be disturbing; as a result, the student was suspended until a psychological evaluation indicated no cause for concern (Keilman and Ford 2007: 10). Writing authentic dialog and capturing genuine vernacular are the marks of a skilled writer. Had Rhett Butler said to Scarlet O'Hara, "Frankly my dear, I don't really care one way or the other," the riveting scene in *Gone With the Wind* would not have had the same compelling intensity.

The reaction to Allen Lee's essay, written according to his teacher's direction, did not respect his right to the expectation of confidentiality in a classroom assignment. He did not intend the essay to be publicly available; he particularly did not expect it to be made public in a way that was intended to support the perspective that he was a dangerous individual with sinister intentions.

The treatment of Allen Lee also calls into question the professionalism of school and public officials. The actions of school personnel and the police destroyed the confidence of Allen Lee and other students that school personnel were committed to their well-being; that is, in failing to act with professional integrity, the school and public officials sullied their respective professions. The failure of integrity undermined students' trust that their teachers would treat them with honesty and respect. The expression of offensive language and disturbing ideas is not a criminal act and should not be prosecuted as such. The teacher's failure to set explicit guidelines for this assignment – in fact, to give instructions that indicated there were no limits to acceptable expression – perhaps should not have been construed by Allen Lee to be carte blanche for writing violent, vulgar prose. However, the response of the school in filing criminal charges against a student who, however inappropriately and literally he followed instructions, is highly unprofessional. To subject the student to arrest without informing or involving the parents or appropriate school personnel qualified to assess the student's emotional state, and instead turning the student over for criminal prosecution, is an egregious and hostile act unworthy of the education profession.

Likewise, the actions of the police and prosecutor were unjustifiable. The charges of disorderly conduct were inappropriate. Disorderly conduct is a public offense, and to bring these charges in response to a private communication that was intended to remain between two people was a mistaken and, thus, an inappropriate application of power. Handing in a writing assignment does not create public disorder. As law-enforcement officials and members of the legal system, both the police and the county court had a duty to protect Allen Lee's rights and freedom. Hence, by acting against him, they failed in their professional duty. Their dereliction is further indicated by the fact that charges were dropped and an evaluation determined that Allen Lee was a threat neither to himself nor to anyone else.

Allen Lee was not treated with equality. Other students were not punished for expressions of violence. Perhaps heightened awareness of campus security was one reason for the response, but can Mr Lee's criticism of his teacher's methods be ruled out as an influencing factor?

In summary, based on the moral principles of consequences, utility, the right to confidentiality, the virtue of professional integrity, the professionals' sworn duties, and equality, Cary-Grove High School administrators and law-enforcement and court officials were not justified in their actions in response to Allen Lee's essay.

Perspective Two

The Cary police and McHenry County Court acted appropriately in arresting and charging Allen Lee with disorderly conduct. Cary-Grove High School officials likewise acted appropriately in removing Mr Lee from other students for instruction. This position is supported by the moral principles of consequences, particularly balancing harms and benefits; utility; rights, including freedoms and well-being; virtue, particularly motive and professional duty; and justice.

While it is true that Allen Lee suffered negative consequences because of his expressions of violence and vulgarity, the harm to Mr Lee must be weighed against the potential harm to his fellow students and the Cary-Grove High School staff. Mr Lee was an honor student and had been accepted into the Marine Corps. Acceptance into the Marine Corps requires successful completion of the Military Entry Processing Station, including a psychiatric evaluation. Although Mr Lee argued that his writing was misinterpreted and taken out of context, given his intelligence and psychological soundness, it is improbable that he was unaware of the carnage that had occurred only a few days earlier at Virginia Tech, and that his violent essay would cause concern in his own school. Even if the response was an overreaction, even given that the essay was a creative-writing class assignment, the actions taken by school and law-enforcement officials were an understandable and prudent response to a deliberate and poorly considered provocation by Mr Lee.

Part of the educational process is learning the consequences of actions. While the consequences for Mr Lee were serious, they were neither disproportionate to his actions nor to the context in which those actions occurred. Neither Ms Capron nor Ms Popp should be blamed for Allen Lee's lack of judgment and respect: he is responsible for what he writes.

Concern for the overall welfare and safety of the school community was the overriding factor that prompted the actions taken in response to Lee's essay. Protecting the safety of more than 2,000 students and school employees from a potential threat by a single individual, even if it means causing some level of harm to the individual, is supported by the moral principle of utility.

Words are powerful. Free speech comes with consequences, good and bad. Gossips are shunned (or sought after), liars are mistrusted, and whiners are avoided. Angry words escalate tension; slurs create blood feuds; courageous words inspire valor; kind words soothe pain. Protection of free expression is a significant right, both in terms of personal freedom and as a safeguard of democracy. Without the protection of free speech, the press could not expose corruption, protestors could not demonstrate, people could not proclaim unpopular views, citizens could not criticize the government, scholars could not accurately record events or interpret history. Distasteful or offensive as some speech is – rap lyrics that denigrate women, malicious gossip, unwarranted public criticism, narrow-minded bigotry, boring lectures, pornography – its protection is the price of freedom. Yet, some limits on free speech are necessary to protect liberties and prevent harm: hate speech, revealing the names of rape victims, slander, publication of medical records, and leaking classified information (such as revealing the name of CIA agent Valerie Plame in retaliation for her husband's criticism of the administration's policy on the Iraq war). We all know not to joke about a bomb in an airport.

Critics of the action of Cary police and school administrators argue that Mr Lee's right to confidentiality was disregarded. The essay was a classroom assignment, intended only for the eyes of his teacher. Students have a reasonable right to expect that their academic assignments will not be released to the public. Indeed, public exposure of academic efforts would likely create paralyzing fear of ridicule among students, undermine trust in teachers, and discourage motivation.

Nonetheless, teachers and administrators are mandated reporters, required by law to report concerns regarding student safety to administrators or other officials. It was not only appropriate for Ms Capron to discuss her concerns with her supervisor; it was legally mandated. Likewise, her department head was required to inform the principal. Certainly, given the circumstances of the preceding week, it would have been irresponsible of Ms Popp to fail to seek appropriate external support when faced with the threat of danger to those entrusted to her.

It is challenging for school administrators to define acceptable boundaries for freedom of expression in the context of educational goals and appropriate pedagogy, for students of a wide range of maturity and academic skills, and educational and social needs. The challenge is made more difficult by the expectation that schools will protect students from violence, and instill tolerance while upholding students' civil rights. The courts offer no clear guidance on free speech rights in schools. Their caution and inconsistency in interpreting the rights of students in the public educational environment add to the difficulty administrators face in trying to accommodate legitimate and competing interests.

Mr Lee's expectation of (and right to) confidentiality was negligible in comparison with the duty of school administrators to guarantee a safe environment for learning. In addition, the principal's motivation to protect members of the school community was morally appropriate. The effort the school took to continue to educate Mr Lee honored both duty and virtue – specifically, the virtues of integrity, faithfulness, and responsibility to him as a student to whom they also had obligations.

Were the police justified in releasing excerpts from Allen Lee's essay? While it is the responsibility of law-enforcement officials to protect the public from harm, from the threat of harm, and – as much as possible – from the fear of harm, arresting a student for a classroom assignment is a serious act. Capricious acts by law-enforcement officials undermine public confidence. And while Allen Lee is among those whom the police have an obligation to protect, they are not required to protect him in every instance from the consequences of his own actions. It was not unreasonable to inform the public of the details of the charges, particularly as civil rights were at issue. The public has a right to know what constitutes legally acceptable behavior, and law-enforcement officials have a duty to inform them of the acceptable limits of free expression.

The charge of unfairness – that is, discrimination on the basis of morally irrelevant factors – is not supportable in defense of Mr Lee. While the actions against him were taken quickly, they were not taken capriciously. Any other student who had written what Mr Lee did in that post-Columbine, post-Virginia-Tech environment of heightened fear for student safety would likely have received the same treatment. The fact that the school continued to educate Mr Lee in the least restrictive reasonable manner, protecting others while the threat he posed was assessed, indicates the school's commitment to the well-being of all students, including Mr Lee.

Finally, restricting Allen Lee's liberty was morally acceptable according to the principle of justice. Investigating this situation took educators and law-enforcement officials nearly a month before charges were dropped and it was determined that Mr Lee was not a threat to himself or others. It would have been ideal if school officials and the police had the luxury of time to investigate the situation thoroughly before they acted. However, with the safety of more than 2,000 students and teachers on their minds, officials chose the course of action they believed to be appropriate and responsible.

In summary, the actions of Cary-Grove High School administrators, the Cary police, and McHenry County Court in response to Allen Lee's essay were morally justifiable, supported by the moral principles of consequences, particularly balancing harms and benefits; utility; rights, including freedoms and confidentiality; virtue, specifically integrity, faithfulness, responsibility, and professional duty; and justice.

Additional Issues to Consider

Other possible moral dilemmas arising within this case:

Q In this situation, how might those involved appropriately balance protecting freedom of expression and protecting the public from potential harm?

Q Are faculty morally obligated to keep confidential the content of assignments that students submit?

Q Are faculty morally obligated to avoid assignments that might evoke socially problematic responses from students?

Q Are law-enforcement officers morally obligated to maintain confidentiality about persons who have been arrested?

Q If Allen Lee had stood up during a public free-speech event and made remarks of the same tenor, would the school have been justifying in taking the same actions that it took in response to his written remarks?

REFERENCES

Keilman, J., and Ford, L. (2007) When students cross the line: writing teachers try to differentiate between creativity and thinly veiled threats in school assignments. *Chicago Tribune* (April 29): 1, 10.

Lee, A. (2007) Allen Lee's essay. *Chicago Sun Times* (April 27). Available at: www.suntimes.com/news/metro/361573,042707lee.article (accessed October 9, 2007).

Pallasch, A. M., Donovan, L., and Rossi, R. (2007) Marines drop essay writer. *Chicago Sun-Times* (April 28): 5.

Rossi, R. (2007) 'Disturbing' essay gets student arrested: teacher alerts principal after seeing "violence" in teen's writing. *Chicago Sun Times* (April 26): 4.

Rozek, D., Rossi, R., and Pallasch, A. M. (2007) Essay arrest baffles experts. *Chicago Sun Times* (April 27): 3.

Swedberg, N., and Olson, E. R. (2007) Disturbing essay details revealed. *Northwest Herald* (April 26). Available at: www.nwherald.com/articles/2007/04/26/news/local/doc4630304f12dd7798473383.txt (accessed October 9, 2007).

Wang, J. (2007) Student graduates after being investigated for explicit essay: Lee wrote essay in class shortly after Virginia Tech massacre. *Student Press Law Center*

(June 7). Available at: www.splc.org/newsflash_archives.asp?id=1533&year=2007 (accessed October 9, 2007).

CASE THIRTY-THREE: THE IDEALISM OF YOUTH – CIVIL DISOBEDIENCE AND THE BYU HONOR CODE

During autumn semester 2002, Caleb Proulx (pronounced "Pru"), a student at privately owned Brigham Young University (BYU), began voicing his opposition to the Iraq war. Proulx silk-screened the phrase "No War In Iraq" on armbands, one of which he wore to class; he disseminated other armbands around the BYU and the nearby state-owned Utah Valley State College campuses. He engaged in public debate (Walch 2003a) and organized "teach-ins." The first teach-in took place on February 13 in a political science course, "War and Peace," which featured presentations from BYU faculty; the second teach-in, on February 28, had to be moved to the Provo City Library after university administrators would not permit it to be conducted on campus. To boos and hisses, he publicly criticized prohibitions by university administrators against addressing the Bush policy of pre-emptive war in open dialogue on campus (Walch 2003b).

Feeling "shut down and hemmed in" by BYU restrictions (Proulx 2007), Proulx joined a group called Utah Citizens for Peace, which advocated nonviolent civil disobedience as a vehicle to fight injustice. The group believed that the US invasion of Iraq was "unnecessary, unjust, illegal, and immoral" (Welling 2003b). "I fundamentally disagree with the way the Bush administration is approaching the problem," Proulx said. "I don't think Saddam Hussein was an immediate threat. There were other options for dealing with him, including tougher inspections and allowing more time for sanctions to weaken his regime. It might take longer and be a harder road, but it wouldn't kill as many people" (Walch 2003b).

To express their moral outrage at the Bush administration foreign policy and the invasion of Iraq, the group attempted for a second time to get arrested in a nonviolent act of civil disobedience (Welling 2003a). On March 24, 2004, they succeeded. Sitting and singing and blocking the entrance of the Wallace F. Bennett Federal Building in downtown Salt Lake City, after 90 minutes they were finally taken into custody by US marshals for disruptive conduct (Sullivan 2003).

Following their arrest, the protestors evoked the tradition of nonviolent civil disobedience of Henry David Thoreau, Mahatma Gandhi, and Martin Luther King, Jr. "When you've exhausted all the tools within the system to fight an injustice, then you turn to civil disobedience," Proulx said (Rooney 2003). The protesters emphasized the importance of abiding by a higher moral law than mere human statutory law. In the words of one of Proulx's fellow protestors: "I did what I had to do for the love of God and country, moved by faith and conscience to voice dissent in the only way left. I could not do otherwise without sinning against God and abandoning my duty as a citizen" (Welling 2003b). Another protester said, referring to the Bush administration's stated rationale for going to war: "I felt a sense of desperation to get my views known and let the public know that I believe they were deceived" (ibid.).

Proulx asserted that in cases where the social contract has been violated, civil disobedience is a justifiable form of democratic engagement. Reflecting on the prospect of getting arrested, Proulx (2003) wrote:

> While the day-to-to administration of the country is in the hands of an elite, ultimate responsibility rests in the hands of the people. . . . If the governing authority breaks the terms it is bound to, the contract is broken. It is the prerogative of those giving consent to exercise the terms of the contract. If we can grant authority by giving our implicit consent through voting and exercising the other few democratic means to affect government policy, how can we manifest our non-compliance? This is the niche wherein civil disobedience finds its natural fit within the scheme of democracy. Civil disobedience is a symbolic retaking of our consent.

Proulx's decision to get arrested was intentional and premeditated. "Getting arrested is not a decision I took lightly," he said. "I understood the repercussions, that it would make it more difficult to get a job in the future and that it would jeopardize my standing at BYU. But I did it out of a deep conviction that I needed to do something and it was the right thing to do" (Walch 2003b). "I accept all the consequences of my actions," he said (Malouf 2003a). "I'm not repentant of it," Proulx stated (Patterson 2003), and he expressed willingness to break the law again in a nonviolent manner if need be (Rooney 2003).

In court, legal counsel explained that civil disobedience was the only recourse left open to the protesters and therefore all charges should be dropped. Repeated letters and petitions to elected officials went unanswered. "This is not just about the war in Iraq," the lawyer said, "but about the ability to be heard. Because my clients do not have the money to go to $100-a-plate dinners, they are not heard by their representatives. Their only means to get their message out is through the media" (Malouf 2003b). In July 2003, the eight protesters pleaded no contest to class C misdemeanors and were fined $50 each (Welling 2003b). Proulx noted a contradiction in the sentencing: "I had to obey this country's laws, but I saw that this country was not obeying international law that it had agreed to go along with" (ibid.).

The story may have ended there, except that BYU is owned by the Church of Jesus Christ of Latter-day Saints (or LDS Church, colloquially known as the Mormon Church). As a private institution, BYU implements an Honor Code which all students must sign upon matriculation. Referencing the body of revelation from God to Mormon prophets, the Honor Code proclaims: "The Lord, through modern revelation, requires of his people . . . obedience and steadfast support of the properly-instituted governments in all lands" (*vide Doctrine and Covenants* 58: 21–2; 98: 4–6; and 134). The Honor Code also cites a precept by the original Mormon prophet, Joseph Smith, which states: "We believe in being subject to kings, presidents, rulers, magistrates, in obeying, honoring, and sustaining the law" (Smith n.d.).

Yet others were troubled by what appeared to be self-contradictions in the BYU Honor Code, making any alleged "violations" by Proulx absurd. In a letter to the BYU student newspaper, one Provo resident mused:

> I find Caleb Proulx's Honor Code violation most ironic. If the Honor Code requires "steadfast support of the properly-instituted governments in all lands," we may all be in violation. Let's think of some properly instituted governments – Iraq, North Korea and Nazi Germany were all properly instituted by their own government mechanisms. . . . If the Honor Code requires me to steadfastly support Saddam Hussein and all his policies, it leaves me in something of a quandary. (Jones 2003)

Within this context, debate over the significance of Proulx's violation of the Honor Code and the possibility of punitive action by BYU became heated. Some scolded Proulx as a scofflaw, dumbfounded that he would be admired as a shining example of constructive civic engagement. One Utahan cynically remarked in a local newspaper: "The only reason I can think of why BYU administrators should not expel Caleb Proulx, the student who was arrested earlier this week for blocking the entrance to a federal building as part of an antiwar demonstration, is to keep him out of our colleges here in Salt Lake City" (Morrison 2003).

Others praised Proulx for his principled commitment to democracy and justice. In another letter to the BYU student newspaper, a correspondent stated:

> Proulx's concern for his country and the world at large is exemplary. He put aside his own personal interests to try to effect positive change in the world. . . . I think the small but vocal number of BYU students who insult and threaten him for acting on his beliefs are a much greater shame to BYU than Proulx himself. Attending BYU with students like Proulx, who act on their beliefs and try to improve the world, makes me more proud to be a BYU student. (Shirts 2003)

A devout Mormon, who served a two-year proselytizing mission for his church following the events of spring 2003, Proulx expressed feelings of internal tension when obedience to human law seemed inconsistent with obedience to higher moral law, as in the situation of voicing opposition to the Iraq war. "The point of . . . civil disobedience is not to destroy or undermine the public order or the operation of the law. It is symbolic and . . . is undertaken in situations where one feels that a law or moral principle is being sacrificed," Proulx argued. "In a case such as this, the citizen is faced with a lose-lose situation, having to choose which law to obey at the disregard of the other. The moral choice is to obey the higher law; that being the one whose breaking would do more damage to humanity" (2003).

Such tension is inevitable if one sees moral law and human law as having two distinct sources: if the source of moral law is taken to be divinity while the source of civil law is taken to be humanity. "I am still working within the system," as Proulx put it. "I'm just working within a bigger system" (Malouf 2003a). Obedience to both civil law and moral law is desirable, but obedience to the latter takes priority over the former when obedience to both is not possible, mandating disobedience of civil law.

Since Proulx saw an inherent inconsistency in the BYU Honor Code between civil law and moral law, he could no longer accept it as a standard for moral guidance. To that end, he withdrew from BYU before any action by the university was taken (Fantin 2003). Explaining his decision, Proulx said: "If I am willing to break the law to promote peace, then I cannot remain in a commitment to an Honor Code which precludes – in many people's minds – civil disobedience" (Walch 2003c).

Was Proulx ethically justified in engaging in nonviolent civil disobedience in his quest to protest against what he perceived to be injustice?

Perspective One

Proulx was not justified in engaging in nonviolent civil disobedience. According to the ethical theory of deontology (the source of autonomy and rights), each citizen has the duty to obey the law. Law defines ethics and determines the scope of moral and immoral behavior.

Proulx voluntarily accepted the BYU Honor Code when he matriculated. His dishonorable violation of the Honor Code mirrors his dishonorable violation of civil law. LDS Church leaders have been unambiguous about the importance of obedience to civil law. Shortly after Proulx's arrest, H. David Burton, a high-ranking church authority, was clear: "Our participation in life's important events may be jeopardized if we fail to follow the rules contained in our Father in Heaven's commands. Involvement in sexual sin, illegal drugs, civil disobedience, or abuse could keep us on the sidelines at key times" (Burton 2003). At the beginning of April 2003, President Gordon B. Hinckley declared, almost as if he were speaking directly to Proulx: "In a democracy we can renounce war and proclaim peace. There is opportunity for dissent. Many have been speaking out and doing so emphatically. That is their privilege. That is their right, so long as they do so legally" (Hinckley 2003).

As leaders of Proulx's church, their moral condemnation of his actions carry significant weight. If Proulx cannot be expected to be a virtuous member of his own religion, he can scarcely be expected to be a role model for civic duty. As Proulx was not an upstanding BYU student, neither were his actions that of an upstanding citizen. In fact, giving him kudos for engaging in civil disobedience is repugnant.

Perspective Two

Proulx was justified in engaging in nonviolent civil disobedience. According to the ethical theory of deontology, each citizen has the duty to work for justice. If this effort takes one to the edge and beyond the bounds of law, then at times one might be ethically obliged to break the law and engage in nonviolent civil disobedience.

Proulx's allusion to Henry David Thoreau and Martin Luther King is instructive. A pervasive theme of Thoreau's writing is the primacy of the individual, and the importance of acting on *conscience*, even if doing so causes the individual to run up against the power of the state. If you believe certain laws sanction injustice, it is your moral *duty* to disobey them; you must follow a higher *moral law* than *civil law*. In the essay "Resistance to Civil Government" (more commonly know as "Civil Disobedience," written in 1849), Thoreau says of the government: "[I]f it is of such a nature that it requires you to be the agent of injustice to another, then, I say, break the law" (1966: 231). Just because something is legal does not mean that it is ethical.

Thoreau believed that the US government's treatment of Native Americans, the practice of slavery, and the invasion of Mexico were all outrageously unethical. He wrote: "[W]hen a sixth of the population of a nation which has undertaken to be the refuge of liberty are slaves, and a whole country is unjustly overrun and conquered by a foreign army, and subjected to military law, I think that it is not too soon for honest men to rebel and revolutionize" (ibid.: 227). Revolution, however, need not be violent. The passivist can effectively counter legislated injustice by simply not cooperating. This is the reasoning behind Thoreau's intentional failure to pay tax for several years. He did not believe, ethically, that he could support a government guilty of injustice. His stay in the Concord jail was the necessary consequence of civil virtue.

The idea of a moral responsibility to resist unjust laws through nonviolent non-cooperation is a defining feature of Martin Luther King's political philosophy. In a tribute to Thoreau entitled "A Legacy of Creative Protest" (1962), King wrote:

> During my early college days I read Thoreau's essay on civil disobedience for the first time. Fascinated by the idea of refusing to cooperate with an evil system, I was so deeply moved that I re-read the work several times. I became convinced then that non-cooperation with evil is as much a moral obligation as is cooperation with good. No other person has been more eloquent and passionate in getting this idea across than Henry David Thoreau. As a result of his writings and personal witness we are the heirs of a legacy of creative protest. It goes without saying that the teachings of Thoreau are alive today, indeed, they are more alive today than ever before. Whether expressed in a sit-in at lunch counters, a freedom ride into Mississippi, a peaceful protest in Albany, Georgia, a bus boycott in Montgomery, Alabama, it is an outgrowth of Thoreau's insistence that evil must be resisted and no moral man can patiently adjust to injustice.

Through this strategy, it is *possible* to change the minds of the violent aggressor (indeed, trying to precipitate such change is actually, to use the language of Kant, a categorical imperative). As King writes in *Stride Toward Freedom*: "To accept passively an unjust system is to cooperate with that system; thereby the oppressed become as evil as the oppressor" (1958: 212).

Given the supremacy of moral law over civil law, inaction may amount to complicity in injustice. As Thoreau wrote in "Civil Disobedience": "The mass of men serve the state thus, not as men mainly, but as machines[;] . . . they are as likely to serve the devil, without intending it, as God" (1966: 226). King saw his identity and his actions as embedded in a community. As he wrote in "Letter from Birmingham Jail": "Injustice anywhere is a threat to justice everywhere. We are caught in an inescapable network of mutuality, tied in a single garment of destiny. Whatever affects one directly, affects all indirectly" (Schulke and McPhee 1986: 226). In light of his willingness to face the consequences of arrest and believing what he did, for Proulx *not* to have taken action would have been unethical.

Two lessons follow. First, equating ethics with law is empirically impossible. Unless we satisfy ourselves with some form of extreme, naive relativism, two cultures with logically contradictory normative standards – such as the maxim that it is never right ritually to compromise the bodily integrity of a human being with the maxim that it is sometimes ethically obligatory ritually to compromise the bodily integrity of a human being, as in female genital "circumcision" (Rosenberg 2004) – then the two standards cannot both be ethically right. If ethics and the law are coextensive, then we are left with an overt logical contradiction.

Second, as philosopher James Rachels argues, equating law with ethics rules out the possibility of moral progress: if what is legal is ethical, then the law needs no improvement, because, by definition, it is already ethically sound (1986: 18). History shows this to be flatly false, and, happily, ethical reasoning provides a corrective for unjust law.

As Proulx's admirable actions demonstrate, following the nuanced guidance of Thoreau and King, ethics and civil law are not coextensive. Where civil law and moral law are inconsonant, higher moral law trumps lower civil law. Then, in order to be ethical, one must, by definition, break the law. To do so is to exhibit virtuous character.

Additional Issues to Consider

Other possible moral dilemmas arising within this case:

- Q In a morally pluralistic society, are *private institutions* that, on the bases of their own moral beliefs, disagree with civil laws morally permitted to disobey them (assuming the disobedience is peaceful)?

- Q From a moral point of view, do faculty have any duty to support students like Proulx?

- Q Do citizens of societies with bad laws or communities with bad rules (whatever the content of these may be) have a moral obligation to work to overturn them?

- Q Does *civil* law ever trump *moral* law? If so, under what conditions? If not, why not?

448   CASES AND COMMENTARIES

REFERENCES

Blake, C. (2003) BYU student quits school, cites commitment to protest. *Daily Herald* (April 2).

Burton, H. D. (2003) And that's the way it is. *Ensign* (May): 48. Available at: www.lds.org/portal/site/LDSOrg/menuitem.b12f9d18fae655bb69095bd3e44916a0/?vgnextoid=2354fccf2b7db010VgnVCM1000004d82620aRCRD&locale=0&sourceId=b7b776e6ffe0c010VgnVCM1000004d82620a___&hideNav=1 (accessed June 9, 2007).

Doctrine and Covenants of the Church of Jesus Christ of Latter-Day Saints, Containing the Revelations Given to Joseph Smith (1971) Westport, CT: Greenwood Press.

Fantin, L. (2003) BYU student quits university. *The Salt Lake Tribune* (April 2): A8.

Hinckley, G. B. (2003) War and peace. Remarks at the 173rd annual General Conference of The Church of Jesus Christ of Latter-day Saints (April 6). Available at: www.lds.org/conference/talk/display/0,5232,49-1-353-27,00.html (accessed June 9, 2007).

Honor Code of Brigham Young University (n.d.) Obey the law. Available at: http://honorcode.byu.edu/index.php?option=com_content&task=view&id=3600&Itemid=4643 (accessed June 9, 2007).

Jones, R. (2003) Honor code ironic. Letter to the editor. *Daily Universe* (April 2).

King, M. L. (1958) *Stride Toward Freedom: The Montgomery Story*. New York: Harper & Brothers.

King, M. L. (1962) A legacy of creative protest. *Massachusetts Review* 4 (Autumn): 43.

Malouf, M. B. (2003a) War protester risks BYU dismissal. *Salt Lake Tribune* (March 27): A1.

Malouf, M. B. (2003b) War protest was only voice for defendants, says attorney. *Salt Lake Tribune* (May 9): B2.

Morrison, E. (2003) Expel BYU protester. Letter to the editor. *The Salt Lake Tribune* (April 2): A13.

Patterson, C. (2003) BYU student protestor arrested. *Daily Universe* (March 27).

Proulx, C. (2003) Unpublished manuscript.

Proulx, C. (2007) Personal conversation with David R. Keller, Salt Lake City, Utah (June 10).

Rachels, J. (1986) *The Elements of Moral Philosophy*. New York: Random House.

Rooney, M. (2003) Arrested education. *Chronicle of Higher Education* 49 (32): A8.

Rosenberg, T. (2004) Mutilating Africa's daughters: laws unenforced, practices unchanged. *New York Times* (July 5): A14.

Schulke, F., and McPhee, P. O. (1986) *King Remembered*. New York: W. W. Norton.

Shirts, K. (2003) Props to protesters. Letter to the editor. *Daily Universe* (April 7).

Smith, J. *Articles of Faith of The Church of Jesus Christ of Latter-day Saints*. (n.d.) Available at: www.lds.org/library/display/0,4945,106-1-2-1,FF.html (accessed June 9, 2007).

Sullivan, T. (2003) Arrests of antiwar protesters just fine with them. *Salt Lake Tribune* (March 25): B6.

Thoreau, H. D. (1966) Civil disobedience. In O. Thomas (ed.), *Walden and Civil Disobedience*. New York: W. W. Norton (orig. pub. 1849).

Walch, T. (2003a) "Arms" debate rages at BYU. *Deseret News* (March 6): B1.

Walch, T. (2003b) BYU may expel protester after his arrest in SL. *Deseret News* (March 27): B1.

Walch, T. (2003c) Anti-war activist to quit Y over arrest. *Deseret News* (April 2): B2.

Welling, A. (2003a) Ex-Y student denies guilt. *Deseret News* (April 11): B1.
Welling, A. (2003b) 8 voice views, get $50 fines. *Deseret News* (July 22): B3.

CASE THIRTY-FOUR: BRITANNIA WAIVES THE RULES – COLLECTING DNA ON ARRESTEES

David, a graduate student in molecular sciences at a university in London, was excited that his 14-year-old sister, Jessica, was visiting for a few days. The weekend started off on a disastrous note, however, when the London police arrested David and Jessica for "participating in an illegal demonstration." David and Jessica had been walking from the tube stop to the laboratory when they passed a campus rally where students were demonstrating against Britain's policies on global warming. Engrossed in explaining his experiment to his sister, neither David nor Jessica even realized the rally was going on until they were arrested and taken to the police station. David believed that he and Jessica were singled out because they were black. Neither was charged but, despite his protests, particularly when the police refused to get consent from their parents for his younger sister's DNA to be taken, David and Jessica were forced to provide genetic samples and personal information. David was distressed over the emotional effect the arrest had on Jessica, and furious that the weekend they had both so looked forward to had been marred by the incident. He was saddened because he knew that the memory of the experience would haunt both Jessica and him for the rest of their lives. He was also concerned about the consequences that could result from misuse of personal information linked with genetic samples. The combined information can reveal a great deal about an individual, such as a genetic malady or predisposition to disease. Given the circumstances under which the information and samples were collected, David was not confident that the information would be protected from misuse.

David was further outraged to learn that Scott and Nalima, his friends and fellow graduate students in the Molecular Sciences Department, had also been arrested and forced to provide DNA samples. Scott and Nalima, who earned enough on weekends as street musicians to pay their rent, were stunned when they were arrested for "begging" and taken to the local police station. They were not charged and were released almost immediately, but not until each had provided – under protest – a DNA sample, along with personal information.

The three friends met with Nalima's sister Vishaka, who was a lawyer. Although they were upset over the violation of their civil liberties in being taken to the police station for such flimsy reasons, they were infuriated that they – and particularly Jessica – had been forced to provide DNA samples and personal information. As molecular biology researchers, they were well aware of the vast amount of highly personal and identifiable information that could be extracted from genetic samples coupled with personal data. They wanted the samples and data returned, or at least destroyed. Vishaka, also upset at the treatment and forced genetic sampling of her sister and her sister's friends, explained that, unfortunately, their options for recourse were negligible.

Since 1995, under the provisions of the Criminal Justice and Public Order Act, the United Kingdom has been collecting DNA samples, linked with personal information, from everyone arrested. Despite concerns about invasion of privacy, unwarranted government intrusion, and violation of civil liberties, the data are collected without consent and kept permanently. The DNA samples are stored in laboratories, and the genetic profiles and personal information in a computer database. The information is kept even if the individuals are not charged with any wrongdoing, or if they are charged, but acquitted.

Initially, the law did not allow the permanent retention of data collected from individuals acquitted or not charged, but the law was revised in 2001 to allow this. Although it is estimated that approximately 50,000 genetic profiles were illegally retained before the law's revision, they have not been removed from the database. The law has been revised several times since it was first passed, each time allowing greater expansion of the world's largest forensic database, and raising questions about harm to vulnerable populations.

It is anticipated that within the next few years the British government will collect and retain genetic profiles on a third of the UK's adult male population and 7 percent of the adult female population (Puri 2001: 368; Wallace 2006: S26–7). Britain's National Black Police Association has expressed concern that the database contains profiles of 37 percent of the black men in the UK and profiles of only 10 percent of white men, suggesting that racial bias is a strong determinant of who is included in the database (BBC 2006). Terri Dowty, the director of Action on Rights for Children (ARCH), is disquieted by the potential harm to children by their inclusion in the database. In a report to the Home Affairs Committee, Ms Dowty (2007) pointed out that, even enlisting the help of members of Parliament, ARCH has not been able to obtain accurate figures for the number of children whose DNA is included in the database. Relying on statistics from the Youth Justice Board, children's advocates have estimated that genetic information on 400,000 children between the ages of 10 and 17 – who did nothing wrong at all or, at most, received a reprimand or warning – was included in the database. The database does not indicate whether the youth was charged with a crime, charged but acquitted, or merely had a DNA sample taken because someone else in the household was arrested. Nonetheless, having their DNA in the database, even if the child was involved in no wrongdoing, may create suspicion and the assumption of guilt in the event of future contact with law-enforcement officials; evidence indicates that police questioning of a child negatively influences behavior, particularly if the police consider the child to be a troublemaker and disproportionately target him or her for future interrogations (Dowty 2007: 20–3). Children may have interactions with the police that allow collection of their DNA for innocent reasons (e.g., being present during a domestic dispute between the parents, playing on school grounds where drugs were found, being separated from parents in a crowd). In spite of such innocuous reasons for collecting DNA, children who are targeted often become criminal suspects.

From a moral point of view, should the UK destroy the DNA samples and personal information collected from those arrested who are not charged or are subsequently found innocent?

Perspective One

The United Kingdom should purge its genetic database of the records of people arrested who are not charged with a crime or who are acquitted of charges against them. This position is supported by the moral principles of nonmaleficence and utility; autonomy; rights; and justice as both equality and fairness.

The collection and retention of DNA from all individuals who have been detained by the police, even if they are not charged with or found guilty of a crime, carries personal and social consequences. In causing a variety of harms, this policy violates the principle of nonmaleficence. Innocent people, particularly members of vulnerable populations, may be perceived as delinquent and subject to police interest without cause (Bieber et al. 2006: 1316). This unwarranted (and often discriminatory) scrutiny not only harms those personally subjected to it; it also more broadly undermines trust in law-enforcement personnel and the government, and discourages cooperation in crime prevention (Wallace 2006: S29).

Handling vast numbers of DNA samples from individuals who have done nothing wrong wastes resources and creates a backlog of data waiting to be entered into the system. The United States FBI genetic laboratory, for example, currently handles about 96,000 samples a year. Legislation passed in 2006 that expanded the authorization of law-enforcement officials to collect DNA samples from anyone they detain is expected to increase the number of DNA samples submitted to the FBI laboratory by as many as one million a year (Preston 2007: A1). It is true that if data collected from convicted criminals are not in the database, police may take longer to identify and apprehend repeat criminal offenders. But the flood of DNA samples has the potential to overwhelm the system or, at the least, seriously delay entry of the samples of genuine criminals. Ultimately this will delay police apprehension of the truly dangerous, thereby increasing the risk to law-abiding residents.

Once data are collected, genetic information may be used for purposes not initially intended. First, hackers and other unauthorized users who compromise security measures and illicitly access the system pose dangers to those whose information is contained in the database: hackers can access personal information contained therein and use that information for commercial or discriminatory purposes (Puri 2001: 360, 364). Second, UK residents who do not want to rely solely on the country's national healthcare program may purchase private health insurance. The British government already allows insurance companies to require that the results of genetic tests for certain conditions be disclosed to insurers, who are then free to refuse coverage or raise premiums significantly for individuals with a genetic predisposition to certain diseases, such as breast cancer. The insurance companies defend the policy as helpful to those who have a relative with a medical condition and who might be denied insurance on that basis. Although no one is required to have a genetic test, taking a test may prove that one is not at risk (BBC 2000) and, thus, can be insured. But a government that allows insurance companies to require genetic test results may feel no compunction about providing that information – available in the national database – to insurance companies or other interested parties such as employers, financial institutions, professional accreditation organizations, the military, and educational institutions. The likelihood of divulging such information is uncertain, but is not inconceivable.

Recent technological advances allow banked DNA to be used for familial screening. Comparing crime scene DNA with the criminal DNA database may not identify a perfect match, but may reveal a match sufficiently close to suggest a biological relationship between DNA on file and a perpetrator. As whole families share similar DNA profiles, innocent family members may – in virtue of merely being related to a (suspected) criminal – be subjected to a lifetime of suspicion and surveillance by authorities, causing great stress and harm, particularly for children (Bieber et al. 2006: 1316).

Finally, DNA testing is not foolproof. The Innocence Project is a national organization that uses DNA analysis to exonerate prisoners wrongfully convicted of felonies. Ironically, almost two-thirds of the 200 prisoners the Innocence Project has helped to free were convicted, at least in part, as a result of faulty scientific evidence (Page 2007: 23). Careless mistakes have enormous consequences when life and death are at stake, and laboratory practices and interpretations of genetic data are not standardized (Puri 2001: 348, 366).

So, summarizing the appeal to consequences, we find that failure to destroy samples from people who were not charged or who were found to be innocent poses significant risks of harm to individuals and to the population at large, thereby violating the principles of nonmaleficence and utility.

Samples taken without probable cause, and without consent, also fail to respect autonomy. Genetic information is more sensitive than other types of personal data, as it reveals intimate and immutable aspects of the individual. Revealing such personal information without the owner's knowledge or consent to third parties, who may use that information to their own advantage, undermines self-determination (Rosen 2003: 39). For example, someone with access to genetic information may dislike a particular political candidate. Revealing to a journalist that the candidate has a predisposition for early-onset Alzheimer's disease, or is related to a criminal, might bias voters against the candidate when they read the information in the newspaper. Because respect for autonomy was disregarded when samples were taken initially without consent, it is also unlikely that consent would be sought to use samples in the future for any number of research or commercial purposes. Respect is compromised when people who are innocent of any wrongdoing are treated as though they were guilty, being used as a convenient means to the end of solving crimes.

In the furor to establish a large DNA database, British police rounded up groups of people, usually selected by geographic area, and asked for "voluntary" DNA samples. The volunteers complained that their participation was coerced (that is, not autonomous). Although the DNA samples collected in the dragnets were kept separate from the national database and later destroyed, the practice was a serious violation of autonomy and of liberty rights (Puri 2001: 368).

The right to privacy may also be compromised for innocent family members who are subject to scrutiny because their DNA is a close match to a relative's DNA that is held in the database. It has been suggested that such families would be good sources for genetic research on genes associated with criminality (Wallace 2006: S29). Freedom itself can be at risk with the use of the database, as one British subject discovered. Based on a comparison of six match points of his DNA with DNA found at the scene of a robbery, the database identified him as the burglar. When his airtight alibi proved he could not have committed the crime, Britain was forced to admit that six match points were too few for accurate comparison, and would become even less accurate as more samples were added to the DNA bank (Puri 2001: 368–9). How many persons had been previously arrested and falsely convicted (or at least harassed) is unknown.

In addition to the United Kingdom, most other industrialized countries maintain a DNA database. The United States and all 50 states have DNA databases, each with its own regulations governing collection, storage, and use. A number of countries, as well as the United States, are following the British example of allowing law-enforcement officials to take samples from all individuals arrested, whether or not they are charged (ibid.: 352). A 2006 amendment to the Violence Against Women Act, introduced by legislators from states on the US–Mexican boarder, allows DNA samples to be collected from all individuals detained by the police or immigration officials (Preston 2007: A1).

Freedom and privacy rights are curtailed as genetic databases are mined for use in ways not envisioned when they were initially established. Shortly before the statute of limitations ran out on a California sexual assault case, a "John Doe" arrest warrant was obtained, not for an individual, but for a DNA profile. Several weeks later, genetic data-mining turned up a match and the suspect was arrested (Davenport 2001: 1893). Privacy rights are also compromised when genetic or non-genetic information contained in the database reveals secrets, such as medical conditions, parentage, or where family members escaping domestic violence are living (Dowty 2007: 24; Bieber et al. 2006: 1316). Florida officials used DNA to identify the fathers of babies conceived during rape (Willing 2006). While this information may be essential for conviction or useful in requesting child support, great care must be taken, as it is information a child should probably never learn.

The UK has agreed to share its database with other European countries, further compromising the privacy of those whose DNA is stored (Puri 2001: 368). DNA reveals the highly intimate aspects of the individual, including susceptibility to physical and emotional disorders. The government's intrusion into these very personal areas is an unwarranted threat to liberty, privacy, and confidentiality, and, thus, a violation of those rights. Privacy is further compromised by lack of quality control over sampling , inconsistencies regarding who has access to information and for what purpose the information may be used (Rosen 2003: 42).

Finally, the DNA database does not honor the principle of equality (justice), as the rules are not applied consistently. The disproportionate number of black men in the UK's database demonstrates an existing racial bias, as it perpetuates ongoing demographic discrimination (Bieber et al. 2006: 1316). Similar inequitable prejudicial profiling has been documented in the United States (Preston 2007: A1).

Justice requires that those with greater power protect those who are most vulnerable (such as children, ethic minorities, and victims of past discrimination), from unfair exploitation. The inclusion of their DNA, against their will and without their consent, when they have not been convicted of a crime, violates the principle of justice.

In conclusion, numerous moral principles are violated by the retention of DNA samples and personal information in the United Kingdoms' genetic database from individuals neither charged with a crime nor convicted of wrongdoing. These data should be destroyed immediately.

Perspective Two

The United Kingdom should retain in its genetic database the records of all people arrested, whether or not charges are brought against them, and whether they are found to be guilty or innocent. This position is supported by the moral principles of beneficence and utility.

DNA allows law-enforcement officers to exonerate those falsely accused of a crime, as well as to identify, apprehend, and convict criminals. One in three FBI suspects is cleared based on DNA samples (Puri 2001: 341, 355). As freeing these innocent persons from suspicion or incarceration is surely a great good for them, the principle of beneficence is satisfied.

Although some who are innocent will be investigated and may suffer harm, including emotional trauma and social stigmatization, this is true in any criminal investigation, whether DNA is used or not. Society is at greater risk if all possible avenues of investigation are not pursued: the principle of utility recognizes that avoiding negative consequences is morally justifiable.

While some call for scaling back DNA databases, others call for a universal DNA bank. DNA identification is important not just in criminal investigations, but also in identifying remains from natural disasters and war, distinguishing victims of ethnic and government oppression discovered in mass graves, and verifying the identity of missing persons (Bieber et al. 2006: 1315). Following the deadly 2004 Asian tsunami, Professor Sir Alec Jeffreys of Leicester University called for an international database that would assist in identifying victims of mass disasters (Jha 2005). Utility requires that individuals be prepared to limit their own interest to benefit the larger community (and even, conceivably, their own interests should they themselves be victims of large-scale disasters).

DNA technology is an important law-enforcement tool (Puri 2001: 341). Law-enforcement officers must be able to use the most advanced technological means to ensure public safety. Denying access to information that would allow identification of criminals would compromise the ability of police to do their jobs. In the balance between public safety and the individual's right to privacy, the principle of utility requires that individuals give up some of their rights for the greater good of society. Having criminals' genetic information on file can hasten investigations and protect the public, particularly from harms caused by repeat offenders. Collecting DNA from everyone who is detained by the police builds a substantial source of information for solving crimes and protecting the public. It is true that during a criminal investigation some innocent people may come to the attention of the police and be inconvenienced by detention and social or emotional consequences. It is unfortunate, but unavoidable, that occasional inconvenience must be accepted as part of the burden that allows us to enjoy the benefits of society.

Some liberty and privacy rights may be temporarily curtailed by inclusion in the database, but restriction of rights is justifiable to accommodate the greater needs of society. In this instance, the need for public safety outweighs the individual's right to privacy and unrestricted liberty. Although familial DNA searches infringe on privacy rights, they are justified by their potential to increase greatly the number of cases solved through DNA matches.

Although retaining the DNA samples and personal information of all those who are detained by the police is morally controversial, it is in the best interest of the public and therefore is morally justifiable through an appeal to the principle of utility.

Additional Issues to Consider

Other possible moral dilemmas arising within this case:

Q Would DNA banking be morally permissible if its contents were kept highly confidential; for example, if the identities of those whose DNA had been banked could only be accessed by very few persons and for very few reasons?

Q Would DNA banking be morally permissible if the DNA were not accompanied by any narrative analysis (e.g., about susceptibility to disease)?

Q How serious must a threat to society be to morally justify violating a person's rights to privacy or confidentiality?

REFERENCES

BBC (2006) Call for inquiry into DNA samples. British Broadcast Corporation (January 5). Available at: http://news.bbc.co.uk/1/hi/uk/4584000.stm (accessed October 9, 2007).

BBC (2000) Genetic test first for UK. British Broadcast Corporation (October 12). Available at: http://news.bbc.co.uk/hi/english/health/newsid_968000/968443.stm (accessed October 9, 2007).

Bieber, F., Brenner, C. H., and Lazer, D. (2006) Finding criminals through DNA of their relatives. *Science* 312 (5778): 315–16.

Davenport, J. R. (2001) Random samples. *Science* 291 (5510): 1893.

Dowty, T. (2007) Submission to the Home Affairs committee inquiry: "A surveillance society?" Action on Rights for Children. Available at: www.arched.org/docs/FINALsubmission070424.doc (accessed May 28, 2007).

Jha, A. (2005) Scientist calls for world DNA database. *Guardian* (UK) (April 11). Available at: www.guardian.co.uk/uk_news/story/0,3604,1456597,00.html (accessed October 9, 2007).

Page, C. (2007) The 200th reason to test DNA. *Chicago Tribune* (April 25): 23.

Preston, J. (2007) US set to begin a vast expansion of DNA sampling. *New York Times* (February 5): A1.

Puri, A. (2001) An international DNA database: balancing hope, privacy, and scientific error. *Boston College International & Comparative Law Review* 24 (2): 341–80.

Rosen, C. (2003) Liberty, privacy, and DNA databases. *The New Atlantis* 1 (1): 37–52.

Wallace, H. (2006) The UK national DNA database: balancing crime detection, human rights and privacy. *European Molecular Biology Organization Reports* 7 (Special issue): S26–30.

Willing, R. (2006) DNA database can flag suspects through relatives. *USA Today* (August 22). Available at: www.usatoday.com/tech/science/genetics/2006-08-22-dna-partial-matches_x.htm (accessed October 9, 2007).

CASE THIRTY-FIVE: LAND OF THE FREE – THE GUN BAN AT THE UNIVERSITY OF UTAH

In 1977, the University of Utah implemented a policy banning firearms on campus. For 24 years the ban received little attention, until in 2001 Utah Attorney General Mark Shurtleff wrote an unsolicited opinion to Governor Mike Leavitt contending that rules banning state employees with concealed-carry permits from bringing their weapons into the workplace violated state law. Early the following year University President Bernie Machen filed a federal lawsuit challenging Shurtleff's opinion (Harrie 2002c). The Utah State legislature rejoined with what seemed to many as a silly act of retribution: a bill by pro-gun legislators to dock the president's pay by half (Harrie 2002b). The gesture turned out to be inconsequential, but it set the tone for a battle about to ensue.

The federal judge sent the suit back to the state court, claiming the issue was outside federal jurisdiction (Welling 2003), and in May 2003, the university filed a claim in the state court. In September 2003 Judge Robert Hilder ruled that, contrary to the Shurtleff opinion, the university ban did not in fact violate state law (Sykes and Stewart 2003). In repudiation of Hilder's decision, in February 2004 the Utah State legislature, acting on Shurtleff's opinion, passed Senate Bill 48, which was intended to reassert the state's authority to establish gun policy (Stewart 2004). In defiance, the university's board of trustees voted unanimously in April to maintain the institution's 27-year ban on guns, a move lauded by the Gun Prevention Center of Utah (Sykes 2004a). The university argued in front of the Utah Supreme Court that it was granted autonomy over its own internal affairs by the state's constitution (Sykes 2004b).

Eventually, in September 2006, the Utah Supreme Court ruled that state law prevents the University of Utah from banning guns on campus (Manson 2006). After this decision, university officials created an informal working group of lawmakers and education officials to address the feasibility of prohibiting guns from five areas: dorms, classrooms, faculty offices, athletic venues, and hospitals (McFarland and Warchol 2007). The outcome was Senate Bill 251, sponsored by a Republican member of the working group as a compromise between higher education administrators and pro-gun lawmakers (McFarland 2007). The bill was virulently opposed by the Gunowners of Utah, a gun-rights advocacy group, who derided it as the work of over-intellectualized "aging ex-hippies" (ibid.). The bill that passed ended up only providing faculty with the choice of declaring their offices to be gun-free zones, and students the choice of not living with a con-cealed weapons permit-holder, despite the fact that the law puts permit-holders under no obligation to reveal that they are armed (Stewart 2007d). After all this (and possibly due to sheer fatigue), university officials dropped the federal lawsuit against Shurtleff that had been initiated by former president Machen five years earlier (*Deseret News* 2007).

As a legal controversy rooted in the politics of an emotional issue, the players were polarized into two opposing camps: those in favor of retaining the ban and those in favor of its revocation. Numerous arguments were enlisted to rally supporters around these two flags.

Proponents of the ban generally advanced five arguments. First, the univer-sity argued that the right of the institution to govern its own internal affairs must be respected. In the 2002 federal lawsuit, the university argued that "in order to maintain the safety, civility, and freedom of expression and debate essential to the University's mission, it must enforce policies prohibiting the use and pos-session of firearms on the University campus" (Harrie 2002b). The lone dissenter of the 2006 Utah Supreme Court decision, Chief Justice Christine Durham, con-curred, stating that:

[The framers of the Utah Constitution] intended to secure the University's "pro-tection and defense" by perpetuating its autonomous control over internal academic affairs. . . . Applying, as they do, only to University employees and students, and only while these individuals are on the University campus, these policies merely reflect the University's judgment on an issue that is within the scope of its aca-demic expertise – namely, the appropriate means by which to maintain an educa-tional environment in its classrooms and on its campus. (Manson 2006)

Allowing the legislature to meddle in the internal affairs of the university, according to attorney Alan Sullivan, would set a dangerous precedent and could result in the legislature tweaking the academic program according to political whim (Fattah 2004). Through not overtly acknowledged, the zealous antagonism to including biological evolution in the public school curriculum by one power-ful legislator was likely a subtext to these concerns (Toomer-Cook 2005).

Second, and following from the first, proponents of the ban argued that the presence of guns on campus is antithetical to the university's mission to foster a healthy learning atmosphere. "Classrooms, libraries, dormitories and cafeterias are no place for lethal weapons," President Machen stated. "Their very presence would interfere with the essential functions of a university" (Harrie 2002a). Removal of the gun ban could provoke an atmosphere of intimidation and keep students from speaking out in class. President Michael K. Young, Machen's suc-cessor, remarked that institutions of higher education are comprised of young people of "varying degrees of maturity" who may not be accustomed to the strains of academic life. "The moment somebody pulls a six-shooter out, it will have a chilling effect" (Shuppy 2006).

It follows that, third, guns are an outright threat to campus safety. As Kim Wirthlin, Vice-President for Government Relations, said: "Coming to a univer-sity can be a stressful experience, and we're concerned that if guns are in some of these areas, there could be accidental discharges. People could be injured – could be killed – and that kind of an environment is one where circumstances could be out of someone's control, so it makes sense not to have guns" (Stewart 2006). Researchers at the Harvard School of Public Health found that college students who own guns are more likely to engage in risky destructive behavior like binge drinking, drunk driving, having unprotected sex, and propensity to violence (Miller et al. 2002), which proponents of the university gun ban cited as evidence supporting their position (Stewart 2002). Education officials argued that guns are particularly inappropriate in dormitories, where students are living in close proximity to each other, away from home for the first time, and learn-ing how to deal with the pressures of college life (Sykes 2004c).

David Richard Keller, a professor at a sister school in the Utah system of higher education, reasoned that armed students do not necessarily make campuses safer and that law-enforcement should be left up to trained professionals: "If our legislative leaders are really serious about reducing the possibility of violence at schools, then they should act to increase the number of armed professionals on campus, rather than incorrectly assume that a heavily-armed citizenry is up to the challenge" (2004). Keller expressed suspicions that gun-rights advocates have an idealized notion of self-defense using firearms, and are unaware that if a person with a gun permit accidentally kills an innocent bystander in an attack, the shooter may be charged with manslaughter.

Students reflected these concerns. At a debate on campus, a sophomore in biochemical engineering speculated: "The presence of guns is what causes gun violence. . . . If enough people are carrying guns on campus, eventually an accid-ent will happen" (Gardiner 2006).

Fourth, given these considerations within the context of Utah law, proponents argued that the university's academic interests outweigh constitutional rights of individuals to carry guns on campus. As Chief Justice Durham wrote, "The university's academic interests must be weighed against individual constitutional rights where these rights are properly invoked. . . . A policy that prohibited students and employees from openly brandishing firearms in classrooms would clearly be legitimate" (Shuppy 2006).

Fifth, and finally, gun opponents pointed to public opinion polls which suggested that the majority of Utahans favor gun control on college campuses. A non-scientific poll of 500 University of Utah students showed that 70 percent support the gun ban (Adams 1999), and a scientific poll of Utah residents showed that 64 percent think guns should probably or definitely not be allowed on campus, with 80 percent saying guns should not be allowed in classrooms (Stewart 2007a).

Opponents of revoking the ban were also armed with five arguments. First, Shurtleff and others argued that the university's ban on guns is illegal. Independently of whether or not guns belong on campus, the proximate concern of lawmakers is conformity to law; the university cannot defy the will of the legislature (Sykes 2004b). "There is no autonomy" for the university from legislative oversight, according to a lawyer from the Attorney General's office (Fattah 2004). The Utah Supreme Court agreed. Writing for the majority, Justice Jill Parrish claimed that case law "is incompatible with the University's position. . . . We simply cannot agree with the proposition that the Utah Constitution restricts the legislature's ability to enact firearms laws pertaining to the University" (Manson 2006).

Second, gun advocates countered the university's claims regarding safety by asserting that the presence of guns lessens the threat of violence, rather than causing it. At the on-campus debate, a Republican representative claimed: "It is well known that criminals migrate to where they are less likely to be confronted by gun owners" (Gardiner 2006).

Third, students – and all citizens entering campus, for that matter – have a (US) constitutional Second Amendment right to arm themselves, opponents contended (Stewart 2007c). Implying that the university cannot guarantee in any substantive way the safety of students and therefore must allow them to protect themselves, a state representative and police officer rhetorically asked: "If I send my daughter to the U. and you take away her right to defend herself, what guarantee of safety can you give me?" (McFarland and Warchol 2007). In a letter to the editor of a local newspaper, a father railed: "My law-abiding daughter, who has a concealed carry permit, stopped carrying when she became a student at the U. Having a lab job there and working well after dark, she was terrified every time she walked to her car, alone and defenseless" (Daniel 2006).

Fourth, according to opponents, a campus ban on guns is totally ineffective. Rules against guns simply restrict the freedoms and rights of law-abiding citizens, which violent criminals ignore anyway. Critics of the only remaining tattered remnant of the controversy, SB251, argued that creating any gun-free zones was only an open invitation for shooters to wreak their havoc, especially in light of the recent massacre at a local shopping mall (Stolz and Lee 2007). As a Republican legislator put it, allowing faculty to declare their offices as gun-free zones "is about as stupid as anything you can do. They're just telling everyone, 'I don't have a gun, so come shoot me'" (Stewart 2007c).

Fifth, gun advocates, seemingly unwilling to concede any point in the debate, argued against SB251 on the grounds that the segregation of gun-owning students from their peers is discriminatory. "There is no reason for a segregated dorm system. That would not be tolerated by any other minority," said the public-policy director for Gunowners of Utah (Associated Press 2007).

Throughout this debate, both sides have criticized the other for lack of balance and called for equipoise. Lambasting the university, Shurtleff said that "for an institution of higher learning, you'd think they'd be more interested in citing fact than just playing to public fear. This type of policy makes students and faculty at the university less safe" (Harrie 2002c). What worried *Deseret News* staff editorial writer, Marjorie Cortez, was that Shurtleff and other pro-gun lawmakers seem to define "fact" as that data which back the pro-gun agenda to the exclusion of other valid considerations. The Utah legislature, for example, invited John Lott, scholar at the conservative American Enterprise Institute and author of well-known research against gun-control (2000) to the state in the role as expert in public gun policy. As Cortez pointed out, crucial components of Lott's analysis are of dubious quality (Noah 2003; Bialik 2007), and Lott has admitted to deceptively using the pseudonym "Mary Rosh" for several years to rebuke his critics and promote his work under the auspices of an independent scholar (Zeller 2006). If Utah lawmakers truly care about balance, they should bone up on the intricate nuances of gun control policy, says Cortez, and not take Lott as the first and last word on the subject.

So the barbs flew from one camp to the other, each accusing the other of the same thing: lack of reason, lack of balance.

Although in Utah the imbroglio over guns on campus may have died down temporarily, it is unlikely to remain quiet for long. Continued gun violence, such as the massacre at Virginia Tech (Broder 2007), only seems to invigorate and embolden participants on each side of the debate.

Should guns be allowed on public university campuses over the objections of higher education officials?

Additional Issues to Consider

Other possible moral dilemmas arising within this case:

Q In a country that recognizes the right of its citizens to bear arms, are gun-free zones *ever* morally justifiable? If so, under what conditions? If not, why not?

Q If universities do elect to permit guns on campus, are faculty, staff, or students morally permitted to make their work or living areas gun-free zones?

Q If universities elect to ban guns on their campuses, are they morally obligated to have much larger security forces than campuses without such bans?

Q If universities elect to ban guns on their campuses, are faculty, staff, and students morally permitted to hire bodyguards?

Q If universities elect to ban guns on their campuses, are they morally obligated to ban all other weapons (e.g., knives, brass knuckles, pepper spray)?

REFERENCES

Adams, B. (1999) U. student survey finds 70% back a campus gun ban. *Salt Lake Tribune* (October 28): B3.

Associated Press State and Local Wire (2007) Compromise emerges on campus guns (February 7).

Bialik, C. (2007) The numbers guy: Gun-policy advocates on both sides of issue push dubious figures. *Wall Street Journal* (April 20): B1.

Broder, J. M. (2007) Thirty-two shot dead in Virginia; worst U.S. gun rampage. *New York Times* (April 17): A1.

Cortez, M. (2006) Legislature should look again at gun law. Staff editorial. *Deseret News* (September 12): A11.

Daniel, B. A. (2006) U. gun ban is pointless. Letter to the editor. *Deseret News* (December 7).

Deseret News (2007) U. drops its lawsuit over campus gun ban (March 18): B2.

Fattah, G. (2004) U. fears fallout on gun ban. *Deseret News* (August 31): A1.

Gardiner, D. (2006) U. Utah students weigh pros, cons of gun ban. *Daily Utah Chronicle* (December 1).

Harrie, D. (2002a) Battle lines: Lawmakers target gun ban. *Salt Lake Tribune* (January 15): A1.

Harrie, D. (2002b) Bill targets U. leaders. *Salt Lake Tribune* (February 2): A4.

Harrie, D. (2002c) U. moves to keep gun ban. *Salt Lake Tribune* (March 13): A1.

Keller, D. R. (2004) No right or need to bear firearms on college campuses. Opinion-editorial. *Salt Lake Tribune* (June 13): AA5.

Lott, J. R., Jr. (2000) *More Guns, Less Crime: Understanding Crime and Gun-control Laws*, 2nd edn. Chicago: University of Chicago Press.

Manson, P. (2006) OK to pack heat at U., says Utah's high court. *Salt Lake Tribune* (September 8): A1.

McFarland, S. (2007) U. campus gun-rights duel erupts again. *Salt Lake Tribune* (February 63).

McFarland, S., and Warchol, G. (2007) U. seeks support for gun control. *Salt Lake Tribune* (January 3): B.

Miller, M., Hemenway, D., and Wechsler, H. (2002) Guns and gun threats at college. *Journal of American College Health* 51 (2): 57–65.

Noah, T. (2003) The Bellesiles of the right? Another firearms scholar whose dog ate his data. *Slate* (February 3). Available at: http://slate.com/?id=2078084 (accessed October 4, 2007).

Shuppy, A. (2006) Utah court rejects campus gun ban. *Chronicle of Higher Education* 53 (6): 30.

Stewart, E. (2006) U. redirects gun right. *Deseret News* (December 2): A1.

Stewart, E. (2007a) Utahns support campus bans on guns. *Deseret News* (January 8).

Stewart, E. (2007b) Proposed campus gun ban unveiled. *Deseret News* (February 7): A1.

Stewart, E. (2007c) Senate OKs on-campus gun limits. *Deseret News* (February 21): B4.

Stewart, E. (2007d) No New restrictions on concealed weapons permits at universities. *Deseret News* (March 1): A19.

Stewart, K. (2002) Student gun ownership linked to poor behaviors. *Salt Lake Tribune* (October 31): B2.

Stewart, K. (2004) House takes shot at U. gun ban. *Salt Lake Tribune* (February 27): C1.

Stolz, M., and Lee, J. (2007) Armed man kills 5 people at mall in Salt Lake City. *New York Times* (February 12): A16.

Sykes, S. A. (2004a) U. to keep ban on guns in challenge to new law. *Salt Lake Tribune* (April 20): A1.

Sykes, S. A. (2004b) U.'s gunfight with state up to high court. *Salt Lake Tribune* (August 29): B1.

Sykes, S. A. (2004c) Campus debate on guns shifts to dorm concerns. *Salt Lake Tribune* (September 16): A16.

Sykes, S. A., and Stewart, K. (2003) Ruling backs gun ban at the U. *Salt Lake Tribune* (August 30): A1.

Toomer-Cook, J. (2005) Buttars plans a bill on evolution. *Deseret News* (November 11): A1.

Welling, A. (2003) U. will file a 2nd suit on gun ban. *Deseret News* (May 12): B1.

Zeller, T., Jr. (2006) Writers on the web, deprived of masks but not their pride. *New York Times* (September 11): C5.

9

SCHOOL DAYS, SCHOOL DAZE

Ethical Issues in Education

Case Thirty-six: Sheepskin or Fleece? – Plagiarism in University Classrooms

Case Thirty-seven: Fire Up the Coffee Pot! Break Out the Ritalin! – Performance-enhancing Drugs in Academia

Case Thirty-eight: When an A is Not an A – Grade Inflation in Universities

Case Thirty-nine: Readin', Writin', and Rx-in' – School Kids with Medical Needs

Case Forty: Promises, Promises – Selling Genetic Material for Institutional Gain

Education is fundamental to social progress and improved quality of life. It is essential for the welfare of future generations. It holds a particular trust as a partner in nurturing the moral development and social consciousness of our children. Even as it is the hope of the future, education grapples with myriad moral dilemmas. Educational institutions, particularly universities, were once entrusted with the creation, preservation, and dissemination of knowledge. Today, educational institutions frequently guard their intellectual property, ideas, data, and tissue banks with a proprietary ferocity. Historically, education has been a vehicle for equitable access to opportunity and a valued means to personal betterment. More recently, education has also become a means to a privileged lifestyle and enhanced social status, as well as a catalyst and opportunity for competition. While competition can promote excellence, it can also create undue pressure to achieve, sometimes at the expense of others. The desire for a competitive edge also sometimes compromises commitment to moral behavior. Plagiarism tempts not only students, but seduces faculty as well. Substance abuse is not confined to athletics and recreation, but also is a means to academic competitive advantage. These concerns raise questions about moral responsibility in educational endeavors.

When the student body is made up of individuals with different cultural heritages and values, does treating all students identically constitute unfair discrimination, or does discrimination consist in treating students differently – particularly in accordance with their own value systems? Is it morally justifiable to disregard either cultural values of collaboration or institutional policies regarding plagiarism when these come into conflict? What hidden lessons do educational institutions teach learners, whether they be children or adults, students or teachers, when consequences for behavior are inconsistent or in conflict with the educational mission? Who should benefit from proprietary knowledge created at public expense in public institutions? In "School Days, School Daze: Ethical Issues in Education" we examine moral dilemmas in education.

CASE THIRTY-SIX: SHEEPSKIN OR FLEECE? – PLAGIARISM IN UNIVERSITY CLASSROOMS

Dr Mary Green teaches at a west coast state university with approximately 20,000 students. Dr Green's junior-level course, "Introduction to Social Ethics," is especially popular. The course draws students from a wide variety of majors, who come from diverse backgrounds and exhibit disparate levels of experience and different skill sets. Over the past decade she has seen steady increases in the number of international students in her courses. The number of US-born students from non-Anglo cultures has also expanded noticeably.

Dr Green welcomes this burgeoning cultural diversity. The plethora of cultures and life experiences significantly enriches discussions of the social issues that constitute the focus of the class. Diverse interpretations of what counts as morally (in)appropriate responses to the social dilemmas the students consider have been particularly exciting. The students consider a range of moral conundrums arising in multiple social contexts (e.g., business, government, healthcare, education, etc.). They read articles that provide them with background information and also theoretical analyses by experts in the relevant fields. They discuss the readings both in the classroom and in small groups designed to give them more opportunities to raise their own particular concerns and questions. Every two weeks, students turn in a written AJ (see chapter 2 in this volume), in which they justify a particular resolution to one of the moral dilemmas.

Like all faculty who assign written work, Dr Green has taken care to caution her students about the problem of plagiarism, which has become the bane of professors' existence. In 2002 the BBC reported that 31 engineering students at Carlton University, Ottawa, Canada, were suspected of cheating on a fourth-year *ethics paper* (BBC 2002). An estimated 14 percent of Australian students and 25 percent of English students are downloading essays from Internet sites and submitting this work as their own (Foster 2002; BBC 2004: para 2); 50 percent of North American university students engage in some form(s) of cheating (McCabe, as cited in Breen and Maassen 2005: para 1). And Szabo and Underwood reported: "Fewer than 50 percent of [U.K. undergraduates] indicated that cheating *was unac*ceptable at any time" (2004: 190).

What types of behavior actually count as plagiarism is currently the topic of much controversy and little consensus. Various definitions include downloading entire papers from the Internet (about which little disagreement exists, actually); submitting papers written by other students who are personally known to the student submitting the paper; copying papers written by other students at the author's university but who are not known to the student (e.g., taking a paper from a fraternity "paper bank"); cutting and pasting comments from several sources, whether on-line or in print (e.g., chat sites, books, journals, etc.); and reproducing ideas from other media sources (newspapers, radio, television). More ambiguous activities include using another writer's words, but translating them into synonyms, changing active voice into passive (or vice versa), omitting a few words or sentences, or just rearranging the order of the original text. Whatever their differences, these activities have three characteristics in common: (1) the ideas originate outside the mind of the student writer, (2) the student fails to acknowledge these external contributions, and (3) the student's presentation of these ideas leads others (typically, the faculty to whom the writings are submitted) to view these ideas as the student's own original intellectual output. Put more felicitously, a plagiarist takes credit for another person's work.

Students offer a variety of explanations for plagiarizing others' work. The most common excuses include lack of time to complete the writing assignment, too much work to complete all their assignments (or to complete them all well), lack of interest in or lack of perceived relevance of subject matter (either in the course generally or the assignment particularly), or a belief that the assignment is somehow unjustly burdensome. Often these concerns are coupled with a need or desire to achieve or maintain a particular grade point average (see, generally, Breen and Maassen 2005; Devlin 2002; Szabo and Underwood 2004).

Some students do not consider downloading material from the Internet to be cheating at all: "These students . . . have become so accustomed to downloading music and reading articles free on the Internet that they see it as acceptable to incorporate passages into their papers without attribution as well" (McCabe 2005: 239; Young 2001: para 8).

To reduce – hopefully, avoid completely – plagiarized work, Dr Green has provided written examples of plagiarism and has discussed in class why these types of writing are unacceptable. She has included in her syllabus and repeatedly posted on the white board the university's web address that details the requirements of academic honesty and that gives further examples of morally problematic work and guidelines for avoiding it. To indicate how seriously she takes the obligation not to plagiarize, she has included a statement in her syllabus that states: "Any student caught plagiarizing any assignment will fail the course and be turned over to the student affairs office with a recommendation that the incident be permanently noted on the student's academic transcript." The syllabus also indicates that, should one student "loan" a paper to another student, both will be considered plagiarists and punished accordingly.

Dr Green is confident that she has taken every possible step to eliminate plagiarism from her students' written work. Thus, she is both surprised and deeply disappointed when the first writing assignments are submitted, including five papers in which students appear to have used the work of others without properly citing their sources. The types of plagiarism demonstrated in the papers, however, look very different. Samuel and Jeff have turned in versions of the same paper: the content and organization are very similar. Samuel's position is very well argued and the paper is very well written, although several passages look familiar to Dr Green. The progression of Jeff's paper closely resembles Samuel's, but the content is much less sophisticated: the ideas are underdeveloped or not developed at all, and the writing lacks polish and is ungrammatical throughout. Georgia's paper is mostly off topic: instead of analyzing – in AJ format – the particular moral dilemma assigned, her paper is a review of the general ethical issues that are raised regarding the dilemma, generally stated. The papers submitted by Sui-fong Ma and Pik-wah Li (two young women from China) have been copied, almost verbatim, from the lecture notes that Dr Green handed out and used to structure the in-class discussions on the issue that formed the initial steps in the analysis. In none of the papers is any source cited, either in the text or in a bibliography at the end of the paper.

In an attempt to determine the motivations of the student authors, Dr Green does some research. Running the papers through "Turnitin" software results in her discovering the original paper, written by a student at another university and posted on a class website, that Georgia lifted and submitted with no revision. She also finds pieces of Samuel's paper in several different articles. No such originals are discovered for the papers of the other three students.

Dr Green meets with all five students individually and learns the following information: Georgia hates the course in general and the (what she considers excessive) writing requirements in particular. She is taking the course to meet a distribution requirement, claims that she will "never, ever use this crap again," and deeply resents "having to work so hard in a course that isn't even in my major." When asked if she understood the prohibition and the consequences, Georgia shrugs and remarks: "Lots of students do it. I didn't think I'd get caught. Anyway, student affairs would never put this on my transcript; that wouldn't be fair." Informed by Dr Green that student affairs regularly makes such a notation on the transcripts of cheating students, Georgia shrugs again and says, "My tough luck, I guess."

Samuel and Jeff pose a different challenge. Jeff explains his poor paper and its similarity to Samuel's more elegant version thus:

> I (Jeff) have really been struggling this semester. I had mononucleosis the first two weeks of class and really got behind. Then my band got a really great opportunity to perform at a regional jazz festival. This will give us much-needed exposure and really open some doors for us. But the practice schedule has been grueling. Sam and I have been friends since first year; we have the same major and lots of similar interests. When I told him how worried I was about this paper, he loaned me his – just to look it over and see how the format worked and how the ideas

tied together. I jotted down some notes and planned to develop those idea in my own way. "But I ran out of time, so I just kind of strung them together and turned that kind of outline in."

When asked if he understood the prohibition and the consequences, Jeff wailed: "Please don't punish Sam! He was just being a good friend! I'll take the F, but please don't hurt him because of what I did. He doesn't even know what I did!"

A conference with Sam immediately after the conference with Jeff (so: no opportunity for Jeff and Sam to confer) confirms that Sam did let Jeff "borrow" his paper. Sam seems genuinely surprised to learn about the content of Jeff's paper. He asserts: "The possibility of plagiarism never even occurred to me when I let Jeff look at the paper. I just hoped he'd see that he had the ideas to do the work, and that would calm him down enough so he could complete the assignment." Sam also seems surprised when Dr Green points out that she discovered portions of his paper, somewhat altered but not really paraphrased, in several journal articles. His explanation is that, never having taken a philosophy course before, he has been struggling with the terminology. He reports that he has finally begun to make sense of the readings, but isn't comfortable enough with the concepts and their expression to put them into his own words. He did think he had done a good job with transitional comments, though, as well as drawing out some practical implications.

Finally, the professor meets with Sui-fong and Pik-wah, one after the other. Both readily admit that the content of their papers – including the actual wording – came directly from Dr Green's lecture notes. Asked why they didn't put the ideas in "their own words" or at least cite the lecture notes, both young women give a version of the following justification. First, both students admit that they are really struggling with the English language in the classroom setting. While their command of conversational English is quite good, they are often unable to understand remarks during class – either by the professor or by other students. They have been struggling with the words themselves, but also with the pace at which the discussions occur. By the time they have made sense of the last point, three more have been made that they have now missed. As to the paper's content, they note that Dr Green is the respected expert whose knowledge about the topics under consideration in the classroom would – of course! – be well thought out, complete, and correct. How could a student hope to improve on those ideas? Wouldn't any sensible student merely reprise them, thereby indicating that the information had been received and remembered? When asked if they understood the prohibition and the consequences, both seem befuddled. What, Sui-fong queries, is learning but understanding and committing to memory the ideas of others who are more qualified to discuss the issue? That anyone would be punished for an activity that, to these women, is the essence of education is completely baffling.

Dr Green believes that she is obligated, in virtue of her commitment to academic honesty and her promise (in the syllabus), to impose some punishments here. But she wonders if she should punish all five students and, if so, whether the punishments should be identical.

From a moral perspective, should Dr Green subject all students to the same punishment?

Perspective One

All students should be punished and all should receive the same punishment.

First, this position is justified by appealing to the concept of autonomy. All students made autonomous choices about plagiarizing material. All students had equal access to the same syllabus, in which the expectations regarding, and the sources explaining, plagiarism were explicitly stated. These expectations were also stated repeatedly by the professor during class periods. As a result, all students knew (or should have known) the requirements for correctly constructing a paper. Those who chose not to examine the resources specified in the syllabus made their autonomous choice earlier than those who examined the rules and elected to ignore them. No one was forced to cheat. Thus all decisions were autonomous and, consequently, the students are responsible for any developments that result from those choices – including punishment.

Second, the virtues of fidelity and honesty require Dr Green to keep her promises. She indicated in the syllabus that plagiarism would be punished and what that punishment would be; nowhere did she indicate that a *range* of punishments (including no punishment at all) was a possibility. If she metes out disparate punishments, she is going back on her word.

Finally, identical punishment is required by the appeal to equality (justice). All students were given the same syllabus, the same assignment, and the same amount of time in which to complete it. All students had the same classroom experience and the same exposure to lectures, readings, and discussions. No student received any particular advantage or disadvantage; the playing field was level. To punish students differently presumes an inequality where none exists. Further, to fail to punish the students treats them unequally when compared to the other students in the class – who took the time to discover, appreciate, and apply the rules regarding plagiarism. To fail to punish students who failed to take the same care would be unjust to the students who were conscientious.

Appeals to the moral principles of autonomy, the virtues of fidelity and honesty, and of justice (equality) demonstrate that all students should be punished, and all should be punished alike.

Perspective Two

Sui-fong Ma and Pik-wah Liu should not be punished; but all other students should receive identical punishment. This disparity is supported by the moral appeals to consequences (particularly nonmaleficence), autonomy, and the virtue of professional integrity.

First, the consequences to Sui-fong Ma and Pik-wah Liu would be considerably worse than for the three US students: they would not only fail the course and be reported to student judicial affairs, but could (assuming student judicial affairs found them guilty) be expelled from the university. If expelled, the young women would be sent back to China and deprived of the possibility of an American education. Expulsion and deportation would deprive them of not just an American education, but any education at all. They would likely be denied all but the most menial jobs for their lifetime. In addition, the shame would affect their families: certainly the disgrace would affect them socially, but economic impacts would eventuate as well. Even if the students were not expelled, the cost of an education for international students is two, three, or even four times as expensive as is the cost to native students. If Sui-fong Ma and Pik-wah Liu have to retake the class or add another semester to complete their academic requirements, the financial burden to their families would be significant.

Second, the virtue of integrity requires Dr Green to make an exception in this case. Although she indicated in the syllabus that plagiarism would be punished and what that punishment would be, the concept of plagiarism is completely foreign to Asian students. As an employee of an institution that actively recruits international students, Dr Green is obligated to familiarize herself with the educational cultures and pedagogical customs of international students, and work with them to insure that they appreciate the differences between their native cultures and Western customs. In cases where she does not anticipate problems, she is obliged to bring cultural sensitivity to the arena after the fact, rather than mechanically punishing students for cultural confusion. Professional integrity requires that Dr Green provide information to her students on the consequences of plagiarism, but, as the consequences are so significant, she is also obligated to insure that students who have language or cultural challenges not only receive the information but understand it. The lack of understanding by these young women renders their behavior inautonomous. If their choices were made inautonomously, they are not morally culpable and, hence, should not be punished but, rather, further educated. In short, these cultural concerns should exempt Sui-fong Ma and Pik-wah Liu from punishment (though not, of course, from education about how to avoid such problems in the future). Conversely, the native students have no reason to be confused about citation conventions and, thus, should be punished as the syllabus and its links have specified.

Perspective Three

Dr Green should punish different students differently. Specifically, she should not punish Sui-fong, Pik-wah, or Sam. None of these students autonomously chose to plagiarize and each of these students *reasonably* believed the assignment was completed in acceptable fashion. Georgia and Jeff, however, should be punished as the syllabus specifies. These students did choose to use others' work deceptively and in full knowledge of the wrongness of their acts.

Step 1: Information-gathering

Implications

- What would happen, in both the short and long term, to the students if they are punished for plagiarism?
- What would happen to other students if the plagiarizing students are punished identically? if they are punished differently? if they are not punished at all?

Psychological

- What were the intentions of (each of) the plagiarizing students?
- Do (and why might) these intentions differ?
- What particular stressors might each of these students face? Would these reach the level of irresistible (i.e., coercive) pressures, thereby rendering their decisions inautonomous?

Sociocultural

- Did different cultural traditions/expectations play a role in the students' behavior?
- Do learning styles differ cross-culturally?
- Does the definition of "good" work differ cross-culturally?
- Does the definition of "plagiarism" differ cross-culturally?
- Does the definition of "plagiarism" differ between students and faculty?

Law/policy

- Does the university have policies governing the treatment of students accused of plagiarizing? If so, what goals or values justify these policies?
- Do faculty codes of ethics indicate appropriate behavior regarding plagiarism? If so, what goals or values justify these positions?

History

- Have the definition of plagiarism and why it causes concern evolved over time?
- Have concerns about plagiarism evolved over time?
- Have methods for plagiarizing evolved over time?

Step 2: Creative problem-solving

A creative solution must treat all students fairly. What fairness will look like in the case of each of the students must be carefully determined.

Step 3: Listing pros and cons

Options	Pros	Cons
Punish students identically.	1. Sends an unambiguous message about plagiarism (C-U) 2. Students will trust faculty to avoid favoritism (C-U) 3. All students chose to omit citing the work of others (A) 4. Promotes honesty (V-H) 5. Professor has announced what the punishment for this behavior will be (V-Fidelity) 6. Behavior is the same (J-E) 7. Different punishment for same behavior unfair (J-F)	8. Thwarts positive learning outcomes (C-NM) 9. Same punishment leads to unequal burdens (J-E) 10. The playing field cannot be truly leveled (J-E)
Punish students differently.	11. Not all students chose to plagiarize (A) 12. Only some students were deliberately dishonest (V-H) 13. Compassionate (V) 14. Promise of supportive environment (V-Fidelity) 15. Intentions differed (J-E, A) 16. Respects culturally distinct learning styles (J-F) 17. Respects culturally distinct values (J-F, C-U)	18. Encourages disrespect for classroom rules (C-NM, C-U) 19. Encourages students to fabricate "good" excuses (C-NM, V-Honesty)

Step 4: Analysis

Factual assumptions

- Learning styles vary across cultures.
- Definitions of plagiarism vary across cultures.
- Definitions of good work vary across cultures.
- Students plagiarize for different reasons.
- Only some students who plagiarize realize they are doing something wrong.
- Only some students who plagiarize intend to do something wrong.
- All students are telling the truth to Dr Green.
- A truly level (educational) playing field is impossible.

Value assumptions

- Students should be punished only if their misbehavior was autonomously chosen.

- An agent's motives should be taken into account when assigning blame or deciding punishment.
- Universities that accept students from different cultures should be sensitive – in deed as well as in word – to the implications of these cultures for the learning experience.
- Students (indeed, all writers) should acknowledge explicitly the intellectual contributions of others.

Step 5: Justification

Dr Green should not punish Sui-fong, Pik-wah, or Sam. She should punish Georgia and Jeff, but her punishments of those students should differ.

The causes for plagiarism are many and, at least in part, are unavoidably subjective or culturally relative (Introna et al. 2003: 9–19). Least charitably, some students are simply lazy: Not wanting to put forth the effort required to write an original paper, they purchase one – from another local student or from a website – or they simply download a paper that they believe fulfills the assignment. Other students have trouble managing their time and, faced with an all-too-rapidly-approaching due date, succumb to the temptation to use someone else's work rather than receive a grade of zero. Still others, faced with a need for better grades than they are capable of achieving through their own unaided efforts, will lift text from books, journals, other students, or the Internet (Handa and Power 2005: 67; Szabo and Underwood 2004). Other justifications offered include the belief that "everyone else" is doing it, which would leave (especially) the novice student at a comparative disadvantage; a belief that the assignment is, for some reason, unfair – so students who plagiarize are behaving no worse than professors who give "unfair" assignments; and the grade is an end in itself (i.e., the grade matters more than learning the material) (Introna et al. 2003: 43–8). Finally, some cases of unintentional plagiarism (i.e., a student inadvertently omitting a source notation, and erroneously thinking she was copying her own idea from an index card) have been identified (Reasons ##11, 12).

Another issue contributes to confusion regarding using the words or ideas of others: plagiarism is not uniformly defined. Definitions not only differ between cultures, but vary within cultures and, indeed, may even be differently understood within single institutions and among the faculty therein employed (Howard 1999: 18–28; Howard 2000b: 473–5; Introna et al. 2003). For example, some laboratories have a policy of listing the laboratory's director as first author on any publications from the lab, whether or not the director did any of the research or contributed to the paper (or even knew of its existence!). Some faculty members use excerpts from student work without acknowledging the student, justifying the student's writing as an extension of the professor's ideas. While some educators see these practices as acceptable, others find them morally and professionally disreputable. Within a single university, faculty may have disparate conceptions of what counts as plagiarism. If this ambiguity reaches students, they may inadvertently plagiarize because they are uncertain about how or when to cite others' work (Howard 1999: xviii).

Third, some students are completely unaware of the need to cite others' work at all. If students are merely uneducated about the rules of writing, education and practice may suffice. But students who are working outside the university's dominant culture may be coming from a background in which the concept of plagiarism simply does not exist (Introna et al. 2003: 7–8). Asian and some European students view knowledge as public property: ideas – and the words that express them – do not belong to particular persons, but to humanity at large (Reasons ##16, 17). Educated persons know these ideas and feel free to share them when occasions to do so arise (ibid.; Graham and Leung 2007–8: para 2).

Finally, even students who do understand and who do wish to comply with particular expectations regarding documentation can go astray. Undergraduate students writing to meet academic requirements may lack the skills to decode course material. Unfamiliarity with course content generally (especially in courses outside their majors or minors) and with discipline-specific jargon particularly can leave students at a loss when asked to "put the ideas in your own words." Many, quite simply, have no words of their own for the topic at hand; others cannot imagine their own words being sufficiently precise, or their own phrasing being acceptably concise or elegant (Breen and Maassen 2005: paras 13–14). Students who are literally speechless often engage in "patchwriting" – cutting and pasting the work of others (sometimes, of many others) to complete a paper assignment – much like a patchwork quilt is assembled from a variety of sources (Howard 1999: xviii–xxi; Introna et al. 2003: 49–50).

The difficulties of manipulating an unfamiliar language are often magnified for international students or students for whom English is a second language (ESL). Although most universities require incoming international students to have passed the TOEFL or TEFL (Test of English as a Foreign Language) exam, phrases encountered in a purely academic environment are often daunting. Many of the terms are fully foreign and have not been encountered previously. Others are used idiomatically or technically, that is, in ways that diverge from their more common usage – which is even more confusing: students think they know the meanings of the words, only to find that this assumption is mistaken. And the usual problems with idiomatic English – often used by faculty and other students during class discussions – add to their perplexity (Introna et al. 2003: 11–12). Of course not all international or ESL students struggle mightily with English (Handa and Power 2005: 67–8), but many do.

For Sui-fong or Pik-wah, the problems associated with working in a second language seem to be an important contributing factor. Lack of facility with English has made learning much more difficult than they had anticipated. Like many international students, their command of conversational English has not transferred without problems into the classroom. Thus, even assuming that both women are highly motivated, conscientious students, the language barriers will, at least for some time, pose a barrier not of their own making. The virtue of compassion recommends "cutting them some slack" (Reason #13). The virtue of professional fidelity (Reason #14) also applies here: any institution that actively recruits international students implicitly promises an environment in which success is possible; the resident faculty owe these students a familiarity with pedagogical divergence between the students' home universities' pedagogical styles and practices and any disparities with Western universities that may pose obstacles to the students' success.

The two women face a second significant problem: what counts as good academic work. Unlike students steeped in the Western tradition, Asian students are unlikely to view ideas or even particular text as owned by an author (Swearingen 1999: 19). Coming as they do from a "Confucian heritage culture," they are likely to believe that knowledge "belongs to society and is for sharing" (Graham and Leung 2007–8: para 2), or "is a common property created by and for human communities to edify and communicate, to advance learning" (Swearingen 1999: 21). In addition, Asian students typically have been schooled to memorize and reiterate verbatim large amounts of material, both from written sources and from professors' lectures: "Knowledge is considered static, something to be mastered through arduous study and preferably memorized, because of the intrinsic moral benefits such discipline imparts. Original thinking should be avoided" (Dryden 1999: 81). This tradition explains why Asian students often meticulously and exactly reproduce material from sources provided: they have been educated to believe that:

> [I]t is proper to mistrust or discount one's own opinion; it is good and virtuous to study, memorize, and imitate proper models. . . . Given such views of learning and morality – that students should, as a matter of correctness, defer to the opinions and models provided by received wisdom – the tendency to copy freely from published sources seems only natural. When students are taught that there is a single correct answer to be obtained from an authority above and beyond their own judgment, they can be expected to seek it out. (Ibid.: 83)

Such practices are "a way of acknowledging one's respect for the received wisdom of their ancestors" (Buranen 1999: 66, 68). Finally, in Asian countries, in-text citations are neither expected of, nor taught to, undergraduate students (Breen and Maassen 2005: para 3; Handa and Power 2005: 70–1, 74–5).

In short, Sui-fong or Pik-wah have provided work that meets their own cultural standards. Yes, they have freely chosen to reiterate – without citing – the remarks of others (Reason #3); but this choice was *not* an autonomous decision *to cheat or to attempt to deceive* Dr Green; nor was it an attempt to avoid the learning process that motivated the assignment (Reasons ##11, 12). Rather, the women chose to follow the standards that they believed applied in this case. Their unfamiliarity with Western standards and protocols suggests that the choice was, in an important sense, inautonomous: the women were unaware of the criteria for good work in the local setting. Although Sui-fong and Pik-wah are responsible and attentive students, who dutifully recorded the information, the values intrinsic in their culture prevented them from integrating those concepts into their behavior. Consequently, the belief that persons should be punished for autonomously chosen misbehavior (Reason #3) simply does not apply to these students. Further, the claim that they "did the same thing" (Reasons ##6, 7) as, for example, Georgia, is untrue in any meaningful sense. They should not be punished at all (though they should be educated about Western writing requirements).

Conversely, Georgia's decision to download a paper from the Internet *was* an autonomous choice to cheat, deceive, and avoid the learning process that motivated the assignment (Reason #3). As she indicated in her conference with Dr Green, she feels the writing requirements are too demanding and that the course content will be of no use to her in her professional career. She seems to believe the paper is an unfair (unjust) demand on her and, thus, that she is morally excused from completing the assignment without plagiarizing. That is, she assumes that her cheating is somehow a permissible way to cancel out the perceived unfairness of the assignment. But even assuming that the assignment were somehow inappropriate, the morally appropriate response would not be a different inappropriate action (viz., cheating). Two wrongs do not make a right. Georgia is being treated no differently from any other student; she is not being unfairly singled out for an unequally onerous assignment. If she feels that some reason exists to treat her differently – that is, that her assignment should be *less* demanding, she should discuss these concerns with Dr Green. At the least she might get a better sense of the paper's purpose and how she might best approach its completion.

In any case, Georgia's choice to lift a paper *in toto* from the Internet was, by her own account, autonomous: she concedes that she understood the prohibition and the consequences for the unacknowledged use of another's work; that is, she was informed and she understood the information provided. Nor does she indicate the presence of any coercive influences (e.g., genuine terror at the possibility of a failing grade) that might even partially excuse her from responsibility for the theft of intellectual property. In fact, she doesn't even appeal to the belief, held by over 50 percent of students, that lifting material from the Internet does not constitute cheating (McCabe 2005: 239; BBC 2006: paras 1, 2). Instead, she indicates that she had undertaken a burden-benefit analysis (one that, no doubt to her dismay, has been shown to be incorrect): "I didn't think I'd get caught." She makes an attempt to justify her behavior with a claim that the practice is common.

Because the paper assigned to Georgia was no different from the paper assigned to the other students, and because she autonomously chose to engage in deceit, she should receive the punishment described in the syllabus. Doing less than that would be a breach of fidelity (and, perhaps, cowardice) on Dr Green's part. (See Kostigen 2006: para 6; BBC 2004: para 15; and McCabe 2003: 15–17 about the reluctance of faculty to actually impose penalties on student plagiarists.)

Like Georgia, Jeff is cognizant of his mistake and appreciates the consequences that he is facing. Like Georgia, Jeff has an explanation for why he turned in someone else's work without citing the true author. Unlike Georgia, Jeff's explanation could generate some sympathy, even compassion, from Dr Green. After all, he never *intended* to steal Jeff's work; he just found himself between a rock and a hard place. Maybe the professor should cut Jeff some slack.

While a lesser punishment might seem appealing, Dr Green should resist this temptation. After all, some of Jeff's choices that contributed to the purloined paper have been autonomous (Reason #3). Like Georgia, Jeff has been warned about the impermissibility of using the work of another person, and we have no reason to think Jeff was uninformed. But was he coerced? Was he forced by his time crunch to turn in the borrowed material without any attempt to develop his own ideas? No. Time crunches are a fact of life for most students. Even those who have been lucky enough to escape them personally are well acquainted with their effects on friends and classmates. As a result, students must be considered informed/forewarned about the need to plan ahead and to get an early start on larger projects. True, Jeff had some bad luck (the mononucleosis); but he also made some unwise choices (putting band practice ahead of completing class requirements). Finally, as a Junior, Jeff can be assumed to know about alternatives – talking to the professor to determine if an extension is possible or just taking the zero being the two most common. In short, Jeff's choice to use Sam's work was informed and unforced, making Jeff morally responsible for the consequences that follow from that choice (a responsibility Jeff seems willing to acknowledge in agreeing to take his "F").

Further, if Dr Green is swayed by Jeff's bad luck and bad choices, she promotes the appearance of being amenable to a good story – an appearance that will travel through the student populace. While some students may merely find this attitude amusing, others will take advantage of it, should the need arise (Reasons ##18, 19). As a result, Dr Green will see more bad, late, and plagiarized papers and hear more tearful stories. Put differently, a sympathetic attitude (or appearance thereof) will unequally reward two groups of students: those who have heard of Dr Green's soft heart and those who can spin a good yarn. The uninformed and the uncreative, having no alternative, will just have to do the work. This violates the principle of equality (justice).

Reluctant as she may be, the appeal to consequences, autonomy, and equality indicate that Dr Green should give Jeff the specified punishment.

Finally, what should be the professor's treatment of Sam?

Sam's just deserts require addressing two issues: Sam's loaning his paper to Jeff and Sam's engaging in patchwriting. The easy way out would be to note quickly and without further investigation that Sam did loan his paper to Jeff, even though the syllabus explicitly warns that such behavior is deemed to be plagiarism, will not be tolerated, and will be punished. Nonetheless, both Jeff and Sam report (truthfully, we have assumed) that the purpose of sharing the paper was to give Jeff an idea of what was involved, an action that would indicate that he did, in fact, have the knowledge and ability to do the assignment. Sam indicates that this was his motive, and Jeff confirms that explanation. Thus it seems reasonable to assume that Sam made no autonomous choice to deceive or to (help Jeff) cheat (Reason #3). Moreover, given the class's use of small-group work, some collaboration between students is to be expected. Granted, a discussion with Jeff in which the same goals – Jeff's appreciation that he was capable of completing the task and, as a result, being able to settle down and write the paper – would likely have been a wiser choice; but Sam's intentions seem compassionate, a response to be expected and hoped-for when the worried student is a friend. Still, the exclusion of sharing in the syllabus gives some reason to punish Sam; after all, he should have thought about that before loaning his paper. But if Dr Green is convinced that Sam "just didn't think," she has some reason to let him off with a warning.

The patchwriting issue raises the issue, somewhat ironically, of Sam himself depending on the ideas of others; it raises the question of the extent to which such dependence is morally acceptable.

Patchwriting is defined as "using a sentence or two, a small paragraph, etc. from one or more sources without attribution" (McCabe 2004: 6) or "copying from a source text and then deleting some words, altering grammatical structures, or plugging in one-for-one synonym-substitutes" (Howard 1993: 233). Broad consensus exists that this method is not only widespread (among faculty as well as student writers), but is common because it is the process by which persons come to appreciate unfamiliar concepts (Howard 2000a: 82–3). When persons are writing about ideas with which they have limited experience or understanding, they are hard-pressed to translate text into different words. An author's patchwriting can be analogous to a speaker learning a new language: when one's vocabulary is limited, the best one can do is to keep repeating the original phrase with different inflections or in different cases (e.g., active to passive, declarative to subjunctive). Consequently, novice writers (or those entering a new discipline or who suffer from dyslexia) may understandably be reluctant to change words or phrases "for fear of distorting" their message (ibid.: 86). Understood in this manner, patchwriting is a temporary stage which should be anticipated by faculty, and through which students can be expected to pass as their mastery of a topic/discipline increases. To punish students who engage in patchwriting is to leave them without any viable options for fulfilling assignments, and to risk thwarting one's own professional goals (Reasons ##8, 14).

This description seems to describe Sam. By his own account, he has been challenged by the language he has encountered in the readings, by the course concepts, and by issues arising in an unfamiliar discipline. He is making some progress in comprehension, but not enough to bravely engage in paraphrasing. Like many students, he is not convinced that incorporating the ideas, or even the language of someone who knows more that he does, is wrong (Rocklin 2005: 172). He notes that his own voice is (he thinks) apparent in other portions of the paper, which (he thinks) he has completed in satisfactory fashion.

Dr Green considers the consequences of punishing Sam for patchwriting. She is worried that punishment will change a conscientious student into a frustrated student who might lose his motivation to master the content and the methodologies the course is designed to instill. Unlike Georgia (Reason #6), who expresses disdain for the subject matter, Sam has been devoted to the class. Unlike Jeff, in whom the professor hopes to stimulate the habit of planning ahead (Reason #6), Sam did plan ahead. So punishment of Sam seems unnecessary as a prompt for promoting good consequences and it runs the risk of incurring negative ones

(Reason #8). Further, Sam apparently made no autonomous decision to avoid the learning process or deceive Dr Green. He understood the assignment and worked to complete it in a thoughtful fashion.

Dr Green should not punish Sam for his patchwriting. She should, of course, educate him that this practice becomes plagiarism when he fails to acknowledge, through citation, the original author, and insure that he acquires familiarity with citation requirements.

The critic will charge that disparate treatment of students is unjust. Because all students received the same directions, the same opportunities for further research into plagiarism, the same in-class instructions, and the same assignment, they are all equally responsible for avoiding illicit practices (Reason #5). True, these students found themselves in different personal situations and faced different stressful conditions. But that can be said of all people in all situations at all times. Individuals just are differently situated and nothing can change that. Moreover, professors cannot hope to know or appreciate all the particular conflicting demands their students face. And if they cannot know and address all relevant stressors, they cannot hope to treat students fairly. Instead, teachers should strive for equality via a common denominator: in whatever other respects you differ, you will be held responsible for complying with the following set of requirements. To that extent, the playing field will be level. This is the best any teacher can do and the most that she should do. Equality of expectations reigns in the classroom.

While this objection has merit, it posits faculty ignorance as more extensive than it actually is. The job of professors is to teach and, toward that end, to familiarize themselves with the conditions under which students learn best and those that pose obstacles to pedagogical goals. Part of professional excellence is to foster the former and eliminate or ameliorate the latter. Pedagogical research has extensively documented the obstacles faced by international students in foreign classrooms (Hamilton et al. 2004, provide a detailed overview of these issues). A burgeoning literature in response to such findings is available to faculty who wish to make their classrooms more user-friendly to students who are struggling with culture shock. Nor is the user-friendly literature limited to problems faced by international students: the conditions under which native students learn better or are inhibited in reaching learning goals is also extensive. Such literature enables Dr Green, for example, to appreciate that punishing Sam's patchwriting is likely to be counterproductive. Pedagogical research is done to enable faculty to promote – through continued self education – the purposes to which they are professionally committed (Reason #14). In short, the playing field will never be truly level for a community of students, but the well-educated, well-motivated, student-friendly teacher can – as she must – ameliorate limiting inequities when she can do so (Reasons ##10, 14).

The critic may raise consequential concerns: different punishments might confuse students about writing requirements (Reason #1), raise concerns about faculty impartiality and reliability (Reasons ##2, 5), and fail to encourage honesty (Reason #4). Note, however, that these outcomes presuppose that other students will discover (1) that their peers have been punished (or not) for plagiarism and (2) that Dr Green's treatment of all candidates for punishment has been unequal. But the probability that students will acquire this information is low. First, we assume that students who are punished will be unlikely to broadcast this fact. Second, we assume that students who are punished are unlikely to know either that other students were punished or what punishment they have received (i.e., that the punishments differed). The possible exception to these assumptions may be in the case of Jeff and Sam who, in virtue of Jeff's using Sam's ideas, might compare Dr Green's treatment of them. But since Jeff admits that he used Sam's paper without Sam's knowledge and that Sam does not deserve punishment, both seem unlikely to publicize the particulars (e.g., by complaining – the most common reason for broadcasting one's suspect behavior – that they have been ill-treated).

In sum, that Dr Green is not aware of every stressor her students face does not mean she is completely ignorant of any of them. Professional integrity requires her to address those that will enhance learning. And because the untoward consequences are unlikely to occur, they do not serve as compelling reasons to the contrary.

In conclusion, Dr Green should not punish Sui-fong, Pik-wah, or Sam. None of these students autonomously chose to plagiarize and, in all three cases, each gave a reasonable (and well-supported by pedagogical research) explanation for her/his belief that the assignment was completed in acceptable fashion. Georgia and Jeff, however, did choose to use others' work deceptively and in full knowledge of the wrongness of their acts. Different punishments are morally warranted.

Additional Issues to Consider

Other possible moral dilemmas arising within this case:

Q Should different grading criteria be applied routinely to international students and native students?

Q Should different grading criteria be applied routinely to students who are majoring or minoring in a subject than to students who are taking the course to meet a distribution requirement?

Q Should all students be required to take and pass (say, with a C – or better) a course in writing techniques (which includes study in plagiarism issues)?

Q Should universities just quit worrying about plagiarism?

REFERENCES

BBC (2002) Students accused of cheating in ethics essay. Available at: http://news.bbc.co.uk/2/hi/uk_news/education/1899731.stm (accessed October 5, 2007).

BBC (2004) "Epidemic" of student cheating? Available at: http://newsvote.bbc.co.uk/
    mpapps/pagetools/print/news.bbc.co.uk/2/hi/uk_news/education/3854465.stm
    (accessed October 5, 2007).
BBC (2006) Net students "think copying OK." Available at: http://news.bbc.co.uk/
    2/hi/uk_news/education/5093286.stm (accessed October 5, 2007).
Breen, L., and Maassen, M. (2005) Reducing the incidence of plagiarism in an
    undergraduate course: the role of education. *Issues in Educational Research* 15
    (1): 1–16. Available at: www.iier.org.au/iier15/breen.html (accessed October 5,
    2007).
Buranen, L. (1999) But I *wasn't* cheating: plagiarism and cross-cultural mythology. In
    L. Buranen and A. M. Roy (eds.), *Perspectives on Plagiarism and Intellectual
    Property in a Postmodern World*. Albany, NY: State University of New York Press,
    pp. 63–74.
Devlin, M. (2002) Australian universities teaching committee. Minimising plagiarism.
    Excerpt from R. James, C. McInnis, and M. Devlin, *Assessing Learning in Austra-
    lian Universities*. Available at: www.cshe.unimelb.edu.au/assessinglearning/docs/
    PlagMain.pdf (accessed October 5, 2007).
Dryden, L. M. (1999) A distant mirror or through the looking glass? Plagiarism and
    intellectual property in Japanese education. In L. Buranen and A. M. Roy (eds.),
    Perspectives on Plagiarism and Intellectual Property in a Postmodern World. Albany,
    NY: State University of New York Press, pp. 75–85.
Foster, A. (2002) Up to 14% of Australian university students may be plagiarizing from
    web, study suggests. *The Chronicle of Higher Education* (November 20). Available
    at: http://chronicle.com/free/2002/11/2002112001t.htm (accessed October 5,
    2007).
Graham, A., and Leung, C. K. (2007–8) Uncovering "blind spots": cultire [*sic*] and copy-
    ing. *Conference 2004 Abstracts*. Northumbria Learning: Joint Information Systems
    Committee Plagiarism Advisory Service (JISCPAS). Available at: www.jiscpas.ac.uk/
    2004abstract_9.php?s=8 (accessed October 5, 2007).
Hamilton, D., Hinton, L., and Hawkins, K. (2004) International students at Australian
    universities: plagiarism and culture. In H. Marsden, M. Hicks, and A. Bundy (eds.),
    *Educational Integrity: Plagiarism and Other Perplexities. Proceedings of the First
    Australasian Educational Integrity Conference*. Adelaide: University of South
    Australia.
Handa, N., and Power, C. (2005) Land and discover! A case study investigating the cul-
    tural context of plagiarism. *Journal of University Teaching and Learning Practice* 2
    (3b): 64–84. Available at: http://jutlp.uow.edu.au/2005_v02_i03b/pdf/handa_
    006.pdf (accessed October 5, 2007).
Howard, R. M. (1993) A plagiarism *pentimento*. *Journal of Teaching Writing* 11 (2),
    233–46.
Howard, R. M. (1999) *Standing in the Shadow of Giants: Plagiarists, Authors, Col-
    laborators*. Stamford, CT: Ablex.
Howard, R. M. (2000a) The ethics of plagiarism. In M. A. Pemberton (ed.), *The
    Ethics of Writing Instruction: Issues in Theory and Practice*. Stamford, CT: Ablex,
    pp. 79–89.
Howard, R. M. (2000b) Sexuality, textuality: the cultural work of plagiarism. *College
    English* 62 (4): 473–91.
Introna, L., and Hayes, N. (2004) Plagiarism, detection and intentionality: on the (un)con-
    struction of plagiarists. Lancaster University, UK. Available at: www.jiscpas.ac.uk/
    documents/papers/2004Papers11.pdf (accessed October 5, 2007).

Introna, L., Hayes, N., Blair, L., et al. (2003) Cultural attitudes towards plagiarism: developing a better understanding of the needs of students from diverse cultural backgrounds relating to issues of plagiarism. Lancaster, UK: Lancaster University. Available at: www.jiscpas.ac.uk/images/bin/lancsplagiarismreport.pdf (accessed October 5, 2007).

Kostigen, T. (2006) MBAs: The biggest cheaters. *Yahoo! Finance Weekend*. Available at: http://biz.yahoo.com/weekend/mbacheat_1.html (accessed October 5, 2007).

McCabe, D. L. (2004) Promoting academic integrity: A US/Canadian perspective. In H. Marsden, M. Hicks, and A. Bundy (eds.), *Educational Integrity: Plagiarism and Other Perplexities. Proceedings of the First Australasian Educational Integrity Conference*. Adelaide: University of South Australia, pp. 3–11.

McCabe, D. L. (2005) Cheating: why students do it and how we can help them stop. In A. Lathrop and K. Foss (eds.), *Guiding Students from Cheating and Plagiarism to Honesty and Integrity: Strategies for Change*. Westport, CT: Libraries Unlimited, pp. 237–40.

Rocklin, T. (2005) Plagiarism, trust, and fraud. In A. Lathrop and K. Foss (eds.), *Guiding Students from Cheating and Plagiarism to Honesty and Integrity: Strategies for Change*. Westport, CT: Libraries Unlimited, pp. 172–3.

Stark, L. J., Perfect, T. J., and Newstead, S. E. (2005) When elaboration leads to appropriation: unconscious plagiarism in a creative task. *Memory* 13 (6), 561–73.

Swearingen, C. J. (1999) Originality, authenticity, imitation, and plagiarism: Augustine's Chinese cousins. In L. Buranen and A. M. Roy (eds.), *Perspectives on Plagiarism and Intellectual Property in a Postmodern World*. Albany, NY: State University of New York Press, pp. 19–30.

Szabo, A., and Underwood, J. (2004) Cybercheats: is information and communication technology fueling academic dishonesty? *Active Learning in Higher Education* 5 (2), 180–99. Available at: http://alh.sagepub.com/cgi/reprint/5/2/180 (accessed October 5, 2007).

Young, J. R. (2001) The cat-and-mouse game of plagiarism detection. *The Chronicle of Higher Education* (July 6). Available at: http://chronicle.com/weekly/v47/i43/43a02601.htm (accessed October 5, 2007).

CASE THIRTY-SEVEN: FIRE UP THE COFFEE POT! BREAK OUT THE RITALIN! – PERFORMANCE-ENHANCING DRUGS IN ACADEMIA

Not too long ago, drugs like Ritalin and Adderall were used exclusively to treat children (and some adults) with Attention Deficit Hyperactivity Disorder (ADHD). Those affected by this disorder have difficulty staying focused and concentrating on particular tasks (WebMD 2006). For instance, children with ADHD are unable to stay on task in school, often have trouble with impulse control (e.g., staying in their seats), or are unable to complete their work at the same pace as other children. Drugs such as Ritalin and Adderall help such children remain focused in school. The drugs work by increasing levels of dopamine, a neurotransmitter, in parts of the brain. Among other things, dopamine controls attention and helps maintain concentration. Children who might otherwise perform poorly in school can benefit tremendously by using such drugs.

However, in recent years, it is not uncommon to find drugs such as Ritalin and Adderall on college campuses, being used by students who are not affected by ADHD (Nichols 2004). Students use the drugs to help them study longer with greater focus and efficiency. For this purpose, Ritalin and Adderall are better than traditional stimulants, such as caffeine. According to Dr Eric Heiligstein, director of clinical psychiatry at the University of Wisconsin: "Students are able to accumulate more information in a shorter time frame. These drugs keep you awake longer. They minimize fatigue and help maintain a high performance level" (Sinderbrand 2005). One Yale University student credited Adderall with allowing him to read the 576-page book, *Crime and Punishment*, and write a 15-page paper on the novel in a mere 30 hours (ABC News 2004).

The practice of taking ADHD medications to enhance academic performance has raised health concerns about side-effects, including increased heart rate, elevated blood pressure and insomnia. Professor Paul Cooper of Leicester University (UK) worries about the danger of taking these drugs without qualified medical supervision: "We are moving into a phase now where informed parents can by-pass the medical profession, go online and prescribe the drug themselves" (BBC News 2007).

Other critics, such as Dr Heiligstein, are concerned about fairness; they worry that using Adderall or Ritalin to improve one's academic performance is simply cheating, just as using steroids in an athletic event is cheating. However, many students reject this view, arguing that Ritalin and Adderall are not unlike other kinds of stimulants or study aids that students routinely use. "These drugs are study tools, just like tutors and caffeine pills," said one Central Florida student. "We use what's available to us. It's not cheating" (ABC News 2004).

Aside from the cheating-related concerns, other worries, held, for example, by Dr Judy Illes, senior research scholar at Stanford University's Center for Biomedical Ethics, include the potential for coercion to keep up with those who enhance their ability through ADHD medications or other available mind-enhancing drugs (Penttila 2007). Pressure to remain competitive in academic life leads students to use ADHD medications, just as athletes use steroids to gain a competitive edge in sports.

Should college students be permitted to take ADHD drugs to enhance their academic performance?

Perspective One

Students should not be permitted to utilize ADHD drugs to enhance their academic performance. Such drugs are simply the academic version of steroids, which have been universally banned in amateur and professional athletic events. The use of steroids harms users and undermines the integrity of athletic competition. Students who take such drugs to enhance their academic ability have an unfair advantage over students who do not have access to those drugs. Moreover, drugs such as Ritalin and Adderall are, in fact, treatments for an actual disorder recognized by the medical community. As such, the only legal way to obtain them is by prescription from a physician who has arrived at a diagnosis of ADHD. Medications of this sort are regulated in this way (i.e., available only by prescription) precisely because they may pose a health risk if taken without medical supervision or by those who have no medical need for them.

Perspective Two

Students should be permitted to utilize ADHD drugs to enhance their academic performance. Those concerned about fairness fail to recognize that there are many other kinds of commonly used resources that are not available to everyone, but are nonetheless not considered unfair. For instance, some students have the financial means to hire tutors for additional help, or to take expensive test-preparation courses. Should we prohibit students from making use of these resources simply because they may not be available to all? Hence, if the use of ADHD medications to enhance academic performance is ethically objectionable, it is not because it creates unfairness (or at least no more unfairness than other resources to which we have no serious ethical objection).

It might be objected that Ritalin and Adderall pose serious health risks. However, the medical evidence suggests just the opposite. There is a very low likelihood of adverse side-effects. One could argue that if Ritalin or Adderall are used without physician supervision, people might take excessive amounts, leading to adverse reactions; but this objections holds for both over-the-counter medications and prescription medications, and access to the former is widely available. For instance, excessive doses of aspirin may lead to stomach bleeding. However, no one would suggest that people should not be free to purchase aspirin and use it as they wish.

Finally, merely because some medications have been used primarily to treat ADHD does not mean that they have no other legitimate uses. Consider again the use of aspirin. Aspirin has historically been used as a pain reliever, but has also proven effective in preventing heart attacks and is believed to help prevent certain kinds of cancer (National Cancer Institute n.d.). Aspirin is also put to non-medical uses. For instance, adding a tablet of aspirin to water in a vase appears to help keep flowers fresh longer (WiseGEEK n.d.). If we agree that the side-effects of Ritalin and Adderall are not so worrisome that they are widely prescribed to both children and adults, and that making use of them can improve academic performance, why prohibit students from making use of them?

Perspective Three

From a moral point of view, should students be permitted to take ADHD drugs to enhance their academic performance?

Step 1: Information-gathering

Medical

- What are the long-term consequences of taking ADHD drugs, such as Ritalin?
- Are some people, such as those with certain medical conditions, at greater risk of serious health effects from ADHD medications?
- Are there other drugs with which ADHD medications should not interact?
- By what kind of mechanism do stimulants such as Ritalin or Adderall operate?

Psychosocial

- What kinds of social or academic pressures do college students face?
- What are the psychological costs of pressure to succeed in college?
- What are the likely extended psychological effects of taking ADHD drugs?
- How do the cognitive and deliberative capacities of traditional college-age students differ from children or older adults? Are ADHD drugs likely to impede these capacities?
- How does the emotional development of traditional college-age students differ from older adults?
- Is the typical college student capable of autonomously choosing to use these drugs?

Legal

- What are the laws related to the use of ADHD drugs?
- What are the laws related to the prescription of ADHD drugs?
- What are the legal restrictions to individual autonomy regarding controlled substances?

Step 2: Creative problem-solving

There does not appear to be any obvious creative way to solve this problem that would not simply amount to choosing one of the original alternatives (listed below). It is possible that the problem would resolve itself if ADHD medications became so safe that they were available without prescription, and so widely accessible and inexpensive that any student could make use of them.

Step 3: Listing pros and cons

Options	Pros	Cons
Permit students to use ADHD medications to enhance their academic performance.	1. Respects students' autonomy (A) 2. Students are able to concentrate longer and study more effectively (C-B) 3. Greater academic success may improve graduate school or employment opportunities (C-B) 4. Students may increase their knowledge and skills (C-B)	5. Could create an unfair disadvantage for students who have no, or less, access to the medications (J-F, J-E) 6. Would create a coercive atmosphere that undermines free choice (A, C-NM)
Prohibit students from using ADHD medications to enhance their academic performance.	7. Protects student from possible harmful side-effects of ADHD medications (C-B) 8. Accords with physician's professional integrity not to prescribe medication for which there is no obvious medical need (V-I)	9. Other risky behaviors are not similarly restricted (J-E) 10. Leads to further restriction (slippery slope) of individual autonomy (C-NM, C-U, A)

Step 4: Analysis

Factual assumptions

- Pressure to take ADHD medications would increase with increased availability.
- A student's academic performance will improve with the aid of ADHD medications.

Value assumptions

- Any restriction on individual autonomy should be avoided.
- A person's autonomy may be restricted to prevent harm to other parties or to prevent violation of their rights.
- All people have a right to make decisions about their lives without coercion.
- Physicians are obligated not to prescribe medication to patients who have no medical need for that medication.

Justification

There is little doubt that college students are under considerable pressure to get good grades in college and, in many cases, perform well on graduate and professional school admissions tests. So they have every reason to look for ways to enhance their academic performance. However, a careful analysis of the issue will suggest that students should not be permitted to take medications intended for people with ADHD.

Consider the consequences of permitting versus the consequences of prohibiting the use of ADHD as a study aid. What harms and benefits are likely? First, these medications may be dangerous for some students. In February 2007, the Food and Drug Administration required that all manufacturers of ADHD medications print warnings regarding possible heart and psychiatric risks (CBC News 2006). For people with heart defects or high blood pressure, drugs such as Ritalin pose a serious risk of harm and may even be fatal. These drugs can also have negative effects in persons with a history of mental illness, such as depression. For these reasons, those taking Ritalin or Adderall should be under the supervision of a physician. A student taking Ritalin to improve his academic performance could put himself in serious danger if he has an undiagnosed heart condition or high blood pressure. Prohibiting students from taking Ritalin would protect them from possible harm (Reason #7). Indeed, such adverse consequences are one of the main reasons why many medications are only available by prescription.

Of course the practice of taking ADHD medications as study aids would not exist if there were no benefits whatsoever. Individual students are, in many cases, able to study longer, with greater focus and comprehension, with the aid of Ritalin or Adderall. It is a fact that students taking these medications have been able to achieve higher scores on examinations. All other things being equal, higher exam scores represent a benefit for these students, both in terms of their resulting in higher course grades (Reason #2), and in terms of expanded graduate school or professional opportunities that attach to a higher grade point average (Reason #3). In response to the argument that the physical risks of taking ADHD medications outweigh the potential benefits, it is important to notice that different people weigh harms and benefits differently. While the slight risk of a heart attack or stroke for one student might be worth a higher score on the MCAT, it might not be worth it for another. These are the sorts of decisions autonomy protects (Reason #1). And certainly, other kinds of stimulants, such as caffeine, when taken in excess, can also pose health risks (Reason #9). Yet we allow people to assess those risks on their own. Therefore, the fact that the use of ADHD comes with some possible serious side-effects cannot, *by itself*, offer a decisive reason against allowing their use on campuses.

However, other kinds of negative consequences accompany the use of Ritalin and Adderall on campus. Consider the kind of coercive academic culture it would create. The freedom to make uncoerced choices is a widely considered to be a fundamental good. It sits at the very foundation of all the other goods people pursue – precisely because it is a precondition to those goods. However, one can readily imagine how this value could be threatened if students believe that they simply *must* take ADHD medication in order to remain competitive in their college courses or in their applications to graduate or professional schools. Hence, while the risk that one individual might freely assume for herself may not alone offer a strong reason for disallowing the use of ADHD medications as study aids, the coercive effect that such a practice would have on academic culture provides a stronger reason (Reason #6).

Our consideration of the consequences of permitting the use of ADHD drugs on campus alluded to personal freedom and the high value we place on it. For this reason, one common strong presumption in ethics is that any restriction of individual autonomy requires justification. That is, there is a presumption in favor of allowing people to do as they wish (Reason #1). Nonetheless, some justifications exist for restricting individual autonomy. One widely accepted justification for restricting autonomy is that one's actions will have a negative impact on the rights or well-being of others. So, people have the right to act as they choose, but not when it interferes negatively with outside parties. A student who takes Ritalin when studying for an exam may admit that he might be hurting himself (with possible negative side-effects of the drug), but believe that is not hurting anyone else. Unfortunately, as discussed above, there is a real sense in which a student's use of Ritalin does harm others. A policy that allowed taking Ritalin would create a coercive atmosphere, and in turn restrict the autonomy of others.

In addition to restricting autonomy to prevent harm to outside parties, it is also frequently permissible to restrict the conduct of those whose capacity for autonomy may be limited. For instance, a hospital may be justified in overriding a patient's refusal of treatment if the patient is cognitively impaired. Similarly, young children are often forced to take medication for their own good because they are incapable of rational burden-benefit analyses. In both cases, we are justified in overriding their wishes (or restricting their conduct) because they lack the autonomy to make sound judgments and choices.

Is there a sense in which the typical college-age student is not fully autonomous? One sense of autonomy refers to a person's ability to make rational judgments (Miller 1981: 170). Anything that limits one's cognitive capacity limits one's autonomy in this sense. Do college students typically lack autonomy in this sense? While it is probably not the case that the average college student has less reasoning capacity than, say, a 35-year-old, it is likely true that they have insufficient life experience to make sound, rational choices about certain things. So, college students might be said to lack some autonomy in this sense.

Another important sense of autonomy refers to a consistency or stability of values, beliefs, and character. A person has autonomy in this sense if his decisions are consistent with his ongoing stable, considered values that make up who he is as a person (ibid.). When a person acts in a way that is inconsistent with his long-held, ongoing values, we say that he is acting "out of character." Might the typical college student lack autonomy in this sense? Most likely, many do. College often is (and ought to be) a time of self-exploration and self-discovery, a time of both losing oneself and finding oneself. College students are often engaged in the process of exploring different beliefs and trying on different selves. In some sense, they are no one in particular yet. To this extent, their choices cannot possibly reflect or be consistent with a stable set of values that define who they are. Certainly it would be an exaggeration to assert that all college students lack autonomy in the sense just described. Nonetheless, many do.

Finally, making good choices, especially difficult choices that might have far-reaching implications, requires emotional maturity. Persons not uncommonly look back on decisions they made earlier in life and realize that they lacked the emotional maturity needed to make *wise* decisions. While some college students are mature for their age, many do not yet possess full or even extensive emotional maturity. All these factors lend support to the view that it may be permissible to restrict their conduct and choices in order to protect them from themselves (Reason #7). Prohibiting the use of ADHD medications as an academic performance-enhancer may be justified in this way.

Much of what has been said can be recast in the language of *rights*: people have a right to do as they wish so long as it does not violate the rights and well-being of others. Sometimes this point is couched in terms of a right to physical privacy – that is, a right to do what one will with one's body without interference (Beauchamp and Childress 1989: 319). However, we have already concluded that permitting college students to use Ritalin and Adderall as a study aid would have a negative effect on others and would violate their right to be free to make uncoerced choices.

An examination of one final common justification for restricting individual autonomy leads us to a consideration of justice, in particular, justice as fairness. It is often alleged that using Ritalin is simply a form of cheating, a way of gaining an unfair advantage over other students. In one sense this allegation is clearly true. If the use of Ritalin is prohibited and one student ignores this prohibition, then she has an unfair advantage over others and can rightly be said to be cheating (Reason #5). For instance, if an exam is graded on a curve, such that one's grade will depend on how well one does compared to others, then someone taking Ritalin will have an advantage over those who did not take the medication. In fact, given that the exam is being graded on a curve, a student taking Ritalin is depending on the other students *not* to take it. Otherwise, she has no advantage. Similarly, a student studying for a graduate or professional school admissions test and competing against other students is hoping that her competitors do not use Ritalin.

If taking these kinds of ADHD drugs is prohibited, and one student ignores the prohibition in order to gain an advantage over those who comply with it, then she has an *unfair* advantage. Indeed, she is cheating. However, whether taking Ritalin as an academic performance-enhancer should be prohibited is exactly the dilemma at hand. So, it sheds no light on this question to point out that it would be unfair to violate the rule in order to gain an advantage over those who follow it. One could argue that if everyone were free to take these drugs, no one would have an advantage. This may or may not be true, but the drugs certainly would offer no advantage if everyone took them. Still, students might respond that they would like the freedom to take Ritalin as a study aid if they choose. That is, even knowing that their advantage might be minimal if everyone is free to take it, they might reason that many students may choose not to do so, creating at least some advantage. How could this be unfair?

Perhaps it might be unfair because not everyone would have equal access to ADHD drugs. Certainly, if students were allowed to use them, but only by prescription, then only those students who could persuade their physicians to prescribe the drugs would have access to them. However, a great number of academic performance-enhancing tools would not be accessible to all students, namely, those who could not afford to see a physician or could not afford to purchase the drugs (Reason #5). Of course, and by analogy, test preparation courses for professional school admissions tests are also prohibitively expensive for some students, and students who complete those courses do have some advantage over those who do not. However, no one would argue that the lack of resources on the part of some warrants a restriction of the autonomy of those students who can afford such course and who want to take them.

Before concluding, we should examine whether a consideration of virtue can shed light on our issue. What can we say about the academic integrity of those who take Ritalin as a study aid? Under the current laws governing such drugs, possessing Ritalin without a prescription is illegal (Pringle 2006). So, perhaps a more fruitful approach would be to consider the professional integrity of physicians who prescribe ADHD drugs to students who have no clinical need (Reason #8)? The answer to this question would depend on what counts as a clinical need, and that would surely be a complicated answer. However, it would seem that, despite society's strong commitment to autonomy, it allows physicians the power to use their judgment regarding what would be reasonably appropriate and safe. A physician would not prescribe weight loss medication to a patient who, from an objective point of view, has no weight problem even though the patient wants to be thinner. The medical community would surely disapprove of a physician who prescribed weight loss medication to a budding model or actress simply because those industries seem to prefer very thin people. Hence, because ADHD medications come with some health risks, professional integrity will require physicians to prescribe these drugs only to those diagnosed with ADHD. Pressure on the medical community to prescribe such drugs to those who have no such diagnosis would threaten the professional integrity of physicians and, for that reason, physicians should refuse to prescribe these drugs for non-medical reasons. Granted, if equally effective drugs that pose no health risks become available, then they may be become available without a prescription. This would certainly affect our present argument.

In conclusion, students should not be permitted to take ADHD drugs, such as Ritalin or Adderall, as academic performance-enhancers. While considerations of the possible harm to students taking the drugs and the possible unfairness to other students did not seem to offer decisive support, the coercive academic culture that would result from the need to remain competitive provides one good reason to prohibit the practice. There is also some reason to question the extent to which the average college student is fully capable of autonomous choice. This provides some support to the view that restricting the choices of college students in order to protect them from themselves may be justified. Finally, we note that society depends on the professional integrity of physicians to prescribe ADHD drugs only to patients who have been diagnosed with the disorder.

Additional Issues to Consider

Other possible moral dilemmas arising within this case:

Q Should campuses ban, and punish students who use, ADHD drugs as study aids?

Q Should physicians who write prescriptions for ADHD drugs to be used as study aids be penalized legally?

Q Should ADHD drugs be regulated as controlled substances?

REFERENCES

ABC News (2004) Students take ADHD drug to boost scores (November 15). Available at: http://abcnews.go.com/WNT/News/Story?id=254123&page=1 (accessed October 23, 2007).

BBC News (2007) Parents accused of exam drug use (May 29). Available at: http://news.bbc.co.uk/2/hi/uk_news/education/6700673.stm (accessed October 23, 2007).

Beauchamp, T., and Childress, J. (1989) *Principles of Biomedical Ethics*, 3rd edn. New York: Oxford University Press.

CBC News (2006) ADHD drugs carry slight risk of psychiatric side-effects (September 21). Available at: www.cbc.ca/health/story/2006/09/21/adhd.html (accessed October 23, 2007).

Miller, B. (1981) Autonomy and the refusal of lifesaving treatment. *Hastings Center Report* 11 (4), 22–8. Repr. in J. Arras and N. Rhoden (eds.), *Ethical Issues in Modern Medicine*, 3rd edn. Mountain View, CA: Mayfield, pp. 167–75.

National Cancer Institute (n.d.) Aspirin and cancer prevention. Available at: www.cancer.gov/cancertopics/aspirin-cancer-prevention (accessed October 23, 2007).

Nichols, K. (2004) The other performance-enhancing drugs. *The Chronicle of Higher Education* 51 (17). Available at: http://chronicle.com/subscribe/login?url=/weekly/v51/i17/17a04101.htm (accessed October 23, 2007).

Penttila, N. (2007) How smart are we about smart drugs? Available at: www.dana.org/events/detail.aspx?id=7854 (accessed October 23, 2007).

Pringle, E. (2006) Adderall on-line: Black market profits in plain sight. Available at: www.lawyersandsettlements.com/articles/adderall_profits.html (accessed October 23, 2007).

Sinderbrand, A. (2005) Need a study boost? *The Daily Northwestern* (October 26). Available at: http://media.www.dailynorthwestern.com/media/storage/paper853/news/2005/10/26/Forum/Need-A.Study.Boost.Try.An.Espresso-1919689.html (accessed October 23, 2007).

WebMD (2006) What is attention deficit hyperactivity disorder (ADHD)? Available at: www.webmd.com/add-adhd/guide/attention-deficit-hyperactivity-disorder-adhd-topic-overview (accessed October 23, 2007).

WiseGEEK (n.d.) What are some uses of aspirin? Available at: www.wisegeek.com/what-are-some-uses-of-aspirin.htm (accessed October 23, 2007).

CASE THIRTY-EIGHT: WHEN AN A IS NOT AN A – GRADE INFLATION IN UNIVERSITIES

As the average SAT and ACT scores remain the same, college grade point averages continue to climb. Once the most common grade on college campuses, the C now only makes a rare appearance; and Ds and Fs are almost unheard of. A grade of C used to represent a satisfactory mastery of the content of a course. It was a respectable grade. However, in the eyes of college students nowadays, a C is an unacceptably bad grade. This trend represents a phenomenon often referred to as "grade inflation." Ivy League institutions, such as Harvard and Princeton, appear to be the worst offenders. No fewer than 91 percent of Harvard's class of 2001 graduated with honors (Gordon 2006: 10). However, the problem of grade inflation is certainly not restricted to Ivy League schools. Indeed, it is a nationwide epidemic, affecting colleges and universities everywhere. Retired Duke University Professor, Stuart Rojstaczer, has compiled years of data-tracking grade inflation across the country: "Every school I can find that has data available shows grade inflation," Rojstaczer reports (Rojstaczer 2003: 37).

Grade inflation is worrisome for a number of reasons. First, assigning higher grades than a student's performance warrants is unfair to students who legitimately do outstanding work. If an A grade is awarded for merely good work, then there is no way to reward the student who does outstanding work. As an analogy, if a panel of Olympic judges were to give perfect scores of ten to very good, but slightly flawed, figure-skating performances, they would be unable to give a legitimate score of ten to a skater who gave a perfect performance. Second, studies show that students tend to underperform when standards are set low (Johnson 2003: 8, 236–7). Hence, grade inflation cheats students educationally, since they get less out of college when grades are inflated, that is, when they are able to get good grades for less effort and achievement. Third, inflated grades also deceive and mislead employers and graduate schools. An impressive undergraduate transcript will suggest an ability to do graduate work, even though the student may be quite under-prepared. Similarly, an employer may hire a college graduate believing that her excellent GPA reflects a set of skills that, in reality, she does not possess.

Most who have studied grade inflation trace its roots back to the late 1960s and the Vietnam War (*USA Today* 2004). Students who were enrolled in college were not subject to the draft. However, flunking out of college almost certainly meant service in the military – often in a war zone. Aware of this, professors became reluctant to assign failing grades. Thus, students who would have received Fs, began to receive Ds and Cs, and students who would have received Cs and Bs, by extension (i.e., inflation), received Bs and As.

Nowadays, the threat of the draft has vanished, but there are other serious negative consequences for students who receive poor grades. Many students depend on financial aid in order to remain in college, and must maintain a certain grade point average in order to continue receiving those monies. A professor who knows that a D or an F will jeopardize a student's ability to pay for and remain in college may be inclined to grade that student more sympathetically. Similarly, a professor who is aware that a student is applying to professional schools or graduate programs may tend to grade generously, so as to increase the student's likelihood of admission. Also, a high rate of acceptance of its students into graduate and professional schools is a point of pride for most colleges, and faculty may be subtly encouraged to do what they can to maintain or raise this rate.

Other factors as well have contributed to grade inflation. Course evaluations, in which students evaluate professors, create a strong incentive for professors to inflate grades. They recognize that strict grading often translates into poor course evaluations. Since course evaluations are taken into consideration in making promotion and tenure decisions, professors are personally rewarded for inflating grades. Aside from this, many simply do not want to face disgruntled students at their doors. Inflating grades is an effective way to avoid uncomfortable confrontations with unhappy, disappointed students.

While there is wide consensus that grade inflation is a serious problem, there is considerable disagreement over what to do about it. Some professors simply take a stand against it and significantly limit the number of As and Bs they award. However, as laudable as this principled approach sounds, some, such as Barbara Walvoord and Virginia Johnson Anderson, authors of *Effective Grading*, worry about the unfairness to the students of such professors (Gordon 2006: 10). These students are placed at a distinct disadvantage on the job market or when applying to graduate or professional schools compared to other students whose professors awarded higher (inflated) grades. Such an approach, they contend, is unlikely to have any impact on the overall grading culture of a university, and even less on higher education in general. Thus, Walvoord and Anderson discourage professors from acting individually against grade inflation.

A few universities have attempted to address the problem by developing grading policies that place limits on the number of As that can be given out. Since fall 2004, Princeton University faculty have been required to restrict the number of As they give to 35 percent for undergraduate courses (Aronauer 2005: 41). Not surprisingly, and despite the evidence that this approach has had an impact on grade inflation at Princeton, 70 percent of Princeton undergraduates surveyed in 2004 disapproved of the policy (Bruno 2007). Among other things, Princeton undergraduates are concerned that the policy may have a negative impact on classroom atmosphere. In particular, students may be reluctant to help one another in a particular course if they know that helping others could result in lowering their own chance of receiving an A for the course. Granted, the Princeton policy does not actually restrict the number of As that can be given in any one class, but rather places restrictions on the number of As given out by departments. Nevertheless, if a department has a limit on the percentage of As it can give, then, realistically, professors are forced to limit the number of As they give out. According to Professor Diana Fuss of Princeton's Department of English, the policy has made professors much more frugal with As. "The mercy A – has disappeared" (Aronauer 2005: 41).

Students at Princeton have also complained that limiting As puts them at an unfair disadvantage when competing against students from other universities for places in graduate and professional programs.

Regardless of these objections, Princeton appears to be pleased with the impact the policy has made and remains committed to curtailing the number of As awarded in undergraduate courses.

From a moral point of view, is Princeton University's strategy to reduce grade inflation justified?

Additional Issues to Consider

Other possible moral dilemmas arising within this case:

> **Q** If an institution does not put in place a policy or procedure to curb grade inflation, should individual faculty be morally required to inflate grades (assuming the majority of their colleagues are doing so)?

> **Q** Is grading on a standard bell curve (i.e., 10 percent As and Fs, 20 percent Bs and Ds, and 40 percent Cs) morally justifiable?

> **Q** Is a "mercy A" ever morally justifiable?

> **Q** From a moral point of view, should students whose course grade is lower than B – be prevented from evaluating the professor?

REFERENCES

Aronauer, R. (2005) Princeton's war on grade inflation drops the number of A's. *Chronicle of Higher Education* 52 (6): 41.
Bruno, L. (2007) Princeton leads in grade inflation. *USA Today*. Available at: www.usatoday.com/news/education/2007-03-27-princeton-grades_N.htm (accessed October 3, 2007).
Gordon, M. E. (2006) When B's are better. *Chronicle of Higher Education* 52 (49): 10.
Johnson, V. E. (2003) *Grade Inflation: A Crisis in College Education*. New York: Springer-Verlag.
Rojstaczer, S. (2003) Professor compiles GPA database to confront grade inflation. *Chronicle of Higher Education* 49 (23): 37.
USA Today (2004) Princeton becomes first to formally combat grade inflation. Available at: www.usatoday.com/news/education/2004-04-26-princeton-grades_x.htm (accessed October 3, 2007).

CASE THIRTY-NINE: READIN', WRITIN', AND RX-IN' – SCHOOL KIDS WITH MEDICAL NEEDS

Justin Jones is a typical second-grader – with one exception: he has type-1 (insul-independent, or "juvenile") diabetes (T-1-D). T-1-D is a genetically inherited disease in which the pancreas fails to produce insulin, a hormone needed to metabolize sugar. In persons with T-1-D, blood sugars can become dangerously high (if not controlled with insulin); extreme elevations of blood sugar can cause coma and death.

With careful management, type-1 diabetics can live near-normal lives. They must, however, scrupulously observe several precautions: they must follow dietary restrictions, exercise regularly, and check their blood sugar levels several times each day. If the blood sugar level is too high, the person must inject more insulin to metabolize the excess sugar; if the level is too low, the person must have a snack to get more sugar into the body. If the blood sugar level is dangerously low, an injection of glucagon (a naturally occurring peptide that stimulates the liver to release stored sugar) is given.

Most diabetics test their own blood sugar and, based on the results, decide how much (if any) insulin, food, or glucagon to take. Very young diabetics typically need adult assistance for blood testing and injection of insulin or glucagon. Their parents assist at home, but other arrangements must be made to carry out these procedures when the child is at school.

Ideally, a school nurse would oversee blood sugar testing and would inject any necessary drugs. The problem is that Justin's school, like increasingly many schools, does not have a nurse. Although the National Association of School Nurses has a goal of one nurse for every 750 students, many school districts, in an attempt to control costs, have eliminated school nurse positions or assigned nurses to more than one school. As a result, a school nurse may only be on site one or two hours a day, one day each week, or some other such part-time arrangement.

Justin, who was diagnosed two years ago, knows how to test his blood sugar. Twice daily he leaves his classroom and goes to the principal's office where he pricks his finger, places a drop of blood on chemically treated paper, and puts the paper into an instrument that reads out his blood sugar level. If his blood sugar is too low, he eats a snack that he carries with him for this purpose; but if he needs insulin he must call his mother, who must leave work (30 minutes away) and come to Justin's school to give him his medicine. She waits with him until he is able safely to return to his classroom and resume his educational activities.

Over the last three years Justin's mother has had to come to his school one to two times each week. Not surprisingly, her employer's patience regarding her absences has worn thin. The employer understands why Ms Jones must leave, but he also has a production schedule to meet and needs his employees to perform their work – as they have contracted to do. To add insult to injury, Ms

Jones is not paid for the time away from her job; in some weeks she loses eight hours of pay. This financial loss is one the family can ill afford.

At her first parent–teacher conference, Ms Jones discussed her worries with Justin's teacher and the school principal. She requested that Justin's teacher be trained to oversee blood sugar testing and insulin administration. Ms Jones volunteered to teach the teacher everything she knows about the disease, how it typically manifests in Justin, how to perform blood sugar testing, how to give insulin injections, and warning signs of too much or too little insulin. Ms Jones shares her concerns about her loss of income and, potentially, the loss of her job; she pleads with the teacher and principal to help her manage the medications that Justin needs to control his T-1-D.

After careful consideration of Ms Jones's request, the principal tells her that the school and its personnel cannot accept the responsibility of caring for Justin's medical needs. They worry that Ms Jones, however well intentioned, is not a healthcare professional trained to educate others about diabetes or its management. If important information is omitted or misinterpreted, Justin's welfare would be jeopardized. Furthermore, testing and injections are medical procedures that neither the principal nor the teacher feels comfortable performing. (Indeed, the teacher stated that blood and needles make her squeamish and she wants nothing at all to do with either.) Prior to making her decision, the principal contacted the state nursing association and was informed that insulin is a "high-alert" medication that requires a dosage check by two licensed nurses before the drug can be administered. Finally, the principal expresses the concern that assuming responsibility for these tasks could place the school in a precarious position regarding legal liability, especially if Justin develops serious problems while at school. In short, neither the principal nor the teacher will agree to Ms Jones's requests.

Ms. Jones replies that neither blood sugar testing nor insulin injection is difficult. She adds that since Justin can do his own testing and knows when to take any needed snacks, all she is asking is that some adult (perhaps another teacher or the school secretary, if Justin's teacher is unable or unwilling) give any injections he needs. She notes that, in any case, Justin's teacher needs to understand his disease and any warning signs of pending crisis, since Justin is under her supervision for seven hours each day. Ms Jones offers to try to find a registered nurse educator to instruct a willing adult (since her educational qualifications have been questioned) about this disease and injection administration. The principal continues to refuse her request.

From a moral point of view, should the principal accede to Ms. Jones' request?

Additional Issues to Consider

Other possible moral dilemmas arising within this case:

Q   Should elementary schools be required to have a registered nurse on the premises during instructional hours?

Q If putting a nurse in each school is cost-prohibitive, should school districts be required to provide a nurse in one or two schools and require all children who are likely to need medical assistance during instructional hours to attend those schools?

Q Should Ms Jones be allowed to take sick time (for which she is paid) for her trips to Justin's school to meet his medical needs?

REFERENCES

American Academy of Pediatrics (2001) The role of the school nurse in providing school health services. *Pediatrics* 108 (5), 1231–2.

American Diabetes Association (2003) Position statement: Insulin administration. *Diabetes Care* 26, S121–S124. Available at: http://care.diabetesjournals.org/cgi/content/full/26/suppl_1/s121 (accessed September 13, 2007).

Association of American Educators (n.d.) Code of ethics. Available at: www.aaeteachers.org/code-ethics.shtml (accessed September 12, 2007).

National Association of School Nurses (2002) Position statement: Using assistive personnel in school health services programs. Available at: www.nasn.org/Portals/0/positions/2002psassistive.pdf (accessed September 13, 2007).

National Association of School Nurses (2003) Medication administration in the school setting. Available at: www.nasn.org/Portals/0/positions/2003psmedication.pdf (accessed September 13, 2007).

National Association of School Nurses (2003) Resolution: Access to a school nurse. Available at: www.nasn.org/Portals/0/statements/resolutionaccess.pdf (accessed September 13, 2007).

National Association of School Nurses (2006) Position statement: School nurse management of students with chronic health conditions. Available at: www.nasn.org/Portals/0/positions/2006pschronic.pdf (accessed September 13, 2007).

National Association of School Nurses (2006) Position statement: School nurse role in care and management of the child with diabetes in the school setting. Available at: www.nasn.org/Portals/0/positions/2006psdiabetes.pdf (accessed September 13, 2007).

National Education Association (1975) Code of ethics of the education profession. Available at: www.aaeteachers.org/code-ethics.shtml (accessed September 12, 2007).

CASE FORTY: PROMISES, PROMISES – SELLING GENETIC MATERIAL FOR INSTITUTIONAL GAIN

In 1988, the National Human Genome Research Institute (NHGRI, originally named the Genome Office) was created as part of the National Institutes of Health (NIH). One of the first acts of its director, Nobel Laureate James Watson, was to recommend to Congress that a percentage of the NIH and Department of

Energy (DOE) genome budgets be set aside to examine moral and humane issues generated by new genetic knowledge, concurrent with its discovery. Congressional approval quickly followed, and ELSI (Ethical, Legal, and Social Implications of the Human Genome Project) was established in 1990 (Cahill 1996: 12, 15).

Intrigued by the challenge of using scientific knowledge in a wise and just way, Sophia earned a double major in biology and philosophy. The Human Genome Project, which began just as she entered college, galvanized her to research the genetic bases of disease. The concept behind ELSI, and its commitment to examine the human consequences of genetic knowledge and its applications, fascinated her. She wanted to be part of it. She received a Master of Science degree in biology, concentrating on genetic research for her thesis. She was hired by a small undergraduate state college to develop a strong student research program in biology. Her enthusiasm for research was contagious, and Sophia soon had a devoted and impassioned team of student researchers working on genetics projects. Some faculty members also caught the research bug, and in a couple of years the college had a small, but respected, genetics research program.

During her second year, Sophia was awarded her first DOE grant, as well as a NHGRI/ELSI grant. To facilitate research on the genetic bases of a number of diseases, Sophia included in the DOE grant application a proposal to create a repository of genetic samples, which would be available for science faculty and their students to use in research. The ELSI grant included three components: analysis of the ethical issues and human consequences of storage and use of genetic materials, a community program for public education and discussion of the potential benefits and consequences of the Human Genome Project, and creation of a task force to develop a code of ethics for the repository of human genetic material. Developing the code of ethics would be a collaborative effort among community members and representatives of the college, including faculty, students, and administrators. When Sophia discussed the two grant applications with Dr Maunders, the biology department chair and vice-president for research, they agreed that the intention was to establish a repository of genetic materials to support a strong genetics research program, incorporating the highest ethical standards in the collection and storage of materials, the research itself, and the practical applications of research outcomes. These ethical standards would include an ongoing process of informed consent that would share information about research goals, methods of collection and storage of samples and data, and potential uses of any discoveries; safeguards to ensure participant anonymity and confidentiality of research data; information about genetic counseling; and forums to update the community on research progress.

Sophia was awarded both grants, enabling her to start a bank for genetic material that was housed in the biology department under Dr Maunder's direction. Community members, faculty, students, and outside ethics advisors participated in the development of ethical guidelines governing the collection, storage, and use of genetic materials. There was tremendous pride in Sophia's accomplishments in the tightly knit college town; and students, faculty, and community members were happy to provide genetic samples and personal and family health histories.

Sophia created a popular research ethics course, and served on the college Institutional Review Board (IRB), the federally mandated independent committee that reviews proposed research with human subjects to minimize risk and harm. Her request to allow research students to attend IRB meetings, unless sensitive subjects were being discussed, was initially greeted with skepticism. When it became evident that the students learned a great deal from the experience and contributed insightful perspectives (when asked), their presence became a valued element in the review process. A student often served as a community member on the IRB.

After four years of teaching and research, Sophia left the college to begin work on her doctoral degree. She was very proud of the college's thriving genetics research program. She was most proud of the genetic repository she had established and the scientific discoveries it enabled, particularly because it had earned the trust of the community. The success of the research program attracted additional grant funding and external partners – resources that enabled more research and research facilities, and attracted more students and more accomplished faculty. Dr Maunders had been selected as the college's new president a few months earlier, due in large part to the success the biology department had achieved under his leadership, and the new resources it brought to the college and community.

A few months after she left the college, Sophia received a disturbing visit from three of her former research students. They were so upset that they had traveled several hundred miles to talk with her in person. Alison, a student community member on the IRB, was distraught by the discussion at the last IRB meeting. She agonized for several days about compromising the meeting's confidentiality, then decided to talk about her concerns with her trusted friends and research partners, David and Julia.

The IRB had discussed whether the informed consent of past donors who had contributed samples and personal information to the genetic repository would be violated by the agreement to sell the genetic bank to Megapharmagen, one of college's research partners. Megapharmagen anticipated a substantial return on investment by securing exclusive access to the samples and data in the genetic repository. The company planned to mine the data and samples and use them in corporate research. Because Megapharmagen's research would be privately funded, it would not be encumbered by the original ethical guidelines and could accelerate the commercialization of end products.

Faculty might still participate in research, but it would be Megapharmagen's research. Among other things, this would mean that faculty would have little or no input into research priorities and methodologies. Megapharmagen would hire scientists from the college at will; that is to say, researchers could be terminated at any time, for any reason – even if they were on the verge of a breakthrough. Faculty would be prohibited from publishing results of their research at Megapharmagen, or bringing students into their research projects without express corporate approval.

In addition to a sizeable sum for the sale of the repository, the college would receive a modest percentage of profits from downstream commercial use of the data and products developed from the repository's genetic samples. The IRB reviewed the original consent form, and with the guidance of the college attorney, agreed that the clause giving consent for future unspecified genetic research with the collection's samples and data allowed the sale of the college's genetic bank to Megapharmagen's genetic research program.

Sophia felt physically ill, devastated by the news. Even though she had been unaware of the sale until Alison, David, and Julia showed up on her doorstep, she felt she had personally betrayed the community. The community had trusted her with their most personal information, and she had promised that the repository would safeguard it. The samples and data could reveal unwanted information, such as predispositions to certain diseases, or parentage different from what the individual believed. Sophia was concerned that confidentiality would be compromised once Megapharmagen had possession of the code to contributors' samples and linked medical information. She was worried that personal information would be used in ways that was neither specified nor intended in the original consent process. What if contributors from a family with a genetic predisposition for early-onset Alzheimer's disease were contacted to find out if any family members had developed symptoms? She reflected deeply on what she would ask Dr Maunders when she called him to hear his perspective on the situation.

The phone call was short and not particularly pleasant, given the years that they had worked closely together. Dr Maunders demanded to know where Sophia had heard the news of the sale.

"It's common knowledge by now," she replied, and then asked: "What about the community? We promised the community that we would safeguard their privacy and the confidentiality of their samples and records. They trusted us and we betrayed that trust. We promised them that our policies would be transparent. The proposed arrangement exploits them: they didn't give permission to be used like this."

"Sophia, have you forgotten that the consent documents allow future unspecified genetic research? You should remember, also, that when we developed the repository's code of ethics, it specifically included the provision for regular review and revision; a provision that I recall you strongly advocated, or more accurately, insisted upon! We have done nothing that was not permitted."

"No, I haven't forgotten; in fact I remember the clause, and the discussions about the code of ethics clearly. The intention of the clause, as you well know, was to allow future researchers to use more advanced techniques than were available at the time samples were collected to re-examine samples and histories. We had public discussions about that issue, and the community agreed that they didn't want their children denied the possibility of scientific and medical advances because the original donors died or moved away. It was never intended to be carte blanche for future research, and certainly never intended that participants' information and biological samples would be sold for commercial gain. The purpose of periodic review was to make sure that confidentiality would be protected as technology allowed us to delve deeper into the secrets of the genome. Allowing revision was meant to protect confidentially, not undermine it!"

"Sophia, I am truly surprised that you are so vested in your own history here that you can't see that the sale is a great benefit to the college, and by extension, the community."

"Dr Maunders, I disagree. This sale can only harm the people of this community. Who will have access to their confidential genetic and family information? Insurance companies or financial institutions might use identifiable health information to deny coverage or a home loan."

Dr. Maunders reminded her that she had no authority at the college any more, certainly not over the genetic repository. He told Sophia that he had made a decision that was in the best long-term interests of the school. The sale would bring a windfall to the college, securing its financial future for decades. Megapharmagen's corporate infrastructure was much more effective than the college's systems for bringing new discoveries and therapies to market, and it had resources far beyond those of the college to speed the process of research. This would only serve to benefit humanity.

"Dr Maunders, the genetic bank was created with public money. Taxpayers provided the funding, and we agreed to fulfill the conditions of our proposal, in exchange for that money. Taxpayers built the repository. It belongs to them, and the college has no right to sell it, or to deny the community a share in the benefit from the profits of research. Some of the money was granted specifically because of the ethical guidelines we promised to establish and follow. Those guidelines are being deliberately misinterpreted to allow the exact opposite of their original intent and promise. We created the research program under federal IRB regulations. The college IRB approved only research specified or allowed by participants' consent. Incidentally, is there any provision for the donors to share in Megapharmagen's profits from commercialization of their bodies?"

From a moral point of view, should the sale of the repository for genetic material proceed?

Additional Issues to Consider

Other possible moral dilemmas arising within this case:

Q Given her separation from the university, was Sophia acting in a morally responsible fashion by involving herself in this controversy?

Q From a moral point of view, do non-specific consent forms, such as the college's form that allowed future unspecified genetic research, imply that anything goes?

Q Given the college's non-specific consent, were the subjects' consents (in this case, to sell the material to a corporation) autonomous?

Q Does anyone have a moral obligation to inform the local community about the agreement?

Q Is the college morally obligated to share profits from the sale and future research with members of the community who donated samples?

Q Did Alison, David, and Julia behave in a morally responsible fashion?

REFERENCE

Cahill, G. F. (1996) A brief history of the human genome project. In B. Gert, E. M. Berger, G. F. Cahill, Jr., et al. *Morality and the New Genetics: A Guide for Students and Health Care Providers.* Sudbury, MA: Jones and Bartlett, pp. 1–28.

PART III

THE INTERCOLLEGIATE ETHICS BOWL

10

HISTORY OF THE ETHICS BOWL

How to engage students in energetic, thoughtful, careful, substantive, and respectful examination of ethics and its practical applications to everyday dilemmas was the challenge that confronted Professor Robert Ladenson and inspired him to create the Ethics Bowl. In particular, Professor Ladenson was concerned by the increased use of aggressive and polarizing invectives that characterized public debate, whether political, religious, or social. Students were often reluctant to engage in vigorous discussions on issues about which they felt deeply because, so often, the nature of exchange on moral issues was belligerent and judgmental, rather than respectful and engaging. Professor Ladenson wanted students to integrate probing debate on relevant moral issues and ethical decision-making into their daily lives. To promote these objectives, he created a method to develop deliberative resolutions to everyday moral dilemmas by building on a solid foundation of moral reasoning. In 1993, he organized the first intramural Ethics Bowl at the Illinois Institute of Technology. The event was an immediate success, growing in popularity each year. In the third year, teams from three nearby universities were invited to participate, and in 1996 a demonstration Ethics Bowl was presented at the annual meeting of the Association for Practical and Professional Ethics (APPE). In 1997, 14 teams competed in the first National Intercollegiate Ethics Bowl (IEB), held in conjunction with the annual APPE meeting, and in 2000, the Ethics Bowl became an official part of the annual meeting. The day-long competition drew 40 teams of students from across the country, and had a waiting list of teams eager to participate. In 2007, because of the explosive growth of the IEB, eight regional competitions were held to determine the final 32 teams that would advance to the national event.

In the complex and changing environment of practical ethics, Ethics Bowl training has proved to be an effective approach to the study of moral decision-making. The training provides grounding in ethical theory and moral reasoning, and practice in applying theories and their principles to real-world moral dilemmas. Many colleges and universities use the Ethics Bowl model as a teaching opportunity, or sponsor their own Ethics Bowl as part of campus programming. Even before

2007, several schools sponsored regional Ethics Bowls. Brigham Young University (BYU) has 32 teams that participate in an intramural Ethics Bowl sponsored each semester by the BYU Student Leadership Council. It is interesting to note that few Ethics Bowl participants are philosophy majors: the Ethics Bowl attracts students from disciplines broadly represented throughout academia.

Students who participate in an Ethics Bowl gain an in-depth understanding of moral dilemmas of social relevance that are of concern to them. They are exposed to and prepared for the ethical behavior expected in their chosen professions. They develop greater sensitivity to other perspectives and become better able to listen critically, evaluate thoughtfully, and advocate effectively. They enhance their appreciation of and respect for the personal values, experiences, cultures, social situations, and beliefs that lead others to embrace ethical perspectives that differ from their own. They learn to understand and respect positions with which they do not agree.

Ethics Bowl training facilitates progression from a position of passionate opinion to one based on intellectually rigorous analysis and independent thought; progression that, while developing a distance necessary for critical examination, does not lose the energetic intensity of personal moral concern. The experience of thoughtful analysis nurtures respect for shared standards of moral reasoning while fostering independent thought and the creation of justifiable responses to practical dilemmas.

11

NATIONAL INTERCOLLEGIATE ETHICS BOWL COMPETITION

The Ethics Bowl begins with three morning sessions of concurrent matches. Teams of up to five members are given two cases per match. Each team both presents a case and responds to the other team's presentation of a different case; teams may not refer to notes. The selected case for each round is announced, and a moderator's question about the case is given to the presenting team (Team One). Team One has two minutes to confer before a team member responds to the question. The response must be tailored to the moderator's question and must articulate and examine the salient moral issues of the case. Ultimately, the analysis must lead to a rationally defensible answer. Next, Team Two responds to Team One, and Team One in turn responds to Team Two's comments. Following both teams' deliberations and comments, a panel of three judges asks questions of Team One. Following the team members' responses to the judges' questions, the judges evaluate and score both teams on intelligibility (logic, consistency, clarity, precision), depth (awareness and understanding of ethical issues central to the case), focus (avoidance of irrelevancies), and judgment (careful, reasonable, comparative assessment of ethically relevant considerations). In the second round of the match the teams reverse roles, with Team Two responding to the moderator's question.

The eight top-scoring teams advance to the quarter-final matches in the afternoon. The four winning teams advance to the semi-final match, and, finally, the two teams that win their semi-final matches advance to the championship match in the evening. Despite the competitive nature of the Ethics Bowl, its goal is not to produce a winning team, but to develop an informed, respectful discourse that creates a deep understanding of moral issues.

Preparation

Immediately following the annual IEB, the case-writing team – professionals from a variety of disciplines and from across the country – begins discussing possible cases for the following year's event. During the next several months, drafts of cases are exchanged for commentary via email, and in December the final cases are sent to Professor Ladenson for distribution. In early January, about six weeks prior to the IEB competition, judges and teams are sent copies of the cases. About 15 are included, of which 12 will be used during the actual competition. Neither the teams nor the judges know which cases will be included in the competition, so they must prepare all of them.

As students begin to analyze the cases, judges also begin to examine each one and to develop questions to be used in the competition. Teams do not know which cases they will have to address, nor whether they will present a particular case or respond to the other team's presentation; students must prepare to do both types of presentation for all cases. Teams report that their members often begin their preparation holding by antithetical positions on several cases. Whether or not the team members reach a consensus of belief on a particular case, they must agree on how the case will be presented.

At this point, the real learning begins. Each team must understand thoroughly the multiple moral values, beliefs, and perspectives suggested by the case, appreciate the practical realities and concerns underlying the dilemma, articulate clear distinctions among the perspectives, identify the strengths and weaknesses of the moral reasoning supporting each position, and present a compelling ethical rationale for the particular resolution that they determine is morally preferable. Team members must also anticipate the philosophical arguments and moral reasoning an opposing team might use, as well as the questions the moderators may pose. Equally important, students must hone their ability to listen carefully and open-mindedly to another's viewpoint, not with the intent of converting the other person to their own perspective, but with the intent of truly understanding the other's values, logic, and perspective, and of examining these within the context of moral reasoning. This critical listening forces students to consider seriously the arguments supporting others' opinions. As the case is studied in depth and the issues examined within the moral context, one position often emerges as more ethically compelling and is eventually supported by (a majority of) the team. In other instances the divergent perspectives remain, but each team member develops a deep understanding and appreciation for the opposing position. Team members who do not personally embrace the majority opinion come to respect it as a morally defensible perspective that principled individuals could reasonably hold and, when called upon to do so, can effectively and compellingly articulate their team's perspective. Students also come to realize that opposing teams, judges, and moderators may offer perspectives they had not considered. The intense preparation the students undergo creates an intellectual rigor that allows them to extrapolate the moral reasoning they have carefully applied to a known situation and utilize their skills to examine unfamiliar dilemmas they will face in the future.

Although the Ethics Bowl is of particular value for education, it also has a lasting impact outside the classroom. Students are required to explore ethical issues and moral reasoning in depth and be able to apply ethical theory to practical situations that have great relevance for their personal, civic, and future professional lives. Rather than presenting views primarily for the approval of the teacher, students are required to engage each other in discourse, actively listening and analyzing responses. Discussions are stimulating, focused, and guided by disciplined scholarship and logical – even when impassioned – discussion. Students learn from their own efforts, as well as from teammates and members of opposing teams. The Ethics Bowl is particularly effective as a tool to refine the habits of thought and discussion that characterize many interpersonal interactions, replacing unexamined opinions with thoughtful, reasoned perspectives.

12

INTERCOLLEGIATE ETHICS BOWL (IEB) RULES

Regional Intercollegiate Ethics Bowl Rules

Rules for school eligibility

1 A school may send unlimited teams to a regional bowl. If it sends multiple teams, it must specify which teams are linked and which are not. Linked teams are closely connected: they may have the same faculty sponsor, prepare together in the same class or ethics bowl club, or participate in the same intramural ethics bowl, etc. Unlinked teams are those without major connections: they may consist of students from different colleges, with significantly different courses of study, within a large university.
2 If any of a group of linked teams is eligible for the national bowl, a single team may be formed with members of any linked teams in the group for the national bowl, but only one space can be earned at the national bowl, no matter how well the linked teams perform at the regional bowl. If teams are not linked, each team is independently eligible for the national bowl, but members may not be switched from one team to another.

Rules for student eligibility

1 Members of a school's team must be undergraduate students currently enrolled at the school.
2 Students who graduate between the regional bowl and the national bowl remain eligible for the national bowl.

Rules for participating in multiple regional bowls

1   A school may take part in more than one regional bowl. However, the school must notify the IEB Executive Board prior to *any* of the bowls which one it will use as a qualifier for the national bowl.

Number of teams at the National Bowl (2007–8)

There will be thirty-two (32) participating teams.

Qualifying rules for teams to advance from regional bowls to the national bowl

1   The number of teams each regional bowl sends to the national bowl each year will depend on the total number of participating regional bowls and the size of the particular regional bowl.
2   The default number of teams sent by a regional bowl will be $D = 32/N$ where N is the number of regional bowls participating, and D is the default number of teams sent.
3   If a regional bowl has fewer than ten (10) unlinked teams, the default number of teams it will send to the national bowl is one ($D = 1$).
4   The remaining spaces will be filled in by the procedure outlined in the appendix.
5   Each regional bowl will therefore have a claim on a particular number of spaces, S. Each bowl will fill those spaces with the top S teams from its region. Should a team be unable to attend the national bowl, its space will go to the next highest ranked team, until all S spaces are filled.
6   Each regional bowl will use scoring rules that make it possible to rank teams from top to bottom.

APPENDIX

The additional spaces up to thirty-two (32) are allocated to the regional bowls based on the odds of a team from that regional bowl moving on. The first space is allocated to the regional bowl with the lowest odds, the second space to the regional bowl with the second lowest odds, and so forth. Ties are broken by counting the number of schools involved (the higher the better), then by totaling the number of unlinked and linked teams (the higher the better), then by coin toss.

Example: Assume that there are eight (8) regional bowls. Assume the following number of unlinked teams in each bowl:

Bowl A 8
Bowl B 8
Bowl C 8

Bowl D 9
Bowl E 11
Bowl F 13
Bowl G 15
Bowl H 18

The initial distribution of spaces for each bowl would be:

Bowl A 3
Bowl B 3
Bowl C 3
Bowl D 3
Bowl E 4
Bowl F 4
Bowl G 4
Bowl H 4

This would leave four (4) open spaces. We calculate the odds of moving on from a particular bowl:

Bowl A 3/8 = 37.5%
Bowl B 3/8 = 37.5%
Bowl C 3/8 = 37.5%
Bowl D 3/9 = 33%
Bowl E 4/11 = 36.3%
Bowl F 4/13 = 30%
Bowl G 4/15 = 26%
Bowl H 4/18 = 22%

So the four spaces would go to the following bowls:

Bowl H 22%
Bowl G 26%
Bowl F 30%
Bowl D 33%

Dates

Regional bowls must be held in time for teams to accept an invitation to the national bowl by December 15. Teams must confirm by this date or risk losing their space.

Rules variations in regional bowls

Regional bowls are expected to use the national bowl's rules, guidelines, and scoring rubric, with the following exceptions:

1   Regional bowls are not required to conduct a straight elimination match of the top scoring teams in the three morning matches, as provided for under the national rules. However, regional bowls must adopt scoring rules that enable them to rank teams from top to bottom.

2   Under certain conditions other alterations will be allowed, such as the following:

Minor adjustments to timing and other rules are allowed without prior approval, but require notification to the IEB Executive Board, and, where appropriate, post-bowl reports about the effects of these adjustments. Pre-approved variations include:

1.   initial presentations may run from seven to twelve minutes
2.   commentary on initial presentations may run from five to eight minutes
3.   ratio of presenting team to opposing team scores may not exceed 5:1
4.   judges' Q&A need not be restricted to one Q and one follow-up
5.   judges' Q&A may be expanded from ten to fifteen minutes
6.   response to commentary may be shortened in favor of lengthening the judges' Q&A period
7.   rules regarding the number of members of a team who may speak during any particular part of the round may be changed without prior consent
8.   regional bowls may allow one minute for initial conferral, and may have any policy they deem appropriate on when teams may use scratch paper, as long as notes are not in from the outside
9.   the winner of a match may be determined by which team received higher scores from the majority of judges rather than the highest points.

Experiments involving more significant changes require approval from the IEB Executive Board and require reports about the effects of these changes. The regional bowls can serve as test beds for useful experimentation, with successful experiments ultimately being adopted by the national bowl (and therefore the other regional bowls). However, changes that alter the essential nature of the event as an academic competition will be turned down by the executive board.

National Intercollegiate Ethics Bowl Championship Rules (2008)

Procedural rules

1   In an Ethics Bowl match each team will be questioned by a moderator on a case. On or about January 10, 2008 each team will receive fifteen (15) cases. Each of the cases will be one to two pages in length. The cases on which teams will be asked questions at the Ethics Bowl will be taken from these fifteen cases. The teams will not know in advance which of the cases they will be asked about at the Ethics Bowl or what the questions will be.

Judges and moderators will also receive the fifteen cases on or about January 10, 2008. Like the teams, they will receive copies of the cases but not copies of the questions. The judges and moderators, like the teams, will not be informed in advance of the specific cases teams will be asked about at the ethics bowl.

2   Teams may be any size but only five or fewer may be active participants at any time. Substitutions may not be made once the initial five or fewer are seated and ready for action. Substitutions *may not* be made once the case is announced. Team members must be undergraduates.

3   During competition books and notes will not be allowed, however, scrap paper to jot down thoughts is permissible. The teams will be given a copy of the case and the question to which they must respond. Teams should wait to use the scratch paper until the case has been announced. Students are permitted to pass notes to one another at any point.

4   The Moderator will indicate the case with which the team that goes first (hereinafter Team One) will deal, and then read Team One's question about the case. (The Moderator will not read aloud the entire case.)

5   Team One will then have two (2) minutes to confer, after which one spokesperson for the team may use up to ten (10) minutes to respond to the Moderator's question.

6   The opposing team (hereinafter Team Two) receives one minute to confer, and then may use up to five minutes to comment about Team One's answer to the Moderator's question. The commentary may include the posing of a question to Team One. More than one team member may contribute to the commentary, but only one team member may speak at a time.

7   Team One receives one minute to confer and then may use up to five minutes to respond to Team Two's commentary. More than one team member may respond to the commentary, but only one team member may speak at a time.

8   The judges then may ask questions to Team One. *Each judge may ask no more than one question with a brief follow-up question. The entire period for judges' questions shall last no more than ten (10) minutes.* Before asking questions the judges may confer with one another to discuss briefly areas that they want to cover during the question period. Different team members may respond to the questions of different judges. Teams may huddle briefly to discuss their answers to the judges' questions.

9   The judges will evaluate Team One and Team Two on score sheets provided to them (see scoring rules below). At this point, however, the judges will not announce to the teams the scores they have given them.

10   Team One and Team Two will reverse roles for a second round with a different case.

11   At the close of the second round the Moderator will ask the judges to announce the teams' scores for the match (see scoring rules below).

Scoring rules

Judges shall evaluate the responses of teams *solely* in terms of the following criteria:

- Clarity and Intelligibility: Was the presentation clear and systematic? Regardless of whether or not you agree with the conclusion, did the team give a coherent argument in a clear and succinct manner?
- Avoidance of Ethical Irrelevance: Did the team avoid ethically irrelevant issues? Or was the team preoccupied with issues that are not ethically relevant or are of minor ethical relevance to the case?
- Identification and Discussion of Central Ethical Dimensions: Did the team's presentation clearly identify and thoroughly discuss the central ethical dimensions of the case?
- Deliberative Thoughtfulness: Did the team's presentation indicate both awareness and thoughtful consideration of different viewpoints, including especially those that would loom large in the reasoning of individuals who disagree with the team's position?

The judges will score each team as follows:

- 0–40 for Team One's answer to the Moderator's question (40 best); in evaluating a team's answer the judges will give the team a score of 0–10 relative to each of the four evaluation criteria indicated above and total the sum.
- 0–10 for Team Two's commentary (10 best).
- 0–10 for Team One's response to Team Two's commentary, and for the response to the judges' questions, by the team that answered the Moderator's question (10 best).
- Both in evaluating a team's commentary, and the other team's response to the commentary, the judges will take into account the four evaluation criteria indicated above, but give the teams an overall score, rather than a separate point score relative to each of the criteria.

The top eight teams in the competition will be determined in the following way:

Morning Competition
Teams will be ranked based on (a) the number of wins, followed by (b) the number of ties, followed by (c) point differentials between the total points awarded by judges. Thus, all teams with three wins will rank ahead of all teams with two wins. All teams with two wins will rank ahead of all teams with one win. Within rankings, a team with more ties ranks above a team with fewer ties. Finally, for teams with the same number of wins and ties, a team with a higher point differential would rank above a team with a lower point differential. For example:

TEAMS	WINS	TIES	POINTS	RANK
School R	3 wins	0 ties	12 point differential	1st
School M	3 wins	0 ties	0 point differential	2nd
School B	2 wins	1 tie	15 point differential	3rd
School S	2 wins	0 ties	–8 point differential	4th
School H	1 win	2 ties	–6 point differential	5th

Note, for example, that School B has a greater point differential than School M, and School H has a lower negative point differential than School S. Nonetheless, M ranks ahead of B because it has more wins, and, likewise, S ranks ahead of H.

Point differentials. Point differentials are the margin of victory or loss. A point differential for each match is determined by taking the team's total points and subtracting the other team's total. Note that point differentials will be negative in the case of a loss. At the end of the morning competition the point differential for a team is simply the sum of the point differentials for that team in each of its three morning matches.

The eight teams with the highest ranking based on the morning competition will enter the evening competition.

Ties at the end of the morning competition:

1   If two teams have the same ranking, then if they played against each other during the three rounds of play, whoever won that competition will win gain the higher ranking.
2   The method in number 1, above, will also apply to a three (or more) way tie in ranking, just in case all teams played each other and transitivity holds (e.g., A beat B, B beat C, but C did not beat A).
3   In case numbers 1 and 2 do not determine a winner, then raw points will be used to determine a winner.
4   Finally, if 1–3 above fail, an impartial random process will determine the final outcome between the teams. In case two teams are still tied, a coin toss will be used. If more than two teams still remain, the high card drawn from a standard deck of playing cards will decide. This process will be repeated until the outcome is decided.

The winner of the Ethics Bowl, among the top eight teams, will be determined as follows:

Evening Competition

- The top eight teams will face each other during the evening in three elimination matches: quarterfinals, semifinals, and finals.
- Judges will use the same numerical scoring guidelines as they did during the morning competition.
- The winner of the Fourteenth Intercollegiate Ethics Bowl will be the team that wins three matches in the evening competition.

Ties during quarterfinal or semifinal matches:
In case of a tie in a quarterfinal or semi final match:

- if the two teams have faced each other in the morning matches, the winner of that match wins the tie-break; or else
- the team with the most wins in the morning wins the tie-break; or else
- the team with the most ties in the morning wins the tie-break; or else
- the team with the most points in the morning wins the tie-break; or else
- a coin toss decides the winner of the tie-break.

In the case of a tie in the final round, the two finalists will be declared co-winners of the Intercollegiate Ethics Bowl.

©2008 Illinois Institute of Technology. 3300 South Federal Street, Chicago, IL 60616-3793. Tel 312.567.3000. Available at: http://ethics.iit.edu/eb/IEBrules07_08.html and http://ethics.iit.edu/eb/IEBrules07_08.html#Regional. [Accessed February 28, 2008].